Practical Guidelines and Best Practices for Microsoft® Visual Basic® and Visual C#® Developers

Francesco Balena

Giuseppe Dimauro

PUBLISHED BY
Microsoft Press
A Division of Microsoft Corporation
One Microsoft Way
Redmond, Washington 98052-6399

Library of Congress Control Number: 2005920002

Printed and bound in the United States of America.

1 2 3 4 5 6 7 8 9   QWT   9 8 7 6 5

Distributed in Canada by H.B. Fenn and Company Ltd.

A CIP catalogue record for this book is available from the British Library.

Microsoft Press books are available through booksellers and distributors worldwide. For further information about international editions, contact your local Microsoft Corporation office or contact Microsoft Press International directly at fax (425) 936-7329. Visit our Web site at www.microsoft.com/mspress. Send comments to mspinput@microsoft.com.

Microsoft, Active Accessibility, Active Directory, ActiveX, IntelliSense, Microsoft Press, MSDN, Visual Basic, Visual Studio, Win32, Windows, and Windows Server are either registered trademarks or trademarks of Microsoft Corporation in the United States and/or other countries. Other product and company names mentioned herein may be the trademarks of their respective owners.

The example companies, organizations, products, domain names, e-mail addresses, logos, people, places, and events depicted herein are fictitious. No association with any real company, organization, product, domain name, e-mail address, logo, person, place, or event is intended or should be inferred.

This book expresses the author's views and opinions. The information contained in this book is provided without any express, statutory, or implied warranties. Neither the authors, Microsoft Corporation, nor its resellers, or distributors will be held liable for any damages caused or alleged to be caused either directly or indirectly by this book.

Acquisitions Editor: Ben Ryan
Project Editor: Kathleen Atkins
Technical Editor: Marco Bellinaso
Indexers: Caroline Parks and Ginny Bess

Body Part No. X11-08652

Contents at a Glance

Part II   .NET Framework Guidelines and Best Practices

Table of Contents

Part I   Coding Guidelines and Best Practices

Part II   .NET Framework Guidelines and Best Practices

Foreword

In software development, it's always the little things that cause all the big problems. Everyone has worked on a huge performance bug that held up the release of a product and that turned out to be nothing more than incorrectly using something innocuous in the system. Anyone who has been on a project team, moreover, has certainly taken part in one of those withering religious debates of tabs versus spaces. Even though I have debugged and tuned countless applications, I have yet to find any root causes that are new, unique, or, for that matter, very big. One thing I have found is that nearly all the problems I've worked on occur in the code construction phase. That's right: when the typing starts, the bugs begin.

Although I do, only rarely, find problems that were introduced during design—such as using server-side cursors in a database when they might kill scalability—those bugs nearly always show up quickly, mainly because on big issues, there are enough "rules of thumb" sites you can Google for. Those lists are also relatively short. However, when you move down into the coding level, those rules of thumb get harder to find, and the number of rules expands exponentially. Given enough time with Google, you might eventually find all the rules, but you rarely have the time when you've got delivery dates to hit.

What makes life even more interesting for Microsoft .NET Framework developers is that .NET is essentially a brand new technology in the overall scheme of Microsoft Windows development. At the time I write this, .NET was announced publicly only four years ago and shipped only two and a half years ago. Even though Microsoft has bet the farm on .NET, less than half of Windows developers are actually using .NET on their projects today. You might think that's a small percentage, but I find it amazing that companies have moved to .NET so quickly, given its relatively short existence.

In any case, because .NET hasn't been around very long, many .NET developers don't have that internal "feeling" that something they are typing in is going to cause performance problems or bugs, like most experienced C++ or Microsoft Visual Basic 6.0 developers do. Because, as I mentioned earlier, most developers make nearly all their mistakes during coding, this potentially presents a big problem. Fortunately, *Practical Guidelines and Best Practices for Microsoft Visual Basic and Visual C# Developers* solves this predicament!

Francesco and Giuseppe have brought together all of those rules for best practices that you absolutely must follow when writing .NET code. The highest compliment I can pay any book is to say that I learned something from it. With this book, I not only learned something; I learned a ton!

Microsoft has promulgated its Design Guidelines, but these fall far short of what's needed in the real world. Francesco and Giuseppe have addressed the entire .NET code construction process and given you the best practices for everything from how to set up your projects to how to best use the XML classes to the best ways to handle ASP.NET state management.

When I'm writing .NET code, I always have the book's table of contents open, and I give it a quick scan when I'm about to loop over a collection to see whether I'm going to do it correctly. *Practical Guidelines and Best Practices* is like having a .NET expert eXtreme Programming pair developing by your side.

Francesco and Giuseppe are true .NET experts because they've written more .NET code than nearly anyone outside of Microsoft. From the moment Microsoft introduced .NET, Francesco, Giuseppe, and the developers in their company, CodeArchitects, have been working on the largest and most complicated .NET applications I've seen. The more than 700 rules in this book have been learned through developing and, more importantly, shipping, big, real-world applications that use every possible feature in the .NET technology tree. With real teams coming up with these rules, you can rest assured that the rules in this book are not just what some theorist *thinks* are correct; they *are* correct.

After glancing through the book, you might think that its sole audience is the software developer down in the trenches. Actually, it's also perfect for development leads and project managers. Although you might be a little confused by that assertion, think about the last code review you sat in. You probably had a group of folks read over the code, but because they weren't looking for anything specific—just the obvious stuff—they didn't find anything useful, and the whole review was probably a waste of time.

Great code reviews should validate two key items: (1) Does the code meet the requirements set up for the developer? and (2) Does the developer use the technologies and approaches in the environment correctly? As long as your team knows the code requirements, checking for compliance should be relatively easy. Now that *Practical Guidelines and Best Practices* gives you the rules for all those hard .NET Framework and technology interactions, ensuring that the code is as correct as possible is just as easy.

No matter how you use *Practical Guidelines and Best Practices*, it will save you a tremendous amount of time by helping to reduce those insidious bugs and performance problems in your code. I've been using it with all my projects, and it's certainly made me a much better developer.

John Robbins

Cofounder, Wintellect

October 2004

Introduction

As weird as it might sound, you are reading a book that was born almost accidentally. When we began to work on this material, we weren't even thinking of writing a book. Our initial, quite unpretentious goal was to define a list of guidelines for internal use in Code Architects, the software company we founded in 2002.

We founded Code Architects when we realized the extent of the Microsoft .NET Framework potential and the impact it would have on the developers' community and on the way enterprise-level applications are designed and implemented. Before long, we found ourselves working on software projects that included half a million lines of code, mainly written in C# but with some portions developed with Visual Basic. Projects of this size are simply too large for just one or two programmers, and you need more than plain good will to write them in an orderly way. Instead, you need coding discipline and, above all, a set of well-defined and proven guidelines. These guidelines are essential when many developers with different expertise levels and knowledge backgrounds work on the same project.

In the long run, our initial checklist of recommended practices grew in size and included special cases and exceptions meant to accommodate the imperfect world of software development. We also added code examples and short sample projects. But foremost, we discussed nearly all the guidelines in our internal forum and weighed the opinions of Code Architects' team of .NET experts, which includes renowned writers and conference speakers (who are mentioned, as they deserve to be, in the acknowledgment section at the end of this introduction).

We finally realized that many developers all around the world might benefit from our efforts, so we proposed the book to Microsoft Press. To our astonishment, they accepted the proposal within a couple of hours. Wow! That was fast, even in the fast world of the Internet!

Mission (Almost) Impossible: Writing Quality Software

The purpose of this book, and of all guideline and best practice collections, for that matter, is to help you write great applications. Which brings up the obvious question: what makes an application a *great* application?

Microsoft Visual Studio and the .NET Framework have simplified the production of software in ways that would have been inconceivable only five years ago. On the other hand, the programming world has become more complex and, above all, more dangerous. In the pre-Internet era, writing a robust program mainly meant protecting your code from end-user mistakes (the mythical *foolproof* code). Today's users are maybe less naive, but you have to defend your application against malicious hackers, exploits, script kiddies, spoofing, SQL injection, and cross-site scripting attacks, just to name a few of the new threats. Writing secure code is now imperative for Web applications and even for applications running in a seemingly and relatively protected environment such as an intranet.

Robustness and security are just the first and most important qualities that great software should have, but there are many other features that combine to make a successful application, for example, scalability and performance. An application should have a coherent user interface and a smooth learning curve so that end users can become productive as soon as possible. Also, a perfect application should be easily customizable and extendable, to meet the end user's expectations and reduce support costs.

Other features aren't visible to the end user, but they are very important from the perspective of the software company that produces it. For example, source code should be written in an orderly and standardized way and should be reusable in other projects if possible. Code reuse is essential in reducing the time-to-market and development costs.

At the end of the day, you see that writing high-quality software isn't impossible, it's only *very* difficult. You need to be an expert in many programming areas, prepare a state-of-the-art test plan, keep yourself up-to-date on freshly discovered issues and bugs, and keep reading about new product releases. But mostly, you must be very serious about adopting a coherent set of coding guidelines and best practices on which all the developers in your team agree.

Once you are convinced that you need a set of guidelines, you have a practical problem to solve: *where can you find such guidelines?* On the Internet, you can find hundreds of articles and white papers of varying quality and depth that discuss .NET Framework best practices. Understandably, no single article can cover all the facets of Visual Studio .NET and the .NET Framework, but worse than missing coverage is that many articles contradict each other. In a few cases you can find white papers that explain the advantages and disadvantages of a given recommendation; only rarely do they mention that there might be important exceptions to a given rule.

Microsoft has published some great articles containing what should be considered *the official guidelines* for all .NET developers, and we used them as the basis of our own recommendations (and you'll find many links pointing to them in this book). For example, all developers agree that the name of attribute types should end with Attribute and that fields should be made private and be wrapped in public properties. Unfortunately, these official guidelines don't really cover all aspects of the code production process, and the existing gray area has fueled the proliferation of all sorts of flames in newsgroups and in blogs.

However, the key word in this book's title is *practical*. We didn't want to create yet another list of guidelines that only the most motivated developers use in their applications. Our goal was to come up with general directives that every developer can customize to fit his or her needs and coding style and to convince you that these rules can help you achieve more than just a pretty-looking piece of code.

We would bet that some developers won't agree with some of our guidelines, but it isn't our intention to fuel endless (and unproductive, in some cases) discussions. To the contrary, we recognize that many guidelines have both advantages and disadvantages, and therefore they shouldn't be considered as absolute rules. In fact, you'll often find a **Why** section that explains the pros of a rule and a **Why not** section that explains its shortcomings so that you can make an informed decision. In some cases, you'll even find an **Exceptions** section, where we list the cases when adopting a given guideline would harm your application's overall quality.

It is sometimes difficult to say which rule is the best rule under any given circumstance. This often happens when you discuss a coding style guideline that has no effect on the code's performance, robustness, or maintainability—for example, the prefix you should use for private fields or whether you should put curly braces on a line of their own. In these cases, we decided to add an **Alternative rule** immediately following our "official" guideline, explaining the whys and whynots of each. Our rationale is, when the overall quality won't suffer, it isn't really important which guideline you decide to abide by. Just pick one that fits your coding style, but after you choose it, use it consistently. Your motto should be: *Any guideline is better than no guideline.*

Once again, you might disagree with some guidelines. If so, drop us an e-mail at *fbalena@codearchitects.com* or *gdimauro@codearchitects.com*. We're also planning to devote a forum or section on *http://www.dotnet2themax.com* from where you can download more material related to this book and guidelines in general. To stay updated, just subscribe to our newsletter at *http://www.dotnet2themax.com/newsletter/subscribe.aspx*.

Guideline Priority

In the first part of this book, we have gathered coding guidelines related to Visual Studio .NET and the two main .NET programming languages, C# and Visual Basic. Here, you'll find naming rules or suggestions about how you might organize your classes, as well as tips about writing code that is both robust and efficient. Most rules apply to both languages, but a few are relevant only under C# or Visual Basic.

In the second part of the book, you can find a vast collection of best practices to be used in the various portions of the .NET Framework, including Windows Forms, ASP.NET, ADO.NET, PInvoke and COM Interop, serviced components, and remoting.

Each of the more than 700 rules in the book can help you in pursuing one of the following objects, listed in decreasing order of importance:

1. **Robustness**   Code must work as intended and must not cause fatal errors.

2. **Security**   The program must not be subject to attacks from malicious users or, in the case of class libraries, used in an improper way.

3. **Scalability**   The application should scale well when the number of users grows, especially in the case of server-side components and database-intensive applications.

4. **Efficiency**   Code must consume few resources and be as fast as possible; it shouldn't unnecessarily stress the CPU, the .NET garbage collector, the file system, and the database engine.

5. **Usability**   The application should be easy to use and learn—for example, menu commands should be organized in a logical way and use standard shortcut key combinations. If it is a class library, its programming interface should be coherent and in line with the .NET Framework guidelines.

6. **Code reuse**   It should be possible to reuse code in other projects easily.

7. **Extensibility**   If necessary, it must be possible to extend a class or the entire application with newer and more powerful versions, customize it for a specific user, or localize for a different language, with minimal or no impact on applications that have already been deployed.

8. **Maintainability**   Source code should be readable; indenting and commenting style should be uniform; member names should be used in a consistent way; code shouldn't rely on undocumented features or behaviors, and so on.

9. **Language interoperability**   A class library should be callable from any .NET programming language without any restriction. As a secondary goal, source code should rely as little as possible on specific language features so that it can be reviewed by as many developers as possible and translated to a different language with minimal effort.

10. **Ease of development**   When all the available alternatives have no impact on any of the previous points, it is always preferable to adopt a technique that helps to deliver code in less time and that has a narrower margin for human errors. (Yes, developers *are* humans, after all.)

Not surprisingly, some of these goals are often mutually exclusive. For example, a robust and secure application can't be the most efficient application at the same time because the action of checking user input data surely slows down execution speed. Whenever we had to make a choice, we gave a higher priority to goals near the top of the list. For this reason, we usually recommend a more efficient technique only if it doesn't decrease the application's scalability.

At the end of the list, you find a goal that many developers—either consciously or not—place at the top of their own priorities. All developers would love to write great code in little time, but this is rarely a realistic goal. The sad truth is: *writing quality software takes time.* On the other hand, you should be convinced that all the energy you spend to design your software and make it as robust, safe, and reusable as possible pays off when it's time to sell it, support it, or release a new version. At least, this is what we have learned in the last two decades spent writing applications of all sorts.

We haven't cataloged our guidelines according to their importance, and we don't distinguish critical rules from simpler style recommendations. Let us explain why. Except for a few uncontroversial cases, the actual value of a rule depends heavily on the context in which the rule is applied and, in some cases, on the kind of end user who will run the application. For example, all the rules that have to do with security should be considered critical, but their actual importance depends on whether they are applied to a Web application that is accessed over the Internet, or in an intranet behind a firewall, or in a Windows Forms application installed on the LAN, or in a simple console application meant to be run from the local hard disk.

Instead of using a label or a number that would establish how critical a rule is, we opted for the many flavors of the English language, for example, using adverbs such as *always* and *never* for stronger recommendations, or verbs such as *favor, consider,* or *avoid* for rules that might or might not be the best choice in a given circumstance. This approach won't delight those who see a black-and-white world, but it is the most correct one in our opinion.

> **Important** All the code Visual Basic and C# code samples that are longer than a few lines can be downloaded from the Internet. Read Appendix C for more details.

Who Should Read This Book

Many expert developers mistakenly believe that abiding by a set of guidelines is a limitation to their creativity because they believe that writing software is a form of art that shouldn't be caged with these sorts of artificial rules.

Granted, writing software is *also* a creative act. If it weren't, our job would be really tedious and unexciting. But it is also true that you must transform this creative act into manufacturing to create a successful software factory and be competitive in the third millennium. With this goal in mind, you should favor standardization over extreme creativity and personal style because the former improves your productivity and flexibility. For example, if all the developers in your company agree on a given coding style, it is easier to move one or more persons from one project to another without any negative impact on deadlines or code quality.

In writing this book we had the following kinds of readers in mind:

- Individual developers who want to write robust, fast, and scalable code and are already proficient with the .NET Framework and either Visual Basic or C#

- Developers who are asked to write enterprise-level, mission-critical applications that must scale well and resist attacks of all sorts

- Team leaders who wish to define a common set of guidelines for a group of developers with varying expertise levels and coding styles

- Consultants who are asked to debug and review code written by other developers and who need a list of all the most common problems and related solutions

> **Important**   One category of developers should *not* buy this book:
>
> This book is neither for beginner developers nor for developers who have never worked with the Microsoft .NET Framework.

Let us state it once again: *This book doesn't teach you the basics of the .NET Framework, Visual Basic, and C#.* Quite the opposite: we expect that you have a good familiarity with these languages, with object-oriented programming in general, and with the most important types in the .NET Framework.

Where to Look for More Information

This book can't replace a real tutorial on .NET Framework programming. If we had written a tutorial-oriented textbook, space constraints would have forced us to leave out too many important topics. However, we tried to explain all the techniques and concepts that, in our opinion, aren't commonly known among developers.

Fortunately, many great sources of information are available for free on the Internet, ranging from introductions to .NET programming techniques to detailed white papers on very specific topics. We routinely scan the Internet for these articles and have scattered many useful links throughout this book. If you think you need more information about a specific topic or technique, we suggest that you pay a visit to one of the following Web sites:

- The MSDN online Web site (*http://www.msdn.microsoft.com*) is the starting point for all searches related to the .NET Framework.

- The MSDN Magazine Web site (*http://msdn.microsoft.com/msdnmag/*) includes hundreds of great articles on .NET-related topics.

- The Visual Studio Magazine's site (*http://www.visualstudiomagazine.com*) provides access to the current issue and all past issues of this popular magazine. You can also read the .NET-2-the-Max monthly column, written by members of the Code Architects team.

- The .NET-2-the-Max Web site (*http://www.dotnet2themax.com*) is where you can find many tips, articles, and ready-to-use routines written by Code Architects experts, available in both Visual Basic and C# flavors. This is the successor of the popular *http://www.vb2themax.com* site, which has been active since 1999. (We recently launched an Italian version of this site, which you can reach at *http://www.dotnet2themax.it*.)

- The Code Project Web site (*http://www.codeproject.com*) has published many great articles on the .NET Framework, mostly written by and for C# developers.

- The CodeGuru Web site (*www.codeguru.com*) is another good repository of C#-oriented articles, and it hosts many contributions from Wintellect guys.

- …And, of course, Google (*http://www.google.com*) is the place to go when everything else fails. Or even before trying anything else!

For a more comprehensive discussion of .NET-related technologies, you might consider the following books:

- *Programming Microsoft Visual Basic .NET 2003* by Francesco Balena (Microsoft Press, 2003), a 1400-page guide for the Visual Basic language and in-depth overview of all portions of the .NET Framework, including Windows Forms, ASP.NET, ADO.NET, serviced components, remoting, and Code Access Security.

- *Applied Microsoft .NET Framework Programming* by Jeffrey Richter (Microsoft Press, 2002), the reference guide for .NET internals such as memory management and exception handling. All examples are written in C#. If you don't feel at ease with curly braces, try out the Visual Basic version: *Applied Microsoft .NET Framework Programming in Microsoft Visual Basic .NET* by Jeffrey Richter and Francesco Balena (Microsoft Press, 2002).

- *Programming Microsoft ASP.NET* by Dino Esposito (Microsoft Press, 2003), a must-have for all serious ASP.NET developers.

- *Windows Forms Programming in C#* by Chris Sells (Addison-Wesley, 2003), with tons of useful techniques for GUI-oriented programmers.

- *Programming .NET Components* by Juval Lowy (O'Reilly, 2003), where you can learn more about components, COM+, and security.

Acknowledgments

First and foremost, we want to thank John Robbins for the most enthusiastic foreword that a book author could ever hope for. Last year, John happened to review a few applications we wrote at Code Architects, so we knew he could prepare an informed foreword. But John went further than that: he actually read every page of the manuscript and provided suggestions and hints, his opinions on controversial guidelines, and ultimately made *Practical Guidelines and Best Practices for Microsoft Visual Basic and Visual C# Developers* a better and more useful book. Having a guru like John Robbins review your book is like having Michael Schumacher give you driving lessons!

Many other persons helped us in creating and polishing this book. At the top of the list is Marco Bellinaso, a great author himself who has also written several bestsellers for the publisher Wrox. Marco tech reviewed the manuscript, tested each and every code snippet (in both Visual Basic and C#, of course), but above all provided countless hints and suggestions about how to improve the material. We think of him more as a coauthor than a tech reviewer.

Other members of the Code Architects team contributed to this book in crucial ways. Enrico Sabbadin helped us to better understand the subtle world of security, remoting, and serviced components, Alberto Falossi supported us in writing many chapters in Part I, and Dino Esposito made great suggestions to improve the ASP.NET section. We are so proud to work with such a great team of experts.

A big thank you also to Natale Fino, who spent many of his evenings and weekends translating the manuscript into Italian and double-checking it for consistency and accuracy at the same time.

Our initial idea would have never become a concrete book without the behind-the-scenes, relentless work of Ben Ryan, our acquisitions editor at Microsoft Press. An acquisitions editor is a bit like the author's advocate in all the meetings when the publisher decides whether a book should be published, how many pages it should have, and so forth. It's to Ben's credit that we could publish exactly the book we had in mind.

Even if it isn't a very large book, we faced many editing challenges in writing *Practical Guidelines and Best Practices*. For example, many rules reference other rules and there is an unusually high number of cross references that had to be checked. Each rule is split into subsections and we needed to maintain a consistent style across completely different topics. We could have never delivered the manuscript on time if it weren't for Kathleen Atkins and Christina Palaia, our editing guardian angels. It was pure pleasure to work with you.

Many friends and readers ask us where we find the time, energy, and motivation to run a company, create applications, teach, consult, manage a couple of Web sites, write articles and books, *and* have a social life at the same time. In this case, the answer is simple: each of us has a wonderful family behind him.

Thank you Adriana, Francesca, Andrea, and Lucia.

—Francesco Balena, Giuseppe Dimauro

Part I
Coding Guidelines and Best Practices

Chapter 1
Projects and Solutions

The first step that you should take to ensure that all the developers in your company produce code that can be easily merged into larger projects is to pay attention to how Microsoft Visual Studio .NET projects and solutions are shaped, how files are named, and where they are stored.

In this first chapter, you can read a few basic rules to keep your projects and files in order as well as some tips to ensure that applications are compiled with the most appropriate settings. All in all, it's very simple stuff, but we must start from somewhere, right?

1.1 Solution name

The name of the solution matches the name of its main project.

1.2 Location of files in single-project solutions

Solution files (.sln and .suo) in single-project solutions are placed inside the main source code directory, together with the main project files.

More details: This is the way Visual Studio .NET arranges files when you create a new project by means of the Project command on the New submenu of the File menu.

1.3 Location of files in multiple-project solutions

Solution files (.sln and .suo) in multiple-project solutions are placed inside the main directory, whereas each individual project goes in a subdirectory of this main solution directory.

How to: Create an empty solution using the Blank Solution command on the New submenu of the File menu in Visual Studio .NET, and then use the Add Project command from the File menu to create one or more projects in the solution's directory.

1.4 Location of files in ASP.NET projects

Don't use the Visual Studio .NET default directory for ASP.NET solutions. Instead, create a blank solution in a directory of your choice, and then make it a virtual Microsoft Internet Information Services (IIS) folder.

Why: By default, Visual Studio .NET places ASP.NET solution files (.sln and .suo) in a directory in the C:\Documents and Settings*CurrentUserName*\My Documents\Visual Studio Projects folder (unless you've changed it on the Projects And Solutions page of the Options dialog box that you reach from the Tools menu), whereas .aspx and other source code files go in a directory under C:\Inetpub\wwwroot (or whatever the IIS installation path is). Having solution files scattered in two different places isn't practical.

Why not: The main limitation of this technique is that you can't reach the solution with the Project From Web command on the Open submenu. This command can display only physical folders in the C:\Inetpub\wwwroot directory.

How to: Follow this procedure to make the solution's directory a virtual IIS folder.

1. In Visual Studio .NET, create a blank solution in a directory (e.g., the AspNetDemo solution in the C:\Projects\AspNetDemo directory) using the Blank Solution command on the New submenu on the File menu.

2. Switch to Windows Explorer, right-click the new directory, and select the Sharing And Security command from the context menu.

3. Switch to the Web Sharing tab, and click the Share This Folder radio button, which displays the Edit Alias dialog box. (See Figure 1-1.)

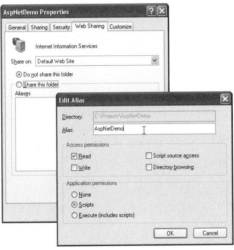

Figure 1-1   The Web Sharing tab of a folder's Properties dialog box (on the left). When you click the Share This Folder radio button, the Edit Alias dialog box appears (on the right).

4. Type a name for the virtual folder or accept the suggested name if you want the virtual folder and the physical directory to have the same name, and then click OK once to close this dialog box and a second time to close the Properties dialog box.

5. Go back to Visual Studio .NET and select the New Project command from the Add Project submenu on the File menu. Select the ASP.NET Web Application item from the Templates pane in the Add New Project dialog box (see Figure 1-2), type the name of the virtual directory in the Location text box (http://localhost/AspNetDemo in this example), and then click OK.

All the files of the project will be created in this folder.

Add New Project

Project Types:

- Visual Basic Projects
- Visual C# Projects
- Visual J# Projects
- Visual C++ Projects
- Setup and Deployment Projects
- Other Projects

Templates:

Smart Device Application   ASP.NET Web Application   ASP.NET Web Service

ASP.NET Mobile W...   Web Control Library   Console Application

A project for creating an application with a Web user interface

Name: AspNetDemo

Location: http://localhost/AspNetDemo   Browse...

Project will be created at http://localhost/AspNetDemo.

OK   Cancel   Help

Figure 1-2   The Add New Project dialog box enables you to select the virtual folder of the ASP.NET project being created.

1.5 Project folders

Use project folders to group source files that define types in a nested namespace (see Figure 1-3). For example, create a folder named DataObjects for all the source files containing types in the *companyname.projectname*.DataObjects namespace.

How to: You can create a project folder by right-clicking a project item in the Solution Explorer window and then selecting the New Folder command from the Add submenu. (You can also create subfolders, if necessary.)

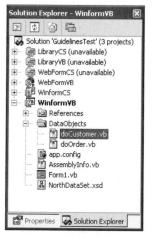

Solution Explorer - WinformVB

- Solution 'GuidelinesTest' (3 projects)
  - LibraryCS (unavailable)
  - LibraryVB (unavailable)
  - WebFormCS (unavailable)
  - WebFormVB
  - WinformCS
  - **WinformVB**
    - References
    - DataObjects
      - doCustomer.vb
      - doOrder.vb
    - app.config
    - AssemblyInfo.vb
    - Form1.vb
    - NorthDataSet.xsd

Properties   Solution Explorer

Figure 1-3   Project folders in the Solution Explorer window

1.6 Source file name

Use PascalCase for source files, and name them after the main type they contain. Never use nonstandard file name extensions (that is, file name extensions other than .vb or .cs).

1.7 Executable EXE files

The name of the executable file of a Console or Windows Forms application should match the name of the project.

1.8 Executable DLL files

The name of the executable file of a Control Library application should match the name of the main namespace of the project.

Example: CodeArchitects.Controls.Validation.dll.

1.9 Source files shared among multiple projects

Enable multiple projects to share files that contain reusable methods and classes and files that contain settings and constants used by all applications of your company.

How to: Use the Add Existing Item command on the File menu, click the arrow to the right of the Open button in the Add Existing Item dialog box, and select the Link File option (see Figure 1-4).

More details: This technique is especially useful to share the same instance of Assembly-Info.vb or AssemblyInfo.cs files and ensure that all the assemblies in a solution have the same version, company information, and so on.

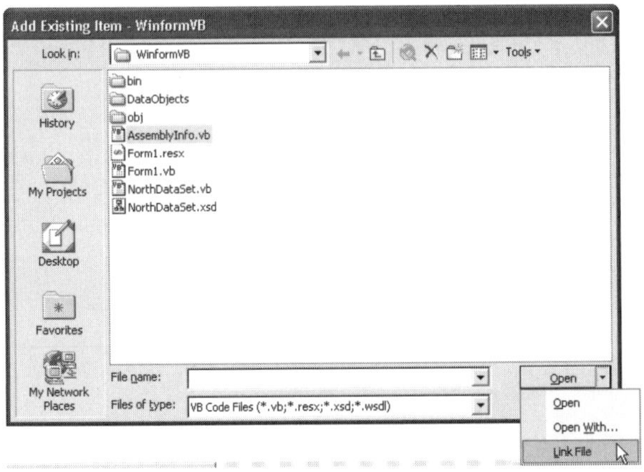

Figure 1-4   The Link File option in the Add Existing Item dialog box

1.10 Configuration files

Always add a configuration file named App.Config to the current project.

How to: Use the Add New Item command on the Project menu, and then select the Assembly Configuration File item.

Why: When you build the project, Visual Studio .NET automatically copies this file in the output directory and renames it *program.exe*.config so you don't have to create the configuration file manually.

1.11 Compiler warnings [Visual Basic]

Always compile with the Enable Build Warnings option enabled. In release mode, also enable the Treat Compiler Warnings As Errors option.

How to: Set both options on the Build page of the Project Properties dialog box (see top portion of Figure 1-5). The former option is the default when compiling from the command line; use the /warnaserror+ switch to enable the latter option.

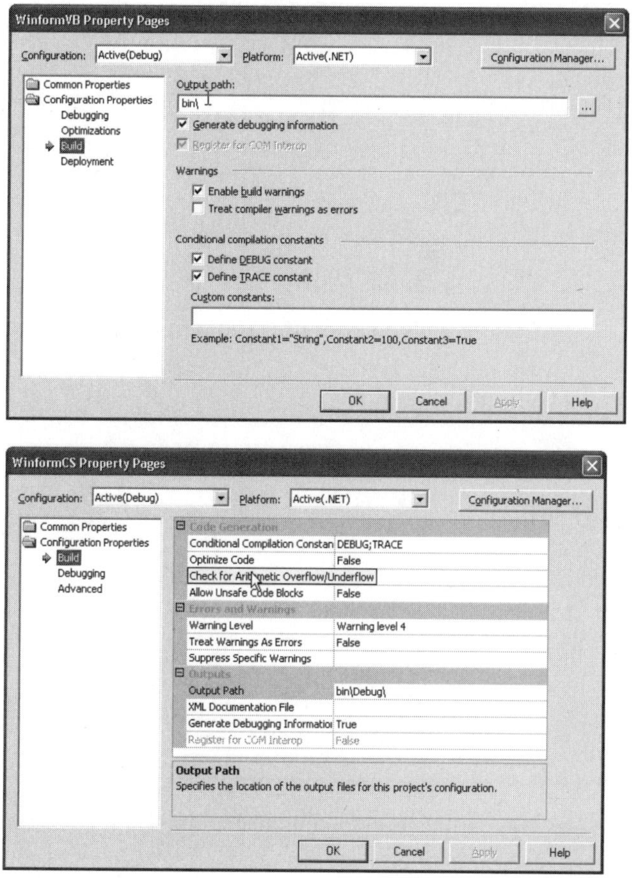

Figure 1-5 The Build page in the Project Properties dialog box in Visual Basic projects (top) and C# projects (bottom)

1.12 Compiler warnings [C#]

Always compile with Warning Level 4. Never suppress specific warnings. In release mode, also enable the Treat Warnings As Errors option.

More details: Treating warnings as errors is a simple way to spot many potential problems and bugs in your code, so you might want to turn this feature on even in debug mode.

How to: Set these options on the Build page of the Project Properties dialog box (see bottom portion of Figure 1-5). Use the /warnaserror+ switch to treat warnings as errors when compiling from the command line.

1.13 Compiler optimizations

Disable compiler optimization and remove the integer overflow checks option in debug mode, but enable them in release mode.

Why: Compiler optimizations can make debugging harder. For example, the JIT compiler can inline a method, in which case following the actual execution flow in the debugger becomes more difficult. Integer overflow exceptions should always be checked in debug mode so that you can fix all programming mistakes; once you have solved these problems, however, disabling integer overflow checks can make your code run remarkably faster.

How to: You can find these options on the Build page of the Project Properties dialog box (see Figure 1-5).

See also: See rule 14.2 for more information about method inlining. See rule 20.4 about using checked blocks in C# programs.

1.14 Debugging information

Always include debug symbols in the executable, both in debug and release modes. Notice that, by default, this option is disabled in release mode.

How to: You can find this option on the Build page of the Project Properties dialog box (see Figure 1-5).

1.15 Base address for DLLs

In class library (DLL) projects, always change the default base address. Ensure that all the DLLs you use in the current solution have different values, and try to keep values far enough apart so that DLLs don't overlap in memory.

How to: You find this option on the Optimizations page (Visual Basic) or the Advanced page (C#) of the Project Properties dialog box (see Figure 1-6).

Why: Windows can load DLLs faster if they don't have to be rebased (i.e., loaded at an address other than their base address). This is especially true if the DLL has been precompiled with the Ngen utility (see rule 4.12).

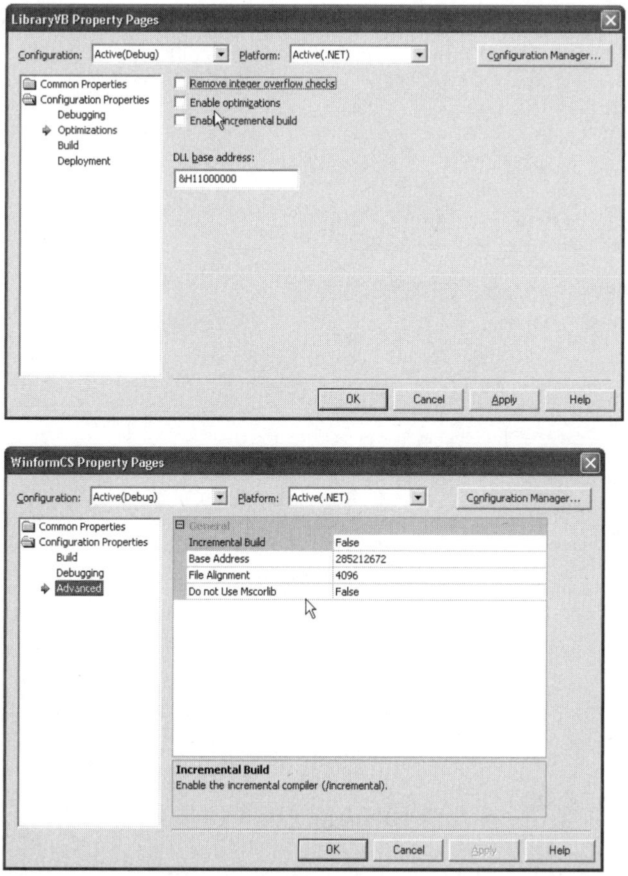

Figure 1-6   You can set the Base Address on two different pages of the Project Properties dialog box: the Optimization page for Visual Basic projects (top) and the Advanced page for C# projects (bottom).

1.16 Option Strict setting for new projects [Visual Basic]

Enforce Option Explicit On, Option Strict On, and Option Compare On for all the new Visual Basic projects you create.

How to: Set these options on the Projects page of the Options dialog box, which you can reach from the Tools menu (see top portion of Figure 1-7).

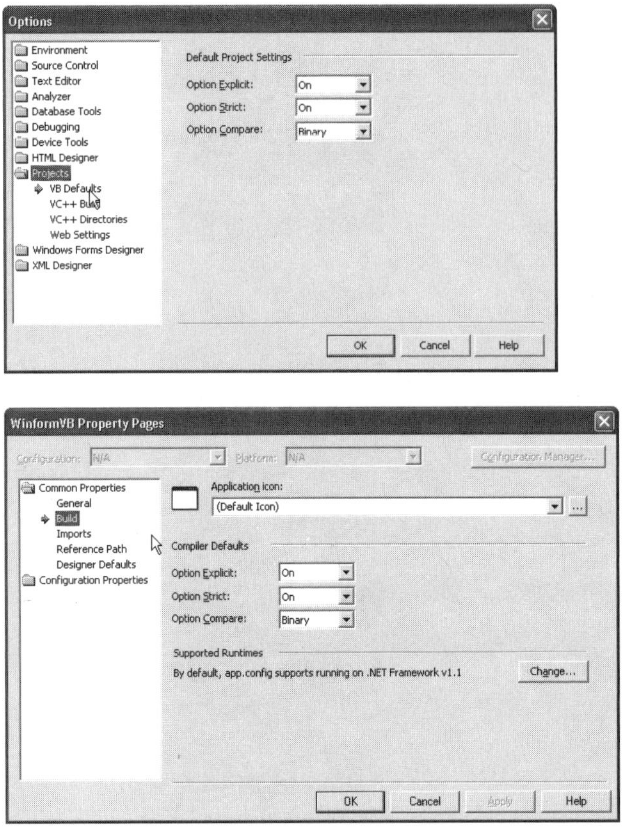

Figure 1-7   The Projects page of the Options dialog box that you reach from the Tools menu (top), and the Build page of the Project Properties dialog box that you reach from the Project menu (bottom)

1.17 Option Strict setting for the current project [Visual Basic]

Enforce Option Explicit On, Option Strict On, and Option Compare On for the Visual Basic projects that you inherit from other developers.

How to: Set these options on the Build page of the Project Properties dialog box (see bottom portion of Figure 1-7).

1.18 The Option Strict directive [Visual Basic]

Insert an Option Strict Off statement at the top of the source files in which you decide to relax strong typing or use late binding to invoke methods and properties using an object variable. Ideally, no more than one source file in the project should include such a statement, and this file should contain only the methods for which Option Strict Off is actually necessary; all these methods should be exposed as static methods of a private type (or a module) and used as helper methods from elsewhere in the project.

1.19 Project-level custom constants

Avoid #const directives in favor of project-level custom constants defined on the Build page of the Project Properties dialog box (see Figure 1-5). Use all caps style for these custom constants.

1.20 VERSION*xyy* custom compilation constant

Define a custom compilation constant named VERSION*xyy*, where *x* and *yy* are the project's major and minor version numbers, respectively.

How to: You can set one or more custom compilation constants on the Build page of the Project Properties dialog box (see Figure 1-5).

Why: This rule makes it easy to include or exclude portions of code in different versions of the project by means of #If directives (Visual Basic) or #if directives (C#).

```
' [Visual Basic]
#If VERSION110 Or VERSION120 Then
    ' Include code for versions 1.10 and 1.20 here.
    ' ...
#End if

// [C#]
#if VERSION110 || VERSION120
    // Include code for version 1.10 and 1.20 here.
    // ...
#endif
```

See also: Visual Basic developers might also want to consider rule 1.21.

1.21 VERSION custom compilation constant [Visual Basic]

Define a custom compilation constant named VERSION on the Build page of the Project Properties dialog box (see Figure 1-5) and assign it a string that matches the *major.minor* version of the project.

Why: This rule makes it easy to include or exclude portions of code in different versions of the project by means of #If directives.

```
' [Visual Basic]
#If VERSION = "1.10" Or VERSION = "1.20" Then
    ' Include code for versions 1.10 and 1.20 here.
    ' ...
#End if
```

More details: This rule can't be adopted in C# projects because that language doesn't support assignment of values to compilation constants.

1.22 Microsoft.VisualBasic project-wide imports [Visual Basic]

Attempt not to use types and methods in the Microsoft.VisualBasic.dll assembly in favor of the Microsoft .NET Framework native counterpart.

Why: Native .NET Framework types offer better performance and added flexibility, and using them consistently makes it easier to convert the source code to other languages.

How to: You can effectively force developers to stay clear of commands that are specific to Visual Basic by removing the Microsoft.VisualBasic namespace from the list of project-wide imports on the Imports page of the Project Properties dialog box (see Figure 1-8). This is a very strong decision, however, which can have a negative short-term impact on your team's productivity.

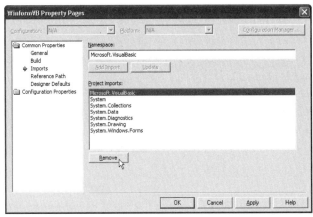

Figure 1-8   The Imports page of the Project Properties dialog box (Visual Basic only)

1.23 Incremental builds [C#]

Disable incremental builds, both in debug and release modes.

Why: Incremental builds can reduce compilation time, but in most cases the speed advantage isn't noticeable. On the other hand, in some cases we have experienced problems and some kinds of malfunctioning that went away after disabling incremental builds.

How to: You can find this option on the Advanced page of the Project Properties dialog box (see bottom portion of Figure 1-6).

Chapter 2
Spaces and Indentation

Many developers don't really care about keeping a consistent style in how they use spaces and indentation in their code. Usually the resulting code is a real mess because it's hard to keep track of where code blocks begin and end. The problem is somewhat less serious in Microsoft Visual Basic because Visual Studio .NET automatically enforces formatting as you type code inside its editor, but even Visual Basic developers must exercise some self-discipline to deliver correctly indented code. (Good news for C# developers: the forthcoming Visual Studio 2005 supports a rich set of formatting options for their language, too.)

2.1 Indent by tabs

Use tabs instead of spaces to indent code.

Why: Using tabs instead of spaces gives you more options when printing the source code. It lets you easily change the indentation level and helps you avoid nonstandard indentation styles.

How to: You can set this option on the Tabs pages under the Text Editor folder in the Options dialog box from the Tools menu (see Figure 2-1). You can also set different settings for each language that Visual Studio .NET supports.

Alternate rule: We know that many developers prefer spaces, mainly because they ensure that code is printed exactly as it appears on screen. Our preference goes to tabs, yet we list this alternate style for the sake of completeness.

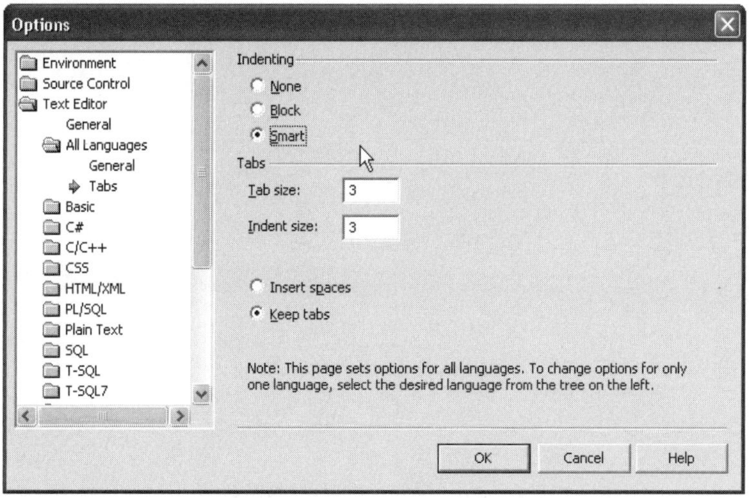

Figure 2-1 The Tabs page in the Text Editor folder in the Options dialog box from the Tools menu

2.2 Indentation width

Use three spaces for each indenting level. Never use spaces to create nonstandard indentation.

How to: Set this option on the Text Editor pages for your language in the Tools dialog box from the Tools menu (see Figure 2-1).

Why: Default Visual Studio .NET settings are four spaces per tab. Using three spaces increases the amount of code visible on the screen and reduces the need to scroll horizontally to browse longer lines.

Tip: You might need to reformat existing code if you change tab width or change the way indentation is rendered (spaces or tabs). You can do this quickly by means of the Format Document or Format Selection command on the Advanced submenu of the Edit menu.

2.3 Consecutive blank lines

Avoid two or more consecutive blank lines. Screen estate is too precious to be wasted. If necessary, use a commented line of dashes or asterisks to separate clearly two sections of the same source file.

2.4 Line length

Manually wrap lines that are longer than 80 characters.

Alternate rule: Manually wrap lines that are longer than the number of characters that fit in your editor window. This value depends on many factors, such as screen resolution, editor font size, and position and size of docked windows in Visual Studio .NET.

More details: Of course, it isn't really important which value you opt for when deciding how long your code lines can be, as long as all the developers on the team agree on such a unique value.

Tip: You can use the Ctrl+R, Ctrl+R key combination to quickly enable and disable word wrapping in the Visual Studio .NET code editor. (This shortcut corresponds to the Word Wrap command on the Advanced submenu of the Edit menu.)

2.5 Line wrapping

Use the following guidelines when deciding where to insert a carriage return character to split a long statement:

   a. Break a long line after a comma but before an operator, if possible. Beginning a physical line with an operator makes it clear that it is the result of a statement splitting.

    b. Avoid wrapping a line in the middle of an expression, especially if in the middle of a parenthesized expression.

    c. Try to keep all items at a given logical nesting level on the same physical line.

    d. Don't create excessively long lines if you later need to split them. For example, consider using temporary variables to reduce expression complexity.

    e. Indent all wrapped lines by one tab.

```
' [Visual Basic]
' *** Wrong: splits a parenthesized expression, leaves the operator on first line.
result = DoSomething(first, second * (third + _
    fourth))

' *** Both correct, the second one is better.
result = DoSomething(first, second _
    * (third + fourth))
result = DoSomething(first, _
    second * (third + fourth))

// [C#]
// *** Wrong: splits a parenthesized expression, leaves the operator on the first line.
result = DoSomething(first, second * (third +
    fourth));

// *** Both correct, the second one is better.
result = DoSomething(first, second
    * (third + fourth));
result = DoSomething(first,
    second * (third + fourth));
```

More details: This rule doesn't apply to statements that contain attributes (see rule 11.1).

Exception: As an exception to point e in the preceding list, Visual Basic developers might consider indenting all lines after the first one by two tabs if the next physical statement is indented by one level, as in the following example:

```
' [Visual Basic]
Public Sub PerformTask(ByVal id As Integer, ByVal userName As String, _
        ByVal password As String)          ' Indented by two tabs.
    ' Here goes the body of this method.
End Sub
```

C# developers don't need to take this case into account because they can use an open curly brace to avoid the ambiguity, as in this code:

```
// [C#]
public void PerformTask(int id, string userName,
    string password)
{
    // Here goes the body of this method.
}
```

2.6 Curly braces [C#]

Type open and close curly braces on a line of their own at the same indenting level as the preceding statement.

```
// [C#]
void PerformTask(int x)
{
    if ( x > 0 )
    {
        ...
    }
    else
    {
        ...
    }
}
```

Alternate rule: Type open curly braces on the same line as the statement that defines the block.

```
// [C#]
void PerformTask(int x) {
    if ( x > 0 ) {
        ...
    }
    else {
        ...
    }
}
```

```
// Also OK, if/else is even more concise.
void PerformTask(int x) {
    if ( x > 0 ) {
        ...
    } else {
        ...
    }
}
```

More details: Deciding between these styles is a matter of personal preference, and we found that many C# developers have very strong opinions about which one is better. The developers' team at Code Architects has standardized on having curly braces on a line of their own, a style that delivers more readable code, and we adopt this style throughout this book. However, you should consider the alternative style if you like concise code and want to maximize the number of statements that are visible in the editor window at any given moment.

Exception: See rule 13.3 for a more compact style that can be used with simple properties.

2.7 Spaces and operators [C#]

Leave one space before and after binary operators such as + and *. Leave one space after commas and semicolons.

```
// [C#]
// *** OK
int x=y+GetValue(y,2);

// *** Better
int x = y + GetValue(y, 2);
```

2.8 Spaces and parentheses [C#]

Add one space after the opening parenthesis and before the closing parenthesis in *if*, *while*, *for*, *foreach*, *switch*, and *lock* statements.

```
// [C#]
// *** OK
while (x == 0)
{}

// *** Better
while ( x == 0 )
{}
```

Chapter 3
Comments

The single factor that can improve code readability more than anything else is the presence of an adequate quantity of comments. Without good comments, it is nearly impossible to understand what a type or a method does. All this considered, it is surprising that most software shops don't adopt any recommendations or guidelines about remarks.

In this chapter, we have gathered a few suggestions that we think can greatly improve the quality of your code and the companion documentation. Some are obvious, some are not, but all of them have been tested in the field. And we also illustrate a few freeware products that nicely complement the excellent features of Microsoft Visual Studio .NET in this area.

3.1 Spell checking and comments

Always spell check all the text in comments.

More details: You might consider using the Spell Checker add-in for Visual Studio .NET 2003, a freeware utility by Dean J. Giovanelli. This tool enables you to spell check both remarks and quoted strings; supports Visual Basic, C#, C++, J#, HTML, XML, and text files; and comes with an integrated and extensible dictionary. You can download it from *www.dotnet2themax.com/goto/SpellCheckerAddin.aspx*.

3.2 Language used for comments

Favor using U.S. English for comments—or, at least, standardize on one language to be used for all comments.

Why: Using one language for all the comments in the application enables you to use automatic spell-checking techniques more easily (see rule 3.1).

3.3 Consistent comment style

Use a consistent imperative comment style. *Imperative* style means that comments sound like commands that you give to the code, as in "Evaluate the application statistics."

Alternative rule: Use a consistent descriptive comment style. *Descriptive* style means that comments sound like descriptions of what the code is doing and uses the singular third person (where the explicit or implicit subject is the code), as in "Evaluates the application statistics."

More details: As with many coding guidelines, it doesn't really matter whether you choose imperative or descriptive comment style as long as you are consistent throughout your code. By mixing different comment styles, you can easily create confusion and, in some cases, make your comments obscure or ambiguous.

3.4 Comment position and indentation

A comment uses the same indenting level as the code block it is related to and immediately precedes that code, without any intervening blank lines.

```vb
' [Visual Basic]
' *** Wrong: not indented and with a blank line
For i As Integer = 0 To arr.Length - 1
' Initialize the array element.

    arr(i) = i
Next

' *** Correct
For i As Integer = 0 To arr.Length - 1
    ' Initialize the array element.
    arr(i) = i
Next
```

```csharp
// [C#]
// *** Wrong: not indented and with a blank line
for ( int i = 0; i <= arr.Length ; i++ )
{
// Initialize the array element.

    arr[i] = i;
}

// *** Correct
for ( int i = 0; i <= arr.Length; i++ )
{
    // Initialize the array element.
    arr[i] = i;
}
```

3.5 XML comments [C#]

Use XML comments to document all public types and their public members in class libraries, Windows Forms control projects, and ASP.NET Web control projects. Use standard class- and method-level comments (as described in rule 3.9) for types and methods that aren't visible from outside the current project, such as types in executable files with the .exe file extension and private types and members in DLL projects.

Why: XML comments have two remarkable advantages. First, you can easily generate an XML documentation file by enabling the XML Documentation File option on the Build page of the Project Properties dialog box (see the right portion of Figure 1-5). By deploying this file in the same directory as the DLL executable, developers using your types or controls can read your comments in Visual Studio .NET's Object Browser (see Figure 3-1). The second advantage is that you can then use the NDoc to create the technical documentation of your class library or control (see rule 3.7).

Why not: The main issues of XML comments are that they take a lot of space on the screen and make comments less readable. However, you can collapse XML comment blocks and display them only when really necessary, so the first issue is rarely a serious problem.

You might want to enable the XML Documentation File option only in release mode, not to slow down all the compilations you run while in the debug and test phases.

```csharp
// [C#]
/// <summary>
/// Send an e-mail message.
/// </summary>
/// <param name="to">The name of person the mail is sent to.</param>
/// <param name="from">The name of sender.</param>
/// <param name="msgText">The text of the message</param>
/// <returns>true if message could be sent.</returns.>
public bool SendMail(string to, string from, string msgText)
{
    ...
}
```

Alternate rule: In a more radical approach, you might use XML comments to document *all* types and all members in the application, including types and members that aren't visible from other assemblies. This alternative guideline can be more convenient if you use the NDoc utility to produce technical documentation for all the types and members in your application (not just the public ones), which might be a requirement if you are a contractor or work for government agencies.

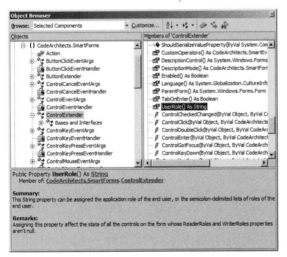

Figure 3-1   The XML documentation for Code Architects' Form Maximizer for .NET control library (*http://www.dotnet2themax.com/formmaximizer*) as displayed in the Object Browser

3.6 XML comments in separate files [C#]

Consider using an <include> tag in XML comments that points to an external .xml file containing the actual descriptions.

Why: Keeping XML comments in a separate file reduces clutter in your source files and enables two developers on the team to work on the main source file and on the XML documentation at the same time.

Why not: If you move XML comments to a separate file, you might need to add regular comments to explain what a type or a method does.

More details: Many developers strongly advise against XML comments in separate files because this technique might encourage bad and broken comments and because an additional effort to keep the two files in sync is required. As we do many times elsewhere in this book, we are listing both choices and leave the final decision to you.

How to: Here's an example of how to use the <include> tag. First, prepare an XML file named docs.xml containing the following text:

```
<?xml version="1.0" encoding="utf-8" ?>
<MyDocs>
    <Doc name="Customer">
        <summary>
            A customer type.
        </summary>
    </Doc>

    <Doc name="Order">
        <summary>
            An order type.
        </summary>
        <remarks>
            This class describes an order and allows you to save it to the data store,

            and optionally send notifications to the admin.

        </remarks>

        <Doc name="ID">
            <summary>
                The order's ID.
            </summary>
            <remarks>
                The ID is autogenerated when a new instance of Order is created.
            </remarks>
        </Doc>

        <Doc name="Description">
            <summary>
                The order's description.
            </summary>
        </Doc>
```

```
    <Doc name="Save">
      <summary>
         Saves the order to the data store.
      </summary>
      <param name="sendNotification">
         Specified whether a notification e-mail is sent to the store's administrator.
      </param>
      <returns>
         A Boolean value indicating whether the operation was completed successfully.
      </returns>
      <example>
         <b>Visual Basic .NET</b>
         <pre>
         Dim o As New Order()<br/>
         o.Description = "My order 1"<br/>
         Dim res As Boolean = o.Save(True)<br/>
         </pre>
         <b>C#</b>
         <pre>
         Order o = new Order();<br/>
         o.Description = "My order 2";<br/>
         bool res = o.Save(true);<br/>
         </pre>
      </example>
    </Doc>
  </Doc>
</MyDocs>
```

As you can see, XML comments support quite a rich grammar and you can even include pieces of HTML text, for example, to include examples in one or more languages.

Here's how you can reference individual descriptions in this XML file from a C# source file:

```
// [C#]
/// <include file='docs.xml' path='MyDocs/Doc[@name="Customer"]/*' />
public class Customer
{
   ...
}

/// <include file='docs.xml' path='MyDocs/Doc[@name="Order"]/*' />
public class Order
{
   public Order() {}

   private Guid _ID = Guid.NewGuid();
   /// <include file='docs.xml' path='MyDocs/Doc[@name="Order"]/Doc[@name="ID"]/*' />
   public Guid ID
   {
      get { return _ID; }
   }

   private string _Description = "";
```

```
/// <include file='docs.xml'
/// path='MyDocs/Doc[@name="Order"]/Doc[@name="Description"]/*' />
public string Description
{
    get { return _Description; }
    set { _Description = value; }
}

/// <include file='docs.xml' path='MyDocs/Doc[@name="Order"]/Doc[@name="Save"]/*' />
public bool Save(bool sendNotification)
{
    // Do something here...
    return true;
}
}
```

Names used for outer tags in the XML file (MyDocs and Doc, in this example) are arbitrary. You can use any name you wish, as long as you provide the correct XPath expression that locates them in the path attribute of the <include> tag.

As with standard XML comments, you must enable the XML Documentation File option on the Build page of the Project Properties dialog box (see bottom portion of Figure 1-5) and recompile the project.

3.7 Producing technical documentation

Use the NDoc utility to produce technical documentation for all the public types and methods in your application (more in general, for all the types and members that you have documented by means of XML comments).

More details: NDoc is a freeware utility that takes one or more Microsoft .NET assemblies and the file containing XML comments and produces documentation in MSDN or HTML Help 2 style, plus other styles (see Figure 3-2). The MSDN documenter creates documentation that is similar to the one that Microsoft uses for the .NET Framework (see Figure 3-3), whereas the HTML documenter generates documentation that can be viewed directly from within Visual Studio .NET 2003. NDoc automatically generates links between a class and its base classes and interfaces and links to types referenced as input or return value by a method or property. It lists inherited members and their descriptions and generates the type/member's signature in both Visual Basic and C# code. It even supports tags in addition to those recognized by the C# compiler, such as the <exclude> tag. Visit *ndoc.sourceforge.net/* to download the latest version of NDoc and read more about its features and options.

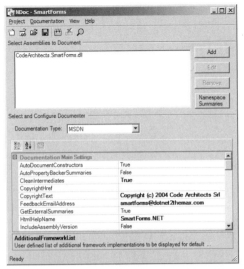

Figure 3-2   NDoc's easy-to-use and intuitive user interface

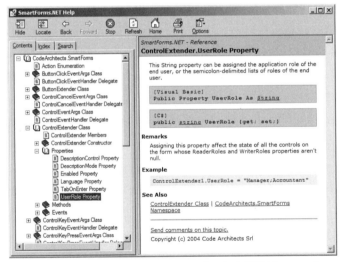

Figure 3-3   The technical documentation in MSDN format that we produced with NDoc for Code Architects' Forms Maximizer for .NET control library

3.8 The VBCommenter add-in [Visual Basic]

Consider using the VBCommenter add-in (*www.gotdotnet.com/team/ide/*) to add the XML documentation file to all types and members, or just public types and members that can be used by other developers.

More details: Visual Basic .NET 2005, in beta as of this writing, supports XML Documentation file. The VBCommenter add-in adds similar capabilities to Visual Basic .NET 2003.

See also: See rules 3.5 and 3.7 for more details on the advantages of XML comments.

3.9 Class- and method-level comments

Add a comment before the definition of a class or a method separated from the class/method code by a blank line. The comment should explain what the class or method does and, in the latter case, what each argument is and what the method returns. Consider using lines of dashes or asterisks to make these comments more visible.

More details: C# developers should ignore this rule in class and control libraries, and even in other types of applications if they decided to follow the alternate version of rule 3.5. Visual Basic developers should ignore this rule if they decided to use XML comments and rely on the VB Commenter add-in (see rule 3.8) to create the documentation for their code.

```vb
' [Visual Basic]
' ----------------------------------------------------
' The User class holds data about a user in the system.
' ----------------------------------------------------

Public Class Person

    ' ------------------------------------------------
    ' Return the complete name of this person.
    ' ------------------------------------------------

    Public Function CompleteName() As String
        ...
    End Function


    ...
End Class
```

```csharp
// [C#]
// ----------------------------------------------------
// The User class holds data about a user in the system.
// ----------------------------------------------------

public class Person
{
    // ------------------------------------------------
    // Return the complete name of this person.
    // ------------------------------------------------

    public string CompleteName()
    {
        ...
    }


    ...
}
```

3.10 Block comments [C#]

Avoid /* */ comments that interrupt the stream of executable code. Optionally, use block comments for comments that span more than three lines.

```
// [C#]
// *** Wrong
void EvalStats(DateTime start /* start of period */,
   DateTime end /* end of period */)
{}

// *** Correct
void EvalStats(DateTime start,      // Start of period
   DateTime end                     // End of period
)
{}

// *** Also correct
/* ****************************************************
 * Evaluate the statistics for the application
 * in the [start,end] date range.
 * ***************************************************/
void EvalStats(DateTime start, DateTime end)
{}

// *** Also correct
// ****************************************************
// Evaluate the statistics for the application
// in the [start,end] date range.
// ***************************************************/
void EvalStats(DateTime start, DateTime end)
{}
```

3.11 File header comments

Consider placing a standard block of comments at the top of all source files. These comments can include a copyright notice, the author's name, the creation date, and so forth. Wrap the comments block with a *#region* directive so that you can easily collapse it and keep it out of sight.

```
' [Visual Basic]
#Region "Copyright Code Architects Srl 2004"
' All rights reserved. Reproduction or transmission of this file, or a portion thereof,
' is forbidden without prior written permission of Code Architects Srl.

' Author: Giuseppe Dimauro
' Date: September 9, 2004
#End Region

// [C#]
#region Copyright Code Architects Srl 2004
/*
 * All rights reserved. Reproduction or transmission of this file, or a portion thereof,
 * is forbidden without prior written permission of Code Architects Srl.
 *
 * Author: Giuseppe Dimauro
 * Date: September 9, 2004
 */
#endregion
```

3.12 Block-level comments

Always describe what a block of statements does, but avoid obvious remarks. Ideally, there should be a line of comments every four to six executable statements.

3.13 Statement-level comments

Avoid statement-level comments (that is, comments on the same line and to the right of executable code), unless you are explaining what a variable or an argument does.

```
' [Visual Basic]
' *** Wrong
Do Until dr.Read()        ' Read all records.
   ...
Loop

' *** Correct
' Read all records .
Do Until dr.Read()
   ...
Loop

' *** Correct
Dim inFile As String      ' Input file
Dim outFile As String     ' Output file

// [C#]
// *** Wrong
while ( dr.Read() )        // Read all records.
{
   ...
}

// *** Correct
// Read all records
while ( dr.Read() )
{
   ...
}

// *** Correct
string inFile;            // Input file
string outFile;          // Output file

// *** Correct
EvalStats(hireDate,      // Begin of period
   DateTime.Now,         // End of period
   true                  // true = show details
   );
```

3.14 Comments at the end of long blocks

Consider adding a remark to the right of the *End* closing statement (Visual Basic) or the closing curly brace (C#) of a block that is longer than 20 lines.

Why: These additional remarks make it easier to follow the flow of execution, even for blocks longer than the number of lines that can be displayed on the screen at one time. The technique is especially effective for C#, which uses a curly brace to close all types of blocks (*if, switch, using, lock, for, while,* etc.).

```vb
' [Visual Basic]
Public Sub PerformTask(ByVal text() As String)
   If Not text Is Nothing Then
      For Each t As String In text
         ...
         ' A lot of statements here...
         ...
      Next      ' For Each t As String In Text
      ...
      ' More statements here...
      ...
   End If     ' If Not text Is Nothing
   ...
   ' More statements here...
   ...
End Sub      ' Sub PerformTask
```

```csharp
// [C#]
public void PerformTask(string[] text)
{
   if ( text != null )
   {
      foreach (string t in text)
      {
         ...
         // A lot of statements here...
         ...
      }        // foreach (string t in text)
      ...
      // More statements here...
      ...
   }          // if ( text != null )
   ...
   // More statements here...
   ...
}            // void PerformTask
```

3.15 Comments for overloaded methods

Don't repeat the same comment for all the versions of an overloaded method. Just use a thorough description for the version with more arguments and include a short comment at the top of simpler methods.

Exception: You can't adopt this technique if you're using XML comments; otherwise, the compiler (for C#) or the external tool (for Visual Basic; see rule 3.8) would create the documentation for just one of the methods in the group.

3.16 Comments for autogenerated code

If you generate code automatically with a tool, include a comment at the top of the source file that clearly explains how the code was created and that it shouldn't be manually edited. A majority of code generators create such header comments automatically. For example, this is the comment that the DataSet designer generates for DataSet types.

```
' [Visual Basic]
' ----------------------------------------------------------------
'  <autogenerated>
'     This code was generated by a tool.
'     Runtime Version: 1.1.4322.573
'
'     Changes to this file may cause incorrect behavior and will
'     be lost if the code is regenerated.
'  </autogenerated>
' ----------------------------------------------------------------

// [C#]
//----------------------------------------------------------------
// <autogenerated>
//     This code was generated by a tool.
//     Runtime Version: 1.1.4322.573
//
//     Changes to this file may cause incorrect behavior and will
//     be lost if the code is regenerated.
// </autogenerated>
//----------------------------------------------------------------
```

3.17 Remarks for commenting out code [C#]

Use single-line comments rather than block comments to comment out a block of code. The // symbol should appear in the first column to make it clear that this isn't a standard comment.

How to: Visual Studio .NET lets you comment and uncomment a selected block of lines by means of two commands on the Advanced submenu of the Edit menu. These commands correspond to the Ctrl+K, Ctrl+C and Ctrl+K, Ctrl+U key combinations, respectively. (Buttons for these commands are also available on the Text Editor toolbar.)

3.18 TODO and HACK comment tokens

Use TODO comment tokens to mark unfinished portions of your code and HACK tokens to tag portions of code that use undocumented or hard-to-read techniques so that you (or another developer on the team) can refine the code later.

Why: You can display these special comment tokens by right-clicking the Task List window and selecting either the Policy or the All command from the Show menu. (See Figure 3-4.)

```
' [visual Basic]
' TODO: Add validation code here.
...

' HACK: Use of undocumented .NET class here.
...

// [C#]
// TODO: Add validation code here.
...

// HACK: Use of undocumented .NET class here.
...
```

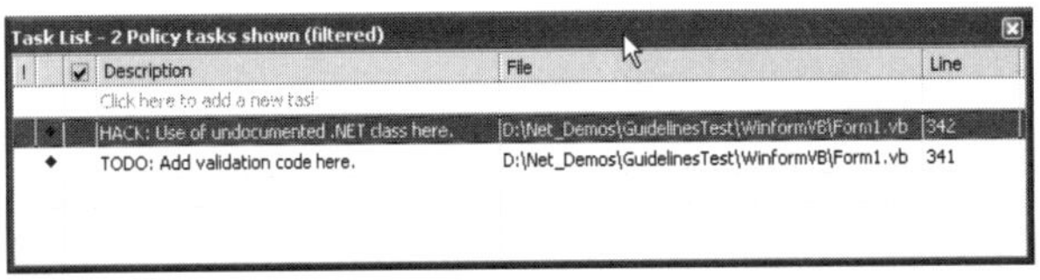

Figure 3-4   TODO and HACK comments in the Task List window. You can navigate to the actual position in the source file by double-clicking the comments.

3.19 Custom policy comment tokens

Consider extending the set of policy comment tokens that are recognized by Visual Studio .NET. For example, you might add the DOC token for code that needs to be better documented, TEST for code that needs to be tested, VALIDATE for code that lacks input argument validation, and OPTIMIZE for code that needs to be fine-tuned.

How to: You can define new policy comment tokens on the Task List page of the Options dialog box from the Tools menu (see Figure 3-5). If you add custom policy tokens, it is essential that they are recognized by all the Visual Studio .NET installed copies in your company.

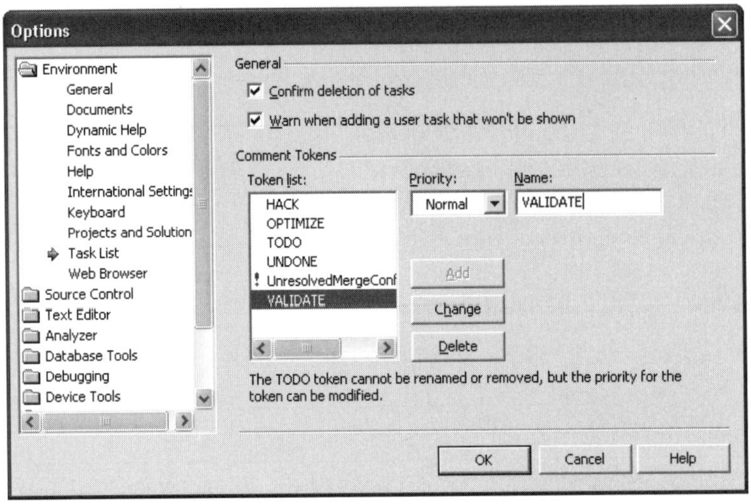

Figure 3-5   The Task List page, after adding a couple of custom policy comment tokens, in the Options dialog box that you can reach from the Tools menu

Chapter 4
Assemblies and Resources

Assemblies are the smallest units of versioning and deployment in the Microsoft .NET Framework, and for this reason it is essential that you decide correctly how to organize your applications in one or more assemblies, how you use version numbers, and how to embed resources in the application's executable files, including strings, images, icons, and sound and video files.

The .NET Framework also supports a special type of assemblies, the so-called *satellite assemblies*, that are meant to contain only resources. In this chapter, you'll see how to create such satellite assemblies from Microsoft Visual Studio .NET and how to reference them from the main application.

> **Note**   One or more code examples in this chapter assume that the following namespaces have been imported by means of *Imports* (Visual Basic) or *using* (C#) statements:
>
> ```
> System
> System.Globalization
> System.IO
> System.Reflection
> System.Resources
> ```

4.1 The AssemblyInfo file

Don't place any assembly-level attribute outside AssemblyInfo.vb or AssemblyInfo.cs files. Don't place any executable code in these files.

4.2 Strong names

Always sign your assemblies with a strong name. This rule applies to both DLL and EXE executables.

How to: Specify the path of your company's .snk file in the AssemblyKeyFile attribute in AssemblyInfo.vb or AssemblyInfo.cs.

Why: This rule offers several long-term advantages: you can register the assembly in the global assembly cache (GAC); the .NET runtime can detect whether the assembly has been tampered with; assemblies called by your assembly can check the caller's identity. Finally, if you use the assembly in a Smart Client application, a strong name enables the administrator of the client computer to relax Code Access Security (CAS) policy for only that specific assembly (or for all the assemblies from your company).

More details: The strong name of an assembly includes the assembly name, version, culture, and publisher's key. If you change any of these values and recompile, the new assembly has a different name (and therefore a different identity, as far as the .NET Framework is concerned).

You can generate the .snk file holding private and public keys of your company by running the SN command-line tool with the -k options. (You find this tool in the C:\Program Files\ Microsoft Visual Studio .NET 2003\SDK\v1.1\Bin directory.)

4.3 Assembly size

In general, favor few large assemblies to many smaller ones. If you have a group of types that are always loaded and used together, place them in the same assembly. If you have two or more assemblies that are always loaded and used together, merge them in a single assembly.

Why: The .NET runtime loads a large assembly faster than several smaller assemblies. A single, larger assembly creates a smaller working set of the application, and Ngen can optimize it more effectively (see rule 4.14).

Why not: You might need to split a larger assembly into multiple smaller ones if the types in it need to be assigned different identities or different trust levels.

Another reason for splitting large DLL assemblies is when building Smart Client applications (a.k.a. Forms-over-HTTP applications). The first time the main application references a type in the DLL, the .NET runtime downloads this DLL to the client's machine. By using many smaller DLL assemblies, you can improve the application's perceived speed.

4.4 Multimodule assemblies

Avoid multimodule assemblies. In most practical cases, you can deploy a Windows Forms application as one main EXE assembly plus zero or more DLL assemblies, without having to create multimodule assemblies.

Why: Compiling these assemblies requires that you link the separate modules using the command-line AL tool, a practice that slows down the build process. (You can't compile a multimodule assembly from inside Visual Studio .NET.)

Why not: The main advantage of having a single assembly made of multiple modules instead of multiple distinct assemblies is that types marked as *internal* (C#) or *Friend* (Visual Basic) are visible by types in other modules. If you have distinct assemblies, you must mark these types as *Public* to make them callable by another assembly, but in this case you can't easily prevent other assemblies from using your types (see rule 33.15).

Exceptions: Multimodule assemblies are necessary when you absolutely must merge modules written in different programming languages in one assembly. However, in such cases you might consider the opportunity of splitting the application into distinct assemblies (one per language), as discussed in rule 4.3.

4.5 CLS-compliant assemblies

Mark the assembly with a CLSCompliant attribute in a class library project to ensure that all its types and members are compliant with the Common Language Specification (CLS) and can be called by any other .NET language.

Why: A CLS-compliant assembly can be accessed by multiple languages.

How to: Visual Studio .NET automatically adds this attribute when you create a new project, so in practice you just need to ensure that you don't accidentally delete it.

More details: The current version of the Visual Basic compiler doesn't actually emit any warning for non-CLS-compliant types or members; therefore, this attribute is currently useless inside Visual Basic libraries.

```
' [Visual Basic]
' Inside AssemblyInfo.vb
' NOTE: This attribute is currently useless.
<Assembly: CLSCompliant(True)>

 // [C#]
// Inside AssemblyInfo.cs
[assembly: CLSCompliant(true)]
```

4.6 Assembly versioning

Edit the AssemblyVersion("1.0.*") attribute that Visual Studio .NET creates in Assembly-Info.vb or AssemblyInfo.cs, and mark the assembly with a specific version number. Change the version number when you publish a new version of the assembly (that is, when you deploy the assembly to your customers' sites).

Why: The version number concurs to create the strong name of an assembly (see rule 4.2). If you omit the AssemblyVersion attribute, the assembly has no version. If you use an asterisk in the version number, the version number changes each time you recompile the assembly, and so does the assembly's identity.

If the assembly's identity changes at each recompilation, you must recompile all the client assemblies as well. Also, the identity of a given type changes if the enclosing assembly's version number changes. Therefore, you have problems when deserializing an object that was serialized by a previous version of the same assembly.

```
' [Visual Basic]
' *** Wrong
<Assembly: AssemblyVersion("1.0.*")>

' *** Correct, but remember to change as needed.
<Assembly: AssemblyVersion("1.0.0.0")>

 // [C#]
// *** Wrong
[assembly: AssemblyVersion("1.0.*")]

// *** Correct, but remember to change as needed.
[assembly: AssemblyVersion("1.0.0.0")]
```

4.7 Manifest resources vs. stand-alone files

Favor using embedded resources for read-only data that will never change during the application's lifetime cycle. Use separate files to store data that the application can modify or that you might want to deploy independently of the main application.

Why: Resources that are embedded in the main assembly's manifest can be located and loaded faster and are protected from accidental deletion. On the other hand, these resources can't be deployed separately and the code in your application can't modify them.

Why not: Don't use the technique discussed in this guideline for resources that are locale-dependent and that should be localized for each different language that you plan to support. (See rule 4.9 for these localized resources.)

How to: You can embed any data file—including text files and images—in the assembly's manifest by following these simple steps:

1. Drag the file from Windows Explorer into the Solution Explorer window to include the file in the project. If the file is already in the project's directory, click the Show All Files button on the Solution Explorer toolbar, right-click the file icon, and select the Include In Project command.

2. Select the file in the Solution Explorer, and press the F4 key (or click the Properties button on the Solution Explorer toolbar) to display the properties of that file.

3. Change the Build Action property from Content to Embedded Resource (see Figure 4-1).

Figure 4-1   The properties of a file include the action to be performed at build time (can be None, Compile, Content, or Embedded Resource).

Example: The following code shows how you can access programmatically a text file named Data.txt from inside an assembly whose default namespace (a.k.a. root namespace in Visual Basic) is CodeArchitects.

```
' [Visual Basic]
Dim resFile As String = "CodeArchitects.Data.txt"
' Get a reference to the current assembly.
Dim asm As [Assembly] = [Assembly].GetExecutingAssembly()
Dim stream As Stream = asm.GetManifestResourceStream(resFile)
' Read the contents of the embedded file, then close it.
Dim reader As New StreamReader(stream)
```

```
Dim text As String = reader.ReadToEnd()
reader.Close()

// [C#]
string resFile = "CodeArchitects.Data.txt";
// Get a reference the current assembly.
Assembly asm = Assembly.GetExecutingAssembly();
Stream stream = asm.GetManifestResourceStream(resFile);
// Read the contents of the embedded file, then close it.
StreamReader reader = new StreamReader(stream);
string text = reader.ReadToEnd();
reader.Close();
```

The name of a resource is formed by the assembly's default namespace (C#) or root namespace (Visual Basic), followed by the filename and extension (without the path). However, if the resource file is stored in a project's folder (see rule 1.5), the rule for forming the resource name depends on the language in use. The C# compiler generates a resource name that includes the folder's name, whereas the Visual Basic compiler ignores the folder and generates the name as if the resource were stored in the project's root folder. For example, if you move the Data.txt file to a project folder named TextFiles, the previous Visual Basic code snippet will continue to work as before, whereas you should edit the C# code as follows:

```
// [C#]
string resFile = "CodeArchitects.TextFiles.Data.txt";
// (The remainder of code example as before.)
```

An important detail: resource names are compared in case-sensitive mode. You can check the exact names of embedded resources by means of the Ildasm tool (see Figure 4-2) or programmatically with the Assembly.GetManifestResourceNames method, which returns a string array that contains the names of all the files you've embedded in the assembly, as well as one .resource file for each Windows Forms class in the application.

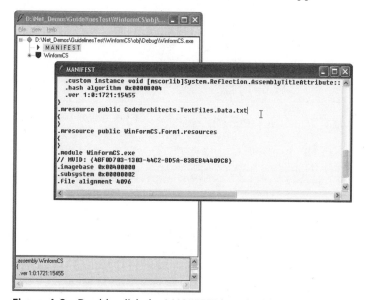

Figure 4-2 Double-click the MANIFEST item in Ildasm to display all the embedded resources of an assembly.

4.8 Resources vs. hard-coded string

Place all your user-interface strings in a resource file rather than burning them in code.

Why: Keeping all your strings in a centralized repository makes it simpler to spell check them or localize them to a different language.

How to: Follow this procedure to embed and use a set of string resources in your application.

1. Select the Add New Item command from the Project menu, highlight the Assembly Resource File element from the template gallery, type the name of the resource file you want to create, and click the Open button. (The following code assumes that the resource file is named Strings.resx.)

2. Create one or more string resources in the file you have just created (see Figure 4-3). You can assign each resource a name of your choice, but you might want to follow the guidelines in rule 4.9. Specify System.String as the type of each element.

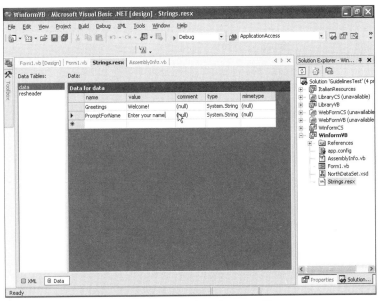

Figure 4-3   The Visual Studio .NET editor for .resx files

Here's how the application can reference a string stored as a resource in the Strings.resx file, assuming that the project's default namespace (C#) or root namespace (Visual Basic) is CodeArchitects:

```
' [Visual Basic]
Dim resFile As String = "CodeArchitects.Strings"
Dim resources As New ResourceManager(resFile, [Assembly].GetExecutingAssembly())
Dim greetings As String = resources.GetString("Greetings")

// [C#]
string resFile = "CodeArchitects.Strings";
ResourceManager resources = new ResourceManager(resFile, Assembly.GetExecutingAssembly());
string greetings = resources.GetString("Greetings");
```

It is usually a good idea to store the ResourceManager reference in a variable that can be accessed by the entire application so that you don't have to re-create it every time you need to retrieve a resource.

An important note: the filename passed to the ResourceManager constructor must be formed by concatenating the name of the project's default (root) namespace and the name of the resource file as it appears in the Solution Explorer window, but without the .resx extension. However, if the .resx file is stored in a project folder, naming rules depend on the language in use; for more information, please read the notes that follow the code example in rule 4.7. Unlike manifest resources, however, .resx files are searched in a case-insensitive way.

More details: Visual Studio .NET doesn't provide a tool to let you easily add nonstring resources to .resx files. However, you can use several freeware tools to add images, icons, video or sound files, or any other type of data to a resource file, for example, Lutz Roeder's Resourcer for .NET (*http://aisto.com/roeder/dotnet/*). The following code shows how you can display an image named Logo.bmp stored in a resource file named Bitmaps.resx:

```
' [Visual Basic]
Dim resFile As String = "CodeArchitects.Bitmaps"
Dim resources As New ResourceManager(resFile, [Assembly].GetExecutingAssembly())
PictureBox1.Image = DirectCast(resources.GetObject("Logo.bmp"), System.Drawing.Bitmap)
```

```
// [C#]
string resFile = "CodeArchitects.Bitmaps";
ResourceManager resources =
    new ResourceManager(resFile, Assembly.GetExecutingAssembly());
pictureBox1.Image = (System.Drawing.Bitmap) resources.GetObject("Logo.bmp");
```

4.9 Resource names

Use PascalCase for resource names. Generally follow the same naming guidelines that you use for a public field (see rules 6.2, 6.3, 6.4, and 12.1): use descriptive names, don't include spaces and punctuation symbols, don't begin the name with a digit, and avoid keyword names such as *Integer* or *long*. For example, CompanyName is a good resource name, whereas companyName and Company:Name aren't.

More details: You can include dots to specify the property of an object (e.g., lblPrompt.Text) or to separate elements in a hierarchy, such as Menus.Edit.Copy.Text.

4.10 Satellite assemblies with localized resources

Use satellite assemblies to hold all the strings and other resources (images, .wav files, and so on) that your main application uses. Satellite assemblies must be marked with an AssemblyCulture attribute, should contain no code, and their names should include the .resources word (as in MyApp.resources.dll for a resource file used by a main assembly named MyApp.dll).

How to: Follow this procedure to create one or more satellite assemblies with localized resources from inside Visual Studio .NET. (In this example, we are going to create a satellite assembly holding Italian resources for an application named MyApp.)

1. Create a new class library project, in the same solution as the main application or in a different solution. The name of this project isn't important, but you might want to use a name formed by appending the name of the main project and the culture identifier. (In this example, you might name the project as MyApp_it_IT because the satellite assembly will contain resources for the it-IT culture.) Delete the Class1.vb or Class1.cs file that Visual Studio .NET creates for a class library project.

2. On the General page of the new project, change the assembly name to match the name of the main application (MyApp, in this example), and change the default namespace (C#) or the root namespace (Visual Basic) to match the default or root namespace of the main application (see Figure 4-4). In this example, we assume that this namespace is CodeArchitects; more in general, it should match your company's name, as per rule 5.1.

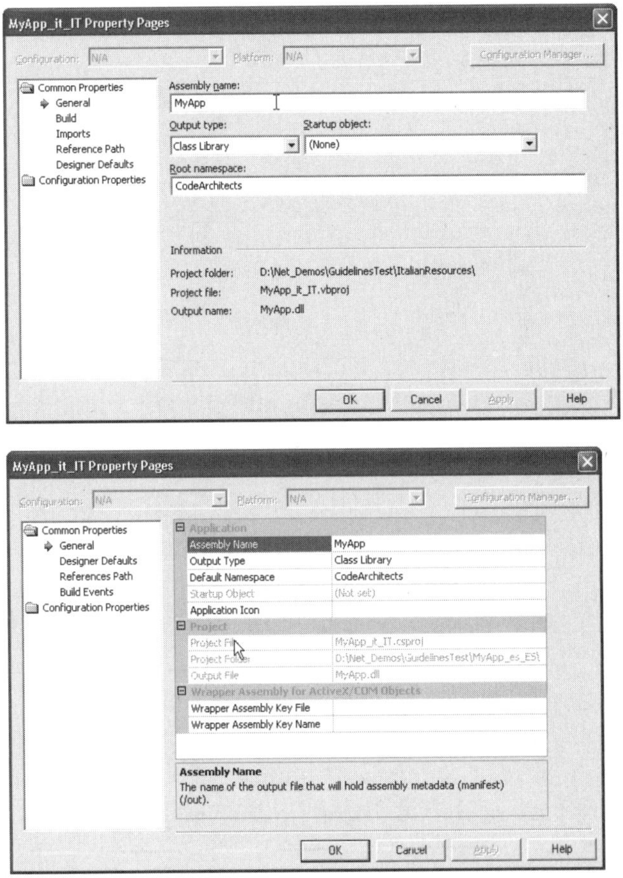

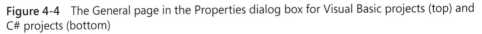

Figure 4-4   The General page in the Properties dialog box for Visual Basic projects (top) and C# projects (bottom)

3. On the Build page of the Project Properties dialog box (see Figure 1-5), change the Output path value to point to the subdirectory where the main application's assembly is created. For example, if the main project is stored in the C:\Projects\MyApp folder, the output directory for both the main and the satellite assemblies should be C:\Projects\MyApp\bin.

4. In the AssemblyInfo.vb or AssemblyInfo.cs file, add an AssemblyCulture attribute that specifies the culture of the satellite assembly.

```
' [Visual Basic]
<Assembly: AssemblyCulture("it-IT")>
```

```
// [C#]
[assembly: AssemblyCulture("it-IT")]
```

5. You are now ready to add one or more resources to the satellite assembly by following the procedure outlined in rule 4.8. However, it is essential that all the .resx files you create embed the culture name in their names. For example, a file containing all the Italian strings should be named Strings.it-IT.resx.

> **Note**   Don't place the resource file in a C# project subfolder. Placing a resource file in a subfolder of a C# project requires that you use a different name when referencing the resource file from the main application as explained at the end of rule 4.8.

You can now compile the satellite assembly as usual. Visual Studio .NET recognizes the AssemblyCulture attribute and correctly creates an assembly named MyApp.resources.dll. (The name of resource-only satellite assemblies must be in the form *MainAssemblyName*.resources.dll.) This assembly is created in a subdirectory named after the assembly culture under the folder you have specified in step 2: in this example, the path of such a folder is C:\Projects\MyApp\bin\it-IT. (This is the folder in which the .NET runtime will look for Italian resources.)

Notice that Visual Studio .NET also creates the "standard" MyApp.dll assembly in the Output folder you specified in step 2 (C:\Projects\MyApp\bin, in this example). This assembly contains no code and no resources and can be deleted before deploying the application.

You can now go back to the main application and write the code that uses the localized resource:

```
' [Visual Basic]
Dim resFile As String = "CodeArchitects.Strings"
Dim resources As New ResourceManager(resFile, [Assembly].GetExecutingAssembly())
Dim greetings As String = resources.GetString("Greetings")
// [C#]
string resFile = "CodeArchitects.Strings";
ResourceManager resources = new ResourceManager(resFile, Assembly.GetExecutingAssembly());
string greetings = resources.GetString("Greetings");
```

This code is exactly the same code that you use to access resources stored in the main application (see rule 4.8). To see how this code behaves on an Italian version of the Windows operating system, you must change the locale used for the current UI thread, which you do by running the following code *before* creating the ResourceManager object:

```
' [Visual Basic]
' Force usage of Italian resources.
Thread.CurrentThread.CurrentUICulture = New CultureInfo("it-IT")
```

```
// [C#]
// Force usage of Italian resources.
Thread.CurrentThread.CurrentUICulture = new CultureInfo("it-IT");
```

If you specify for the UI thread a locale for which you didn't provide any satellite assembly, the ResourceManager object will fall back to the Strings.resx resource file embedded in the main assembly. If this resource file is missing, an exception is thrown.

Interestingly, you can also retrieve a resource for a specific culture by passing a CultureInfo object to the GetString or GetObject method of the ResourceManager class, as in this code:

```
' [Visual Basic]
Dim esCi As New CultureInfo("es-ES")      ' Resources for Spanish.
Dim greetings As String = resources.GetString("Greetings", esCi)

// [C#]
CultureInfo esCi = new CultureInfo("es-ES");      // Resources for Spanish.
string greetings = resources.GetString("Greetings", esCi);
```

4.11 Culture for main assembly

Apply the NeutralResourcesLanguage attribute to the main assembly to inform the resource manager about the language for the neutral resources that are embedded in the main assembly.

Why: This attribute speeds up resource loading when the current user's locale matches the culture used for the resources in the main assembly.

```
' [Visual Basic]
' This main assembly contains resources for US English culture.
<Assembly: NeutralResourcesLanguage("en-US")>

// [C#]
// This main assembly contains resources for US English culture.
[assembly: NeutralResourcesLanguage("en-US")]
```

More details: Never use the AssemblyCultureAttribute in the main assembly. The main assembly should contain only neutral resources (e.g., strings and bitmaps related to the default language).

4.12 Configuration settings

Consider using the Microsoft Configuration Management Application Block to store and retrieve all your configuration settings.

Why: This library lets you store configuration settings in various data stores, such as the Windows registry, Microsoft SQL Server, or XML files, and enables you to add support for other storage types. It promotes location transparency (you can opt for a different data store at deployment time or runtime) and can save and load any object that can be serialized by means of the XmlSerializer type. It supports a set of optional features, including authentication (to ensure that data hasn't been tampered with), encryption (to keep data secret), and caching (to speed up access to data read frequently).

How to: You can download this library from MSDN at *http://msdn.microsoft.com/library/ default.asp?url=/library/en-us/dnbda/html/cmab.asp.*

More details: The .NET Framework programming guidelines recommend against storing data in the Windows registry or in INI files.

4.13 GAC registration

Carefully consider the pros and cons of registering your DLL assemblies in the GAC.

Why: The .NET runtime finds GAC assemblies more quickly and loads them faster because it doesn't have to check them for integrity. Also, assemblies in the GAC are protected from accidental deletes because only the Administrator can access the GAC directory.

Why not: Registration in the GAC makes deployment slightly more complicated because you can't rely on XCOPY deployment any longer. Also, you must remember to uninstall the previous version from the GAC before you recompile.

More details: Don't use the GAC with only the purpose of sharing one or more types among different applications because there are better ways to pursue this goal. For example, you can share a DLL assembly (including a private assembly) among different applications if all the applications' executable files are deployed in the same directory. Or you can reference a strong-named assembly that is located outside the application's main directory by means of a <codeBase> element in the application's configuration file. (See *http://msdn.microsoft.com/ library/en-us/cpgenref/html/gngrf/CodeBase* for more information.)

You can make GAC registration simpler by running the GacUtil utility from the External Tools command on the Tools menu, or you can create a Visual Studio .NET macro that automatically runs GacUtil after a successful compilation. C# developers can also run GacUtil by means of a postbuild event command defined on the Build Events page of the Project Properties dialog box (see Figure 4-5). Use the following command line to install the current assembly in the GAC after a successful build:

```
"C:\Program Files\Microsoft Visual Studio .NET
    2003\SDK\v.1.1\GacUtil.exe" /i $(TargetPath)
```

Note that the previous command has been split in two lines for typographical reasons. You must enter it as a single line in the Visual Studio .NET dialog box.

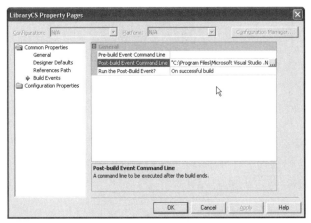

Figure 4-5   The Build Events page in the Properties dialog box of a C# project

4.14 The Ngen utility

Use Ngen to precompile Windows Forms applications and Windows Forms Control library DLLs. As a rule of thumb, don't use Ngen with other application types.

Why: Precompiling applications of these types can remarkably speed up loading time. Also, precompiled applications can run faster on computers with less RAM because the operating system can share a single copy of an Ngen-compiled assembly among different processes. (This optimization technique isn't possible with JIT-compiled assemblies.)

Why not: Ngen-compiled assemblies aren't as optimized as JIT-compiled assemblies and can run slower than standard.

More details: Each application reacts differently to Ngen compilation; therefore, you should always perform some benchmarks to see whether the Ngen-compiled version actually loads more rapidly and runs fast enough for your purposes. Note that Ngen supports multiple assemblies on its command line, as in the following:

```
Ngen mainapp.exe assembly1.dll assembly2.dll assembly3.dll
```

 When this syntax is used, Ngen compiles all the DLLs and optimizes them for executing in the main application's context, taking the application's configuration file into account.

 You can run the Ngen utility from the External Tools command on the Tools menu, or you can create a Visual Studio .NET macro that automatically runs Ngen after a successful compilation. C# developers can also run Ngen by means of a postbuild event command defined on the Build Events page of the Project Properties dialog box. (See rule 4.13 for an example of this technique.)

Chapter 5
Namespaces

All types live (or should live, at least) inside a namespace. However, you should keep in mind that the namespace is a programming language concept, not a Microsoft .NET Framework concept, at least in the sense that there is no keyword in the Intermediate Language (IL) that is similar to the *Namespace, Imports* (Visual Basic), *namespace*, or *using* (C#) keyword. When the compiler generates IL code, all types are referenced with their complete names.

Regardless of what happens to your namespaces when they are compiled, it is important that you organize your types in a logical namespace hierarchy, at the top of which there should be a namespace named after your company (see rule 5.1). Most other guidelines in this chapter are just recommendations and suggestions that don't impact performance or other essential features, yet they can be useful to reduce typing and make your code more readable.

5.1 Primary namespace name

The name of the default namespace (C#) or root namespace (Visual Basic) should match the name of the company (see Figure 4-4).

Example: CodeArchitects.

More details: Keep in mind that the name of the default or root namespace can affect the way the application uses or exposes its resources, as explained in rules 4.7 and 4.8.

5.2 Second-level namespace

The secondary namespace for classes in main executable projects (that is, the project that generates the main executable of a console, Windows Forms, or ASP.NET application) is the same as the name of the project itself.

Example: CodeArchitects.Invoicing.

5.3 Logical organization of types inside namespace

A namespace should contain types that are related to each other. A namespace should never contain types that are mutually exclusive and that are never used together in the same application, such as types used in either Windows Forms or ASP.NET applications.

5.4 Number of types in each namespace

Avoid namespaces with fewer than five types. If you end up with scarcely populated namespaces, consider merging two or more namespaces. However, don't define namespaces that contain types that are mutually exclusive (see rule 5.3).

5.5 Reduce namespace block nesting

Avoid nested namespace blocks. Instead, use disjointed namespace blocks and use dotted arguments.

Why: The purpose of this guideline is to avoid statements that are indented too much to the right and to reduce the need to scroll the page to see longer statements.

Example: The following code defines a type named Order in the CodeArchitects.Invoicing. BusinessObjects namespace. It assumes that the root namespace for the Visual Basic project is equal to CodeArchitects.

```
' [Visual Basic]
Namespace Invoicing.BusinessObjects
   Public Class Order
      ...
   End Class
End Namespace

// [C#]
namespace CodeArchitects.Invoicing.BusinessObjects
{
   public class Order
   {
      ...
   }
}
```

5.6 Types belong to namespaces

Always place a type inside a namespace block.

Why: Namespaces let you organize your types in a logical manner and help prevent name collisions.

More details: Visual Basic types always live in the project's root namespace, as defined on the General page of the Project Properties dialog box, so any nonempty value for such a root namespace automatically makes you comply with this rule. C# developers must abide by this rule by explicitly placing the type definition inside a *namespace* block.

5.7 One namespace for each source file

Don't define multiple namespace blocks inside a single source file.

Exception: See rules 8.2 and 10.1 for exceptions to this rule.

5.8 .NET Framework namespace naming conventions

If your types resemble a type defined in the .NET Framework, use the .NET namespace name, except use your company's name instead of System as the first-level namespace.

Example: Gather your Windows Forms custom controls in the *CompanyName*.Windows.Forms namespace, your custom Web controls in *CompanyName*.Web.UI.WebControls namespace, your utility types that work with the Microsoft SQL Server .NET Data Provider in the *CompanyName*.Data.SqlClient namespace, and so on.

5.9 Type dependency in nested namespaces

Types in a nested namespace can depend on types defined in the enclosing namespace. However, types in the enclosing namespace should never depend on—that is, derive from, take as an argument, or return as the result of a method—types defined in the nested namespace.

Example: Types in System.Web.UI.WebControls depend on types defined in System.Web.UI, but types in the latter namespace don't depend on types in the former namespace.

5.10 Nested namespaces for special types

Use the following guidelines for namespaces containing specific types:

   a. Modules and utility classes that might be easily reused in other applications by compiling them in a DLL or by adding them to a project by means of the Link File option in the Open dialog box (see rule 1.9) should be grouped in a second-level namespace named Utilities. Example: CodeArchitects.Utilities.

   b. Modules and utility classes that are unique to the current application and that can hardly be reused in other projects should be grouped in a third-level namespace named Helpers. Example: CodeArchitects.Invoicing.Helpers.

   c. Design-time types, such as types used to implement custom designers, should be grouped in a nested namespace named Design. Example: CodeArchitects.Windows.Forms.Design.

   d. Data object types and business object types in a project should be grouped in third-level namespaces named DataObjects and BusinessObjects, respectively. Example: CodeArchitects.Invoicing.DataObjects, CodeArchitects.Invoicing.BusinessObjects.

   e. Types that are public but that shouldn't be used by other assemblies should be grouped in a nested namespace named Internal. Example: CodeArchitects.Invoicing.Internal.

   f. Custom permission types should be grouped in a nested namespace named Permissions. Example: CodeArchitects.Invoicing.Permissions.

   g. Types that are used to configure your application should be grouped in a nested assembly named Configuration. Example: CodeArchitects.Invoicing.Configuration.

5.11 Namespace-qualified member types

Avoid fully qualified type names and make statements shorter by adding suitable *Imports* (Visual Basic) or *using* (C#) statements at the top of the source file. List all .NET Framework namespaces first and then namespaces imported from third-party libraries. Always list nested namespaces after their enclosing namespace.

```
' [Visual Basic]
Imports System.Security
Imports System.Security.Permissions     ' Nested namespace
Imports System.Text
Imports CodeArchitects.Utilities        ' 3rd-party namespace

// [C#]
using System.Security;
using System.Security.Permissions;      // Nested namespace
using System.Text;
using CodeArchitects.Utilities;         // 3rd-party namespace
```

5.12 Namespace aliasing

If you are using types with the same name from two different namespaces, alias both namespaces when importing them with an *Imports* (Visual Basic) or *using* (C#) statement.

Example: The .NET Framework contains the System.Windows.Forms.Control and the System.Web.UI.Control types. In some cases, for example, when writing a class library, you might need to work with both types, so you need to import both namespaces (according to rule 5.11). You might solve the ambiguity by aliasing just one of the two namespaces, but it is recommended that you alias both.

```
' [Visual Basic]
' *** OK: only one namespace is aliased.
Imports System.Windows.Forms
Imports Web = System.Web.UI
...
' Reference the two Control classes.
Dim c1 As Control       ' This is System.Windows.Forms.Control.
Dim c2 As Web.Control    ' This is System.Web.UI.Control.

' *** Better: both namespaces are aliased.
Imports Win = System.Windows.Forms
Imports Web = System.Web.UI
...
' Reference the two Control classes.
Dim c1 As Win.Control    ' This is System.Windows.Forms.Control.
Dim c2 As Web.Control    ' This is System.Web.UI.Control.

// [C#]
// *** OK: only one namespace is aliased.
using System.Windows.Forms;
using Web = System.Web.UI;
...
// Reference the two Control classes.
Control c1;        // This is System.Windows.Forms.Control.
Web.Control c2;    // This is System.Web.UI.Control.

// *** Better: both namespaces are aliased.
using Win = System.Windows.Forms;
using Web = System.Web.UI;
...
// Reference the two Control classes
Win.Control c1;    // This is System.Windows.Forms.Control.
Web.Control c2;    // This is System.Web.UI.Control.
```

Chapter 6
Types

A Microsoft .NET Framework type is a more general concept than a .NET class. More specifically, a class is what is also called a *reference type*, whereas a structure is known as a *value type*. The difference between these two flavors of the type concept is particularly important and is thoroughly explained in many articles and books. In this chapter, we focus on *when* you should render a type as a class or a structure and also cover many other guidelines related to types, including how to name them, how to group their members, how to apply scope qualifiers, and when to use nested types.

> **Note** One or more code examples in this chapter assume that the following namespace has been imported by means of an *Imports* (Visual Basic) or *using* (C#) statement:
>
> `System.Diagnostics`

6.1 Type names

Use the following guidelines for type names:

   a. Use PascalCase for type names. Example: Customer, ForeignCustomer.

   b. Don't use underscores inside type names.

   c. Try to avoid class and structure names with a leading I character to minimize confusion with interface types; use casing if you can't help having a name beginning with the I character. Example: Invoice.

6.2 U.S. English for identifiers

Use American English for type and member names. For example, use Color (U.S. English) rather than Colour (U.K. English).

Why: Developers outside the United States might consider this rule as quite arbitrary and too U.S.-centric, but it undoubtedly has one important benefit: type and member U.S. English names can look like names used in the .NET Framework, thus many developers will feel at ease with these identifiers.

6.3 Abbreviations and acronyms

Follow these guidelines to decide how you should render abbreviations and acronyms:

   a. Don't use abbreviations in type and member names.

b. Use acronyms only if they are well known among the developer community.

c. Use all-uppercase style for acronyms of two characters.

d. Use PascalCase for acronyms with three characters or more.

Example: UIThread, AsciiDocument, HtmlParser.

More details: Even though these guidelines come from Microsoft, notice that some class names in the .NET Framework incorrectly use uppercase for acronyms, for example, ASCIIEncoding and CLSCompliant.

6.4 Words to avoid

Avoid using the words listed in Table 6-1 as type or member names. The table includes all Visual Basic and C#, including keywords from their 2005 versions (in beta version as of this writing).

Table 6-1   Words to Avoid

abstract	AddHandler	AddressOf	Alias	And
AndAlso	Ansi	As	Assembly	Auto
Base	bool	Boolean	break	ByRef
Byte	ByVal	Call	Case	Catch
CBool	CByte	CChar	CDate	CDec
CDbl	Char	checked	CInt	Class
CLng	CObj	Const	continue	CSByte
CShort	CSng	CStr	CType	CUInteger
CULong	CUShort	Custom	Date	Decimal
Declare	Default	Delegate	Dim	Do
Double	Each	Else	ElseIf	End
Enum	Erase	Error	eval	Event
Exit	explicit	extends	extern	ExternalSource
False	Finalize	Finally	fixed	float
For	foreach	Friend	Function	Get
GetType	Global	Goto	Handles	If
Implements	implicit	Imports	In	Inherits
instanceof	int	Integer	Interface	internal
Is	IsFalse	IsNot	IsTrue	Let
Lib	Like	lock	Long	Loop
Me	Mod	Module	MustInherit	MustOverride
My	MyBase	MyClass	Namespace	Narrowing
New	Next	Not	Nothing	NotInheritable
NotOverridable	null	Object	Of	On

Table 6-1   Words to Avoid

operator	Option	Optional	Or	OrElse
out	Overloads	Overridable	override	Overrides
package	ParamArray	params	Partial	Preserve
Private	Property	Protected	Public	RaiseEvent
ReadOnly	ReDim	ref	Region	Rem
RemoveHandler	Resume	Return	sbyte	sealed
Select	Set	Shadows	Shared	Short
Single	sizeof	stackalloc	Static	Step
Stop	String	struct	Structure	Sub
switch	SyncLock	Then	this	Throw
To	True	Try	TryCast	TypeOf
uint	UInteger	ulong	ushort	unchecked
Unicode	unsafe	Until	using	var
virtual	void	volatile	When	While
Widening	With	WithEvents	WriteOnly	Xor
yield				

More details: You should also avoid names that match .NET Framework namespaces, such as System, Forms, Web, UI, Collections, Win32, and so on.

6.5 One type per source file

Each source file should contain only one type definition.

Exception: See rules 6.7, 8.2, and 10.1 for exceptions to this rule.

6.6 Type complexity

Consider splitting a type with many methods and properties into one main class and one or more dependent classes. A simple rule of thumb is to consider a type as a candidate for splitting when it exposes many properties or methods with similar names.

Why: Code in smaller types can be reused more easily.

Example: Let's say you have a Person class that exposes many similar properties such as HomeAddress, HomeCity, HomeZipCode, HomeState, and HomeCountry. Such an entity can be better represented by two distinct types, Person and Location, where Person exposes one property of type Location.

```
' [Visual Basic]
Public Class Person
   Public Property Home() As Location

     ...
   End Property
End Class
```

```
// [C#]
public class Person
{
    public Location Home
    {
        ...
    }
}
```

The benefit of having a separate Location type becomes apparent if you later decide to implement other similar properties, such as Work (for the office's address), Vacation, and so forth.

6.7 Dependency on external variables

Ensure that code inside a type doesn't reference any external variable, including global variables defined in a module (Visual Basic) or static fields or properties exposed by another type. All the values that a type needs should be assigned to the type's properties or passed as arguments to its constructors or methods.

Why: Self-containment is the key to code reuse: if the type doesn't depend on any other type, you can drop it in a different project with fewer or no side effects. Besides, the code in the type can't be broken by accidentally or purposely assigning an invalid value to the external variable, and you don't have to synchronize access to the global variable in a multithreaded environment.

Why not: In many complex object hierarchies, you must be prepared to relax this rule to an extent. For example, you might decide to have one class that contains all the configuration settings of the assembly, in which case many types in the assembly have to read values from static fields of the configuration class.

More details: If you can't help breaking this rule, you can at least ensure that external values are implemented as properties (as opposed to fields) so that you can validate them and ensure that they are never invalid. Also, if just two or three types depend on one another, you can mitigate this rule by having all of them stored in the same source file.

6.8 Module names [Visual Basic]

Don't use any special suffix or naming convention for Visual Basic modules.

Why: Modules are just types whose members are all static, so they shouldn't be dealt with in a different way.

6.9 App type or module

Use App name for the module (Visual Basic) or the class (C#) that contains the Main procedure. Don't place the Main procedure in a Windows Forms class.

6.10 Globals class

Use Globals for the type that contains all the global variables of the current application. Global variables are implemented as static fields of this type. (Visual Basic developers can also use a module.)

Why: References to those variables are in the form Globals.*VariableName* and are therefore more readable and easier to spot.

See also: See rule 6.7 about why you should avoid dependency on global variables. Visual Basic developers should also read rule 18.4 about referencing members of a module.

6.11 Member names from common interfaces

Avoid names used in common .NET interfaces if your property or method doesn't implement that interface.

Example: Examples of such methods are Count, Clone, Dispose, CompareTo, Compare, GetEnumerator, and GetObjectData.

6.12 Case sensitivity in member names [C#]

Never define public members using names that differ only in the casing of the characters. Private members using names that differ only in casing aren't recommended either.

Why: Names that differ only in their case make it harder to read the source code. In addition, if you have two or more public members that differ only in their casing, only one of them is visible to client applications written in Visual Basic or another case-insensitive .NET language.

Example: Examples of members that should be avoided are count and Count, UserName and userName.

6.13 Member ordering and grouping

Group members of the same kind (fields, properties, methods, etc.), and use a #region directive to collapse them easily. Always adopt the same order when defining members.

Example: Always define type members in this order:

1.   Event and delegate definitions
2.   Private and public fields, except those wrapped by properties (see rule 12.17)
3.   Constructors, including static constructors
4.   Instance public properties (and the private fields they wrap)
5.   Instance public methods

6. Static public methods and properties

7. Methods in interfaces

8. Private (helper) methods

6.14 Language-specific member types

Use the language-specific keywords when defining the type of fields, properties, and methods. For example, use *Integer* (Visual Basic) or *int* (C#) rather than Int32 or System.Int32.

Why: Developers feel it is more natural to use keywords that they know well. Besides, the Microsoft Visual Studio .NET code editor renders language-specific types with a different color, thus increasing code readability.

```
' [Visual Basic]
' *** OK
Dim total As Int32
' *** Better
Dim total As Integer
```

```
// [C#]
// *** OK
private Int32 total;
// *** Better
private int total;
```

Alternative rule: Many .NET developers prefer using names specific to .NET (e.g., Int32) in the definition of a field, property, method, or parameter. The rationale behind this guideline is that, everything being an object in the .NET Framework, integer and string values shouldn't be dealt with in any special way and shouldn't be rendered with a different color in the code editor. Arguably, this style makes the source code more readable for developers who work in other languages. Another good point in favor of this style is that it works well with methods whose names contain the name of the .NET type they return, as in this example:

```
' [Visual Basic]
' *** OK, but return type doesn't match suffix in method name.
Function GetDataInt32() As Integer
    ...
End Function
```

```
' *** Better
Function GetDataInt32() As Int32
    ...
End Function
```

```
// [C#]
// *** OK, but return type doesn't match suffix in method name.
public int GetDataInt32()
{}
```

```
// *** Better
public Int32 GetDataInt32()
{}
```

More details: Both guidelines have their merits; therefore, we list both of them. In this book, we have used language-specific types because we believe that most readers are more familiar with this style.

6.15 Nested types

Use a private or internal (*Friend* in Visual Basic) scope qualifier for nested types.

Why: A type should be nested if it is used only by the type that encloses it; therefore, in most cases there is no reason for making the nested type public.

Exception: Nested enumerators and comparers can be given public scope.

6.16 Member scope

Don't make a field, a property, or a method public if that isn't necessary. Mark it with the *Friend* (Visual Basic) or *internal* (C#) keyword if it isn't meant to be invoked from other assemblies; mark it as private if it isn't meant to be invoked from other types in the current assembly.

6.17 Explicit scope qualifier

Always explicitly use a scope keyword for all types and members.

Why: The default scope for Visual Basic type members is *Public*, whereas the default scope for C# is *private*. Omitting the scope keyword might disorient developers who are more familiar with other languages.

```
' [Visual Basic]
' *** OK
Sub PerformTask()
   ...
End Sub

' *** Better
Public Sub PerformTask()
   ...
End Sub

// [C#]
// *** OK
void PerformTask()
{}

// *** Better
private void PerformTask()
{}
```

More details: Visual Basic developers shouldn't use the *Dim* keyword to define type-level fields because this keyword implies a private scope if used inside a class, but it implies a public scope if used inside a structure. Favor using explicit *Private* and *Public* keywords so that you can later change the class to a structure (and vice versa) with minimal impact on the remainder of the application.

```
' [Visual Basic]
' *** Wrong
Structure Person
   Dim FirstName As String       ' These are public fields.
   Dim LastName As String
End Function

' *** Better: explicit Public keyword
Structure Person
   Public FirstName As String
   Public LastName As String
End Function
```

6.18 Shadowed members

Avoid *Shadows* (Visual Basic) or *new* (C#) keywords in favor of *Overridable* and *virtual* keywords, respectively, to redefine methods and properties in derived types.

6.19 Non-CLS-compliant types [C#]

Try to avoid public methods or properties that take or return object types that aren't compliant with Common Language Specifications (CLS), such as unsigned integers. If you can't avoid these members, mark them with the CLSCompliant(false) attribute.

Why: Methods that take or return unsigned integers aren't callable from Visual Basic and some other .NET languages.

```
// [C#]
public class SampleClass
{
   [CLSCompliant(false)]
   public void PerformTask(uint x)
   {}
}
```

More details: The C# compiler checks the CLS compliance and honors the CLSCompliant attribute only for public members in public types and emits a compilation error if a member is incorrectly marked as CLS-compliant. You can't mark a type or a member as CLS-compliant unless the assembly is also marked with a CLSCompliant(true) attribute (see rule 4.5).

6.20 The *Me/this* keyword

Avoid the *Me* (Visual Basic) or *this* (C#) keyword to reference a field or a property unless it helps make the code less ambiguous.

Exception: Using the *Me* or *this* keyword is OK in a method or a constructor that has a parameter or a local variable whose name is the same or is similar to the name of a class-level field or property.

```
' [Visual Basic]
Class Person
   ' These would be properties in a real-world application.
   Public FirstName As String
   Public LastName As String

   Sub New(ByVal firstName As String, ByVal lastName As String)
      Me.FirstName = firstName
      Me.LastName = lastName
   End Sub
End Class

// [C#]
class Person
{
   // These would be properties in a real-world application.
   public string FirstName;
   public string LastName;

   public Person(string firstName, string lastName)
   {
      this.FirstName = firstName;
      this.LastName = lastName;
   }
}
```

6.21 "New" member [C#]

Don't use public member names that match Visual Basic keywords, more specifically the *New* keyword.

Why: Visual Basic developers would need to enclose the name in square brackets to access a method named *New*:

```
' [Visual Basic]
' MyType is a C# type that exposes a New void method.
Dim o As New MyType
' This is the syntax required to access that method from Visual Basic.
o.[New]()
```

6.22 The Conditional attribute

Use the Conditional attribute instead of the *#If* (Visual Basic) or *#if* (C#) compiler directive to exclude a method and all the statements that invoke it.

```
' [Visual Basic]
' *** Wrong
#If DEMOVERSION Then
   ShowNagScreen()
#End If

Sub ShowNagScreen()
   ...
End Sub
```

```
' *** Correct
ShowNagScreen()              ' No need for #If directive

<Conditional("DEMOVERSION")> _
Sub ShowNagScreen()
   ...
End Sub

// [C#]
// *** Wrong
#if DEMOVERSION
   ShowNagScreen();
#endif

void ShowNagScreen()
{
   ...
}

// *** Correct
ShowNagScreen();             // No need for #If directive

[Conditional("DEMOVERSION")]
void ShowNagScreen()
{
   ...
}
```

More details: The Conditional attribute can discard all the statements that invoke the method, but it doesn't discard the method definition itself, so you can still invoke it through reflection. The Visual Basic developer should also keep in mind that the Conditional attribute is ignored when applied to methods that return a value: in other words, *Function* methods are always included, even if they're marked with a Conditional attribute. (The C# compiler correctly flags these cases as compilation errors.) If you need to receive a value back from a method marked with the Conditional attribute, you must use an argument passed with the *ByRef* (Visual Basic) or *ref* (C#) keyword. You shouldn't use an *out* parameter because the compiler would flag the passed variable as unassigned if the Conditional attribute discards the method call that initializes the variable.

6.23 The Serializable attribute

As a rule, apply the Serializable attribute to all nonsealed classes, but mark all nonserializable fields with the NonSerialized attribute.

Why: This technique ensures that instances of this class (and of all types that inherit from it) can be passed as arguments to remote methods.

See also: See rule 12.26 about nonserializable fields and rule 17.23 about events in serializable types.

6.24 The Obsolete attribute

Mark deprecated types and members with the Obsolete attribute so that clients receive a compile warning when they use the deprecated member. The attribute's Message property should describe why the code element is obsolete and what should be used in its place. In later versions of your class library, consider passing True as the second argument of the Obsolete attribute to cause a compile error and therefore force clients to remove any reference to the member.

More details: You should never remove a type (or a member of a type) without marking it obsolete in at least one or two versions of your library.

```
' [Visual Basic]
' Cause a compilation warning.
<Obsolete("Call ShellSort instead")> _
Sub BubbleSort()
   ...
End Sub

' Cause a compilation error.
<Obsolete("Call ShellSort instead", True)> _
Sub BubbleSort()
   ...
End Sub

// [C#]
// Cause a compilation warning.
[Obsolete("Call ShellSort instead")]
void BubbleSort()
{
   ...
}

// Cause a compilation error.
[Obsolete("Call ShellSort instead", true)]
void BubbleSort()
{
   ...
}
```

Chapter 7
Inheritance

Type inheritance is arguably one of the most important features of object-oriented languages such as Visual Basic and C# and can dramatically simplify the design of new types. Method overriding is strictly related to inheritance and enables you to redefine the way a derived class behaves, while letting it reuse code in the base class—thanks to the *MyBase* (Visual Basic) or *base* (C#) keyword.

Unfortunately, it is also true that these features are often used incorrectly. When reviewing someone else's code, we often notice that types are marked as sealed (*NotInheritable* in Visual Basic) and methods are marked as virtual (*Overridable* in Visual Basic) without any apparent logic. We also see code that uses interfaces when a base class would be more appropriate, or vice versa. And we never find any criterion by which base and derived types are named. That's why we decided that type inheritance deserved a chapter of its own.

7.1 Object hierarchies

Favor wide and shallow object hierarchies over narrow and deep ones. Ideally, object hierarchies shouldn't be more than three levels deep.

7.2 Abstract classes

Use the Base suffix for abstract (*MustInherit* in Visual Basic) types.

Example: DocumentBase.

More details: Many abstract types in the Microsoft .NET Framework follow this guideline, including ButtonBase (in System.Windows.Forms), CollectionBase, and DictionaryBase (in System.Collections).

7.3 Derived class names

Use a compound name for a derived class if possible, with the second part of the name equal to the base class's name.

Why: This naming convention emphasizes the inheritance relation with the base class.

Example: The names of HatchBrush and SolidBrush classes make it clear that they inherit from Brush (in System.Drawing).

7.4 Base classes vs. interfaces

Favor using base abstract classes to interfaces when defining a set of methods that a group of types must expose.

Why: If you use base classes, you can later extend a base class with new properties and methods without breaking existing clients. Just as important, members in an abstract class can include a default implementation, which reduces the amount of code that is necessary when inheriting from the base class.

Why not: When writing an application that uses .NET remoting, an interface can be a better and cleaner choice. (See rules 32.16 and 32.17.)

7.5 Mandatory features in base classes

If a feature can't be implemented in a base class but it's illegal for derived classes not to implement it, make both the class and the corresponding method abstract.

```
' [Visual Basic]
Public MustInherit Class Document
    ' Print is a mandatory feature, but it can't be implemented in the base class.
    Public MustOverride Sub Print()
End Class

Public Class InvoiceDocument
    Inherits Document

    Public Overrides Sub Print()
        ' Implement the print feature here.
        ...
    End Sub
End Class

// [C#]
public abstract class Document
{
    // Print is a mandatory feature, but it can't be implemented in the base class.
    public abstract void Print();
}

public class InvoiceDocument : Document
{
    public override void Print()
    {
        // Implement the print feature here.
        ...
    }
}
```

See also: See rule 7.6 about the correct way to implement optional features in a base class.

7.6 Optional features in base classes

If a feature can't be implemented in a base class and it's legal for derived classes not to implement it, make the corresponding method virtual and have it throw a NotSupportedException. In addition, consider the opportunity to expose a Can-prefixed, virtual Boolean method that enables clients to test whether the feature is implemented in derived classes.

Exception: If you anticipate that only a small number of inherited classes will actually implement a given optional feature, consider gathering all its corresponding methods in an interface.

```vb
' [Visual Basic]
Public Class Document
    ' Print is an optional feature.
    Public Overridable Sub Print()
        Throw New NotSupportedException("Printing isn't supported.")
    End Sub

    Public Overridable Function CanPrint() As Boolean
        Return False
    End Function
End Class

Public Class InvoiceDocument
    Inherits Document

    Public Overrides Sub Print()
        ' Implement the print feature here.
        ...
    End Sub

    Public Overrides Function CanPrint() As Boolean
        ' Let clients now that the Print feature is available.
        Return True
    End Function
End Class
```

```csharp
// [C#]
public class Document
{
    // Print is an optional feature.
    public virtual void Print()
    {
        throw new NotSupportedException("Printing isn't supported.");
    }

    public virtual bool CanPrint()
    {
        return false;
    }
}

public class InvoiceDocument : Document
{
    public override void Print()
    {
        // Implement the print feature here.
        ...
```

```
    }

    public override bool CanPrint()
    {
        // Let clients now that the Print feature is available.
        return true;
    }
}
```

See also: See rule 7.5 about mandatory features.

7.7 Sealed classes

Consider using the *NotInheritable* (Visual Basic) or *sealed* (C#) keyword to mark a type as sealed, if you are certain that you'll never need to inherit from it.

Why: A sealed type performs slightly better because all its properties and methods are implicitly sealed and the compiler can often inline them.

See also: See rule 14.2 for more information about method inlining.

7.8 Static classes

Consider using a static class for types that should neither be instantiated nor inherited from. A *static class* is a sealed class that has a private constructor and has only static fields, properties, and methods.

Why: A static class is typically used to achieve one of the following goals:

   a. To implement the singleton design pattern. An example is the Console class: each application can display data in only one console window, and it makes sense to expose its functionality to the developer as a singleton class.

   b. To provide a container for methods. An example is the System.Math class, whose static methods can be accessed by any .NET application to perform math-related tasks.

   c. To provide a container for global variables in the current application.

```
' [Visual Basic]
' A static class
Public NotInheritable Class Helpers
    ' Private empty constructor to prevent instantiation
    Private Sub New()
    End Sub

    ' One or more static members
    Public Shared Sub ShowMessage(ByVal msg As String)
        ...
    End Sub
End Class

// [C#]
// A static class
public sealed class Helpers
```

```
{
    // Private empty constructor to prevent instantiation
    private Helpers()
    {}

    // One or more static members
    public static void ShowMessage(string msg)
    {
        ...
    }
}
```

More details: Visual Basic developers can use the *Module* keyword to create a static class with less code. This keyword prevents the compiler from adding a constructor (not even a private constructor) and makes all the class members static (*Shared*).

```
' [visual Basic]
' Another, simpler way to reach a similar result
Public Module Helpers
    Public Sub ShowMessage(ByVal msg As String)
        ...
    End Sub
End Module
```

In addition to these two features, a module also supports the so-called *static imports*, a term that indicates that Visual Basic clients can reference methods in the module without having to specify the module name, as if they had an *Imports* statement that imports the class itself:

```
' [visual Basic]
' (Inside an application that uses the Helpers module.)
'  These two statements are equivalent.
Helpers.ShowMessage("Hello world!")
ShowMessage("Hello world!")
```

Thanks to static imports, a Visual Basic program can use all the methods in the modules belonging to the Microsoft.VisualBasic namespace as if they were language keywords, a precious feature when migrating projects written in Visual Basic 6 or earlier versions.

7.9 Constructors in abstract types

An abstract class (*MustInherit* in Visual Basic) must have a constructor with protected scope.

Why: The constructor in an abstract class is meant to be called only by derived types; therefore, it should have protected visibility.

More details: You must add an explicit protected constructor in an abstract class to keep the Visual Basic compiler from mistakenly creating a parameterless public constructor. The C# compiler correctly creates a protected constructor in abstract classes; however, it is recommended that you add an explicit constructor in this case as well.

```
' [Visual Basic]
' *** Wrong: the compiler mistakenly creates a default public constructor.
Public MustInherit Class Document
   ...
End Class

' *** Correct
Public MustInherit Class Document
   Protected Sub New()
      ' You can leave this constructor empty.
   End Sub
   ...
End Class

// [C#]
// *** OK: C# creates a protected default constructor anyway.
public abstract class Document
{
   ...
}

// *** Better: the explicit protected constructor makes your intention more evident.
public abstract class Document
{
   // You can leave this constructor empty.
   protected Document()
   {}
   ...
}
```

7.10 Protected members in sealed classes [Visual Basic]

Don't define protected members in a sealed (*NotInheritable*) class.

Why: A sealed type can't be inherited from; thus, no other class can access or override a protected member. Declare the member as private instead. (Notice that this rule applies to *new* members; a sealed type can override protected methods that are inherited from its base class, as in the case of the Finalize method.)

More details: Interestingly, the C# compiler correctly emits a warning in this case.

```
' [Visual Basic]
Public NotInheritable Class Person
   ' *** Wrong
   Protected Sub SendEmail()
      ...
   End Sub

   ' *** Correct: scope is private.
   Private Sub SendEmail()
      ...
   End Sub
End Class
```

7.11 Virtual members

Don't mark a method or a property with the *Overridable* (Visual Basic) or *virtual* (C#) keyword, unless you can predict a scenario in which derived classes need to modify the behavior of this method.

Alternative rule: Mark public and protected members in a nonsealed class as *Overridable* (Visual Basic) or *virtual* (C#) unless you have a specific reason to make them sealed.

More details: We are providing two rules that glaringly contrast with each other to reflect the fact that many developers believe that the author of a type should anticipate all possible uses of the type as a base class (and therefore the author is responsible for marking each method as virtual or sealed), whereas others think that it's impossible to predict which derived classes can be inherited from a given type.

Another way to express the differences in the two approaches is as follows: the first rule puts more responsibility on the author of the base class and tends to reduce the chance that inheritors can misuse the properties and methods in the base class; the alternative rule puts more responsibility on the inheritor but simplifies the development of the base class.

In general, we prefer the first coding style because we believe that spending more time in the design phase of an object hierarchy saves times later, but we occasionally adopt the second approach when we believe that we can't really know in advance how the base class will be used in real-world applications.

One additional but secondary benefit of the first approach is performance: invoking a virtual member is slightly slower than invoking a nonvirtual (sealed) member; therefore, you should have as few virtual members as possible. However, the higher speed of sealed members becomes an important factor only in time-critical loops that are repeated hundreds of thousands of times. In most real-world cases, you shouldn't make a choice based on the better performance provided by sealed methods.

7.12 Split long tasks in overridable methods

In nonsealed classes, split long and complex tasks in two or more protected and overridable methods.

Example: The following code shows how you can split a complex print operation in three stages and why you should do it.

```
' [Visual Basic]
' *** Wrong
Public Class Report
    Public Overridable Sub Print()
        ' Print report's header here.
        ...
        ' Print report's body here.
        ...
        ' Print report's footer here.
```

```vb
        ...
    End Sub
End Class


' *** Correct
Public Class Report
    ' Notice that this method isn't overridable.
    Public Sub Print()
        PrintHeader()
        PrintBody()
        PrintFooter()
    End Sub

    Protected Overridable Sub PrintHeader()
        ' Print report's header here.
        ...
    End Sub

    Protected Overridable Sub PrintBody()
        ' Print report's body here.
        ...
    End Sub

    Protected Overridable Sub PrintFooter()
        ' Print report's footer here.
        ...
    End Sub
End Class
```

```csharp
// [C#]
// *** Wrong
public class Report
{
    public virtual void Print()
    {
        // Print report's header here.
        ...
        // Print report's body here.
        ...
        // Print report's footer here.
        ...
    }
}


// *** Correct
public class Report
{
    // Notice that this method isn't overridable.
    public void Print()
    {
        PrintHeader();
        PrintBody();
        PrintFooter();
    }

    protected virtual void PrintHeader()
    {
        // Print report's header here.
        ...
```

```
    }

    protected virtual void PrintBody()
    {
       // Print report's body here.
       ...
    }

    protected virtual void PrintFooter()
    {
       // Print report's footer here.
       ...
    }
}
```

Splitting a complex method enables inherited classes to redefine individual subtasks with a minimal amount of code. For example, here's how you can define a new type that behaves like the Report class but adds totals to each report:

```
' [Visual Basic]
Public Class ReportWithTotals
   Inherits Report

   Protected Overrides Sub PrintBody()
      ' First, print the report's body.
      MyBase.PrintBody()
      ' Then print totals.
      ...
   End Sub
End Class

// [C#]
public class ReportWithTotals : Report
{
    protected override void PrintBody()
    {
       // First, print the report's body.
       base.PrintBody();
       // Then print totals.
       ...
    }
}
```

7.13 Overloaded virtual methods

If you have overloaded a method and also want to let developers override it in derived types, mark only the most complete version of the method as virtual, and have all the other versions of the method call it.

Why: This technique simplifies the task of redefining what the method does in derived classes because inheritors have to override only one method.

```
' [Visual Basic]
Public Sub PerformTask(ByVal arg1 As String)
```

```
    ' Call the other overload.
    PerformTask(arg1, 0)
  End Sub

  ' This is the only method that needs to be overridden in a derived class.
  Public Overridable Sub PerformTask(ByVal arg1 As String, ByVal arg2 As Integer)
      ' Do something here...
  End Sub
```

```
// [C#]
public void PerformTask(string arg1)
{
    // Call the other overload.
    PerformTask(arg1, 0);
}

// This is the only method that needs to be overridden in a derived class.
public virtual void PerformTask(string arg1, int arg2)
{
    // Do something here...
}
```

Alternate rule: Make the overloaded versions sealed—that is, not explicitly marked with *Overridable* (Visual Basic) or *virtual* (C#)—and have all of them call a protected overridable method named *MethodName*Core. This alternative pattern requires that you write slightly more code, but it makes clearer the relation between public sealed and protected overridable methods. This pattern is used often in the .NET Framework. For example, all the overloaded versions of the SetBounds method of the Form object delegate to the SetBoundsCore protected method. A variation of this pattern is often used for properties as well: for example, the set block of the Form's Visible property invokes the SetVisibleCore method.

```
' [Visual Basic]
Public Sub PerformTask(ByVal arg1 As String)
    ' Call the protected method.
    PerformTaskCore(arg1, 0)
End Sub

Public Sub PerformTask(ByVal arg1 As String, ByVal arg2 As Integer)
    ' Call the protected method.
    PerformTaskCore(arg1, arg2)
End Sub

' This is the only method that needs to be overridden in a derived class.
Protected Overridable Sub PerformTaskCore(ByVal arg1 As String, ByVal arg2 As Integer)
    ' Do something here...
End Sub
```

```
// [C#]
public void PerformTask(string arg1)
{
    // Call the protected method.
    PerformTaskCore(arg1, 0);
}
```

```
public void PerformTask(string arg1, int arg2)
{
    // Call the protected method.
    PerformTaskCore(arg1, arg2);
}

// This is the only method that needs to be overridden in a derived class.
protected virtual void PerformTaskCore(string arg1, int arg2)
{
    // Do something here...
}
```

7.14 ToString method overriding

Override the ToString method to provide a standard way for an object to display its value.

```
' [Visual Basic]
Public Class Person
    ' These would be properties in a real-world class.
    Public FirstName As String
    Public LastName As String

    Public Overrides Function ToString() As String
        Return Me.FirstName & " " & Me.LastName
    End Function
End Class

// [C#]
public class Person
{
    // These would be properties in a real-world class.
    public string FirstName;
    public string LastName;

    public override string ToString()
    {
        return this.FirstName + " " + this.LastName;
    }
}
```

7.15 Equals method overriding

Consider overriding the Equals instance method if two objects can be considered equal even if they aren't the same instance of the type. Keep in mind that the Equals method should never throw an exception and that it should always return false if the argument is a null object reference or is of a type other than the current type.

More details: As an example of how this guideline is used in the .NET Framework, notice that the String class overrides the Equals method to compare the individual characters in a string rather than comparing the pointer to the string.

Example: The following class redefines the Equals method so that two Square instances can be considered equal when the value of their Side property is the same. You can use the same skeleton code for your classes.

```vb
' [Visual Basic]
Public Class Square
    ' This would be a property in a real-world class.
    Public Side As Double

    Public Overloads Overrides Function Equals(ByVal obj As Object) As Boolean
        If Me Is obj Then
            ' This is actually the same object reference.
            Return True
        ElseIf obj Is Nothing OrElse Not obj.GetType() Is Me.GetType() Then
            ' Argument is null or is of a different type.
            Return False
        Else
            ' Compare the actual properties (just one in this example).
            Dim other As Square = DirectCast(obj, Square)
            Return (Me.Side = other.Side)
        End If
    End Function
End Class
```

```csharp
// [C#]
public class Square
{
    // This would be a property in a real-world class.
    public double Side;

    public override bool Equals(object obj)
    {
        if ( this == obj )
        {
            // Argument is actually the same object as this.
            return true;
        }
        else if ( obj == null || obj.GetType() != this.GetType() )
        {
            // Argument is null or is of a different type.
            return false;
        }
        else
        {
            Square other = (Square) obj;
            return (this.Side == other.Side);
        }
    }
}
```

7.16 GetHashCode method overriding

If you override the Equals method, also override the GetHashCode method so that equal objects also have equal hash codes.

More details: The C# compiler correctly emits a warning if you override the Equals method but not the GetHashCode method. The Visual Basic compiler doesn't, so it's left to the developer to abide by this rule.

7.17 GetHashCode method immutability

The value returned by the GetHashCode method must not change during the object's lifetime. If you override this method, ensure that the value you return doesn't change over the object's lifetime.

How to: You can return a constant value by combining the hash codes of two or more immutable fields, or you can evaluate a random value at creation time and store it in a private field.

More details: Regardless of how you evaluate the hash code for an object, ensure that two equal objects also have the same hash code (see rule 7.18).

```vbnet
' [Visual Basic]
Public Class User
    ' These values are immutable after the object has been created
    ' (in real-world code we would use properties).
    Public ReadOnly UserName As String
    Public ReadOnly Domain As String

    Private hashCode As Integer

    Sub New(ByVal userName As String, ByVal domain As String)
        Me.UserName = userName
        Me.Domain = domain
        ' Users with same name from same domain also have identical
        ' hash codes. (We use bitwise Xor to avoid overflow.)
        hashCode = userName.GetHashCode() Xor domain.GetHashCode()
    End Sub

    Public Overrides Function GetHashCode() As Integer
        Return hashCode
    End Function
End Class
```

```csharp
// [C#]
public class User
{
    // These values are immutable after the object has been created
    // (in real-world code we would use properties).
    public readonly string UserName;
    public readonly string Domain;

    private int hashCode;

    public User(string userName, string domain)
    {
        this.UserName = userName;
        this.Domain = domain;
        // Users with same name from same domain also have identical
        // hash codes. (We use bitwise Xor to avoid overflow.)
        hashCode = userName.GetHashCode() ^ domain.GetHashCode();
    }

    public override int GetHashCode()
```

```
    {
        return hashCode;
    }
}
```

More details: When overriding the GetHashCode method, avoid calling the Object.GetHash-Code method, which is relatively inefficient. Instead, evaluate the hash code by combining the values and hash codes of fields as shown in the previous example.

7.18 GetHashCode method and equality

Never use the value returned by the GetHashCode method as a quick way to determine whether two objects are equal (whatever *equal* means for that specific type). The only conclusion you can infer by comparing the hash codes of two objects is that the objects are surely different if their hash codes differ.

Why: Inferring equality for objects from the fact that they have the same hash code is incorrect. It is true that the Object.GetHashCode method returns different values for different instances. However, this consideration is true only for the Object class because the GetHash-Code method is often overridden in derived types. For this reason, you should never assume that two object variables with the same hash code also point to the same object. Additionally, the Object.GetHashCode implementation might change in future versions of the .NET Framework, so similar assumptions can be broken even for types that derive directly from Object and don't override the GetHashCode method.

7.19 *MyClass* keyword [Visual Basic]

Use the *MyClass* keyword to call an overridable method defined in the same class as the caller code, if you want to be sure that that specific version of the method is invoked even if the method is redefined in a derived class.

Why: The main reason for using *MyClass* is to ensure that the local version of the method is invoked (as opposed to the redefined version in a derived class) as explained in the previous paragraph. In addition to this main reason, the *MyClass* keyword can improve performance slightly.

More details: When compiling a method call, the Visual Basic compiler can emit two different IL opcodes: the *callvirt* opcode when the called method is virtual (*Overridable* in Visual Basic) or the *call* opcode when the target method is nonvirtual or when you use a *MyClass* keyword in the method call. When the IL code is compiled into native code, the JIT compiler can optimize the *call* IL instruction but not the *callvirt* opcode; therefore, using the *MyClass* keyword can generate a slightly faster code.

```
' [Visual Basic]
Overridable Function GetResult() As Integer
    Return 123
End Function
```

```
Sub Test()
    ' Next statement calls GetResult above even if it has been overridden in a derived class.
    Dim result As Integer = MyClass.GetResult()
End Sub
```

The C# language doesn't have a keyword that corresponds to *MyClass*.

7.20 Equals and Compare strong-typed static methods

Consider providing static, strong-typed versions of the Equals and Compare methods to simplify comparisons among instances of a custom type.

Why: Methods that take arguments of a specific type (as opposed to a generic Object instance) can make your code more robust. Static methods are often preferable to instance methods because you don't need to check whether an object reference is *Nothing* (Visual Basic) or *null* (C#) before invoking the method.

Example: The String class exposes two overloads of the Equals static method, the version inherited from Object (which takes two object arguments) and a strong-typed version that takes two strings. The String class also exposes several overloads of the Compare static method, which enable developers to test the entire string or a portion of it in both case-sensitive and case-insensitive modes.

```
' [Visual Basic]
Public Class Person
    ' These would be properties in a real-world class.
    Public FirstName As String
    Public LastName As String

    Public Sub New(ByVal firstName As String, ByVal lastName As String)
        Me.FirstName = firstName
        Me.LastName = lastName
    End Sub

    ' This is the strongly typed version of the static Equals method.
    Public Overloads Shared Function Equals(ByVal o1 As Person, ByVal o2 As Person) _
            As Boolean
        If o1 Is Nothing AndAlso o2 Is Nothing Then
            ' Two null objects are equal.
            Return True
        ElseIf o1 Is Nothing OrElse o2 Is Nothing Then
            ' If only one object is null, they can't be equal.
            Return False
        Else
            ' If neither is null, delegate to the String.Equals method.
            Return (String.Equals(o1.FirstName, o2.FirstName) AndAlso _
                String.Equals(o1.LastName, o2.LastName))
        End If
    End Function

    ' This is the strongly typed version of the static Compare method.
    ' In this case we compare persons on their (lastname,firstname).
```

```vb
      Public Shared Function Compare(ByVal o1 As Person, ByVal o2 As Person) As Integer
         If o1 Is Nothing AndAlso o2 Is Nothing Then
            ' Two null objects are equal.
            Return 0
         ElseIf o1 Is Nothing Then
            ' A null object is less than any non-null object.
            Return -1
         ElseIf o2 Is Nothing Then
            ' A non-null object is greater than any null object.
            Return 1
         Else
            ' Delegate the comparison to the String.Compare method.
            Dim res As Integer = String.Compare(o1.LastName, o2.LastName)
            If res = 0 Then
               res = String.Compare(o1.FirstName, o2.First Name)
            End If
            Return res
         End If
      End Function
End Class
```

```csharp
// [C#]
public class Person
{
   // These would be properties in a real-world class.
   public string FirstName;
   public string LastName;

   public Person(string firstName, string lastName)
   {
      this.FirstName = firstName;
      this.LastName = lastName;
   }

   // This is the strongly typed version of the static Equals method.
   public static bool Equals(Person o1, Person o2)
   {
      if ( o1 == null && o2 == null )
         // Two null objects are equal.
         return true;
      else if ( o1 == null || o2 == null )
         // If only one object is null, they can't be equal.
         return false;
      else
         // If neither is null, delegate to the String.Equals method.
         return ( string.Equals(o1.FirstName, o2.FirstName) &&
             String.Equals(o1.LastName, o2.LastName) );
   }

   // This is the strongly typed version of static Compare method.
   // In this case we compare persons on their (lastname,firstname).
   public static int Compare(Person o1, Person o2)
   {
      if ( o1 == null && o2 == null )
         // Two null objects are equal.
```

```
            return 0;
        else if ( o1 == null )
            // A null object is less than any non-null object.
            return -1;
        else if ( o2 == null )
            // A non-null object is greater than any null object.
            return 1;
        else
        {
            // Delegate the comparison to the String.Compare method.
            int res = String.Compare(o1.LastName, o2.LastName);
            if ( res == 0 )
                res = String.Compare(o1.FirstName, o2.FirstName);
            return res;
        }
    }
}
```

More details: If a type exposes a static Compare method and performance isn't an issue, you can simplify the implementation of the Equals method as follows:

```
' [Visual Basic]
Public Overloads Shared Function Equals(ByVal o1 As Person, ByVal o2 As Person) _
      As Boolean
   Return Compare(o1, o2) = 0
End Function

// [C#]
public static bool Equals(Person o1, Person o2)
{
    return Compare(o1, o2) == 0;
}
```

7.21 Inheriting from MarshalByRefObject

Don't inherit a new type from MarshalByRefObject (or from types that derive from Marshal-ByRefObject, such as Component and Control) unless you plan to use the additional features that this type provides.

Why: Instantiating types that derive from MarshalByRefObject takes longer than a regular type. Besides, the JIT compiler can't inline methods in such types; therefore, method calls execute slightly slower.

More details: You might want to split a complex object into two distinct types, one of which exposes all the methods that don't require the features provided by the MarshalByRefObject base type, so that the JIT compiler can optimize calls to methods in this latter object.

Example: Consider a type that exposes methods to log messages to a custom logging system. You would like to derive this type from Component, so that users of your class can drop an instance of the type on a designer's surface and assign its properties at design time in

Microsoft Visual Studio .NET's Properties window. Because this type inherits from Component, the JIT compiler can't optimize calls to the type's methods.

However, if you do so, you effectively disable inline optimization even if you use the type as a regular class and instantiate it in code. You can get the best of both worlds by defining two classes: the Logger type that inherits from Object and that actually performs the various log operations; and the LoggerComponent type that inherits from Component and exposes the same methods as the Logger class. Each method in LoggerComponent delegates to the method with the same name of a private instance of the Logger class; therefore, you don't really duplicate any code. The following code illustrates this concept:

```vb
' [Visual Basic]
Public Class LoggerComponent
   Inherits System.ComponentModel.Component

   ' The private instance of the Logger type
   Private logger As New Logger

   Public Sub LogMessage(ByVal text As String)
      ' Delegate to the private Logger instance.
      logger.LogMessage(text)
   End Sub
End Class
```

```csharp
// [C#]
public class LoggerComponent : System.ComponentModel.Component
{
   // The private instance of the Logger type
   private Logger logger = new Logger();

   public void LogMessage(string text)
   {
      // Delegate to the private Logger instance.
      logger.LogMessage(text);
   }
}
```

Chapter 8
Interfaces

Although the Microsoft .NET Framework is heavily based on inheritance, some of its key features can be exploited only by means of interfaces. For example, you can compare objects by means of the IComparable interface, and you can enumerate collections through the IEnumerable interface. You often must implement the ISerializable interface to create serializable types correctly, which in turn are necessary when communicating with .NET applications running in a different AppDomain.

Defining your own interfaces correctly can be as important as implementing the interfaces that the .NET Framework exposes. For example, most real-world applications based on .NET remoting rely on interfaces as a software protocol through which two applications can communicate (see Chapter 34).

All in all, being familiar with interfaces and using them appropriately are of paramount importance for any Visual Basic and C# developer. In this chapter we cover many common programming techniques based on interfaces and show how to correctly implement some of the most common interfaces exposed by the .NET Framework.

 Note One or more code examples in this chapter assume that the following namespaces have been imported by means of *Imports* (Visual Basic) or *using* (C#) statements:

```
System.Collections
System.IO
System.Runtime.Serialization
System.Runtime.Serialization.Formatters.Binary
```

8.1 Interface names

Use the I prefix for interface names. Except for this initial character, apply the same naming guidelines explained for types: use PascalCase, don't use abbreviations, use all-uppercase for acronyms of two characters, and so on. (See rule 6.1.)

Example: IPlugIn, IAsciiEncoder.

8.2 Interface types in one source file

Gather all the interface types in a file named Interfaces.vb or Interfaces.cs.

Why: Interface definitions are usually quite short. Using a single file for all interfaces reduces the number of files in the solution and enables you to find any interface type in the source code quickly.

Why not: This rule might contradict rules 5.7 and 6.5.

8.3 Number of members in interface types

Avoid interfaces with more than six methods. If more methods are required, consider creating base interfaces from which you derive more complex interfaces.

Example: The IList interface (in the System.Collections namespace) provides a great example of the interface inheritance concept. This interface contains as many as 15 methods, 5 of which are inherited from the ICollection interface. The ICollection interface, in turn, inherits one method from the IEnumerable interface (see Figure 8-1).

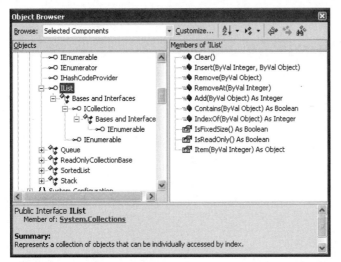

Figure 8-1　Interface inheritance as shown in the Object Browser

8.4 Events in interface types

Don't include events in interface types.

Why: Events are legal in interfaces, but they are seldom useful and tend to confuse developers.

8.5 Interface immutability

Consider interfaces as immutable entities. You should never change an interface in any way after you publish it—that is, after you make the interface available to other developers, who might implement it in the types they author. Forbidden changes include adding or removing members and changing the type of a parameter or the return value of a method. (All these changes would break existing clients.)

More details: If you absolutely must add members to an interface, consider creating a new interface that inherits from the existing one. The new interface might have a version number appended to it (as in IPlugins2) to emphasize the relationship with the current interface.

8.6 Name of classes implementing an interface

Use the following naming guidelines for types that implement an interface:

a.   Use the Comparer suffix for types that implement the IComparer interface. Example: PersonComparer.

b.   Use the Formatter suffix for types that implement the IFormatter interface. Example: PersonFormatter.

c.   When defining a type whose only purpose is implementing an interface, use the interface name (but without the I prefix) as a suffix for the type name. Example: A class that implements the IHashCodeProvider interface might be named CaseInsensitiveHashCodeProvider.

8.7 Interface implementation in *#region* blocks

Enclose the implementation of any interface in *#region* blocks to collapse and expand it easily.

See also: See rule 6.13 on member ordering and grouping.

```vb
' [Visual Basic]
#Region "IDisposable implementation"
    Public Sub Dispose() Implements IDisposable.Dispose
        ...
    End Sub
#End Region
```

```csharp
// [C#]
#region IDisposable implementation
    public void Dispose()
    {
        ...
    }
#endregion
```

8.8 Public vs. private members in interface implementation

Both the Visual Basic and C# languages enable you to implement an interface with either public or private members. In Visual Basic, you change the visibility of an interface member simply by applying the desired scope keyword; in C#, you can implement an interface as a private member by adopting the so-called *explicit* (or *private*) *interface implementation*:

```vb
' [Visual Basic]
Public Class Person
    Implements ICloneable, IComparable

    ' ICloneable is implemented by means of public members.
    Public Function Clone() As Object Implements ICloneable.Clone
        ...
    End Function

    ' IComparable is implemented by means of private members.
    Private Function CompareTo(ByVal obj As Object) As Integer _
```

```
      Implements IComparable.CompareTo
      ...
   End Function
End Class
```

```
// [C#]
public class Person : ICloneable, IComparable
{
    // ICloneable is implemented by means of public members.
    public object Clone()
    {
        ...
    }

    // IComparable is implemented by means of private members.
    int IComparable.CompareTo(object obj)
    {
        ...
    }
}
```

In general, you should favor using public interface members to interfaces that are implemented privately, even though there are several exceptions to this rule.

Why: If a type implements an interface by means of private members, clients can call a method in the interface only after casting the object to an interface variable. In addition to being more verbose, method calls that flow through an interface variable can't be inlined and therefore run slightly slower. Worse, if the object that exposes the interface is a value type (a user-defined structure, for example), the cast operation requires a boxing operation, so you get less-than-optimal performance.

Why not: One good reason to implement an interface privately is to avoid polluting a type with many public methods that are seldom used. (This is the reason all numeric types implement the IConvertible interface as private methods.) Another reason for using private interface implementation is when you also want to provide a public method that performs the same operation in a strongly typed fashion (see rule 8.11 for an example of this technique).

8.9 Private interface implementation in inheritable types

If you implement an interface with nonpublic members in a nonsealed class, ensure that derived types can access and override these members.

How to: Visual Basic developers can achieve this simply by marking those members with the *Protected Overridable* keywords. C# developers must adopt a different coding style, however, because explicit interface members can be private only, and it's therefore necessary to define a *protected virtual* method and call this method from the interface method.

```
' [Visual Basic]
Public Class Person
   Implements IComparable
```

```
    ' IComparable is implemented by means of protected members
    ' that can be overridden by inherited types.
    Protected Overridable Function CompareTo(ByVal obj As Object) As Integer _
        Implements IComparable.CompareTo
        ...
    End Function
End Class

// [C#]
public class Person : IComparable
{
    // IComparable is implemented privately.
    int IComparable.CompareTo(object obj)
    {
        // Delegate to the protected virtual method.
        return CompareTo(obj);
    }

    // A protected method that can be overridden by derived types.
    protected virtual int CompareTo(object obj)
    {
        // Do the actual comparison here.
        ...
    }
}
```

8.10 ICloneable interface

Implement the ICloneable interface for types that might need to be cloned. Make the Clone method public if possible. Add documentation that explains whether your Clone method performs a shallow copy or a deep copy.

How to: If you are returning a shallow copy of the object, often you can simplify the code in the Clone method by invoking the protected MemberwiseClone method.

```
' [Visual Basic]
Public Class Person
    Implements ICloneable

    ' Return a shallow copy of this Person object.
    Public Function Clone As Object Implements ICloneable.Clone
        Return Me.MemberwiseClone()
    End Function
End Class

// [C#]
public class Person : ICloneable
{
    // Return a shallow copy of this Person object.
    public object Clone()
    {
        return this.MemberwiseClone();
    }
}
```

How to: Read rule 8.12 for more information about shallow and deep copies.

8.11 Strong-typed cloning

When implementing the ICloneable interface, consider having both a public strongly typed Clone method that returns an instance of the current type and a private Clone method that implements the interface and returns a generic object.

```
' [Visual Basic]
Public Class Person
   Implements ICloneable

   ' The public Clone method returns a Person object.
   Public Function Clone() As Person
      Return DirectCast(Me.Clone2(), Person)
   End Function

   ' The private Clone method returns a generic object.
   Private Function Clone2 As Object Implements ICloneable.Clone
      Return Me.MemberwiseClone()
   End Function
End Class

// [C#]
public class Person : ICloneable
{
    // The public Clone method returns a Person object.
    public Person Clone()
    {
        return (Person) (this as ICloneable).Clone();
    }

    // The private Clone method returns a generic object.
    object ICloneable.Clone()
    {
        return this.MemberwiseClone();
    }
}
```

8.12 Shallow and deep cloning

Understand the difference between shallow copies and deep copies. You have a shallow copy when a reference to a child object is copied as is, without creating a clone of that child object; you have a deep copy when all child objects are cloned and you end up with a completely separate copy of the entire object graph.

More details: You see the difference between shallow and deep copying if the object contains fields and properties pointing to other objects. A *shallow copy* creates a copy of the main object only. A *deep copy* creates a copy of the object and of all its child objects. Let's say that you have a 100-element System.Array containing references to Person objects: a shallow copy of this array would create a new array in which elements point to the same Person objects referenced by the original array; a deep copy of this array would create a copy of the original array in which elements point to a copy of each Person object referenced by the original array (101 new objects in total).

In most cases, the ICloneable.Clone method returns a shallow copy of the object, but it doesn't have to be so. As the author of the class, it's up to you to decide whether a deep copy is more appropriate.

How to: If the object is marked as serializable and all its child objects are also serializable, you can perform a deep copy with this reusable method:

```vb
' [Visual Basic]
Public Function CloneObject(ByVal obj As Object) As Object
   ' Create a memory stream and a formatter.
   Dim ms As New MemoryStream
   Dim bf As New BinaryFormatter(Nothing, _
      New StreamingContext(StreamingContextStates.Clone))
   ' Serialize the object into the stream.
   bf.Serialize(ms, obj)
   ' Deserialize into a different object and release memory.
   Dim res As Object = bf.Deserialize(ms)
   ms.Close()
   Return res
End Function
```

```csharp
// [C#]
public object CloneObject(object obj)
{
   // Create a memory stream and a formatter.
   MemoryStream ms = new MemoryStream();
   BinaryFormatter bf = new BinaryFormatter(null,
      new StreamingContext(StreamingContextStates.Clone));
   // Serialize the object into the stream.
   bf.Serialize(ms, obj);
   // Deserialize into a different object and release memory.
   object res = bf.Deserialize(ms);
   ms.Close();
   return res;
}
```

8.13 Cloning immutable objects

If your object is immutable, the Clone method can simply return a reference to the object itself.

More details: A type is *immutable* if clients can initialize its properties and fields only at creation time. (Strings and delegates are immutable objects, for example.)

```vb
' [Visual Basic]
' An immutable object
Public Class Location
   Implements ICloneable

   Public ReadOnly X As Double
   Public ReadOnly Y As Double

   Public Sub New(ByVal x As Double, ByVal y As Double)
      Me.X = x
      Me.Y = y
   End Sub
```

```
    ' The Clone method can just return a reference to self.
    Public Function Clone() As Object Implements ICloneable.Clone
        Return Me
    End Function
End Class
```

```
// [C#]
// An immutable object
public class Location : ICloneable
{
    public readonly double X;
    public readonly double Y;

    public Location(double x, double y)
    {
        this.X = x;
        this.Y = y;
    }

    // The Clone method can just return a reference to self.
    public object Clone()
    {
        return this;
    }
}
```

8.14 IComparable interface

Implement the IComparable interface if instances of the type can be compared to each other.
Make the CompareTo method public if possible. Always account for null arguments in the
CompareTo method.

```
' [Visual Basic]
Class Square
    Implements IComparable

    ' This would be a property in a real-world class.
    Public Side As Double

    ' Squares can be compared by their width property.
    Public Function CompareTo(ByVal obj As Object) As Integer _
            Implements IComparable.CompareTo
        ' Throw if other object can't be cast to Square.
        Dim other As Square = DirectCast(obj, Square)
        ' Any square is greater than a null square.
        If other Is Nothing OrElse Me.Side > other.Side Then
            Return 1
        Else If Me.Side < other.Side Then
            Return -1
        Else
            Return 0
        End If
    End Function
End Class
```

```csharp
// [C#]
class Square : IComparable
{
    // This would be a property in a real-world class.
    public double Side;

    // Squares can be compared by their width property.
    public int CompareTo(object obj)
    {
        // Throw if other object can't be cast to Square.
        Square other = (Square) obj;
        // Any square is greater than a null square.
        if ( other == null || this.Side > other.Side )
            return 1;
        else if ( this.Side < other.Side )
            return -1;
        else
            return 0;
    }
}
```

8.15 Leverage IComparable fields and properties

When implementing the IComparable or IComparer interface, delegate to the IComparable and/ or IComparer interface exposed by objects referenced by inner fields and properties, if possible.

Example: When you compare objects on their string, numeric, and date/time elements, leverage the fact that all these types implement the IComparable interface.

```vbnet
' [Visual Basic]
Public Class Person
    Implements IComparable

    ' This would be a property in a real-world class.
    Public Age As Integer

    ' Compare Person instances on their age.
    Public Function CompareTo(ByVal obj As Object) As Integer _
          Implements IComparable.CompareTo
        ' Throw if other object can't be cast to Person.
        Dim other As Person = DirectCast(obj, Person)
        ' Any person is greater than a null object.
        If other Is Nothing Then
            Return 1
        Else
            ' Build on IComparable interface for strings.
            Return Me.Age.CompareTo(other.Age)
        End If
    End Function
End Class
```

```csharp
// [C#]
public class Person : IComparable
{
    // This would be a property in a real-world class.
    public int Age;
```

```
    // Compare Person instances on their age.
    public int CompareTo(object obj)
    {
        // Throw if other object can't be cast to Person.
        Person other = (Person) obj;
        // Any Person is greater than a null object.
        if ( other == null )
            return 1;
        else
            // Build on IComparable interface for strings.
            return this.Age.CompareTo(other.Age);
    }
}
```

8.16 IComparer interface

If the instances of a type can be compared and sorted along multiple keys, create a nested type named *Typename*Comparer that implements the IComparer interface. The constructor of this comparer class takes one or more enum types that specify which fields are used as sort keys and the direction of the sort.

```
' [Visual Basic]
Public Class Person
    ' These would be properties in a real-world class.
    Public FirstName As String
    Public LastName As String

    ' The Enum type used when creating a PersonComparer
    Public Enum SortKey
        LastName        ' LastName, then FirstName
        FirstName       ' FirstName, then LastName
    End Enum

    ' A nested comparer for Person instances.
    Public Class PersonComparer
        Implements IComparer

        ' No need to define a public property
        Private ReadOnly Key As SortKey
        Private ReadOnly Descending As Boolean

        Public Sub New(ByVal key As SortKey, ByVal descending As Boolean)
            If key <> SortKey.LastName AndAlso key <> SortKey.FirstName Then
                Throw New ArgumentException("Invalid SortKey value")
            End If
            Me.Key = key
            Me.Descending = descending
        End Sub

        Public Function Compare(ByVal o1 As Object, ByVal o2 As Object) As Integer _
                Implements IComparer.Compare
            Dim p1 As Person = DirectCast(o1, Person)
            Dim p2 As Person = DirectCast(o2, Person)
```

```vb
        ' Rule out the simplest cases.
        If p1 Is Nothing AndAlso p2 Is Nothing Then
            Return 0
        Else If p1 Is Nothing Then
            Return -1
        Else If p2 Is Nothing Then
            Return 1
        End If
        Dim res As Integer = 0

        ' For simplicity's sake, we assume that FirstName
        ' and LastName properties can't be Nothing.
        Select Case Me.Key
            Case SortKey.LastName
                res = p1.LastName.CompareTo(p2.LastName)
                If res = 0 Then
                    res = p1.FirstName.CompareTo(p2.FirstName)
                End If
            Case SortKey.FirstName
                res = p1.FirstName.CompareTo(p2.FirstName)
                If res = 0 Then
                    res = p1.LastName.CompareTo(p2.LastName)
                End If
            Case Else
                Throw New ArgumentException("Invalid sort key")
        End Select
        ' Account for descending sort.
        If Me.Descending Then res = -res
        Return res
    End Function
  End Class
End Class
```

```csharp
// [C#]
public class Person
{
    // These would be properties in a real-world class.
    public string FirstName;
    public string LastName;

    // The Enum type used when creating a PersonComparer
    public enum SortKey
    {
        LastName,      // LastName, then FirstName
        FirstName      // FirstName, then LastName
    }

    // A nested comparer for Person instances
    public class PersonComparer : IComparer
    {
        // No need to create a public property
        private readonly SortKey Key;
        private readonly bool Descending;

        public PersonComparer(SortKey key, bool descending)
        {
```

```
        if ( key != SortKey.LastName && key != SortKey.FirstName )
           throw new ArgumentException("Invalid SortKey value");
        this.Key = key;
        this.Descending = descending;
     }

     public int Compare(object o1, object o2)
     {
        Person p1 = (Person) o1;
        Person p2 = (Person) o2;

        // Rule out the simplest cases.
        if ( p1 == null && p2 == null )
           return 0;
        else if ( p1 == null )
           return -1;
        else if ( p2 == null )
           return 1;

        int res = 0;

        // For simplicity's sake, we assume that FirstName
        // and LastName properties can't be null.
        switch ( this.Key )
        {
           case SortKey.LastName:
              res = p1.LastName.CompareTo(p2.LastName);
              if ( res == 0 )
                 res = p1.FirstName.CompareTo(p2.FirstName);
              break;
           case SortKey.FirstName:
              res = p1.FirstName.CompareTo(p2.FirstName);
              if ( res == 0 )
                 res = p1.LastName.CompareTo(p2.LastName);
              break;
           default:
              throw new ArgumentException("Invalid sort key");
        }
        // Account for descending sort.
        if ( this.Descending )
           res = -res;
         return res;
     }
   }
}
```

Thanks to the PersonComparer class, it is now easy to compare and sort Person instances.

```
' [Visual Basic]
' persons is an array of Person objects.
Array.Sort(persons, New Person.PersonComparer(Person.SortKey.FirstName, False))
```

```
// [C#]
// persons is an array of Person objects.
Array.Sort(persons, new Person.PersonComparer(Person.SortKey.FirstName, false));
```

To help developers use your comparer classes even more, consider exposing static read-only fields that return preinstantiated references of the comparer class:

```vb
' [Visual Basic]
Public Class Person
   ...
   Public Class PersonComparer
      Implements IComparer

      Public Shared ReadOnly ByLastName As PersonComparer = _
         New PersonComparer(SortKey.LastName, False)
      Public Shared ReadOnly ByFirstName As PersonComparer = _
         New PersonComparer(SortKey.FirstName, False)
      ...
   End Class
End Class
```

```csharp
// [C#]
public class Person
{
   ...
   public class PersonComparer : IComparer
   {
      public static readonly PersonComparer ByLastName =
         new PersonComparer(SortKey.LastName, false);
      public static readonly PersonComparer ByFirstName =
         new PersonComparer(SortKey.FirstName, false);
      ...
   }
}
```

These static fields enable clients to use the comparer class as follows:

```vb
' [Visual Basic]
' persons is an array of Person objects.
Array.Sort(persons, Person.PersonComparer.ByFirstName)
```

```csharp
// [C#]
// persons is an array of Person objects.
Array.Sort(persons, Person.PersonComparer.ByFirstName);
```

8.17 IEnumerable and IEnumerator types

Use the *Typename*Enumerator name for a type that implements the IEnumerator interface and that is meant to enumerate objects of the *Typename* type. Make the class private and nest it inside the definition of the IEnumerable type it enumerates.

Why: Using a private nested type for enumerator classes makes sense because such classes are used only in conjunction with their enclosing type and are rarely (if ever) used explicitly in code.

Example: The following code shows how you can define an IEnumerable type that enables you to enumerate prime numbers in a loop.

```vb
' [Visual Basic]
Public Class PrimeNumbers
    Implements IEnumerable

    Private ReadOnly MaxPrime As Integer

    Public Sub New(ByVal maxPrime As Integer)
        Me.MaxPrime = maxPrime
    End Sub

    ' The IEnumerable interface
    Public Function GetEnumerator() As IEnumerator Implements IEnumerable.GetEnumerator
        Return New PrimeNumbersEnumerator(Me)
    End Function


    Private Class PrimeNumbersEnumerator
        Implements IEnumerator

        ' A reference to the enclosing object
        Private Parent As PrimeNumbers
        ' The last prime found
        Private currentValue As Integer = -1
        ' This holds all the prime (odd) numbers found so far. (2 isn't included.)
        Private primes As New ArrayList

        ' The constructor
        Public Sub New(ByVal parent As PrimeNumbers)
            ' Keep a reference to the object being enumerated.
            Me.Parent = parent
        End Sub

        ' The IEnumerator interface
        Public Function MoveNext() As Boolean Implements IEnumerator.MoveNext
            If currentValue < 0 Then
                ' First prime number is 2.
                currentValue = 2
            ElseIf currentValue = 2 Then
                ' Second prime number is 3.
                currentValue = 3
                primes.Add(currentValue)
            Else
                ' Test all odd numbers after currentValue value.
                Dim n As Integer = currentValue
                Do
                    n += 2
                    Dim isPrime As Boolean = True      ' Assume N is prime.

                    ' Check whether N can be divided by one of the prime numbers
                    ' found so far.
                    For Each prime As Integer In primes
                        If (n Mod prime) = 0 Then
                            ' Exit if we found a divisor. (N isn't prime.)
                            isPrime = False
                            Exit For
                        ElseIf prime * prime > n Then
                            ' Exit if it is useless to test more divisors. (N is prime.)
                            Exit For
```

```
                              End If
                          Next

                          ' Check whether we found a divisor.
                          If isPrime Then
                              ' Remember N, add it to the list of found prime numbers.
                              currentValue = n
                              primes.Add(currentValue)
                              Exit Do
                          End If
                    Loop
                End If

                ' Return true if the prime we've found is within the desired range.
                ' (Notice that a nested type can access private members in the enclosing type.)
                Return currentValue <= Parent.MaxPrime
            End Function

            Public ReadOnly Property Current() As Object Implements IEnumerator.Current
                Get
                    ' Return the last prime found.
                    Return currentValue
                End Get
            End Property

            ' This method is never invoked by the .NET runtime.
            Public Sub Reset() Implements IEnumerator.Reset
            End Sub

        End Class
    End Class

    // [C#]
    public class PrimeNumbers : IEnumerable
    {
        private readonly int MaxPrime;

        public PrimeNumbers(int maxPrime)
        {
            this.MaxPrime = maxPrime;
        }

        // The IEnumerable interface
        public IEnumerator GetEnumerator()
        {
            return new PrimeNumbersEnumerator(this);
        }

        private class PrimeNumbersEnumerator : IEnumerator
        {
            // A reference to the enclosing object
            private PrimeNumbers Parent;
            // The last prime found
            private int currentValue = -1;
            // This holds all the prime (odd) numbers found so far. (2
            // isn't included.)
            private ArrayList primes = new ArrayList();

            // The constructor
```

```
public PrimeNumbersEnumerator(PrimeNumbers parent)
{
    // Keep a reference to the object being enumerated.
    this.Parent = parent;
}

// The IEnumerator interface
public bool MoveNext()
{
    if ( currentValue < 0 )
    {
        // First prime number is 2.
        currentValue = 2;
    }
    else if ( currentValue == 2 )
    {
        // Second prime number is 3.
        currentValue = 3;
        primes.Add(currentValue);
    }
    else
    {
        // Test all odd numbers after current value.
        int n = currentValue;
        while ( true )
        {
            n += 2;
            bool isPrime = true;      // Assume N is prime.

            // Check whether N can be divided by one of the prime numbers found so far.
            foreach ( int prime in primes )
            {
                if ( (n % prime) == 0 )
                {
                    // Exit if we found a divisor. (N isn't prime.)
                    isPrime = false;
                    break;
                }
                else if ( prime * prime > n )
                {
                    // Exit if it is useless to test more divisors. (N is prime.)
                    break;
                }
            }

            // Check whether we found a divisor.
            if ( isPrime )
            {
                // Remember N, add it to the list of found prime numbers.
                currentValue = n;
                primes.Add(currentValue);
                break;
            }
        }
    }

    // Return true if the prime we've found is within the desired range.
    // (Notice that a nested type can access private members in the enclosing type.)
    return currentValue <= Parent.MaxPrime;
```

```
      }

      public object Current
      {
         get
         {
            // Return the last prime found.
            return currentValue;
         }
      }

      // This method is never invoked by the .NET runtime.
      public void Reset()
      {}
   }
}
```

Here's how you can use the PrimeNumbers type to display all prime numbers that are less than 1000:

```
' [Visual Basic]
For Each n As Integer In New PrimeNumbers(1000)
   Console.WriteLine(n)
Next
```

```
// [C#]
foreach ( int n in new PrimeNumbers(1000) )
   Console.WriteLine(n);
```

8.18 Strong-typed members in interface implementation

Types implementing the IEnumerator, ICollection, and IList interfaces should implement weakly typed members as private members and expose public strong-typed members with the same name. The members that are candidates for this rule are Current (in the IEnumerator interface), CopyTo (in the ICollection interface), Item, Add, Insert, Remove, Contains, and IndexOf (in the IList interface).

Why: By providing strong-typed methods, you reduce the amount of code that clients need to access the interface and indirectly make the type more usable.

Example: This code illustrates how you can provide both a weakly and a strongly typed version of the ICollection.CopyTo method.

```
' [Visual Basic]
Class PersonCollection
   Implements ICollection

   ' The ArrayList that holds the Person objects
   Dim persons As New ArrayList

   ' Private implementation of the CopyTo method
   Private Sub ICollection_CopyTo(ByVal array As Array, ByVal index As Integer) _
         Implements ICollection.CopyTo
      persons.CopyTo(array, index)
   End Sub
```

```
    ' Public strong-typed version of CopyTo method
    Public Sub CopyTo(ByVal array() As Person, ByVal index As Integer)
        ICollection_CopyTo(array, index)
    End Sub

    ' (Other ICollection members omitted)...
End Class
```

```
// [C#]
class PersonCollection : ICollection
{
    // The ArrayList that holds the Person objects
    ArrayList persons = new ArrayList();

    // Private implementation of the CopyTo method
    void ICollection.CopyTo(Array array, int index)
    {
        persons.CopyTo(array, index);
    }

    // Public strong-typed version of CopyTo method
    public void CopyTo(Person[] array, int index)
    {
        (this as ICollection).CopyTo(array, index);
    }

    // (Other ICollection members omitted)...
}
```

8.19 ISerializable interface

Types implementing the ISerializable interface must be marked with the Serializable attribute.

Why: A type that implements ISerializable but isn't marked with the Serializable attribute might not be serialized under all circumstances and might not be recognized as serializable by reflection code that only checks for the presence of the attribute.

Example: For examples of types implementing the ISerializable interface, see rule 17.23 on serializing types exposing events and rule 19.26 on serializable exceptions.

Chapter 9

Structures

All the types in the Microsoft .NET Framework can be grouped in two broad categories: reference types and value types. Reference types behave like objects: when you assign a reference to an object variable, the object's address is copied and no new object is created. (All reference type variables take 4 bytes on 32-bit systems.) Value types behave like scalar values and assignments create a *copy* of the original value. Value type variables are as large as the value itself. (For example, Double variables take 8 bytes.)

In most cases, value types are more efficient than reference types because value types are usually allocated on the stack, don't take memory from the managed heap (unless they are fields of a reference type), and can be released immediately. Reference types are less efficient because the .NET garbage collection needs to reclaim a block of memory in the managed heap when the object isn't in use any longer. Finally, accessing data in a value type is slightly more efficient because the variable *contains* the value, whereas a reference type variable *points* to the actual value and therefore an additional indirection is required at the CPU level.

Even though value types are usually more efficient, there are cases when a reference type can be a better choice, so there aren't fixed rules and you must weigh the pros and cons of value and reference types when you have a choice between the two. This can happen both when two .NET types can solve the problem (is it better to use a String object or an array of Chars?) and when you are defining a new type that might be implemented as a regular class (a reference type) or a structure (a value type).

This chapter contains several guidelines that can help you make the most appropriate decision in these cases.

9.1 Value types vs. reference types

Consider defining a structure instead of a regular class if all the following conditions are met:

   a. You don't need to inherit your type from a specific .NET Framework class.

   b. The type can be sealed—in other words, you'll never need to inherit from the type.

   c. You don't need to initialize the type's fields to any value other than their default state; that is, zero for numbers and null for objects. (See rule 9.4 for more details.)

   d. Expected semantics are such that assignments are expected to copy the value, not the pointer, to the object.

   e. You don't need to implement a finalizer. (See the "More details" section.)

In addition to these required properties, you should consider defining a structure rather than a class when one or more of the following conditions are also true:

a. The fields in the type take 16 bytes of memory or fewer. (See rule 9.3.)

b. All the fields in the type are value types (see rule 9.2 for more details).

c. The type doesn't have to implement interfaces, or at least you rarely need to cast instances of this type to an interface variable.

d. You plan to create arrays containing a large number of instances of this type (see rule 9.2 for more details).

Why: You should define a structure rather than a class when possible because, in addition to the increased speed deriving from being sealed, structures are typically accessed faster because the variable *contains* the data rather than *points* to it. Therefore, no indirection is necessary. Finally, structures are allocated and released faster than reference types.

Why not: Large structures that are often assigned to variables or passed by value to methods require a lot of memory copy operations.

More details: The Visual Basic compiler doesn't complain if you override the Finalize method in a structure, yet the .NET runtime never invokes this method. More correctly, the C# compiler emits a compilation error if you define a destructor in a structure.

9.2 Structures instead of classes with value type members

Use a structure to implement types with few members, all of which are value types such as numeric, Char, and DateTime values. This guideline is especially effective if you plan to create arrays of these objects.

Why: Structures don't take memory from the managed heap and reduce the number of garbage collections. An array of structures takes contiguous memory locations, can be created with a single allocation operation, can be released faster, and often can be accessed more efficiently because consecutive elements tend to fit into the CPU's secondary cache.

9.3 Structure size

Attempt to define structures so that their size is an integer multiple of 4 bytes, and sort their fields in such a way so that the CLR need not insert hidden padding bytes to keep elements aligned. Ideally, a structure should be 16 bytes or smaller.

Why: Arrays of structures take a block of contiguous memory. By making the structure size a multiple of 4 bytes (on 32-bit operating systems), you make the best use of memory. Also, a structure should be small in size because assignments cause all the internal data to be copied to a new structure, unlike assignments between reference types. Remember that you have a hidden assignment, and therefore a memory copy, when you pass a structure to a method argument that isn't marked with the *ByRef* (Visual Basic) or *ref* or *out* (C#) keyword.

More details: You can calculate the memory taken by a structure using the information in Table 9-1.

Table 9-1   Size and Alignment of Primitive .NET Types on 32-Bit Platforms

Data Type	Size	Alignment
Byte, SByte	1 byte	1 byte
Int16, UInt16, Char	2 bytes	2 bytes
Int32, UInt32, Single, all reference values	4 bytes	4 bytes
Double, DateTime, TimeSpan	8 bytes	4 bytes
Decimal, Guid	16 bytes	4 bytes

By default, the CLR automatically arranges the layout of all the fields in a class to avoid padding bytes, but it doesn't perform this type of optimization on structures unless the structure is marked with a StructLayout attribute with the value set to LayoutKind.Auto. (The reason why the CLR doesn't automatically optimize structure layout is because structures are often used to pass values to an external method using PInvoke or COM Interop, and the external method obviously expects the data with a given layout.)

```vb
' [Visual Basic]
' *** Wrong: this structure appears to take 8 bytes, but
' it actually takes 12 bytes because of hidden padding bytes.
Structure MyStruct
    Public a As Byte        ' This is followed by 3 hidden padding bytes.
    Public b As Integer
    Public c As Byte        ' This is followed by a hidden padding byte.
    Public d As Short
End Structure

' *** Correct: no hidden padding bytes are inserted.
Structure MyStruct
    Public a As Byte
    Public c As Byte
    Public d As Short
    Public b As Integer
End Structure
```

```csharp
// [C#]
// *** Wrong: this structure appears to take 8 bytes, but
// it actually takes 12 bytes because of hidden padding bytes.
struct MyStruct
{
    public byte a;          // This is followed by 3 hidden padding bytes.
    public int b;
    public byte c;          // This is followed by a hidden padding byte.
    public short d;
}

// *** Correct: no hidden padding bytes are inserted.
struct MyStruct
{
    public byte a;
    public byte c;
    public short d;
    public int b;
}
```

9.4 Default state of structure members

Define a structure in such a way that it is in a valid state when all its members are zero or null.

More details: You can define constructors with parameters in a structure type, but it is illegal to define a default (parameterless) constructor. Likewise, it is illegal to define an initial value for fields in a structure. When the CLR creates a structure, it zeros all its fields. Therefore, such "all zeros" fields must represent a valid instance of the structure.

Example: If the structure contains a Boolean field or property, ensure that the false state is a valid initial value for it. (If it doesn't, reverse the meaning of the Boolean field.)

9.5 Equals overload in value types

Value types (structures) should overload the Equals method to provide both an instance version and a static version that take typed arguments.

Why: Typed versions of the Equals method avoid boxing and improve performance. This is especially important because the ValueType.Equals method (that all value types inherit) internally uses reflection to compare all fields and is therefore quite inefficient.

More details: If you redefine the Equals method, you should also override the GetHashCode method so that equal objects have an equal hash code (see rule 7.16). In addition, C# developers should also override the == and != operators when redefining the Equals method (see rule 14.31).

```
' [Visual Basic]
Public Structure Point
   ' These should be properties in a real-world application.
   Public ReadOnly X As Double
   Public ReadOnly Y As Double

   Sub New(ByVal x As Double, ByVal y As Double)
      Me.X = x
      Me.Y = y
   End Sub

   ' Strong-typed version of the instance Equals method.
   Public Overloads Function Equals(ByVal p As Point) As Boolean
      Return Me.X = p.X AndAlso Me.Y = p.Y
      ' You might also return Equals(Me, p).
   End Function

   ' Strong-typed version of the static Equals method.
   Public Overloads Shared Function Equals(ByVal p1 As Point, ByVal p2 As Point) _
         As Boolean
      Return p1.X = p2.X AndAlso p1.Y = p2.Y
   End Function
End Structure
```

```csharp
// [C#]
public struct Point
{
    // These should be properties in a real-world application.
    public readonly double X;
    public readonly double Y;

    public Point(double x, double y)
    {
        this.X = x;
        this.Y = y;
    }

    // Strong-typed version of the instance Equals method.
    public bool Equals(Point p)
    {
        return this.X == p.X && this.Y == p.Y;
        // You might also return Equals(this, p).
    }

    // Strong-typed version of the static Equals method.
    public static bool Equals(Point p1, Point p2)
    {
        return p1.X == p2.X && p1.Y == p2.Y;
    }
}
```

9.6 Interface implementation in structures

Avoid defining structures that implement interfaces. However, if you must implement an interface in a structure, ensure that you never assign one or more fields from inside the interface methods.

Why: Both Visual Basic and C# transparently box a structure when they access it through an interface variable, and you should avoid boxing operations because they consume memory and add overhead. Worse, when you access a method through an interface variable, the method runs in the context of the boxed *copy* of the structure rather than the original structure. If the code in the method modifies a field, these changes aren't propagated to the original structure, as this code demonstrates:

```vb
' [Visual Basic]
Interface IUser
    Sub SetName(ByVal name As String)
End Interface

Structure User
    Implements IUser

    Public UserName As String

    ' This interface method modifies a field.
    Public Sub SetName(ByVal name As String) Implements IUser.SetName
        Me.UserName = name
    End Sub
End Structure
```

```
Module MainModule
    Sub Main()
        Dim u As New User
        InitializeUser(u, "John")        ' Hidden box operation
        Console.WriteLine(u.UserName)  ' UserName is still empty!
    End Sub

    Public Sub InitializeUser(ByVal u As IUser, ByVal name As String)
        u.SetName(name)
    End Sub
End Module

// [C#]
interface IUser
{
    void SetName(string name);
}

struct User : IUser
{
    public string UserName;

    // This interface method modifies a field.
    public void SetName(string name)
    {
        this.UserName = name;
    }
}

class App`
{
    static void Main()
    {
        User u = new User();
        InitializeUser(u, "John");          // Hidden box operation
        Console.WriteLine(u.UserName);      // UserName is still empty!
    }

    static void InitializeUser(IUser u, string name)
    {
        u.SetName(name);
    }
}
```

9.7 IDisposable structures [C#]

If a structure implements the IDisposable interface, you should implement this interface by means of a public Dispose method (as opposed to using explicit interface implementation).

Why: Using explicit interface implementation for the Dispose method would force the C# compiler to box the structure if used in a using block (see rule 9.6).

Chapter 10
Enum Types

Enum types can make your code more readable and more robust at the same time, thus we recommend that you use enum types in lieu of "magic" integer values—that is, integer values to which you assign a special meaning.

Defining enum types is quite simple, but a few little-known facts might affect the way you use them. For example, what happens to an application that uses an enum type in a DLL if you later change the definition of the enum and redeploy the DLL? What is the most efficient way to validate an enum value? In this chapter we answer these and other recurring questions about enum types.

10.1 Enum types in one source file

Gather all the enum types in a file named Enums.vb or Enums.cs.

Why: Enum definitions are usually quite short. Using a single file for all enums reduces the number of files in the solution and enables you to find any enum type in the source code quickly.

Why not: You might decide that enum types for different namespaces should go in different source files, to comply with rule 5.7.

Exception: See rule 10.2 for an exception to this rule.

10.2 Enum types nested in another type

If an enum type is used only to define arguments or return values in one or more methods in a given type, it is acceptable to nest the enum type inside that type's definition.

Example: An example of this method is the System.Environment.SpecialFolder enum type, which is used only as an argument of the GetFolderPath method of the System.Environment type.

10.3 Enum type names

Use the following rules when assigning names to enum types:

- **a.** Use a singular name for an enum type whose members are never combined with the *Or*, |, or + operator.
- **b.** Use a plural name for a *bit-coded* enum type—that is, an enum type whose members are meant to be combined with the *Or*, |, or + operator.

    c.   Don't use any special suffix for enum types, such as Enum or Flags.

Enter each enum value on a line of its own so that you can add a remark to its right if necessary.

```
' [Visual Basic]
Public Enum Gender
    Unknown              ' This value means "missing data."
    Male
    Female
End Enum

<Flags()> _
Public Enum LoadOptions
    SingleUser = 1
    MultiUser = 2
    UseCache = 4
End Enum

// [C#]
public enum Gender
{
    Unknown,            // This value means "Missing data."
    Male,
    Female
}

[Flags()]
public enum LoadOptions
{
    SingleUser = 1,
    MultiUser = 2,
    UseCache = 4
}
```

10.4 Flags attribute for bit-coded enum types

Mark bit-coded enum types with the Flags attribute.

Why: This attribute affects the way the ToString method displays the enum value.

Example: See the code example in rule 10.3.

10.5 Base type for enum types

Don't specify the base type for enum types; rely on the default Int32 base type.

Exception: You might have a specific reason to specify a nondefault base type; for example, you can use Byte or Int16 if you anticipate that you will create large arrays of enum values. Or you can use Int64 for bit-coded enum values if you anticipate that you need more than 32 distinct values. However, never use a non-CLS-compliant integer type as the base type, such as UInt32 or UInt64.

```vb
' [Visual Basic]
' Use this 16-bit enum only to save memory.
Public Enum OrderStatus As Short
    Pending
    Processing
    Completed
End Enum
```

```csharp
// [C#]
// Use this 16-bit enum only to save memory.
public enum OrderStatus : short
{
    Pending,
    Processing,
    Completed
}
```

10.6 Member names in enum types

Members in an enum type must not have a common prefix.

```vb
' [Visual Basic]
' *** Wrong
Enum Format
    FormatNormal
    FormatCompressed
End Enum
```

```vb
' *** Correct
Enum Format
    Normal
    Compressed
End Enum
```

```csharp
// [C#]
// *** Wrong
enum Format
{
    FormatNormal,
    FormatCompressed
}
```

```csharp
// *** Correct
enum Format
{
    Normal,
    Compressed
}
```

10.7 Values in non-bit-coded enum types

Explicitly assign values to non-bit-coded values only if you want to insert out-of-order special values, for example, negative numbers for error codes. It's preferable that you place these special values after regular ones.

```
' [Visual Basic]
Public Enum ControlState
    Visible              ' = 0, the default value
    Disabled
    Hidden
    Unknown = -1
    Invalid = -2
End Enum

// [C#]
public enum ControlState
{
    Visible,             // = 0, the default value
    Disabled,
    Hidden,
    Unknown = -1,
    Invalid = -2
}
```

10.8 Values in bit-coded enum types

Use powers of two for values in bit-coded enum types. Consider including values that represent common bitwise-Or combinations of simpler values. Never use negative values.

Why: Negative values should be avoided because they behave in unexpected ways when combined with the bitwise-Or operator.

See also: See rule 10.10 about defining a zero enum value named None.

```
' [Visual Basic]
<Flags()> _
Public Enum AccessModes
    None = 0
    Read = 1
    Write = 2
    ReadWrite = Read Or Write
End Enum

// [C#]
[Flags()]
public enum AccessModes
{
    None = 0,
    Read = 1,
    Write = 2,
    ReadWrite = Read | Write
}
```

10.9 Default value for enum types

Ensure that the default value for a non-bit-coded enum type is zero.

Why: This rule ensures that an enum value is valid even if you don't explicitly assign it in code.

```
' [Visual Basic]
Public Enum ControlState
    Visible          ' = 0, the default value
    Disabled
    Hidden
End Enum
```

```
// [C#]
public enum ControlState
{
    Visible,         // = 0, the default value
    Disabled,
    Hidden
}
```

10.10 Default value for bit-coded enum types

Add a value named None equal to 0 for bit-coded enum types.

```
' [Visual Basic]
<Flags()> _
Public Enum LoadOptions
    None = 0              ' Default value
    SingleUser = 1
    MultiUser = 2
    UseCache = 4
End Enum
```

```
// [C#]
[Flags()]
public enum LoadOptions
{
    None = 0,            // Default value
    SingleUser = 1,
    MultiUser = 2,
    UseCache = 4
}
```

10.11 Reserved enum values

Don't include "reserved for future use" values in an enum value.

Why: Defining such reserved values is a holdover from COM programming. A later version of a Microsoft .NET Framework class library can simply add new values as and when required, without breaking existing clients, provided that you don't change the numeric value of existing values.

```
' [Visual Basic]
'*** Wrong
Public Enum Behavior
    CloseOnExit
    ReadSingleRow
    Reserved1
    Reserved2
End Enum
```

```
// [C#]
// *** Wrong
public enum Behavior
{
   CloseOnExit,
   ReadSingleRow,
   Reserved1,
   Reserved2
}
```

More details: When you compile a .NET application that uses an enum type whose definition is stored in a library (DLL) assembly, the enum value is burned in the application's IL code, even though the application still needs to access the DLL to retrieve the enum's metadata. Therefore, you can later *append* new values to the enum type (so that you don't change the numeric representation of existing values) and redeploy the DLL without breaking the main application's code—provided that the DLL assembly isn't strong-named or that you haven't changed its version number.

10.12 Validation of enum values

Always validate a non-bit-coded enum value passed to properties or method arguments. You can validate against a range, but only if all the numbers in the range are valid enum values.

Why: Defining an enum parameter only ensures that the value being passed to the method is an integer, but it doesn't guarantee that it is one of the constants defined for the enum type. For example, it is possible to define an illegal DayOfWeek enum value as follows:

```
' [Visual Basic]
Dim dow As DayOfWeek = CType(123, DayOfWeek)
```

```
// [C#]
DayOfWeek dow = (DayOfWeek) 123;
```

How to: The following code shows how to implement correctly a property that takes and returns a non-bit-coded enum type with members that form a range containing no invalid values:

```
' [Visual Basic]
Private m_WeekDay As DayOfWeek = DayOfWeek.Sunday

Public Property WeekDay() As DayOfWeek
   Get
      Return m_WeekDay
   End Get
   Set(ByVal Value As DayOfWeek)
      If Value < DayOfWeek.Sunday OrElse Value > DayOfWeek.Saturday Then
         Throw New ArgumentException("Invalid DayOfWeek")
      End If
      m_WeekDay = Value
   End Set
End Property
```

```
// [C#]
private DayOfWeek m_WeekDay = DayOfWeek.Sunday;
```

```
public DayOfWeek WeekDay
{
   get
   {
      return m_WeekDay;
   }
   set
   {
      if ( value < DayOfWeek.Sunday || value > DayOfWeek.Saturday )
         throw new ArgumentException("Invalid DayOfWeek");
      m_WeekDay = value;
   }
}
```

More details: You should avoid using the Enum.IsDefined static method to validate an enum value. This method uses reflection and must load metadata, thus its performance is less than optimal.

10.13 Validation of bit-coded enum values

The following code shows the recommended way to test a bit-coded enum value:

```
' [Visual Basic]
Dim fa As FileAttributes = GetFileAttributes()

' *** Wrong: fails if fa has more than one bit set.
If fa = FileAttributes.Hidden Then ...

' *** Wrong: can't be applied to test multiple bits at once.
If (fa And FileAttributes.Hidden) <> 0 Then ...

' *** Correct
If (fa And FileAttributes.Hidden) = FileAttributes.Hidden Then ...

' Example: test whether the file is System AND hidden.
Dim mask As FileAttributes = FileAttributes.System Or FileAttributes.Hidden
If (fa And mask) = mask Then ...

// [C#]
FileAttributes fa = GetFileAttributes();

// *** Wrong: fails if fa has more than one bit set.
if ( fa == FileAttributes.Hidden )
   ...

// *** Wrong: can't be applied to test multiple bits at once.
if ( (fa & FileAttributes.Hidden) != 0 )
   ...

// *** Correct
if ( (fa & FileAttributes.Hidden) == FileAttributes.Hidden )
   ...

// Example: test whether the file is System AND hidden.
FileAttributes mask = FileAttributes.System | FileAttributes.Hidden;
if ( (fa & mask) == mask )
   ...
```

Chapter 11
Attribute Types and Reflection

Attributes are an important feature of all the Microsoft .NET Framework programming languages and offer a standard yet generic way to store metadata in an assembly. The .NET Framework defines hundreds of attributes for various purposes, and it is important that you use a coherent style when you apply them. In addition to these attributes, you can define your own custom attributes, and it is important that you adhere to the guidelines in this chapter when you do so.

Attributes are in close relationship with reflection because reflection is the part of the .NET Framework that enables you to extract metadata from an assembly. For this reason, we have included a few guidelines related to reflection at the end of this chapter.

> **Note** One or more code examples in this chapter assume that the following namespaces have been imported by means of *Imports* (Visual Basic) or *using* (C#) statements:
>
> ```
> System.Diagnostics
> System.Reflection
> System.Runtime.CompilerServices
> ```

11.1 Applying attributes

Apply attributes on a separate line. Don't indent the line that follows the attribute.

Why: This technique enables you to remove the attribute by simply adding a remark symbol in front of it.

```
' [Visual Basic]
' *** Wrong
<Conditional("TRACE")> Sub DisplayMessage(ByVal msg As String)
   ...
End Sub

' *** Also wrong: the line after the attribute must not be indented.
<Conditional("TRACE")> _
   Sub DisplayMessage(ByVal msg As String)
   ...
End Sub

' *** Correct
<Conditional("TRACE")> _
Sub DisplayMessage(ByVal msg As String)
   ...
End Sub
```

```
// [C#]
// *** Wrong
[Conditional("TRACE")] void DisplayMessage(string msg)
{
    ...
}

// *** Also wrong: the line after the attribute must not be indented.
[Conditional("TRACE")]
    void DisplayMessage(string msg)
{
    ...
}

// *** Correct
[Conditional("TRACE")]
void DisplayMessage(string msg)
{
    ...
}
```

11.2 Applying multiple attributes to the same member [C#]

If a type member takes multiple attributes, enclose each attribute in square brackets and type it on a line of its own.

Why: In addition to making the code more readable, this technique enables you to remove one of the attributes temporarily by simply adding a remark symbol in front of it.

```
// [C#]
// *** OK
[Conditional("TRACE"), DebuggerStepThrough]
void DisplayMessage(string msg)
{
    ...
}

// *** Better
[Conditional("TRACE")]
[DebuggerStepThrough]
void DisplayMessage(string msg)
{
    ...
}
```

11.3 Custom attribute type names

Use the Attribute suffix for attribute types, that is, types that inherit from System.Attribute.

Example: AllowedUserAttribute.

11.4 Sealed custom attribute types

Use sealed (*NotInheritable* in Visual Basic) classes for custom attributes, unless you anticipate the need to inherit from the custom attribute (something that is rarely necessary).

11.5 Constructors in custom attribute types

When defining a custom attribute type, expose one public constructor that takes all the required (positional) arguments and expose these values as public read-only properties. Expose all the remaining, optional (named) arguments as read-write properties. Don't expose the same value as both a positional and a named value.

```vb
' [Visual Basic]
Public NotInheritable Class AllowedUserAttribute
    Inherits System.Attribute

    ' The constructor takes one positional (required) value.
    Public Sub New(ByVal name As String)
        m_Name = name
    End Sub

    ' The positional Name value corresponds to a read-only property.
    Private m_Name As String

    Public ReadOnly Property Name() As String
        Get
            Return m_Name
        End Get
    End Property

    ' The named Group value corresponds to a read-write property.
    Private m_Group As String

    Public Property Group() As String
        Get
            Return m_Group
        End Get
        Set(ByVal Value As String)
            m_Group = Value
        End Set
    End Property
End Class
```

```csharp
// [C#]
public sealed class AllowedUserAttribute: System.Attribute
{
    // The constructor takes one positional (required) value.
    public AllowedUserAttribute(string name)
    {
        m_Name = name;
    }

    // The positional Name value corresponds to a read-only property.
    private string m_Name;

    public string Name
    {
        get
        {
            return m_Name;
        }
    }
}
```

```
// The named Group value corresponds to a read-write property.
private string m_Group;

public string Group
{
   get
   {
      return m_Group;
   }
   set
   {
      m_Group = value;
   }
}
}
```

11.6 Overloaded constructors in custom attribute types

Avoid multiple constructors in attribute classes.

Why: Attributes can take optional (named) arguments, thus in general you rarely need multiple constructors to provide clients with the ability to initialize the attribute correctly.

More details: Although Microsoft recommends against multiple constructors in attributes, it should be noted that many attributes in the .NET Framework don't abide by this rule, for example, the StructLayoutAttribute and ClassInterfaceAttribute types (both in the System.Runtime.InteropServices namespace).

11.7 The AttributeUsage attribute

Mark custom attribute types with an AttributeUsage attribute that specifies to which code members the custom attribute can be applied. Explicitly set the Inherited and AllowMultiple named arguments, even if they could be omitted because their value is false.

Why: If you omit the AttributeUsage attribute, developers can apply your custom attribute to any kind of code members and indirectly cause malfunctioning. By explicitly setting the Inherited and AllowMultiple named arguments, you make it clear that you have pondered how the attribute should be used.

More details: You should set the Inherited named argument to true if the custom attribute type should be automatically inherited in derived classes and members. You should set the AllowMultiple named argument to true if multiple instances of this custom attribute can be applied to the same code element.

```
' [Visual Basic]
' A custom attribute that can be applied to properties and methods
<AttributeUsage(AttributeTargets.Property Or AttributeTargets.Method, _
   Inherited:=False, AllowMultiple:=True)> _
Public Class AllowedUserAttribute
   Inherits Attribute
   ...
End Class
```

```csharp
// [C#]
// A custom attribute that can be applied to properties and methods
[AttributeUsage(AttributeTargets.Property | AttributeTargets.Method,
    Inherited=false, AllowMultiple=true)]
public class AllowedUserAttribute: Attribute
{
    ...
}
```

11.8 Attribute vs. marker interfaces

Favor custom attributes instead of empty interfaces to mark types.

More details: Before the .NET Framework was released, developers would use empty interfaces (that is, interfaces that don't contain any member, a.k.a. *marker interfaces*) to mark types that implement a given functionality; for example, they would use an empty ISqlServer-DataObject interface to mark data objects that work with Microsoft SQL Server and an IOracleDataObject interface to mark data objects that work with Oracle. In the .NET environment, it is recommended that a custom attribute be used in lieu of such marker interfaces.

Why: Custom attributes can convey additional information and are more granular than interfaces in that they can be applied to both type and type members.

Why not: The compiler can't check the presence of an attribute at compile time: for example, you can't define a method parameter that can take only a type marked with a given custom attribute. In such cases, you should use a marker interface instead.

11.9 Checking for a custom attribute

Favor the IsDefined method over the GetCustomAttribute and GetCustomAttributes methods when checking the presence of a given attribute.

Why: The IsDefined method simply looks for the custom attribute in the assembly's metadata; conversely, the GetCustomAttribute and GetCustomAttributes methods actually instantiate the attribute by calling its constructor, which takes CPU cycles and memory in the managed heap.

```vbnet
' [Visual Basic]
' *** Wrong
Dim attr As FlagsAttribute = DirectCast(Attribute.GetCustomAttribute(GetType(Actions), _
    GetType(FlagsAttribute)), FlagsAttribute)
If Not attr Is Nothing Then
    ' Actions type is marked with the Flags attribute.
End If


' *** Correct
If GetType(Actions).IsDefined(GetType(FlagsAttribute), False) Then
    ' Actions type is marked with the Flags attribute.
End If
```

```
// [C#]
// *** Wrong
FlagsAttribute attr = (FlagsAttribute) Attribute.GetCustomAttribute(typeof(Actions),
    typeof(FlagsAttribute));
if ( attr != null )
{
    // Actions type is marked with the Flags attribute.
}

// *** Correct
if ( typeof(Actions).IsDefined(typeof(FlagsAttribute), false) )
{
    // Actions type is marked with the Flags attribute.
}
```

11.10 Loading an assembly for reflection purposes

Favor using the Load static method of the Assembly type when you want to inspect through reflection an assembly with a given identity. If loading an assembly given its path, favor using the LoadFrom method over the LoadFile method. Never use the LoadWithPartialName method.

More details: The Assembly class exposes four static methods for loading an assembly for reflection purposes:

■ The Load method takes an assembly identity and loads the corresponding assembly. The assembly identity is formed by the assembly name, version, culture, and public key token, or just the assembly name if the assembly doesn't have a strong name. This method follows the same rules that the CLR uses when loading an assembly, thus it looks into the GAC first (if the assembly is strongly named) and then in the application's path. It honors any redirection tags found in the application's configuration file; therefore, you can be absolutely sure that the assembly you load with this method is the same assembly that the application would load when referencing one of the types in the assembly.

■ The LoadFrom method takes a file path and loads the assembly with that name or throws an exception if the assembly can't be found. The method resolves any dependency using the load path and loads the assembly in a load context. (You can't load two assemblies with the same identity in this load context.) You should favor the LoadFrom method when loading an assembly from a given path.

■ The LoadFile method also takes a filename and loads the assembly with that name. This method doesn't load the assembly in the context created by the LoadFrom method and doesn't resolve dependencies using the load path. You should use the LoadFile method only when loading two or more assemblies with the same identity and different paths, for example, when you need to compare them.

■ The LoadWithPartialName enables you to load an assembly by providing an incomplete set of identity values (for example, just the name and the culture). This method is marked as obsolete in version 2.0 of the .NET Framework (in beta as of this writing) and should be avoided.

```vb
' [Visual Basic]
' Load an assembly given its identity.
Dim asmName As String = "System, Version=1.0.5000.0, Culture=neutral, " _
    & "PublicKeyToken=b77a5c561934e089"
Dim asm As [Assembly] = [Assembly].Load(asmName)
' Load an assembly given its path.
Dim asm2 As [Assembly] = [Assembly].LoadFrom("c:\myapp\library.dll")
```

```csharp
// [C#]
// Load an assembly given its identity.
string asmName = "System, Version=1.0.5000.0, Culture=neutral, "
    + "PublicKeyToken=b77a5c561934e089"
Assembly asm = Assembly.Load(asmName);
// Load an assembly given its path.
Assembly asm2 = Assembly.LoadFrom(@"c:\myapp\library.dll");
```

11.11 Using the StackTrace object

Use the StackTrace object only for diagnostic purposes. Never use the content of the call stack to make any decision or change the execution flow.

Why: When you compile with optimizations turned on, the JIT compiler can decide to inline a method; when this happens, the actual content of the call stack is different from what you expect, therefore any decision based on the call stack content would be wrong.

More details: You can prevent the JIT compiler from inlining a method by marking the method with a MethodImpl attribute:

```vb
' [Visual Basic]
<MethodImpl(MethodImplOptions.NoInlining)> _
Sub DumpTheCallStack()
    Dim st As New StackTrace
    For i As Integer = 0 To st.FrameCount - 1
        Dim mb As MethodBase = st.GetFrame(i).GetMethod()
        Debug.WriteLine(mb.Name)
    Next
End Sub
```

```csharp
// [C#]
[MethodImpl(MethodImplOptions.NoInlining)]
void DumpTheCallStack()
{
    StackTrace st = new StackTrace();
    for ( int i = 0; i < st.FrameCount; i++ )
    {
        MethodBase mb = st.GetFrame(i).GetMethod();
        Debug.WriteLine( mb.Name );
    }
}
```

11.12 Invoking a method through reflection

Favor the methods of the FieldInfo, PropertyInfo, MethodInfo, ConstructorInfo, and EventInfo types to perform an action through reflection instead of the InvokeMember method of the Type object.

Why: The InvokeMember method must perform two distinct actions: first, it must check whether the actual member being accessed exists (the discovery step), and then it executes the method, or assigns the field, or reads the property, and so forth. When repeatedly accessing the same member, you can avoid the discovery step (and therefore produce more efficient code) by getting a reference to the actual FieldInfo, PropertyInfo, MethodInfo, ConstructorInfo, and EventInfo type.

More details: The following example shows how you can iterate over all the characters of a string by means of reflection.

```vb
' [Visual Basic]
Dim s As String = "Code Architects"
Dim ty As Type = GetType(String)
' First method repeats the discovery step at each loop iteration.
For i As Integer = 0 To s.Length - 1
   Dim args() As Object = {i}
   Dim c As Char = CType(ty.InvokeMember("Chars", _
      BindingFlags.GetProperty, Nothing, s, args), Char)
   Console.WriteLine(c)
Next
' The second method performs the discovery step just once.
Dim pi As PropertyInfo = ty.GetProperty("Chars")
For i As Integer = 0 To s.Length - 1
   Dim args() As Object = {i}
   Dim c As Char = CType(pi.GetValue(s, args), Char)
   Console.WriteLine(c)
Next

// [C#]
string s = "Code Architects";
Type ty = typeof(string);
// First method repeats the discovery step at each loop iteration.
for ( int i = 0; i < s.Length; i++ )
{
   object[] args = { i };
   char c = (char) ty.InvokeMember("Chars", BindingFlags.GetProperty,
      null, s, args);
   Console.WriteLine(c);
}
// The second method performs the discovery step just once.
PropertyInfo pi =ty.GetProperty("Chars");
for ( int i = 0; i < s.Length; i++ )
{
   object[] args = { i };
   char c = (char) pi.GetValue(s, args);
   Console.WriteLine(c);
}
```

Chapter 12
Fields and Variables

In this book, we make a distinction between fields and variables. A field is always declared at the type level and can have a scope keyword (public, private, and so on); a variable is always local to a procedure. Public fields are visible from outside the type; therefore, they have different naming rules from private fields and local variables.

In general, you should never expose a public field, even though there are exceptions to this general rule. You should keep all your fields private and wrap them in public properties to ensure that the field is assigned only valid values and to enable inheritors to change the behavior of the property in derived classes. However, please note that many code examples in this book use public fields in lieu of properties to save space and keep code complexity to a minimum. In other words, do as we say, not as we do.

12.1 Field and variable names

Use the following guidelines when assigning a name to a class-level field or a local variable:

   a. Use PascalCase for public fields. Example: File, FileName.

   b. Use camelCase for private fields and local variables. Example: file, fileName.

   c. Avoid underscores and names longer than 15 characters in public fields. (Private fields and variable names have no limitation in length and can contain underscores; see rule 12.16.)

   d. Use meaningful names for fields and variables. Don't use abbreviations that would make the name ambiguous. However, it is usually acceptable to use short names for the controlling variables in loops.

   e. Use letters and digits in field and variable names, but keep in mind that some letters and digits look similar, such as uppercase letter O and digit 0, or lowercase L and digit 1. If using these characters, at least avoid defining other fields that differ only by characters that look alike. For example, if you already have defined fields named al and ROI, avoid creating variables named a1 and R0I.

12.2 Constant names

Use the following guidelines when assigning a name to a constant:

   a. Use all uppercase for constants of one or two characters. Example: PI.

   b. Use PascalCase for constant names of three characters or longer. Example: DoublePI.

   c. Optionally, use all-uppercase naming style for private constants. This style is especially appropriate for constants used when calling methods in the Microsoft Windows API. Example: WM_MOVE.

12.3 Hungarian notation

Don't use Hungarian notation to imply the type of variables. (Hungarian notation uses different prefixes for different types, as in strName or intValue.)

Why: In general, a variable name should describe the semantics of the variable, not its type. Hungarian notation is a leftover from the days when developers worked with very primitive editors and tools. The Microsoft Visual Studio .NET editor enables you to determine the type of a variable by simply hovering the mouse over it or by highlighting the variable name and pressing the F12 function key (in the default keyboard mapping scheme). Hungarian notation gets in the way when you later wish to change the type of a variable, prevents you from getting the best of IntelliSense (all variables of the same type have the same prefix), and can't be applied consistently without introducing many exceptions.

Exception: Even though Hungarian notation isn't recommended in general, it's quite common and acceptable to use it in a loose way for collections, controls, and other common objects (see rule 12.4 on naming rules for common objects, and rules 27.4 and 29.1 on control names).

12.4 Common prefixes for variable names

Use a prefix from Table 12-1 for variables that reference generic Microsoft .NET Framework objects.

Table 12-1   Prefixes for Generic Types

Prefix	Type	Prefix	Type
att	attribute	han	Win32 handle
buf	buffer	obj	object
del	delegate	per	CAS permission
ex	exception	st	stream

```
' [Visual Basic]
Dim perFileIO As New FileIOPermission(PermissionState.Unrestricted)
perFileIO.Assert()
```

```
// [C#]
FileIOPermission perFileIO = new FileIOPermission(PermissionState.Unrestricted);
perFileIO.Assert();
```

Use a prefix from Table 12-2 for variables that reference the most common .NET Framework objects.

Table 12-2   Prefixes for Common .NET Framework Types

Prefix	Type	Prefix	Type
dom	AppDomain	mi	MemberInfo
asm	Assembly	re	Regex
br	BinaryReader	sb	StringBuilder
bw	BinaryWriter	thr	Thread

Table 12-2   Prefixes for Common .NET Framework Types

Prefix	Type	Prefix	Type
ci	CultureInfo	ty	Type
dir	DirectoryInfo	xdoc	XmlDocument
fil	FileInfo	xelm	XmlElement
fs	FileStream	xnod	XmlNode
ma	Match		

```
' [Visual Basic]
Dim tyPerson As Type = GetType(Person)
For Each mi As MemberInfo In tyPerson.GetMembers()
   ...
Next

// [C#]
Type tyPerson = typeof(Person);
foreach ( MemberInfo mi in tyPerson.GetMembers() )
{
   ...
}
```

12.5 Explicit private scope for fields

Use the explicit *Private* (Visual Basic) or *private* (C#) keyword to define the scope of a type-level field. Neither use *Dim* for such fields (in Visual Basic) nor omit their scope to make them implicitly private (in C#).

More details: Using the Visual Basic *Dim* keyword for type-level fields should be avoided because it gives private visibility to fields exposed by a class and public visibility to fields exposed by a structure. This keyword makes the code less readable and gets in the way if you later want to change a class into a structure, or vice versa. (See rule 6.17.)

12.6 Multiple declarations on same line

Don't declare multiple variables or fields on the same line.

```
' [Visual Basic]
' *** Wrong
Public FirstName, LastName As String
' *** Wrong, but more readable
Public FirstName As String, LastName As String

' *** Correct
Public FirstName As String
Public LastName As String

// [C#]
// *** Wrong
public string FirstName, LastName;
// *** Wrong, but more readable
public string FirstName; string LastName;
```

```
// *** Correct
public string FirstName;
public string LastName;
```

12.7 Constant values

Never hard code a numeric or string value in code. Instead, use a read-only field or a constant. Use the *Const* (Visual Basic) or *const* (C#) keyword only for values that will *never* change in future versions of the application, such as natural math constants.

```
' [Visual Basic]
Const DoublePI As Double = Math.PI * 2
```

```
// [C#]
const double DoublePI = Math.PI * 2;
```

12.8 Read-only fields

Mark a field with the *ReadOnly* (Visual Basic) or *readonly* (C#) keyword if the value of the field must not change after instantiation.

```
' [Visual Basic]
Private ReadOnly CreationDate As Date = Date.Now
```

```
// [C#]
private readonly DateTime CreationDate = DateTime.Now;
```

Why: Marking a field as read-only even if the field is private ensures that code in the class doesn't mistakenly assign a value to the field and that code outside the class can't change the value of a private field using reflection.

12.9 Public instance fields

Never define public instance fields. Instead use a private field and wrap it inside a public property so that you can validate the incoming value before it's assigned to the private field. Unless the enclosing type is sealed (*NotInheritable* in Visual Basic), consider whether the property should be marked as virtual (*Overridable* in Visual Basic).

Why: Properties enable you to validate values; fields don't. Even if you don't need to validate the value in the current class, using a property enables inheritors to apply more restrictive validation criteria.

See also: See rules 12.10 and 12.11 for other guidelines related to fields.

```
' [Visual Basic]
' *** Wrong
Public Name As String

' *** Correct
Private m_Name As String
```

```
Public Property Name() As String
   Get
      Return m_Name
   End Get
   Set(ByVal Value As String)
      If Value Is Nothing OrElse Value.Length = 0 Then
         Throw New ArgumentException("Invalid Name")
      End If
      m_Name = Value
   End Set
End Property

// [C#]
// *** Wrong
Public string Name;

// *** Correct
private string m_Name;

public string Name
{
   get
   {
      return m_Name;
   }
   set
   {
      if ( value == null || value.Length == 0 )
         throw new ArgumentException("Invalid Name");
      m_Name = Value;
   }
}
```

12.10 Public static fields

All the static fields in a type should be marked as constant or read-only.

Why: Access to writeable static fields isn't thread-safe and requires synchronization techniques; therefore, you should never make them writable.

More details: Public static read-only fields are often used to return an "empty" instance of the current type, whatever "empty" means for a given type, as in the following code:

```
' [Visual Basic]
Public Shared ReadOnly Empty As Rect = New Rect(0, 0)

// [C#]
public static readonly Rect Empty = new Rect(0, 0);
```

12.11 Protected fields

Never define protected instance fields. Instead, use a private field and wrap it inside a protected and virtual (*Overridable* in Visual Basic) property.

Why: By defining a protected virtual property, you let inheritors redefine how the field is used or validated.

```vbnet
' [Visual Basic]
' *** Wrong
Public Class User
   Protected Name As String
End Class

' *** Correct
Public Class User
   Private m_Name As String

   Protected Overridable Property Name() As String
      Get
         Return m_Name
      End Get
      Set(ByVal Value As String)
         m_Name = Value
      End Set
   End Property
End Class
```

```csharp
// [C#]
// *** Wrong
public class User
{
   protected string Name;
}

// *** Correct
public class User
{
   private string m_Name;

   protected virtual string Name
   {
      get
      {
         return m_Name;
      }
      set
      {
         m_Name = value;
      }
   }
}
```

Because the field is wrapped in a protected and overridable property, a derived class can change the way the Name value is used or validated, for example, by enforcing a more robust validation policy:

```vbnet
' [Visual Basic]
Public Class PowerUser
   Inherits User

   Protected Overrides Property Name() As String
      Get
         Return MyBase.Name
```

```
        End Get
        Set(ByVal Value As String)
            ' Power users' passwords must be 8 characters or longer.
            If Value Is Nothing OrElse Value.Length < 8 Then
                Throw New ArgumentException("Null or too short password")
            End If
            ' Let the base class validate the value and assign it to a private field.
            MyBase.Name = Value
        End Set
    End Property
End Class

// [C#]
public class PowerUser : User
{
    protected override string Name
    {
        get
        {
            return base.Name;
        }
        set
        {
            // Power users' passwords must be 8 characters or longer.
            if ( value == null || value.Length < 8 )
                throw new ArgumentException("Null or too short password");
            // Let the base class validate the value and assign it to a private field.
            base.Name = value;
        }
    }
}
```

12.12 Local variables

Declare all the local variables near the top of the method and comment them adequately.

Exception: This rule doesn't apply to block variables (see rule 12.14).

12.13 *Static* local variables [Visual Basic]

Don't use *Static* local variables. Instead, replace them with standard class-level variables.

Why: The Visual Basic compiler supports static local variables only for backward compatibility with previous versions of the language. For each local variable marked as *Static*, the compiler generates a hidden class-level variable and extra IL code to ensure that the variable is correctly initialized only the first time the method is executed.

```
' [Visual Basic]
' *** Wrong
Sub PerformTask
    Static firstTime As Boolean
    If Not firstTime Then
        ' Initialize values here.
        ...
        firstTime = True
```

```
      End If
      ...
End Sub

' *** Correct
Private firstTime As Boolean

Sub PerformTask
    If Not firstTime Then
        ' Initialize values here.
        ...
        firstTime = True
    End If
    ...
End Sub
```

12.14 Block variables

Take advantage of block variables. If a variable is used only in a loop or a conditional block, declare the variable in that block.

Why: This rule ensures that the variable declaration is close to its first use and enables you to later remove the block or change its contents without having to delete or modify the code elsewhere in the method.

```
' [Visual Basic]
If x > 0 Then
    Dim tmp As Integer = x * 10
    ' Use tmp here...
    ...
End If

// [C#]
if ( x > 0 )
{
    int tmp = x * 10;
    // Use tmp here...
    ...
}
```

12.15 Block variable initialization [Visual Basic]

Always explicitly initialize block variables.

Why: A block can be reentered (for example, if it is nested in a loop); therefore, you should make no assumption on the value that the block variable holds at any moment. By explicitly assigning a value to a block variable, you can avoid many common programming bugs. (The C# compiler correctly flags uninitialized block variables as errors; therefore C# developers don't need to be reminded of this guideline.)

```
' [Visual Basic]
For i As Integer = 1 To 100
    Dim s As String = ""      ' Explicitly initialize block variable.
    ...
Next
```

12.16 Name of fields wrapped by properties

Use m_*PropertyName* name for a private field that is wrapped by a property named *PropertyName*. Notice that *PropertyName* is PascalCase and matches exactly the name of the property. Don't use this convention for any other kind of private field.

Why: Wrapped variables are more easily recognizable and are grouped together in the IntelliSense list.

Example: Use m_UserName for a field wrapped by the UserName property, as the following code demonstrates.

```
' [Visual Basic]
Private m_UserName As String

Public Property UserName() As String
    Get
        Return m_UserName
    End Get
    Set(ByVal Value As String)
        m_UserName = Value
    End Set
End Property

// [C#]
private string m_UserName;

public string UserName
{
    get
    {
        return m_UserName;
    }
    set
    {
        m_UserName = value;
    }
}
```

Alternative rule: Use _*PropertyName* names for private fields that are wrapped by a property named *PropertyName*. Don't use this convention for any other kind of private field. For example, use _FileName for a field wrapped by the FileName property.

More details: Choosing one of these two styles is mainly a matter of personal preference. Many developers prefer the em-underscore style because they find it unnatural to begin a variable name with an underscore. Also, Visual Basic developers might have problems detecting a leading underscore if they enable the Show Procedure Line Separators option (in the Visual Basic Specific page of the Text Editor folder in the Options dialog box). Advocates of the latter rule find it more convenient to have all the fields wrapped by properties grouped together at the top of the IntelliSense list. We have listed both rules and recommend only that you consistently use the same style in all your listings.

12.17 Location of fields wrapped by properties

Always place the definition of the private field wrapped by a property immediately before the property.

Why: You can remove a property or change its name and type more easily because all the relevant code elements are grouped together.

Example: See rule 12.16 for a code example of this guideline.

12.18 References to fields wrapped by properties

Never directly access private fields from inside methods and constructors if the field is wrapped by a public property. Instead, reference the property.

Why: You can change the implementation of the property by editing just one portion of code.

Exception: You can't follow this rule when you must assign a field that is wrapped by a read-only property. In such cases, you have no other choice but to reference the field directly. See rule 15.4 for more details and a code example.

Example: The following code assumes that elsewhere in the current class you have defined the UserName property as in rule 12.16.

```
' [Visual Basic]
' *** Wrong: it references the private field.
Public Sub DisplayUserName()
   Console.WriteLine(m_UserName)
End Sub

' *** Correct: it references the public property.
Public Sub DisplayUserName()
   Console.WriteLine(UserName)
End Sub

// [C#]
// *** Wrong: it references the private field.
public void DisplayUserName()
{
   Console.WriteLine(m_UserName);
}

// *** Correct: it references the public property.
public void DisplayUserName()
{
   Console.WriteLine(UserName);
}
```

12.19 Field initialization

Use the following guidelines when deciding how to initialize private and public fields to their default values:

1. Favor initializers to explicit assignments in the constructor if you have only one constructor.

```
' [Visual Basic]
Public ReadOnly CreationDate As Date = Date.Now
```

```
// [C#]
public readonly DateTime CreationDate = DateTime.Now;
```

2. Initialize fields in the constructor if assignment order is relevant.

3. If the type has multiple constructors, ensure that each given field is assigned in only one constructor. Use constructor chaining so that all fields are initialized correctly.

```
' [Visual Basic]
Public Class Person
    Public ReadOnly FirstName As String
    Public ReadOnly LastName As String
    Public ReadOnly Country As String

    Public Sub New(ByVal firstName As String, ByVal lastName As String)
       ' Delegate to the other constructor, use default value for Country.
      Me.New(firstName, lastName, Nothing)
    End Sub

    ' This is the only constructor that initializes fields.
    Public Sub New(ByVal firstName As String, ByVal lastName As String, _
        ByVal country As String)
      Me.FirstName = firstName
      Me.LastName = lastName
      Me.Country = country
    End Sub
End Class
```

```
// [C#]
public class Person
{
    public readonly string FirstName;
    public readonly string LastName;
    public readonly string Country;

    // Delegate to the other constructor, use default value for Country.
    public Person(string firstName, string lastName)
       : this(firstName, lastName, null)
    {}

    // This is the only constructor that initializes fields.
    public Person(string firstName, string lastName, string country)
    {
       this.FirstName = firstName;
       this.LastName = lastName;
       this.Country = country;
    }
}
```

Why: Field initializers make your code more concise and should be used when possible. However, when the type contains multiple constructors, the Visual Basic and C# compilers create a duplicate hidden assignment for each field and each constructor. For example, if you have

10 initialized fields and 4 constructors, the compiler creates as many as 40 hidden assignments, thus unnecessarily bloating your executable file and the application's working set in memory. By explicitly assigning the fields in just one of the constructors, you avoid these additional hidden statements and reduce overhead.

See also: Read rules 15.13, 15.14, and 15.15 for more information on how to use field initializers in conjunction with constructors.

12.20 Simplified syntax for object instantiation [Visual Basic]

Use the concise syntax when declaring an object variable and instantiating an object in the same statement.

```
' [Visual Basic]
' *** OK
Dim p As Person = New Person("Joe", "Smith")

' *** Better
Dim p As New Person("Joe", "Smith")
```

12.21 The *DirectCast* operator [Visual Basic]

Use the *DirectCast* operator instead of *CType* when you unbox a value type, cast an object to an interface variable, or cast an object to a derived-type variable.

Why: Unlike *CType*, the *DirectCast* operator is never translated to a call into the language runtime library and is therefore more efficient. The *CType* operator should be used only to perform conversions—for example, from strings to numbers or DateTime values.

```
' [Visual Basic]
' Let's box an integer into the obj variable.
Dim obj As Object = 123

' *** Wrong (inefficient) ways of doing unboxing
Dim n As Integer = CInt(obj)
Dim n2 As Integer = CType(obj, Integer)

' *** Correct way of doing unboxing
Dim n As Integer = DirectCast(obj, Integer)
```

12.22 The assignment operator inside expressions [C#]

Avoid using the = (assignment) operator to embed a variable assignment inside an expression.

Why: This guideline makes for more readable code because assignments inside complex expressions can be confusing and might be mistakenly read as the == equality operator. Besides, if the variable is used multiple times in the same expression, you might introduce bugs by accidentally reordering the expression's operands.

```
// [C#]
// *** Wrong
int i;
if ( ( i = k+1 ) != 0 )
```

```
{
    // Use i here...
}

// *** Correct
int i = k + 1;
if ( i != 0 )
{
    // Use i here...
}
```

Exception: It is acceptable to use assignments in expressions to assign the same value to multiple variables, as in this code:

```
// [C#]
int x, y, z;
x = y = z = 0;
```

12.23 The *as* operator [C#]

Use the *as* operator instead of combining the *is* operator with casting.

Why: This approach speeds up execution because the type of the object is queried only once.

```
// [C#]
// *** Wrong
void PerformTask(object obj)
{
    if ( obj is Person )
    {
        Person p = (Person) obj;
        // Use p here...
    }
}

// *** Correct
void PerformTask(object obj)
{
    Person p = obj as Person;
    if ( p != null )
    {
        // Use p here...
    }
}

// *** Also correct, but less readable
void PerformTask(object obj)
{
    Person p;
    if ( (p = obj as Person) != null )
    {
        // Use p here...
    }
}
```

12.24 The *With* keyword [Visual Basic]

When repeatedly accessing a nested object, use a *With* block to make the code more concise and efficient at the same time.

```
' [Visual Basic]
With daOrders.SelectCommand.Parameters(0)
    .ParameterName = "OrderID"
    .Value = 123
    .Direction = ParameterDirection.Input
End With
```

12.25 Temporary variables for nested objects [C#]

When repeatedly accessing a nested object, use a temporary variable to make the code more concise and efficient at the same time.

```
// [C#]
// *** Wrong
daOrders.SelectCommand.Parameters[0].ParameterName = "OrderID";
daOrders.SelectCommand.Parameters[0].Value = 123;
daOrders.SelectCommand.Parameters[0].Direction = ParameterDirection.Input;

// *** Correct
System.Data.OleDb.OleDbParameter par = daOrders.SelectCommand.Parameters[0];
par.ParameterName = "OrderID";
par.Value = 123;
par.Direction = ParameterDirection.Input;
```

12.26 Nonserializable fields

Always mark nonserializable fields with the NonSerialized attribute, regardless of whether the class is marked as serializable.

Why: This technique enables you later to apply the Serializable attribute to the type without having to check individual fields.

More details: Delegates aren't serializable, so you must mark all delegate fields with the Non-Serialized attribute. If your C# type exposes one or more events, you must mark them with the NonSerialized attribute as well because events are based on delegates:

```
// [C#]
[field: NonSerialized]
public event EventHandler NameChanged;
```

See also: See rule 17.23 for a technique that works with Visual Basic as well.

12.27 IntPtr fields and properties

Fields and properties of type IntPtr or UIntPtr containing memory addresses should be marked as private, internal (*Friend* in Visual Basic), or read-only.

Why: This rule ensures that no malicious client can change the value of these fields to read and/or write arbitrary memory locations.

Chapter 13
Properties

Most types expose one or more properties that can be read or written to. If a type has neither properties nor fields, the type doesn't actually have a state, so it should be used only as a container for static methods. (An example of such a type is System.Activator.)

Because properties are so common in object-oriented programming, it is essential that you use them appropriately by following the guidelines illustrated in this chapter to meet the expectations that most developers have when they read or assign properties.

One thing to bear in mind about properties is that they are only an abstraction ("syntactical sugar") that the compiler provides for us. In fact, the compiler generates for each property a get_*PropertyName* and a set_*PropertyName* method, and therefore many rules that apply to methods apply to properties as well (and aren't repeated in this chapter).

> **Note** One or more code examples in this chapter assume that the following namespace has been imported by means of an *Imports* (Visual Basic) or *using* (C#) statement:
>
> ```
> System.Runtime.CompilerServices
> ```

13.1 Property names

Use PascalCase for property names. Avoid underscores, names longer than 15 characters, and names that start with Get or Set.

Why: Developers perceive properties as smart fields; thus, properties' names follow the same rules as public fields (see rule 12.1). Get and Set prefixes should be avoided because they are usually associated with methods (see rules 1.24, 14.25, and 14.26).

13.2 Property size

Keep the body of a property as short as possible. Ideally, the get block should just return the private field, whereas the set block should only assign the private field (or throw an exception if the incoming value isn't valid).

Why: Properties should be regarded as smart fields and should be read and written as fast as possible. In addition, the JIT compiler can inline short nonvirtual properties more frequently, thus improving the overall performance.

Example: This example shows how to implement a simple property that doesn't need to validate the incoming value.

```
' [Visual Basic]
Private m_Enabled As Boolean = True

Public Property Enabled() As Boolean
   Get
       Return m_Enabled
   End Get
   Set(ByVal Value As Boolean)
      m_Enabled = Value
   End Set
End Property

// [C#]
private bool m_Enabled = true;

public bool Enabled
{
   get
   {
      return m_Enabled;
   }
   set
   {
      m_Enabled = value;
   }
}
```

13.3 Compact formatting for properties [C#]

Consider using a more compact style only for properties that simply wrap a private field without performing any form of validation, for example, Boolean properties.

See also: This is an exception to rule 2.6; the purpose of this rule is making the code more concise and increasing the amount of code visible on the screen.

```
// [C#]
private bool m_Enabled = true;

public bool Enabled
{
   get { return m_Enabled; }
   set { m_Enabled = value; }
}
```

13.4 Validation and assignment in properties

The set block of a property procedure should validate the incoming value and throw an exception if necessary. Then it should compare the incoming value with the current value and do the assignment only if the values are different.

Why: By actually performing the assignment only if the new value is different, you reduce undesirable side effects, simplify debugging, and prepare your code to raise a *PropertyName*Changed event, should you later wish to do so.

See also: See rule 17.15 for more information on raising events when a property changes.

```vb
' [Visual Basic]
' A property that validates the incoming value
Private m_UserName As String

Public Property UserName() As String
    Get
        Return m_UserName
    End Get
    Set(ByVal Value As String)
        If Value Is Nothing OrElse Value.Length = 0 Then
            Throw New ArgumentException("Invalid UserName")
        ElseIf m_UserName <> Value Then
            m_UserName = Value
            ' Raise the UserNameChanged event here, if desired.
        End If
    End Set
End Property
```

```csharp
// [C#]
// A property that validates the incoming value
private string m_UserName;

public string UserName
{
    get
    {
        return m_UserName;
    }
    set
    {
        if ( value == null || value.Length == 0 )
            throw new ArgumentException("Invalid UserName");
        else if ( m_UserName != value )
            m_UserName = value;
            // Raise the UserNameChanged event here, if desired.
    }
}
```

13.5 Properties vs. methods

Use the following guidelines when deciding whether you should return a value by means of a read-only property or a method:

   a. Use a read-only property when returning the value of a private field.

   b. Use a read-only property when returning the result of a simple calculation based on private fields.

   c. Use a method when producing the result requires complex calculations.

   d. Use a method when the read operation might throw an exception.

   e. Use a method when performing a conversion.

   f. Use a method when returning an array.

g. Use a method when the operation has an observable side effect.

h. Use a method when invoking it twice might deliver different results.

i. Use a method to assign multiple fields when assignment order is important.

Generally, you should use a property when the member behaves like a field; otherwise, use a method.

Why: Most programmers assume that they can read properties as they read fields; this operation should execute quickly, have no side effects, and not throw exceptions.

More details: Properties should be implemented in such a way that clients can assign them in any order without changing the final result. If you can't guarantee this behavior, consider exposing a method for setting a group of properties in one operation and make the corresponding values available as read-only properties.

Example: Assume you wish to return clients a list of colors that are available for a given operation. You should define an AvailableColors read-only property if the value is held in a private collection field and can be returned immediately; otherwise, define a GetAvailableColors method. See rules 14.24 and 14.25 for guidelines on using Get-prefixed methods.

13.6 Read-only properties

Define a *SetPropertyName* method for each read-only public property defined in a type. This method should have private, *Friend* (Visual Basic), or *internal* (C#) scope and should validate the value before assigning it to the private field wrapped by the property. Consistently use this Set-prefixed method from constructors and other methods in the class whenever you need to assign a value to the private field. You can also consider using a protected scope for this method and marking it as *Overridable* (Visual Basic) or *virtual* (C#) if the class isn't sealed so that inherited types can write the private field and can enforce different validation criteria if necessary.

```
' [Visual Basic]
' The public read-only property that wraps a private field.
Private m_UserName As String

Public ReadOnly Property UserName() As String
    Get
        Return m_UserName
    End Get
End Property

' The private method that validates the value and assigns it to private field.
Private Sub SetUserName(ByVal name As String)
    If name = "" Then
        Throw New ArgumentException("Invalid UserName ")
    End If
    m_UserName = name
End Sub
```

```csharp
// [C#]
// The public read-only property that wraps a private field.
private string m_UserName;

public string UserName
{
   get
   {
      return m_UserName;
   }
}

// The private method that validates the value and assigns it to private field.
private void SetUserName(string name)
{
   if ( name == null || name.Length == 0 )
      throw new ArgumentException("Invalid UserName");
   m_UserName = name;
}
```

13.7 Write-only properties

Never define a write-only property. Use a Set-prefixed method instead, or pass the property value as an argument for the constructor and don't provide any other method or property that grants code outside the current type access to the private field that holds the value.

Why: Developers assume that a property is always writable and perceive a write-only property as unnatural.

```vb
' [Visual Basic]
' A private field
Private m_Password As String

' *** Wrong
Public WriteOnly Property Password() As String
   Set(ByVal Value As String)
      m_Password = Value
   End Set
End Property

' *** Correct
Public Sub SetPassword(ByVal newPassword As String)
   m_Password = newPassword
End Sub
```

```csharp
// [C#]
// A private field
private string m_Password;

// *** Wrong
public string Password
{
   set
   {
```

```
        m_Password = value;
    }
}

// *** Correct
public void SetPassword(string newPassword)
{
    m_Password = newPassword;
}
```

13.8 Properties with arguments

Avoid properties that take more than one argument. Use arguments of type Int32 or String exclusively.

Why: Properties with more than one argument or with arguments of types other than integers or strings tend to confuse users and reduce the usability of your types.

More details: The C# language allows only one property with arguments in each type; this property is often dubbed as the *indexer* of the type. The indexer property must be named *this* and can be overloaded to support different sets of arguments.

```
// [Visual Basic]
Private arItems() As String = {"zero", "one", "two", "three"}

Public Default Property Item(ByVal index As Integer) As String
    Get
        Return arItems(index)
    End Get
    Set(ByVal Value As String)
        arItems(index) = Value
    End Set
End Property

// [C#]
private string[] arItems = new string[] {"zero", "one", "two", "three"};

public string this[int index]
{
    get
    {
        return arItems[index];
    }
    set
    {
        arItems[index] = value;
    }
}
```

13.9 Default properties [Visual Basic]

If defining a property with arguments, name it Item and mark it with the *Default* keyword. Don't define more than one public property with arguments in a public class. (Overloaded properties with the same name and private properties with different names are fine, though.) Don't define *Shared* properties with arguments unless the type contains only static members.

Why: The *Default* keyword enables clients to omit the name of the property, which often makes client code easier to read. (This technique is especially effective with collection-like classes.) Just as important, the *Default* keyword makes a public property callable from C# clients, which see the property as an indexer.

More details: C# clients can directly call a Visual Basic public property with arguments only if the property is marked with the *Default* keyword; all other instance and static properties with parameters can be read and written only by means of get_*PropertyName* and set_*PropertyName* accessor methods, which make the usage of the property less natural.

Example: See the code example in rule 13.8.

13.10 The *value* keyword [C#]

Use the keyword *value* only in the set block of a property.

Why: This keyword has no special value outside a property's set block, but its usage is confusing and should be avoided. (Confusion can arise also because the Microsoft Visual Studio .NET editor uses a different color for this keyword even when it appears outside a property block.)

Why not: Sometimes this guideline contradicts other rules, so you might decide to ignore it. Ignoring this guideline might be necessary, for example, when the type has a property named Value (initial capped) and you are passing the property's initial value in the constructor (whose argument should be lowercase, according to rule 14.4).

13.11 Alternate friendly names for indexers [C#]

Use the IndexerName attribute to expose an indexer to Visual Basic clients as a property with a name other than Item.

More details: By default, a C# indexer appears to Visual Basic clients as a property named Item. This default name is OK in most cases, for example, when the type is a custom collection and the indexer provides access to one of its elements. In other cases, however, this default name isn't appropriate, and you might want to expose the indexer under a different name. (For example, the String type's indexer appears to Visual Basic users as a read-only property named Chars, not Item.)

```
// [C#]
// This property appears to Visual Basic clients as "Value" rather than "Item."
private object[] arValues;

[IndexerName("Value")]
public object this[int index]
{
   get
   {
      return arValues[index];
   }
   set
   {
      arValues[index] = value;
   }
}
```

13.12 Is-prefixed Boolean read-only properties

Use the Is prefix for read-only properties that return a Boolean value. Don't use the Is prefix if the property is writable.

Example: Use Visible for a read-write property, but use IsVisible if the property is read-only.

13.13 Properties that return arrays

Don't define a read-only array property if clients shouldn't be allowed to change individual elements in the returned array. Instead, use a read-only scalar property with an index argument (Visual Basic) or an indexer (C#). If the array has few elements, you can define a property that takes no arguments and returns a clone of the private array.

Why: You typically define a read-only property to prevent clients from modifying the value of the private field that the property wraps. However, if a property returns an array reference, clients can still modify all the array elements, regardless of whether the property is marked as read-only. This ability can lead to programming mistakes or security problems, and therefore it should be avoided.

More details: C# doesn't support properties with arguments, so you can only use an indexer. However, an index appears to C# clients as a nameless member and appears to Visual Basic clients as a property named Item; therefore, you should consider whether the semantics implied by indexers is feasible. If not, consider using a Get-prefixed method that takes an index argument.

See also: See rule 13.9 about default properties in Visual Basic.

```
' [Visual Basic]
' A private array
Private m_FileNames() As String

' *** Wrong: a read-only property that returns an array
```

```vb
Public ReadOnly Property FileNames() As String()
   Get
       Return m_FileNames
   End Get
End Property

' *** Slightly better: it is more secure, but it is less efficient
' if the array has many elements.
Public ReadOnly Property FileNames() As String()
   Get
       Return DirectCast(m_FileNames.Clone(), String())
   End Get
End Property

' *** Correct: note the singular name and the Default keyword.
Default Public ReadOnly Property FileName(ByVal index As Integer) As String
   Get
       Return m_FileNames(index)
   End Get
End Property

' *** Also correct
Public Function GetFileName(ByVal index As Integer) As String
   Return m_FileNames(index)
End Function
```

```csharp
// [C#]
// A private array
private string[] m_FileNames;

// *** Wrong: a read-only property that returns an array
public string[] FileNames
{
   get
   {
      return m_FileNames;
   }
}

// *** Slightly better: it is more secure, but it is less efficient
// if the array has many elements.
public string[] FileNames
{
   get
   {
      return string[] m_FileNames.Clone();
   }
}

// *** Correct
public string this[int index]
{
   get
   {
      return m_FileNames[index];
```

```
    }
}

// *** Also correct
public string GetFileName(int index)
{
    return m_FileNames[index];
}
```

13.14 Properties that return collections

If a property returns a collection (in general, a type that implements the ICollection interface), the property should be marked as read-only.

More details: By making the property read-only, you prevent clients from replacing the collection with a new one or from setting it to a null object reference, which might cause problems elsewhere in the type.

Chapter 14
Methods

In a sense, methods are the backbone of types and object-oriented programming. Even if the class exposes just properties, under the hood those properties are read and written by means of hidden methods that the Visual Basic and C# compilers generate transparently, as we explained in Chapter 13. (These methods are named get_*PropertyName* and set_*PropertyName*; they don't appear in the object browser, but you can see them if you disassemble the code with the Ildasm tool.) Events are closely related to methods as well because when an object raises an event, it actually invokes one or more methods by means of a delegate. Finally, even constructors are akin to methods in that they can take arguments and throw exceptions.

For these reasons, the guidelines we've gathered in this chapter can be applied in many cases, including constructors and the get and set blocks in a property definition.

> **Note**   One or more code examples in this chapter assume that the following namespace has been imported by means of an *Imports* (Visual Basic) or *using* (C#) statement:
>
> `System.IO`

14.1 Method names

Use the following guidelines for method names:

a.   Use PascalCase for both public and private methods.

b.   Avoid underscores and names longer than 25 characters if the method is public.

c.   Use a consistent verb-noun syntax. Example: EvalTotals, UpdateStats (rather than TotalsEval or StatsUpdate, respectively).

d.   Maintain consistent naming for methods that perform similar (or opposite) operations. For example, define a SaveFile method if you have a LoadFile method; define a Close method if you have an Open method, and so on.

14.2 Method size

Try to avoid methods longer than 50 executable statements. If necessary, split longer methods into multiple procedures.

Why: Shorter methods improve code readability. In addition, the JIT compiler can inline short nonvirtual methods (fewer than 32 bytes of IL code) that don't contain *Try* (Visual Basic) or *try* (C#) blocks or conditional or loop statements and that don't receive a structure as an argument.

More details: Method inlining is an optimization technique that eliminates a method call by moving the code of the called method inside the body of the caller.

See also: See rule 7.12 on how you can split longer methods contained in nonsealed classes.

14.3 Number of arguments

Avoid methods with more than six arguments. If a method requires more arguments, consider defining an auxiliary class or structure to be used as one of the arguments.

If you define a method with two or more arguments, to simplify common cases when default values would be passed, consider the opportunity to provide overloaded methods with the same name that take fewer arguments (see rule 14.20).

14.4 Parameter names

Use camelCase for parameter names. Use names that reflect the meaning of the parameter and avoid prefixes and suffixes that indicate the type of a parameter, such as intValue or short-Value.

```vbnet
' [Visual Basic]
' *** Wrong: uses incorrect casing, type is embedded in parameter name.
Sub PerformTask(ByVal UserName As String, ByVal boolIsAdmin As Boolean)
    ...
End Sub

' *** Correct
Sub PerformTask(ByVal userName As String, ByVal isAdmin As Boolean)
    ...
End Sub
```

```csharp
// [C#]
// *** Wrong: uses incorrect casing, type is embedded in parameter name.
void PerformTask(string UserName, bool boolIsAdmin)
{
    ...
}

// *** Correct
void PerformTask(string userName, bool isAdmin)
{
    ...
}
```

14.5 Reserved parameters

Don't reserve one or more parameters for future use. Define only the parameters that are actually currently used by the method. If additional parameters are required in future versions of the class, you can later define an overloaded method.

14.6 Parameters typed as base classes

Consider using parameters typed after base classes or interfaces (as opposed to parameters of a specific type) to improve the usability of your methods.

Exception: You can't apply this rule to parameters marked with the *ByRef* (Visual Basic), *ref*, and *out* (C#) keywords. Also, you shouldn't apply this rule to delegate parameters and array parameters.

Example: The following code shows a simple method named SetFormColors, which sets the foreground and background colors of a form. Because the method's body only accesses properties in the Form base class, it is a mistake to declare the parameter as a frmMain object. By defining the parameter as generically as possible, you can make this code reusable with any kind of form.

```
' [Visual Basic]
' *** Wrong: the method doesn't access specific frmMain members.
Sub SetFormColors(ByVal frm As frmMain)
    frm.ForeColor = Color.Black
    frm.BackColor = Color.White
End Sub

' *** Correct: uses the base Form class and is therefore reusable.
Sub SetFormColors(ByVal frm As Form)
    frm.ForeColor = Color.Black
    frm.BackColor = Color.White
End Sub

// [C#]
// *** Wrong: the method doesn't access specific frmMain members.
void SetFormColors(frmMain frm)
{
    frm.ForeColor = Color.Black;
    frm.BackColor = Color.White;
}

// *** Correct: uses the base Form class and is therefore reusable.
void SetFormColors(Form frm)
{
    frm.ForeColor = Color.Black;
    frm.BackColor = Color.White;
}
```

14.7 Argument validation

Always validate arguments near the top of the procedure and throw an exception if they are invalid. You should throw an ArgumentException object and set its Message property to explain why the argument has been rejected. Or throw an ArgumentNullException object if the method receives a null object and null references aren't acceptable.

More details: The ArgumentNullException type inherits from ArgumentException; thus, clients that only explicitly catch the latter exception will transparently catch the former exception as well.

```vb
' [Visual Basic]
Sub PerformTask(ByVal text As String, ByVal width As Integer)
   ' Validate all arguments before proceeding.
   If text Is Nothing Then
      Throw New ArgumentNullException("text")
   ElseIf width <= 0 Then
      Throw New ArgumentException("Width can't be zero or negative", "width")
   End If
   ...
End Sub
```

```csharp
// [C#]
void PerformTask(string text, int width)
{
   // Validate all arguments before proceeding.
   if ( text == null )
      throw new ArgumentNullException("text");
   else if ( width <= 0 )
      throw new ArgumentException("Width can't be zero or negative", "width");
   ...
}
```

14.8 The *ByVal* keyword [Visual Basic]

Use the explicit *ByVal* keyword for arguments that are passed by value even if the by-value passing mechanism is the default behavior for Visual Basic. Microsoft Visual Studio .NET automatically adds the *ByVal* keyword if you omit it, so in practice you must actively apply this rule only when you use a different editor that doesn't exhibit this behavior or when you paste or convert code from Microsoft Visual Basic 6 projects.

More details: The default argument-passing mechanism under Visual Basic 6 is by reference. When importing an entire Visual Basic 6 project into Visual Studio .NET, all arguments lacking an explicit *ByVal* keyword are rendered with the *ByRef* keyword to preserve semantics. However, this conversion doesn't take place when you manually paste Visual Basic 6 code into the Visual Studio .NET editor, in which case implicit *ByRef* keywords are mistakenly morphed into *ByVal*. The bottom line: never paste Visual Basic 6 code directly in the editor; instead, use the Upgrade Visual Basic 6 Code utility that you can run from the Tools menu (see Figure 14-1).

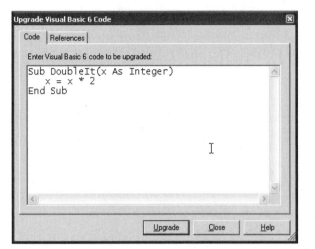

Figure 14-1   The Upgrade Visual Basic 6 Code utility

14.9 Reference types passed by reference

Avoid defining methods that take arguments passed by reference—that is, by means of the *ByRef* (Visual Basic) or *ref* (C#) keyword—if the argument is a reference type.

Why: There is rarely the need to pass a reference type to a by-reference parameter because a by-value parameter still lets the method read and modify all the fields and properties of the object.

Exception: The only exception to this rule is when the method must be allowed to set the parameter to a null object reference or to make it point to a different object.

```vb
' [Visual Basic]
' *** Wrong: the method doesn't need to modify the pointer.
Sub ClearProperties(ByRef p As Person)
    p.FirstName = Nothing
    p.LastName = Nothing
End Sub

' *** Correct: the object is passed by value.
Sub ClearProperties(ByVal p As Person)
    p.FirstName = Nothing
    p.LastName = Nothing
End Sub

' *** Correct: the method assigns a new object reference.
Sub ClearProperties(ByRef p As Person)
    p = New Person
End Sub
```

```csharp
// [C#]
// *** Wrong: the method doesn't need to modify the pointer.
void ClearProperties(ref Person p)
```

```
{
    p.FirstName = null;
    p.LastName = null;
}

// *** Correct: the object is passed by value.
void ClearProperties(Person p)
{
    p.FirstName = null;
    p.LastName = null;
}

// *** Correct: the method assigns a new object reference.
void ClearProperties(ref Person p)
{
    p = new Person();
}
```

More details: It is essential that you understand the difference between passing an argument by value or by reference as well as the implications of passing reference types rather than value types. There are four cases in total:

a. **Passing value types by value**   A copy of the value type is created and passed to the method. This argument-passing style is commonly used and exhibits no side effects because the callee can't change any member of the original value type.

b. **Passing reference types by value**   A copy of the pointer to the object is created and passed to the method. In most cases, this is the correct way to pass a reference type: the method can use the parameter to access and change the fields and properties of the object. If the method changes the parameter (for example, it assigns it a null value or makes it point to a different instance), the original object variable isn't affected.

c. **Passing value types by reference**   A pointer to the original value is passed to the method. When a value type argument is passed by reference, the code in the method can modify fields and properties in the value type. This case is less common than case a, and it's mostly used in nonvoid methods (*Function* methods in Visual Basic jargon) when you want to return additional information to the caller or in PInvoke/COM Interop scenarios.

d. **Passing reference types by reference**   The address of the pointer to the object is passed to the method. This is the least common scenario: the callee can change the object's fields and properties, as in case b, plus all the changes to the pointer are reflected in the original object variable. For example, if the method sets the argument to a null object reference, the original object variable is set to a null reference as well.

> **Note**   Reference types passed to by-reference parameters are quite common in Visual Basic projects hastily and carelessly converted from Visual Basic 6 because *ByRef* was the default passing mechanism under previous versions of Visual Basic. You should carefully scrutinize any code ported from Visual Basic 6 to Visual Basic .NET, looking for unnecessary *ByRef* arguments. (See also rule 14.8.)

14.10 *ref* and *out* arguments [C#]

When a value is returned to the caller by means of a by-reference parameter, use the *ref* keyword if the called method needs to access the passed object's current state; in all other cases, use the *out* keyword.

Why: Using the *out* keyword makes your code faster and less verbose because it doesn't force the client to initialize the argument before invoking the method.

More details: Notice that the *out* keyword is a C# feature; parameters marked with this keyword appear as *ByRef* arguments to Visual Basic clients.

14.11 Multiple by-reference arguments

If a public method definition includes more than one *ByRef* (Visual Basic), *ref*, or *out* (C#) argument, consider having the method return values using an object or a structure.

Example: The following code shows a hypothetical GetCustomerData method that reads data related to a customer from a database. In the former (wrong) case, the data is returned using by-reference arguments; in the latter (correct) case, the data is returned in an instance of the CustomerData type that has been defined just for this purpose.

```
' [Visual Basic]
' *** Wrong: too many by-reference arguments.
Sub GetCustomerData(ByVal id As Integer, ByRef name As String, ByRef address As String, _
      ByRef city As String, ByRef country As String)
   ' Use the ID value to query the database (omitted).
   ...
   ' Assign to arguments. (cust-prefixed values were from the database.)
   name = custName: address = custAddress: city = custCity: country = custCountry
End Sub

' *** Correct: The method returns an instance of the CustomerData type.
Function GetCustomerData(ByVal id As Integer) As CustomerData
   ' Use the ID value to query the database.
   ...
   ' Return a CustomerData object. (cust-prefixed values were read from the database.)
   Return New CustomerData(custName, custAddress, custCity, custCountry)
End Function

' The definition of the CustomerData type (can be a nested type)
Public Structure CustomerData
   ' These might be properties in a real-world application.
   Public Name As String
   Public Address As String
   Public City As String
   Public Country As String

   Public Sub New(ByVal name As String, ByVal address As String, _
      ByVal city As String, ByVal country As String)
      Me.Name = name
      Me.Address = address
```

```
        Me.City = city
        Me.Country = country
    End Sub
End Structure
```

```csharp
// [C#]
// *** Wrong: too many by-reference arguments.
public void GetCustomerData(int id, out string name, out string address,
    out string city, out string country)
{
    // Use the ID value to query the database (omitted).
    ...
    // Assign to arguments. (cust-prefixed values were from the database.)
    name = custName; address = custAddress; city = custCity; country = custCountry;
}

// *** Correct: The method returns an instance of the CustomerData type.
public CustomerData GetCustomerData(int id)
{
    // Use the ID value to query the database.
    ...
    // Return a CustomerData object. (cust-prefixed values were read from the database.)
    return new CustomerData(custName, custAddress, custCity, custCountry);
}

// The definition of the CustomerData type (can be a nested type)
public struct CustomerData
{
    // These might be properties in a real-world application.
    public string Name;
    public string Address;
    public string City;
    public string Country;

    public CustomerData(string name, string address, string city, string country)
    {
        this.Name = name;
        this.Address = address;
        this.City = city;
        this.Country = country;
    }
}
```

14.12 Optional parameters [Visual Basic]

Don't use the *Optional* keyword in the definition of a public method in a public type. Use overloading to support methods with different numbers of arguments. If the method really requires a variable number of arguments and using overloading isn't practical, use a *ParamArray* parameter.

Why: Even though optional parameters are CLS-compliant, they aren't visible to C# clients. For example, if a Visual Basic method takes one regular argument and three optional ones, a C# client always must pass four arguments.

More details: Optional parameters are OK in private methods.

```
' [Visual Basic]
' *** Wrong: a public method with an optional argument
Public Class SampleType
   Public Sub PerformTask(ByVal name As String, Optional ByVal pwd As String = Nothing)
      ...
   End Sub
End Class

' *** Correct: method overloading is used instead.
Public Class SampleType
   Public Sub PerformTask(ByVal name As String)
      ' Invoke the more complete overload.
      PerformTask(name, Nothing)
   End Sub

   Public Sub PerformTask(ByVal name As String, ByVal pwd As String)
      ...
   End Sub
End Class
```

14.13 Variable number of parameters

When defining the *ParamArray* (Visual Basic) or *params* (C#) parameter, always define a typed array if possible (as opposed to using an object array). This rule is especially effective if the elements of the array are of value-typed objects.

Why: When the elements in the array are reference types, this rule avoids casting to the specific type and therefore makes the call statement code less verbose. When the elements in the array are value types, this rule helps you avoid boxing value types; therefore, it makes the call statement less verbose *and* faster.

Example: See rule 14.15 for an example of a method that takes a variable number of arguments.

14.14 Multiple parameters of same type

If a method has the last three or more arguments of the same type, consider extending the method to an undefined number of parameters by means of a *ParamArray* (Visual Basic) or *params* (C#) parameter.

Example: See rule 14.15 for an example of an Avg method that uses a parameter array.

14.15 Special-case methods with a variable number of parameters

When defining a method that uses the *ParamArray* (Visual Basic) or *params* (C#) keyword to take a variable number of arguments, consider defining one or more overloaded versions that take a small number of arguments.

Why: Accessing a regular parameter is faster than accessing an array; therefore, this guideline provides better performance for time-critical code. For example, the String.Concat method can take a variable number of arguments, but it also has special cases for two, three, and four arguments.

Example: This code shows how you can define a method that can calculate the average value of any number of floating-point arguments and that uses overloading to define more efficient special cases when you have just two or three arguments.

```vb
' [Visual Basic]
' The average of two or more values
Function Avg(ByVal n1 As Double, ByVal n2 As Double) As Double
   Return (n1 + n2) / 2
End Function

Function Avg(ByVal n1 As Double, ByVal n2 As Double, ByVal n3 As Double) As Double
   Return (n1 + n2 + n3) / 3
End Function

Function Avg(ByVal ParamArray values() As Double) As Double
   Dim sum As Double = 0
   For i As Integer = 0 To values.Length - 1
      sum += values(i)
   Next
   Return sum / values.Length      ' Throws if no arguments are passed.
End Function
```

```csharp
// [C#]
// The average of two or more values
double Avg(double n1, double n2)
{
   return (n1 + n2) / 2;
}

double Avg(double n1, double n2, double n3)
{
   return (n1 + n2 + n3) / 3;
}

double Avg(params double[] values)
{
   double sum = 0;
   for ( int i = 0; i < values.Length; i++ )
      sum += values[i];
   return sum / values.Length;      // Throws if no arguments are passed.
}
```

14.16 Single exit point

Methods should have a single exit point. *Sub* procedures (Visual Basic) should have no *Exit Sub* statement; *void* methods (C#) should have no *return* keywords. Methods that return values should contain only one *Return* (Visual Basic) or *return* (C#) keyword.

Why: Having a single exit point is considered to be good design and enables you to add tracing statements or assertions easily.

Exception: If special cases can be dealt with at the top of the method, it is OK to exit earlier by means of additional *Exit Sub*, *Return* (Visual Basic), or *return* (C#) keywords.

14.17 The *Return* keyword [Visual Basic]

Return a value to the caller by means of the *Return* keyword (as opposed to assigning the return value to the implicit local variable named after the current property or method).

Why: The *Return* keyword often enables the compiler to optimize your code more effectively.

```
' [Visual Basic]
' *** Wrong
Function GetUserName() As String
   GetUserName = m_UserName
End Function

' *** Correct
Function GetUserName() As String
    Return m_UserName
End Function
```

More details: Visual Basic programmers can also use the *Return* keyword (without any argument) to replace an *Exit Sub* statement.

```
' [Visual Basic]
Sub PerformTask()
    ' *** OK
   If x = 0 Then Exit Sub

    ' *** Better
   If x = 0 Then Return
End Sub
```

14.18 Returning the result of an expression

If returning an expression from a method, optionally enclose the expression in parentheses if it helps readability. Don't use parentheses when returning a single value.

```
' [Visual Basic]
' *** OK
Return (123)
Return x = 0

' *** Better
Return 123
Return (x = 0)

// [C#]
// *** OK
return (123);
return x == 0;

// *** Better
return 123;
return ( x == 0 );
```

14.19 Method overloading to reduce boxing

Provide overloaded versions of the same method if the method can take arguments of different types rather than using a single method that takes Object arguments.

Why: This guideline helps you avoid the boxing operation that would occur if a value-type argument were passed to an Object parameter.

How to: Provide specific overloaded methods for most common types (numbers, strings, date/time), plus a more generic method that takes an object argument. At the very minimum, provide one version for 64-bit integers (which also serves 16- and 32-bit integers), one version for double floating-point numbers, one version for string values, and one generic version that takes an object argument.

More details: It is essential that the overloaded methods that serve value types don't delegate to the more generic method that takes an object; otherwise, you would have a boxing operation anyway.

```
' [Visual Basic]
Public Sub WriteLine(ByVal arg As Long)
   ' This version serves Short, Integer, and Long arguments.
End Sub
Public Sub WriteLine(ByVal arg As Double)
   ' This version serves Single and Double arguments.
End Sub
Public Sub WriteLine(ByVal arg As Decimal)
   ' This version serves Decimal arguments.
End Sub
Public Sub WriteLine(ByVal arg As DateTime)
   ' This version serves DateTime arguments.
End Sub
Public Sub WriteLine(ByVal arg As String)
   ' This version serves String arguments.
End Sub
Public Sub WriteLine(ByVal arg As Object)
   ' This version serves arguments of any other type.
End Sub

// [C#]
public void WriteLine(long arg)
{
   // This version serves short, int, and long arguments.
}
public void WriteLine(double arg)
{
   // This version serves float and double arguments.
}
public void WriteLine(decimal arg)
{
   // This version serves decimal arguments.
}
public void WriteLine(DateTime arg)
{
```

```
    // This version serves DateTime arguments.
}
public void WriteLine(string arg)
{
    // This version serves string arguments.
}
public void WriteLine(object arg)
{
    // This version serves arguments of any other type.
}
```

14.20 Method overloading to reduce number of arguments

Provide overloaded versions of the same method if the method can take a variable number of arguments to reduce the number of arguments that clients have to pass in the most common scenarios.

More details: It is essential that you define the order of arguments passed to methods in a consistent way and that you select the semantics of each argument so that when omitted, the argument defaults to its zeroed value (false for Boolean values, zero for numbers, null object reference for objects).

See also: See rule 14.22 about how you can chain overloaded methods.

```
' [Visual Basic]
Public Sub FormatText(ByVal text As String)
    FormatText(text, 0, Nothing)
End Sub

Public Sub FormatText(ByVal text As String, ByVal indent As Integer)
    FormatText(text, indent, Nothing)
End Sub

Public Sub FormatText(ByVal text As String, ByVal indent As Integer, _
        ByVal formatter As Object)
    ' Process the format text request.
    ...
End Sub

// [C#]
public void FormatText(string text)
{
    FormatText(text, 0, null);
}

public void FormatText(string text, int indent)
{
    FormatText(text, indent, null);
}

public void FormatText(string text, int indent, object formatter)
{
    // Process the format text request.
    ...
}
```

14.21 Method overloading based on argument-passing style [C#]

Don't define overloaded public methods that differ by only the *ref* or *out* (or no) keyword applied to their arguments.

Why: Languages such as Visual Basic can't distinguish among such overloaded methods.

```
// [C#]
// Wrong: overloaded methods differ only by ref/out keywords.
public void PerformTask(ref int id)
{
    ...
}

public void PerformTask(out int id)
{
    ...
}
```

14.22 Overloaded method chaining

If overloaded variations of a given method contain more than three lines of code, have all the method variations call the overloaded version that has more arguments. If there is no public method that could serve all such calls, consider defining a private method that can.

Why: You can later change the behavior of all the overloaded methods by editing a single block of code.

```
' [Visual Basic]
' The simpler method delegates to the more complex one,
' passing the default value for the 2nd argument.
Sub LoginUser(ByVal userName As String)
    LoginUser(userName, False)
End Sub

' The more complex method actually processes the data.
Sub LoginUser(ByVal userName As String, ByVal isAdmin As Boolean)
    ' Process arguments here...
    ...
End Sub
```

```
// [C#]
// The simpler method delegates to the more complex one,
// passing the default value for the 2nd argument.
public void LoginUser(string userName)
{
    LoginUser(userName, false);
}

// The more complex method actually processes the data.
public void LoginUser(string userName, bool isAdmin)
{
    // Process arguments here...
    ...
}
```

14.23 Number of local variables

Don't define more than 64 local variables in a method.

Why: When more than 64 local variables are defined, the JIT compiler must use a more sophisticated (and slower) flow analysis algorithm to decide which variables can be enregistered (that is, kept in faster CPU registers); thus, defining a large number of local variables has a negative impact on runtime performance.

14.24 Get-prefixed methods

Use the Get prefix for methods whose primary function is to evaluate and return a value; the portion of the name following Get should describe what the method returns.

Example: GetUpdatedStats.

14.25 Get-prefixed methods matching property names

Don't have a type expose a method named Get*PropertyName*, where *PropertyName* is the name of a property exposed by the same type.

Why: Exposing a property and a Get-prefixed method that apparently return the same information can be very confusing to users of your type and should be avoided.

Example: Don't expose the GetUserName method if the type already exposes a UserName property.

14.26 Set-prefixed methods

Consider the opportunity to define one or more Set-prefixed methods that take arguments and that assign multiple properties in one shot.

Why: Such methods simplify the structure of client code and speed up execution when the type is accessed from a different AppDomain because they require one single cross-domain method call instead of one call for each property.

```
' [Visual Basic]
Public Sub SetCustomerData(ByVal id As Integer, ByVal name As String, _
    ByVal address as String, ByVal city As String, ByVal country As String)
    ...
End Sub

// [C#]
public void SetCustomerData(int id, string name, string address,
    string city, string country)
{
    ...
}
```

14.27 Method names that include type of returned value

Use the *BaseMethodName+TypeName* syntax when you have multiple methods that return the same information but convert it to a given type. Notice that the type name should be the Microsoft .NET Framework official name, not the language-specific name for that type.

```
' [Visual Basic]
' Two similar methods return the same value as an integer or a string.
Public Function GetResultInt32() As Integer
   ...
End Function

Public Function GetResultString() As String
   ...
End Function

// [C#]
// Two similar methods return the same value as an integer or a string.
public int GetResultInt32()
{
   ...
}

public string GetResultString()
{
   ...
}
```

14.28 Factory method names

Use the Create prefix for factory methods. (A *factory method* is a method that creates and returns an instance of the defining type or an instance of a type that inherits from a defining type.) Use the CreateInstance name for static factory methods that create an instance of the current type; use the CreateFrom prefix to differentiate among different ways to create the object.

Why: Factory methods are especially useful when overloaded constructors can't capture all the possible ways to create an instance or when you need to run a piece of code *before* calling the constructor of a given type.

More details: Consider that when you pass invalid arguments to a standard constructor and the constructor throws an exception, the object is unusable, but the .NET runtime has already allocated it in the managed heap and must therefore destroy it. If the object has a Finalize method, the .NET runtime must execute this method and must postpone the complete destruction of the object. If you expect that many attempts to create the object will fail, you should make the constructor private and expose a public static factory method that checks all arguments and creates the object only if they are all correct. This arrangement makes the application run faster (because no memory is allocated and no finalizer is run without a reason) and simplifies the structure of the Finalize method as well because it is guaranteed that it runs only if the object was allocated correctly. (See rule 16.7 for more details.)

Factory methods are widely used in all versions of the .NET Framework. For example, see the CreateCaseInsensitiveHashtable and CreateCaseInsensitiveSortedList methods of the CollectionUtils class, the CreateCommand method of ADO.NET connection types, and the CreateDomain method of the AppDomain class.

Example: Suppose you have a Parser class that can parse data in a string, a stream, or a file. You can define a constructor that takes a string argument and another constructor that takes a Stream object, but you can't also define a third constructor that takes a filename because there is no way to differentiate it from the constructor that takes a string. (You might use additional arguments to create different method signatures, but similar signatures for completely distinct semantics should be avoided because they can be quite confusing.) In such a case, you might define a static CreateFromFile factory method.

See also: See rule 14.29 about parameter types that should be used in factory methods.

```vbnet
' [Visual Basic]
Public Class Parser
   ' The text to be parsed
   Public ReadOnly Text As String

   ' Parse the characters in a string.
   Public Sub New(ByVal text As String)
      Me.Text = text
   End Sub

   ' Parse the characters in a stream.
   Public Sub New(ByVal stream As Stream)
      Dim sr As New StreamReader(stream)
      Me.Text = sr.ReadToEnd()
      sr.Close()
   End Sub

   ' A static factory method that returns a parser that reads data in a file.
   Public Shared Function CreateFromFile(ByVal fileName As String) As Parser
      Dim fs As New FileStream(fileName, FileMode.Open)
      Dim obj As New Parser(fs)
      fs.Close()
      Return obj
   End Function

   ' More methods to perform the actual parsing
   ...
End Class

// [C#]
public class Parser
{
   // The text to be parsed
   public readonly string Text;

   // Parse the characters in a string.
   public Parser(string text)
```

```
   {
      this.Text = text;
   }

   // Parse the characters in a stream.
   public Parser(Stream stream)
   {
      StreamReader sr = new StreamReader(stream);
      this.Text = sr.ReadToEnd();
      sr.Close();
   }

   // A static factory method that returns a parser that reads data in a file.
   public static Parser CreateFromFile(string fileName)
   {
      FileStream fs = new FileStream(fileName, FileMode.Open);
      Parser obj = new Parser(fs);
      fs.Close();
      return obj;
   }

   // More methods to perform the actual parsing
   ...
}
```

14.29 Factory method parameters

Don't define factory methods that take System.Type parameters to specify which object should be created. Instead, use a string or a bit-coded enum value that represents the set of services the returned object should expose. (A string is preferable to an enum value because you can later expand the set of valid values without any versioning problem.)

Why: Factory methods are often used in multitiered architectures as black boxes that create an object that provides a given set of features. In such cases, the client doesn't really know which object will be returned, and the result from the factory method is usually assigned to an interface variable or a base class variable. If the client application passes a Type argument to the factory method, the client must be able to access the assembly where that type is defined, a condition that would defy one of the purposes of multitier architectures.

Example: The following abridged example shows how to write a factory method that returns a data object that can access a given table of a database, using one of the data providers that .NET supports (Microsoft Access, Microsoft SQL Server, Oracle, etc.). Because the client doesn't necessarily have a reference to the assembly that contains the actual data object types, the returned object is returned as an interface pointer. The following code assumes that all data object types implement the custom IDbDataObject interface, which should be defined in a separate assembly that both the following code and the client code can access.

```
' [Visual Basic]
Public Function CreateDataObject(ByVal provider As String, ByVal dbName As String, _
      ByVal tableName As String) As IDbDataObject
```

```
      Select Case provider.ToLower()
        Case "access"
            Return New AccessDataObject(dbName, tableName)
        Case "sqlserver"
            Return New SqlServerDataObject(dbName, tableName)
        Case "oracle"
            Return New OracleDataObject(dbName, tableName)
        Case Else
            Throw New ArgumentException("Unsupported provider")
    End Select
End Function

// [C#]
public IDbDataObject CreateDataObject(string provider, string dbName, string tableName)
{
    switch ( provider.ToLower() )
    {
        case "access":
            return new AccessDataObject(dbName, tableName);
        case "sqlserver":
            return new SqlServerDataObject(dbName, tableName);
        case "oracle":
            return new OracleDataObject(dbName, tableName);
        default:
            throw new ArgumentException("Unsupported provider");
    }
}
```

14.30 Operator overloading in reference types [C#]

In general, avoid overloading binary operators in reference types. (Operator overloading is OK with value types.)

Why: Binary operators return a new instance of the type in which they are defined but shouldn't modify either operator (see rule 14.32). Such semantics are what developers expect from a value type, but differ from what most developers expect from a reference type. Consider this example:

```
// [C#]
// *** Wrong: operator overloading in a reference type
public class Fraction
{
    // In a real-world class these would be properties.
    public int Numerator;
    public int Denominator;

    public Fraction(int numerator, int denominator)
    {
        this.Numerator = numerator;
        this.Denominator = denominator;
    }

    // Operator overloading
    public static Fraction operator*(Fraction f, int multiplier)
```

```
    {
        return new Fraction(f1.Numerator * multiplier, f1.Denominator);
    }
}

// Demo app that uses the Fraction class
public class App
{
    static void Main()
    {
        Fraction f1 = new Fraction(1, 10);
        DoubleIt(f1);
        Console.WriteLine("{0}/{1}", f.Numerator, f.Denominator);  // 1/10 (hasn't changed!)
    }

    void DoubleIt(Fraction f)
    {
        f *= 2;
    }
}
```

The problem in the preceding code example is that the DoubleIt method doesn't change the actual argument but creates a new Fraction, which is eventually subjected to garbage collection. To have the code work correctly, the DoubleIt method should take a *ref* argument, but it would then conflict with rule 14.9 (reference types shouldn't be passed by reference).

14.31 == and != operator overloading [C#]

If you overload the == and *!=* operators, ensure that you also override the Equals method so that results are consistent. Because of rule 7.16, you must override GetHashCode as well to ensure that equal objects also have equal hash codes.

14.32 Modifying arguments in overloaded operators [C#]

Never modify the properties of arguments passed to a method that overload an operator.

Why: Developers expect that operators don't modify their operands. The only operators that modify their operands are the = (assignment), ++, and -- operators, which aren't overloadable.

14.33 Alternative methods for operator overloading [C#]

When you overload one or more operators, define alternative methods that perform the same operation as the overloaded operators.

Why: Visual Basic and other .NET languages don't support operator overloading and don't recognize operators defined in a C# assembly; therefore, these languages can access the operations that these operators implement only if you expose a standard static or instance method.

Example: When overloading the + operator, you should also expose an Add method that performs the same operation.

```
// [C#]
public struct Fraction
{
   // Operator overloading
   public static Fraction operator+(Fraction f1, Fraction f2)
   {
      // The code that adds two fractions goes here...
   }

   // Alternative method for Visual Basic clients
   public static Fraction Add(Fraction f1, Fraction f2)
   {
      return f1 + f2;
   }
}
```

For each overloadable operator, Table 14-1 lists the special method that the C# compiler creates and the name of the alternative method that you should expose to make the functionality available to clients that don't support operator overloading.

Table 14-1   Suggested Names for Methods Alternative to Operator Overloads

Operator	Special op_ method	Alternative Method
− (unary)	op_UnaryNegation	Negate
+ (unary)	op_UnaryPlus	Plus
+ (binary)	op_Addition	Add
− (binary)	op_Subtraction	Subtract
*	op_Multiply	Multiply
/	op_Division	Divide
%	op_Modulus	Mod
&	op_BitwiseAnd	BitwiseAnd
|	op_BitwiseOr	BitwiseOr
^	op_ExclusiveOr	Xor
~	op_OnesComplement	OnesComplent
>>	op_RightShift	RightShift
<<	op_LeftShift	LeftShift
==	op_Equality	Equals
!=	op_Inequality	Compare
<	op_LessThan	Compare
<=	op_LessThanOrEqual	Compare
>	op_GreaterThan	Compare
>=	op_GreaterThanOrEqual	Compare
Implicit conversion	op_Implicit	To*Xxx* or From*Xxx*
Explicit conversion	op_Explicit	To*Xxx* or From*Xxx*

14.34 Conversion and parsing methods

Apply the following guidelines when defining methods that perform type conversions:

a. Override the ToString method to return a textual representation of the current state of a type.

b. Implement an instance To*Xxxx* method to provide a way to convert the value in the current object to another type.

c. Implement a static From*Xxxx* method to convert from another type into a new instance of the current type.

d. Use the Parse name for a static method that converts a string into an instance of the current type (or throws an exception if the string doesn't represent a valid object).

e. Use the TryParse name for a static method that converts a string into an instance of the current type and returns true if the conversion succeeds; the last argument of this method is a *ByRef* (Visual Basic) or *out* (C#) value that receives the parsed value.

```vb
' [Visual Basic]
Public Class Fraction
    ' The numerator and denominator of this fraction
    Private num As Long
    Private den As Long

    ' This constructor takes numerator and denominator.
    Public Sub New(ByVal numerator As Long, ByVal denumerator As Long)
        Me.num = numerator
        Me.den = denumerator
    End Sub

    ' An instance method that converts to String
    Public Overrides Function ToString() As String
        Return num.ToString() & "/" & den.ToString()
    End Function

    ' An instance method that converts to Double
    Public Function ToDouble() As Double
        Return num / den
    End Function

    ' A static method that converts from Double
    Public Shared Function FromDouble(ByVal val As Double) As Fraction
        ' For simplicity's sake, we assume we never get an overflow.
        Const Precision As Long = 10000000
        Return New Fraction(CLng(val * Precision), Precision)
    End Function

    ' A static method that parses a string in the "X/Y" format
    Public Shared Function Parse(ByVal text As String) As Fraction
        Dim result As Fraction
        ' Delegate to the TryParse method.
```

```vbnet
        If TryParse(text, result) Then
            Return result
        Else
            ' Unlike TryParse, this method throws if parsing fails.
            Throw New FormatException("Invalid format for fraction")
        End If
    End Function

    ' A static method that attempts to parse a string in the "X/Y" format
    Public Shared Function TryParse(ByVal text As String, ByRef result As Fraction) As Boolean
        result = Nothing
        Try
            ' Split the X/Y string, exit if not 2 operands.
            Dim numbers() As String = text.Split("/"c)
            If numbers.Length <> 2 Then Return False
            ' Get the numerator and denominator.
            Dim num As Long = Long.Parse(numbers(0).Trim())
            Dim den As Long = Long.Parse(numbers(1).Trim())
            ' Create a fraction and return true if everything was OK.
            result = New Fraction(num, den)
            Return True
        Catch ex As Exception
            ' Return false if either Long.Parse method failed.
            Return False
        End Try
    End Function
End Class

// [C#]
public class Fraction
{
    // The numerator and denominator of this fraction
    private long num;
    private long den;

    // A constructor that takes numerator and denominator
    public Fraction(long numerator, long denumerator)
    {
        this.num = numerator;
        this.den = denumerator;
    }

    // An instance method that converts to String
    public override string ToString()
    {
        return num.ToString() + "/" + den.ToString();
    }

    // An instance method that converts to Double
    public double ToDouble()
    {
        return Convert.ToDouble(num) / Convert.ToDouble(den);
    }
}
```

```csharp
// A static method that converts from Double
public static Fraction FromDouble(double val)
{
    const long Precision = 10000000;
    return new Fraction(Convert.ToInt64(val * Precision), Precision);
}

// A static method that parses a string in the "X/Y" format
public static Fraction Parse(string text)
{
    Fraction result;
    // Delegate to the TryParse method.
    if ( TryParse(text, out result) )
    {
        return result;
    }
    else
    {
        // Unlike TryParse, this method throws if parsing fails.
        throw new FormatException("Invalid format for fraction");
    }
}

// A static method that attempts to parse a string in the "X/Y" format
public static bool TryParse(string text, out Fraction result)
{
    result = null;
    try
    {
        // Split the X/Y string, exit if not 2 operands.
        string[] numbers = text.Split('/');
        if ( numbers.Length != 2 )
            return false;
        // Get the numerator and denominator.
        long num = long.Parse(numbers[0].Trim());
        long den = long.Parse(numbers[1].Trim());
        // Create a fraction and return true if everything was OK.
        result = new Fraction(num, den);
        return true;
    }
    catch ( Exception ex )
    {
        // Return false if either Long.Parse method failed.
        return false;
    }
}
}
```

14.35 URI values

Use properties, parameters, and return values of the System.Uri type instead of string values when the value represents a Uniform Resource Identifier (URI).

More details: You can use a string parameter instead of a System.Uri parameter if an overload of the same method has a System.Uri parameter in the same position.

```vb
' [Visual Basic]
' *** Wrong
Sub PerformTask(ByVal uri As String)
   ...
End Sub

' *** Correct
Sub PerformTask(ByVal uri As System.Uri)
   ...
End Sub
```

```csharp
// [C#]
// *** Wrong
void PerformTask(string uri)
{
   ...
}

// *** Correct
void PerformTask(System.Uri uri)
{
   ...
}
```

Chapter 15
Constructors

The code in the constructor runs when an object hasn't been completely initialized yet, so it is essential that you take special precautions when defining which constructors a type exposes and what kind of actions you should perform inside them.

Many of the guidelines in this chapter are evident and intuitive, but a few might surprise you at first. For example, few programmers realize that the finalizer method runs even if the constructor has thrown an exception; therefore, you should pay even more attention than usual to the constructor of a finalizable class, or you should consider replacing a public constructor with a static factory method that checks arguments before invoking a private constructor.

> **Note** One or more code examples in this chapter assume that the following namespace has been imported by means of an *Imports* (Visual Basic) or *using* (C#) statement:
>
> ```
> System.IO
> ```

15.1 Parameter names

The names of all the parameters of a constructor should be equal to the name of the property or field they are assigned to, except for casing. (Fields and properties are PascalCase, parameters are camelCase.)

Example: See the code example in rule 15.4.

15.2 Constructor size

Attempt to keep constructors as simple and short as possible. Ideally, a constructor should initialize (and indirectly validate) only the minimum number of properties that define a valid object. If more complex initializations need to be performed, postpone them until the user makes use of a specific feature.

15.3 Assignments to writable properties

Never validate arguments inside a constructor if the value is assigned to a property. Instead, assign values to public properties and rely on the validation code inside the property procedure.

15.4 Assignments to read-only properties

When assigning a read-only property, you must discern between two cases: if the property wraps a read-only field, you can only access the field directly and you must do that from inside the constructor. In all other cases, define a private Set-prefixed method that writes the private field and assign the property from your constructor by means of such a Set-prefixed method.

See also: See rule 13.6 for more information about Set-prefixed methods that wrap read-only properties.

```vb
' [Visual Basic]
Public Class User
    Public Sub New(ByVal userName As String, ByVal group As String)
        ' Assign properties instead of wrapped fields.
        Me.Group = group
        ' Assign the read-only property by means of private SetUserName method.
        SetUserName(userName)
        ' Read-only fields can only be accessed directly, though.
        m_CreationDate = DateTime.Now
    End Sub

    ' Group is a regular writable property.
    Private m_Group As String

    Public Property Group() As String
        Get
            Return m_Group
        End Get
        Set(ByVal Value As String)
            m_Group = Value
        End Set
    End Property

    ' CreationDate is a read-only property that wraps a read-only field.
    Private ReadOnly m_CreationDate As Date

    Public ReadOnly Property CreationDate() As Date
        Get
            Return m_CreationDate
        End Get
    End Property

    ' UserName is a read-only property that wraps a writable field and is
    ' therefore paired by a SetUserName private method.
    Private m_UserName As String

    Public ReadOnly Property UserName() As String
        Get
            Return m_UserName
        End Get
    End Property

    Private Sub SetUserName(ByVal userName As String)
        m_UserName = userName
    End Sub
End Class
```

```csharp
// [C#]
public class User
{
    public User(string userName, string group)
    {
        // Assign properties instead of wrapped fields.
        this.Group = group;
        // Assign the read-only property by means of private SetUserName method.
        SetUserName(userName);
        // Read-only fields can only be accessed directly, though.
        m_CreationDate = DateTime.Now;
    }

    // Group is a regular writable property.
    private string m_Group;

    public string Group
    {
        get
        {
            return m_Group;
        }
        set
        {
            m_Group = value;
        }
    }

    // CreationDate is a read-only property that wraps a read-only field.
    private readonly DateTime m_CreationDate;

    public DateTime CreationDate
    {
        get
        {
            return m_CreationDate;
        }
    }

    // UserName is a read-only property that wraps a writable field and is
    // therefore paired by a SetUserName private method.
    private string m_UserName;

    public string UserName
    {
        get
        {
            return m_UserName;
        }
    }

    private void SetUserName(string userName)
    {
        m_UserName = userName;
    }
}
```

15.5 Explicit parameterless constructor

Add an explicit parameterless public constructor instead of relying on the default public constructor that the compiler implicitly creates.

Why: You can easily add and remove other constructors without any side effects or versioning problems.

More details: Both the Visual Basic and the C# compilers automatically generate a parameterless (default) constructor if and only if you don't define one explicitly. If your clients rely on this default constructor and you later add another constructor (with parameters), these clients will cease to work correctly. Adding an explicit, empty, parameterless constructor to the type avoids this sort of programming error.

Exception: Don't define such a parameterless constructor if the object requires one or more arguments to be instantiated in a valid state (see rule 15.6).

15.6 Main constructor for robust instances

Define a public constructor that takes the smaller set of arguments so that clients can create an instance in a valid state.

Why: This guideline ensures that the object is in a valid state immediately after being created.

```vb
' [Visual Basic]
Public Class Person
    ' A Person object is in a robust state if its FirstName and
    ' LastName properties have been assigned correctly.
    Public Sub New(ByVal firstName As String, lastName As String)
        Me.FirstName = firstName
        Me.LastName = lastName
    End Sub

    ' Code for FirstName, LastName properties omitted...
End Class
```

```csharp
// [C#]
public class Person
{
    // A Person object is in a robust state if its FirstName and
    // LastName properties have been assigned correctly.
    public Person(string firstName, string lastName)
    {
        this.FirstName = firstName;
        this.LastName = lastName;
    }

    // Code for FirstName, LastName properties omitted...
}
```

15.7 Additional constructors for ease of use

Define one or more constructors that take additional arguments, even if these arguments aren't strictly necessary to instantiate the object in a valid state. The constructors with fewer arguments should delegate to more complex constructors if possible (see rules 15.13 and 15.14).

Why: Such additional constructors help keep client code as concise as possible.

```vb
' [Visual Basic]
Class Person
    ' A Person object is in a robust state if its FirstName and
    ' LastName properties have been assigned correctly.
    Public Sub New(ByVal firstName As String, lastName As String)
       ' Delegate to the more complex constructor, pass 0 for extra argument.
       Me.New(firstName, lastName, 0)
    End Sub

    Public Sub New(ByVal firstName As String, lastName As String, ByVal age As Integer)
       Me.FirstName = firstName
       Me.LastName = lastName
       Me.Age = age
    End Sub

    ' Code for FirstName, LastName, Age properties omitted...
End Class
```

```csharp
// [C#]
class Person
{
    // A Person object is in a robust state if its FirstName and
    // LastName properties have been assigned correctly.
    // Delegate to the more complex constructor, pass 0 for extra argument.
    public Person(string firstName, string lastName) : this(firstName, lastName, 0)
    {}

    public Person(string firstName, string lastName, int age)
    {
       this.FirstName = firstName;
       this.LastName = lastName;
       this.Age = age;
    }

    // Code for FirstName, LastName, Age properties omitted...
}
```

15.8 Private constructors

Define a private constructor to prevent instantiation of types that contain only static members or types that should be instantiated only by means of one or more static factory methods.

15.9 *Friend* and *internal* constructors

Define a *Friend* (Visual Basic) or *internal* (C#) constructor in a public type that you want to use freely from inside the current project but that must appear as noninstantiable (sealed) to code in other assemblies. This constructor can be empty.

More details: Instances of a public type that doesn't expose public constructors can be passed to external assemblies only by means of methods exposed by the type itself or by other types in the same assembly.

15.10 *Protected Friend* and *protected internal* constructors

Define a *Protected Friend* (Visual Basic) or *protected internal* (C#) constructor in a public type that you want to use without any limitation from inside the current project but that must appear as an abstract type (*MustInherit* in Visual Basic) to other assemblies. This constructor can be empty.

More details: External assemblies can declare variables of this type (because the type is public) and can inherit from this type, but they can't directly create an instance of the type.

```
' [Visual Basic]
Public Class Person
   Protected Friend Sub New()
      ...
   End Sub
End Class

// [C#]
public class Person
{
   protected internal Person()
   {}
}
```

15.11 Static constructors in reference types

Favor assigning static fields by means of initializers instead of a static contructor (a.k.a. type constructor) in reference types. Initialize static fields in a static type constructor only if initialization order is important.

Why: Direct initialization of static fields can yield better performance.

```
' [Visual Basic]
' *** OK
Public Class Person
   Private Shared ID As Integer

   Shared Sub New()
      ID = 1
   End Sub
   ...
End Class
```

```
' *** Better
Public Class Person
    Private Shared ID As Integer = 1
    ...
End Class

// [C#]
// *** OK
public class Person
{
    private static int ID;

    static Person()
    {
        ID = 1;
    }
    ...
}

// *** Better
public class Person
{
    private static int ID = 1;
    ...
}
```

15.12 Static constructors in value types

Always avoid static (type) constructors in value types.

Why: Static constructors in value types are not guaranteed to be called before instance members on the value type are called; therefore, the instance might use uninitialized static fields.

15.13 Delegating to constructors with more parameters

If a type has multiple constructors, have constructors with fewer parameters invoke constructors with more parameters if the missing parameters have a default value. Ideally, the body of constructors with fewer parameters should be empty (C#) or should contain only the Me.New statement that delegates to a constructor with more arguments (Visual Basic).

Why: This guideline ensures that all the initialization code is kept in one place and the class is more easily maintained and debugged. Creating a chain of constructors also reduces the amount of IL code generated by the compiler if the source code includes one or more field initializers.

Why not: This approach causes an additional method call and unnecessary field assignments when a client invokes a constructor with fewer arguments. In general, this overhead is negligible, though, at least compared with the activity that is undertaken when a new object is initialized.

Exception: See rules 15.14 and 15.15.

```vb
' [Visual Basic]
Public Class User
    ' These would be properties in a real-world class.
    Public ReadOnly UserName As String
    Public ReadOnly IsAdministrator As Boolean

    ' Simpler constructor delegates to the more complex constructor
    ' because isAdministrator has a default value.
    Public Sub New(ByVal userName As String)
        Me.New(userName, False)
    End Sub

    Public Sub New(ByVal userName As String, ByVal isAdministrator As Boolean)
        Me.UserName = userName
        Me.IsAdministrator = isAdministrator
    End Sub
End Class
```

```csharp
// [C#]
public class User
{
    // These would be properties in a real-world class.
    public readonly string UserName;
    public readonly bool IsAdministrator;

    // Simpler constructor delegates to the more complex constructor
    // because isAdministrator has a default value.
    public User(string userName) : this(userName, false)
    {}

    public User(string userName, bool isAdministrator)
    {
        this.UserName = userName;
        this.IsAdministrator = isAdministrator;
    }
}
```

15.14 Delegating to constructors with fewer parameters

If a type has multiple constructors and it isn't practical to have constructors with fewer parameters invoke constructors with more parameters, have the more complex constructor call simpler constructors and then continue by processing the additional parameters.

Why: You need this approach if the additional arguments that appear in more complex constructors don't have a default value or when the sole presence of an argument affects the behavior of the constructor.

See also: See rules 15.13 and 15.15.

```vb
' [Visual Basic]
Class User
    ' This would be a property in a real-world class.
    Public ReadOnly UserName As String
```

```
    ' The simpler constructor doesn't set up an account.
    Public Sub New(ByVal userName As String)
        Me.UserName = userName
    End Sub

    ' The more complex constructor delegates to the simpler
    ' constructor, then continues with its own chores.
    Public Sub New(ByVal userName As String, ByVal password As String)
        Me.New(userName)
        ' Set up the account using provided password.
        ...
    End Sub
End Class

// [C#]
class User
{
    // This would be a property in a real-world class.
    public readonly string UserName;

    // The simpler constructor doesn't set up an account.
    public User(string userName)
    {
        this.UserName = userName;
    }

    // The more complex constructor delegates to simpler
    // constructor, then continues with its own chores.
    public User(string userName, string password) : this(userName)
    {
        // Set up the account using provided password.
        ...
    }
}
```

15.15 Private parameterless constructor to help delegation

If a type has multiple constructors, each one with completely different sets of arguments, define a private parameterless constructor and have all the constructors in the class delegate to it.

Why: This approach ensures that no duplicate IL code is generated for fields with initializers and provides a single point at which to specify actions that must be performed whenever an instance of the type is created.

See also: See rules 15.13 and 15.14.

```
' [Visual Basic]
Public Class User
    ' No duplicate IL code is generated for these initializers.
    Private Id As Integer = 1
    Private CreationDate As Date = Now

    Public Sub New(ByVal userName As String)
        ' Invoke the private constructor, then continue.
```

```
        Me.New()
        Me.UserName = userName
    End Sub

    Public Sub New(ByVal isAdministrator As Boolean)
        ' Invoke the private constructor, then continue.
        Me.New()
        Me.IsAdministrator = isAdministrator
    End Sub

    Private Sub New()
        ' Empty private constructor.
    End Sub
End Class
```

```
// [C#]
public class User
{
    // No duplicate IL code is generated for these initializers.
    private int Id = 1;
    private DateTime CreationDate = DateTime.Now;

    // Invoke the private constructor, then continue.
    public User(string userName) : this()
    {
        this.UserName = userName;
    }

    // Invoke the private constructor, then continue.
    public User(bool isAdministrator) : this()
    {
        this.IsAdministrator = isAdministrator;
    }

    // Empty private constructor
    private User()
    {}
}
```

15.16 Constructors that take a disposable object

If a class exposes one or more constructors that take a disposable object as an argument (e.g., a Stream or a Connection), the class should implement the IDisposable interface and close the stream or the connection in the Dispose method.

If disposing of the inner object in the Dispose method might not be desirable under all circumstances, the class should also expose an overloaded constructor that takes an additional Boolean argument named leaveOpen so that clients can pass true to override the default behavior.

See also: See rule 16.1 for more information about the IDisposable interface.

```vbnet
' [Visual Basic]
Public Class Document
   Implements IDisposable

   Private stream As Stream
   Private leaveOpen As Boolean

   Public Sub New(ByVal stream As Stream)
      Me.New(stream, False)
   End Sub

   Public Sub New(ByVal stream As Stream, ByVal leaveOpen As Boolean)
      Me.stream = stream
      Me.leaveOpen = leaveOpen
   End Sub

   Public Sub Dispose() Implements IDisposable.Dispose
      If Not leaveOpen AndAlso Not stream Is Nothing Then
         stream.Close()
      End If
      ' Process other disposable objects here.
      ...
   End Sub
End Class
```

```csharp
// [C#]
public class Document : IDisposable
{
   Stream stream;
   bool leaveOpen;

   public Document(Stream stream) : this(stream, false)
   {}

   public Document(Stream stream, bool leaveOpen)
   {
      this.stream = stream;
      this.leaveOpen = leaveOpen;
   }

   public void Dispose()
   {
      if ( ! leaveOpen && stream != null )
         stream.Close();
      // Process other disposable objects here.
      ...
   }
}
```

15.17 Calling virtual methods from inside a constructor

Code in a constructor must not invoke a virtual method defined in the same type.

Why: If you instantiate a derived class, the first thing that its constructor does is invoke its base type's constructor; if this constructor invokes a virtual method and this method is overridden in the derived type, the code in the method runs when the derived type's constructor hasn't completed its execution and the type isn't properly initialized yet. This situation can lead to unexpected behaviors or exceptions.

Example: The following code shows an example of the kind of problem you might incur if you don't abide by this rule. When you instantiate the DerivedClass type, the base type's constructor calls a virtual overridden method that should display the alElements.Count property; instead, it causes a NullReferenceException because the alElements object hasn't been created yet.

```
' [Visual Basic]
Public Class BaseClass
    Public Sub New()
        ShowData()        ' Error: calls an overridable method.
    End Sub

    Public Overridable Sub ShowData()
        Console.WriteLine("No data available")
    End Sub
End Class

Public Class DerivedClass
    Inherits BaseClass

    Private alElements As ArrayList

    Public Sub New()
        alElements = New ArrayList
    End Sub

    Public Overrides Sub ShowData()
        ' Next line throws a NullReferenceException during object instantiation.
        Console.WriteLine("{0} elements found", alElements.Count)
    End Sub
End Class

// [C#]
public class BaseClass
{
    Public BaseClass()
    {
        ShowData();    // Error: Calls an overridable method.
    }
```

```
    public virtual void ShowData()
    {
        Console.WriteLine("No data available");
    }
}

public class DerivedClass : BaseClass
{
    private ArrayList alElements;

    public DerivedClass()
    {
        alElements = new ArrayList();
    }

    public override void ShowData()
    {
        // Next line throws a NullReferenceException during object instantiation.
        Console.WriteLine("{0} elements found", alElements.Count);
    }
}
```

15.18 Exceptions in constructors

Throw an exception in the constructor if provided parameters are incorrect or if, for any reason, it is impossible to create a valid instance. However, attempt to initialize all fields correctly before throwing the exception if the class has a Finalize method.

More details: The CLR invokes the class's Finalize method even if the constructor throws an exception. For this reason, the code in the Finalize method should never assume that all type members are correctly initialized.

See also: See rule 16.7 for more information about accessing members from the Finalize method; see rule 14.28 about using factory methods to validate arguments before they are passed to a constructor.

15.19 Exceptions in static constructors

Ensure that you catch all the exceptions that might be thrown in the static (type) constructor.

Why: If an exception in the type constructor isn't caught inside the constructor itself and is thrown to the caller, the Microsoft .NET runtime considers the type to be uninitialized. Any further attempt to access the type's static members or to instantiate the type results in a TypeInitializationException.

Chapter 16
Dispose and Finalize Methods

One of the most intricate characteristics of the Microsoft .NET Framework is its memory management and the way it deals with memory allocation and object destruction. Many developers switching from Visual Basic 6 or C++ can find the new rules in the .NET world contorted and counterintuitive, especially when compared with the relatively simple mechanism used by COM and based on reference counting. When authoring and using a managed object, you must account for so many issues, especially if the object uses or allocates resources that should be released in an orderly way, or if the object is meant to be used from different clients and threads. Many developers refer to these issues as the *underdeterministic finalization* problem: you have no control over when a .NET object is removed from memory.

The situation is so confusing that we decided to devote one entire chapter to the best practices you should apply when working with objects that allocate any system resource other than plain memory. We haven't covered all the possible cases, however, and decided not to discuss some advanced techniques—for example, object resurrection—that aren't used frequently in real-world applications.

> **Note** One or more code examples in this chapter assume that the following namespace has been imported by means of an *Imports* (Visual Basic) or *using* (C#) statement:
>
> ```
> System.Data.OleDb
> ```

16.1 The IDisposable interface

Implement the IDisposable interface if a method in the type creates one or more instances of other disposable objects (a disposable object is an object that implements the IDisposable interface) and the method doesn't invoke the objects' Dispose method before returning to the caller.

More details: In practice, you should implement the IDisposable interface only if you have one or more fields (either private or public) that hold a reference to a disposable object. You don't need to implement the IDisposable interface if all methods create disposable objects, assign them to local variables (as opposed to type-level fields), and invoke these objects' Dispose method before exiting.

Also, you don't need to implement this interface if the only resource that your object allocates is memory.

Example: The following code contains the definition of two types. Both of them use a connection object (which is disposable), but only the former keeps a reference to the connection in a class-level field and therefore needs to implement the IDisposable interface. Notice that the EndTask method does close the connection, but the class's author has no warrant that the client code will actually call this method after each call to StartTask.

```vb
// [Visual Basic]
Public Class TypeOne
    Public Sub PerformTask()
        ' Create and use the connection, then close it.
        ' (In a real class a Try...Finally block should be used; see rule 16.5.)
        Dim cn As New OleDbConnection()
        ...
        cn.Close()
    End Sub
End Class

Public Class TypeTwo
    Implements IDisposable

    Private cn As OleDbConnection

    Public Sub StartTask()
        ' Create and use the connection, leave it open.
        cn = New OleDbConnection
        ...
    End Sub

    Public Sub EndTask()
        ' Use the connection left open by StartTask, then close it.
        If Not cn Is Nothing Then
            ...
            cn.Close()
        End If
    End Sub

    Public Sub Dispose() Implements IDisposable.Dispose
        If Not cn Is Nothing Then cn.Close()
    End Sub
End Class
```

```csharp
// [C#]
public class TypeOne
{
    public void PerformTask()
    {
        // Create and use the connection, then close it.
        // (In a real class a using block should be used; see rule 16.4.)
        OleDbConnection cn = new OleDbConnection();
        ...
        cn.Close();
```

```
        }
}

public class TypeTwo : IDisposable
{
    private OleDbConnection cn;

    public void StartTask()
    {
        // Create and use the connection, leave it open.
        cn = new OleDbConnection();
        ...
    }

    public void EndTask()
    {
        // Use the connection left open by StartTask, then close it.
        if ( cn != null )
        {
            ...
            cn.Close();
        }
    }

    public void Dispose()
    {
        if ( cn != null )
            cn.Close();
    }
}
```

16.2 Dispose and Finalize methods

Implement both the IDisposable interface and the protected Finalize method only if the type must release one or more unmanaged resources that it has directly allocated. If the object allocates only disposable managed resources, implementing the IDisposable interface will suffice.

More details: It is a common programming mistake to implement the Finalize method unnecessarily, which results in overhead at instantiation and suboptimal usage of memory. The rule is simple, though: you must implement both IDisposable and the Finalize method only if the object allocates unmanaged resources, for example, if one of its methods invokes the CreateFile method in the Windows API and doesn't close the file before returning from the method.

Ideally, a type with a Finalize method should handle only one resource, and that resource should be an unmanaged resource. If you follow this guideline, the code in the Dispose and Finalize methods is quite simple and the margin for mistakes is greatly reduced.

16.3 Implementing only the Finalize method

Implement only the protected Finalize method (but not the IDisposable interface) for those (rare) cases in which you need to perform an action when the object is about to be finalized by the garbage collector but the type doesn't use any disposable object.

16.4 *using* blocks for disposable objects [C#]

Use *using* blocks to dispose of IDisposable objects automatically when you're done with them.

```csharp
// [C#]
using ( OleDbDataAdapter da = new OleDbDataAdapter() )
{
   // Use the data adapter here...
}
```

16.5 Invoking Dispose in the *Finally* block [Visual Basic]

Always allocate disposable objects in a *Try* block and invoke their Dispose method in the *Finally* clause to ensure that the object is disposed of even if an unhandled exception is thrown.

```vb
' [Visual Basic]
Dim da As OleDbDataAdapter
Try
   da = New OleDbDataAdapter
   ' Use the data adapter here...
   ...
Catch ex As Exception
   ' Deal with exceptions here (optional).
Finally
   ' Dispose of the data adapter.
   If Not da Is Nothing Then da.Dispose()
End Try
```

16.6 Dispose vs. Close method

By default, disposable objects should have a public Dispose method. However, if the type exposes an Open method (or a method with a similar name), as is the case with streamlike and connectionlike types, you should implement a public Close method that maps to a private Dispose method.

```vb
' [Visual Basic]
Public Class EncryptedStream
   Implements IDisposable

   Public Sub Close() Implements IDisposable.Dispose
      ' Release resources here.
      ...
   End Sub
End Class
```

```
// [C#]
public class EncryptedStream : IDisposable
{
    public void Close()
    {
        (this as IDisposable).Dispose();
    }

    void IDisposable.Dispose()
    {
        // Release resources here.
        ...
    }
}
```

16.7 Field access in Finalize method

Never access reference type fields from inside the Finalize method because those fields might be pointing to objects that have already been finalized. Even better, code in the Finalize method should access only unmanaged resources.

More details: Accessing a value type variable from the Finalize method is always safe. However, you can't assume that value type variables contain a valid value because an exception thrown in the constructor might have interrupted the standard initialization sequence before all the fields were correctly initialized.

```
' [Visual Basic]
Public Class SampleType
    Private ID As Integer        ' Value type
    Private Name As String       ' Reference type

    Protected Overrides Sub Finalize()
        Dim msg As String = String.Format("ID={0}", ID)      ' This reference is OK.
        msg &= String.Format(" Name={0}", Name)              ' This might cause a problem.
        ...
    End Sub
End Class

// [C#]
public class SampleType
{
    private int ID;            // Value type
    private string Name;       // Reference type

    ~SampleType()
    {
        string msg = String.Format("ID={0}", ID);        // This reference is OK.
        msg += String.Format(" Name={0}", Name);         // This might cause a problem.
        ...
    }
}
```

See also: See rule 15.18 about throwing exceptions in constructors.

16.8 Error handling in the Finalize method [Visual Basic]

Always wrap the body of the Finalize method in a *Try* block, and invoke the base type's Finalize method from inside the *Finally* block.

Why: It is essential that exceptions in the Finalize method are caught, else some objects might not be finalized correctly or at all. (C# developers don't need to adopt this approach because the code in the finalizer method runs inside a hidden *try* block.)

```
' [Visual Basic]
Protected Overrides Sub Finalize()
   Try
      ' Finalization code here...
      ...
   Catch ex As Exception
      ' Catch errors here...
      ...
   Finally
      ' Invoke the base object's Finalize method.
      MyBase.Finalize()
   End Try
End Sub
```

16.9 Throwing DisposedObjectException

The Dispose method (and its Close alias, if present) shouldn't throw an exception if the object has already been disposed of. All other methods in a disposable type must throw an Object-DisposedException object if called after the Dispose method.

How to: To keep track of whether the object has been disposed of, define a protected field named disposed and a protected nonvirtual method (named CheckDisposed in the following example) that test the field and throw if the Dispose or Close method has already been invoked.

```
' [Visual Basic]
Public Class DisposableType
   Implements IDisposable

   Protected disposed As Boolean = False

   ' Helper method that checks the disposed field
   Protected Sub CheckDisposed()
      If disposed Then
         Throw New ObjectDisposedException(Me.GetType().FullName)
      End If
   End Sub

   Public Sub Dispose() Implements IDisposable.Dispose
      ' Exit right now if resources have already been released.
      If disposed Then Exit Sub
      ' Release resources here.
      ...
      ' Remember that this instance has been disposed of.
```

```
        disposed = True
    End Sub


    ' Throw when any other method is invoked on a disposed object.
    Public Sub PerformTask()
        CheckDisposed()
        ' Continue with regular execution.
        ...
    End Sub
End Class
```

```
// [C#]
public class DisposableType : IDisposable
{
    private bool disposed = false;

    // Helper method that checks the disposed field
    protected void CheckDisposed()
    {
        if ( disposed )
            throw new ObjectDisposedException(this.GetType().FullName);
    }

    public void Dispose()
    {
        // Exit right now if resources have already been released.
        if ( disposed )
            return;
        // Release resources here.
        ...
        // Remember that this instance has been disposed of.
        disposed = true;
    }

    // Throw when any other method is invoked on a disposed object.
    public void PerformTask()
    {
        CheckDisposed();
        // Continue with regular execution.
        ...
    }
}
```

16.10 The Dispose-Finalize pattern

Types exposing both the Finalize method and the IDisposable interface must adopt the recommended Dispose-Finalize pattern and include a protected Dispose method that takes a Boolean argument. If the type is meant to be used by clients in different threads, you must protect the Dispose methods from concurrent access by means of a suitable *SyncLock* (Visual Basic) or *lock* (C#) statement.

```
' [Visual Basic]
Public Class DisposableType
    Implements IDisposable

    Protected disposed As Boolean = False
```

```vb
Protected Overridable Sub Dispose(ByVal disposing As Boolean)
    SyncLock Me
        ' Do nothing if the object has already been disposed of.
        If disposed Then Exit Sub

        If disposing Then
            ' Release disposable objects used by this instance here.
            ...
        End If
        ' Release unmanaged resources here. Don't access reference type fields.
        ...
        ' Remember that the object has been disposed of.
        disposed = True
    End SyncLock
End Sub

Public Sub Dispose() Implements IDisposable.Dispose
    Dispose(True)
    ' Unregister object for finalization.
    GC.SuppressFinalize(Me)
End Sub

Protected Overrides Sub Finalize()
    Try
        Dispose(False)
    Catch
        ' Deal with errors or just ignore them.
    Finally
        ' Invoke the base object's Finalize method.
        MyBase.Finalize()
    End Try
End Sub
End Class

// [C#]
public class DisposableType : IDisposable
{
    protected bool disposed = false;

    protected virtual void Dispose(bool disposing)
    {
        lock (this)
        {
            // Do nothing if the object has already been disposed of.
            if ( disposed )
                return;

            if ( disposing )
            {
                // Release disposable objects used by this instance here.
                ...
            }
            // Release unmanaged resources here. Don't access reference type fields.
            ...
            // Remember that the object has been disposed of.
            disposed = true;
        }
    }
}
```

```
public void Dispose()
{
   Dispose(true);
   // Unregister object for finalization.
   GC.SuppressFinalize(this);
}

~DisposableType()
{
   Dispose(false);
}
}
```

16.11 The Dispose-Finalize pattern in derived types

Override the protected Dispose method when deriving from a disposable type that correctly implements the Dispose-Finalize pattern (as described in rule 16.10).

```
' [Visual Basic]
Protected Overloads Overrides Sub Dispose(ByVal disposing As Boolean)
   SyncLock Me
      ' Do nothing if the object has already been disposed of.
      If disposed Then Exit Sub

      If disposing Then
         ' Release disposable objects used by this instance here.
         ...
      End If
      ' Release unmanaged resources here. Don't access reference type fields.
      ...
      ' Call the base object's Dispose protected method.
      MyBase.Dispose(disposing)
   End SyncLock
End Sub
```

```
// [C#]
protected override void Dispose(bool disposing)
{
   lock (this)
   {
      // Do nothing if the object has already been disposed of.
      if ( disposed )
         return;

      if ( disposing )
      {
         // Release disposable objects used by this instance here.
         ...
      }
      // Release unmanaged resources here. Don't access reference type fields.
      ...
      // Call the base object's Dispose protected method.
      base.Dispose(disposing);
   }
}
```

Chapter 17
Delegates and Events

Events in the Microsoft .NET Framework are implemented by means of delegates. This fact explains why these two concepts are so closely related and why we decided to deal with both these topics in the same chapter. This correlation is evident if you write C# code but isn't if you are a Visual Basic programmer because many implementation details on events are hidden from you.

In this chapter, we illustrate some recommended coding patterns to be used with events—for example, how to deal with events raised by different threads or how to serialize correctly types that expose one or more delegate variables.

 Note   One or more code examples in this chapter assume that the following namespaces have been imported by means of *Imports* (Visual Basic) or *using* (C#) statements:

```
System.ComponentModel
System.IO
System.Reflection
System.Runtime.Serialization
System.Threading
```

17.1 Delegate and event names

Use PascalCase for delegate and event names. Avoid underscores and names longer than 25 characters.

17.2 EventArgs-derived type names

Use the *EventName*EventArgs name for types that derive from System.EventArgs and that are meant to be used as the second argument of an event named *EventName* (and therefore the second argument of the delegate named *EventName*EventHandler; see rule 17.3).

Example: Define a NameChangedEventArgs and use it with a delegate named NameChangedEventHandler to define an event named NameChanged.

17.3 Delegate naming style

Use the following suffixes when defining delegate types:

a.   Use the *EventName*EventHandler name for a delegate type that is meant to be used in the definition of an event named *EventName* (see rule 17.2). Example: NameChanged-EventHandler to define the NameChanged event.

b. Use the *ProcName*Filter name for a delegate type that defines a callback method used by a procedure named *ProcName* to let the main program filter the procedure's results. Example: GetResultsFilter.

c. Use the *ProcName*Callback name for a delegate type that defines a callback method used by a procedure named *ProcName* to notify the main program that something has happened. Example: PerformTaskCallback.

d. Don't use any specific suffix for a generic delegate type that doesn't fall in any of the event handler, filter, or callback categories defined earlier. More specifically, don't use Delegate as a suffix for these types.

More details: The distinction between a filter delegate and a callback delegate is often blurred because you can always use a filter delegate to perform an action in addition to returning a value to the main program. You can decide to standardize on just the Callback suffix if you prefer.

Example: The following code shows a reusable method named GetFiles that returns all the files in a given directory tree. This method takes a GetFilesFilter delegate that points to a Boolean method that lets you filter results and decide which files are included in the array returned by GetFiles.

```
' [Visual Basic]
Delegate Function GetFilesFilter(ByVal fileName As String) As Boolean

Sub Main()
   For Each file In GetFiles("c:\data", AddressOf FilterFiles)
      Console.WriteLine(file)
   Next
End Sub

Function FilterFiles(ByVal file As String) As Boolean
   ' Include only files created in year 2004.
   Return ( File.GetCreationTime(file).Year = 2004 )
End Function

' Reusable recursive routine that takes a delegate to filter results.
Function GetFiles(ByVal path As String, ByVal filter As GetFilesFilter) As String()
   Dim res As New ArrayList
   For Each file As String In Directory.GetFiles(path)
      ' Include this file in result only if filter routine says it's OK to do so.
      If Not filter Is Nothing AndAlso filter(file) Then res.Add(file)
   Next
   ' Recurse on all subfolders.
   For Each dir As String In Directory.GetDirectories(path)
      res.AddRange(GetFiles(dir, filter))
   Next
   Return DirectCast(res.ToArray(GetType(String)), String())
End Function
```

```csharp
// [C#]
public delegate bool GetFilesFilter(string file);

static void Main()
{
    foreach ( string file in GetFiles(@"c:\data", new GetFilesFilter(FilterFiles)) )
        Console.WriteLine(file);
}

bool FilterFiles(string file)
{
    // Include only files created in year 2004.
    return ( File.GetCreationTime(file).Year == 2004 );
}

// Reusable recursive routine that takes a delegate to filter results.
public string[] GetFiles(string path, GetFilesFilter filter)
{
    ArrayList res = new ArrayList();
    foreach ( string file in Directory.GetFiles(path) )
    {
        // Include this file in result only if filter routine says it's OK to do so.
        if ( filter == null || filter(file) )
            res.Add(file);
    }
    // Recurse on all subfolders.
    foreach ( string dir in Directory.GetDirectories(path) )
        res.AddRange( GetFiles(dir, filter) );
    return (string[]) res.ToArray(typeof(string));
}
```

17.4 Event naming style

Use gerund tense (the "ing" form) for events that are raised before something happens; use past tense for events that are raised after something has happened. More specifically, don't use On*Xxxx* or Before*Xxxx*/After*Xxxx* names for events.

More details: When documenting an event, you should use the phrase *raise the event*. Events are neither triggered nor fired nor invoked.

Example: The Update method of a class might raise the Updating event before performing the action and an Updated event after the action has been performed. Often preaction events have an EventArgs-derived argument that exposes a Boolean property named Cancel; clients of the event can set this property equal to true to cancel the event.

See also: See rule 17.15 for an example of a cancelable event.

17.5 Name of event-handling methods

Use the *VariableName_EventName* naming pattern for methods that handle events.

Why: This is the pattern used by Microsoft Visual Studio .NET when it creates handlers for events raised by Windows Forms and Web Forms controls.

Example: Use the currentUser_SessionEnded method to handle the SessionEnded event raised by the User object referenced by the currentUser variable.

More details: Some developers prefer the On*EventName* name pattern for event handlers; we advise against using it because On-prefixed names should be reserved for methods that *raise* events and also because this naming scheme creates confusion when you have multiple methods that handle events with the same name but raised by different objects.

17.6 Scope of event-handling methods

Event-handling methods must be marked as private or internal (*Friend* in Visual Basic).

17.7 Delegate invocation

Always assign a delegate object to a temporary variable before invoking the delegate, and check that the temporary variable isn't null before invoking the delegate.

Why: This technique enables you to avoid race conditions in multithreaded environments.

```
' [Visual Basic]
Dim handler As EventHandler

' *** Wrong
handler(Me, EventArgs.Empty)

' *** Correct
Dim tmpHandler As EventHandler = handler
If Not tmpHandler is Nothing Then
    tmpHandler(Me, EventArgs.Empty)
End If

// [C#]
EventHandler handler;

// *** Wrong
handler(this, EventArgs.Empty);

// *** Correct
EventHandler tmpHandler = handler;
if ( tmpHandler != null )
    tmpHandler(this, EventArgs.Empty);
```

17.8 Delegates vs. interfaces for callback methods

In time-critical code, favor using interfaces instead of delegates to implement a means to receive a callback notification.

Why: The invocation of a method by using a delegate is slower than a call through an interface method.

More details: In some cases, delegates and interfaces can solve similar programming problems. For example, both can achieve a degree of polymorphism in your code and provide a means to receive callback notifications from a method. If performance is critical, consider defining and using an interface instead of a delegate. Even though an interface method invocation is slower than a direct call, it is faster than a delegate invocation. Never achieve polymorphism by means of techniques based on reflection.

Example: You might change the GetFiles method defined in rule 17.3 to take an interface argument rather than a delegate argument:

```
' [Visual Basic]
Interface IGetFilesFilter
    Function Filter(ByVal file As String) As Boolean
End Interface

Function GetFiles(ByVal path As String, ByVal filter As IGetFilesFilter) As String()
    ...
End Function
```

```
// [C#]
interface IGetFilesFilter
{
    bool Filter(string file);
}

public string[] GetFiles(string path, IGetFilesFilter filter)
{
    ...
}
```

where the GetFiles method calls the IGetFilesFilter.Filter method instead of the GetFilesFilter delegate to decide whether a file should be included in the result.

Some types in the .NET Framework implement callback method invocation by means of delegates; others use an interface. In general, the approach based on interfaces is more efficient and flexible because one interface can define multiple callback methods.

17.9 Instantiation of delegate objects [Visual Basic]

Don't explicitly instantiate a delegate object. Instead, directly assign the address of the target method to the delegate variable or pass it to the delegate argument of a method.

Example: The following code shows a verbose and a concise technique to instantiate a Thread object. (The PerformTask method must be a *Sub* without parameters to comply with the signature implied by the ThreadStart delegate.)

```
' [Visual Basic]
' *** OK
Dim thr As New Thread(New ThreadStart(AddressOf PerformTask))

' *** Better
Dim thr As New Thread(AddressOf PerformTask)
```

17.10 Event syntax

All events must define two parameters. The first parameter is an Object named sender; the second parameter is an instance of the EventArgs type (or a type that derives from EventArgs) and must be named e.

```
' [Visual Basic]
Public Event ApplicationStart(ByVal sender As Object, ByVal e As EventArgs)
Public Event Progress(ByVal sender As Object, ByVal e As ProgressEventArgs)
```

```
// [C#]
public delegate void ProgressEventHandler(object sender, ProgressEventArgs e);
// Events with an EventArgs argument can be defined by means of the EventHandler delegate.
public event EventHandler ApplicationStart;
public event ProgressEventHandler Progress;
```

See also: See rule 17.11 about using delegates to define events in Visual Basic.

17.11 Event definition through delegates [Visual Basic]

Favor defining events in terms of delegate types rather than by directly stating the event syntax. If possible, use common delegate types as defined in the .NET Framework (e.g., EventHandler or CancelEventHandler); otherwise, define a delegate explicitly.

Why: If you use the *Event* keyword without a delegate, the Visual Basic compiler defines a hidden delegate type named *EventName*EventHandler; such a hidden delegate makes it less natural to subscribe to the event from C# or other languages and unnecessarily increases the application's footprint in memory.

```
' [Visual Basic]
' *** OK
Event ApplicationStart(ByVal sender As Object, ByVal e As EventArgs)
Event Progress(ByVal sender As Object, ByVal e As ProgressEventArgs)

' *** Better
Event ApplicationStart As EventHandler
Event Progress As ProgressEventHandler
' Here's the explicit declaration of the delegate.
Delegate Sub ProgressEventHandler(ByVal sender As Object, ByVal e As ProgressEventArgs)
```

17.12 Event return type

Events must have no return type. The C# compiler lets you define an event by means of a non-void delegate, but this practice must be avoided.

Why: Multiple clients can subscribe to a given event; therefore, the object raising the event would access only the value returned by the last client who handled the event. If clients are expected to return a value when handling an event, they should set a property of the EventArgs-derived object passed in the second argument.

More details: The Visual Basic compiler lets you define an event with or without an explicit delegate. The latter syntax implicitly defines a delegate that doesn't return any value and therefore complies with this rule. If you explicitly use a delegate to define an event (see rule 17.11), the compiler emits an error when a *Function* delegate is used.

```
' [Visual Basic]
'*** Wrong: compiler error
Delegate Function MyHandler(ByVal sender As Object, ByVal e As MyEventArgs) As Integer
Event MyEvent As MyHandler      ' <-- Compiler error

'*** Correct
Delegate Sub MyHandler(ByVal sender As Object, ByVal e As MyEventArgs)
Event MyEvent As MyHandler

'*** Also correct, but not recommended. (See rule 17.11.)
Event MyEvent(ByVal sender As Object, ByVal e As MyEventArgs)
```

```
// [C#]
//*** Wrong: the delegate returns a value.
public delegate int MyHandler(object sender, MyEventArgs e);
public event MyHandler MyEvent;

//*** Correct
public delegate void MyHandler(object sender, MyEventArgs e);
public event MyHandler MyEvent;
```

17.13 Event raising [C#]

Assign an event variable to a temporary delegate variable and compare it with *null* before raising the event.

Why: This approach avoids race conditions if the object is used in a multithreading environment (see rule 17.7).

```
// [C#]
public event EventHandler UserChanged;

// *** Wrong
void ChangeUser()
{
   if ( UserChanged != null )
      UserChanged(this, EventArgs.Empty);
}

// *** Correct
void ChangeUser()
{
   EventHandler handler = UserChanged;
   if ( handler != null )
      handler(this, EventArgs.Empty);
}
```

17.14 Event unsubscription

Always unsubscribe an event you've subscribed to as soon as you no longer need to receive event notifications. An object should unsubscribe all events it has subscribed to even if the object is about to go out of scope and be reclaimed by the garbage collector.

Why: When a client object X subscribes to an event of another object Y, then Y has a delegate pointing to a method in X. For this reason, the X object won't really go out of scope until Y is reclaimed by the garbage collector. The net result is that the X object might live longer than you think, which prevents optimal memory usage and might cause unexpected behavior. (For example, if the client object X has created a timer that activates in the background, the time will continue to tick until the Y object is also reclaimed.)

```
' [Visual Basic]
Dim user As New User
AddHandler user.UserNameChanged, AddressOf user_UserNameChanged
' Use the User object here.
...
' Unregister the event before clearing the object variable.
RemoveHandler user.UserNameChanged, AddressOf user_UserNameChanged
user = Nothing

// [C#]
User user = new User();
user.UserNameChanged += new EventHandler(user_UserNameChanged);
// Use the User object here.
...
// Unregister the event before clearing the object variable.
user.UserNameChanged -= new EventHandler(user_UserNameChanged);
user = null;
```

17.15 Events that notify a property change

Use *PropertyName*Changing and *PropertyName*Changed names for events that notify when a property named *PropertyName* changes. The *PropertyName*Changing event is raised before the property changes and takes a CancelEventArgs object (or an object that derives from CancelEventArgs) so that clients can cancel the change of the property's value.

Example: The following code shows how to raise events immediately before and after a property named UserName is changed. For simplicity's sake, the UserNameChanging event uses the CancelEventHandler delegate and the CancelEventArgs class, both of which are defined in the .NET Framework. In a real application, however, you should define a UserNameChangingEventArgs type that inherits from the CancelEventArgs type and that exposes a NewValue property. Clients of the event can query this property to accept or reject the value that is about to be assigned to the UserName property.

```vb
' [Visual Basic]
Public Event UserNameChanging As CancelEventHandler
Public Event UserNameChanged As EventHandler

Private m_UserName As String

Public Property UserName() As String
   Get
      Return m_UserName
   End Get
   Set(ByVal Value As String)
      If m_UserName <> Value Then
         ' Let clients know that the property is about to change.
         Dim e As New CancelEventArgs
         RaiseEvent UserNameChanging(Me, e)
         If e.Cancel Then Exit Property
         ' If change wasn't canceled, proceed with it.
         m_UserName = Value
         RaiseEvent UserNameChanged(Me, EventArgs.Empty)
      End If
   End Set
End Property
```

```csharp
// [C#]
public event CancelEventHandler UserNameChanging;
public event EventHandler UserNameChanged;

private string m_UserName;

public string UserName
{
   get
   {
      return m_UserName;
   }
   set
   {
      if ( m_UserName != value )
      {
         // Let clients know that the property is about to change.
         CancelEventHandler handler = UserNameChanging;
         if ( handler != null )
         {
            CancelEventArgs e = new CancelEventArgs();
            handler(this, e);
            if ( e.Cancel )
               return;
         }
         // If change wasn't canceled, proceed with it.
         m_UserName = value;
         EventHandler handler2 = UserNameChanged;
         if ( handler2 != null )
            handler2(this, EventArgs.Empty);
      }
   }
}
```

17.16 Raising events from inside overridable methods

Always raise events from inside a protected overridable method named *OnEventName* whose only argument is the EventArgs-derived argument that would be passed to the event.

Why: This technique enables the derived class to override the event and cancel it if necessary.

```
' [Visual Basic]
Public Event UserChanging As CancelEventHandler

' *** Wrong
Sub ChangeUser()
   Dim e As New CancelEventArgs
   RaiseEvent UserChanging(Me, e)
   ' Exit if change has been canceled.
   If e.Cancel Then Exit Sub
   ' Change user here.
   ...
End Sub

' *** Correct
Sub ChangeUser()
   Dim e As New CancelEventArgs
   OnUserChanging(e)
   ' Exit if change has been canceled.
   If e.Cancel Then Exit Sub
   ' Change user here.
   ...
End Sub

Protected Overridable Sub OnUserChanging(ByVal e As CancelEventArgs)
   RaiseEvent UserChanging(Me, e)
End Sub

// [C#]
public event CancelEventHandler UserChanging;

// *** Wrong
void ChangeUser()
{
   CancelEventHandler handler = UserChanging;
   if ( handler != null )
   {
      CancelEventArgs e = new CancelEventArgs();
      handler(this, e);
      // Exit if change has been canceled.
      if ( e.Cancel )
         return;
   }
   // Change user here.
   ...
}
```

```csharp
// *** Correct
void ChangeUser()
{
   if (UserChanging != null )
   {
      CancelEventArgs e = new CancelEventArgs();
      OnUserChanging(e);
      // Exit if change has been canceled.
      if ( e.Cancel )
         return;
   }
   // Change user here.
   ...
}

protected virtual void OnUserChanging(CancelEventArgs e)
{
   CancelEventHandler handler = UserChanging;
   if ( handler != null )
      handler(this, e);
}
```

17.17 The hidden event variable [Visual Basic]

Compare the hidden *EventName*Event field with *Nothing* before calling the On*EventName* protected overridable method that raises the event.

Why: This technique enables you to optimize execution speed, especially because you don't have to create an EventArgs-derived object if no client has registered for the event.

More details: When a Visual Basic class exposes a public event, the compiler creates a hidden field named *EventName*Event and two methods named add_*EventName* and remove_*EventName* (see Figure 17-1). These members don't appear in the object browser, so you can't count on IntelliSense and must type their names correctly.

```vbnet
' [Visual Basic]
Event UserChanging As CancelEventHandler

Sub ChangeUser()
   If Not UserChangingEvent Is Nothing Then
      Dim e As New CancelEventArgs
      OnUserChanging(e)
      ' Exit if change has been canceled.
      If e.Cancel Then Exit Sub
   End If
   ' Change user here.
   ...
End Sub

Protected Overridable Sub OnUserChanging(ByVal e As CancelEventArgs)
   RaiseEvent UserChanging(Me, e)
End Sub
```

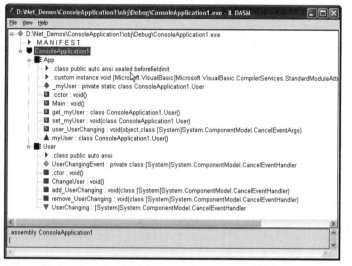

Figure 17-1 The Visual Basic compiler creates a hidden *Xxxx*Event delegate variable for each event exposed by a class (UserChangingEvent in the User class) and a property for each WithEvents variable (myUser in the App class).

17.18 *WithEvents* variables [Visual Basic]

Favor explicit event subscriptions by means of *AddHandler* and *RemoveHandler* operators instead of *WithEvents* variables and *Handles* clauses.

Why: *WithEvents* variables are implemented as properties; therefore, accessing them is slower than accessing a regular variable, especially when the variable is assigned a value. (Reading a *WithEvents* variable isn't noticeably slower than reading a regular field, however.) Also, *WithEvents* variables must be declared at the class level, and they can't handle events from objects used locally in a procedure, objects stored in an array or collection, or static events raised from noncreatable types such as System.Windows.Forms.Application.

More details: The Visual Basic compiler generates a property for each variable marked with the *WithEvents* keyword (see Figure 17-1). Such a property wraps a private field named *_VariableName*. The set block in the property procedure transparently subscribes to all the events exposed by the event source (by calling the hidden add_*EventName* method) when the property is assigned a non-null object reference and unsubscribes (by calling the hidden remove_*EventName* method) when the property is assigned a null reference.

```vb
' [Visual Basic]
' *** OK
Private WithEvents user As New User

' This event handler requires the Handles keyword.
Sub user_UserNameChanged(ByVal sender As Object, ByVal e As EventArgs) _
      Handles user.UserNameChanged
    ...
End Sub
```

```
' *** Better
Private user As New User

' You must subscribe to events manually if you don't use WithEvents variables.
Sub SubscribeEvents()
    AddHandler user.UserNameChanged, AddressOf user_UserNameChanged
    ' Use the object here.
    ...
    RemoveHandler user.UseNameChanged, AddressOf user_UserNameChanged
End Sub

' This event handler doesn't require the Handles keyword.
Sub user_UserNameChanged(ByVal sender As Object, ByVal e As EventArgs)
    ...
End Sub
```

17.19 Reentrancy issues when raising events

The code that raises the event shouldn't assume that the state of the object hasn't changed after the event; therefore, you shouldn't cache property values and return values from methods in local variables while the event is being raised.

Why: All clients listening for the event can modify the state of the object that is raising the event; therefore, the code that raises the event should read again all the object's properties it uses after raising the event.

17.20 Raising events from secondary threads

Avoid raising events from threads other than the thread that created the object. If you do raise an event from a different thread, clearly document this detail.

Why: Clients of the object typically implement event handlers under the assumption that code in these handlers runs in the client's main thread. This detail is especially important if the client can be a Windows Forms object because code in a non-UI thread can't directly access the form itself and its controls.

More details: This rule applies to events raised by methods invoked asynchronously, by code running in the Elapsed event of a System.Timers.Timer object, and by code running in a thread started by means of a ThreadPool.QueueUserWorkItem method.

See also: See rule 17.21 for a technique that solves this issue.

17.21 Implementing the SynchronizingObject property

If an object is capable of raising an event from a different thread, you should expose a property named SynchronizingObject (of type System.ComponentModel.ISynchronizeInvoke). If the client code assigns an object to this property, all events should be raised in the thread implied by this object.

More details: This pattern is used by several components in the .NET Framework, including System.IO.FileSystemWatcher, System.Timers.Timer, and System.Diagnostics.EventLog.

```vb
' [Visual Basic]
Public Class User
    Public Event UserNameChanged As EventHandler

    ' The SynchronizingObject property
    Private m_SynchronizingObject As ISynchronizeInvoke

    Public Property SynchronizingObject() As ISynchronizeInvoke
        Get
            Return m_SynchronizingObject
        End Get
        Set(ByVal Value As ISynchronizeInvoke)
            m_SynchronizingObject = Value
        End Set
    End Property

    ' The UserName property raises an event when changed.
    Private m_UserName As String

    Public Property UserName() As String
        Get
            Return m_UserName
        End Get
        Set(ByVal Value As String)
            If m_UserName <> Value Then
                m_UserName = Value
                OnUserNameChanged(EventArgs.Empty)
            End If
        End Set
    End Property

    ' This method runs in the User object's thread.
    Protected Overridable Sub OnUserNameChanged(ByVal e As EventArgs)
        If m_SynchronizingObject Is Nothing OrElse _
                Not m_SynchronizingObject.InvokeRequired Then
            OnUserNameChangedThreadSafe(Me, e)
        Else
            Dim args() As Object = {Me, e}
            m_SynchronizingObject.Invoke( _
                New EventHandler(AddressOf OnUserNameChangedThreadSafe), args)
        End If
    End Sub

    ' This method runs in the client's thread (if a synchronizing object was provided).
    Private Sub OnUserNameChangedThreadSafe(ByVal sender As Object, ByVal e As EventArgs)
        RaiseEvent UserNameChanged(sender, e)
    End Sub
End Class

// [C#]
public class User
{
    public event EventHandler UserNameChanged;
```

```csharp
// The SynchronizingObject property
private ISynchronizeInvoke m_SynchronizingObject;

public ISynchronizeInvoke SynchronizingObject
{
   get
   {
      return m_SynchronizingObject;
   }
   set
   {
      m_SynchronizingObject = value;
   }
}

// The UserName property raises an event when changed.
private string m_UserName;

public string UserName
{
   get
   {
      return m_UserName;
   }
   set
   {
      if ( m_UserName != value )
      {
         m_UserName = value;
         OnUserNameChanged(EventArgs.Empty);
      }
   }
}

// This method runs in the User object's thread.
protected virtual void OnUserNameChanged(EventArgs e)
{
   if ( m_SynchronizingObject == null || ! m_SynchronizingObject.InvokeRequired )
   {
      OnUserNameChangedThreadSafe(this, e);
   }
   else
   {
      object[] args = new object[]{this, e};
      m_SynchronizingObject.Invoke(new EventHandler(OnUserNameChangedThreadSafe), args);
   }
}

// This method runs in the client's thread (if a synchronizing object was provided).
private void OnUserNameChangedThreadSafe(object sender, EventArgs e)
{
   EventHandler handler = UserNameChanged;
   if (handler!= null )
      handler (sender, e);
}
}
```

See also: See rule 17.20 for details about issues that might be caused by raising events from secondary threads.

17.22 Events in Finalize methods

Never raise an event in the Finalize method.

Why: Clients expect that an event is raised in the same thread that registered it. The Finalize method runs in a different thread; therefore, an event raised from inside this method might fail to work correctly. (For example, the code can't access variables marked with the Thread-Static attribute.)

17.23 Events in serializable classes

Implement the ISerializable interface for serializable classes that expose events.

Why: For each event, both the Visual Basic and the C# compiler define a hidden delegate field; delegate types aren't serializable and any attempt to serialize an instance that contains non-null delegates will fail. By implementing custom serialization, you can skip these delegate fields in the serialization process.

See also: See rule 12.26 for a simple technique that enables C# developers to mark event delegates as nonserialized.

How to: The simplest solution is retrieving all the MemberInfo objects corresponding to serializable fields (which you can do by means of the FormatterServices.GetSerializableMembers static method) and discard those fields that have a delegate type. Consider the following three helper methods:

```
' [Visual Basic]
Public Class SerializationHelpers        ' (Can also be a module)

   ' Helper routine for serializing objects
   Public Shared Sub GetObjectDataHelper(ByVal info As SerializationInfo, _
        ByVal context As StreamingContext, ByVal obj As Object)
      ' Get the list of serializable members.
      Dim members() As MemberInfo = GetFilteredSerializableMembers(obj.GetType())
      ' Read the value of each member.
      Dim values() As Object = FormatterServices.GetObjectData(obj, members)
      ' Store in the SerializationInfo object, using the member name.
      For i As Integer = 0 To members.Length - 1
         info.AddValue(members(i).Name, values(i))
      Next
   End Sub

   ' Helper routine for deserializing objects
   Public Shared Sub ISerializableConstructorHelper(ByVal info As SerializationInfo, _
        ByVal context As StreamingContext, ByVal obj As Object)
      ' Get the list of serializable members for this object.
      Dim members() As MemberInfo = GetFilteredSerializableMembers(obj.GetType())
```

```vb
    Dim values(members.Length - 1) As Object
    ' Read the value for each member.
    For i As Integer = 0 To members.Length - 1
        ' Retrieve the type for this member.
        Dim member As MemberInfo = members(i)
        If member.MemberType = MemberTypes.Field Then
            Dim memberType As Type = CType(member, FieldInfo).FieldType
            values(i) = info.GetValue(member.Name, memberType)
        End If
    Next
    ' Assign all serializable members in one operation.
    FormatterServices.PopulateObjectMembers(obj, members, values)
End Sub


' Return an array of serializable MemberInfo for a given type. (Same as
' FormatterServices.GetSerializableMembers, but filters out delegate fields.)
Private Shared Function GetFilteredSerializableMembers(ByVal ty As Type) As MemberInfo()
    Dim al As New ArrayList
    ' Get the list of serializable members.
    For Each mi As MemberInfo In FormatterServices.GetSerializableMembers(ty)
        If Not (TypeOf mi Is FieldInfo AndAlso GetType([Delegate]).IsAssignableFrom( _
                DirectCast(mi, FieldInfo).FieldType)) Then
            al.Add(mi)
        End If
    Next
    Return DirectCast(al.ToArray(GetType(MemberInfo)), MemberInfo())
End Function
End Class

// [C#]
public class SerializationHelpers
{
    // Helper routine for serializing objects
    public static void GetObjectDataHelper(SerializationInfo info, StreamingContext context,
        object obj)
    {
        // Get the list of serializable members.
        MemberInfo[] members = GetFilteredSerializableMembers(obj.GetType());
        // Read the value of each member.
        object[] values = FormatterServices.GetObjectData(obj, members);
        // Store in the SerializationInfo object, using the member name.
        for ( int i = 0; i < members.Length; i++ )
            info.AddValue(members[i].Name, values[i]);
    }

    // Helper routine for deserializing objects
    public static void ISerializableConstructorHelper(SerializationInfo info,
        StreamingContext context, object obj)
    {
        // Get the list of serializable members.
        MemberInfo[] members = GetFilteredSerializableMembers(obj.GetType());
        object[] values = new object[members.Length];
        // Read the value for each member.
        for ( int i = 0; i < members.Length; i++ )
        {
```

```
            // Retrieve the type for this member.
            FieldInfo fi = members[i] as FieldInfo;
            if ( fi != null )
                values[i] = info.GetValue(fi.Name, fi.FieldType);
        }
        // Assign all serializable members in one operation.
        FormatterServices.PopulateObjectMembers(obj, members, values);
    }

    // Return an array of serializable MemberInfo for a given type. (Same as
    // FormatterServices.GetSerializableMembers, but filters out delegate fields.)
    private static MemberInfo[] GetFilteredSerializableMembers(Type ty)
    {
        ArrayList al = new ArrayList();
        // Get the list of serializable members.
        foreach ( MemberInfo mi in FormatterServices.GetSerializableMembers(ty) )
        {
            FieldInfo fi = mi as FieldInfo;
            if ( fi == null || ! typeof(Delegate).IsAssignableFrom(fi.FieldType) )
                al.Add(mi);
        }
        return (MemberInfo[]) al.ToArray(typeof(MemberInfo));
    }
}
```

These helper procedures greatly simplify the implementation of the ISerializable interface:

```
' [Visual Basic]
<Serializable()> _
Class Person
    Implements ISerializable

    ' Some public fields and a (nonserializable) event
    Public FirstName As String
    Public LastName As String
    Public Event GotEmail As EventHandler

    Sub New(ByVal firstName As String, ByVal lastName As String)
        Me.FirstName = firstName
        Me.LastName = lastName
    End Sub

    Public Sub GetObjectData(ByVal info As SerializationInfo, _
            ByVal context As StreamingContext) Implements ISerializable.GetObjectData
        SerializationHelpers.GetObjectDataHelper(info, context, Me)
    End Sub

    Protected Sub New(ByVal info As SerializationInfo, ByVal context As StreamingContext)
        SerializationHelpers.ISerializableConstructorHelper(info, context, Me)
    End Sub
End Class
```

```csharp
// [C#]
[Serializable]
class Person : ISerializable
{
    // Some public fields and a (nonserializable) event
    public string FirstName;
    public string LastName;
    public event EventHandler GotEmail;

    public Person(string firstName, string lastName)
    {
        this.FirstName = firstName;
        this.LastName = lastName;
    }

    public void GetObjectData(SerializationInfo info, StreamingContext context)
    {
        SerializationHelpers.GetObjectDataHelper(info, context, this);
    }

    protected Person(SerializationInfo info, StreamingContext context)
    {
        SerializationHelpers.ISerializableConstructorHelper(info, context, this);
    }
}
```

Chapter 18
Execution Flow

In this chapter, we continue our exploration of all the elements that make up an application at the single-statement level.

Most of the rules in this chapter are coding guidelines that can affect only the readability of your code, not its performance. Here, we handle hot topics such as where to place curly braces (in C#) or whether you should use the hideous *GoTo* statement (in Visual Basic). Over the years, thousands of developers have debated these details without reaching any definitive conclusion; thus, we decided to mention the whys and why-nots and exceptions to all the approaches.

In addition to style issues, this chapter also includes many tips on how you can help your favorite compiler produce the most efficient code and avoid some common programming mistakes at the same time.

18.1 Multiple statements on one line

Don't include multiple statements on a single line.

Why: Lines containing single statements make the code more readable and enable you to add a comment for each individual variable.

```
' [Visual Basic]
' *** Wrong
x = 1: y = 1

' *** Correct
x = 1           ' (You can explain what x is here.)
y = 1           ' (You can explain what y is here.)

// [C#]
// *** Wrong
x = 1; y = 1;

// *** Correct
x = 1;          // (You can explain what x is here.)
y = 1;          // (You can explain what y is here.)
```

18.2 Empty parentheses in method calls [Visual Basic]

Use an empty pair of parentheses when invoking a method that takes no argument.

Why: This rule helps distinguish properties from parameterless methods and is consistent with the way you invoke methods in other languages, including C#.

```
' [Visual Basic]
' *** Wrong
Dim res As String = obj.ToString

' *** Correct
Dim res As String = obj.ToString()
```

18.3 Invoking static methods [Visual Basic]

Always use a type name (as opposed to an instance variable) as a prefix when invoking a static (*Shared*) method.

Why: This style makes it clear that you are calling a static member and is consistent with how static members are used in other languages.

```
' [Visual Basic]
Dim n As Double

' *** Wrong
n = n.Parse("123.45")          ' Parse is a static method.

' *** Correct
n = Double.Parse("123.45")
```

18.4 Invoking methods in modules [Visual Basic]

Include the module name when invoking methods in modules.

Why: This style makes it evident that the method is defined in a different type; besides, modules are just types whose members are all static (*Shared*), and this rule ensures that module members and static members in regular types are dealt with consistently (see rule 18.3).

```
' [Visual Basic]
' This code makes the following assumptions:
'    (a) The Helpers module contains a procedure named ShowMessage.
'    (b) following code is outside the Helpers module.

' *** OK
ShowMessage("hello world")

' *** Better
Helpers.ShowMessage("hello world")
```

18.5 Single-statement *If* blocks [Visual Basic]

Avoid single-line *If* statements. Always close an *If* statement with an *End If* keyword. By doing so, it is easier to add remarks and other statements in the *If* block.

```
' [Visual Basic]
' *** OK
If x > 0 Then y = 0

' *** Better
```

```
If x > 0 Then
    y = 0
End If
```

Alternate rule: Single-line *If...Then* and *If...Then...Else* blocks are accepted if they contain only one statement. The rationale for this alternate rule is that this style uses only one line of code instead of three (or five) lines, and therefore makes better use of screen real estate.

```
' [Visual Basic]
' *** OK, if you accept single-line If blocks.
If x > 0 Then z = x
If x > 0 Then z = x Else z = y
```

18.6 Single-statement conditional and loop blocks [C#]

Use curly braces also for *if*, *else if*, *for*, *foreach*, and *while* blocks that contain a single line.

```
// [C#]
if ( obj != null )
{
    msg = obj.ToString();
}
```

Alternate rule: Don't use curly braces for *if*, *else if*, *for*, *foreach*, and *while* blocks that contain a single line, but ensure that the statement is correctly indented. (This alternate rule affects readability but maximizes the amount of code that is visible on the screen in a given moment.)

```
// [C#]
// *** OK, if you accept single-statement ifs without curly braces.
if ( obj != null )
    msg = obj.ToString();
```

More details: C, C++, and now C# developers have debated so far endlessly about whether conditional and loop statements should use curly braces if they contain only a single statement. We don't want to fuel the debate even further, thus we list the two options and leave the choice up to you.

In general, we prefer using curly braces because this style is more consistent and makes it simpler to add new statements later in the development and debugging process. However, we have often used the more concise style in this book to keep listings to an acceptable size.

The one thing that we never do in our code (and never in this book) is mix the two styles in the same method or, worse, the same block. For example, *never* write this kind of code:

```
// [C#]
// *** Wrong: mixes the two styles in same block.
if ( x >= 0 )
    Console.WriteLine(x);
else
{
    Console.WriteLine("x is zero");
    Console.WriteLine("Please enter a new value:");
}
```

18.7 Nested conditional and loop blocks

Don't nest conditional and loop blocks to more than three levels—or four levels in exceptional cases. If more levels are required, move the innermost code into a separate private method.

18.8 *AndAlso* and *OrElse* operators [Visual Basic]

Use *AndAlso* and *OrElse* operators when combining Boolean conditions.

Why: These operators perform better than *And* and *Or* operators, which should be reserved for bit-field manipulation.

Exception: Use the *And* and *Or* operators on Boolean values when migrating Visual Basic 6 code and the second operand is a call of a function that has *ByRef* arguments or that has side effects, such as changing the value of global variables.

```
' [Visual Basic]
' *** Wrong
If x > 0 And y < 10 Then Console.Write("ok")
' *** Correct
If x > 0 AndAlso y < 10 Then Console.Write("ok")

' Use Or instead of OrElse because Increment function modifies its argument.
If x > 0 Or Increment(y) > 10 Then Console.Write("ok")
...
Function Increment(ByRef n As Integer) As Integer
    n += 1
    Return n
End Function
```

18.9 Comparisons with *true/false*

Avoid comparisons with true and false Boolean values.

```
' [Visual Basic]
' *** Wrong
Sub PerformTask(ByVal condition1 As Boolean, ByVal condition2 As Boolean)
    If condition1 = True Then
        ...
    ElseIf condition2 = False Then
        ...
    End If
End Sub

' *** Correct
Sub PerformTask(ByVal condition1 As Boolean, ByVal condition2 As Boolean)
    If condition1 Then
        ...
    ElseIf Not condition2 Then
        ...
    End If
End Sub
```

```csharp
// [C#]
// *** Wrong
void PerformTask(bool condition1, bool condition2)
{
   if ( condition1 == true )
      ...
   else if ( condition2 == false )
      ...
}

// *** Correct
void PerformTask(bool condition1, bool condition2)
{
   if ( condition1)
      ...
   else if ( ! condition2)
      ...
}
```

18.10 Conditional blocks to assign a Boolean value

Use a direct assignment of the result of a Boolean expression instead of an *If...Then...Else* block.

```vb
' [Visual Basic]
' *** Wrong: too verbose
Dim ok As Boolean
If x > 0 Then
   ok = True
Else
   ok = False
End If

' *** OK
Dim ok As Boolean = (x > 0)
```

```csharp
// [C#]
// *** Wrong: too verbose
bool ok ;
if ( x > 0 )
   ok = true;
else
   ok = false;

// *** OK
bool ok = (x > 0);
```

18.11 The ternary operator *(? :)* [C#]

Avoid using the *? :* ternary operator inside expressions because it makes the expression logic harder to follow. Instead, assign the result of the ternary operator to a temporary variable and use that variable in the expression.

```
// [C#]
// *** OK
Console.WriteLine( (x == 0 ? "equal to" : "different from") + " zero");

// *** Better
string tmp = ( x == 0 ? "equal to" : "different from" );
Console.WriteLine(tmp + " zero");
```

Alternate rule: Never use the ternary operator, not even for simple assignments; use an *if...else* block instead. (Many C# developers believe that the ternary operator is always a bad thing, so we list this alternate rule for the sake of completeness.)

18.12 The IIf function [Visual Basic]

Avoid using the IIf function in time-critical code or if one of its operands is a function call. Instead, use an explicit *If...Then...Else* block.

Why: This function is not part of the language. Instead, it is just one method defined in the Microsoft.VisualBasic.dll library and is always slower than an explicit *If* block. Also, all its operands are always evaluated; therefore, you might add unncessary overhead (and undesired side effects, in some cases) if one of them is a method call.

```
' [Visual Basic]
' *** Wrong: method call is involved.
Dim s As String = IIf(Name <> "", Name, GetUsername())

' *** OK
Dim s As String = IIf(Name <> "", Name, "Unknown")

' (Next code assumes that names is an array of strings.)
' *** Wrong: uses IIf inside a loop
For i As Integer = 0 To names.Length - 1
   Console.WriteLine(IIf(names(i) <> "", names(i), "Unknown"))
Next

' *** Correct
For i As Integer = 0 To names.Length - 1
   If names(i) <> "" Then
      Console.WriteLine(names(i))
   Else
      Console.WriteLine("Unknown")
   End If
Next
```

18.13 Testing and comparing object types

Consider all the alternatives you have when testing the type of an object or when comparing the types of two objects. Remember that the *TypeOf...Is* (Visual Basic), *is*, and *as* (C#) operators test the existence of an inheritance relationship, as in this code:

```
' [Visual Basic]
If TypeOf obj Is Person Then
   ' obj is an instance of Person or of another type that derives from Person.
End If
```

```
// [C#]
if ( obj is Person )
{
    // obj is an instance of Person or of another type that derives from Person.
}
```

In most cases, the previous code is OK. In some cases, however, you really need to check whether an object is of a given type. In this case, you must compare the result returned by the GetType method, as in the following code:

```
' [Visual Basic]
If Not obj Is Nothing AndAlso obj.GetType() Is GetType(Person) Then
    ' obj is an instance of the Person type.
End If
```

```
// [C#]
if ( obj != null && obj.GetType() == typeof(Person) )
{
    // obj is an instance of the Person type.
}
```

The following technique should be used to check whether two objects are of the same type:

```
' [Visual Basic]
Function AreSameType(ByVal obj1 As Object, ByVal obj2 As Object) As Boolean
    Return (Not obj1 Is Nothing AndAlso Not obj2 Is Nothing _
        AndAlso obj1.GetType() Is obj2.GetType())
End Function
```

```
// [C#]
bool AreSameType(object obj1, object obj2)
{
    return ( obj1 != null && obj2 != null && obj1.GetType() == obj2.GetType() );
}
```

More details: Explicitly testing the type of an object in a series of *If...ElseIf* (Visual Basic) or *if...else if* (C#) blocks can be the symptom of a badly designed piece of code because such a piece of code can't be expanded to work with other types without modifying and recompiling the method. In such cases it is preferable to test against an interface or the presence of a custom attribute.

18.14 Testing a variable for multiple values [Visual Basic]

Favor a *Select Case* block instead of an *If* statement when testing the same variable against four or more values or ranges of values.

```
' [Visual Basic]
' *** Wrong
If x = 1 OrElse x = 3 OrElse (x >= 6 AndAlso x <= 9) Then
   Console.WriteLine("OK")
End If
```

```
' *** Correct
Select Case x
    Case 1, 3, 6 To 9
        Console.WriteLine("OK")
End Select
```

18.15 Statements in *Case* blocks [Visual Basic]

Never include multiple statements on the same line as the *Case* keyword.

It is acceptable to have a *Case* clause followed by a single statement on the same line, but only if all the *Case* clauses in the *Select Case* block are followed by a single statement.

```
' [Visual Basic]
' *** Wrong
Select Case x
    Case 1: y = 2
    Case 2: y = 5: z = 8
End Select

' *** Correct
Select Case x
    Case 1
        y = 2
    Case 2
        y = 4
        z = 8
End Select

' *** Also correct: all Case blocks contain one statement.
Select Case x
    Case 1: y = 2
    Case 2: y = 5
    Case 3: y = 8
End Select
```

18.16 Order of *Case* blocks

Always check the most frequent values near the top of a *Select Case* (Visual Basic) or *switch* (C#) statement.

Why: This arrangement improves execution speed because values in the block are usually tested in the order they appear.

More details: In Visual Basic, this guideline is especially effective with *Select Case* blocks containing a large number of *Case* blocks.

In C#, this guideline might be less effective than you think because the compiler can often optimize a *switch* block by means of a jump table (if values to be tested are consecutive integers), hidden String.IsInterned methods calls (if testing against a small number of string constants), or an auxiliary Hashtable object. However, even if in some cases the order of *case* blocks doesn't improve performance, it doesn't harm it either; therefore, we suggest that more frequent cases always be tested near the top of a *switch* block.

18.17 Asserting the default case

Always have a *Case Else* clause in a *Select Case* block (Visual Basic) or a *default* clause in a *switch* block (C#). If you expect that this clause is never executed, your code should include a Debug.Assert statement or it should throw an exception.

```vb
' [Visual Basic]
Select Case x
   Case 1
      y = 2
   Case 2
      y = 5
   Case Else
      Throw New ArgumentException("Invalid value for x")
End Select
```

```csharp
// [C#]
switch ( x )
{
   case 1:
      y = 2;
      break;
   case 2:
      y = 5;
      break;
   default:
      throw new ArgumentException("Invalid value for x");
}
```

18.18 *GoTo* keyword [Visual Basic]

Never use the *GoTo* statement except in the following case: to jump to the end of a loop if this jump style saves you from defining deeply nested *If* statements.

More details: This use of the *GoTo* statement remedies the lack of the *Continue* statement in the current version of Visual Basic. Notice, however, that you shouldn't have more than three nested *If* statements, as per rule 18.7.

```vb
' [Visual Basic]
' *** OK, but flow is hard to follow.
For i As Integer = 1 To 1000
   Dim a As Integer = GetData()
   If a = i Then
      Dim b As Integer = GetData()
      If b <> a Then
         Dim c As Integer = GetData()
         If c <> a And c <> b Then
            ' Use a, b, c variables here.
            ...
         End If
      End if
   End if
Next
```

```
' *** More readable, even if it uses the dreaded GoTo keyword.
For i As Integer = 1 To 1000
   Dim a As Integer = GetData()
   If a <> i Then GoTo ContinueFor
   Dim b As Integer = GetData()
   If b = a Then GoTo ContinueFor
   Dim c As Integer = GetData()
   If c = a Or c <> b Then GoTo ContinueFor
   ' Use a, b, c variables here.
   ...
ContinueFor:
Next
```

18.19 *goto* keyword [C#]

Never use the *goto* statement except to jump to another *case* block or to the *default* block in a *switch* statement.

18.20 Variable declaration in *For* and *For Each* loops [Visual Basic]

Always declare the controlling variable of a *For* and *For Each* loop inside the loop.

Why: This syntax (available with Visual Basic 2003 and later versions) is more concise and, above all, ensures that the variable isn't accidentally used after the last iteration of the loop.

```
' [Visual Basic]
' *** Wrong
Dim i As Integer
For i = 1 To 100
   ...
Next
Dim p As Person
For Each p In colPersons
   ...
Next

' *** Correct
For i As Integer = 1 To 100
   ...
Next
For Each p As Person in colPersons
   ...
Next
```

18.21 Array upper limit in *For* loops

Always explicitly test the controlling variable in *For* loops against the array's Length property. Don't attempt to optimize code by storing the Length property's value in a temporary variable.

Why: The C# compiler recognizes this special pattern and produces code that doesn't test the variable at each iteration. The Visual Basic compiler doesn't currently adopt this optimization technique, but it will presumably in a future version.

```
' [Visual Basic]
' *** Wrong: uses a function in the Microsoft.VisualBasic library.
Dim arr(99) As Integer
For i As Integer = 0 To UBound(arr)
   ...
Next

' *** Wrong: caches the upper limit in a variable.
Dim arr(99) As Integer
Dim maxIndex As Integer = arr.Length - 1
For i As Integer = 0 To maxIndex
   ...
Next

' *** Correct
Dim arr(99) As Integer
For i As Integer = 0 To arr.Length - 1
   ...
Next
```

```
// [C#]
// *** Wrong
int[] arr = new int[100];
int maxIndex = arr.Length - 1;
for ( int i = 0; i <= maxIndex; i++ )
{
   ...
}

// *** Correct
int[] arr = new int[100];
for ( int i = 0; i < arr.Length; i++ )
{
   ...
}
```

18.22 Modifying the controlling variable in *For* loops

Don't modify the controlling variable in the body of a *For* (Visual Basic) or *for* (C#) loop.

```
' [Visual Basic]
Dim oddProd As Integer = 1
Dim evenProd As Integer = 1

' *** Wrong
For i As Integer = 1 To 100
   oddProd *= i
   i += 1
   evenProd *= i
Next
```

```
' *** Correct
For i As Integer = 1 To 100 Step 2
    oddProd *= i
    evenProd *= (i + 1)
Next
```

```
// [C#]
int oddProd = 1;
int evenProd = 1;
```

```
// *** Wrong
for ( int i = 1; i <= 100; i++ )
{
    oddProd *= i++;
    evenProd *= i;
}
```

```
// *** Correct
for ( int i = 1; i <= 100; i += 2 )
{
    oddProd *= i;
    evenProd *= (i + 1);
}
```

18.23 Floating-point variables in *For* loops

Never use a floating-point variable as the controlling variable of a *For* (Visual Basic) or *for* (C#) loop because rounding errors might cause the loop to execute a wrong number of times. Instead, use two distinct variables: an integer variable to control the loop and a floating-point variable that is manually incremented in the loop.

```
' [Visual Basic]
' *** Wrong: this loop executes only 100 times (it should be 101).
For d As Double = 0 To 1 Step 0.01
    ...
Next
```

```
' *** Correct
Dim d As Double = 0
For i As Integer = 0 To 100
    ...
    d += 0.01
Next
```

```
// [C#]
// *** Wrong: this loop executes only 100 times (it should be 101).
for ( double d = 0; d <= 1; d+=0.01 )
{
    ...
}
```

```
// *** Correct
double d = 0;
for ( int i = 0; i <= 100; i++, d+=0.01 )
{
    ...
}
```

18.24 Constant subexpressions in loops

If a subexpression doesn't change inside a loop, assign it to a temporary variable outside the loop and use the temporary variable inside the loop.

Why: The JIT compiler isn't able to enforce constant folding optimization techniques, thus this coding style makes the code faster and more readable at the same time (because it shortens expressions in loops).

```
' [Visual Basic]
' *** OK
Dim arr(10, 20) As Integer
For r As Integer = 0 To arr.GetUpperBound(0)
   For c As Integer = 0 To arr.GetUpperBound(1)
      arr(r, c) = r * r + c * c + 1
   Next
Next

' *** Better
Dim arr(10, 20) As Integer
For r As Integer = 0 To arr.GetUpperBound(0)
   Dim tmp As Integer = r * r + 1
   For c As Integer = 0 To arr.GetUpperBound(1)
      arr(r, c) = tmp + c * c
   Next
Next

 // [C#]
// *** OK
int[,] arr = new int[10, 20];
for ( int r = 0; r <= arr.GetUpperBound(0); r++ )
{
   for ( int c = 0; c <= arr.GetUpperBound(1); c++ )
   {
      arr[r, c] = r * r + c * c + 1;
   }
}

// *** Better
int[,] arr = new int[10, 20];
for ( int r = 0; r <= arr.GetUpperBound(0); r++ )
{
```

```
    int tmp = r * r + 1;
    for ( int c = 0; c <= arr.GetUpperBound(1); c++ )
    {
        arr[r, c] = tmp + c * c;
    }
}
```

18.25 *While* loops [Visual Basic]

Don't use *While...End While* loops.

Why: This kind of loop can have a test condition only at its top, so it's less flexible than the more modern *Do...Loop* statement, which can have the test condition at either the top or the bottom (or even no test condition at all).

18.26 Unsafe code [C#]

Avoid unsafe code if possible. If you must use unsafe code, place all your unsafe methods in a a separate assembly.

Why: Unsafe code can't be guaranteed to be safe; therefore, it requires that the application be fully trusted. For example, a Windows Forms application containing unsafe code can run from a local disk but throws a security exception if run from an intranet or Internet server (unless the client computer's administrator defines a nonstandard code policy to grant the application full trust).

More details: Unsafe code is usually valuable in the following cases: in performance-critical code (as in image processing), in advanced PInvoke and COM Interop scenarios, and when dealing with existing structures on disk. However, in most cases you can achieve the same result with safe and verifiable code, even if at the expense of slower code.

All the unsafe methods should be gathered in a separate DLL, and the main application should use methods in the DLL only when running as a fully trusted application. In all other cases the application should degrade to less efficient but verifiable code (compiled in the main executable or in a different DLL) or disable the functionality. If the unsafe code method is triggered by a user interface element, this element should be disabled or it should display a message box that explains why the requested functionality isn't available.

Chapter 19
Exception Handling

Exceptions play quite an important role in the Microsoft .NET Framework as well as in all .NET applications. As a Visual Basic or C# developer, you are expected to correctly throw and catch exceptions and even define custom exception types if the exception classes in the .NET Framework don't suit your needs.

To begin with, you should keep in mind one golden rule: the fewer exceptions your application throws or catches, the faster it runs. If a piece of code runs slower than you expected, the very first thing to do is check the value of these two performance counters in the .NET CLR Exceptions category (see Figure 19-1).

- # of Exceps Thrown (the total number of exceptions thrown since the start of the application)

- # of Exceps Thrown / sec (the number of exceptions thrown per second)

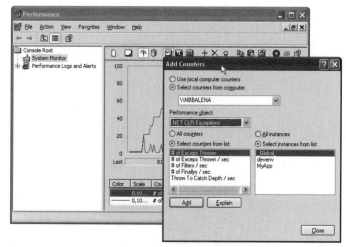

Figure 19-1   The Performance utility can display the total number of exceptions thrown and the rate of exceptions per second.

> **Note**   One or more code examples in this chapter assume that the following namespaces have been imported by means of *Imports* (Visual Basic) or *using* (C#) statements:
>
> ```
> System.Diagnostics
> System.IO
> System.Reflection
> System.Resources
> System.Runtime.Serialization
> ```

19.1 Exception variable names

Use ex as the name of any exception caught in a *Try* (Visual Basic) or *try* (C#) block. Use ex as the prefix for variables explicitly referencing an Exception object outside these blocks. (Notice that you shouldn't use e to reference exceptions in these blocks because you would have a name collision inside event handlers.)

```
' [visual Basic]
Try
   ' Here goes the code to be protected from exceptions.
   ...
Catch ex As NullReferenceException
   ...
Catch ex As Exception
   ...
End Try

// [C#]
try
{
   // Here goes the code to be protected from exceptions.
   ...
}
catch ( NullReferenceException ex )
{
   ...
}
catch ( Exception ex )
{
   ...
}
```

19.2 Custom exception type names

Use the Exception suffix for custom exception types, namely, types that inherit directly or indirectly from System.Exception.

Example: IniFileNotFoundException.

19.3 The *On Error* statement [Visual Basic]

Don't use the *On Error Goto* or *On Error Resume Next* statements. Instead, use *Try* blocks, which are more structured and far more efficient.

Exception: *On Error Resume Next* statements are tolerated only when migrating an application from Visual Basic 6 because there is no way to tell the compiler "ignore all errors" by using *Try* blocks. Even in this case, however, you should get rid of these *On Error* statements as soon as possible and use *Try* blocks exclusively.

19.4 Using exceptions to control execution flow

Exceptions are extremely time-consuming, so you shouldn't use them as a way to control execution flow, for example, to exit a procedure prematurely.

Throw an exception only if you want to be sure that client code can't absolutely miss the error condition. If it isn't the case, consider returning a special value (e.g., a negative number or a null object reference) instead of throwing an exception.

19.5 Throwing specific exception objects

Always use the most specific exception type that describes more closely the error condition of which you want to notify callers. Favor throwing an exception that isn't used as the base class for other exception types. Never throw a generic Exception object.

Why: Throwing the most specific exception provides callers with richer information and enables them to catch only the exceptions they can handle.

Example: Don't throw an ArithmeticException object if one of the types that inherit from this class—namely, DivideByZeroException, OverflowException, or NotFiniteNumberException—describe better what went wrong in your code.

19.6 Throwing on Dispose and Close methods

Never throw an exception from inside a Close or Dispose method, even if the object has been already closed or been disposed of.

Why: The Close method exposed by many .NET Framework objects—for example, ADO.NET connections—doesn't throw an exception if the object is already closed. You should apply the same guideline when designing your own types.

19.7 Exception message style

Use complete sentences in exception messages, include a trailing period, and provide enough information for the client to solve the problem. Don't expose information that should be regarded as private (e.g., filenames and user names) because the error message might be displayed to remote and unauthorized users (for example, remote callers of a Web service).

19.8 Localized error messages

Consider the opportunity to use satellite assemblies to store localized versions of your error messages. This rule is especially effective if error messages are displayed to the end user.

How to: See rules 4.8 and 4.10 for more information about storing localized resources in localized assemblies. Once all the satellite assemblies are in place you can read the actual messages by means of a ResourceManager object.

More details: Names for resource elements holding strings to be used for the Message property of an exception should be named as *ExceptionTypeName.MessageShortName*. For example, you can use ArgumentOutOfRangeException.NegativeValue as the name of the string resource that is displayed when a method receives a negative argument and you throw an ArgumentOutOfRangeException object.

```VisualBasic
' [Visual Basic]
' Define this variable somewhere in your application.
Friend resources As New ResourceManager("CodeArchitects.Strings", _
    [Assembly].GetExecutingAssembly())

' Here's how you throw an exception with a localized message string.
Sub PerformTask(ByVal x As Integer)
    If x < 0 Then
        Throw New ArgumentOutOfRangeException("x", resources.GetString( _
            "ArgumentOutOfRangeException.NegativeValue"))
    End If
    ...
End Sub
```

```csharp
// [C#]
// Define this variable somewhere in your application.
internal ResourceManager resources = new ResourceManager(
    "CodeArchitects.Strings", Assembly.GetExecutingAssembly());

// Here's how you throw an exception with a localized message string.
void PerformTask(int x)
{
    if ( x < 0 )
    {
        throw new ArgumentOutOfRangeException("x", resources.GetString(
            "ArgumentOutOfRangeException.NegativeValue"));
    }
    ...
}
```

19.9 XML remarks documenting which exceptions a method can throw [C#]

Use XML remarks to document which exceptions a method can throw. List all the exceptions explicitly thrown by your code and, if possible, those thrown by the .NET runtime and that your code doesn't catch.

```csharp
// [C#]
/// <summary>
/// Multiply a fraction by an integer value.
/// </summary>
/// <exception cref="NullReferenceException">
/// The <paramref name="f1"/> argument was null.
/// </exception>
/// <exception cref="OverflowException">
/// The numerator of the result is too high for 32-bit precision.
/// </exception>
```

```
/// <param name="f">The fraction to be multipled.</param>
/// <param name="factor">The integer multiplier.</param>
/// <returns>
/// A new Fraction object that is the result of the multiplication.
/// </returns>
public static Fraction Multiply(Fraction f, int factor)
{
    return new Fraction(f.Numerator * factor, f.Denominator);
}
```

19.10 Remarks documenting which exceptions a method can throw [Visual Basic]

Add a comment at the top of the method that lists which exceptions the method is known to throw, and specify under which conditions this happens. You can rarely anticipate all the exceptions that can be thrown by the .NET runtime, but at least developers calling the method may have an idea of the most common exceptions for which they must account.

More details: If you use XML remarks in your Visual Basic applications (see rule 3.8), you should also use XML remarks to document the exceptions your methods throw, as explained in rule 19.9.

19.11 Can-prefixed read-only properties to prevent exceptions

Consider exposing one or more Can-prefixed read-only properties marked as virtual (*Overridable* in Visual Basic) to let clients test whether a given operation can be completed without throwing an exception. You should have one such property for each public method that might throw an exception.

Why: Exposing these Can-prefixed read-only properties can improve the overall performance because they enable clients to avoid exceptions. This pattern is especially useful for classes meant to work as base classes because derived classes can override the read-only property and return a different value. (See rule 7.6.)

Example: If your type exposes a method named EvalResults that might throw an exception under certain conditions (for example, when other properties haven't been set correctly), you can expose a CanEvalResults property that returns true if the EvalResults method can be invoked without throwing any exception. Notice that, in practice, you don't write more code than you would anyway because the EvalResults method can invoke the CanEvalResults property and throw if the latter returns false.

```
' [Visual Basic]
Public Class Foo
    Public Overridable ReadOnly Property CanEvalResults() As Boolean
        Get
            ' Return True if results are available, else return False.
            ...
        End Get
    End Property
End Class
```

```
' This is the method that might throw an exception.
Sub EvalResults()
    If Not Me.CanEvalResults Then
        Throw New ArgumentException("Results aren't available")
    End If
    ...
End Sub
End Class

// [C#]
public class Foo
{
    public virtual bool CanEvalResults
    {
        get
        {
            // Return true if results are available, else return false.
            ...
        }
    }

    // This is the method that might throw an exception.
    public void EvalResults()
    {
        if ( ! this.CanEvalResults )
            throw new ArgumentException("Results aren't available");
        ...
    }
}
```

More details: You might think of exposing a single Can-prefixed read-only property that takes an enum argument instead of one property for each method. However, such an approach might cause versioning issues if you later add more methods to the type.

19.12 Order of *Catch* blocks [Visual Basic]

Sort *Catch* blocks so that more specific exceptions are tested before more generic ones.

Why: If you put more generic exceptions on top, subsequent exceptions will never be tested.

```
' [Visual Basic]
' *** Wrong: FileNotFoundException inherits from IOException.
Try
    ...
Catch ex As IOException
    ...
Catch ex As FileNotFoundException
    ' This block will never be executed.
    ...
End Try


' *** Correct
Try
    ...
```

```
Catch ex As FileNotFoundException
   ...
Catch ex As IOException
   ...
End Try
```

More details: C# developers don't have to worry about this issue because the C# compiler refuses to compile a *try...catch* block containing inaccessible *catch* blocks.

19.13 The *When* keyword [Visual Basic]

Take advantage of the *When* keyword in *Catch* blocks to refine the filter condition and avoid the need to rethrow an exception.

```
' [Visual Basic]
' *** OK
Try
   ...
Catch ex As FileNotFoundException
   If Path.GetFileName(ex.FileName) = "data.ini" Then
      ' Catch the exception if the .ini file hasn't been found.
      InitializeData()
   Else
      ' Rethrow the exception in all other cases.
      Throw
   End If
End Try

' *** Better
Try
   ...
Catch ex As FileNotFoundException When Path.GetFileName(ex.FileName) = "data.ini"
   ' Catch the exception if the .ini file hasn't been found.
   InitializeData()

   ' (Other FileNotFound exceptions are automatically rethrown.)
End Try
```

19.14 Setting return values in *Finally* blocks [Visual Basic]

Don't assign a value to the local variable named after the current method from inside a *Finally* block.

Why: The Visual Basic compiler correctly flags *Return* keywords in *Finally* blocks as errors because they would override any *Return* statements in the *Try* block or in any *Catch* block. However, the compiler doesn't flag as an error the assignment to the variable named as the method.

```
' [Visual Basic]
' *** Wrong
Function GetValue() As Integer
   Try
      ...
      Return 123
   Finally
```

```
        GetValue = 456           ' This statement assigns the return value.
    End Try
End Function


' *** Correct: Use a variable to hold the return value.
Function GetValue() As Integer
    Dim result As Integer
    Try
        ...
        result = 123
    Finally
        result = 456
    End Try
    Return result
End Function
```

19.15 Undoing state in *Catch* blocks

If you catch an exception, you should restore the program state to what it was before the code attempts the operation that caused the exception. Examples of program state to be restored include variable values, current position in streams, state of database tables and connections, and state of individual rows in a DataSet.

How to: In general, you can adopt one of the following two strategies to restore the previous state of an object:

- You remember the initial state in local variables and restore these values if an exception is caught.

- You clone an object and perform all the operations on the cloned object. If an exception is thrown, you don't need to do anything special because the original object hasn't been affected; if the operation is successful, you replace the original object with the cloned object.

Example: The following code is an example of the former of the two preceding strategies:

```
' [Visual Basic]
Sub AppendToFile(ByVal fileName As String, ByVal lines() As String)
    Dim fs As FileStream
    Dim saveLength As Long = -1           ' -1 means "file didn't exist."

    Try
        If File.Exists(fileName) Then
            ' If the file exists, open it in append mode.
            fs = New FileStream(fileName, FileMode.Append, FileAccess.Write)
            saveLength = fs.Position
        Else
            ' If the file doesn't exist, create it.
            fs = New FileStream(fileName, FileMode.Create, FileAccess.Write)
        End If

        Dim sw As New StreamWriter(fs)
        For Each s As String In lines
            sw.WriteLine(s)
```

```
            Next
            ' Close the file stream if everything was OK.
            sw.Flush()
            sw.Close()

        Catch ex As Exception
            ' Log the exception.
            Debug.WriteLine("EXCEPTION: " & ex.Message)
            If fs Is Nothing Then
                ' Nothing to undo if the file stream wasn't even created.
            ElseIf saveLength >= 0 Then
                ' The file existed: trim it to previous size and close it.
                fs.SetLength(saveLength)
                fs.Close()
            Else
                ' The file didn't exist: close it and delete it.
                fs.Close()
                File.Delete(fileName)
            End If
        End Try
    End Sub

// [C#]
void AppendToFile(string fileName, string[] lines)
{
    FileStream fs = null;
    long saveLength = -1;           // -1 means "file didn't exist."

    try
    {
        if ( File.Exists(fileName) )
        {
            // If the file exists, open it in append mode.
            fs = new FileStream(fileName, FileMode.Append, FileAccess.Write);
            saveLength = fs.Position;
        }
        else
        {
            // The file doesn't exist-close it and delete it.
            fs = new FileStream(fileName, FileMode.Create, FileAccess.Write);
        }

        StreamWriter sw = new StreamWriter(fs);
        foreach ( string s in lines )
            sw.WriteLine(s);
        // Close the file stream if everything was OK.
        sw.Flush();
        sw.Close();
    }
    catch ( Exception ex )
    {
        // Log the exception.
        Debug.WriteLine("EXCEPTION: " + ex.Message);
        if ( fs == null )
        {
```

```
            // Nothing to undo if the file stream wasn't even created.
        }
        else if ( saveLength >= 0 )
        {
            // The file existed: trim it to previous size and close it.
            fs.SetLength(saveLength);
            fs.Close();
        }
        else
        {
            // The file didn't exist: close it and delete it.
            fs.Close();
            File.Delete(fileName);
        }
    }
}
}
```

19.16 Catching SystemException and ApplicationException

Don't catch SystemException and ApplicationException objects.

Why: According to .NET Framework guidelines, all the .NET Framework exceptions should derive from SystemException, whereas all user-defined exception types should derive from ApplicationException. These guidelines were issued to help developers catch all application-specific exceptions in a single *catch* block. Unfortunately, Microsoft developers didn't closely follow these rules and a few exceptions in the .NET Framework mistakenly derive directly from Exception or from ApplicationException. Because of these nonstandard exceptions, a *catch* block for ApplicationException might catch system exceptions instead of just user-defined exceptions. Likewise, a catch block for SystemException isn't guaranteed to catch all the system exceptions.

See also: See rule 19.29 for a solution to this problem.

19.17 Catching DivideByZeroException

Avoid catching DivideByZeroException objects.

Why: There are two reasons for this guideline. First, it's more efficient to compare the second operand of a division with zero rather than letting the CLR runtime throw the exception. Second, this exception is thrown only for integer division. (A floating-point division whose second operand is zero creates a PositiveInfinity or NegativeInfinity value but doesn't throw any exception.)

```vb
' [Visual Basic]
' *** Wrong
Try
    Dim d As Double = 0
    ' This statement doesn't throw, m becomes PositiveInfinity.
    Dim m As Double = 1 / d
```

```
    Dim i As Integer = 0
    Dim k As Integer = 1 \ i          ' This throws, but is inefficient.
Catch ex As DivideByZeroException
    ...
End Try

' *** Correct
Dim d As Double = 0
Dim m As Double = 1 / d
If Double.IsInfinity(m) Then
    ' Catch the divide-by-zero condition on floating-point values.
End If

Dim i As Integer = 0
Dim k As Integer = 1
If i <> 0 Then
    ' Perform the division only if denominator is nonzero.
    k = k \ i
End If

// [C#]
// *** Wrong
try
{
    double d = 0;
    // This statement doesn't throw, m becomes PositiveInfinity.
    double m = 1 / d;

    int i = 0 ;
    int k = 1 / i;            // This throws, but is inefficient.
}
catch ( DivideByZeroException ex )
{
    ...
}

// *** Correct
double d = 0;
double m = 1 / d;
if ( Double.IsInfinity(m) )
{
    // Catch the divide-by-zero condition on floating-point values.
}

int i = 0;
int k = 1;
if ( i != 0 )
{
    // Perform the division only if denominator is nonzero.
    k = k / i;
}
```

19.18 Catching special .NET exceptions

Don't catch the following special .NET exceptions except for logging reasons: OutOfMemoryException, StackOverflowException, ThreadAbortException, and ExecutionEngineException. If you catch these exceptions, you should always rethrow them.

Why: After the .NET runtime throws one of these exceptions, the application is usually in an unstable or undetermined state and it's quite unlikely that you can recover from these exceptions gracefully. In addition, you can't actually catch the ExecutionEngineException object and (in some cases) the OutOfMemoryException object, so you don't really have a choice.

19.19 Throwing NotSupportedException vs. NotImplementedException

In an interface method or a method that overrides a base class method, throw a NotSupportedException if your type isn't expected to implement the corresponding feature and clients should never invoke the method; throw a NotImplementedException if the current version of your type hasn't yet implemented the corresponding feature, but a future version (or a derived type) might do it.

Example: Let's say that you have a type named MyCollection that implements the IList interface but doesn't support insertion of an element between existing items. In this case the Insert method should throw the NotSupportedException because it's a programming mistake to invoke this method on this type and on all the types that derive from MyCollection.

Let's further suppose that you don't want to implement the Remove method but you want to allow inherited classes to implement it. In this case, the Remove method should throw the NotImplementedException.

19.20 Catching exceptions in class libraries

In general, don't catch exceptions inside class libraries unless you rethrow them.

Why: You should catch an exception without rethrowing it only if you are sure that the caller never needs to know what happened. Although this condition can be true inside an application, it is rarely true in a class library.

19.21 Rethrowing original exceptions

For debugging and reporting purposes, the last *Catch* (Visual Basic) or *catch* (C#) block should handle generic Exception objects and should rethrow the original exception so that stack information isn't altered.

How to: You rethrow the original exception by executing a *Throw* (Visual Basic) or *throw* (C#) command without any argument.

```vb
' [Visual Basic]
Try
   ...
Catch ex As FileNotFoundException
   ...
Catch ex As Exception
   Debug.WriteLine(ex.Message)
   Throw                          ' No argument
End Try
```

```csharp
// [C#]
try
{
   ...
}
catch ( FileNotFoundException ex )
{
   ...
}
catch ( Exception ex )
{
   Debug.WriteLine(ex.Message);
   throw;                         // No argument
}
```

19.22 Rethrowing exceptions of a different type

When you rethrow an exception that is different from the exception that the .NET Framework threw at your code, ensure that you pass the original exception to the new exception's constructor.

Why: This guideline ensures that the code that catches your exception can inspect the Inner-Exception property and follow the chain of exceptions to understand precisely what went wrong, and where.

Exception: In some cases you can't follow this rule because a few .NET Framework exception types don't expose a constructor that takes the inner exception. Examples of such classes are ArgumentOutOfRangeException and InvalidExpressionException.

```vb
' [Visual Basic]
Sub ProcessFile(ByVal fileName As String)
   Try
      ' Process the file.
      ...
   Catch ex As FileNotFoundException
      ' Throw ArgumentException but keep track of the original exception.
      Throw New ArgumentException("Invalid file", ex)
   End Try
End Sub
```

```csharp
// [C#]
void ProcessFile(string fileName)
{
   try
   {
      // Process the file.
      ...
   }
   catch ( FileNotFoundException ex )
   {
      // Throw ArgumentException but keep track of the original exception.
      throw new ArgumentException("Invalid file", ex);
   }
}
```

19.23 Exception logging

All handled exceptions should be logged so that they can be reviewed while the application is running. All fatal exceptions should be logged to a durable medium so that they can be reviewed after the program has terminated.

More details: Consider using the Microsoft Exception Management Application Block, which you can download from MSDN at *http://msdn.microsoft.com/library/default.asp?url=/library/en-us/dnbda/html/emab-rm.asp*. This library lets you decide which exceptions should be logged and where log data should be stored. You can affect the library's behavior by editing its settings in the application's configuration file; therefore, you can change its behavior after deploying the executable files. With this library installed, you can log an exception just by calling one method, as in the following code:

```vb
' [Visual Basic]
Try
   ...
Catch ex As Exception
   ExceptionManager.Publish(ex)
End Try
```

```csharp
// [C#]
try
{
   ...
}
catch ( Exception ex )
{
   ExceptionManager.Publish(ex);
}
```

Visual Basic programmers can simplify exception logging even further by having a first *Catch* block with the *When* filter that invokes a method that does the logging and then returns false, as in the following code:

```
' [Visual Basic]
Sub PerformTask()
   Try
      ...
   Catch ex As Exception When LogException(ex)
   Catch ex As FileNotFoundException
      ' Add other Catch blocks here...
   End Try
End Sub

Public Shared Function LogException(ByVal ex As Exception) As Boolean
   ExceptionManager.Publish(ex)
   Return False
End Function
```

19.24 Defining custom exception types

Don't define a custom exception type if you can get along with the exception classes defined in the .NET Framework. More specifically, you should define a custom exception type only in the following cases:

a.   No .NET exception can reasonably be used to imply the semantics of a user-defined exception.

b.   You want to run some custom code when the exception is created, for example, to log exception details or update a custom performance counter.

c.   You want to extend the exception type with additional methods. (For example, a custom exception type might expose a Recover method that recovers from the problem.)

d.   You need a safe and robust way to discern exceptions thrown by the application and those thrown by the .NET Framework when you catch an exception.

Why: By throwing .NET Framework exceptions exclusively, you simplify the error-handling code in clients. Also, defining a custom exception type correctly isn't a trivial task, as you can see in rules 19.25 through 19.28.

19.25 Overall structure of custom exception types

A custom exception type must inherit from ApplicationException and be marked with the Serializable attribute. If you don't plan on using the class as the base class for other custom exception types, mark the class as *NotInheritable* (Visual Basic) or *sealed* (C#).

Why: A custom exception might be thrown across AppDomain boundaries, and only serializable objects can be passed between different AppDomains.

Example: The following code shows how to implement a very basic exception type that has no properties and only one constructor.

```
' [Visual Basic]
<Serializable()> _
Public NotInheritable Class WrongSyntaxException
   Inherits ApplicationException
```

```
    Sub New()
       ' Provide a default message for this custom exception.
       MyBase.New("Wrong syntax")
    End Sub
End Class

// [C#]
[Serializable]
public sealed class WrongSyntaxException : ApplicationException
{
    // Provide a default message for this custom exception.
    public WrongSyntaxException() : base("Wrong syntax")
    {}
}
```

See also: See rule 19.26 for more details about constructors in custom exception types and rule 19.29 about using a base class other than ApplicationException for custom exceptions.

19.26 Constructors in custom exception types

A custom exception type should expose four public constructors (including the constructor implied by ISerializable, an interface that all exception types inherit from their base class).

Example: The following code is an example of a serializable exception type that exposes all four constructors. For simplicity's sake, this type doesn't define any field or property in addition to those inherited from its base class.

```
' [Visual Basic]
<Serializable()> _
Public NotInheritable Class WrongSyntaxException
   Inherits ApplicationException

   Sub New()
      ' Provide a default message for this custom exception.
      MyBase.New("Wrong syntax")
   End Sub

   Sub New(ByVal message As String)
      MyBase.New(message)
   End Sub

   Sub New(ByVal message As String, ByVal innerException As Exception)
      MyBase.New(message, innerException)
   End Sub

   ' The constructor implied by the ISerializable interface
   ' is private because the class is sealed.
   Private Sub New(ByVal info As SerializationInfo, ByVal context As StreamingContext)
      MyBase.New(info, context)
   End Sub
End Class
```

```csharp
// [C#]
[Serializable]
public class WrongSyntaxException : ApplicationException
{
    // Provide a default message for this custom exception.
    public WrongSyntaxException() : base("Wrong syntax")
    {}

    public WrongSyntaxException(string message) : base(message)
    {}

    public WrongSyntaxException(string message, Exception innerException)
        : base(message, innerException)
    {}

    // The constructor implied by the ISerializable interface
    // is private because the class is sealed.
    private WrongSyntaxException(SerializationInfo info, StreamingContext context)
        : base(info, context)
    {}
}
```

See also: See rule 19.25 for basic requirements in a custom type and rule 19.28 for the correct way to serialize and deserialize fields in custom exception types.

19.27 Exceptions in constructors of custom exception types

Ensure that constructors of a custom exception type don't throw any exceptions. If you can't guarantee that code in a constructor doesn't throw any exception, wrap the constructor's body in a *Try* (Visual Basic) or *try* (C#) block.

Why: If the constructor in a custom exception type throws an unhandled exception, the code that is instantiating the exception type—typically, a *Throw* (Visual Basic) or *throw* (C#) command—does throw an exception, yet it throws an exception of a different type, a situation that can be confusing and can lead to hard-to-diagnose bugs.

Example: If a client throws an instance of your custom WrongSyntaxException type but the constructor of your custom type throws an ArgumentException object, the client incorrectly throws an instance of the latter exception type.

19.28 Serialization in custom exception types

If a custom exception type defines one or more additional fields, you should expose these values as read-only properties and provide one or more constructors that accept these values as arguments. If these values appear in the exception message, you should also override the Message property. Finally, if these fields are to be serialized, you must also override the GetObject-Data method and add code in the special constructor implied by the ISerializable interface.

Example: The following code is an example of a custom exception type that defines an additional field named FileName.

```vb
' [Visual Basic]
<Serializable()> _
Public Class IniFileNotFoundException
   Inherits ApplicationException

   ' The private field and the related read-only property
   Private m_FileName As String

   Public ReadOnly Property FileName() As String
      Get
         Return m_FileName
      End Get
   End Property

   ' Override the Message property to include filename.
   Public Overrides ReadOnly Property Message() As String
      Get
         Dim msg As String = MyBase.Message
         If Not m_FileName Is Nothing AndAlso m_FileName.Length > 0 Then
            msg &= Environment.NewLine & "FileName = " & m_FileName
         End If
         Return msg
      End Get
   End Property

   ' The three constructors that all exception types should expose

   Sub New()
      ' Provide a default message for this custom exception.
      MyBase.New("Initialization file not found")
   End Sub

   Sub New(ByVal message As String)
      MyBase.New(message)
   End Sub

   Sub New(ByVal message As String, ByVal innerException As Exception)
      MyBase.New(message, innerException)
   End Sub

   ' Additional constructors that initialize the FileName property
   Sub New(ByVal message As String, ByVal fileName As String)
      MyBase.New(message)
      m_FileName = fileName
   End Sub

   Sub New(ByVal message As String, ByVal fileName As String, _
         ByVal innerException As Exception)
      MyBase.New(message, innerException)
      m_FileName = fileName
   End Sub

   ' Support for serialization

   ' This constructor is protected because the class isn't sealed.
```

```vb
    Protected Sub New(ByVal info As SerializationInfo, ByVal context As StreamingContext)
       MyBase.New(info, context)
       ' Deserialize the additional field(s).
       m_FileName = info.GetString("FileName")
    End Sub

    Public Overrides Sub GetObjectData(ByVal info As SerializationInfo, _
          ByVal context As StreamingContext)
       ' Serialize the additional field(s).
       info.AddValue("FileName", m_FileName)
       ' Let the base class serialize its fields.
       MyBase.GetObjectData(info, context)
    End Sub
End Class
```

```csharp
// [C#]
[Serializable]
public class IniFileNotFoundException : ApplicationException
{
    // The private field and the related read-only property
    private string m_FileName;

    public string FileName
    {
        get
        {
            return m_FileName;
        }
    }

    // Override the Message property to include filename.
    public override string Message
    {
        get
        {
            string msg = base.Message;
            if ( m_FileName != null && m_FileName.Length > 0 )
                msg += Environment.NewLine + "FileName = " + m_FileName;
            return msg;
        }
    }

    // The three constructors that all exception types should expose

    // Provide a default message for this custom exception.
    public IniFileNotFoundException() : base("Initialization file not found")
    {}

    public IniFileNotFoundException(string message) : base(message)
    {}

    public IniFileNotFoundException(string message, Exception innerException)
      : base(message, innerException)
    {}

    // Additional constructors that initialize the FileName property

    public IniFileNotFoundException(string message, string fileName) : base(message)
```

```
    {
        m_FileName = fileName;
    }

    public IniFileNotFoundException(string message, string fileName,
        Exception innerException) : base(message, innerException)
    {
        m_FileName = fileName;
    }

    // Support for serialization

    // This constructor is protected because the class is sealed.
    protected IniFileNotFoundException(SerializationInfo info, StreamingContext context)
        : base(info, context)
    {
        // Deserialize the additional field(s).
        m_FileName = info.GetString("FileName");
    }

    public override void GetObjectData(SerializationInfo info, StreamingContext context)
    {
        // Serialize the additional field(s).
        info.AddValue("FileName", m_FileName);
        // Let the base class serialize its fields.
        base.GetObjectData(info, context);
    }
}
```

See also: See rule 19.29 about using a base class other than ApplicationException for your custom exceptions.

19.29 Base class for custom exception types

If you define one or more custom exception types, define a serializable custom exception class named *CompanyName*Exception that inherits from ApplicationException, and make all your exception types inherit from this class.

Why: By having all your exception types inherit from a specific class, you achieve two goals. First, you can easily catch all your custom exceptions by means of a single *Catch* (Visual Basic) or *catch* (C#) block. Second, you have a single place for adding code that you wish to execute inside all your custom exception types, for example, the code that logs the exception to a file or a database.

More details: According to .NET Framework guidelines, all custom exception types should inherit from ApplicationException to distinguish them from system exceptions (most of which derive from the SystemException class). The idea behind the Microsoft guideline is that code in your application should be able to distinguish immediately between system and user-defined exceptions in catch blocks. Unfortunately, some .NET Framework exceptions derive directly from Exception and a few inherit from ApplicationException; thus, you can't easily catch all application exceptions with a single catch block unless you define a base class for all your exception classes.

Example: Here's the code for a class that you can use as the base type for your custom exceptions.

```vbnet
' [Visual Basic]
<Serializable()> _
Public Class CodeArchitectsException
   Inherits ApplicationException

   Sub New()
      MyBase.New()
   End Sub
   Sub New(ByVal message As String)
      MyBase.New(message)
   End Sub
   Sub New(ByVal message As String, ByVal innerException As Exception)
      MyBase.New(message, innerException)
   End Sub

   ' This constructor is protected because it should be
   ' callable only from inherited types.
   Protected Sub New(ByVal info As SerializationInfo, ByVal context As StreamingContext)
      MyBase.New(info, context)
   End Sub

   ' This method isn't strictly necessary because it just delegates to the base class.
   ' However, in a real-world class you might add tracing code here.
   Public Overrides Sub GetObjectData(ByVal info As SerializationInfo, _
         ByVal context As StreamingContext)
      MyBase.GetObjectData(info, context)
   End Sub
End Class
```

```csharp
// [C#]
[Serializable]
public class CodeArchitectsException : ApplicationException
{
    public CodeArchitectsException() : base()
    {}
    public CodeArchitectsException(string message) : base(message)
    {}
    public CodeArchitectsException(string message, Exception innerException)
       : base(message, innerException)
    {}

    // This constructor is protected because it should be
    // callable only from inherited types.
    protected CodeArchitectsException(SerializationInfo info, StreamingContext context)
       : base(info, context)
    {}
    // This method isn't strictly necessary because it just delegates to the base class.
    // However, in a real-world class you might add tracing code here.
    public override void GetObjectData(SerializationInfo info, StreamingContext context)
    {
        base.GetObjectData (info, context);
    }
}
```

Chapter 20
Numeric Types

In this chapter, we have gathered many coding guidelines related to how you use integer and floating-point variables and how you can use operators correctly. For example, we often see Visual Basic code that uses the floating-point division operator in lieu of the integer division operator (see rule 20.11), a mistake that makes your code run several times slower.

Applying optimized techniques to process numbers doesn't make a difference in many real-world applications, which are typically slowed down by the interaction with the database or a narrow network bandwidth. In some performance-critical portions of your code, however, selecting the right operator, suppressing an unnecessary conversion, or adopting an optimized math algorithm can make a big difference.

20.1 Constants in lieu of "magic" numbers

Define and use constants instead of numbers other than natural constants such as zero or one. Use constants only if the number isn't expected to change in a future version of the application.

Why: Constants exposed by a library are burned in the code of client applications that use it. If you later change the constant without recompiling the client application as well, the code in the client application uses the old value. For this reason, if you expect the value to change in a future value, use a read-only static field instead of a constant.

How to: Constants make your code more readable and become handy when you later need to change the "magic" number value.

```
' [Visual Basic]
' *** Wrong
Dim arr(99) As Integer

' *** Correct
Const NumItems As Integer = 100
Dim arr(NumItems - 1) As Integer

// [C#]
// *** Wrong
int[] arr = new int[100];

// *** Correct
const int NumItems = 100;
int[] arr = new int[NumItems];
```

20.2 Integer field width

Use 32-bit integer variables unless you have a specific reason to use 16-bit or 64-bit variables.

Why: 32-bit values are processed faster by 32-bit CPUs.

Exception: One reason for using 16-bit integers is to save memory when defining a large array. Integers that are 64-bit are necessary only when you need their larger range. Also, you have no choice when you are passing an integer to unmanaged code in PInvoke or COM Interop scenarios.

20.3 Unsigned integers [C#]

Use Common Language Specifications (CLS)–compliant integer types (*byte, short, int, long*) unless you have a compelling reason for using non-CLS-compliant integer types (*sbyte, ushort, uint, ulong*).

20.4 The *checked* and *unchecked* keywords [C#]

Compile with the Check For Arithmetic Overflow/Underflow option disabled (on the Build page of the Project Properties dialog box), but use the *checked* keyword to create *checked contexts* in which arithmetical errors throw an exception. This keyword can be applied to an individual expression or can be used to define a block of checked statements.

More details: In a checked context, the compiler emits statements that check the result from the four math operations, the unary minus, the ++ and -- operators, and explicit conversions between integer types and from *double* or *float* to an integer type. If for any reason you have compiled with the Check For Arithmetic Overflow/Underflow option enabled, you can disable it locally by using the *unchecked* keyword. Bear in mind, however, that the *checked* and *unchecked* keywords affect only the math operators that they enclose directly: if the expression or the block invokes a method, exceptions in that method are dealt with according to the current compiler settings (or any *checked* or *unchecked* keyword in use in that method).

```
// [C#]
// A checked expression that can throw an exception
int a = checked( b * c );

// A checked block
checked
{
   short res = 0 ;
   for ( short i = 1; i<=times; i++ )
      res += (short) (i * ( i / 10000));
}

// Important: if the GetValue throws an OverflowException that isn't checked,
// the exception is ignored in spite of the checked keyword.
int a = checked( b * GetValue(c));

// An unchecked expression
int a = unchecked( b * c );
```

20.5 Language-specific math functions [Visual Basic]

Don't use Visual Basic–specific math functions, such as Abs and Sqr. Instead, exclusively use methods of Microsoft .NET Framework types.

Why: Language-specific functions perform slightly worse than .NET native methods, are less flexible, and make the translation to another language more difficult.

```
' [Visual Basic]
' *** Wrong
If Abs(x) > 1 Then ok = True

' *** Correct
If Math.Abs(x) Then ok = True
```

20.6 Shortened notation for common math operations

Use shortened notation when incrementing/decrementing a numeric variable or when appending characters to a string variable.

Why: This technique improves code readibility and can speed up execution if the target is a property of an object.

```
' [Visual Basic]
' *** OK
x = x + 1
' *** Better
x += 1

' *** Wrong
TextBox1.MaxLength = TextBox1.MaxLength + 1
' *** Correct
TextBox1.MaxLength += 1

// [C#]
// *** OK
x++;
// *** Also OK
x = x + 1;
// *** Better
x += 1;

// *** Wrong
textBox1.MaxLength = textBox1.MaxLength + 1;
// *** Correct
textBox1.MaxLength += 1;
```

20.7 ++ and – – operators [C#]

Use ++ and –– operators only inside expressions that are located in performance-critical portions of code or in loops.

Why: When used on a statement on its own, these operators don't offer any speed benefit over += and −=.

```
// [C#]
// *** OK
x++;
// *** Better
x += 1;

// OK
int total = 0;
int j = arr.Length;
for ( int i = 0; i < arr.Length; i++ )
    total += arr[i] * arr[--j];
```

20.8 Multiple ++ and − − operators in same expression [C#]

Avoid using ++ and −− operators on a variable that appears more than once in the expression.

Why: If you allow multiple uses of the variable, the expression would deliver different results if you (or another developer) later change the order of operands.

```
// [C#]
// *** Wrong: j appears twice in the expression.
int total = 0;
int j = arr.Length;
for ( int i = 0; i < arr.Length; i++ )
    total += arr[i] * arr[--j] + j;

// *** Correct
int total = 0;
int j = arr.Length;
for ( int i=0; i < arr.Length; i++ )
{
    j -= 1;
    total += arr[i] * arr[j] + j;
}

// Also correct, but slightly less readable
int total = 0;
for ( int i=0, j=arr.Length; i < arr.Length; i++, --j )
    total += arr[i] * arr[j] + j;
```

20.9 Conversion of Boolean values to integers

Avoid converting Boolean values to integers for use in expressions. Favor explicit assignments in conditional statements.

Why: Most languages convert the true value to 1, whereas Visual Basic's *CInt* operator converts it to −1 for backward compatibility with previous versions of the language; thus, the result of explicit conversions from Boolean to integers is language-dependent.

```
' [Visual Basic]
' The task: decrement k if k is positive.

' *** Wrong: relies on CInt returning -1 if argument is True.
k = k + CInt(k > 0)

' *** Wrong, but at least relies on .NET official documentation.
k = k - Convert.ToInt32(k > 0)

' *** Correct
If k > 0 Then k = k - 1

// [C#]
// The task: decrement k if k is positive.

// *** Wrong
k = k - Convert.ToInt32(k > 0);

// *** Correct
if ( k > 0 )
    k--;
```

20.10 Shift operators [Visual Basic]

Use >> and << shift operators (added in Visual Basic 2003) instead of * and \ to process bit-coded values.

Why: Shift operators are more efficient because you don't have to check for overflow and they perform especially well on 64-bit integers.

```
' [Visual Basic]
' The task: shift a bit-coded value to the right by one position.

' *** Both wrong
val = val \ 2
val \= 2

' *** Both correct
val = val >> 1
val >>= 1
```

20.11 Division operators [Visual Basic]

Use the division operator that fits your needs. The / (slash) operator promotes its operands to Double and performs a floating-point division; the \ (backslash) operator truncates its operand to the nearest integer, performs an integer division, and discards the remainder.

Why: Using the / operator with integer operands involves two unnecessary conversions, which can slow down your code.

```
' [Visual Basic]
' The task: Divide two integers and truncate the remainder.
```

```
' *** Wrong: does rounding.
Dim res As Integer = CInt(n1 / n2)

' *** Correct
Dim res As Integer = n1 \ n2
```

20.12 Decimal variables

Use the Decimal type when it is essential that rounding errors be avoided. In practice, you should use the Decimal type whenever you deal with currency values. Keep in mind that Decimal values can be added and subtracted quickly, but other operations are relatively slow on this type.

20.13 Floating-point variables

Use double-precision floating-point numbers unless you have a particular reason to use single-precision numbers.

Why: Double-precision operations are slightly faster than single-precision operations, are more accurate, and have a broader range.

Exception: One reason for using single-precision values is to save memory when defining a large array.

20.14 Equality test for floating-point values

Avoid using the equality operator (or the Equals method) to compare single-precision or double-precision values because rounding errors might make the test fail. Instead, check whether the absolute difference between the two values is below a threshold you define.

```
' [Visual Basic]
Dim number As Double = 0
' Process the variable as needed, then compare it with 100.
...
' *** Wrong
If number = 100 Then ok = True
' *** Correct
If Math.Abs(number - 100) < 0.0000000001 Then ok = True

// [C#]
double number = 0.0;
// Process the variable as needed, then compare it with 100.
...
// *** Wrong
if ( number == 100 )
   ok = true;
// *** Correct
if ( Math.Abs(number - 100) < 0.0000000001 )
   ok = true;
```

20.15 Floating-point temporary results [Visual Basic]

Avoid floating-point intermediate values in expressions on integer operands. For example, both the ^ (exponentiation) operator and the Int function return a Double value. You should use the *CShort, CInt,* and *CLng* built-in conversion operators to convert a number to an integer.

See also: See rules 20.16 and 20.17 for optimization techniques that can be used with floating-point values.

20.16 Multiplication instead of division

Use multiplications instead of divisions in performance-critical code sections.

Why: Multiplications are about twice as fast as divisions on single- and double-precision numbers. Therefore, you can make your code faster if you replace a division by N with a multiplication by the reciprocal of N.

Example: The following code shows how you can optimize a code snippet that divides all the elements in an array by the same number.

```
' [Visual Basic]
' (This code assumes that arr is an initialized Double array.)

' *** OK
Dim divisor As Double = 125
For i As Integer = 0 To arr.Length - 1
   arr(i) = arr(i) / divisor
Next

' *** Better
Dim factor As Double = 1 / 125
For i As Integer = 0 To arr.Length - 1
   arr(i) = arr(i) * factor
Next

// [C#]
// arr is an initialized Double array.

// *** OK
double divisor = 125;
for ( int i = 0; i < arr.Length; i++ )
   arr[i] = arr[i] / divisor;

// *** Better
double factor = 1 / 125;
for ( int i = 0; i < arr.Length; i++ )
   arr[i] = arr[i] * factor;
```

20.17 Multiplication instead of exponentiation

In performance-critical code, use multiplication instead of the Math.Pow method (or Visual Basic's ^ operator) when the exponent is a small integer and when the number to be raised is an integer.

Why: The Math.Pow method must work with fractional and negative exponents, so it internally uses an algorithm that isn't particularly efficient with small integer exponents. A floating-point multiplication can be 3 to 4 times faster than the Math.Pow method, and an integer multiplication can be even 50 times faster.

```
' [Visual Basic]
' *** OK
Dim num as Double = 123.45
Dim result As Double = Math.Pow(num, 4)        ' Same as 123.45^4

' *** Better
Dim num as Double = 123.45
Dim result As Double = num * num * num * num
' *** Slightly faster, relies on n^4 = (n^2)^2.
Dim num as Double = 123.45
Dim num2 As Double = num * num
Dim result As Double = num2 * num2
```

```
// [C#]
// *** OK
double num = 123.45;
double result = Math.Pow(num, 4);

// *** Better
double num = 123.45;
double result = num * num * num * num;
// *** Slightly faster, relies on n^4 = (n^2)^2.
double num = 123.45;
double num2 = num * num;
double result = num2 * num2;
```

Chapter 21
Strings

One of the great advantages of teaching programming classes is that we can talk to so many different programmers, each one working on different sorts of applications. Some developers are interested in the user interface, others in browser-based applications; some have to deal with huge databases, others with complex COM+ or remoting architectures. The one thing that we found that all developers have in common is their need to work with text and strings. They must validate strings typed by the end user, efficiently parse large text files, or produce log files as quickly as possible.

Microsoft .NET strings are immutable, which means that once you've assigned a sequence of characters to a string variable and the .NET runtime has allocated a block of memory for them in the managed heap, you can't change them anyway. As a matter of fact, when you append one character to the string, a new block of memory is allocated and the new string is copied there. The old block is then made available for garbage collection (unless another string variable is pointing to it). Needless to say, all this memory activity can slow down your code remarkably; therefore, you should be careful not to create new strings unnecessarily, including temporary strings. In this chapter, you'll see how.

> **Note** One or more code examples in this chapter assume that the following namespaces have been imported by means of *Imports* (Visual Basic) or *using* (C#) statements:
>
> ```
> System.Configuration
> System.Globalization
> System.Text
> System.Text.RegularExpressions
> System.Threading
> ```

21.1 Strings used in the user interface

Avoid hard coding a value that might appear in the user interface; use a value read from a resource file instead.

Why: You can later change details in the user interface without recompiling, and it is easier to localize the application for another country and language.

21.2 The & Operator [Visual Basic]

Use the & operator to concatenate strings instead of the + operator.

Why: The + operator is supported as a string concatenation operator only for historical reasons. This guideline makes your code more readable and less ambiguous.

21.3 Char variables

Use Char variables rather than String variables if you are sure you need to store only individual characters.

Why: Char variables are more efficient because they take less memory than a 1-char String object and because they are value types rather than reference types.

21.4 String variable initialization

Explicitly initialize string fields and variables to a zero-length string.

Why: Explicit assignment avoids NullReferenceException errors when referencing the string and simplifies code (because the string doesn't have to be tested against null).

More details: Contrary to what some developers believe, using either "" or the String.Empty value when initializing a string doesn't waste memory because all strings initialized in this way point to the only zero-length string that is allocated in the string intern heap.

```vbnet
' [Visual Basic]
' *** Wrong
Dim x As String
...
If Not x Is Nothing Then
    ' Must check for Nothing before processing the string.
End If

' *** Correct
Dim x As String = ""
' *** Also correct
Dim x As String = String.Empty
...
' Process the string (no need to check it first).

' This code proves that "" and String.Empty are perfectly equivalent.
Dim x As String = ""
Dim y As String = String.Empty
Console.WriteLine(String.ReferenceEquals(x, y))     ' Displays "True".
```

```csharp
// [C#]
// *** Wrong
string x;
...
if ( x != null )
{
    // Must check for Nothing before processing the string.
}

// *** Correct
string x = "";
' *** Also correct
string x = String.Empty;
...
```

```
// Process the string (no need to check it first).

// This code proves that "" and String.Empty are perfectly equivalent.
string x = "";
string y = String.Empty;
Console.WriteLine(String.ReferenceEquals(x, y));    // Displays "True".
```

21.5 Long string expressions

When splitting a long string expression over multiple lines, have each line after the first one begin with the concatenation operator.

Why: This coding style makes it more evident that the statement is split over more lines even if the line is too long to fit in the editor window and you can't see whether the first statement ends with a semicolon (C#) or an underscore character (Visual Basic).

```
' [Visual Basic]
Dim s As String = "A long string expression " _
   & 'that is split over two lines'

// [C#]
string s = "A long string expression "
   + "that is split over two lines";
```

21.6 Methods and properties that return strings

When defining a method or property that returns a string, return an empty string rather than a null object reference when the result string has no characters.

Why: You simplify the task of the caller code, which can use the returned string without having to test it first for a *Nothing* (Visual Basic) or *null* (C#).

```
' [Visual Basic]
Function Spaces(ByVal n As Integer) As String
   If n <= 0 Then
      Return ""           ' Empty string rather than Nothing
   Else
      Return New String(" "c, n)
   End If
End Function

// [C#]
string Spaces(int n)
{
   if ( n <= 0 )
      return "";          // Empty string rather than null
   else
      return new String(" ", n);
}
```

21.7 Language-specific string functions [Visual Basic]

Don't use Visual Basic–specific string functions, such as Len, Left, and Mid. Instead, exclusively use methods and properties of the String type or other .NET types.

Why: Language-specific functions perform worse than .NET native methods, are less flexible (for the most part, at least), and make the translation to another language more difficult.

```
' [Visual Basic]
' *** Wrong
If Len(x) = 0 Then isEmpty = True

' *** Correct
If x.Length = 0 Then isEmpty = True
```

Table 21-1 helps you replace language-specific functions with .NET native methods and properties.

Table 21-1   Correspondence Between Visual Basic and .NET String Methods

Visual Basic	.NET Framework	Notes and Examples
Asc, AscW	Convert.ToChar	
Chr, ChrW	Convert.ToInt16	
Format	String.Format	

FormatCurrency	String.Format, *number*.ToString	`res = String.Format("{0:C2}", num)`
		
		`res = num.ToString("C2")`

FormatDateTime	String.Format, *datetime*.ToString, DateTime.ToShortDateString, DateTime.ToShortTimeString, DateTime.ToLongDateString, DateTime.ToLongTimeString	`res = String.Format("{0:d}", date)`
		
		`res = date.ToString("d")`

FormatNumber	String.Format, *number*.ToString	`res = String.Format("{0:#,###}", num)`
		
		`res = num.ToString("#,###")`

FormatPercent	String.Format, *number*.ToString	
Hex, Oct	Convert.ToString(num, base)	*base* can be 2, 8, 10, or 16.
Instr	String.IndexOf	Result is zero-based.
InstrRev	String.LastIndexOf	Result is zero-based.
Join	String.Join	
LCase	String.ToLower	
Left	String.Substring(0,n)	
Len	String.Length	
LSet (function)	String.PadRight	PadRight never trims.

Table 21-1   Correspondence Between Visual Basic and .NET String Methods

Visual Basic	.NET Framework	Notes and Examples
LTrim	String.TrimStart	
Mid	String.Substring(m,n)	Indices are zero-based.
Mid (command)	n/a	
Replace	String.Replace	
Right	String.Substring	`res = s.SubString(s.Length - n)`
RSet (function)	String.PadLeft	PadLeft never trims.
RTrim	String.TrimEnd	
Space	New String(" "c, n)	Create a new string by invoking the string constructor.
Split	String.Split	The .NET method can take only 1-char separators, but supports multiple separators.
StrComp	String.Compare	
StrConv	n/a	Use ToLower or ToUpper for lower/uppercase conversions; use a custom method for other cases.
StrDup	New String(char, n)	Corresponds to Visual Basic 6 String function.
StrReverse	n/a	Must replace with custom method.
Trim	String.Trim	
UCase	String.ToUpper	
Val	Convert.To*Xxx*	`res = Convert.ToInt32(mystring)`
	CInt, *CDbl*, and other conversion operators	
vbCrLf and other constants	ControlChars members	

21.8 Verbatim (@) string constants [C#]

Use verbatim strings when defining a string constant that contains the backslash (\) character or spans multiple lines and that doesn't contain any control character other than CR-LF.

Why: @ strings improve code readability.

```
// [C#]
string fileName = @"c:\data.txt";

// A string that contains CR-LF characters and spans multiple lines.
string msg =
@"First line
Second line
Third line";
```

21.9 Strings containing control characters [Visual Basic]

Visual Basic doesn't support control characters in strings, so you must use string concatenation when defining strings containing control characters.

```
' [Visual Basic]
Dim s As String = "First line" & ControlChars.CrLf _
   & ControlChars.Tab & "Second line" & ControlChars.CrLf _
   & "Third line"
```

The compiler resolves all string constants at compile time, so the preceding line defines only one long constant string in the managed heap.

More details: You can opt to make the code more readable at the expense of efficiency by using the Regex.Unescape static method, which takes a string that can contain C#-like escape sequences such as \n (newline) or \t (tab).

```
' [Visual Basic]
Dim s As String = Regex.Unescape("First line\n\tSecond line\nThird line")
```

21.10 ChrW vs. Chr function [Visual Basic]

Favor the ChrW function over the Chr function.

Why: The ChrW function is faster because it simply returns the Unicode character with given numeric code and its result is independent of the culture and code page settings for the current thread. The Chr function must determine internally whether the current thread is using a single-byte character set (SBCS) or a double-byte character set (DBCS) and then performs the conversion accordingly.

21.11 Looping over all the characters of a string [Visual Basic]

Use the Chars property in a *For* loop instead of a more elegant, but slower *For Each* loop.

More details: This guideline doesn't apply to the C# language because the C# compiler recognizes a *foreach* loop that iterates over all the characters in a string and generates more efficient code. (As a matter of fact, it generates a *for* loop that uses the Chars property.)

```
' [Visual Basic]
Dim companyName As String = "Code Architects Srl"

' *** OK
For Each c As Char In companyName
   Console.Write(c)
Next

' *** Better: nearly twice as fast
For index As Integer = 0 To companyName.Length - 1
   Console.Write(companyName.Chars(index))
Next
```

21.12 Checking for null strings

Always check that string arguments aren't null object references to prevent NullReferenceException errors. In most cases you can test the string for emptyness in the same statement because null and empty strings often need to be processed in the same way.

```vb
' [Visual Basic]
Sub DisplayMessage(ByVal msg As String)
   If msg Is Nothing OrElse msg.Length = 0 Then Exit Sub
   ' Display the message here.
   ...
End Sub
```

```csharp
// [C#]
public void DisplayMessage(string msg)
{
   if ( msg == null || msg.Length == 0 )
      return;
   // Display the message here.
   ...
}
```

21.13 Checking for empty strings

Compare the Length property with zero rather than comparing a string with "" or String.Empty.

Why: This technique delivers better performance.

```vb
' [Visual Basic]
' *** Wrong
If s = "" Then isEmpty = True
If s = String.Empty Then isEmpty = True
If s.Equals("") Then isEmpty = True
If s.Equals(String.Empty) Then isEmpty = True
If String.Equals(s, "") Then isEmpty = True
If String.Equals(s, String.Empty) Then isEmpty = True

' *** Correct
If s.Length = 0 Then isEmpty = True
```

```csharp
// [C#]
// *** Wrong
if ( s == "" ) isEmpty = true;
if ( s == string.Empty ) isEmpty = true;
if ( s.Equals("") ) isEmpty = true;
if ( s.Equals(String.Empty) ) isEmpty = true;
if ( string.Equals(s, "") ) isEmpty = true;
if ( string.Equals(s, String.Empty) ) isEmpty = true;

' *** Correct
if ( s.Length == 0 ) isEmpty = true;
```

21.14 Case-insensitive comparisons

Use the String.Compare static method to compare strings in case-insensitive mode. Don't perform case-insensitive comparisons by means of the equality operator after converting both operands to uppercase or lowercase.

Why: The ToLower and ToUpper methods create a new string; therefore, they impact the memory heap and, indirectly, performance. The Compare static method is much faster.

More details: The Compare method is especially convenient when comparing only a substring because one of its overloads takes the initial index and number of characters to compare.

```
' [Visual Basic]
' *** Wrong
If s1.ToLower() = s2.ToLower() Then
    ' Strings are equal in case-insensitive mode.
End If
If s1.Substring(0, 1).ToLower() = s2.Substring(0, 1).ToLower() Then
    ' Strings begin with same character (in case-insensitive mode).
End If


' *** Correct
If String.Compare(s1, s2, True) = 0 Then
    ' Strings are equal in case-insensitive mode.
End If
If String.Compare(s1, 0, s2, 0, 1, True) = 0 Then
    ' Strings begin with same character (in case-insensitive mode).
End If


// [C#]
// *** Wrong
if ( s1.ToLower() == s2.ToLower() )
{
    // Strings are equal in case-insensitive mode.
}
if ( s1.Substring(0, 1).ToLower() == s2.Substring(0, 1).ToLower() )
{
    // Strings begin with same character (in case-insensitive mode).
}


// *** Correct
if ( String.Compare(s1, s2, true) == 0 )
{
    // Strings are equal in case-insensitive mode.
}
if ( String.Compare(s1, 0, s2, 0, 1, true) == 0 )
{
    // Strings begin with same character (in case-insensitive mode).
}
```

21.15 Three-case string comparisons

Always use the Compare static method when checking whether a string is less than, equal to, or greater than another string.

Why: The Compare method compares the two strings in a single operation and is faster than making two distict comparisons.

```vbnet
' [Visual Basic]
' *** Wrong
If s1 < s2 Then
    Console.WriteLine("s1 < s2")
ElseIf s1 > s2 Then
    Console.WriteLine("s1 > s2")
Else
    Console.WriteLine("s1 = s2")
End If

' *** Correct
Select Case String.Compare(s1, s2)
    Case -1
        Console.WriteLine("s1 < s2")
    Case 1
        Console.WriteLine("s1 > s2")
    Case Else
        Console.WriteLine("s1 = s2")
End Select
```

```csharp
// [C#]
// *** Wrong
if ( s1 < s2 )
    Console.WriteLine("s1 < s2");
else if ( s1 > s2 )
    Console.WriteLine("s1 > s2");
else
    Console.WriteLine("s1 = s2");

// *** Correct
switch ( String.Compare(s1, s2) )
{
    case -1:
        Console.WriteLine("s1 < s2");
        break;
    case 1:
        Console.WriteLine("s1 > s2");
        break;
    default:
        Console.WriteLine("s1 = s2");
        break;
}
```

21.16 String comparisons with CompareOrdinal

Consider using the CompareOrdinal static method when comparing strings for equality in case-sensitive, locale-independent mode.

Why: This method compares the numeric values of individual characters and returns a result when the characters differ. No locale-aware conversion is performed, hence this method is typically faster than Compare and CompareTo methods. However, you should never use CompareOrdinal to check whether a string is greater than or less than another string.

```
' [Visual Basic]
' *** OK
If String.Compare(s1, s2) = 0 Then
   ' Strings are equal in case-sensitive mode.
End If

' *** Better
If String.CompareOrdinal(s1, s2) = 0 Then
   ' Strings are equal in case-sensitive mode.
End If

// [C#]
// *** OK
if ( String.Compare(s1, s2) == 0 )
{
    // Strings are equal in case-sensitive mode.
}

// *** Better
if ( String.CompareOrdinal(s1, s2) == 0 )
{
    // Strings are equal in case-sensitive mode.
}
```

21.17 Searching and replacing with regular expressions

Use the Regex type and the other classes in the System.Text.RegularExpressions namespace to perform nontrivial string search and replace operations.

Example: The following code snippet shows how you can find consecutive repeated words. The regular expression passed to the constructor of the Regex object finds a word (that is, a sequence of alphanumerical characters, or \w+) and captures it by enclosing it in parentheses, followed by one or more white spaces (\s+), and finally followed by the same word captured previously (\k<word>). The entire regular expression is enclosed in \b to avoid false matches as in "knight night" or "a an."

```
' [Visual Basic]
Dim re As New Regex("\b(?<word>\w+)\s+\k<word>\b")
Dim text As String = "The cat on the the roof."
For Each m As Match In re.Matches(text)
   Console.WriteLine(m.Value)          ' Displays "the the".
```

```
Next
' Replace the repeated word with a single occurrence.
Dim result As String = re.Replace(text, "${word}")
Console.WriteLine(result)              ' Displays "The cat on the roof".
```

```
// [C#]
Regex re = new Regex(@"\b(?<word>\w+)\s+\k<word>\b");
string text = "The cat on the the roof.";
foreach ( Match m in re.Matches(text) )
{
    Console.WriteLine(m.Value);         // Displays "the the".
}
// Replace the repeated word with a single occurrence.
string result = re.Replace(text, "${word}");
Console.WriteLine(result);              // Displays "The cat on the roof".
```

See also: See rule 21.18 for a list of the most common regular expressions.

21.18 Validating with regular expressions

Use the Regex type to validate strings typed by the user or read from files.

How to: In general, you can transform any Regex-based search code routine into a validation code routine by enclosing the regular expression between the ^ character (matches the beginning of the string) and $ character (matches the end of the string).

Example: The following code shows how to ensure that a control contains a valid floating-point number.

```
' [Visual Basic]
Dim re As New Regex("^[+-]?\d+(\.\d+)?$")
If re.IsMatch(txtWidth.Text) Then
   ' Text in txtWidth is a valid floating-point number.
   ...
End If
```

```
// [C#]
Regex re = new Regex(@"^[+-]?\d+(\.\d+)?$");
if ( re.IsMatch(txtWidth.Text) )
{
    // Text in txtWidth is a valid floating-point number.
    ...
}
```

Here's a list of some common regular expressions:

- **\d+** matches a positive integer.

- **[+-]?\d+** matches a positive or negative integer whose sign is optional.

- **[+-]?\d+(\.\d+)?** matches a floating-point number whose sign and decimal portion are optional.

- [+-]?\d+(\.\d+)?(E[+-]?\d+)? matches a floating-point number that can be optionally expressed in exponential format (e.g., 1.23E+12); the mantissa sign and the exponent sign are optional.

- [0-9A-Fa-f]+ matches a hexadecimal number.

- \w+ matches a sequence of alphanumerical and underscore characters; it's the same as [A-Za-z0-9_]+.

- [A-Z]+ matches an all-uppercase word.

- [A-Z][a-z]+ matches a proper name (initial capped, then all lowercase characters).

- [A-Z][A-Za-z']+ matches a last name (initial capped, can contain other uppercase characters and apostrophes, as in O'Brian).

- \b[A-Za-z]{1,10}\b matches a word of 10 characters or fewer.

- \b[A-Za-z]{11,}\b matches a word of 11 characters or more.

- [A-Za-z_]\w* matches a valid Visual Basic and C# identifier that begins with a letter or underscores and optionally continues with letters, digits, or underscores.

- \b(10|11|12|0?[1-9])(?<sep>[-/])(30|31|2\d|1\d|0?[1-9])\k<sep>(\d{4}|\d{2})\b matches a U.S. date in the format *mm-dd-yyyy* or *mm/dd/yyyy*. Month and day numbers can have a leading zero; month number must be in the range 1–12; day number must be in the range 1–31 (but invalid dates such as 2/30/2004 are matched); year number can have two or four digits and isn't validated.

- \b(30|31|2\d|1\d|0?[1-9])(?<sep>[-/])(10|11|12|0?[1-9])\k<sep>(\d{4}|\d{2})\b is similar to the previous regular expression, but matches a European date in the form *dd-mm-yyyy* or *dd/mm/yyyy*.

- (2[0-3]|1\d|0?\d):[0-5]\d matches a time value in the 24-hour format *hh:mm*; leading zero for hour value is optional.

- \(\d{3}\)-\d{3}-\d{4} matches a phone number such as (123)-456-7890.

- ([0-9A-Fa-f]{32}|[0-9A-Fa-f]{8}-([0-9A-Fa-f]{4}-){3}[0-9A-Fa-f]{12}) matches a 32-digit GUID, with or without embedded dashes, as in 00000304-0000-0000-C000-000000000046.

- ((\d{16}|\d{4}(-\d{4}){3})|(\d{4}(\d{4}){3})) matches a 16-digit credit card number that can embed optional dashes or spaces to define four groups of four digits, for example, 1234567812345678, 1234-5678-1234-5678, or 1234 5678 1234 5678. (Needless to say, it doesn't validate whether it is a *valid* credit card number.)

- ([A-Za-z]:)?\\?([^/:*?<>"|\\]+\\)*[^/:*?<>"|\\]+ matches a Windows filename, with or without a drive and a directory name.

- **(http|https)://([\w-]+\.)+[\w-]+(/[\w- ./?%&=]*)?** matches an Internet URL; you should use the regular expression in case-insensitive mode to match prefixes such as HTTP or Https also.

- **\w+([-+.]\w+)*@\w+([-.]\w+)*\.\w+([-.]\w+)*** matches an Internet e-mail address.

- **((\(\d{3}\) ?)|(\d{3}-))?\d{3}-\d{4}** matches a U.S. phone number.

- **\d{5}(-\d{4})?** matches a U.S. ZIP code.

- **\d{3}-\d{2}-\d{4}** matches a U.S. Social Security number (SSN).

You can find more regular expressions in Microsoft Visual Studio .NET's Regular Expression Editor dialog box (see Figure 21-1) or by browsing the huge regular expression library you can find at *http://www.regexlib.com*. If you are serious about regular expressions, don't miss The Regulator free utility, which you can download from *http://royo.is-a-geek.com/iserializable/regulator*.

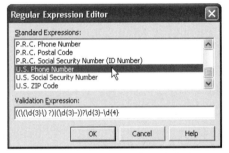

Figure 21-1   You can set the ValidationExpression property of a RegularExpressionValidator ASP.NET control by selecting one of the common regular expressions you find in the Regular Expression Editor dialog box.

21.19 Concatenating a fixed number of strings

Use the String.Format method as the preferred way to concatenate a fixed number of string constants and variables.

Why: This approach makes your code more readable and maintainable and has the added advantage of not requiring you to convert numbers and data to strings explicitly before concatenating them.

```vb
' [Visual Basic]
' *** OK
Dim msg As String = "Time=" & DateTime.Now.ToString() & ", Value=" & total.ToString()
' *** Better
Dim msg As String = String.Format("Time={0}, Value={1}", DateTime.Now, total)
```

```csharp
// [C#]
// *** OK
string msg = "Time=" + DateTime.Now.ToString() + ", Value=" + total.ToString();
// *** Better
string msg = string.Format("Time={0}, Value={1}", DateTime.Now, total);
```

More details: A little-known feature of the String.Format enables you to insert literal curly braces by doubling them. However, this behavior can cause unexpected behavior if the pair of curly braces happens to be contiguous to a {} placeholder that specifies a format.

```
' [Visual Basic]
' *** OK: next statement assigns the string "{number is 123}".
Dim s As String = String.Format("{{number is {0}}}", 123)
' *** Error: next statement assigns the string "{number is G2}".
s = String.Format("{{number is {0:G2}}}", 123)
' *** OK: next statement assigns the string "{number is 1.2E+02 }"
' (Note the space before }} ).
s = String.Format("{{number is {0:G2} }}", 123)
```

```
// [C#]
// *** OK: next statement assigns the string "{number is 123}".
string s = String.Format("{{number is {0}}}", 123);
// *** Error: next statement assigns the string "{number is G2}".
s = String.Format("{{number is {0:G2}}}", 123);
// *** OK : next statement assigns the string "{number is 1.2E+02 }"
// (Note the space before }} ).
s = String.Format("{{number is {0:G2} }}", 123);
```

21.20 Concatenating a variable number of strings

Use the StringBuilder object as the preferred way to concatenate string values inside a loop or strings whose number isn't known at compile time. Never create temporary strings when appending to a StringBuilder because they would defeat the purpose of using the StringBuilder in the first place.

Why: The StringBuilder.Append method is *much* more efficient than the regular string concatenation operator.

Example: The following code shows the most efficient way to create a comma-delimited list of integers in the range of 1 to 100. Notice that, unlike what many developers believe, the assignment to the separator variable inside the loop doesn't cause any allocation because all constant strings are created by the compiler in a region of memory known as *string intern heap*, and these assignments do nothing but copy the address of the constant string into the variable.

```
' [Visual Basic]
Dim sb As New StringBuilder()
Dim separator As String = ""
For i As Integer = 1 To 100
   sb.Append(separator)
   sb.Append(i)
   separator = ", "
Next
Dim res As String = sb.ToString()
```

```
// [C#]
StringBuilder sb = new StringBuilder();
string separator = "";
```

```
for ( int i = 1; i <= 100; i++)
{
   sb.Append(separator);
   sb.Append(i);
   separator = ", ";
}
string res = sb.ToString();
```

You can also leverage the fact that most StringBuilder methods return a reference to the String-Builder itself to make your code more concise (but not faster). Here's how you can rewrite the loop in the previous example:

```
' [Visual Basic]
For i As Integer = 1 To 100
   sb.Append(separator).Append(i)
   separator = ", "
Next

// [C#]
for ( int i = 1; i <= 100; i++)
{
   sb.Append(separator).Append(i);
   separator = ", ";
}
```

21.21 StringBuilder initialization

Initialize the StringBuilder's internal buffer if you know in advance a reasonable upper limit to the number of characters in the result.

Why: By default, the internal buffer's length is 16 characters and doubles each time the string gets longer than the maximum number of available characters. This means that a result of 1030 characters would cause eight memory reallocations and a final length of 2048 characters, with an overhead of almost 2 KB (each Unicode character takes 2 bytes). By specifying a suitable size when creating the StringBuilder object, you can avoid both the reallocations and the wasted bytes.

```
' [Visual Basic]
' Allocate 1030 characters for this StringBuilder.
Dim sb As New StringBuilder(1030)

// [C#]
// Allocate 1030 characters for this StringBuilder.
StringBuilder sb = new StringBuilder(1030);
```

21.22 StringBuilder reuse

If possible, don't append more characters to a StringBuilder after you've invoked its ToString method because this impacts performance and memory usage.

Why: If you call the Insert, Append, or Remove methods after the ToString method, a new buffer is created and all existing characters are copied there. (This new buffer is needed to preserve immutability of the string returned by the call to the ToString method.)

21.23 Configuration-dependent strings

Never hard code a string or a number in the code if its value might change when the application is deployed on a different machine, as is often the case with filenames, connection strings, and user preferences. Instead, store these values in the application's config file.

Example: Here's a configuration file that stores one value in the appSettings section:

```
<?xml version="1.0" encoding="utf-8"?>
<configuration>
   <appSettings>
      <!-- User application and configured property settings -->
      <add key="DataFilePath" value="c:\MyData\data.txt" />
   </appSettings>
</configuration>
```

You can then read values stored in the configuration file by using the following code:

```
' [Visual Basic]
Dim configReader As New AppSettingsReader()
Dim DataFilePath As String = DirectCast(configReader.GetValue("DataFilePath", _
   GetType(String)), String)

// [C#]
AppSettingsReader configReader = new AppSettingsReader();
string DataFilePath = (string) (configReader.GetValue("DataFilePath", typeof(string)));
```

If the configuration value corresponds to a property of a Windows Forms control, you can leverage the Visual Studio .NET form designer's ability to mark a property as dynamic; if you do so, Visual Studio .NET generates code that reads the configuration file automatically for you.

21.24 Setting the culture for the current thread

When writing or parsing numeric, date, or time values in a well-defined format that doesn't depend on the current regional settings—for example, when reading or writing a text file containing numbers and dates in a culture-independent format—you have two options: you can set a specific culture for the current thread or you can pass a CultureInfo object to each format and parse operation.

How to: Setting the culture for the current thread is the simplest technique because it doesn't affect the way you invoke ToString, Parse, and TryParse methods of numeric, String, and DateTime types. You can override the computer's regional settings by assigning a proper CultureInfo object to the current thread's CurrentCulture property.

```
' [Visual Basic]
' Ensure that all formatting and parsing methods use U.S. settings.
Thread.CurrentThread.CurrentCulture = New CultureInfo("en-US")
```

```
// [C#]
// Ensure that all formatting and parsing methods use U.S. settings.
Thread.CurrentThread.CurrentCulture = new CultureInfo("en-US");
```

Exception: You can't use this technique when you need to deal with data formatted along two or more different cultures. See rule 21.25 for a solution to this issue.

21.25 Culture-aware parsing and formatting

Create a global CultureInfo object, and pass it to all ToString and Parse methods that need to work with nondefault locale settings.

More details: In some cases, setting the current thread's CurrentCulture property doesn't offer the granularity you need (see rule 21.24). In such cases, the recommended technique is to create a global CultureInfo object and pass it as an argument to all the ToString and Parse methods (more generally, to all methods that take an IFormatProvider object).

```
' [Visual Basic]
' Define a global CultureInfo object for Italian culture.
Dim ci As New CultureInfo("it-IT")
...
' Write data using the global CultureInfo object.
Dim number As Double = 123.45
Dim res As String = num.ToString(ci)              ' res = 123,45
' Parse an Italian date (July 4, 2004) .
Dim startDate As Date = Date.Parse("4 Luglio 2004", ci)
```

```
// [C#]
// Define a global CultureInfo object for Italian culture.
CultureInfo ci = new CultureInfo("it-IT");
...
// Write data using the global CultureInfo object.
double number = 123.45;
string res = number.ToString(ci);                 // res = 123,45
// Parse an Italian date (July 4, 2004).
DateTime startDate = DateTime.Parse("4 Luglio 2004", ci);
```

Chapter 22
Arrays and Collections

Arrays and collections are ubiquitous in Microsoft .NET Framework programming; thus, it always surprises us how relatively few developers seem to be very familiar with them and exploit their great features fully. For this reason, we have gathered many important tips and recommendations in this chapter so that you can easily determine which object fits your needs and how you can squeeze the best performance out of arrays and collections.

It's interesting to notice that one-dimensional arrays (a.k.a. *vectors*) are dealt with differently than multidimensional arrays. The C# compiler is able to understand when it meets a loop that iterates over all the elements of a vector and can produce better Intermediate Language (IL) code, and in fact, as counterintuitive as it might sound, your attempts to optimize code might actually make it slower (see rule 18.21). Also, the JIT compiler deals with vectors in a special way and produces code that is extremely efficient, to the point that using a vector of vectors delivers better performance than a two-dimensional array and can save memory as well (see rule 22.6).

> **Note** One or more code examples in this chapter assume that the following namespaces have been imported by means of *Imports* (Visual Basic) or *using* (C#) statements:
>
> ```
> System.Collections
> System.Collections.Specialized
> ```

22.1 Array and collection object names

Use a prefix from Table 22-1 for array and collection variables. Use plural names for the array or collection name.

Example: alPersons, matValues, htNames.

Table 22-1   Prefixes for Common Collection Types

Prefix	Type	Prefix	Type
arr	Array and jagged array	sl	SortedList
mat	Matrix (two-dimensional array)	st	Stack
al	ArrayList	qu	Queue
ht	HashTable	col	Generic collection

22.2 Custom collection type names

Use the following naming guidelines for custom collection types defined in your application:

  a.   Use the Collection suffix for collection types that inherit from CollectionBase or Read-OnlyCollectionBase, for types that implement the IList interface, and, more generally, for types that behave like ArrayList and whose members can be indexed by their position. Example: PersonCollection.

  b.   Use the Dictionary suffix for collection types that inherit from DictionaryBase, for types that implement the IDictionary interface, and, more generally, for types that behave like Hashtable and whose members can be indexed by their key. Example: PersonDictionary.

  c.   Use the Queue suffix for collection types that behave like Queue and whose members can be manipulated with Enqueue and Dequeue methods. Example: PersonQueue.

  d.   Use the Stack suffix for collection types that behave like Stack and whose members can be manipulated with Push and Pop methods. Example: PersonStack.

22.3 Nonzero bound arrays

Don't use arrays with a nonzero lower index.

Why: Elements in non-CLS-compliant arrays can be accessed only through methods of the Array class.

More details: You can create such arrays by means of the Array.CreateInstance method. See *http://msdn.microsoft.com/library/en-us/cpref/html/frlrfsystemarrayclasscreateinstancetopic.asp* for more information.

22.4 Arrays and collections in performance-critical code

Favor one-dimensional arrays to collections in performance-critical code, especially when storing value type elements.

Why: The .NET runtime can access vector elements much faster than elements in a collection. Also, arrays are strongly typed; therefore, you never need a cast or an unbox operation when reading elements.

More details: If performance is essential, you should consider using an array that is large enough for your data rather than a collection object that grows as you add elements to it. When used with value types, vectors can be 3 times as fast as ArrayList objects and even 20 times faster than Hashtable objects.

22.5 Array initialization

Initialize array elements in the array declaration if possible.

```
' [Visual Basic]
Dim arr() As Integer = {1, 1, 2, 3, 5, 8, 13}

// [C#]
int[] arr = new int[] {1, 1, 2, 3, 5, 8, 13};
```

22.6 Jagged arrays

Favor jagged arrays (arrays of arrays) to standard two-dimensional arrays, especially if the array is nonrectangular (i.e., its rows contain different numbers of items).

Why: The reason for jagged arrays' superior performance is that the CLR is optimized to access elements of vectors and, even if accessing a jagged array's element requires two vector accesses, the combined operation is still faster than accessing a two-dimensional array. Besides, jagged arrays consume less memory and their elements can be referenced faster than standard two-dimensional arrays. Finally, jagged arrays offer some extra flexibility, for example, by letting you assign an entire row in one operation.

How to: The following code shows how you can create and use a jagged array.

```
' [Visual Basic]
' Initialize an array of arrays.
Dim arr()() As String = {New String() {"a00"}, _
   New String() {"a10", "a11"}, _
   New String() {"a20", "a21", "a22"}, _
   New String() {"a30", "a31", "a32", "a33"}}

' This is how you can reference an element.
Console.WriteLine(arr(3)(1))                    ' => a31
' Assign an entire row.
arr(0) = New String() {"a00", "a01", "a02"}
' Read an element just added.
Console.WriteLine(arr(0)(2))                    ' => a02

' Expand one of the rows.
ReDim Preserve arr(1)(3)
' Assign the new elements. (Currently they are Nothing.)
arr(1)(2) = "a12"
arr(1)(3) = "a13"
' Read back one of them.
Console.WriteLine(arr(1)(2))                    ' => a12

// [C#]
string[][] arr = new string[][] { new string[]{"a00"},
   new string[]{"a10", "a11"},
   new string[]{"a20", "a21", "a22"},
   new string[]{"a30", "a31", "a32", "a33"}};
// This is how you can reference an element.
Console.WriteLine(arr[3][1]);                    // => a31
// Assign an entire row.
arr[0] = new string[] {"a00", "a01", "a02"};
// Read an element just added.
Console.WriteLine(arr[0][2]);                    // => a02
```

22.7 The Collection object [Visual Basic]

Avoid using the Collection object defined in the Microsoft.VisualBasic library. Instead, use the ArrayList or Hashtable .NET native objects (in the System.Collections namespace), depending on whether you need to access individual elements by their index or their key.

More details: For the rare cases when you really need the ability to index a collection's elements both by their index and their key, you can inherit a custom collection type from the NameObjectCollectionBase class. See *http://msdn.microsoft.com/library/default.asp?url=/ library/en-us/cpref/html/frlrfsystemcollectionsspecializednameobjectcollectionbaseclasstopic.asp* for more information.

22.8 Methods and properties that return arrays and collections

When defining a method or property that returns an array or a collection, return a zero-length array or collection rather than a null object reference when the result has no elements.

Why: You simplify the task of the caller code, which can directly use the result in a loop without having to check it.

```vb
' [Visual Basic]
Function GetNaturalNumbers(ByVal max As Integer) As Integer()
   If max < 1 Then
      Return New Integer() {}            ' A 0-item array
   Else
      Dim arr(max - 1) As Integer
      For i As Integer = 1 To max
         arr(i - 1) = i
      Next
      Return arr
   End if
End Function
```

```csharp
// [C#]
int[] GetNaturalNumbers(int max)
{
   if ( max < 1 )
      return new int[0];                 // A 0-item array
   else
   {
      int[] arr = new int[max];
      for (int i = 1; i <= max; i++)
         arr[i-1] = i;
      return arr;
   }
}
```

If the function can't return a null object, the client code can use its result value in a *For Each* (Visual Basic) or *foreach* (C#) loop without having to test it first:

```vbnet
' [Visual Basic]
' If the function can return Nothing, you must do this.
Dim arr() As Integer = GetNaturalNumbers(10)
If Not arr Is Nothing Then
    For Each n As Integer in arr
        ...
    Next
End If

' If Nothing can't be returned, you can simplify the code as follows.
For Each n As Integer In GetNaturalNumbers(10)
    ...
Next
```

```csharp
// [C#]
// If the function can return null, you must do this.
int[] arr = GetNaturalNumbers(10);
if ( arr != null )
{
    foreach ( int n in arr )
    {
        ...
    }
}

// If null can't be returned, you can simplify the code as follows.
foreach ( int n in GetNaturalNumbers(10) )
{
    ...
}
```

22.9 Loops over array and collection elements

Use *For* (Visual Basic) or *for* (C#) loops when processing all the elements in an array. Use *For Each* (Visual Basic) or *foreach* (C#) loops to iterate over all elements in a collection.

Why: Direct indexing is faster with standard arrays, but using an enumerator object (which is transparently created and used in *For Each* and *foreach* loops) is faster with collections.

22.10 Looping over two-dimensional matrices

When using two nested loops to visit all the elements in a two-dimensional array, have the outer loop iterate over rows and the inner loop iterate over columns.

Why: .NET arrays (unlike pre-.NET arrays) are stored in row-wise order; therefore, the suggested loop visits elements in the order in which they are stored in memory. This technique is especially effective with arrays of value types because they take contiguous memory locations.

```vbnet
' [Visual Basic]
' *** OK
Dim sum As Long = 0
For c As Integer = 0 To numCols
```

```vb
    For r As Integer = 0 To numRows
        sum += arr(r, c)
    Next
Next

' *** Better
Dim sum As Long = 0
For r As Integer = 0 To numRows
    For c As Integer = 0 To numCols
        sum += arr(r, c)
    Next
Next
```

```csharp
// [C#]
// *** OK
long sum = 0;
for ( int c = 0; c < numCols; c++ )
{
    for ( int r = 0; r < numRows; r++ )
    {
        sum += arr[r, c];
    }
}

// *** Better
long sum = 0;
for ( int r = 0; r < numRows; r++ )
{
    for ( int c = 0; c < numCols; c++ )
    {
        sum += arr[r, c];
    }
}
```

More details: If performance isn't an issue, you can visit all the elements of a multidimensional array with a single *For Each* or *foreach* loop, as the following code demonstrates:

```vb
' [Visual Basic]
Dim arr(,) As Integer = {{1, 2, 3, 4}, {5, 6, 7, 8}}
For each n As Integer In arr
    Console.WriteLine(n)
Next
```

```csharp
// [C#]
int[,] arr = new int[,] { {1,2,3,4}, {5,6,7,8}};
foreach ( int n in arr )
    Console.WriteLine(ni);
```

22.11 Large arrays of Boolean values

Consider using a BitArray object instead of a large array of Boolean values.

Why: BitArray objects consume 32 times less memory than a Boolean array.

22.12 Generic vs. strong-typed collections

When implementing a one-to-many relationship between two types, use a public read-only property that returns a strong-typed collection rather than a generic collection.

Why: Strong-typed collections force users of your class to pass objects of the right type, thus making your code more robust.

Example: Let's say that you have a Customer type that exposes a property named Orders, which is a collection of Order objects. Exposing the collection as a generic ArrayList or Dictionary collection, as in the following code, is wrong and must be avoided:

```vb
' [Visual Basic]
' *** Wrong
Class Customer
    Private m_Orders As New ArrayList

    Public ReadOnly Property Orders() As ArrayList
        Get
            Return m_Orders
        End Get
    End Property

    ' Evaluate the total of all orders for this customer.
    Public Function GetOrderTotal() As Decimal
        Dim res As Decimal = 0
        For Each o As Order In Me.Orders
            res += o.Quantity * o.UnitPrice
        Next
        Return res
    End Function
End Class
```

```csharp
// [C#]
// *** Wrong
class Customer
{
    private ArrayList m_Orders = new ArrayList();

    public ArrayList Orders
    {
        get
        {
            return m_Orders;
        }
    }

    // Evaluate the total of all orders for this customer.
    public decimal GetOrderTotal()
    {
        decimal res = 0;
        foreach ( Order o in this.Orders )
            res += o.Quantity * o.UnitPrice;
        return res;
    }
}
```

The problem with the previous code is that a client might accidentally pass objects for the wrong type to the Add method of the Orders property, without causing an error. (A runtime error will occur when the client invokes the GetOrderTotal method, though.) For a more robust implementation you must define a strong-typed collection class named OrderCollection, which derives from CollectionBase and which can contain only Order objects:

```vb
' [Visual Basic]
' *** Correct
Class Customer
    Private m_Orders As New OrderCollection

    Public ReadOnly Property Orders() As OrderCollection
        Get
            Return m_Orders
        End Get
    End Property

    ' Remainder of class as before...
End Class

' The strongly typed collection
Class OrderCollection
    Inherits CollectionBase

    Public Sub Add(ByVal order As Order)
        Me.List.Add(order)
    End Sub

    Public Sub Remove(ByVal order As Order)
        Me.List.Remove(order)
    End Sub

    Public Default Property Item(ByVal index As Integer) As Order
        Get
            Return DirectCast(Me.List(index), Order)
        End Get
        Set(ByVal Value As Order)
            Me.List(index) = Value
        End Set
    End Property
End Class
```

```csharp
// [C#]
// *** Correct
class Customer
{
    private OrderCollection m_Orders = new OrderCollection();

    public OrderCollection Orders
    {
        get
        {
            return m_Orders;
        }
    }
```

```
    // Remainder of class as before...
}

// The strongly typed collection
class OrderCollection : CollectionBase
{
   public void Add(Order order)
   {
      this.List.Add(order);
   }

   public void Remove(Order order)
   {
      this.List.Remove(order);
   }

   public Order this[int index]
   {
      get
      {
         return (Order) this.List[index];
      }
      set
      {
         this.List[index] = value;
      }
   }
}
```

22.13 Collection initial capability

Specify an initial capability for ArrayList, Hashtable, SortedList, Queue, and Stack objects, if you know in advance how many items the collection will hold.

Why: This technique reduces the number of memory reallocations.

```
' [Visual Basic]
Dim al As New ArrayList(1000)
```

```
// [C#]
ArrayList al = new ArrayList(1000);
```

22.14 Collection growth factor

Avoid specifying the growth factor argument in the constructor of collection objects that accept it, such as Hashtable and Queue, unless you know exactly what you're doing.

Why: A default growth factor performs well in most cases, and specifying an arbitrary value can lead you to waste memory or create underoptimized objects.

22.15 Adding multiple elements to a collection

Use the AddRange and InsertRange methods to add multiple elements to an ArrayList object and other .NET collections that expose these methods, such as the Nodes collection of the TreeView control or the Columns collection of the DataTable object.

Example: See how the following code merges two ArrayList objects and returns a third Array-List that contains all the items from both arguments:

```
' [Visual Basic]
Function MergeArrayList(ByVal al1 As ArrayList, ByVal al2 As ArrayList) As ArrayList
    Dim al As New ArrayList(al1.Count + al2.Count)
    al.AddRange(al1)
    al.AddRange(al2)
    Return al
End Function
```

```
// [C#]
ArrayList MergeArrayList(ArrayList al1, ArrayList al2)
{
    ArrayList al = new ArrayList(al1.Count + al2.Count);
    al.AddRange(al1);
    al.AddRange(al2);
    return al;
}
```

22.16 The SortedList object

Use the SortedList object only when you must display all the elements in sorted order between consecutive add or remove operations. If you need to sort elements only after a large number of insertions, first add elements to a Hashtable and then pass the Hashtable to the SortedList constructor.

Why: Adding and removing SortedList elements is a relatively inefficient operation. It's much faster to add elements to a Hashtable object and then sort all of them in one operation by using the technique described in the following code:

```
' [Visual Basic]
' *** Wrong
Dim sl As New SortedList
' Fill the SortedList (omitted)
...
' You can now display elements in sort order...

' *** Correct
Dim ht As New Hashtable
' Fill the Hashtable (omitted)...
...
' Sort all the elements in one operation.
Dim sl As New SortedList(ht)
' You can now display elements in sort order...
```

```csharp
// [C#]
// *** Wrong
SortedList sl = new SortedList();
// Fill the SortedList (omitted)...
...
// You can now display elements in sort order...

// *** Correct
Hashtable ht = new Hashtable();
// Fill the Hashtable (omitted)
...
// Sort all the elements in one operation.
SortedList sl = new SortedList(ht);
// You can now display elements in sort order...
```

22.17 Case-insensitive Hashtable and SortedList collections

Don't convert all keys of a Hashtable or SortedList to lowercase or uppercase if you need to use case-insensitive keys. Instead, use the methods of the CollectionsUtil class to create a case-insensitive dictionary.

```vbnet
' [Visual Basic]
Dim ht As Hashtable = CollectionsUtil.CreateCaseInsensitiveHashtable()
Dim sl As SortedList = CollectionsUtil.CreateCaseInsensitiveSortedList()
```

```csharp
// [C#]
Hashtable ht = CollectionsUtil.CreateCaseInsensitiveHashtable();
SortedList sl = CollectionsUtil.CreateCaseInsensitiveSortedList();
```

22.18 Iterating over Hashtable or SortedList collections

Iterate over an IDictionary object by means of a *For Each* (Visual Basic) or *foreach* (C#) loop whose control variable is a DictionaryEntry object.

```vbnet
' [Visual Basic]
' *** Wrong: requires indexing in the loop.
For Each key As Object In ht.Keys
   ' Read the value associated with current key.
   Dim val As Object = ht(key)
   ...
Next

' *** Correct
For Each de As DictionaryEntry In ht
   Dim key As Object = de.Key
   Dim val As Object = de.Value
   ...
Next
```

```csharp
// [C#]
// *** Wrong: requires indexing in the loop.
foreach (object key in ht.Keys )
{
```

```
   // Read the value associated with current key.
   object val = ht[key];
   ...
}

// *** Correct
foreach ( DictionaryEntry de in ht )
{
   object key = de.Key;
   object val = de.Value;
   ...
}
```

22.19 Custom collection classes

At the very minimum, classes that derive from CollectionBase should implement the Add, Remove, and Item members (or the indexer for C#) and should override the OnValidate protected method. The members should access the internal IList object by means of the List protected property.

```
' [Visual Basic]
' A collection that can hold Document objects
Class DocumentCollection
   Inherits CollectionBase

   Public Sub Add(ByVal doc As Document)
      Me.List.Add(doc)
   End Sub

   Public Sub Remove(ByVal doc As Document)
      Me.List.Remove(doc)
   End Sub

   Default Public Property Item(ByVal index As Integer) As Document
      Get
         Return DirectCast(Me.List.Item(index), Document)
      End Get
      Set(ByVal Value As Document)
         Me.List.Item(index) = Value
      End Set
   End Property

   Protected Overrides Sub OnValidate(ByVal obj As Object)
      If Not TypeOf obj Is Document Then
         Throw New ArgumentException("A Document is expected ")
      End If
   End Sub
End Class

// [C#]
// A collection that can hold Document objects
class DocumentCollection : CollectionBase
{
   public void Add(Document doc)
```

```
    {
        this.List.Add(doc);
    }

    public void Remove(Document doc)
    {
        this.List.Remove(doc);
    }

    public Document this[int index]
    {
        get
        {
            return (Document) this.List[index];
        }
        set
        {
            this.List[index] = value;
        }
    }

    protected override void OnValidate(object obj)
    {
        if ( ! (obj is Document) )
            throw new ArgumentException("A Document is expected");
    }
}
```

Custom collection classes that expose methods such as Sort and IndexOf should delegate to the inner ArrayList object, which they can reference by means of the InnerList protected property.

```
' [Visual Basic]
' Inside the DocumentCollection class
Public Sub Sort()
    Me.InnerList.Sort()
End Sub

// [C#]
// Inside the DocumentCollection class
public void Sort()
{
    this.InnerList.Sort();
}
```

More details: Creating custom collection and dictionary types will be much easier in .NET 2.0, thanks to the introduction of generic types.

22.20 Custom dictionary classes

At the very minimum, classes that derive from DictionaryBase should implement the Add, Remove, Contains, and Item members (or the indexer for C#) and should override the OnValidate protected method. The members should access the internal IDictionary object by means of the Dictionary protected property.

```vbnet
' [Visual Basic]
' A dictionary that can hold Document objects
Class DocumentDictionary
    Inherits DictionaryBase

    Public Sub Add(ByVal key As String, ByVal doc As Document)
        Me.Dictionary.Add(key, doc)
    End Sub

    Public Sub Remove(ByVal key As String)
        Me.Dictionary.Remove(key)
    End Sub

    Default Public Property Item(ByVal key As String) As Document
        Get
            Return DirectCast(Me.Dictionary.Item(key), Document)
        End Get
        Set(ByVal Value As Document)
            Me.Dictionary.Item(key) = Value
        End Set
    End Property

    Function Contains(ByVal key As String) As Boolean
        Return Me.Dictionary.Contains(key)
    End Function

    Protected Overrides Sub OnValidate(ByVal key As Object, ByVal obj As Object)
        If Not TypeOf obj Is Document Then
            Throw New ArgumentException("A Document is expected ")
        End If
    End Sub
End Class

// [C#]
// A dictionary that can hold Document objects
class DocumentDictionary : DictionaryBase
{
    public void Add(string key, Document doc)
    {
        this.Dictionary.Add(key, doc);
    }

    public void Remove(string key)
    {
        this.Dictionary.Remove(key);
    }

    public Document this[string key]
    {
        get
        {
            return (Document) this.Dictionary[key];
        }
        set
        {
```

```
            this.Dictionary[key] = value;
        }
    }

    public bool Contains(string key)
    {
        return this.Dictionary.Contains(key);
    }

    protected override void OnValidate(object key, object obj)
    {
        if ( ! (obj is Document) )
            throw new ArgumentException("A Document is expected");
    }
}
```

Custom dictionary classes that expose methods such as ContainsValue and CopyTo should delegate to the inner Hashtable object, which they can reference by means of the InnerHashtable protected property.

```
' [Visual Basic]
' (Inside the DocumentDictionary class.)
Public Function ContainsValue(ByVal doc As Document) As Boolean
    Return Me.InnerHashtable.ContainsValue(doc)
End Function

// [C#]
// (Inside the DocumentDictionary class.)
public bool ContainsValue(Document doc)
{
    return this.InnerHashtable.ContainsValue(doc);
}
```

More details: Creating custom collection and dictionary types will be much easier in .NET 2.0, thanks to the introduction of generic types.

22.21 Zero-based indexers

Use zero-based indexers when implementing a custom collection class. In other words, valid index values that can be passed to the indexer (C#) or the default Item property (Visual Basic) should range from zero to the number of items in the collection minus one.

Why: All .NET collections are zero-based; therefore, a custom collection that uses a different index base will confuse developers.

Chapter 23
Memory Usage

The garbage collector is one of the most sophisticated pieces of the Microsoft .NET Framework architecture. Each time an application runs short of memory, the .NET runtime fires a garbage collection (GC) and examines all the objects that are in use, either because the application has a reference to them (these are known as *roots*) or because the object is referenced by another object in use. All the objects in the managed heap that aren't reachable are candidates for the GC. If the object has no finalizer, the object is immediately reclaimed and the heap is compacted; if the object has a Finalize method, the .NET runtime runs the method but doesn't reclaim the object until the next GC. (Actually, it might take more than one GC to collect an object with a finalizer because the object has been promoted to Generation 1 or Generation 2 and won't be reclaimed by a Generation-0 GC.) When all unreachable objects have been reclaimed, the managed heap can be compacted and the garbage collector can update all object references to point to the new position of the object in the heap.

This very concise description of what the garbage collector does explains why a GC is a relatively time-consuming operation. All .NET developers worth their salt should feel the responsibility of reducing the number of GCs that occur during the application's lifetime. We have illustrated several techniques that guarantee optimal usage of memory elsewhere in the book; in this chapter we focus on how you can help the garbage collector perform its job as efficiently as possible.

The simplest way to check whether your application uses memory efficiently is to have a look at a few counters of the .NET CLR Memory performance object:

- # Bytes in all Heaps (the sum of the four heaps used by the application, that is, Generation-0, Generation-1, Generation-2, and Large Object heaps)

- Gen 0 heap size, Gen 1 heap size, Gen 2 heap size, Large Object Heap size (the size of the four heaps used by the garbage collector)

- Gen 0 Collections, Gen 1 Collections, Gen 2 Collections (the number of GCs fired by the runtime)

- % Time in GC (the percentage of CPU time spent performing GCs)

Note One or more code examples in this chapter assume that the following namespaces have been imported by means of *Imports* (Visual Basic) or *using* (C#) statements:

```
System.IO
System.Runtime.InteropServices
```

23.1 Early creation of long-lasting objects

As a rule of thumb, objects that are meant to live for the entire duration of the application lifetime should be created earlier, if possible immediately after starting the application, and shouldn't be reallocated during the application lifetime.

Why: This simple technique has a twofold benefit. First, after a couple of garbage collections these objects will be promoted to Generation 2 and the garbage collector will ignore them during all Generation-0 and Generation-1 collections. (Having fewer objects to scan speeds up the garbage collection step.) Second, these objects will be allocated near the beginning of the managed heap and the .NET runtime won't need to move them in memory when the heap is compacted.

More details: For the aforementioned reason, fields in long-lasting objects shouldn't point to short-term objects; otherwise, these short-term objects will quickly be promoted to Generation 2 and, even if your code later sets them to *Nothing* (Visual Basic) or *null* (C#), they will take memory until the .NET runtime fires a Generation-2 collection.

23.2 Boxing

Ensure that you don't box value types without a good reason. You have a boxing operation when you assign a value type (for example, a number, a DataTime value, a structure) to an Object variable, pass it as an argument to a method that takes Object parameters, or assign it to an interface variable.

Why: Boxing consumes memory in the managed heap and indirectly causes the garbage collection process to run more frequently, thus slowing down the application.

See also: Read 8.8, 9.5, 9.6, and 14.19 for techniques that allow you to reduce the number of boxing operations in your applications.

23.3 Clearing object references

Don't explicitly set an object reference to null when you don't need it any longer inside a method.

Why: When optimizations are enabled, both Visual Basic and C# compilers can detect when an object variable isn't used later in the method and the garbage collector can reclaim the memory without the developer's assistance.

```
' [Visual Basic]
Sub PerformTask()
   Dim p As New Person
   ' Use the object.
   ...
   ' No need to explicitly set the variable to Nothing
End Sub
```

```csharp
// [C#]
void PerformTask()
{
    Person p = new Person();
    // Use the object.
    ...
    // No need to explicitly set the variable to null
}
```

Exception: See rule 23.4 for an exception to this rule.

23.4 Clear object references explicitly in loops

Explicitly set an object reference to null if you are inside a loop and want the .NET runtime to collect the object before the loop ends.

Why: When compiling a loop, the Visual Basic and C# compilers can't automatically detect whether the variable is going to be used during subsequent iterations of the loop, and therefore the garbage collector can't automatically reclaim the memory used by the object. By clearing the object variable explicitly, you can help the garbage collector understand that the object can be reclaimed.

```vb
' [Visual Basic]
Sub PerformTask()
    Dim p As New Person
    ' Use the object inside the loop.
    For i As Integer = 1 To 100
        If i <= 50 Then
            ' Use the object only in the first 50 iterations.
            Console.WriteLine(p.CompleteName)
            ' Explicitly set the variable to Nothing after its last use.
            If i = 50 Then p = Nothing
        Else
            ' Do something else here, but don't use the p variable.
            ...
        End If
    Next
End Sub
```

```csharp
// [C#]
void PerformTask()
{
    Person p = new Person();
    // Use the object inside the loop.
    for ( int i=1; i <= 100; i++ )
    {
        if ( i <= 50 )
        {
            // Use the object only in the first 50 iterations.
            Console.WriteLine(p.CompleteName);
```

```
         // Explicitly set the variable to null after its last use.
         if ( i == 50 )
            p = null;
      }
      else
      {
         // Do something else here, but don't use the p variable.
         ...
      }
   }
}
```

23.5 Keeping objects alive

Because the .NET runtime can collect objects even if they haven't been set explicitly to null (see rule 23.3), you must use the GC.KeepAlive method to keep an object alive if the object is supposed to continue to run until the current method completes.

More details: You might need to adopt this technique if the object uses a timer to perform background operations or if the object wraps an unmanaged resource that shouldn't be released until the method completes. You should notice, however, that in both these cases the object should implement the IDisposable interface and it should be used inside a *using* block (see rule 16.4) or a *Try...Finally* block (see rule 16.5). For this reason, in practice you rarely need to keep an object alive by means of the GC.KeepAlive method.

```
' [Visual Basic]
Sub PerformTask()
   Dim p As New Person
   ' Use the object.
   ...
   ' Keep the object alive until the end of the method.
   GC.KeepAlive(p)
End Sub

// [C#]
void PerformTask()
{
   Person p = new Person();
   // Use the object.
   ...
   // Keep the object alive until the end of the method.
   GC.KeepAlive(p);
}
```

23.6 Explicit garbage collections in server applications

Never explicitly invoke the GC.Collect method in server-side applications except for testing and debugging purposes. (Server-side applications include Web Forms, Web Services, Serviced Components, and Windows Services projects.)

23.7 Explicit garbage collections in client applications

Use the GC.Collect method judiciously in client-side applications and only at the conclusion of a time-consuming operation such as file load or save. (Client-side applications include Console and Windows Forms projects.)

Never use the GC.Collect method in a class library or a control library unless you clearly document under which conditions a garbage collection is fired. In other words, induced garbage collections should always be under the control of the main application.

23.8 Waiting for finalizers after explicit garbage collections

Always use the GC.WaitForPendingFinalizers method after invoking the GC.Collect method.

Why: Finalizer methods run in a separate thread; by calling the GC.WaitForPendingFinalizers method, you ensure that all finalizers have completed and your objects are destroyed before continuing.

```
' [Visual Basic]
' The correct way to force a garbage collection
GC.Collect()
GC.WaitForPendingFinalizers()

// [C#]
// The correct way to force a garbage collection
GC.Collect();
GC.WaitForPendingFinalizers();
```

23.9 Large object heap fragmentation

Don't frequently create and destroy *large objects*, that is, objects that occupy more than 85,000 bytes. Consider splitting large objects into two or more smaller (regular) objects.

Why: Large objects are stored in a separate managed heap that is never compacted (because moving such large memory blocks would be too time-consuming). If you frequently allocate and free large objects, this separate heap can become fragmented, so even though you have enough free memory in the heap overall, you might run out of memory if there isn't a block large enough for the object you're trying to create.

More details: The majority of large objects are arrays. In some cases you can avoid the creation of a large object by using alternate but equivalent objects, such as an ArrayList or a BitArray. Likewise, you can often replace a large two-dimensional array with a jagged array whose constituent subarrays are smaller than 85,000 bytes.

You can control how the .NET runtime uses the large object heap by monitoring the Large Object Heap size counter of the .NET CLR Memory performance object.

23.10 Compound finalizable objects

If you have a finalizable object that occupies a lot of memory, consider splitting the definition of the object into two separate types: one type that contains the unmanaged resource and the Finalize method, and another type that contains other variables.

Why: The garbage collector requires at least two collections to reclaim entirely the memory of an object that overrides the Finalize method. (Often, more collections are required because after the first collection the object is promoted to Generation 1.) By splitting the type into two classes, you enable the garbage collector to reclaim the memory of the nonfinalizable portion of the type during the first collection.

Example: The following code shows a naive implementation of a class that opens the system Clipboard and implements the Dispose-Finalize pattern to ensure that the Clipboard is closed when the object is disposed or when the garbage collector finalizes the object.

```vb
' [Visual Basic]
Public Class SimpleObject
   Implements IDisposable

   ' Windows API declarations
   Private Declare Function OpenClipboard Lib "User32" (ByVal hWnd As Integer) As Integer
   Private Declare Function CloseClipboard Lib "User32" () As Integer

   ' This array takes a lot of memory.
   Dim arr() As Integer

   Sub New(ByVal hWnd As Integer, ByVal elements As Integer)
      ReDim arr(elements - 1)
      OpenClipboard(hWnd)
   End Sub

   ' Close the Clipboard when the object is disposed.
   Public Sub Dispose() Implements System.IDisposable.Dispose
      CloseClipboard()
      GC.SuppressFinalize(Me)
   End Sub

   ' Close the Clipboard when the object is finalized.
   Protected Overrides Sub Finalize()
      Dispose()
   End Sub
End Class

// [C#]
public class SimpleObject : IDisposable
{
   // Windows API declarations
   [DllImport("User32")]
   private static extern int OpenClipboard (int hWnd);
   [DllImport("User32")]
   private static extern int CloseClipboard ();

   // This array takes a lot of memory.
```

```
   int[] arr;

   public SimpleObject(int hwnd, int elements)
   {
      arr = new int[elements];
      OpenClipboard(hwnd);
   }

   // Close the Clipboard when the object is disposed.
   public void Dispose()
   {
      CloseClipboard();
      GC.SuppressFinalize(this);
   }

   // Close the Clipboard when the object is finalized.
   ~SimpleObject()
   {
      Dispose();
   }
}
```

In the following improved version, we have split the previous type into two disposable classes, with only one of them containing the Finalize method. This new version can run remarkably faster than the previous one if many objects are created and destroyed frequently.

```
' [Visual Basic]
Public Class CompoundObject
   Implements IDisposable

   ' This array takes a lot of memory.
   Dim arr() As Integer
   ' An instance of the inner (finalizable) object
   Dim clipWrapper As ClipboardWrapper

   Sub New(ByVal hwnd As Integer, ByVal elements As Integer)
      ReDim arr(elements - 1)
      clipWrapper = New ClipboardWrapper(hwnd)
   End Sub

   ' Dispose of the inner object.
   Public Sub Dispose() Implements System.IDisposable.Dispose
      clipWrapper.Dispose()
   End Sub

   ' The inner type that wraps the Finalize method
   Private Class ClipboardWrapper
      Implements IDisposable

      ' Windows API declarations
      Private Declare Function OpenClipboard Lib "User32" (ByVal hwnd As Integer) _
         As Integer
      Private Declare Function CloseClipboard Lib "User32" () As Integer

      Sub New(ByVal hwnd As Integer)
         OpenClipboard(hwnd)
      End Sub
```

```vb
        Public Sub Dispose() Implements System.IDisposable.Dispose
            CloseClipboard()
            GC.SuppressFinalize(Me)
        End Sub

        Protected Overrides Sub Finalize()
            Dispose()
        End Sub
    End Class
End Class
```

```csharp
// [C#]
public class CompoundObject : IDisposable
{
    // This array takes a lot of memory.
    int[] arr = null;
    // An instance of the inner (finalizable) object
    ClipboardWrapper clipWrapper = null;

    public CompoundObject(int hWnd, int elements)
    {
        arr = new int[elements];
        clipWrapper = new ClipboardWrapper(hWnd);
    }

    // Close the Clipboard when the object is disposed.
    public void Dispose()
    {
        clipWrapper.Dispose();
    }

    // The inner type that wraps the Finalize method.
    private class ClipboardWrapper : IDisposable
    {
        // Windows API declarations
        [DllImport("User32")]
        private static extern int OpenClipboard (int hWnd);
        [DllImport("User32")]
        private static extern int CloseClipboard ();

        public ClipboardWrapper(int hWnd)
        {
            OpenClipboard(hWnd);
        }

        public void Dispose()
        {
            CloseClipboard();
            GC.SuppressFinalize(this);
        }

        ~ClipboardWrapper()
        {
            Dispose();
        }
    }
}
```

23.11 WeakReference objects

Always wrap WeakReference objects in a custom type so other developers can use them safely and in a robust way.

More details: Weak references enable you to mantain a reference to another object (typically, an object that consumes a lot of memory) but don't prevent that object from being reclaimed when a garbage collection occurs. Weak references are therefore very useful for creating a cache of large objects: the object stays in memory only until there is a need to reclaim them. Wrapping these weak references in a custom type enables clients to use them in a more robust way.

Example: The following CachedTextFile class wraps a WeakReference object and enables clients to read the contents of a text file (which is supposed to be immutable during the application's lifetime) without having to reload it from the file each time the application uses it.

```
' [Visual Basic]
Public Class CachedTextFile
   ' The name of the file cached
   Public ReadOnly Filename As String
   ' A weak reference to the string that contains the text
   Dim wrText As WeakReference

   ' The constructor takes the name of the file to read.
   Sub New(ByVal fileName As String)
      Me.Filename = fileName
   End Sub

   ' Read the contents of the file.
   Private Function ReadFile() As String
      Dim sr As New StreamReader(Me.Filename)
      Dim text As String = sr.ReadToEnd()
      sr.Close()
      ' Create a weak reference to the return value.
      wrText = New WeakReference(text)
      Return text
   End Function

   ' Return the textual content of the file.
   Public Function GetText() As String
      Dim text As Object
      ' Retrieve the target of the weak reference.
      If Not (wrText Is Nothing) Then text = wrText.Target
      If Not (text Is Nothing) Then
         ' If non-null, the data is still in the cache.
         Return text.ToString()
      Else
         ' Otherwise, read it and put it in the cache again.
         Return ReadFile()
      End If
   End Function
End Class
```

```csharp
// [C#]
public class CachedTextFile
{
    // The name of the file cached
    public readonly string Filename;
    // A weak reference to the string that contains the text
    WeakReference wrText;

    // The constructor takes the name of the file to read.
    public CachedTextFile (string fileName)
    {
        this.Filename = fileName;
    }

    // Read the contents of the file.
    private string ReadFile()
    {
        StreamReader sr = new StreamReader(Me.Filename);
        string text = sr.ReadToEnd();
        sr.Close();
        // Create a weak reference to the return value.
        WeakReference wrText = new WeakReference(text);
        return text;
    }

    // Return the textual content of the file.
    public string GetText()
    {
        object text = null;
        // Retrieve the target of the weak reference.
        if ( wrText != null )
            text = wrText.Target;
        if ( text != null )
        {
            // If non-null, the data is still in the cache.
            return text.ToString();
        }
        else
        {
            // Otherwise, read it and put it in the cache again.
            return ReadFile();
        }
    }
}
```

Here's how you can use this class.

```vbnet
' [Visual Basic]
' Read and cache the contents of the "c:\alargefile.txt" file.
Dim cf As New CachedTextFile("c:\alargefile.txt")
Console.WriteLine(cf.GetText())
...
' Uncomment next line to force a garbage collection.
' GC.Collect(): GC.WaitForPendingFinalizers()
...
```

```
' Read the contents again some time later. (No disk access
' is performed, unless a GC has occurred in the meantime.)
Console.WriteLine(cf.GetText())

// [C#]
// Read and cache the contents of the "c:\alargefile.txt" file.
CachedTextFile cf = new CachedTextFile(@"c:\alargefile.txt");
Console.WriteLine(cf.GetText());
...
// Uncomment next line to force a garbage collection.
// GC.Collect(); GC.WaitForPendingFinalizers();
...
// Read the contents again some time later. (No disk access
// is performed, unless a GC has occurred in the meantime.)
Console.WriteLine(cf.GetText());
```

By examining the CachedTextFile class, you can easily prove that in most cases the file contents can be retrieved through the weak reference and that the disk isn't accessed again. By uncommenting the statement in the middle of the previous code snippet, you force a garbage collection, in which case the internal WeakReference object won't keep the String object alive and the code in the class will read the file again. The key point in this technique is that the client code doesn't know whether the cache object is used or not: the client just uses the CachedTextFile object as a "black box" that deals with large text files in an optimized way.

Remember that you create a weak reference by passing your object (a string, in this example) to the constructor of a System.WeakReference object. However, if the object is also referenced by a regular, nonweak reference, it survives any intervening garbage collection. In our example, the code using the CachedTextFile class should not store the return value of the GetText method in a string variable because that would prevent the string from being garbage collected. The following code snippet illustrates the incorrect way to use the CachedTextFile class:

```
' [Visual Basic]
Dim cf As New CachedTextFile("c:\alargefile.txt")
Dim text As String = cf.GetText()

// [C#]
CachedTextFile cf = new CachedTextFile(@"c:\alargefile.txt");
string text = cf.GetText();
```

23.12 Garbage collector settings

Carefully consider using nondefault settings for the garbage collector.

More details: The .NET Framework comes with two different garbage collectors: the workstation garbage collector and the server garbage collector. These garbage collectors are implemented in two different DLLs: the workstation garbage collector (in mscorwks.dll) is used on single-processor systems, whereas the server garbage collector (in mscorsvr.dll) is used on multiprocessor systems.

The server garbage collector pauses the application during GCs and uses one thread and one managed heap for each CPU; these settings guarantee the best overall throughput, even if an individual client might be slowed down if a GC occurs during a method call. The workstation garbage collector minimizes pauses by running the garbage collector concurrently with the application's worker threads.

On a single-CPU computer, both the server and the workstation garbage collectors behave in the same way and perform collections concurrently. For particular applications, however, you might slightly improve the overall performance by suppressing concurrency at the expense of longer delays in user interface operations. You can do this by using the <gcConcurrent> element in machine.config or the application's config file.

```
<configuration>
   <runtime>
      <gcConcurrent enabled="false" />
   </runtime>
</configuration>
```

You can also change the garbage collector behavior at the machine level by means of the Microsoft .NET Framework version 1.1 Configuration utility, which you can run from the Windows Administrative Tools menu.

By default, noninteractive .NET applications (such as a Windows service or an application that uses remoting) running on a multiprocessor system use the workstation GC and might perform poorly. You can force such applications to use the server GC by adding a <gcServer> element in the configuration file:

```
<configuration>
   <runtime>
      <gcServer enabled="true" />
   </runtime>
</configuration>
```

See also: For more information about this issue, read the MSDN Knowledge Base article at *http://support.microsoft.com/default.aspx?scid=kb;en-us;840523*. To configure an ASP.NET application to use the workstation GC, read *http://msdn.microsoft.com/library/ default.asp?url=/library/en-us/dnpag/html/scalenetchapt06.asp*.

Part II
.NET Framework Guidelines and Best Practices

Chapter 24

Files, Streams, and XML

Working with files in the Microsoft .NET Framework is often as easy as opening a file stream, reading from or writing to it, and then closing it. However, well-behaved applications should do more than just open and close files. For example, they should ensure that data files are stored in the correct location, and depending on whether these files should be shared among users, they should register file associations and add opened data files to the list of recent documents. The first portion of this chapter illustrates these and other guidelines related to files and streams, whereas in the second half you'll find a few important best practices related to XML, including a little-known detail about XML serialization that might cause some serious headaches.

> **Note** One or more code examples in this chapter assume that the following namespaces have been imported by means of *Imports* (Visual Basic) or *using* (C#) statements:
>
> ```
> Microsoft.Win32
> System.IO
> System.IO.IsolatedStorage
> System.Reflection
> System.Runtime.InteropServices
> System.Runtime.Serialization.Formatters.Soap
> System.Text
> System.Xml
> System.Xml.Serialization
> ```

24.1 Custom stream names

Use the Stream suffix for types that inherit from System.IO.Stream.

Example: CompressionStream.

24.2 Working with file and directory names

Always use the static methods in the Path type to extract, modify, and combine directory and filenames.

```vbnet
' [Visual Basic]
' Determine the path of the "Data" folder under the application's directory.
Dim assemblyFile As String = [Assembly].GetExecutingAssembly().Location
Dim assemblyPath As String = Path.GetDirectoryName(assemblyFile)
Dim subdir As String = Path.Combine(assemblyPath, "Data")
```

```csharp
// [C#]
// Determine the path of the "Data" folder under the application's directory.
string assemblyFile = Assembly.GetExecutingAssembly().Location;
string assemblyPath = Path.GetDirectoryName(assemblyFile);
string subdir = Path.Combine(assemblyPath, "Data");
```

24.3 Absolute file paths

Never burn absolute file paths in code. Always use paths that are relative to the application's directory (see the example in rule 24.2) or one of the directories returned by the GetFolder-Path method of the System.Environment type.

```
' [Visual Basic]
' Determine the directory to be used for templates by current user.
Dim templateDir As String = Environment.GetFolderPath(Environment.SpecialFolder.Templates)
```

```
// [C#]
// Determine the directory to be used for templates by current user.
string templateDir = Environment.GetFolderPath(Environment.SpecialFolder.Templates);
```

You can also use the value returned by the Environment.SystemDirectory property:

```
' [Visual Basic]
' Determine the Windows System directory (e.g., C:\Windows\System32).
Dim sysDir As String = Environment.SystemDirectory
' Determine the Windows main directory (e.g., C:\Windows).
Dim winDir As String = Path.GetDirectoryName(Environment.SystemDirectory)
```

```
// [C#]
// Determine the Windows System directory (e.g., C:\Windows\System32).
string sysDir = Environment.SystemDirectory;
// Determine the Windows main directory (e.g., C:\Windows).
string winDir = Path.GetDirectoryName(Environment.SystemDirectory);
```

24.4 User data files

Never place user files in the application's directory. Instead, use the directory returned by the Environment.GetFolderPath method when called with one of the following values from the Environment.SpecialFolder enum type:

- **LocalApplicationData**   The directory that serves as a common repository for application-specific data used by the current, nonroaming user. Example: C:\Application and Settings\Francesco\Local Settings\Application Data.

- **ApplicationData**   This directory serves as a common repository for application-specific data used by the current roaming user. (A roaming user works on more than one computer on a network; a roaming user's profile is kept on a server on the network and is loaded onto a system when the user logs on.) Example: C:\Application and Settings\Francesco\Application Data.

- **CommonApplicationData**   The directory that serves as a common repository for application-specific data used by all users. Example: C:\Application and Settings\All Users\Application Data.

Why: This technique ensures that all users keep their data in distinct directories and that data belonging to one user doesn't overwrite data related to another user. Using these folders to store user data promotes confidentiality, because users without administrative privileges can't read data belonging to other users, and ensures that the application can access user files even if it is running under a less privileged account that might not have access to the folder where the application has been installed (typically, a folder under the C:\Program Files directory).

More details: Even files that are created when the application starts and that are deleted when the application terminates should abide by this rule (unless they are created in the Windows temporary folder) because the Fast User Switching feature in Microsoft Windows XP and the remote desktop feature allow multiple users to be logged on at the same application at the same time.

24.5 Temporary files

Use the GetTempFileName method of the Path type to create a unique temporary file. Remember to delete this temporary file when you don't need it any longer or when the application terminates.

Example: The following TemporaryFileStream class creates a temporary file in the correct folder and automatically deletes the file when the stream is closed.

```vb
' [Visual Basic]
Public Class TemporaryFileStream
   Inherits FileStream

   Public Sub New()
      ' Delegate to the private constructor.
      Me.New(Path.GetTempFileName())
   End Sub

   Private Sub New(ByVal fileName As String)
      MyBase.New(fileName, FileMode.Open)
      m_FileName = fileName
   End Sub

   ' The FileName read-only property
   Private m_FileName As String

   ReadOnly Property FileName() As String
      Get
         Return m_FileName
      End Get
   End Property

   ' Delete the temporary file when the stream is disposed of.
   Protected Overrides Sub Dispose(ByVal disposing As Boolean)
      MyBase.Dispose(disposing)
      If Not FileName Is Nothing Then
         ' Note: You might decide to wrap next statement in Try...Catch block.
         File.Delete(FileName)
         m_FileName = Nothing
      End If
   End Sub
End Class
```

```csharp
// [C#]
public class TemporaryFileStream : FileStream
{
    // Delegate to the private constructor.
    public TemporaryFileStream() : this(Path.GetTempFileName())
    {}

    private TemporaryFileStream(string fileName) : base(fileName, FileMode.Open)
    {
        m_FileName = fileName;
    }

    // The FileName read-only property
    private string m_FileName;

    public string FileName
    {
        get { return m_FileName; }
    }

    // Delete the temporary file when the stream is disposed of.
    protected override void Dispose(bool disposing)
    {
        base.Dispose(disposing);
        if ( FileName != null )
        {
            // Note: You might decide to wrap next statement in Try...Catch block.
            File.Delete(FileName);
            m_FileName = null;
        }
    }
}
```

You can use a TemporaryFileStream object as you'd use a regular FileStream object.

```vbnet
' [Visual Basic]
' Open a temporary file and store data in it.
Dim tfs As New TemporaryFileStream
Dim sw As New StreamWriter(tfs)
sw.WriteLine("abcde")
sw.Flush()
' Rewind the stream and read the data back in memory.
tfs.Position = 0
Dim sr As New StreamReader(tfs)
Dim data As String = sr.ReadLine()
' Close the stream and delete the temporary file.
tfs.Close()
```

```csharp
// [C#]
// Open a temporary file and store data in it.
TemporaryFileStream tfs = new TemporaryFileStream();
StreamWriter sw = new StreamWriter(tfs);
sw.WriteLine("abcde");
sw.Flush();
// Rewind the stream and read the data back in memory.
```

```
tfs.Position = 0;
StreamReader sr = new StreamReader(tfs);
string data = sr.ReadLine();
// Close the stream and delete the temporary file.
tfs.Close();
```

24.6 Reading files

Favor reading files in one operation, for example, using the ReadToEnd method of the Stream-Reader object. If the file is larger than 8 KB and doesn't need to be held in memory all at once, you should read it in chunks or line by line.

Why: Reading a small file in one operation is faster than reading it line by line. However, keeping a large file in memory can slow down your application; therefore, if a large file can be processed in chunks or by individual lines, you should process its contents in chunks. (The actual size threshold above which it is more convenient to read the file in sections depends on how the application uses memory.)

Example: The following reusable method shows how you can read an entire text file in one operation.

```vbnet
' [Visual Basic]
Public Function ReadTextFile(ByVal fileName As String) As String
   Dim sr As StreamReader
   Try
      sr = New StreamReader(fileName)
      Return sr.ReadToEnd()
   Finally
      If Not sr Is Nothing Then sr.Close()
   End Try
End Function
```

```csharp
// [C#]
public string ReadTextFile(string fileName)
{
   using ( StreamReader sr = new StreamReader(fileName)
   {
      return sr.ReadToEnd();
   }
}
```

24.7 Closing StreamWriter and BinaryWriter objects

Always explicitly close a StreamWriter or a BinaryWriter object when you are done with it, rather than just closing the underlying Stream object.

Why: The StreamWriter and BinaryWriter types maintain the data being written to them in an internal buffer. Their Close method flushes the buffered data and then closes the underlying Stream-derived object. If you just invoke the Close method of the underlying Stream, the internal buffer in the StreamWriter or BinaryWriter object isn't flushed correctly and data can be lost.

More details: If you have completed a write operation with the StreamWriter and a Binary-Writer object but you don't want to close the stream, you should call the Flush method.

```
' [Visual Basic]
Dim fs As New FileStream("c:\data.txt", FileMode.OpenOrCreate)
Dim sw As New StreamWriter(fs)
' Write to the file here.
...

' *** Wrong: closing the stream doesn't flush buffered data.
fs.Close()

' *** Correct: closing the StreamWriter flushes the buffered data.
sw.Close()
fs.Close()              ' This statement is optional.

' *** Also correct
sw.Flush()
fs.Close()              ' This statement is not optional.

// [C#]
FileStream fs = new FileStream(@"c:\data.txt", FileMode.OpenOrCreate);
StreamWriter sw = new StreamWriter(fs);
// Write to the file here.
...

// *** Wrong: closing the stream doesn't flush buffered data.
fs.Close();

// *** Correct: closing the StreamWriter flushes the buffered data.
sw.Close();
fs.Close();             // This statement is optional in this case.

// *** Also correct
sw.Flush();
fs.Close();             // This statement is not optional in this case.
```

C# developers can also define a *using* block to ensure that the StreamWriter object is correctly closed when the write operation has completed.

```
// [C#]
FileStream fs = new FileStream(@"c:\data.txt", FileMode.OpenOrCreate);
using ( StreamWriter sw = new StreamWriter(fs) )
{
   // Write to the file here. No need to close the StreamWriter explicitly.
}
```

24.8 Creating file associations

Consider creating file associations for data files created and processed by your application, especially if these files can be created outside the application's folder (see Figure 24-1).

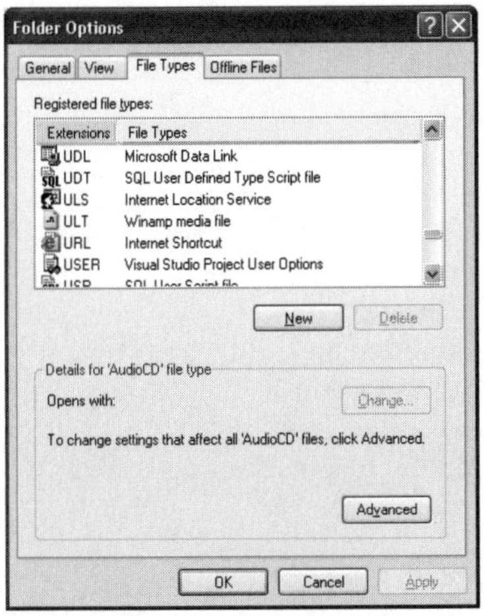

Figure 24-1 Users can use the Options command on the Windows Explorer Tools menu to display and change file associations.

How to: You can create file associations by means of a Visual Studio .NET Setup project, or you can use the following methods to create and delete file associations from inside your application. Notice that these methods access the Windows registry and might fail if the application is running under the identity of a user that doesn't have enough privileges to write to these registry keys.

```
' [Visual Basic]
<DllImport("shell32.dll")> _
Private Sub SHChangeNotify(ByVal wEventId As Integer, ByVal uFlags As Integer, _
    ByVal dwItem1 As Integer, ByVal dwItem2 As Integer)
End Sub
Const SHCNE_ASSOCCHANGED As Integer = &H8000000
Const SHCNF_IDLIST As Integer = 0


' Create the new file association.
'
' Extension is the extension to be registered (e.g., ".cad").
' ClassName is the name of the associated class (e.g., "CADDoc").
' Description is the textual description (e.g., "CAD Document").
' ExeProgram is the app that manages that extension (e.g., "c:\Cad\MyCad.exe").
Public Shared Function CreateFileAssociation(ByVal extension As String, _
        ByVal className As String, ByVal description As String, _
        ByVal exeProgram As String) As Boolean
    ' Ensure that extension has a leading period.
    If Not extension.StartsWith(".") Then extension = "." & extension
    ' Ensure that exeProgram is within double quotes.
    If Not exeProgram.StartsWith("""") Then
        exeProgram = """" & exeProgram & """"
    End If

    Dim key1, key2, key3 As RegistryKey
    Try
        ' Create a value for this key that contains the class name.
```

```vbnet
            key1 = Registry.ClassesRoot.CreateSubKey(extension)
            key1.SetValue("", className)
            ' Create a new key for the class name.
            key2 = Registry.ClassesRoot.CreateSubKey(className)
            key2.SetValue("", description)
            ' Associate the program with this extension.
            key3 = Registry.ClassesRoot.CreateSubKey(className & "\Shell\Open\Command")
            key3.SetValue("", exeProgram & " ""%1""")
        Catch e As Exception
            Return False
        Finally
            If Not key1 Is Nothing Then key1.Close()
            If Not key2 Is Nothing Then key2.Close()
            If Not key3 Is Nothing Then key3.Close()
        End Try

        ' Notify Windows that file associations have changed.
        SHChangeNotify(SHCNE_ASSOCCHANGED, SHCNF_IDLIST, 0, 0)
        Return True
    End Function

    ' Delete a file association.
    Public Shared Sub DeleteFileAssociation(ByVal extension As String)
        ' Ensure that extension has a leading period.
        If Not extension.StartsWith(".") Then extension = "." & extension

        ' Read the associated class name.
        Dim regKey As RegistryKey
        Try
            regKey = Registry.ClassesRoot.OpenSubKey(extension)
            If Not regKey Is Nothing Then
                ' Delete the file's class name.
                Dim className As String = regKey.GetValue("").ToString()
                If className.Length > 0 Then
                    Registry.ClassesRoot.DeleteSubKeyTree(className)
                End If
            End If
        Catch e As Exception
            ' Ignore errors.
        Finally
            If Not regKey Is Nothing Then regKey.Close()
        End Try
        Registry.ClassesRoot.DeleteSubKey(extension, False)

        ' Notify Windows that file associations have changed.
        SHChangeNotify(SHCNE_ASSOCCHANGED, SHCNF_IDLIST, 0, 0)
    End Sub

// [C#]
[DllImport("shell32.dll")]
static extern void SHChangeNotify(int wEventId, int uFlags, int dwItem1, int dwItem2);
const int SHCNE_ASSOCCHANGED = 0x8000000;
const int SHCNF_IDLIST = 0;

// Create the new file association.
//
```

```
// Extension is the extension to be registered (e.g., ".cad").
// ClassName is the name of the associated class (e.g., "CADDoc").
// Description is the textual description (e.g., "CAD Document").
// ExeProgram is the app that manages that extension (e.g., @"c:\Cad\MyCad.exe").
public static bool CreateFileAssociation(string extension, string className,
    string description, string exeProgram)
{
    // Ensure that extension has a leading period.
    if ( ! extension.StartsWith(".") )
        extension = "." + extension;
    // Ensure that exeProgram is within double quotes.
    if ( ! exeProgram.StartsWith("\"") )
        exeProgram = "\"" + exeProgram + "\"";

    RegistryKey key1 = null;
    RegistryKey key2 = null;
    RegistryKey key3 = null;
    try
    {
        // Create a value for this key that contains the class name.
        key1 = Registry.ClassesRoot.CreateSubKey(extension);
        key1.SetValue("", className);
        // Create a new key for the class name.
        key2 = Registry.ClassesRoot.CreateSubKey(className);
        key2.SetValue("", description);
        // Associate the program to open the files with this extension.
        key3 = Registry.ClassesRoot.CreateSubKey(className + @"\Shell\Open\Command");
        key3.SetValue("", exeProgram + @" ""%1""");
    }
    catch (Exception ex)
    {
        return false;
    }
    finally
    {
        if (key1 != null)
            key1.Close();
        if (key2 != null)
            key2.Close();
        if (key3 != null)
            key3.Close();
    }

    // Notify Windows that file associations have changed.
    SHChangeNotify(SHCNE_ASSOCCHANGED, SHCNF_IDLIST, 0, 0);
    return true;
}

// Delete a file association.
public static void DeleteFileAssociation(string extension)
{
    // Ensure that extension has a leading period.
    if ( ! extension.StartsWith(".") )
        extension = "." + extension;
```

```
   // Read the associated class name.
   RegistryKey regKey = null;
   try
   {
      regKey = Registry.ClassesRoot.OpenSubKey(extension);
      if (regKey != null )
      {
         // Delete file's class name.
         string className = (string) regKey.GetValue("");
         if (className.Length > 0)
            Registry.ClassesRoot.DeleteSubKeyTree(className);
      }
   }
   catch (Exception)
   {}
   finally
   {
      if (regKey != null)
         regKey.Close();
   }
   Registry.ClassesRoot.DeleteSubKey(extension, false);

   // Notify Windows that file associations have changed.
   SHChangeNotify(SHCNE_ASSOCCHANGED, SHCNF_IDLIST, 0, 0);
}
```

24.9 Adding data files to the recent document list

If you have registered the extension for your data files (see rule 24.8), add each data file that the end user opens or saves to the recent document list maintained by the operating system.

Why: This technique ensures that end users can launch your application and load one of the files in the recent document list in a single operation.

How to: You can add a file to the list by means of the following reusable method:

```
' [Visual Basic]
<DllImport("shell32")> _
Shared Function SHAddToRecentDocs(ByVal uFlags As Integer, ByVal filePath As String) _
   As Integer
End Function

' Add a file to the list of recent documents. If the parameter is
' an empty string, the function clears all documents from the list.
Public Sub AddToRecentDocs(ByVal fileName As String)
   Const SHARD_PATH As Long = 2
   If fileName Is Nothing OrElse fileName.Length = 0 Then
      SHAddToRecentDocs(SHARD_PATH, Nothing)
   Else
      SHAddToRecentDocs(SHARD_PATH, fileName)
   End If
End Sub
```

```
// [C#]
[DllImport("shell32")]
static extern int SHAddToRecentDocs(int uFlags, string filePath);

// Add a file to the list of recent documents. If the argument is
// an empty string, the function clears all documents from the list.
public void AddToRecentDocs(string fileName)
{
    const int SHARD_PATH = 2;
    if ( fileName == null || fileName.Length == 0 )
        SHAddToRecentDocs(SHARD_PATH, null);
    else
        SHAddToRecentDocs(SHARD_PATH, fileName);
}
```

24.10 Using isolated storage

Consider using isolated storage for saving user preferences and other configuration data.

Why: Isolated storage is a .NET Framework feature that enables assemblies to access a well-defined area of the file system, even if they don't have full permissions on the entire file system. If you are designing a Windows Forms application that might be running from a place other than the local hard disk you should attempt to use isolated storage instead of regular files.

More details: Assemblies manage isolated storage by means of *stores*. Each store contains one or more files or subdirectories and is distinct from the store that another user (or even another assembly running in the same user account) uses. This isolation ensures that an untrusted assembly can't read or modify the store used by another assembly. In addition, the system administrator can set a higher limit to the amount of data that can be written to a store (the so-called *quota*) so that an assembly can't compromise the client system by writing too much data to its hard drive.

How to: All the classes you need to use isolated storage in your applications can be found in the *System.IO.IsolatedStorage* namespace. The most important of such classes are *IsolatedStorageFile* (which represents a store) and *IsolatedStorageFileStream* (which represents an open file in the store).

The following example shows how you get a reference to a store, write a text file into it, and then read the file back. For more information about isolated storage, isolation scope, and quotas, read the MSDN documentation.

```
' [Visual Basic]
' Create a store for current user/assembly.
Dim store1 As IsolatedStorageFile = IsolatedStorageFile.GetStore( _
    IsolatedStorageScope.User Or IsolatedStorageScope.Assembly Or _
    IsolatedStorageScope.Domain, Nothing, Nothing)
' Create a file in the store.
Dim ifs1 As New IsolatedStorageFileStream("file1.txt", FileMode.Create, store1)
' Write a string to it.
```

```
Dim sw As New StreamWriter(ifs1)
sw.WriteLine("This is a test string")
sw.Close()
' This statement ensures that the store is written to disk.
store1.Close()

' Create another store for current user/assembly.
Dim store2 As IsolatedStorageFile = IsolatedStorageFile.GetStore( _
   IsolatedStorageScope.User Or IsolatedStorageScope.Assembly Or _
   IsolatedStorageScope.Domain, Nothing, Nothing)
' Read a file in the store.
Dim ifs2 As New IsolatedStorageFileStream("file1.txt", FileMode.Open, store2)
' Display its contents.
Dim sr As New StreamReader(ifs2)
Console.WriteLine(sr.ReadToEnd())
sr.Close()
store2.Close()

// [C#]
// Create a store for current user/assembly.
IsolatedStorageFile store1 = IsolatedStorageFile.GetStore(IsolatedStorageScope.User |
   IsolatedStorageScope.Assembly | IsolatedStorageScope.Domain, null, null);
// Create a file in the store.
IsolatedStorageFileStream ifs1 = new IsolatedStorageFileStream("file1.txt", FileMode.Create,
 store1);
// Write a string to it.
StreamWriter sw = new StreamWriter(ifs1);
sw.WriteLine("This is a test string");
sw.Close();
// This statement ensures that the store is written to disk.
store1.Close();

// Create another store for current user/assembly.
IsolatedStorageFile store2 = IsolatedStorageFile.GetStore(IsolatedStorageScope.User |
   IsolatedStorageScope.Assembly | IsolatedStorageScope.Domain, null, null);
// Read a file in the store.
IsolatedStorageFileStream ifs2 = new IsolatedStorageFileStream("file1.txt", FileMode.Open, s
tore2);
// Display its contents.
StreamReader sr = new StreamReader(ifs2);
Console.WriteLine(sr.ReadToEnd());
sr.Close();
store2.Close();
```

Note   Isolated data is perfect for storing user preferences but not for configuration set-tings—such as an ADO.NET connection string—because the latter type of settings should be under the control of the administrator, not the end user. Likewise, isolated storage should not be used to store secret data because any unmanaged or fully trusted application can access the area of the file system where the store is held.

24.11 Writing XML text

Always use the XmlTextWriter object to produce XML text.

Why: This technique ensures that the result complies with XML syntax rules and that special characters (such as < and >) are correctly rendered as character entities.

Example: The following code shows how you can use the XmlTextWriter type to generate an XML file containing information about all the Person objects in an array. (The definition of the Person type and the declaration of the arrPersons array are omitted.)

```
' [Visual Basic]
' Create the output XML file.
Dim xtw As New XmlTextWriter("persons.xml", Encoding.UTF8)
' Indent tags by 2 spaces.
xtw.Formatting = Formatting.Indented
xtw.Indentation = 2
' Enclose attributes' values in double quotes.
xtw.QuoteChar = """"c
' Create the following XML declaration for this XML document:
'    <?xml version="1.0" standalone="yes" ?>
xtw.WriteStartDocument(True)
' Add a comment.
xtw.WriteComment("Data converted from Persons array")
' The root element is <Persons>.
xtw.WriteStartElement("Persons")
' This variable will provide a unique ID for each Person element.
Dim id As Integer = 0

For Each p As Person In arrPersons
    ' Write a new <Person id="nnn"> element.
    id += 1
    xtw.WriteStartElement("Person")
    xtw.WriteAttributeString("id", id.ToString())
    ' Write fields as nested elements containing text.
    xtw.WriteElementString("firstName", p.FirstName)
    xtw.WriteElementString("lastName", p.LastName)
    ' Close the <Person> element.
    xtw.WriteEndElement()
Next
' Close the root element (and all pending elements, if any).
xtw.WriteEndDocument()
' Close the underlying stream (never forget this).
xtw.Close()

// [C#]
// Create the output XML file.
XmlTextWriter xtw = new XmlTextWriter("persons.xml", Encoding.UTF8);
// Indent tags by 2 spaces.
xtw.Formatting = Formatting.Indented;
xtw.Indentation = 2;
// Enclose attributes' values in double quotes.
xtw.QuoteChar = '\"';
// Create the following XML declaration for this XML document:
```

```
//     <?xml version="1.0" standalone="yes" ?>
xtw.WriteStartDocument(true);
// Add a comment.
xtw.WriteComment("Data converted from Persons array");
// The root element is <Persons>.
xtw.WriteStartElement("Persons");
// This variable will provide a unique ID for each Person element.
int id = 0 ;

foreach (Person p in arrPersons )
{
    // Write a new <Person id="nnn"> element.
    id += 1;
    xtw.WriteStartElement("Person");
    xtw.WriteAttributeString("id", id.ToString());
    // Write fields as nested elements containing text.
    xtw.WriteElementString("firstName", p.FirstName);
    xtw.WriteElementString("lastName", p.LastName);
    // Close the <Person> element.
    xtw.WriteEndElement();
}
// Close the root element (and all pending elements, if any).
xtw.WriteEndDocument();
// Close the underlying stream (never forget this).
xtw.Close();
```

24.12 Reading and writing XML files

Use the XmlTextReader and the XmlTextWriter objects to process large XML files instead of the XmlDocument object. (This guideline is especially effective in server-side applications.)

Why: The XmlDocument object loads the entire file in memory; therefore, all techniques based on this object don't scale well if used in server-side components and ASP.NET applications.

24.13 Searching XML nodes

Use the SelectNodes or the SelectSingleNode method to find specific nodes in an XmlDocument object.

How to: The XmlNode class exposes two search methods that take an XPath expression. Use the SelectNodes method if the XPath expression can return more than one match or the SelectSingleNode method if it can return only one node (or you're only interested in its first matching node).

```
' [Visual Basic]
' Select the firstName node of the Employee element whose lastName node is 'Davolio'.
Dim xpath As String = "//Employee[lastName='Davolio']/firstName"
Dim xn As XmlNode = xmldoc.SelectSingleNode(xpath)
' Display its text content.
Console.WriteLine(xn.InnerText)
```

```
' Select all Employee elements whose id attribute is <= 4.
Dim xnl As XmlNodeList = xmldoc.SelectNodes("//Employee[@id <= 4]")
' Display number of matches.
Console.WriteLine(xnl.Count)
For Each xmlEl As XmlElement In xnl
    ' Display the InnerText property of the <lastName> child element.
    ' (We know that there is only one <lastName> child node.)
    Console.WriteLine(xmlEl.GetElementsByTagName("lastName")(0).InnerText)
Next

// [C#]
// Select the firstName node of the Employee element whose lastName node is 'Davolio'.
string xpath = "//Employee[lastName='Davolio']/firstName";
XmlNode xn = xmldoc.SelectSingleNode(xpath);
// Display its text content.
Console.WriteLine(xn.InnerText);

// Select all Employee elements whose id attribute is <= 4.
XmlNodeList xnl = xmldoc.SelectNodes("//Employee[@id <= 4]");
// Display number of matches.
Console.WriteLine(xnl.Count);
foreach (XmlElement xmlEl in xnl )
{
    // Display the InnerText property of the <lastName> child element.
    // (We know that there is only one <lastName> child node.)
    Console.WriteLine(xmlEl.GetElementsByTagName("lastName")[0].InnerText);
}
```

24.14 DateTime serialization

Account for time zone information when serializing and deserializing DateTime values by means of a SoapFormatter or XmlSerializer object.

More details: The SoapFormatter and XmlSerializer objects serialize DateTime values together with the time zone information. When data is deserialized in a different time zone, the DateTime value is adjusted to reflect the new time zone. This behavior is often OK, but it can cause problems in some cases. For example, a person born in Italy on January 1, 1970, at 2 A.M. appears to be born on December 31, 1969, at 8 P.M. when the information is saved as XML and deserialized on a computer in New York. Other problems can arise if the DateTime value being serialized happens to be on Daylight Saving Time (DST) in the area where it is serialized but not in the area where it is deserialized, or vice versa.

How to: There are several solutions to this issue, depending on which behavior you want to implement and which serializer you're dealing with. The simplest case is when you are working with the XmlSerializer object and you don't want changes in the time portion to affect the date portion. To solve this problem you just need to decorate the DateTime field or property with an XmlElement attribute that specifies that only the date portion must be stored in the file:

```vbnet
' [Visual Basic]
Public Class Person
   Public FirstName As String
   Public LastName As String
   <XmlElement(DataType:="date")> _
   Public BirthDate As Date
End Class
```

```csharp
// [C#]
public class Person
{
   public string FirstName;
   public string LastName;
   [XmlElement(DataType="date")]
   public DateTime BirthDate;
}
```

In the most general cases you might want to adopt one of the following alternative approaches:

■ You implement the ISerialization interface and convert the DateTime value to a string during the serialization phase. Of course, you must convert the string back to a date during the deserialization step. (This approach works for the SoapFormatter object only.)

■ You suppress serialization for the DateTime field by marking it with an XmlIgnore attribute, but define a public string property that serializes the value as a string in the get block and then deserialize it to a DateTime value in the set block. (This approach works for the XmlSerializer object only.)

■ You define a custom class that wraps a DateTime object and that you use whenever a date or time value is used. This class should implement ISerializable so that you are in full control of how date and time portions are serialized, and you might also include a field that keeps track of time zone information so that you can easily move an instance of this class to another time zone without losing information. (This approach works for both the SoapFormatter and the XmlSerializer object.)

Chapter 25

PInvoke and COM Interop

PInvoke is the portion of the Microsoft .NET Framework that enables you to execute code embedded in traditional, non-COM DLLs, such as user32.dll and other Microsoft Windows API DLLs. COM Interop is the portion of the .NET Framework that enables you to create COM objects and invoke their methods and that lets you expose .NET types to COM clients such as Visual Basic 6 programs. These two portions have much in common—for example, the code that marshals data between the managed and the unmanaged worlds—therefore, it makes sense to discuss PInvoke and COM Interop in the same chapter.

There are many reasons for interacting with non-.NET code from your applications. For example, you might need to invoke a Windows API function whose functionality hasn't been included in the.NET Framework; or you might need to interact with a program in the Microsoft Office suite or other applications that expose their objects through COM; or you are converting a large Visual Basic 6 or C++ application to the .NET world, and you want to reuse portions of the old application because it would be too time-consuming or expensive to rewrite them in a .NET language.

Here's a tip for whoever wants to do serious PInvoke and COM Interop programming: download and install Adam Nathan's excellent CLR SPY tool (from *http://www.gotdotnet.com/Community/UserSamples/Details.aspx?SampleGuid=c7b955c7-231a-406c-9fa5-ad09ef3bb37f*). This utility is capable of detecting and diagnosing several runtime problems that might cause inconsistent results or unexpected exceptions caused by wrong method signatures or premature garbage collections.

Also from Adam Nathan is the great *http://www.pinvoke.net* Web site, where you can find the correct declaration of virtually all Windows API functions, both in Visual Basic and C#. You can even download an add-in that enables you to query the site's database without leaving the Microsoft Visual Studio .NET editor.

Note One or more code examples in this chapter assume that the following namespaces have been imported by means of *Imports* (Visual Basic) or *using* (C#) statements:

```
Microsoft.Win32
System.Runtime.InteropServices
System.Text
```

25.1 The DllImport attribute [Visual Basic]

Favor using the DllImport attribute over using a *Declare* statement.

Why: The DllImport attribute offers a few options that aren't available with the *Declare* statement, for example, the SetLastError option (see rule 25.4).

```
' [Visual Basic]
' *** OK
Private Declare Ansi Function FindWindow Lib "user32" Alias "FindWindowA" _
   (ByVal lpClassName As String, ByVal lpWindowName As String) As Integer

' *** Better
<DllImport("user32")> _
Private Shared Function FindWindow(ByVal lpClassName As String, _
   ByVal lpWindowName As String) As Integer
   ' No code here
End Function
```

25.2 All external methods in one type

Expose all the external procedures as public methods of a type with *Friend* (Visual Basic) or *internal* (C#) visibility. If the external procedure takes StringBuilder arguments or other arguments that require initialization, define the external procedure as private and wrap it in a public method (using the same name) that correctly marshals the arguments.

```
' [Visual Basic]
Friend Class WindowsFunctions
   <DllImport("user32")> _
   Private Shared Function GetClassName (ByVal hWnd As IntPtr, _
      ByVal buffer As StringBuilder, ByVal charcount As Integer) As Integer
   End Function

   Public Shared Function GetClassName(ByVal hWnd As IntPtr) As String
      Dim buffer As New StringBuilder(512)
      GetClassName(hWnd, buffer, buffer.Capacity)    ' Call the private overload.
      Return buffer.ToString()
   End Function
End Class

// [C#]
internal class WindowsFunctions
{
   [DllImport("user32")]
   static extern int GetClassName(IntPtr hWnd, StringBuilder buffer, int charcount);

   public static string GetClassName(IntPtr hWnd)
   {
      StringBuilder buffer = new StringBuilder(512);
      GetClassName(hWnd, buffer, buffer.Capacity);    // Call the private overload.
      return buffer.ToString();
   }
}
```

If you are building a class library that is marked with an assembly-level AllowPartiallyTrusted-Callers attribute and that is meant to be called by untrusted clients, all the methods marked with the DllImport attribute should be marked also with the SuppressUnmanagedCodeSecurity attribute and should demand specific permissions. (Read rule 33.11 for more information.)

25.3 IntPtr parameters

Use the IntPtr type for parameters and return values that correspond to Windows handles and system integers.

Why: This technique enables you to pass the value returned by the Handle property of forms and controls to the external routine without the need to cast it to Int32.

Example: This code uses the GetClassName external method defined in rule 25.2 to read the caption of the current Windows Forms object.

```
' [Visual Basic]
Dim className As String = WindowsFunctions.GetClassName(Me.Handle)

// [C#]
string className = WindowsFunctions.GetClassName(this.Handle);
```

25.4 The SetLastError option

Set the SetLastError option to true when invoking an external method that sets the Win32 error. Otherwise, leave it as the false (default) value.

Why: When this option is enabled, the compiler must emit additional code that saves the error code and makes it available through the Marshal.GetLastWin32Error method. Leaving it to false can slightly improve performance if the external method doesn't actually set the Win32 error.

More details: The Visual Basic *Declare* statement always saves the Win32 error code and makes it available by means of the Marshal.GetLastWin32Error or Err.LastDllError method. You must use the DllImport attribute and set the SetLastError option to false to disable this feature.

```
' [Visual Basic]
<DllImport("myfunctions.dll", SetLastError:=True)> _
Shared Sub PerformTask(ByVal s1 As String)
   ' No implementation code
End Sub

Sub TestExternalMethod()
   PerformTask("tryme")
   If Marshal.GetLastWin32Error() <> 0 Then
      ' Deal with the Win32 error code here.
      ...
   End If
End Sub
```

```
// [C#]
[DllImport("myfunctions.dll", SetLastError=true)]
static extern void PerformTask(string s1);

void TestExternalMethod()
{
    PerformTask("tryme");
    if ( Marshal.GetLastWin32Error() != 0 )
    {
        // Deal with the win32 error code here.
        ...
    }
}
```

25.5 Explicitly release COM objects

Use the Marshal.ReleaseComObject method to release and destroy a COM object explicitly as soon as you're done with it.

Why: If you don't invoke this method, the COM object is released only at the next garbage collection and consumes unmanaged memory until then. Worse, if the COM object has a user interface (for example, a Microsoft Office component), it might continue to be visible even after the .NET application has set it to a null object reference.

```
' [Visual Basic]
Dim msword As New Word.Application
' Use the COM object here.
...
msword.Quit()
Marshal.ReleaseComObject(msword)
msword = Nothing

// [C#]
Word.Application msword = new Word.Application();
// Use the COM object here.
...
object saveChanges = false;
object missing = null;
msword.Quit(ref saveChanges, ref missing, ref missing);
Marshal.ReleaseComObject(msword);
msword = null;
```

25.6 Signed interop assemblies

Use the TlbImp tool to generate a strong-name interop assembly with a version number.

More details: The Visual Studio .NET Add Reference dialog box can create an interop assembly that wraps a COM component, but it doesn't give you the flexibility that you often need in real-world applications. For example, it doesn't let you create an assembly with a version and a strong name, and it doesn't let you generate the classes in namespaces other than the default one.

Example: The following command generates an interop assembly for the source.dll COM component, puts all its types in the CodeArchitects namespace, assigns it the 2.0.0.0 version number, and signs it with the public/private key pair held in the c:\codearchitects.snk file:

```
TLBIMP source.dll /KEYFILE:c:\codearchitects.snk /ASMVERSION:2.0.0.0
  /NAMESPACE:CodeArchitects
```

25.7 Using Primary Interop Assemblies

Before using a third-party COM component, always check whether the publisher of that component has released a Primary Interop Assembly (PIA) for the component.

Why: A PIA is the "official" interop assembly for a COM component. It should be created by the manufacturer of the COM component, and it should be installed in the GAC and registered in the registry. If you don't use a PIA, you might not be able to pass references to an object in the COM component to another application because your application and the other application would assign different identities to the same COM component.

More details: Microsoft provides the PIAs for a few important type libraries, such as adodb, Microsoft.mshtml, Microsoft.stdformat, office, and stdole. Other PIAs might be available on the Microsoft Web site.

25.8 Building Primary Interop Assemblies

Always provide a PIA for all COM components that you have authored. Notice that a PIA can reference only other PIAs.

Why: See rule 25.7 for an explanation of why using PIAs is recommended.

How to: Here's how you can create a PIA for a COM component that you've authored:

1. Use the /primary option of TlbImp to create the PIA, as follows:

    ```
    TLBIMP mylib.dll /OUT:mypia.dll /PRIMARY /KEYFILE:mycompany.snk
    ```

2. Run the AsmReg utility to add the PrimaryInteropAssembly registry key under the HKEY_CLASSES_ROOT\TypeLib\{tlbguid}\Version key related to the COM component:

    ```
    ASMREG mypia.dll
    ```

3. Run the GacUtil tool to install the interop assembly in the GAC:

    ```
    GACUTIL -i mypia.dll
    ```

4. Copy the assembly file to the C:\Program Files\Microsoft.NET\Primary Interop Assemblies folder to make it appear in the Visual Studio .NET Add Reference dialog box. (This step is optional; see the following paragraph.)

More details: Visual Studio .NET deals with PIAs in a special way: when you add a reference to a type library for which a PIA exists, Visual Studio .NET doesn't import the type library as it normally would; instead, it uses the PIA installed in the system.

25.9 Setting properties vs. invoking methods

Reduce the number of calls between .NET and COM applications. If possible, invoke a method that reads or sets multiple properties in one call rather than reading or setting each property individually.

Why: Crossing the border between the managed and unmanaged worlds has a fixed cost in terms of performance penalty, plus a variable cost that depends on how many arguments you're passing (and the type of each argument). By setting multiple properties through one method call, you can substantially reduce the overall overhead.

More details: When interacting with a third-party COM component, you must abide by the programming interface that the component's author has implemented. However, if you are calling a COM component that you've authored yourself, you should consider the opportunity of expanding the component with methods that are able to set or read multiple properties in one shot. (Methods that read multiple properties must have their arguments marked with the *ByRef* or *out* keyword.)

25.10 Blittable arguments and return values

If possible, call PInvoke and COM Interop methods that take and return values of blittable types.

More details: Many data types can be passed from managed to unmanaged code without much concern on your part because these data types have the same memory representation in the two worlds. These types are known as *blittable* types, a group that includes numeric and DateTime values, as well as one-dimensional arrays thereof and structures that contain only blittable elements. You should pass blittable types if possible because they can cross the boundary between managed and unmanaged code very efficiently.

Nonblittable types are those that have a different representation in the two worlds, or that might have many representations in the unmanaged world, and must undergo marshaling when they cross the border between the managed and unmanaged worlds. The most common nonblittable types are Boolean, Char, String, Decimal, and Array. The Boolean type is nonblittable because it can be 1, 2, or 4 bytes in the unmanaged world and because the true value can be represented as either 1 or –1. The Char type can be translated to either an ANSI or a Unicode character. The String type can be transformed into a variety of unmanaged formats, including null-terminated strings or length-prefixed BSTRs (each with the ANSI and Unicode variants). The Decimal type must be converted to Currency. Arrays are nonblittable because they can be translated either to SAFEARRAYS or to C-style arrays. You can determine exactly how nonblittable data is passed to or returned from managed code by means of the MarshalAs attribute.

25.11 Variant arguments

Use the CurrencyWrapper, UnknownWrapper, DispatchWrapper, or ErrorWrapper auxiliary types to pass a value correctly to a Variant argument in a COM method that expects a Currency, IUnknown, IDispatch, or Error value, respectively.

Why: The .NET runtime is capable of correctly passing most kinds of values to a COM method and can perform all the necessary marshaling if the .NET and the COM representation differ. However, when passing a .NET System.Object reference to a COM Variant argument that expects a value in one of the aforementioned types, you must give .NET a hint, by using one of these wrapper classes.

Example: The following example assumes that the ProcessCurrency method receives a Variant that is expected to contain a Currency value. Similar examples can be provided for the other wrapper classes.

```
' [Visual Basic]
' *** Wrong
Dim o As Object = 123.45
comobj.ProcessCurrency(o)

' *** Correct
Dim cw As New CurrencyWrapper(123.45)
comobj.ProcessCurrency(cw)

// [C#]
// *** Wrong
object o = 123.45;
comobj.ProcessCurrency(o);

// *** Correct
CurrencyWrapper cw = new CurrencyWrapper(123.45);
comobj.ProcessCurrency(cw);
```

25.12 Delegate arguments

Never create a delegate object and pass it on the fly to an external procedure using PInvoke or COM Interop. Instead, assign the delegate to a variable, pass the variable to the external procedure, and ensure that you protect the delegate variable from garbage collection.

Why: Delegates passed to external procedures might be garbage collected any time, unless a reference to them is stored in a class-level field or in a local variable. (In the latter case, you must also protect the variable from garbage collection by means of a GC.KeepAlive method.)

Example: The following code assumes that PerformTask is an external procedure that takes an instance of a delegate of the MyDelegate type:

```
' [Visual Basic]
' *** Wrong, might throw an ExecutionEngineException.
PerformTask(New MyDelegate(AddressOf CallbackProc))
```

```
' *** Correct
Dim deleg As New MyDelegate(AddressOf CallbackProc)
PerformTask(deleg)
GC.KeepAlive(deleg)

// [C#]
' *** Wrong, might throw an ExecutionEngineException.
PerformTask(new MyDelegate(CallbackProc));

' *** Correct
MyDelegate deleg = new MyDelegate(CallbackProc);
PerformTask(deleg);
GC.KeepAlive(deleg);
```

25.13 COM-friendly .NET components

.NET components that are meant to be exposed to COM clients shouldn't use features that COM-based clients can't see. Or they should provide alternative ways for COM clients to access those features. Here's a brief summary of the dos and don'ts of COM-friendly .NET components:

a. Only public and nonabstract classes can be exposed to COM; ensure that public abstract (*MustInherit* in Visual Basic) classes are marked with a ComVisible(false) attribute (see rule 25.14).

b. Avoid deep hierarchies in .NET classes, such as nested classes or namespaces with more than two levels.

c. The class must expose an implicit or explicit parameter-less constructor because COM clients can't access constructors with parameters. (The class might expose a public Initialize method that COM clients can call immediately after instantiation to ensure that the object is in a valid state before using it.)

d. The class shouldn't expose shared members because they aren't visible to COM clients.

e. The class shouldn't expose methods or properties that take or return Int64 values because they can't be handled by Visual Basic 6 clients.

f. The class shouldn't expose overloaded members because they can create confusion when used by COM clients.

g. Use custom exception classes that set the HResult property for returning nonstandard error codes to COM clients.

25.14 The ComVisible attribute

When designing a .NET component that is meant to be visible to COM clients, use an assembly-level ComVisible(false) attribute, and explicitly select which types are visible to clients by marking them with a ComVisible(true) attribute. Inside each of these classes, mark with ComVisible(false) attributes the methods that shouldn't be visible to COM clients.

Why: Whether to expose a .NET type to COM clients is an important, and sometimes difficult, decision, and it shouldn't be the default behavior for all the classes in an assembly.

```vb
' [Visual Basic]
<Assembly: ComVisible(False)>

<ComVisible(True)> _
Public Class Person                 ' This class is visible to COM.
    ...
    <ComVisible(False)> _
    Public Sub DoSomething()        ' This method isn't visible to COM.
        ...
    End Sub
End Class

Public Class Employee               ' This class isn't visible to COM.
    ...
End Class
```

```csharp
/ [C#]
[assembly: ComVisible(false)]

[ComVisible(true)]
public class Person              // This class is visible to COM.
{
    ...
    [ComVisible(false)]
    public void DoSomething()    // This method isn't visible to COM.
    {
        ...
    }
}

public class Employee            // This class isn't visible to COM.
{
    //...
}
```

25.15 The DispId attribute

Mark the default property or method of the .NET class with the DispId(0) attribute to make it the default member for COM clients as well.

```vb
' [Visual Basic]
<DispId(0)> _
Public Property Name() As String
    ...
End Property
```

```csharp
// [C#]
[DispId(0)]
public string Name
{
    ...
}
```

25.16 The ComClass attribute [Visual Basic]

If possible, use the ComClass attribute with classes that you want to expose to COM clients.

Why: The ComClass attribute tells the Visual Basic compiler to generate all the necessary interfaces that the .NET class must expose to be successfully exposed to COM. Without any further intervention on your part, the class exposes all public properties, methods, and events to COM clients through both early binding and late binding.

Why not: The ComClass attribute doesn't give you full control of how the .NET class is exposed to COM clients. When this attribute is applied, the class exposes neither public fields nor methods inherited from System.Object (including the all-important ToString method). If you can't accept these limitations, see rules 25.17 and 25.18.

How to: You can generate the code that uses this attribute by selecting the Com Class template from the Add New Item dialog box in Visual Studio .NET.

```
' [Visual Basic]
<ComClass(NetComponent.ClassId, NetComponent.InterfaceId, NetComponent.EventsId)> _
Public Class NetComponent
    ' (These GUIDs will surely be different in your case.)
    Public Const ClassId As String = "FC0B96B3-E719-4CD7-816B-BB3DCAD8BD97"
    Public Const InterfaceId As String = "7B8BA729-6B1D-4AB2-9FDE-75632CFC200E"
    Public Const EventsId As String = "948576A4-15BB-4EE3-A8AE-C22CF652CC56"

    Public Sub New()
        MyBase.New()
    End Sub
End Class
```

25.17 The ClassInterface attribute

Mark a class with the ClassInterface(ClassInterfaceType.AutoDual) attribute to make it accessible to COM clients by means of both early binding and late binding.

Why: If you omit this attribute, the class exposes only the IDispatch interface and can be accessed only by means of late-bound method calls.

Why not: Letting COM clients access the .NET component using early binding might create versioning issues if you later release a newer version of the component.

More details: This attribute doesn't automatically expose events to COM clients; see rule 25.18 to see how events can be exposed.

```
' [Visual Basic]
<ClassInterface(ClassInterfaceType.AutoDual)> _
Public Class NetComponent
    ...
End Class
```

```
// [C#]
[ClassInterface(ClassInterfaceType.AutoDual)]
public class NetComponent
{
    ...
}
```

25.18 Exposing .NET events to COM clients

Define all the events of a class in a separate interface, mark that interface with a proper InterfaceType attribute, and mark the actual class with a ComSourceInterfaces attribute that tells COM Interop which interface defines the outgoing events.

```
' [Visual Basic]
<InterfaceType(ComInterfaceType.InterfaceIsIDispatch)> _
Public Interface Person_Events
    Sub GotEmail(ByVal sender As Object, ByVal e As EventArgs)
    Sub PhoneCall(ByVal sender As Object, ByVal e As CancelEventArgs)
End Interface

<ClassInterface(ClassInterfaceType.AutoDual), _
    ComSourceInterfaces(GetType(Person_Events))> _
Public Class Person
    Public Event GotEmail(ByVal sender As Object, ByVal e As EventArgs)
    Public Event PhoneCall(ByVal sender As Object, ByVal e As CancelEventArgs)
    ...
End Class

// [C#]
[InterfaceType(ComInterfaceType.InterfaceIsIDispatch)]
public interface Person_Events
{
    void GotEmail(object sender, EventArgs e);
    void PhoneCall(object sender, CancelEventArgs e);
}

[ClassInterface(ClassInterfaceType.AutoDual)]
[ComSourceInterfaces(typeof(Person_Events))]
public class Person
{
    public event EventHandler GotEmail;
    public event CancelEventHandler PhoneCall;
    ...
}
```

25.19 The ComRegisterFunction and ComUnregisterFunction attributes

If a method of a type that is exposed to COM is marked with the ComRegisterFunction attribute, there must be another method in the same type marked with the ComUnregisterFunction attribute.

Why: The code in the register function typically adds one or more keys to the registry, creates a file, or performs another kind of action that needs to be undone when the COM component is unregistered.

Example: The following code shows how you can use these two attributes to create a registry key when the .NET component is registered as a COM component and remove the registry key when the component is unregistered.

```vb
' [Visual Basic]
Const CompanyKey As String = "Software\CodeArchitects\MyApp"

<ComRegisterFunction()> _
Private Shared Sub Register(ByVal ty As Type)
    Dim key As RegistryKey = Registry.CurrentUser.CreateSubKey(CompanyKey)
    key.SetValue("InstallDate", Now.ToLongDateString())
    key.Close()
End Sub

<ComUnregisterFunction()> _
Private Shared Sub UnRegister(ByVal ty As Type)
    Registry.CurrentUser.DeleteSubKey(CompanyKey)
End Sub
```

```csharp
// [C#]
const string CompanyKey = @"Software\CodeArchitects\MyApp";

[ComRegisterFunction]
private static void Register(Type ty)
{
    RegistryKey key = Registry.CurrentUser.CreateSubKey(CompanyKey);
    key.SetValue("InstallDate", DateTime.Now.ToLongDateString());
    key.Close();
}

[ComUnregisterFunction]
private static void UnRegister(Type ty)
{
    Registry.CurrentUser.DeleteSubKey(CompanyKey);
}
```

Both these procedures must be static (*Shared* in Visual Basic) and should be public. Both of them take a System.Type argument; this argument identifies the class being registered or unregistered.

Chapter 26
Threading

The Microsoft .NET Framework offers full support for building multithreaded applications, and in fact you can execute an operation in at least four different ways: by instantiating a Thread object, by means of one of the three timers that the .NET Framework defines, by calling one of the static methods of the ThreadPool type, or by invoking an asynchronous delegate. The last two techniques always use the .NET thread pool and scale quite well even when adopted in a server-side component, whereas you should use a Thread object only in Windows Forms applications. (For a guideline about timers, see rule 26.23.)

Even though creating a multithreaded .NET application is easy, there are so many details to account for that the job can quickly become a source of headaches. In fact, you must account for race conditions, resource sharing, non-thread-safe objects, thread synchronization, and more. In this chapter, we have gathered several basic (or not-so-basic) rules for creating multithreaded code that runs well both in client-side and server-side applications.

> **Note** One or more code examples in this chapter assume that the following namespaces have been imported by means of *Imports* (Visual Basic) or *using* (C#) statements:
>
> ```
> System.Collections
> System.ComponentModel
> System.IO
> System.Reflection
> System.Runtime.CompilerServices
> System.Text
> System.Threading
> System.Windows.Forms
> ```

26.1 Thread name

Assign the Name property of the Thread.CurrentThread object and all the Thread objects you create. Ensure that you never assign this property more than once because this operation would cause an invalid operation exception.

Why: Assigning a name to all your threads makes debugging much simpler because it enables you to identify the thread in the Threads window (see Figure 26-1).

```
' [Visual Basic]
Thread.CurrentThread.Name = "Main thread"
Dim thrWorker As New Thread(AddressOf PerformTask)
thrWorker.Name = "Worker thread"
thrWorker.Start()
```

```
// [C#]
Thread.CurrentThread.Name = "Main thread";
Thread thrWorker = new Thread(new ThreadStart(PerformTask));
thrWorker.Name = "Worker thread";
thrWorker.Start();
```

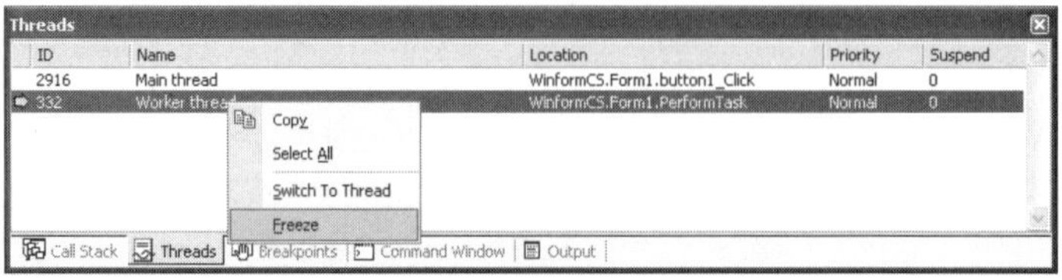

Figure 26-1   The Threads window lists all the threads running in the current application and enables you to freeze and restart them.

26.2 The IsBackground property

Set the IsBackground property of a Thread object to true for low-priority threads that don't need to keep the application running.

```
' [Visual Basic]
Dim thrWorker As New Thread(AddressOf PerformTask)
thrWorker.IsBackground = True
thrWorker.Start()
```

```
// [C#]
Thread thrWorker = new Thread(new ThreadStart(PerformTask));
thrWorker.IsBackground = true;
thrWorker.Start();
```

26.3 The Suspend, Resume, and Abort methods

Never suspend or abort the current thread. Also, in general, avoid Suspend, Resume, and Abort methods of the Thread object.

Why: These methods can easily cause deadlocks in your applications. Also, the Suspend and Resume methods have been marked as obsolete in .NET Framework 2.0.

More details: If you invoke the Abort method, ensure that you also call the Join method to stop processing until the thread has completed its cleanup operations (see rule 26.6).

26.4 The AppDomain.GetCurrentThreadId method

Avoid using the GetCurrentThreadId method of the AppDomain class to retrieve the operating system's ID of the current thread.

Why: This method doesn't return a stable ID when the managed thread runs on fibers (a.k.a. *lightweight* threads). Also, this method has become obsolete in .NET Framework 2.0, in beta as of this writing.

26.5 The Sleep method

Pass a zero argument to the Thread.Sleep method to give up remaining CPU time and force a thread context switch; pass a nonzero argument to pause the program for a given amount of time and during tests that simulate lengthy processing, but never use this method to synchronize threads (that is, to suspend the current thread until another thread completes a job).

26.6 The Join method

Use the Join method to wait until a different thread completes its job. Always ensure that you aren't invoking this method on the current thread (because this operation would freeze the thread), that the thread is alive, and that two different threads don't call the Join method on the other thread in a cyclic fashion (because this operation would cause a deadlock).

```
' [Visual Basic]
If thr.IsAlive AndAlso Not thr Is Thread.CurrentThread Then
   thr.Join()
End If

// [C#]
if ( thr.IsAlive && thr != Thread.CurrentThread )
   thr.Join();
```

More details: Be careful when using the Join method from the main thread of a Windows Forms application; this method freezes the main thread and you can't use the technique described in rule 26.15 to access user interface elements from the other thread. (Any attempt to do so would result in a deadlock.)

26.7 The ThreadAbortException type

Don't catch the ThreadAbortException. Never delay the abortion of the thread by staying inside the *Finally* (Visual Basic) or *finally* (C#) block.

More details: When the .NET runtime unloads an AppDomain inside which one or more threads are still running, a ThreadAbortException object is thrown in those threads. (This exception is also thrown when threads are manually aborted by a call to the Abort method.) This exception is special in that you can catch it, but the CLR throws it again at the end of the catch block. However, the CLR correctly executes the code in any finally block; therefore, a thread might delay its abortion indefinitely. We strongly recommend that you never adopt this technique.

26.8 *SyncLock* and *lock* blocks

Favor *SyncLock* (Visual Basic) or *lock* (C#) statements instead of Monitor's static methods to synchronize access to a shared resource.

Why: These statements internally use the Enter and Exit methods of the Monitor objects, but wrap all calls in a hidden *Try* (Visual Basic) or *try* (C#) block to ensure that the lock is released in case of an unhandled exception.

Why not: *SyncLock* and *lock* statements don't allow you to specify a timeout; therefore, in some cases, they might bring the system to a deadlock (see rule 26.10). When a timeout must be provided, you have no choice other than to use the static methods of the Monitor type.

```vb
' [Visual Basic]
' *** OK, uses the SyncLock block.
SyncLock Me
   ...
End SyncLock

' *** OK, uses the Monitor type because a timeout is specified.
If Monitor.TryEnter(Me, 1000) Then
   ' The thread managed to acquire the lock within 1000 milliseconds.
   Try
      ' Perform the actual operation.
      ...
   Finally
      ' Release the lock.
      Monitor.Exit(Me)
   End Try
End If
```

```csharp
// [C#]
// *** OK, uses the lock block.
lock ( this )
{
   ...
}

// *** OK, uses the Monitor type because a timeout is specified.
if ( Monitor.TryEnter(this, 1000) )
{
   // The thread managed to acquire the lock within 1000 milliseconds.
   try
   {
      // Perform the actual operation.
      ...
   }
   finally
   {
      // Release the lock.
      Monitor.Exit(this);
   }
}
```

26.9 Synchronized methods

Consider using a MethodImpl attribute to mark a method as synchronized, as opposed to using a *SyncLock* (Visual Basic) or *lock* (C#) block that wraps all the statements in the method.

If a type contains two or more methods marked with this attribute, only one thread at a time can be running inside any of the methods at a given instant.

More details: Using the MethodImpl attribute with the MethodImplOptions.Synchronized argument has the same effect as wrapping all the statements in the method with a *SyncLock* or *lock* block that uses the current object (*Me* in Visual Basic, *this* in C#) as the locking object.

Why not: This technique might not be granular enough in some circumstances. Besides, you should never use this attribute with static methods because the current Type object would be used as the locking object (see rule 26.12).

```vb
' [Visual Basic]
' *** OK
' Only one thread at a time can run inside either PerformTask1 or PerformTask2.
Public Sub PerformTask1()
   SyncLock Me

      ...
   End SyncLock
End Sub

Public Sub PerformTask2()
   SyncLock Me

      ...
   End SyncLock
End Sub


' *** Better: same effect with less code.
' Note that you can replace previous code because both methods
' use the current object (Me) for locking purposes.
<MethodImpl(MethodImplOptions.Synchronized)> _
Public Sub PerformTask1()
   ...
End Sub

<MethodImpl(MethodImplOptions.Synchronized)> _
Public Sub PerformTask2()
   ...
End Sub
```

```csharp
// [C#]
// *** OK
// Only one thread at a time can run inside either PerformTask1 or PerformTask2.
public void PerformTask1()
{
   lock ( this )
   {
      ...
   }
}

public void PerformTask2()
{
   lock ( this )
```

```
    {
        ...
    }
}

// *** Better: same effect with less code.
// Note that you can replace previous code because both
// methods use the current object (this) for locking purposes.
[MethodImpl(MethodImplOptions.Synchronized)]
public void PerformTask1()
{
    ...
}

[MethodImpl(MethodImplOptions.Synchronized)]
public void PerformTask2()
{
    ...
}
```

26.10 Nested synchronization blocks

When using nested *SyncLock* (Visual Basic) or *lock* (C#) statements to synchronize access to multiple objects, ensure that you follow the identical nesting sequence everywhere in your application. (And ensure that you use private locking objects; see rule 26.11.)

Why: Acquiring locks in identical order avoids deadlocks among different portions of your application. Notice that this guideline applies also to those cases when code in a *SyncLock* or *lock* block calls a method containing another *SyncLock* or *lock* block.

```
' [Visual Basic]
' Always use this sequence when locking objLock1 and objLock2.
SyncLock objLock1
    SyncLock objLock2
        ...
    End SyncLock
End SyncLock

// [C#]
// Always use this sequence when locking objLock1 and objLock2.
lock ( objLock1 )
{
    lock ( objLock2 )
    {
        ...
    }
}
```

26.11 Objects in synchronization blocks

Favor using objects with private or internal (*Friend* in Visual Basic) scope as arguments in *SyncLock* (Visual Basic) or *lock* (C#) statements or in Enter, TryEnter, and Exit methods of the Monitor type.

Why: By using a private object, you ensure that no code outside the type can cause a deadlock by using the same object for locking purposes.

More details: This guideline implies that you shouldn't use the *Me* (Visual Basic) or *this* (C#) reference in synchronization statements if the current object is public and is visible from another assembly.

```
' [Visual Basic]
Public Class Person
    Private objLock As New Object

    Public Sub PerformTask()
        SyncLock objLock
            ...
        End SyncLock
    End Sub
End Class

// [C#]
public class Person
{
    private object objLock = new Object();

    public void PerformTask()
    {
        lock ( objLock )
        {
            ...
        }
    }
}
```

26.12 System.Type objects in synchronization blocks

Avoid using a Type object to synchronize access to static members of a class. Instead, use a private static field as the argument to *SyncLock* (Visual Basic) and *lock* (C#) blocks that protect global resources.

Why: In some circumstances, two applications running in different AppDomains (but inside the same Win32 process) can share the same Type object. In such cases, two applications loaded in different AppDomains can deadlock if they use the same Type object in synchronization statements. Another reason for following this guideline is that getting a reference to Type objects is a relatively slow operation.

More details: Many developers mistakenly use the current object's Type object in synchronization statements as a simple way to synchronize access to static resources shared by all instances of a class. Even some Microsoft samples use it, even though Microsoft is now deprecating this technique.

```vb
' [Visual Basic]
' *** Wrong
Public Class Person
    Public Shared Sub PerformTask()
        SyncLock GetType(Person)
            ...
        End SyncLock
    End Sub
End Class

' *** Correct
Public Class Person
    Private Shared objLock As New Object()

    Public Shared Sub PerformTask()
        SyncLock objLock
            ...
        End SyncLock
    End Sub
End Class
```

```csharp
// [C#]
// *** Wrong
public class Person
{
    public void PerformTask()
    {
        lock ( typeof(Person) )
        {
            ...
        }
    }
}

// ** Correct
public class Person
{
    private static object objLock = new object();

    public void PerformTask()
    {
        lock ( objLock )
        {
            ...
        }
    }
}
```

26.13 Synchronizing on arrays and collections

Never use an array or a collection object as an argument of a *SyncLock* (Visual Basic) or *lock* (C#) block. Instead, use the object returned by the SyncRoot property that arrays and collections expose.

```
' [Visual Basic]
' *** Wrong
SyncLock alPersons        ' alPersons is an ArrayList.
    ...
End SyncLock

' *** Correct
SyncLock alPersons.SyncRoot
    ...
End SyncLock

// [C#]
// *** Wrong
lock ( alPersons )        // alPersons is an ArrayList.
{
    ...
}

// *** Correct
lock ( alPersons.SyncRoot )
{
    ...
}
```

More details: In practice, you never really need to use an array or a collection as a synchronization object because you can use a regular object instance for this purpose.

26.14 Synchronized collections

Use the Synchronized static method exposed by most collection types (and a few other .NET types, such as TextReader and TextWriter) to create a thread-safe wrapper object that can be accessed without any problem by clients in different threads.

Why: The synchronized wrapper simplifies code structure.

Why not: Accessing the synchronized wrapper instead of the actual collection can make your code significantly slower. When you need to perform operations on multiple elements of a collection, it is preferable to embed all the involved statements in a *SyncLock* (Visual Basic) or *lock* (C#) block.

```
' [Visual Basic]
Dim al As New ArrayList()
' Create a synchronized wrapper.
Dim syncAl As ArrayList = ArrayList.Synchronized(al)

// [C#]
ArrayList al = new ArrayList();
// Create a synchronized wrapper.
ArrayList syncAl = ArrayList.Synchronized(al);
```

26.15 Synchronizing access to Windows Forms objects

Never directly access a property or invoke a method of a System.Windows.Forms.Control object or any object that inherits from this class if there is any chance that the code is running in a thread different from the thread that created the control. If in doubt, check whether the InvokeRequired property of the form returns true and, if this is the case, perform the call using the Invoke method. (You can use the InvokeRequired and Invoke members of either the specific control or the parent form.)

```vb
' [Visual Basic]
Delegate Function GetStringProperty(ByVal ctrl As Control) As String

' This method might run on a non-UI thread.
Sub PerformTask()
   ' Read the Text property of txtUserName control.
   Dim userName As String

   If Not Me.InvokeRequired Then
      ' It is safe to invoke the method directly.
      userName = GetControlText(txtUserName)
   Else
      ' Call the method indirectly by using a delegate.
      Dim args() As Object = {txtUserName}
      userName = CStr(Me.Invoke(New GetStringProperty(AddressOfGetControlText), args))
   End If
   ' userName now contains the value of txtUserName.Text.
   ...
End Sub

Function GetControlText(ByVal ctrl As Control) As String
   Return ctrl.Text
End Function
```

```csharp
// [C#]
delegate string GetStringProperty(Control ctrl);

// This method might run on a non-UI thread.
void PerformTask()
{
   // Read the Text property of txtUserName control.
   string userName;

   if ( ! this.InvokeRequired )
   {
      // It is safe to invoke the method directly.
      userName = GetControlText(txtUserName);
   }
   else
   {
      // Call the method indirectly by using a delegate.
      object[] args = new object[] {txtUserName};
      userName = (string) this.Invoke(new GetStringProperty(GetControlText), args);
   }
```

```
    // userName now contains the value of txtUserName.Text.
    ...
}

string GetControlText(Control ctr)
{
    return ctrl.Text;
}
```

More details: Accessing a control from a thread other than the thread that created it results in an exception under version 2.0 of the .NET Framework (in beta as of this writing). If you consistently query the InvokeRequired property before accessing the control, your code is guaranteed to work also in future versions of the .NET Framework.

26.16 *volatile* fields [C#]

Use the *volatile* keyword to mark fields that should be considered as volatile in a multithread environment. A volatile field is a memory location that can be modified by a hardware device, the operating system, or another thread.

Why: The JIT compiler can (and usually does) use CPU registers to cache values stored in regular (nonvolatile) fields. This optimization technique can deliver wrong results if a value can be modified by a different thread without the compiler knowing. By marking the field as volatile, you disable this optimization and ensure that the value is always read from memory immediately before being used and is immediately written to memory as soon as the corresponding field is assigned.

More details: You can use the *volatile* keyword only with Boolean values, with 8-bit, 16-bit, and 32-bit signed and unsigned integers (and enum types based on one of these integer types), with single-precision floating-point numbers (*float* in C#), with reference values, and with pointer types (in an unsafe context). A volatile field can't be marked with the *readonly* keyword and can't be passed to a method as a *ref* or *out* parameter.

Visual Basic developers and developers working with .NET languages that don't support the *volatile* keyword (or an equivalent keyword) can achieve the same result by means of the Thread.MemoryBarrier method, which flushes the contents of the cache memory to the main memory for the CPU executing the current thread. (See MSDN documentation for more details.)

```
// [C#]
// A volatile field
private volatile int ID = 0;
```

26.17 Thread-safe singleton objects

When authoring a singleton type that exposes static properties and that might be used by multiple threads, use the following coding pattern to ensure that no concurrency issues exist.

```vbnet
' [Visual Basic]
Public Class Singleton
   ' Private constructor to prevent instantiation
   Private Sub New()
   End Sub

   Private Shared m_Value As Singleton
   Private Shared lockObj As New Object

   ' This static property always returns the same Singleton object.
   Public Shared ReadOnly Property Value() As Singleton
      Get
         If m_Value Is Nothing Then
            SyncLock lockObj
               If m_Value Is Nothing Then m_Value = New Singleton
            End SyncLock
         End If
         Return m_Value
      End Get
   End Property
End Class
```

```csharp
// [C#]
public class Singleton
{
   // Private constructor to prevent instantiation
   private Singleton()
   {}

   private static volatile Singleton m_Value;
   private static object lockObj = new object();

   // This static property always returns the same Singleton object.
   public static Singleton Value
   {
      get
      {
         if ( m_Value == null )
         {
            lock ( lockObj )
            {
               if ( m_Value == null )
                  m_Value = new Singleton();
            }
         }
         return m_Value;
      }
   }
}
```

26.18 Synchronizing on multiple objects

Use multiple Mutex objects to synchronize on multiple resources (one Mutex for each resource), and use the WaitAll static method to wait until all of them release the lock.

Why: Using Mutex objects gives you more flexibility than using nested synchronization blocks. Also, you can use the Mutex.WaitAny method to acquire a lock on any object, as soon as any of the resources releases the lock.

Why not: You can't invoke the WaitAll method from Single-Threaded Apartment (STA) threads, such as the threads used in Console or Windows Forms applications.

```
' [Visual Basic]
' These Mutex objects correspond to 3 different resources.
' (They must be visible to the other thread.)
Public m1 As New Mutex()
Public m2 As New Mutex()
Public m3 As New Mutex()

' Acquire and release a Mutex (you can pass an optional timeout).
If m1.WaitOne() Then
    ' The critical section
    ...
    ' Release the Mutex when you're done.
    m1.ReleaseMutex()
End If

' (This code should run in a different thread.)
' Wait until all resources are available.
Mutex.WaitAll(New Mutex() {m1, m2, m3})
```

```
// [C#]
// These Mutex objects correspond to 3 different resources.
// (They must be visible to the other thread.)
public Mutex m1 = new Mutex();
public Muetex m2 = new Mutex();
public Mutex m3 = new Mutex();

// Acquire and release a Mutex (you can pass an optional timeout).
if ( m1.WaitOne() )
{
    // The critical section
    ...
    // Release the Mutex when you're done.
    m1.ReleaseMutex();
}

// (This code should run in a different thread.)
// Wait until all resources are available.
Mutex.WaitAll(new Mutex[] {m1, m2, m3});
```

26.19 ReaderWriterLock objects

User ReaderWriterLock objects instead of Mutex objects when the resource to be synchronized complies with "read-write" semantics and multiple clients can read from the resource even though only one client can write to it.

Why: ReaderWriterLock objects consume fewer resources than Mutex objects.

```vb
' [Visual Basic]
' This object must be visible to all threads.
Public rwl As New ReaderWriterLock()

' This is how you perform a read operation.
rwl.AcquireReaderLock(Timeout.Infinite)
Try
    ' The critical section
    ...
Finally
    rwl.ReleaseReaderLock()
End Try

' This is how you perform a write operation.
rwl.AcquireWriterLock(Timeout.Infinite)
Try
    ' The critical section
    ...
Finally
    rwl.ReleaseWriterLock()
End Try
```

```csharp
// [C#]
// This object must be visible to all threads.
public ReaderWriterLock rwl = new ReaderWriterLock();

// This is how you perform a read operation.
rwl.AcquireReaderLock(Timeout.Infinite);
try
{
    // The critical section
    ...
}
finally
{
    rwl.ReleaseReaderLock();
}

// This is how you perform a write operation.
rwl.AcquireWriterLock(Timeout.Infinite);
try
{
    // The critical section
    ...
}
finally
{
    rwl.ReleaseWriterLock();
}
```

26.20 Base class for threading

Consider using a custom base class to encapsulate all low-level details in thread creation, argument passing, and access to resources that aren't thread-safe. Define a derived class for each job that you want to run in a thread other than the main thread.

More details: In version 1.1 of the .NET Framework, the Thread class doesn't offer a simple way to pass arguments to the routine. (This limitation will be lifted in version 2.0.) The simplest way to work around this limitation is to define a wrapper class that exposes one or more public fields so that you can create an instance of such class, assign its fields, and then start a thread that runs inside that instance. The following code defines a class that you can use as the base type for these wrapper classes.

```vb
' [Visual Basic]
Public MustInherit Class WorkerThreadBase
    ' The argument passed to the Start method
    Private argument As Object

    Public Sub New()
        m_Thread = New Thread(AddressOf StartThread)
    End Sub

    ' The Thread in which this instance is running.
    Private m_Thread As Thread

    Public ReadOnly Property Thread() As Thread
        Get
            Return m_Thread
        End Get
    End Property

    ' Invoke method calls account for any object assigned to this property.
    Private m_SynchronizingObject As ISynchronizeInvoke

    Public Property SynchronizingObject() As ISynchronizeInvoke
        Get
            Return m_SynchronizingObject
        End Get
        Set(ByVal Value As ISynchronizeInvoke)
            m_SynchronizingObject = Value
        End Set
    End Property

    ' Clients call this method to start the thread without any argument.
    Public Sub Start()
        Me.Thread.Start()
    End Sub

    ' Clients call this method to start the thread and pass an argument to it.
    Public Sub Start(ByVal argument As Object)
        Me.argument = argument
        Me.Thread.Start()
    End Sub

    ' This private procedure runs when the secondary thread starts.
    Private Sub StartThread()
        OnStart(argument)
    End Sub

    ' A protected method that can be called from inheritors. If a nonnull object reference
    ' is assigned to SynchronizingObject, the method is invoked in that object's thread.
```

```vb
   Protected Function InvokeMember(ByVal type As Type, ByVal name As String, _
       ByVal invokeAttr As BindingFlags, ByVal target As Object, _
       ByVal args() As Object) As Object
     If m_SynchronizingObject Is Nothing OrElse _
          Not m_SynchronizingObject.InvokeRequired Then
        Return type.InvokeMember(name, invokeAttr, Nothing, target, args)
     Else
        Dim method As New InvokeMemberDelegate(AddressOf InvokeMember)
        Dim args2() As Object = {type, name, invokeAttr, target, args}
        Return m_SynchronizingObject.Invoke(method, args2)
     End If
   End Function


   ' A private delegate that can point to InvokeMember.
   Private Delegate Function InvokeMemberDelegate(ByVal type As Type, ByVal name As String,
_
       ByVal invokeAttr As BindingFlags, ByVal target As Object, _
       ByVal args() As Object) As Object


   ' Inheritors must override this method.
   Protected MustOverride Sub OnStart(ByVal argument As Object)
End Class
```

```csharp
// [C#]
public abstract class WorkerThreadBase
{
   // The argument passed to the Start method
   private object argument;

   protected WorkerThreadBase()
   {
      m_Thread = new Thread(new ThreadStart(StartThread));
   }


   // The Thread in which this instance is running.
   private Thread m_Thread;

   public Thread Thread
   {
      get { return m_Thread; }
   }


   // Invoke method calls account for any object assigned to this property.
   private ISynchronizeInvoke m_SynchronizingObject;

   public ISynchronizeInvoke SynchronizingObject
   {
      get { return m_SynchronizingObject; }
      set { m_SynchronizingObject = value; }
   }


   // Clients call this method to start the thread without any argument.
   public void Start()
   {
      this.Thread.Start();
   }
```

```
// Clients call this method to start the thread and pass an argument to it.
public void Start(object argument)
{
   this.argument = argument;
   this.Thread.Start();
}

// This private procedure runs when the secondary thread starts.
private void StartThread()
{
   OnStart(argument);
}

// A protected method that can be called from inheritors. If a nonnull object reference
// is assigned to SynchronizingObject, the method is invoked in that object's thread.
protected object InvokeMember(Type type, string name,  BindingFlags invokeAttr, object
target, object[] args )
{
   if ( m_SynchronizingObject == null || ! m_SynchronizingObject.InvokeRequired )
   {
      return type.InvokeMember(name, invokeAttr, null, target, args);
   }
   else
   {
      InvokeMemberDelegate method = new InvokeMemberDelegate(InvokeMember);
      object[] args2 = new object[] {type, name, invokeAttr, target, args};
      return m_SynchronizingObject.Invoke(method, args2);
   }
}

// A private delegate that can point to InvokeMember.
private delegate object InvokeMemberDelegate(Type type, string  name,
   BindingFlags invokeAttr, object target, object[] args);

// Inheritors must override this method.
protected abstract void OnStart(object argument);
}
```

The two most intriguing features of the WorkerThreadBase class are its Start method, which can take an argument, and its InvokeMember protected method, which can be used by code in derived classes to access user interface elements in a thread-safe manner (see rule 26.15). Here's a class that inherits from WorkerThreadBase, performs a background operation and displays a message in a Label control when the operation is complete. (See rule 17.21 for more information about the SynchronizingObject property.)

```
' [Visual Basic]
Class MyWorkerThread
   Inherits WorkerThreadBase

   ' This method runs when the client invokes the Start method.
   Protected Overrides Sub OnStart(ByVal argument As Object)
      Dim lbl As Label = DirectCast(argument, Label)
      ' Do something here in the secondary thread
      ...
```

```
                ' Assign the Label's Text property in a thread-safe manner.
                Dim args() As Object = {"Completed"}
                InvokeMember(lbl.GetType(), "Text", BindingFlags.SetProperty, lbl, args)
            End Sub
End Class
```

```
// [C#]
class MyWorkerThread : WorkerThreadBase
{
    // This method runs when the client invokes the Start method.
    protected override void OnStart(object argument )
    {
        Label lbl = (Label) argument;
        // Do something here in the secondary thread
        ...
        // Assign the Label's Text property in a thread-safe manner.
        object[] args = new object[] {"Completed"};
        InvokeMember(lbl.GetType(), "Text", BindingFlags.SetProperty, lbl, args);
    }
}
```

The main application can use the MyWorkerThread class from inside a Windows Forms object as follows:

```
' [Visual Basic]
Dim wt As New MyWorkerThread
' Specify which UI object it must be synchronized with.
wt.SynchronizingObject = Me
' Start the thread, pass a Label as an argument.
wt.Start(Me.lblMessage)
```

```
// [C#]
MyWorkerThread wt = new MyWorkerThread();
// Specify which UI object it must be synchronized with.
wt.SynchronizingObject = this;
// Start the thread, pass a Label as an argument.
wt.Start(this.lblMessage);
```

An important note: A Windows Forms application should never invoke the Join method on the Thread property exposed by a WorkerThreadBase-derived object, because this action would deadlock the application when the code in the secondary thread calls InvokeMember to access user interface elements.

26.21 Asynchronous delegates

Use asynchronous delegates instead of Thread objects in server-side applications and components.

Why: Asynchronous delegates implicitly use threads taken from the thread pool; the thread pool offers higher scalability than Thread objects. (We recommend that you use asynchronous delegates instead of methods of the ThreadPool class.)

More details: Each delegate class exposes three methods in addition to those inherited from the System.MulticastDelegate type: Invoke (for synchronous invocations), BeginInvoke (for asynchronous invocations), and EndInvoke (for completing an asynchronous invocation). The BeginInvoke method takes all the input arguments for the method and returns an IAsync-Result object that you can later pass to the EndInvoke method to complete the method call. (It is mandatory that you call the EndInvoke method even if the method doesn't return a value; otherwise, you'll leak resources.)

Asynchronous delegates offer at least four ways to wait for the completion of a method that runs in a different thread.

   a. **Blocking**   The main thread can invoke the EndInvoke method, which causes the current thread to stop until the other thread terminates.

   b. **Polling**   The main thread can periodically test the IAsynchResult.IsCompleted read-only property to detect when the other thread terminates.

   c. **Waiting**   The main thread can invoke the WaitOne method on the object returned by the IAsyncResult.AsyncWaitHandle property to wait until the other thread terminates (this method takes an optional timeout). Alternatively, the main thread can pass the value returned by the AsyncWaitHandle property as an argument to the WaitAny or WaitAll static methods of the WaitHandle type, if it is necessary to synchronize multiple threads.

   d. **Callback**   The main thread can pass a delegate in the last-but-one argument of the BeginInvoke method; when this delegate is specified, the .NET runtime calls back the application when the other thread terminates.

The following code illustrates how you can implement all the four techniques:

```
' [Visual Basic]
' This is the method that you want to run asynchronously.
Public Function GetAllFiles(ByVal path As String) As String()
   Dim al As New ArrayList
   ' Add all files in this directory and in child directories.
   al.AddRange(Directory.GetFiles(path))
   For Each dir As String In Directory.GetDirectories(path)
      al.AddRange(GetAllFiles(dir))
   Next
   Return DirectCast(al.ToArray(GetType(String)), String())
End Function

' This is a delegate that can point to the GetFiles method.
Delegate Function InvokeGetFiles(ByVal path As String) As String()

' This routine shows how to implement the blocking technique.
Private Sub ShowFiles_Blocking()
   Dim deleg As New InvokeGetFiles(AddressOf GetAllFiles)
   Dim ar As IAsyncResult = deleg.BeginInvoke("c:\windows", Nothing, Nothing)
   ' Next statement blocks the current thread until the other thread terminates.
   Dim files() As String = deleg.EndInvoke(ar)
```

```
      For Each file As String In files
         Console.WriteLine(file)
      Next
   End Sub

   ' This routine shows how to implement the polling technique.
   Private Sub ShowFiles_Polling()
      Dim deleg As New InvokeGetFiles(AddressOf GetAllFiles)
      Dim ar As IAsyncResult = deleg.BeginInvoke("c:\Windows", Nothing, Nothing)
      Do Until ar.IsCompleted
         '  Do something else until the other thread completes.
         ...
      Loop
      Dim files() As String = deleg.EndInvoke(ar)
      For Each file As String In files
         Console.WriteLine(file)
      Next
   End Sub

   ' This routine shows how to implement the waiting technique.
   Private Sub ShowFiles_Waiting()
      Dim deleg As New InvokeGetFiles(AddressOf GetAllFiles)
      Dim ar As IAsyncResult = deleg.BeginInvoke("c:\Windows", Nothing, Nothing)
      Do Until ar.AsyncWaitHandle.WaitOne(100, False)
         ' Do something else until the other thread completes.
         ...
      Loop
      Dim files() As String = deleg.EndInvoke(ar)
      For Each file As String In files
         Console.WriteLine(file)
      Next
   End Sub

   ' This routine shows how to implement the callback technique.
   Private Sub ShowFiles_Callback()
      Dim deleg As New InvokeGetFiles(AddressOf GetAllFiles)
      ' Notice that the last argument is the delegate itself.
      Dim ar As IAsyncResult = deleg.BeginInvoke("c:\Windows", AddressOf GetAllFilesCallback, d
eleg)
   End Sub

   ' This method is called when the asynchronous delegate completes.
   Private Sub GetAllFilesCallback(ByVal ar As IAsyncResult)
      ' Retrieve the delegate object and complete the asynchronous call.
      Dim deleg As InvokeGetFiles = DirectCast(ar.AsyncState, InvokeGetFiles)
      Dim files() As String = deleg.EndInvoke(ar)
      For Each file As String In files
         Console.WriteLine(file)
      Next
   End Sub

// [C#]
// This is the method that you want to run asynchronously.
public string[] GetAllFiles(string path)
{
   ArrayList al = new ArrayList();
   // Add all files in this directory and in child directories.
   al.AddRange(Directory.GetFiles(path));
```

```
      foreach ( string dir in Directory.GetDirectories(path) )
         al.AddRange( GetAllFiles(dir) );
      return (string[]) al.ToArray(typeof(string));
   }

   // This is a delegate that can point to the GetFiles method.
   delegate string[] InvokeGetFiles(string path);

   // This routine shows how to implement the blocking technique.
   private void ShowFiles_Blocking()
   {
      InvokeGetFiles deleg = new InvokeGetFiles(GetAllFiles);
      IAsyncResult ar = deleg.BeginInvoke(@"c:\Windows", null, null);
      // Next statement blocks the current thread until the other thread terminates.
      string[] files = deleg.EndInvoke(ar);
      foreach ( string file in files )
         Console.WriteLine(file);
   }

   // This routine shows how to implement the polling technique.
   private void ShowFiles_Polling()
   {
      InvokeGetFiles deleg = new InvokeGetFiles(GetAllFiles);
      IAsyncResult ar = deleg.BeginInvoke(@"c:\Windows", null, null);
      while ( ! ar.IsCompleted )
      {
         // Do something else until the other thread completes.
         ...
      }
      string[] files = deleg.EndInvoke(ar);
      foreach ( string file in files )
         Console.WriteLine(file);
   }

   // This routine shows how to implement the waiting technique.
   private void ShowFiles_Waiting()
   {
      InvokeGetFiles deleg = new InvokeGetFiles(GetAllFiles);
      IAsyncResult ar = deleg.BeginInvoke(@"c:\Windows", null, null);
      while ( ! ar.AsyncWaitHandle.WaitOne(100, false) )
      {
         // Do something else until the other thread completes.
         ...
      }
      string[] files = deleg.EndInvoke(ar);
      foreach ( string file in files )
         Console.WriteLine(file);
   }

   // This routine shows how to implement the callback technique.
   private void ShowFiles_Callback()
   {
      InvokeGetFiles deleg = new InvokeGetFiles(GetAllFiles);
      // Notice that the last argument is the delegate itself.
      IAsyncResult ar = deleg.BeginInvoke(@"c:\Windows", new AsyncCallback(GetAllFilesCallback)
, deleg);
   }
```

```
// This method is called when the asynchronous delegate completes.
private void GetAllFilesCallback(IAsyncResult ar)
{
   // Retrieve the delegate object and complete the asynchronous call.
   InvokeGetFiles deleg = (InvokeGetFiles) ar.AsyncState;
   string[] files = deleg.EndInvoke(ar);
   foreach ( string file in files )
      Console.WriteLine(file);
}
```

26.22 Expose asychronous methods in your classes

Consider exposing Begin*xxxx* and End*xxxx* variants for each method that clients might want to invoke asynchronously and a Cancel*xxxx* method to let clients abort the operation.

Why: Exposing asynchronous methods (as opposed to forcing clients to call your methods from other threads or using generic asynchronous delegates) simplifies the code that uses your classes. Also, generic asynchronous delegates offer no safe way to cancel an operation, so an explicit Cancel*xxxx* method would actually give clients more flexibility.

Example: The following TextFileReader class exposes a Read method for reading a text file in a synchronous manner and the BeginRead, EndRead, and CancelRead methods to perform the same operation asynchronously.

```
' [Visual Basic]
Public Class TextFileReader
   ' This private delegate matches the signature of the Read method.
   Private Delegate Function InvokeRead(ByVal fileName As String) As String

   ' True if the asynchronous operation has been canceled
   Private canceled As Boolean
   ' A delegate that points to the Read method
   Private deleg As InvokeRead
   ' The object used to control asynchronous operations
   Private ar As IAsyncResult

   ' The Read method (synchronous)
   Public Function Read(ByVal fileName As String) As String
      canceled = False
      Dim sb As New StringBuilder
      Dim sr As StreamReader
      Try
         sr = New StreamReader(fileName)
         While sr.Peek() <> -1
            sb.Append(sr.ReadLine()).Append(ControlChars.CrLf)
            If canceled Then Return Nothing
         End While
         Return sb.ToString()
      Catch ex As Exception
         If Not sr Is Nothing Then sr.Close()
      End Try
   End Function
```

```vbnet
' The following methods add support for asynchronous operations.
Public Sub BeginRead(ByVal fileName As String)
   deleg = New InvokeRead(AddressOf Read)
   ar = deleg.BeginInvoke(fileName, Nothing, Nothing)
End Sub

Public Function EndRead() As String
   If canceled OrElse deleg Is Nothing Then
      Return Nothing
   Else
      Return deleg.EndInvoke(ar)
   End If
End Function

Public Sub CancelRead()
   ' Cause the Read method to exit prematurely.
   canceled = True
End Sub
End Class
```

```csharp
// [C#]
public class TextFileReader
{
    // This private delegate matches the signature of the Read method.
    private delegate string InvokeRead(string fileName);

    // True if the asynchronous operation has been canceled
    private bool canceled;
    // A delegate that points to the Read method
    private InvokeRead deleg;
    // The object used to control asynchronous operations
    private IAsyncResult ar;

    // The Read method (synchronous)
    public string Read(string fileName)
    {
        canceled = false;
        StringBuilder sb = new StringBuilder();

        using ( StreamReader sr = new StreamReader(fileName) )
        {
            // Read the text file one line at the time, exit if canceled.
            while ( sr.Peek() != -1 )
            {
                sb.Append(sr.ReadLine()).Append("\n");
                if ( canceled )
                    return null;
            }
        }
        return sb.ToString();
    }

    // The following methods add support for asynchronous operations.
    public void BeginRead(string fileName)
```

```
      {
         deleg = new InvokeRead(Read);
         ar = deleg.BeginInvoke(fileName, null, null);
      }

      public string EndRead()
      {
         if ( canceled || deleg == null )
            return null;
         else
            return deleg.EndInvoke(ar);
      }

      public void CancelRead()
      {
         // Cause the Read method to exit prematurely.
         canceled = true;
      }
   }
}
```

Here's how you can use the TextFileReader class:

```
' [Visual Basic]
Dim tfr As New TextFileReader
tfr.BeginRead("c:\mydata.txt")
' Perform other tasks while the file is being read.
...
' Retrieve the file contents. (Blocks until the read operation is complete.)
Dim text As String = tfr.EndRead()

// [C#]
TextFileReader tfr = new TextFileReader();
tfr.BeginRead(@"c:\mydata.txt");
// Perform other tasks while the file is being read.
...
// Retrieve the file contents. (Blocks until the read operation is complete.)
string text = tfr.EndRead();
```

26.23 Timers

Favor the System.Threading.Timer type over the System.Timers.Timer type when instantiating a timer object that must truly run in a background thread. Use the System.Windows.Forms.Timer type when you must periodically access a Windows Forms control.

Why: The System.Windows.Forms.Timer type raises its Tick event in the UI-thread, so it is safe to access forms and controls. However, this timer fails to raise events if the UI-thread is busy doing something else. When you absolutely must execute a piece of code periodically, you should use one of the other two timers.

More details: Version 1.1 of the .NET Framework supports as many as three timer types, two of which work similarly and offer the same features (even though they support a different syntax). The beta version of .NET Framework 2.0 that is available as of this writing marks the System.Timers.Timer type as obsolete; therefore, it is recommended that all new applications use the System.Threading.Timer type.

Chapter 27
Windows Forms Applications

System.Windows.Forms is one of the most densely populated namespaces in the Microsoft .NET Framework, so it shouldn't be a surprise that this chapter has so many guidelines. Here we deal with naming conventions as well as programming techniques for beginners and experts. We also cover a few user interface guidelines and illustrate a few tips to avoid common programming mistakes when developing a Windows Forms application.

> **Note** One or more code examples in this chapter assume that the following namespaces have been imported by means of *Imports* (Visual Basic) or *using* (C#) statements:
>
> ```
> Microsoft.Win32
> System.ComponentModel
> System.Diagnostics
> System.Drawing
> System.Drawing.Drawing2D
> System.Globalization
> System.IO
> System.Threading
> System.Windows.Forms
> ```

27.1 Form names

Use the following guidelines for naming form classes:

a. Use the MainForm name for the main form of a Windows Forms application.

b. Use the Form suffix for Windows Forms types that are displayed in modeless fashion (that is, end users can activate other forms in the same application). Example: InvoiceForm.

c. Use the Dialog suffix for Windows Forms types that are displayed modally (that is, end users can't activate other forms in the same application until they dismiss this form). Example: OptionsDialog.

27.2 Loading startup form from Main method

Include an App class that contains a Main static method, and display the startup form from there. Visual Basic developers can use a module instead of a class.

Why: C# developers can start a Windows Forms project only by loading the main form from inside the Main method, as described in this guideline. Putting the Main method inside a class named App (instead of inside the main form's class) enables you to find the method quickly even if you later decide to run another form at startup (for example, when you display a splash screen window).

More details: A Visual Basic project can have a startup form. Creating and displaying the main form of an application explicitly enables you to control additional features—for example, you can invoke the EnableVisualStyles method of the Application object (see rule 27.19).

```
' [Visual Basic]
Module App
   <STAThread()> _
   Sub Main()
      Dim frm As New MainForm
      Application.Run(frm)
   End Sub
End Module

' [C#]
class App
{
   [STAThread]
   static void Main()
   {
      MainForm frm = new MainForm();
      Application.Run(frm);
   }
}
```

27.3 The STAThread attribute

Always mark the entry point of a Windows Forms application with the STAThread attribute.

Why: If this attribute is omitted, the application uses the Multithreaded Apartment Model (MTA) and both Windows Forms and ActiveX controls might not work correctly.

Example: See code example in rule 27.2.

27.4 Windows Forms object and control names

Use prefixes from Table 27-1 for form and control names. (The table includes a couple of ActiveX controls and some components that don't have a user interface.)

Example: frmMain, txtUserName, btnOK.

Table 27-1   Suggested Prefixes for Windows Forms Types

Prefix	Type	Prefix	Type
bnd	Binding	mnu	MainMenu and MenuItem
btn	Button	msk	MaskEditBox (ActiveX)
chk	CheckBox	cal	MonthCalendar
clst	CheckedListBox	not	NotifyIcon
cbo	ComboBox	num	NumericUpDown
ctrl	Control	pnl	Panel
cmnu	ContextMenu	pdoc	PrintDocument
crv	CrystalReportViewer	pic	PictureBox

Table 27-1 Suggested Prefixes for Windows Forms Types

Prefix	Type	Prefix	Type
cur	Cursor	ppc	PrintPreviewControl
dgr	DataGrid	pba	ProgressBar
dgrc	DataGridColumn	pgrd	PropertyGrid
dtp	DateTimePicker	rad	RadioButton
dlg	Dialog controls (OpenFile, etc.)	rtb	RichTextBox
dom	DomainUpDown	spl	Splitter
err	ErrorProvider	sba	StatusBar
frm	Form	tab	TabControl
gbx	GroupBox	txt	TextBox
hlp	HelpProvider	tmr	Timer
hsb	HScrollBar	tba	ToolBar
iml	ImageList	tbtn	ToolBarButton
lbl	Label	tip	ToolTip
lnk	LinkLabel	tba	TrackBar
lst	ListBox	tvn	TreeNode
lvw	ListView	tvw	TreeView
litm	ListViewItem	vsb	VScrollBar
mnu	MainMenu and MenuItem	web	WebBrowser (ActiveX)

27.5 Menu item names and shortcuts

Use a menu structure that resembles popular Windows applications if possible, and use standard text and shortcut values for your MenuItem objects.

Table 27-2 lists some common menu commands and shortcuts that are used in Microsoft Office programs and Visual Studio .NET and that you should attempt to adopt in your applications. Notice that MenuItem names include the name of their parent menu.

Table 27-2 Suggested Names, Captions, and Shortcuts for Common Menu Commands

MenuItem Name	Text	Shortcut
mnuFile	&File	
mnuFileNew	&New	Ctrl+N
mnuFileOpen	&Open ...	Ctrl+O
mnuFileSave	&Save	Ctrl-S
mnuFileSaveAs	Save &As ...	
mnuFileClose	&Close	Ctrl+F4
mnuFileImport	Impor&t and Export ...	
mnuFilePageSetup	Page Set&up	
mnuFilePrintPreview	Print pre&view	
mnuFilePrint	&Print...	Ctrl+P

Table 27-2 **Suggested Names, Captions, and Shortcuts for Common Menu Commands**

MenuItem Name	Text	Shortcut
mnuFileSendTo	Sen&d To	
mnuFileProperties	Propert&ies ...	
mnuFileExit	E&xit	
mnuEdit	&Edit	
mnuEditUndo	&Undo	Ctrl+Z
mnuEditRedo	&Redo	Ctrl+Y
mnuEditCut	Cu&t	Ctrl+X
mnuEditCopy	&Copy	Ctrl+C
mnuEditPaste	&Paste	Ctrl+V
mnuEditPasteSpecial	&Paste &Special ...	
mnuEditDelete	&Delete	Del
mnuEditSelectAll	Select &All	Ctrl+A
mnuEditFind	&Find ...	Ctrl+F
mnuEditReplace	R&eplace ...	Ctrl+H
mnuEditGoto	&Go To ...	Ctrl+G
mnuView	&View	
mnuViewRefresh	&Refresh	F5
mnuViewToolbar	&Toolbar	
mnuViewStatusBar	&StatusBar	
mnuViewHeader	&Header and Footer	
mnuViewRuler	Ru&ler	
mnuViewZoom	&Zoom ...	
mnuViewFullScreen	&Full Screen	Shift+Alt+Enter
mnnuTools	&Tools	
mnuToolsSpelling	&Spelling ...	F7
mnuToolsLanguage	&Language ...	
mnuToolsAddins	&Add-ins ...	
mnuToolsMacros	&Macro	
mnuToolsCustomize	&Customize ...	
mnuToolsOptions	&Options ...	
mnuWindow	&Window	
mnuWindowNew	&New window	
mnuWindowSplit	&Split	
mnuWindowCascade	&Cascade	
mnuWindowTileHor	Tile &Horizontally	
mnuWindowTileVer	Tile &Vertically	

Table 27-2   Suggested Names, Captions, and Shortcuts for Common Menu Commands

MenuItem Name	Text	Shortcut
mnuHelp	&Help	
mnuHelpContents	&Contents ...	Ctrl+Alt+F1
mnuHelpIndex	&Index ...	Ctrl+Alt+F2
mnuHelpSearch	&Search ...	Ctrl+Alt+F3
mnuHelpCheckUpdates	Chec&k for Updates ...	
mnuHelpAbout	&About *appname*	

27.6 GDI+ object names

Use prefixes from Table 27-3 for variables and private fields holding a reference to a GDI+ object.

Example: bmpLogo, clrInk, pntStart.

Table 27-3   Suggested Prefixes for GDI+ Types

Prefix	Type	Prefix	Type
bmp	Bitmap	mfi	Metafile
bru	Brush and derived types	pags	PageSettings
clr	Color	pen	Pen
pal	ColorPalette	pnt	Point, PointF
fnt	Font	pcon	PrintController
gra	Graphics	prns	PrinterSettings
grp	GraphicsPath	rec	Rectangle, RectangleF
ico	Icon	reg	Region
img	Image	siz	Size, SizeF

27.7 Windows component names

Use prefixes from Table 27-4 for variables and private fields holding a reference to common Windows components.

Example: prcWord, repMonthly.

Table 27-4   Suggested Prefixes for Common Windows Components

Prefix	Type	Prefix	Type
ade	DirectoryEntry	pco	PerformanceCounter
ads	DirectorySearcher	prc	Process
fsw	FileSystemWatcher	rep	ReportDocument
evl	EventLog	svc	ServiceController
msq	MessageQueue	tmr	Timer

27.8 ADO.NET Components

Don't drop ADO.NET components on the form's surface. Instead, define one or more classes that expose all the methods you need to query and modify data in the database.

Why: This guideline promotes code reuse and makes it easier to change the application's design later from a traditional client/server, two-tiered architecture into an N-tiered application whose components can be optionally deployed on different computers on the network or even access the database across the Internet.

More details: Visual Studio .NET makes it very simple to create an ADO.NET component—such as a connection or a data adapter—right on the form's surface at design time by dragging it from the Server Explorer window or selecting an element from the Data tab in the Toolbox. Accessing the ADO.NET component from code in the form, however, impedes code reuse and should be avoided even for applications that don't need to be migrated to a more scalable multitiered architecture.

27.9 Control scope

Never expose controls as public members of the form class. Use a public property to let clients access the contents of the control.

Why: Hiding implementation details is one of the axioms of healthy object-oriented programming. By wrapping the control in a property, you can later change the user interface, and possibly use a different kind of control, without affecting the code in clients.

More details: The default control scope is *private* for C# (which is correct) and *Friend* for Visual Basic (which should be changed). Use the Modifiers property of each control to change its scope. (Tip: Select all the controls on the form, and change their Modifiers property in one operation.)

Example: The following code defines a public property that wraps the contents of a TextBox control with private scope. If you later change the implementation of this property (for example, to use a ComboBox control instead of a TextBox control), you need only change the code in this property.

```
' [Visual Basic]
Public Property UserName() As String
   Get
      Return txtUserName.Text
   End Get
   Set(ByVal Value As String)
      txtUserName.Text = Value
   End Set
End Property

// [C#]
public string UserName
{
   get
   {
```

```
        return txtUserName.Text;
    }
    set
    {
        txtUserName.Text = value;
    }
}
```

27.10 Autogenerated code

Never modify the autogenerated code in the InitializeComponent method in a form type. (It is OK to add code in the form's constructor, though, before or after the call to InitializeComponent.)

Why: Your edits would be overwritten as soon as you modify one of the properties in the Visual Studio .NET form designer.

27.11 Business logic

Don't place business logic in form classes. Move business logic code into separate classes.

Why: This technique improves code reuse and prepares for multitiered solutions.

27.12 Resizable forms

Ensure that all the controls resize and move correctly when the end user resizes the form.

How to: Visual Studio .NET and the .NET Framework provide several means to help you manage form resizing with little or no code. You can use the Anchor and Dock properties of child controls for basic resizing; add Panel controls to create containers; handle the form's Resize event; and use Splitter controls to enable the end user to resize one or more controls manually.

27.13 Scrolling and tabbed forms

Use scrolling forms only if you need a large workable area, for example, when displaying images or a print preview. Use a tabbed form—that is, a form with a TabControl on it—to accommodate a large number of controls.

How to: You can create a scrolling form just by setting the form's AutoScroll property to true, and you can adjust its scrolling behavior by means of the AutoScrollMargin and AutoScroll-MinSize properties. At run time, you can ensure that a control is in the viewable window by invoking the form's ScrollControlIntoView method, and you can programmatically scroll the form by setting the AutoScrollPosition property:

```
' [Visual Basic]
' Reset the scroll position.
Me.AutoScrollPosition = New Point(0, 0)

// [C#]
// Reset the scroll position.
this.AutoScrollPosition = new Point(0, 0);
```

27.14 Read control properties from resource files

Consider setting the form's Localizable design-time property to true to force Visual Studio .NET to generate code that reads control properties from resource files, even if you don't need to localize the application.

Why: Even if you don't plan to localize the application for another language any time soon, having all the controls' properties stored in a separate satellite assembly makes it trivial to modify the user interface without recompiling the application. Besides, this technique would enable you to provide different customers with a completely different user interface, again without recompiling your code.

How to: Visual Studio .NET can easily generate a different satellite assembly for each different human language your application supports. Just set the Localizable property to true at design time and Visual Studio .NET 2003 will create a default .resx file named after the form's name (for example, Form1.resx for the Form1 form). If you then change the value of the Language property (see Figure 27-1), Visual Studio .NET creates one or two additional .resx files. More precisely, it creates one .resx file if you select a generic language (e.g., Form1.en.resx for English), or it creates two .resx files if you select a specific language (e.g., Form1.en.resx and Form1.en-US.resx for American English). An important detail: each .resx file contains the values of all the localizable properties (e.g., string, color, position, size values) only if the value for a given locale is different from the value stored in the default .resx.

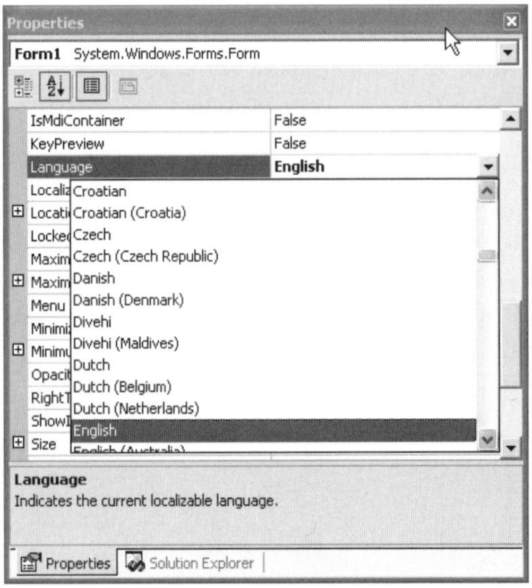

Figure 27-1 Setting the Language property in a localizable form

When the current project is compiled, Visual Studio .NET creates one satellite DLL for each language supported in your application and places these DLLs in appropriate subdirectories of the directory that hosts the main executable. For example, it creates a folder named en for generic English resources and a folder named en-US for American English resources. As explained previously, each satellite assembly contains the resources for a given locale only if the resource value is different from the value stored by the locale-neutral .resx file.

This is how the mechanism works: at run time, the ResourceManager object used to retrieve the actual resource values checks the culture of the current UI thread and looks for the requested resource in the most specific satellite assembly, for example, the one stored in the en-US folder. If not found, the search proceeds with the assembly holding en resources. If the resource isn't found in these two satellite assemblies, the ResourceManager uses the resource stored in the main executable.

By default, the current UI thread's culture is defined as the language used by all operating system menus and resources; for example, it generally is en-US for users in the United States. You can force the ResourceManager to use resources for a specific language by setting the Current-UICulture property of the current thread. For example, the following code forces usage of Italian resources, regardless of which localized version of the Windows operating system has been installed:

```
' [Visual Basic]
<STAThread()> _
Sub Main()
    Thread.CurrentThread.CurrentUICulture = New CultureInfo("it-IT")
    Application.Run(New SplashForm)
End Sub

// [C#]
[STAThread]
static void Main()
{
    Thread.CurrentThread.CurrentUICulture = new CultureInfo("it-IT");
    Application.Run(new SplashForm());
}
```

Resource files aren't just for localization purposes, though. In fact, they are also valuable for customizing the appearance of your forms for different customers without changing the main program, as well as for applying minor visual changes (such as position, size, color, and captions of controls) to meet a given customer's requests without having to redeploy the main executable (see Figure 27-2).

Figure 27-2 You can change the appearance of one or more forms in your applications by deploying a different satellite assembly.

See also: See rule 4.10 for more information about localized resource files.

27.15 Common logic in base forms

Have all the forms in your applications inherit from a base form class you have defined.

Why: This arrangement makes it easier to add common behavior to all the forms in the application. For example, the base form can host a ToolTip and a HelpProvider control, if you want to provide their functionality in all the forms in your application.

Example: The following example illustrates how you can create a base class for your data entry forms in an application (or all your applications, if you define this base class in a shared DLL). The base class defines a new property, named FocusBackColor, and contains an event handler that changes the BackColor property of the control that has the focus and resets it when the focus leaves the control. To create the base class, add a new form and name it DataEntryFormBase, and then add this code to the statements that Visual Studio .NET creates on its own:

```vb
' [Visual Basic]
Public Class DataEntryFormBase
    Inherits System.Windows.Forms.Form

    ...

    ' The FocusBackColor property
    Private m_FocusBackColor As Color

    <Description("The background color of the control that has the input focus")> _
    Public Property FocusBackColor() As Color
        Get
            Return m_FocusBackColor
        End Get
        Set(ByVal Value As Color)
            m_FocusBackColor = Value
        End Set
    End Property

    ' Prepare all event handlers when the form loads.
    Private Sub DataEntryFormBase_Load(ByVal sender As Object, ByVal e As EventArgs) _
            Handles MyBase.Load
        For Each ctrl As Control In GetAllControls(Me)
            ' This condition is true for text box, list box, combo box controls.
            If Color.Equals(ctrl.BackColor, SystemColors.Window) Then
                AddHandler ctrl.Enter, AddressOf Control_Enter
                AddHandler ctrl.Leave, AddressOf Control_Leave
            End If
        Next
    End Sub

    ' Change the background color when the control gets the focus.
    Private Sub Control_Enter(ByVal sender As Object, ByVal e As EventArgs)
        DirectCast(sender, Control).BackColor = Me.FocusBackColor
    End Sub
```

```
    ' Restore the background color when the control loses the focus.
    Private Sub Control_Leave(ByVal sender As Object, ByVal e As EventArgs)
        DirectCast(sender, Control).BackColor = SystemColors.Window
    End Sub

    ' Helper routine that returns all the controls in a container,
    ' including controls nested in other controls
    Private Function GetAllControls(ByVal container As Control) As Control()
        Dim al As New ArrayList
        For Each ctrl As Control In container.Controls
            al.Add(ctrl)
            al.AddRange(GetAllControls(ctrl))
        Next
        Return DirectCast(al.ToArray(GetType(Control)), Control())
    End Function
End Class

' [C#]
public class DataEntryFormBase : System.Windows.Forms.Form
{
    // The FocusBackColor property
    private Color m_FocusBackColor = Color.Yellow;

    [Description("The background color of the control that has the input focus")]
    public Color FocusBackColor
    {
        get { return m_FocusBackColor; }
        set { m_FocusBackColor = value; }
    }

    // (This is the handler of the Form.Load event.)
    // Prepare all event handlers when the form loads.
    private void DataEntryFormBase_Load(object sender, EventArgs e)
    {
        foreach ( Control ctrl in GetAllControls(this) )
        {
            // This condition is true for text box, list box, combo box controls.
            if ( Color.Equals(ctrl.BackColor, SystemColors.Window) )
            {
                ctrl.Enter += new EventHandler(Control_Enter);
                ctrl.Leave += new EventHandler(Control_Leave);
            }
        }
    }

    // Change the background color when the control gets the focus.
    private void Control_Enter(object sender, EventArgs e)
    {
        (sender as Control).BackColor = this.FocusBackColor ;
    }
```

```
// Restore the background color when the control loses the focus.
private void Control_Leave(object sender, EventArgs e)
{
    (sender as Control).BackColor = SystemColors.Window ;
}

// Helper routine that returns all the controls in a container,
// including controls nested in other controls
private Control[] GetAllControls(Control container)
{
    ArrayList al = new ArrayList();
    foreach ( Control ctrl in container.Controls )
    {
        al.Add(ctrl);
        al.AddRange(GetAllControls(ctrl));
    }
    return (Control[]) al.ToArray(typeof(Control));
}
}
```

Compile the current project, select Add Inherited Form from the Project menu, enter the name of the form that you want to inherit from DataEntryFormBase, for example, OrderForm, and click the Open button. In the Inheritance Picker window that appears (see Figure 27-3), select the DataEntryFormBase element, and click the OK button.

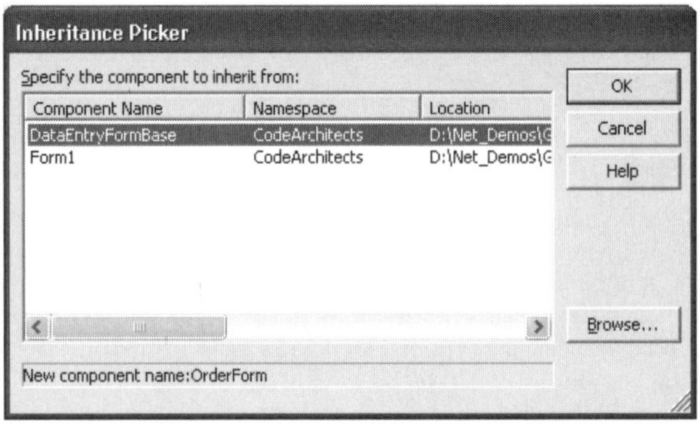

Figure 27-3   The Inheritance Picker dialog box

The form that you have just created exposes a property named FocusBackColor, which specifies the background color of the control that has the input focus (see Figure 27-4). You can now drop controls on this form as you'd do with a standard form. When the application runs, the control that has the focus will be highlighted with the color you've assigned to the FocusBackColor property (see Figure 27-5).

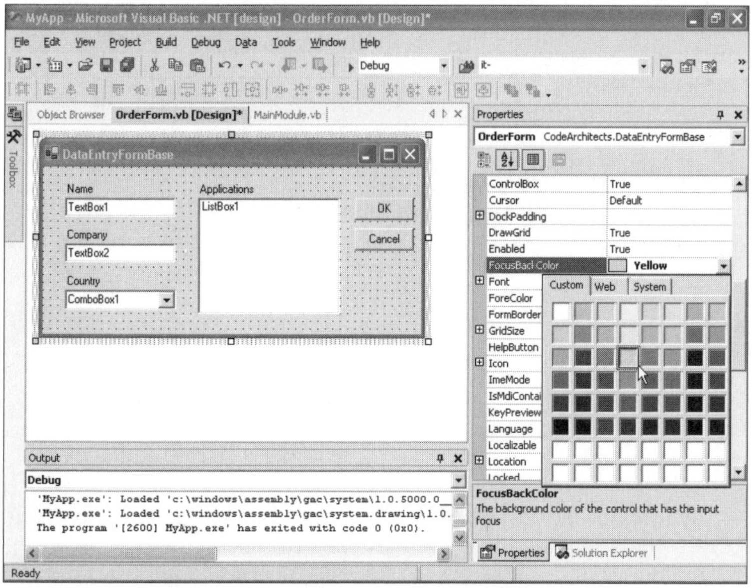

Figure 27-4   All forms that derive from DataEntryFormBase expose the FocusBackColor property.

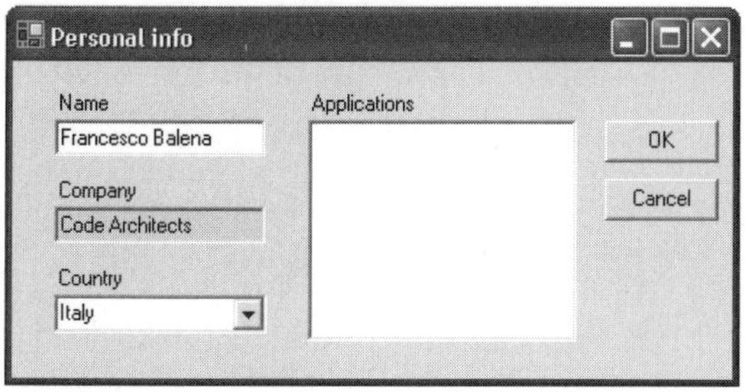

Figure 27-5   The control with the input focus has a different background color at run time.

27.16 Tool windows

Display floating tool windows and palette windows by invoking the main form's AddOwned-Form method.

Why: An owned form always appears in front of its owner, and it is automatically closed when the owner form is closed (see Figure 27-6).

More details: Forms used as floating tool windows should have their FormBorderStyle property set to either FixedToolWindow or SizableToolWindow. You can set this property at design time or run time.

```
' [Visual Basic]
Dim frm As New ColorPaletteForm
frm.FormBorderStyle = FormBorderStyle.FixedToolWindow
Me.AddOwnedForm(frm)
frm.Show()
```

```
// [C#]
ColorPaletteForm frm = new ColorPaletteForm();
frm.FormBorderStyle = FormBorderStyle.FixedToolWindow;
this.AddOwnedForm(frm);
frm.Show();
```

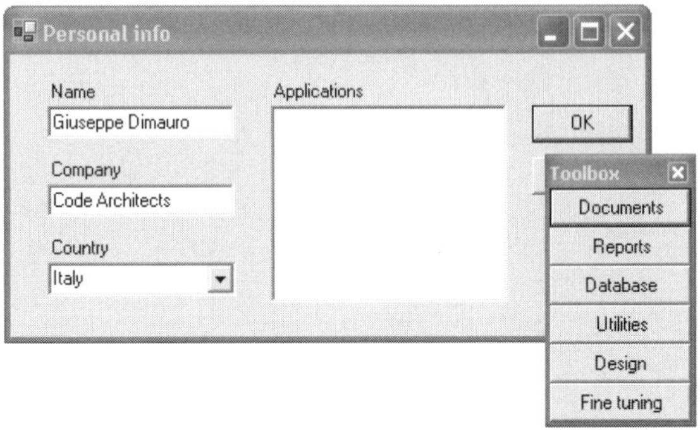

Figure 27-6   An owned window always appears in front of the owner window and is automatically closed when the owner window closes.

27.17 The DialogResult property

Favor setting the form's DialogResult property from the code that handles a Button Click event rather than assigning a value to the DialogResult property of the Button control at design time.

Why: Setting the DialogResult property in code is preferable, especially when creating a form that might be used as a base class for other forms (see rule 27.15). For example, consider the following code:

```
' [Visual Basic]
Private Sub btnOK_Click(ByVal sender As Object, ByVal e As EventArgs) Handles btnOK.Click
   OnButtonOKClick(e)
End Sub

Protected Overridable Sub OnButtonOKClick(ByVal e As EventArgs)
   ' Process data in form's fields here...
   ...
   ' Close the form, let clients know that the OK button was clicked.
   Me.DialogResult = DialogResult.OK
End Sub

// [C#]
private void btnOK_Click(object sender, EventArgs e)
{
   OnButtonOKClick(e);
}

protected virtual void OnButtonOKClick(EventArgs e)
{
   // Process data in form's fields here...
   ...
```

```
    // Close the form, let clients know that the OK button was clicked.
    this.DialogResult = DialogResult.OK;
}
```

Because you process the fields on the form inside a virtual method, a derived class can override the OnButtonOKClick procedure and perform other tasks or additional validation code, as in this example:

```
' [Visual Basic]
' (In a derived form class)
Protected Overrides Sub OnButtonOKClick(ByVal e As EventArgs)
    ' Check whether the password field is long enough.
    If txtPassword.Text.Length > 8 Then
        ' Process fields as usual, then close the form.
        MyBase.OnButtonOKClick(e)
    Else
        ' Display a message, keep the form open.
        MessageBox.Show("Password is too short")
    End If
End Sub
```

```
// [C#]
// (In a derived form class)
protected override void OnButtonOKClick(EventArgs e)
{
    // Check whether the password field is long enough.
    if ( txtPassword.Text.Length > 8 )
    {
        // Process fields as usual, then close the form.
        base.OnButtonOKClick(e);
    }
    else
    {
        // Display a message, keep the form open.
        MessageBox.Show("Password is too short");
    }
}
```

27.18 The MsgBox command [Visual Basic]

Avoid MsgBox commands (located in the Microsoft.VisualBasic assembly) in favor of .NET native MessageBox.Show methods.

27.19 Support for Windows XP Themes

Invoke the Application.EnableVisualStyles method to display forms and controls according to the current Microsoft Windows XP theme.

More details: As a cautionary measure, invoke the Application.DoEvents method immediately after the EnableVisualStyles method. If you omit this step, you might experience strange behaviors, including memory leaks and unexpected exceptions. You can read more about this bug at *http://www.codeproject.com/buglist/EnableVisualStylesBug.asp.*

```
' [Visual Basic]
<STAThread()> _
Sub Main(ByVal args() As String)
   Application.EnableVisualStyles()
   Application.DoEvents()
   Application.Run(New MainForm)
End Function

// [C#]
[STAThread]
static void Main(string[] args)
{
   Application.EnableVisualStyles();
   Application.DoEvents();
   Application.Run(new MainForm());
}
```

After invoking the EnableVisualStyles method, the majority of Windows Forms controls adopt the Windows XP style automatically, including the TextBox, ListBox, ComboBox, Data-Grid, TreeView, ListView, ProgressBar, TrackBar, DateTimePicker, MonthCalendar, TabControl, and the two scroll bar controls. The four controls that inherit from ButtonBase class—namely, Button, CheckBox, RadioButton, and GroupBox—take the new style only if you set their FlatStyle property to System. Notice that a few controls aren't affected at all by the EnableVisualStyles method, including the Label, LinkLabel, NumericUpDown, DomainUp-Down, and CheckListBox. (See Figure 27-7.)

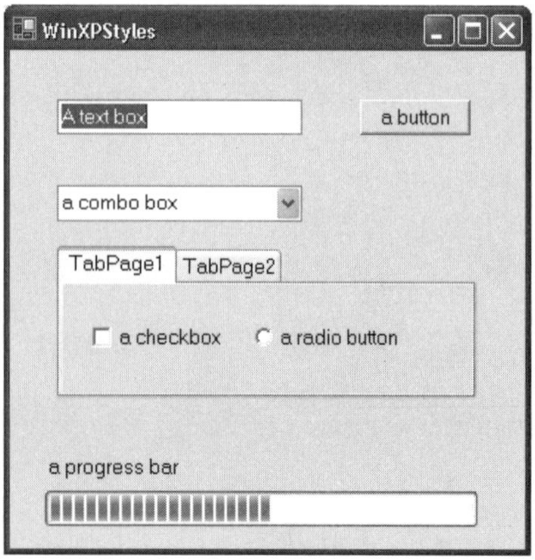

Figure 27-7   A form that uses Windows XP themes

27.20 Caption for MDI forms

Display the name of the current document followed by a dash and the name of the application in the title bar of MDI parent windows. Use a generic name for documents that haven't been saved yet, for example, Document1 or Project1.

How to: Assign the new caption in the handler of the MdiChildActivate event in the form class.

27.21 Menu and toolbar commands

Avoid performing an action in the Click event handler of MenuItem controls. Instead, the code inside such handlers should just delegate to a protected overridable method.

Why: This technique ensures that you can also invoke the menu action from the ButtonClick event of a Toolbar control, and it also ensures that inherited forms can override the protected method to redefine what the menu command or the toolbar command does.

More details: You should also consider the opportunity of having a single method that handles the Click event for all the menus in your form and that delegates to the protected overridable method. Such an arrangement reduces the amount of code that you write for each form. Here's a code example that uses a centralized handler for all menu items, a handler for clicks on all the buttons in a toolbar, and a set of On-prefixed methods that contain the actual code that serves these clicks:

```vb
' [Visual Basic]
' A recursive method that sets the handler for the Click event
' of all the menu items in a form
Private Sub SetMenuHandlers(ByVal parentMenu As Menu, ByVal handler As EventHandler)
    For Each mnu As MenuItem In parentMenu.MenuItems
        AddHandler mnu.Click, handler
        SetMenuHandlers(mnu, handler)
    Next
End Sub


' Set all the menu handlers when the form loads.
Private Sub Form1_Load(ByVal sender As Object, ByVal e As EventArgs) Handles MyBase.Load
    SetMenuHandlers(Me.Menu, AddressOf MenuItem_Click)
End Sub


' This is where all menu clicks are served.
Private Sub MenuItem_Click(ByVal sender As Object, ByVal e As EventArgs)
    If sender Is mnuFileOpen Then
        OnFileOpenClick(e)
    ElseIf sender is mnuFileSave Then
        OnFileSaveClick(e)
    ElseIf sender is mnuFileExit Then
        ' Serve all remaining menu items here.
        ...
    Else
        MessageBox.Show("Not yet implemented")
    End If
End Sub


' This is where all buttons in the toolbar control are served.
Private Sub tbaMain_ButtonClick(ByVal sender As Object, _
        ByVal e As ToolBarButtonClickEventArgs) Handles tbaMain.ButtonClick
    If e.Button Is tbtnFileOpen Then
        OnFileOpenClick(e)
    ElseIf e.Button Is tbtnFileSave Then
        OnFileSaveClick(e)
```

```
      ElseIf e.Button Is tbtnFileExit Then
         ' Serve all remaining toolbar buttons here.
         ...
      Else
         MessageBox.Show("Not yet implemented")
      End If
   End Sub

   Protected Overridable Sub OnFileOpenClick(ByVal e As EventArgs)
      ' Code for the File-Open command here.
   End Sub

   Protected Overridable Sub OnFileSaveClick(ByVal e As EventArgs)
      ' Code for the File-Save command here.
   End Sub

   // [C#]
   // A recursive method that sets the handler for the Click event
   // of all the menu items in a form
   private void SetMenuHandlers(Menu parentMenu, EventHandler handler)
   {
      foreach ( MenuItem mnu in parentMenu.MenuItems )
      {
         mnu.Click += handler;
         SetMenuHandlers(mnu, handler);
      }
   }

   // Set all the menu handler when the form loads.
   private void Form1_Load(object sender, EventArgs e)
   {
      SetMenuHandlers(this.Menu, new EventHandler(MenuItem_Click));
   }

   // This is where all menu clicks are served.
   private void MenuItem_Click(object sender, EventArgs e)
   {
      if ( sender == mnuFileOpen )
         OnFileOpenClick(e);
      else if ( sender == mnuFileSave )
         OnFileSaveClick(e);
      else if ( sender == mnuFileExit )
         // Serve all remaining menu items here.
      else
         MessageBox.Show("Not yet implemented");
   }

   // This is where all buttons in the toolbar control are served.
   private void tbaMain_ButtonClick(object sender, ToolBarButtonClickEventArgs e)
   {
      if ( e.Button == tbtnFileOpen )
         OnFileOpenClick(e);
      else if ( e.Button == tbtnFileSave )
         OnFileSaveClick(e);
      else if ( e.Button == tbtnFileExit )
         // Serve all remaining toolbar buttons here.
      else
```

```
        MessageBox.Show("Not yet implemented");
}

protected virtual void OnFileOpenClick(EventArgs e)
{
    // Code for the File-Open command here.
}

protected virtual void OnFileSaveClick(EventArgs e)
{
    // Code for the File-Save command here.
}
```

27.22 Help for individual controls

All forms should host a HelpProvider control that displays the description of the current control on the form when the end user presses the F1 key (see Figure 27-8).

Tip: You can use a base form that hosts the HelpProvider control and inherits all the forms in your application, as explained in rule 27.15.

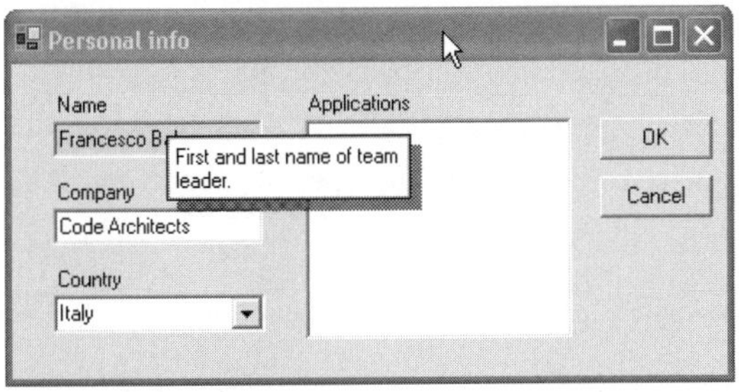

Figure 27-8   Providing field-level help with the HelpProvider control

27.23 TabIndex ordering

Ensure that controls on the form have a correct value for their TabIndex property.

Tip: You can use the Tab Order command on the View menu to assign the TabIndex property quickly and in a visual manner (see Figure 27-9).

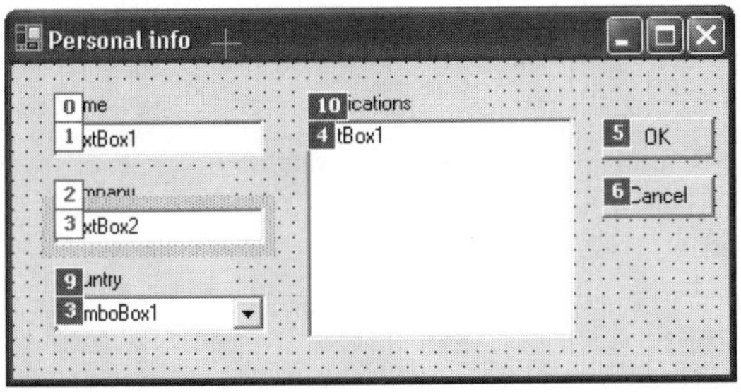

Figure 27-9   The Tab Order command enables you to assign the TabIndex property by clicking each control on the form at design time.

27.24 Control accelerator keys

Ensure that controls on a form have a unique accelerator key and that the accelerator key doesn't clash with the hot key associated with one of the top-level menus.

More details: Hot keys are the Alt+*key* combinations that are assigned by embedding an & (ampersand) character in the control's Text property; don't confuse them with shortcuts, which are key combinations assigned to menu commands (such as the Ctrl+N key that is often associated with the New command on the File menu).

For the following controls, a control's accelerator key is the character that follows the & character in its Text property: Label, LinkLabel, CheckBox, Button, RadioButton, and GroupBox. The TabControl has multiple accelerator keys, one for each of its tab pages. For all other visible controls, the accelerator key is equal to the accelerator key of the Label or LinkLabel control that comes immediately before it in the TabIndex order.

27.25 The UseMnemonic property

Set the UseMnemonic property to false for all Label controls whose value is bound to a data source or, more generally, is assigned at run time.

Why: If you leave this property set to true (the default value), any ampersand character in the data source is mistakenly interpreted as a way to define that the character that follows it is a hot key (see rule 27.24).

27.26 Control validation

Use the Validating event to validate the contents of each control when the user moves the focus away from it, but never omit validating all the controls on the form when the end user clicks the OK or Save button. Use an ErrorProvider control to mark controls visually whose content is invalid, but never cancel the focus shift.

Why: The Validating event is raised only if the control receives and then loses the input focus. If the end user never visits the control, this event is never raised and you might mistakenly consider empty fields as valid.

See also: See rule 27.27.

27.27 The CausesValidation property

Set the CausesValidation property to false for all the controls that shouldn't cause a Validating event for the control that currently has the input focus.

Example: The Cancel, Close, and Help push buttons should have their CausesValidation property set to false.

27.28 Appending text to a text box

Use the AppendText method instead of string concatenation to append text to the current contents of a TextBox or RichTextBox control.

Why: This method is much faster than string concatenation and doesn't tax the garbage collector.

```
' [Visual Basic]
' *** Wrong
txtNotes.Text &= "--- end of notes"
' *** Correct
txtNotes.AppendText("--- end of notes")

// [C#]
// *** Wrong
txtNotes.Text += "--- end of notes";
// *** Correct
txtNotes.AppendText("--- end of notes");
```

27.29 Multilined text boxes

Set the AcceptsTabs and AcceptsReturns properties of a multilined TextBox control or a Rich-TextBox control to enable users to enter tabs and carriage returns in the control.

More details: The RichTextBox control supports only the AcceptsTabs property.

27.30 Global error handlers

Implement global error handlers for Windows Forms applications to recover from (or just ignore) unhandled exceptions. Alternatively, use a global error handler to display a Send Report dialog box to end users, asking them whether they want to send a detailed report of the error condition by e-mail (as many Microsoft applications do).

How to: You can intercept exceptions that would otherwise be fatal for the application by handling the ThreadException event of the Application object. The event handler must account for cases when the application is so unstable that even message boxes can't be displayed correctly and should adopt the technique described in the following code example:

```
' [Visual Basic]
Function Main(ByVal args() As String) As Integer
    ' Install the event handler and run the startup form.
    AddHandler Application.ThreadException, AddressOf Application_ThreadException
    Application.Run(New MainForm)
End Sub

' This is the global error handler.
Sub Application_ThreadException(ByVal sender As Object, _
      ByVal e As ThreadExceptionEventArgs)
    Try
        ' Prepare an informative message.
```

```vb
        Dim msg As String = String.Format("An error has occurred:{0}{0}{1}{0}{0}{2}", _
            ControlChars.Cr, e.Exception.Message, e.Exception.StackTrace)
        ' Ask users whether they want to terminate the application.
        Dim result As DialogResult = MessageBox.Show(msg, "Application Error", _
            MessageBoxButtons.AbortRetryIgnore, MessageBoxIcon.Error)
        ' End the application if the end user said so.
        If result = DialogResult.Abort Then Application.Exit()
    Catch
        ' If the message box couldn't be displayed (presumably because
        ' the Exception object wasn't available), try with a simpler
        ' message, and then close the application anyway.
        Try
            MessageBox.Show("The application will be terminated", "Fatal Error", _
                MessageBoxButtons.OK, MessageBoxIcon.Error)
        Finally
            Application.Exit()
        End Try
    End Try
End Sub


// [C#]
static int Main(string[] args)
{
    // Install the event handler and run the startup form.
    Application.ThreadException +=
        new ThreadExceptionEventHandler(Application_ThreadException);
    Application.Run(new MainForm());
}


// This is the global error handler.
static void Application_ThreadException(object sender, ThreadExceptionEventArgs e)
{
    try
    {
        // Prepare an informative message.
        string msg = String.Format("An error has occurred:\n\n{0}\n\n{1}",
            e.Exception.Message, e.Exception.StackTrace);
        // Ask users whether they want to terminate the application.
        DialogResult result = MessageBox.Show(msg, "Application Error",
            MessageBoxButtons.AbortRetryIgnore, MessageBoxIcon.Error);
        // End the application if the end user said so.
        if ( result == DialogResult.Abort )
            Application.Exit();
    }
    catch
    {
        // If the message box couldn't be displayed (presumably because
        // the Exception object wasn't available), try with a simpler
        // message, and then close the application anyway.
        try
        {
            MessageBox.Show("The application will be terminated", "Fatal Error",
                MessageBoxButtons.OK, MessageBoxIcon.Error);
        }
        finally
```

```
        {
            Application.Exit();
        }
    }
}
```

More details: Global error handlers don't work when the application runs inside a debugger. To see this feature in action, you should run the program using the Start Without Debugging command on the Debug menu (which corresponds to the Ctrl+F5 key combination) or run it from Windows Explorer or the command prompt.

27.31 React to screen resolution changes

Use the SystemEvents object to run code when the screen resolution changes if the application is expected to resize its forms and controls when this happens.

More details: If your application is meant to run on Tablet PCs, you should be ready to handle nonstandard resolutions in which the screen is rotated by 90 degrees (typically, this corresponds to the 768×1024 resolution). For example, your dialog boxes should be never larger than 768×768 pixels. (Better, they shouldn't even approach this size.)

```vb
' [Visual Basic]
Private Sub Form1_Load(ByVal sender As Object, ByVal e As EventArgs) Handles MyBase.Load
    AddHandler SystemEvents.DisplaySettingsChanged, AddressOf DisplaySettingsChanged
End Sub

Private Sub DisplaySettingsChanged(ByVal sender As Object, ByVal e As EventArgs)
    ' React to screen resolution changes here...
End Sub
```

```csharp
// [C#]
private void Form1_Load(object sender, EventArgs e)
{
    SystemEvents.DisplaySettingsChanged += new EventHandler(DisplaySettingsChanged);
}

private void DisplaySettingsChanged(object sender, EventArgs e)
{
    // React to screen resolution changes here...
}
```

27.32 Lengthy operations

Display the hourglass cursor while performing an operation that might last for more than a couple of seconds. If the operation lasts for more than 5 seconds, use a ProgressBar control to display completion status.

```vb
' [Visual Basic]
Try
    Me.Cursor = Cursors.WaitCursor
    ' Lengthy operation here.
    ...
```

```
Finally
   Me.Cursor = Cursors.Default
End Try

// [C#]
try
{
   this.Cursor = Cursors.WaitCursor;
   // Lengthy operation here.
   ...
}
finally
{
   this.Cursor = Cursors.Default;
}
```

You can also write a disposable type that remembers the current cursor shape and restores it when the object is disposed:

```
' [Visual Basic]
Public Class HourglassCursor
   Implements IDisposable
   Private saveCursor As Cursor

   Public Sub New()
      saveCursor = Cursor.Current
      Cursor.Current = Cursors.WaitCursor
   End Sub

   Public Sub Dispose() Implements Idisposable.Dispose
      Cursor.Current = saveCursor
   End Sub
End Class

// [C#]
public class HourglassCursor : IDisposable
{
   private Cursor saveCursor;

   public HourglassCursor()
   {
      saveCursor = Cursor.Current;
      Cursor.Current = Cursors.WaitCursor;
   }

   public void Dispose()
   {
      Cursor.Current = saveCursor;
   }
}
```

You can use the HourglassCursor class from all .NET languages, but it is especially effective from inside C# applications, thanks to the *using* keyword:

```
' [Visual Basic]
Dim cur As New HourglassCursor
Try
   ' Lengthy operation here
   ...
Finally
   cur.Dispose()
End Try

// [C#]
using ( new HourglassCursor() )
{
   // Lengthy operation here
   ...
}
```

27.33 The DoEvents method

Don't use the Application.DoEvents method as a cheap way not to freeze the user interface during lengthy operations. Instead, run the operation on a separate thread.

Why: The DoEvents method allows the Windows operating system to process messages in the message queue, which in turn can raise events in your application and cause reentrancy issues.

More details: If you call the Application.DoEvents method, at least ensure that the end user can't reenter the same code that is executing the lengthy operation. The simplest way to do so is by disabling all the buttons and menu commands that might reenter the method that is executing the lengthy operation.

See also: See rule 26.15 for an example of how to access user interface elements from a non-UI thread.

27.34 The AccessibleName property

Always assign a unique value to the AccessibleName property of all the TextBox, ComboBox, and other editable controls in your application.

Why: This guideline has two benefits. First, it ensures that your application complies with the Microsoft Active Accessibility architecture and works well with users that use alternative input devices. Second, a unique value for the AccessibleName property makes it possible to associate the control with a specific input scope by means of a context mapping (.ctm) file. An *input scope* defines what kind of text a control can contain (numbers, dates, words, etc.) and helps the Tablet PC handwriting recognizer to interpret input from the end user.

More details: You can create a .ctm file by means of the Context Tagging tool, which ships with the Table PC Platform SDK. The great thing about this tool is that it extends your application with support for the Tablet PC without even the need to recompile it. You can read more about context mapping files and the Context Tagging tool at this address: *http://msdn.microsoft.com/mobility/tabletpc/default.aspx?pull=/library/en-us/dntab101/html/tab101c02.asp.*

27.35 Using the registry

Favor configuration files instead of the system registry as a place for storing application-related data that doesn't change often.

Why: Storing data in the registry makes installation more complicated (it doesn't comply with XCOPY deployment). Also, if the program isn't running in a fully trusted context, code might not have the permission to read from or write to the registry.

More details: If you decide to use the registry, account for the following guidelines, excerpted from the Designed for Microsoft Windows XP specifications:

- The HKEY_CURRENT_USER (HKCU) registry hive is appropriate for storing small amounts of data (approximately 64 KB) and for policy settings that are per user.

- Avoid writing to HKEY_LOCAL_MACHINE (HKLM) at run time because limited users have read-only access to the entire HKLM tree by default. In addition, HKLM does not support roaming.

- Larger, file-based data should be placed in the Application Data folder (see rule 24.4). For example, Microsoft Internet Explorer's Temporary Internet cache is stored within the user profile and not in the registry.

- At installation time, the application must not store more than a total of 128 KB across HKCU and HKLM.

- Don't store any data in the HKEY_CLASSES_ROOT key, except for keys that create file associations (see rule 24.8).

27.36 Previous application instances

Define the behavior of the application if the user launches it when another instance of the application is already running, possibly in a desktop associated with another local user (if the Windows XP Fast Switching User feature is enabled) or a remote user.

More details: At the very minimum, an application that claims to support multiple users at the same time should save user data in different directories (see rule 24.4). In addition, you must also define exactly what happens when a user runs the application when another instance is already running. The following list shows some of the possibilities:

a. The new instance runs with all its features enabled.

b. The new instance runs with some features disabled; in this case you should display a message that explains which features aren't available and why. You should also disable the corresponding UI items (such as menu and toolbar items).

c. The new instance exits immediately but passes its command line to the previous instance so that the previous instance can process the data. (This option is especially useful if the application has registered a file extension and the user can run the application by double-clicking a file in Windows Explorer.)

d. The new instance can't run; in this case you should display a message that explains what is happening and why.

These four cases become eight if you also want to account for the Windows XP Fast Switching User feature and for remote users using Terminal Services, because you must define what happens if another instance is running in a different desktop.

How to: The first thing you need to do to comply with this guideline is detect whether another instance of the same application is running. Traditionally, developers have used the FindWindow API function to detect whether a window with a given caption is already opened, but this technique fails to reveal instances running in a different user's session under Windows XP. The Process.GetProcessesByName static method provides an alternative approach that doesn't require a call to unmanaged code and can detect application instances in different user sessions. The following function returns the Process instance that represents a previous instance of the current application; if there is no previous instance, it returns *Nothing* (Visual Basic) or *null* (C#):

```
' [Visual Basic]
Public Function PreviousInstance() As Process
   For Each p As Process In Process.GetProcessesByName(Application.ProductName)
      If p.Id <> Process.GetCurrentProcess().Id Then Return p
   Next
   Return Nothing
End Function

// [C#]
Public Process PreviousInstance()
{
   foreach (Process p in Process.GetProcessesByName(Application.ProductName))
   {
      if ( p.Id != Process.GetCurrentProcess().Id )
         return p;
   }
   return null;
}
```

Notifying the previous instance that a new instance has been launched is slightly more difficult. You can implement a data-passing mechanism based on the TcpClient and TcpListener classes, provided that you can ensure that the IP port used by the communication mechanism isn't used by any other program (you should let the user select the port number by modifying an entry in the .config file). Alternatively, you can use the SendMessage Windows API function to send a string to the other application's main window by means of a WM_COPYDATA message; in this case, the application's main window must override the WndProc procedure to intercept this message and process the incoming data appropriately.

See also: Read the Microsoft Knowledge Base article at *http://support.microsoft.com/?kbid=841291* for more information about how your code can receive session-switch notifications and activate a previous instance by using the MainWindowHandle property of the Process type and a few Windows API functions. (This article covers only Visual Basic.)

27.37 Browsable properties in controls and components

Either mark a public property in a component class or Windows Forms control class with the Browsable(false) attribute or decorate it with the Description and Category attributes.

More details: All read-only properties should be marked with the Browsable(false) attribute; otherwise, they will be unavailable in the Properties window.

```
' [Visual Basic]
<Description("The name of current user"), _  Category("Data")> _
Public Property UserName() As String    ...
End Property

// [C#]
[Description("The name of current user")]
[Category("Data")]
public string UserName
{    ...
}
```

Chapter 28

ADO.NET Programming

Virtually all business applications have to deal with databases. ADO.NET can access databases in two different modes: the connected approach (mostly based on Command and DataReader objects) and the disconnected approach (where you typically use DataAdapter and DataSet objects). The information in this chapter should help you to decide which approach is more suitable in any given situation and how you can leverage ADO.NET to its full potential.

In this chapter, you'll also learn about some common programming mistakes that might have far-reaching consequences, for example, omitting using transactions when you update the database (and in some cases even when you read it). We also cover a few guidelines that are more related to database design, such as how to properly select a primary key or decide whether to use a stored procedure. There are a lot of hard-learned lessons in this chapter, and we hope this information can save you some time and help you build more robust applications.

> **Note** One or more code examples in this chapter assume that the following namespaces have been imported by means of *Imports* (Visual Basic) or *using* (C#) statements:
>
> ```
> System.Data
> System.Data.OleDb
> System.Data.SqlClient
> System.Globalization
> System.IO
> ```

28.1 ADO.NET object names

Use a prefix from Table 28-1 for variables and private fields holding a reference to common ADO.NET objects.

Example: dsNorthwind, cmdSelect.

Table 28-1   Prefixes for Common ADO.NET Types

Prefix	Type	Prefix	Type
clm	ColumnMapping	ds	DataSet
cn	Connection (generic)	dt	DataTable
cmd	Command (generic)	dv	DataView
da	DataAdapter	par	Parameter (generic)
dc	DataColumn	tran	Transaction (generic)
dr	DataReader (generic)	tbm	TableMapping
dro	DataRow		

Notice that the same prefix is used for all objects of the same type (for example, OleDbConnection, SqlConnection), regardless of the specific provider they belong to.

28.2 Error handling for database operations

Always protect database operations from unhandled exceptions. Never assume that the database server is running and is reachable. If you open a connection in a *Try* (Visual Basic) or *try* (C#) block, close it in the *Finally* or *finally* block, respectively.

More details: C# developers can use *using* blocks to ensure that the connection is correctly closed, even if an exception is thrown.

> **Note**   Many ADO.NET objects expose the IDisposable interface and should be explicitly closed after use. The list of such objects includes Connection, Command, DataReader, and DataAdapter. You should always use these objects in *Try...Finally* (Visual Basic), *try...finally* or *using* (C#) blocks to ensure that the object is disposed of as soon as possible.

28.3 Native .NET data providers

Favor using native Microsoft .NET Framework data providers—such as the Microsoft SQL Server .NET Data Provider and the Oracle .NET Data Provider—instead of the more generic OLEDB and ODBC data providers.

Why: Native .NET data providers perform better and enable you to leverage the full potential of the target database.

28.4 Provider-agnostic code

Use ADO.NET base classes and interfaces where possible to create provider-agnostic code.

Why: By definition, provider-agnostic code works well with different .NET data providers and therefore simplifies code reuse and the migration to other databases.

Why not: Not all the features of a given database are available through a generic base class or interface. For example, when working with a SqlTransaction object using an IDbTransaction variable, you can't use named transactions.

In most cases you can't use a generic provider-agnostic approach because the SQL syntax is too different among databases and providers. For example, the syntax for command parameters is different (? for OleDbCommand objects, @-prefixed names for SqlCommand objects), as is the way stored procedures are handled.

Example: The following method is an example of how you can implement provider-agnostic coding techniques. The method checks whether the input connection string references the Microsoft.Jet.OleDb provider, and in that case it creates and returns an OleDbConnection;

otherwise, it interprets the connection string as pointing to a Microsoft SQL Server database, and thus returns a SqlConnection object. You can easily expand this code to support other databases and providers, including the ODBC and the Oracle .NET data providers.

```vbnet
' [Visual Basic]
Function CreateConnection(ByVal connString As String) As IDbConnection
    If connString.ToLower().IndexOf("microsoft.jet.oledb") > -1 Then
        Return New OleDbConnection(connString)
    Else
        Return New SqlConnection(connString)
    End If
End Function
```

```csharp
// [C#]
IDbConnection CreateConnection(string connString)
{
    if ( connString.ToLower().IndexOf("microsoft.jet.oledb") > -1 )
        return new OleDbConnection(connString);
    else
        return new SqlConnection(connString);
}
```

The following code passes a valid connection string to the CreateConnection method and then performs some basic read operations in a provider-agnostic fashion:

```vbnet
' [Visual Basic]
Dim cn As IDbConnection = CreateConnection(connString)
cn.Open()
' Create a command on that connection.
Dim cmd As IDbCommand = cn.CreateCommand()
cmd.CommandText = "SELECT ContactName, ContactTitle FROM Customers"
' Create a DataReader.
Dim dr As IDataReader = cmd.ExecuteReader(CommandBehavior.CloseConnection)
Do While dr.Read()
    ' Process the resultset here...
Loop
dr.Close()
```

```csharp
// [C#]
IDbConnection cn = CreateConnection(connString);
cn.Open();
// Create a command on that connection.
IDbCommand cmd = cn.CreateCommand();
cmd.CommandText = "SELECT ContactName, ContactTitle FROM Customers";
// Create a DataReader.
IDataReader dr = cmd.ExecuteReader(CommandBehavior.CloseConnection);
while ( dr.Read() )
{
    // Process the resultset here...
}
dr.Close();
```

28.5 Connection strings

Never hard code connection strings. Instead, store them in the application's configuration file. Don't store ADODB connection strings in .udl files.

Why: Besides simplifying deployment, using configuration files to store connection strings indirectly ensures that the same exact string is used throughout the application, and therefore that all connections will share the same connection pool.

More details: The OLEDB .NET Data Provider lets you store a connection string in a .udl file, which you can specify in the connection string by means of the File Name attribute. (This option isn't available with other .NET data providers.) Storing a connection string in a .udl file isn't recommended because it requires that the file be read each time a connection is opened, an operation that adds overhead to your application.

Please notice that both configuration files and .udl files pose a security concern, and you should protect them using access control lists (ACLs) to prevent unauthorized users from reading and possibly modifying them.

See also: See rule 21.23 for an example of how you can read a string from the configuration file.

28.6 ADO.NET object constructors

Take advantage of the many overloaded constructors that the Connection and Command types expose. Favor using a constructor with many arguments so that you don't have to assign individual properties later.

```vbnet
' [Visual Basic]
' *** OK, but too verbose
Dim cn As New SqlConnection
cn.ConnectionString = connString
cn.Open()
Dim tran As SqlTransaction = cn.BeginTransaction()
Dim cmd As New SqlCommand
cmd.CommandText = sqlText
cmd.Connection = cn
cmd.Transaction = tran

' *** Better
Dim cn As New SqlConnection(connString)
cn.Open()
Dim tran As SqlTransaction = cn.BeginTransaction()
Dim cmd As New SqlCommand(sqlText, cn, tran)

// [C#]
// *** OK, but too verbose
SqlConnection cn = new SqlConnection();
cn.ConnectionString = connString;
cn.Open();
```

```
SqlTransaction tran = cn.BeginTransaction();
SqlCommand cmd = new SqlCommand();
cmd.CommandText = sqlText;
cmd.Connection = cn;
cmd.Transaction = tran;

// *** Better
SqlConnection cn = new SqlConnection(connString);
cn.Open();
SqlTransaction tran = cn.BeginTransaction();
SqlCommand cmd = new SqlCommand(sqlText, cn, tran);
```

28.7 Authentication mode for SQL Server databases

Favor Windows authentication to SQL Server security, especially in Windows Forms applications. *Never* use the sa account when adopting SQL Server security.

Why: Windows authentication is safer than SQL Server authentication because the username and password for logging in the database doesn't travel over the wire.

Why not: SQL Server authentication might be preferable in ASP.NET applications (see rule 29.27). More generally, SQL Server authentication is OK when you have already authenticated the user and you are running in a middle-tier component that communicates with the database over a secure line.

Example: Here's an example of Windows authentication:

```
Data Source=.;Integrated Security=SSPI;Initial catalog=Pubs
```

This is an example of SQL Server authentication:

```
Data Source=.;User ID=username;Password=pwd;Initial catalog=Pubs
```

More details: Regardless of which kind of authentication you're using, you don't need to take any special step to pool your SQL Server connections because this is the default behavior of the SQL Server .NET Data Provider. You can monitor how your application uses the connection pool by monitoring the following performance counters:

- SqlClient: Current # connection pools (current number of pools associated with the process)

- SqlClient: Current # pooled and nonpooled connections (current number of connections, pooled or not)

- SqlClient: Current # pooled connections (current number of connections in all pools associated with the process)

- SqlClient: Peak # pooled connections (the highest number of connections in all pools since the process started)

28.8 The PacketSize property

Consider changing the default value of the SqlConnection.PacketSize property to improve your application's efficiency.

More details: This property corresponds to the size of network packets used to communicate with SQL Server. It's default value is 8192 (8 KB), but you might want to increase it when performing bulk operations or dealing with large binary or text fields, or reduce it when you plan to work with small records or retrieve individual values by means of ExecuteScalar methods.

How to: The SqlConnection.PacketSize property is read-only and returns a value in the range 512 to 32,767. You can set it in the connection string that you pass to a SqlConnection object; any value outside the valid range throws an exception.

```
' [Visual Basic]
Dim cn As New SqlConnection("Data Source=(local);Integrated Security=SSPI;" _
   & "Initial Catalog=Pubs;Packet Size=16392")

// [C#]
SqlConnection cn = new SqlConnection("Data Source=(local);Integrated Security=SSPI;"
   + "Initial Catalog=Pubs;Packet Size=16392");
```

28.9 Primary keys in database tables

Consider the following guidelines when deciding which column should be the primary key of a database table.

   a. Don't use primary keys that have a meaning for the end user, such as the invoice number or the ISBN value. By using a primary key that isn't entered by the user, you can easily ensure that the value is non-null and unique and that you can later change any value in the row without affecting other records in the same or a different database table (as it would happen if you use a primary key that is meaningful information and that also appears as a foreign key in another table).

   b. Use an autoincrementing (identity) integer column as the primary key of a table. Opt for the int data type (4 bytes), or use the bigint data type (8 bytes) for huge tables and tables that might require a larger range (for example, large tables whose rows are frequently inserted or deleted). Smaller identity fields keep row size small and, more important, reduce the size and the depth of indexes, which in turn makes searches and JOIN operations faster. Identity fields are especially efficient with clustered indexes.

   c. Consider using uniqueidentifier (GUID) columns as primary keys in disconnected architectures, especially when working over slow networks (including WAN and WiFi LANs) or with databases that are partitioned over several servers that aren't continuously connected to each other.

   d. Avoid primary keys consisting of two or more fields.

More details: When inserting a row that has an identity field, you typically need to issue a SELECT query after the INSERT statement so that the application can retrieve the value of the identity value that SQL Server has assigned to the new row. This roundtrip to the server can add noticeable overhead if the application connects to the database server over a slow connection. In this case, using a client-side-generated GUID might be a better choice.

28.10 Asynchronous database operations

Consider using asynchronous delegates when opening a connection from inside a Windows Forms application to prevent the user interface from freezing for several seconds if the database isn't reachable or there isn't any available connection in the pool. (This rule doesn't apply to Microsoft Access databases stored on a local disk.)

How to: See rule 26.21 for an example of using asynchronous delegates.

More details: Keep in mind that you can't perform more than one operation on an open connection. For example, you must open a second connection if you want to query multiple database tables at the same time.

28.11 DataReader vs. DataSet

Read database data into a DataSet in the following cases:

 a.   You must update the database and you want to implement an optimistic update strategy.

 b.   You must account for relations existing in different tables.

 c.   You are binding data to one or more Windows Forms controls.

 d.   You are binding data to two or more Web Forms controls.

 e.   You need to store data between consecutive postbacks in an ASP.NET application.

 f.   You need to pass data between layers in a multitiered application.

 g.   You want to cache data, for example, to reduce traffic on a slow network and improve database performance and scalability.

In all other cases, use a DataReader for processing data coming from a database.

More details: In general, processing data by means of a DataReader is faster than using a Data-Adapter to fill a DataTable in a DataSet. Also, the DataReader doesn't take any memory either on the server or on the client; therefore, it is potentially capable of improving scalability. (The DataSet can also improve scalability and performance by means of caching; see point g in the previous list.)

When binding data from a database table to a *single* Web Forms control, you can use a Data-Reader object. If two or more Web Forms controls are bound to different columns of the same database table, a DataSet or a DataTable is a better choice because a DataReader would force you to read the same table more than once.

28.12 Filtering data

Never read more data that you strictly need. Use a WHERE clause to reduce the number of rows and list the columns that you absolutely need. Avoid using * to read all fields in the table, especially if the table includes one or more large binary or text columns.

Why: The less data you transfer over the network, the faster your application runs.

See also: Read rules 28.27 and 28.28 for guidelines related to large text and binary columns.

28.13 Sorting, and grouping

Favor ORDER BY, GROUP BY, and HAVING clauses in SQL statements to have the database engine sort and group rows in the result, instead of performing these operations on the client.

Why: Performing these operations on the server is typically faster because the database engine can leverage indexes and cached results.

Why not: Sorting and grouping data on the client can be faster if the database has no index defined for the sort key. When working with SQL Server, use the Query Analyzer to understand how a query is carried out.

More details: When the data has already been read in a DataTable object in the client application, you can filter and sort it by means of an auxiliary DataView object without posting a new query to the database. If the DataView is already sorted on the search key, you can use the DataView.Find method to locate a given row quickly. (This method is quite efficient because it uses the internal index that the DataView used to sort rows.)

28.14 Reading individual rows

Use the CommandBehavior.SingleRow enumerated value as an argument of the ExecuteReader method if you know in advance that the result can't include more than one row.

```vb
' [Visual Basic]
' Read a specific row in the Customers table.
' (cn is an open SqlConnection object.)
Dim sql As String = "SELECT ContactName, ContactTitle FROM Customers " _
   & "WHERE CustomerID='ALFKI'"
Dim cmd As New SqlCommand(sql, cn)
Dim dr As SqlDataReader = cmd.ExecuteReader(CommandBehavior.SingleRow)
```

```csharp
// [C#]
// Read a specific row in the Customers table.
// (cn is an open SqlConnection object.)
string sql = "SELECT ContactName, ContactTitle FROM Customers WHERE CustomerID='ALFKI'";
SqlCommand cmd = new SqlCommand(sql, cn);
SqlDataReader dr = cmd.ExecuteReader(CommandBehavior.SingleRow);
```

28.15 Reading individual values

Use the ExecuteScalar method instead of the ExecuteReader method when reading individual database fields or computed values.

Why: This technique is faster because it doesn't require that a DataReader object be created just to read an individual value.

```vb
' [Visual Basic]
' Read number of records in Customers table.
' (cn is an open SqlConnection object.)
Dim sql As String = "SELECT COUNT(*) FROM Customers"
Dim cmd As New SqlCommand(sql, cn)

' *** Wrong
Dim dr As SqlDataReader = cmd.ExecuteReader()
dr.Read()
Dim result As Integer = CInt(dr(0))
dr.Close()

' *** Correct
Dim result As Integer = CInt(cmd.ExecuteScalar())
```

```csharp
// [C#]
// Read number of records in Customers table.
// (cn is an open SqlConnection object.)
string sql = "SELECT COUNT(*) FROM Customers";
SqlCommand cmd = new SqlCommand(sql, cn);

// *** Wrong
SqlDataReader dr = cmd.ExecuteReader();
dr.Read();
int result = (int) dr[0]:
dr.Close();

// *** Correct
int result = (int) cmd.ExecuteScalar();
```

28.16 Limit the number of rows in a resultset

Use a TOP keyword or issue a SET ROWCOUNT command to limit the number of rows in a SELECT command. When displaying resultsets with a large number of rows (say, more than 500 rows), use pagination techniques to read only the rows that you plan to show to the end user.

See also: See rule 28.29 for more information about pagination techniques.

28.17 NULL values in queries

When querying a database on a nullable column, account for NULL values in the WHERE clause of the SELECT statement.

More details: By default, most T-SQL operators return NULL when their arguments are NULL values, and these NULL values can easily propagate to the entire WHERE expression. A row for which the WHERE expression is NULL won't be included in the resultset, a behavior that might introduce bugs in your application. For example, consider these two queries:

```
SELECT * FROM Customers WHERE Country = 'USA'
SELECT * FROM Customers WHERE Country <> 'USA'
```

You might believe that, taken together, these queries return all the rows in the Customers table, but this isn't the case because rows for which Country is NULL aren't returned by either query.

How to: A few T-SQL keywords can avoid the NULL propagation in WHERE expressions: the IS NULL and IS NOT NULL operators, the ISNULL function, and the logical operators AND and OR. For example, the following query returns all customers not residing in the USA, including rows for which the Country field is NULL:

```
SELECT * FROM Customers WHERE Country <> 'USA' OR Country IS NULL
SELECT * FROM Customers WHERE ISNULL(Country, '?') <> 'USA'
```

Notice that you can't use the = and <> operators to test a field for a NULL value because by default all comparison operators return false when either argument is NULL.

You can modify the behavior of comparison operators by issuing a SET ANSI_NULLS OFF command over the connection. However, we don't recommend this practice because it impedes code reusability.

28.18 Special characters in LIKE queries

Ensure that you correctly encode special characters in arguments meant to pass to LIKE operands in SELECT queries.

Why: A few characters have a special meaning when they appear as the right-hand operand of a LIKE operator in a T-SQL query. For example, the _ (underscore) character means "any single character," the % (percent) symbol means "any group of zero or more characters," and square brackets are used to create a list of matching characters.

More details: Most developers are aware that single quote characters should be doubled when they appear in dynamic SQL queries, and they have learned to use parameterized commands to avoid any sort of issues deriving from mishandled single quotes (see rule 28.21). However, when working with LIKE queries, as is often the case in Query by Example (QBE) forms, you should account for other symbols that have a special meaning to the SQL parser. For example, the code in QBE forms typically appends a % symbol to whatever the end user has typed in a search field for the query to return all rows containing a value that begins with the search string. Alas, this simplified approach means that the user can't enter a search string that contains the % symbol itself, or any other symbol that has a special meaning to the LIKE operator.

How to: The easiest way to force the T-SQL parser to consider %, _, and [symbols as literal characters in LIKE operands is to embed them in a pair of square brackets. The following example shows how you can perform a QBE search on the CompanyName field of the Customers table in the sample Northwind database that comes with SQL Server. It assumes that cn is an open SqlConnection object and that the txtCompanyName control contains the search string.

```
' [Visual Basic]
' Read search string, process special symbols.
Dim search As String = txtCompanyName.Text
search = search.Replace("%", "[%]").Replace("_", "[_]").Replace("[", "[[]")
' Create the command object.
Dim sql As String = "SELECT * FROM Customers WHERE CompanyName LIKE @search"
Dim cmd As New SqlCommand(sql, cn)
' Append a % symbol to search for values that begin with given string.
cmd.Parameters.Add("@search", search & "%")
' Proceed with reading data.
...
```

```
' [C#]
// Read search string, process special symbols.
string search = txtCompanyName.Text;
search = search.Replace("%", "[%]").Replace("_", "[_]")"[_]").Replace("[", "[[]");
// Create the command object.
string sql = "SELECT * FROM Customers WHERE CompanyName LIKE @search";
SqlCommand cmd = new SqlCommand(sql, cn);
// Append a % symbol to search for values that begin with given string.
cmd.Parameters.Add("@search", search + "%");
// Proceed with reading data.
...
```

28.19 Close a connection automatically

Consider using the CommandBehavior.CloseConnection enumerated value when invoking the ExecuteReader method of a Command object; this option causes the connection to be automatically closed when the returned DataReader is also closed.

Why: This technique ensures that the connection is returned to the pool as soon as possible. Also, you must use this technique when you implement a method that opens the connection and returns the DataReader because in such cases the caller has no Connection object that can be explicitly closed.

Why not: This technique isn't viable when you must perform multiple queries on the same connection and you aren't working with SQL Server. (See rule 28.30 for an example of sending multiple queries to SQL Server.)

Example: The following method opens a connection and returns a DataReader object. The Connection object isn't exposed to the caller, yet it will be automatically closed when the DataReader is closed.

```vb
' [Visual Basic]
Function GetDataReader(ByVal connString As String, ByVal sqlQuery As String) _
      As SqlDataReader
   Dim cn As New SqlConnection(connString)
   cn.Open()
   Dim cmd As New SqlCommand(sqlQuery, cn)
   Dim dr As SqlDataReader = cmd.ExecuteReader(CommandBehavior.CloseConnection)
   cmd.Dispose()
   Return dr
End Function
```

```csharp
// [C#]
SqlDataReader GetDataReader(string connString, string sqlQuery)
{
   SqlConnection cn = new SqlConnection(connString);
   cn.Open();
   SqlCommand cmd = new SqlCommand(sqlQuery, cn);
   SqlDataReader dr = cmd.ExecuteReader(CommandBehavior.CloseConnection);
   cmd.Dispose();
   return dr;
}
```

28.20 Cancel a DataReader query

Invoke the Cancel method of the Command object before closing a DataReader, if you don't want to read any remaining rows.

Why: If you fail to cancel the query, the Close method of the DataReader object reads all remaining rows, even if you aren't interested in them.

28.21 Parameterized commands vs. dynamic SQL queries

Favor commands with parameters over dynamic SQL queries built by appending pieces of strings and values taken from controls in the user interface.

Why: Parameterized commands can improve performance (see rule 28.23). Just as important, parameterized commands minimize the risk of SQL injection attacks and are especially effective with ASP.NET applications. They also make your code more readable and maintainable.

More details: Another benefit of parameterized commands over dynamic SQL queries is that you don't have to manually double single quote characters in string values.

Example: The following code example assumes that cn is an open SqlConnection object and shows how to read a row whose ID is entered by the end user in the txtCustomerID TextBox control:

```vb
' [Visual Basic]
' *** Wrong
Dim sql As String = "SELECT * FROM Customers WHERE CustomerID = '" _
   & txtCustomerID.Text & "'"
Dim cmd As New SqlCommand(sql, cn)
```

```
' *** Correct
Dim sql As String = "SELECT * FROM Customers WHERE CustomerID=@CustomerID"
Dim cmd As New SqlCommand(sql, cn)
Dim parID As SqlParameter = cmd.Parameters.Add("@CustomerID", SqlDbType.VarChar)
parID.Value = txtCustomerID.Text

// [C#]
// *** Wrong
string sql = "SELECT * FROM Customers WHERE CustomerID = '" + txtCustomerID.Text + "'";
SqlCommand cmd = new SqlCommand(sql, cn);

// *** Correct
string sql = "SELECT * FROM Customers WHERE CustomerID=@CustomerID";
SqlCommand cmd = new SqlCommand(sql, cn);
SqlParameter parID = cmd.Parameters.Add("@CustomerID", SqlDbType.VarChar);
parID.Value = txtCustomerID.Text;
```

28.22 Reusing SqlCommand objects

Invoke the Prepare method of all the SqlCommand objects that you plan to reuse multiple times in the application lifetime.

Why: The Prepare method enables SQL Server to cache the query plan and other information related to the command so that all subsequent queries can be completed faster.

Example: The following code assumes that cn is an open connection to the Northwind database:

```
' [Visual Basic]
Dim sql As String = "INSERT INTO Region (RegionID, RegionDescription) VALUES (@id, @desc)"
Dim cmd As SqlCommand(sql, cn);
' The first query
Dim id As Integer = 20
Dim desc As String = "myFirstRegion"
Dim par As SqlParameter = cmd.Parameters.Add("@id", id)
par.DbType = DbType.Int32
par.Size = 4
par = cmd.Parameters.Add ("@desc", desc)
par.DbType = DbType.String
par.Size = desc.Length
cmd.Prepare()               ' The Prepare statement
cmd.ExecuteNonQuery()
' Change parameter values and call ExecuteNonQuery again.
cmd.Parameters(0).Value = 21
cmd.Parameters(1).Value = "mySecondRegion"
' Uncomment next statement to solve a bug (see note following code examples).
' cmd.Parameters(1).Size = cmd.Parameters(1).Value.ToString().Length
cmd.ExecuteNonQuery()

// [C#]
string sql = "INSERT INTO Region (RegionID, RegionDescription) VALUES (@id, @desc)";
SqlCommand cmd = new SqlCommand(sql, cn);
// The first query
int id = 20;
```

```
string desc = "myFirstRegion";
SqlParameter par = cmd.Parameters.Add("@id", id);
par.DbType = DbType.Int32;
par.Size = 4;
par = cmd.Parameters.Add ("@desc", desc);
par.DbType = DbType.String;
par.Size = desc.Length;
cmd.Prepare();                  // The Prepare statement
cmd.ExecuteNonQuery();
// Change parameter values and call ExecuteNonQuery again.
cmd.Parameters[0].Value = 21;
cmd.Parameters[1].Value = "mySecondRegion";
// Uncomment next statement to solve a bug (see note following code examples).
// cmd.Parameters[1].Size = cmd.Parameters[1].Value.ToString().Length;
cmd.ExecuteNonQuery();
```

The provider sends two groups of commands to SQL Server. As you see, all queries after the first one are shorter. Depending on several factors (including number of rows in the table and existing indexes and their selectivity), prepared queries can be noticeably faster than regular ones.

```
-- First query
declare @P1 int
set @P1=1
exec sp_prepexec @P1 output, N'@id int,@desc nvarchar(13)',
    N'insert into Region (RegionID, RegionDescription)
    values (@id, @desc)', @id = 20, @desc = N'myFirstRegion'
select @P1
-- Second and all subsequent queries. (Notice that second value is truncated.)
exec sp_execute 1, @id = 21, @desc = N'mySecondRegio'
```

> **Note**   You should always update the Size property of a variable-length parameter to match the length of the actual value; otherwise, you might send more data than is strictly needed or, much worse, truncate values, as happens in the previous example. (Read the remarks and uncomment the next to last statement in Visual Basic or C# code to solve this problem.)

28.23 Parameterized commands vs. stored procedures

Consider all the pros and cons of using stored procedures in lieu of parameterized SQL queries.

More details: Developers have debated for years about whether stored procedures are to be preferred to SQL queries that are created dynamically by the application. We believe that there isn't a one-size-fits-all rule and that each approach can meet different requirements and solve different kinds of problems. Here's an (incomplete) list of considerations that can help you make a more informed decision:

   a.   Stored procedures typically offer better performance because SQL Server can cache their query plans even across sessions. (The actual speed advantage can vary greatly, and it can be negligible in some cases.)

b.   Stored procedures can reduce network traffic if they include a batch of SQL commands that should be sent to the database individually.

c.   Stored procedures offer better security (see rule 28.25).

d.   Stored procedures can help the transition to another programming language or another data access technology (for example, from ADO to ADO.NET).

e.   Stored procedures (as well as views; see rule 28.25) provide an additional level of indirection and in some cases enable you to change the structure of the database without impacting the application.

f.   Writing and maintaining nontrivial stored procedures requires dedicated programming skills and familiarity with T-SQL or other SQL dialects.

g.   Dynamic and parameterized SQL queries can help the migration to another kind of database (for example, from Microsoft Access to SQL Server).

h.   Both stored procedures and parameterized SQL queries are virtually immune to SQL injection attacks.

i.   Parameterized SQL queries that are built dynamically by the application offer a degree of flexibility that stored procedures don't have. (For example, dynamic SQL queries are better at implementing complex Query by Example searches.)

j.   The T-SQL language excels at processing data but can't compete with most .NET programming languages for general-purpose tasks. When you implement complex validation rules, dynamic queries embedded in a Visual Basic or C# class can be preferable to stored procedures. (This consideration will be void under SQL Server 2005, in beta as of this writing, because this version allows you to write stored procedures using Visual Basic or C#.)

k.   Stored procedures should never embed business rules; stored procedures should be used exclusively to implement the functions that are part of the data layer of a multi-tiered application.

l.   A stored procedure can run only on the database server, whereas a .NET component that uses dynamic queries can be deployed on a different server, if necessary. In some cases, this flexibility can improve the application's overall scalability.

28.24 SQL Server stored procedure names

Use the usp_ prefix for user-defined SQL Server stored procedures instead of the more common sp_ prefix.

Why: Many developers use the sp_ prefix for their stored procedures, a naming convention that can hurt performance; sp_ stored procedures are meant to be system stored procedures and should reside in the master database. When asked to run an sp_ stored procedure, SQL Server searches for it in the master database first, even if you specify the location and name of the procedure.

28.25 Access tables through views and stored procedures

Consider using SQL Server views or stored procedures to access database tables instead of accessing the tables directly.

Why: Views and stored procedures add a level of indirection to all database operations without adding any overhead. This indirection enables you to change the structure of the database table (to an extent, at least) without breaking existing clients. Just as important, you can implement better security by making the view or the stored procedure accessible only to users who can legally use it. (See also rule 28.23.)

28.26 Stored procedures that return a value

When you use the ExecuteReader method to read the resultset produced by a stored procedure, you must close the DataReader object before attempting to read the return value or the output arguments of the stored procedure, if any.

Why: While the DataReader is open, the query is still executing and the stored procedure hasn't completed yet; therefore, its output arguments and return values aren't available yet. By closing the DataReader, you force the termination of the query, and only then do these values become available through parameters of the Command object.

28.27 Large binary and text fields

Pass the CommandBehavior.SequentialAccess enumerated value as an argument of the ExecuteReader method if you use the returned DataReader to read one or more large binary or text columns. Also, ensure that these large columns are listed at the end of the columns list in the SELECT statement. This technique is especially effective if you need to display or process the large binary or text fields only for a subset of the rows being read.

Why: The SequentialAccess option causes the DataReader to retrieve columns in the order in which they appear in the SELECT statement; if the column is never referenced in code, it is never requested from the database.

More details: This technique forces you to read column values in a specific order. It's just too easy to read columns in an order that is different from the one used in the SQL statement, so you must always use extra care to synchronize these two portions of code.

```
' [Visual Basic]
Dim cmd As New SqlCommand("SELECT pub_id,pr_info,logo FROM pub_info", cn)
Dim dr As SqlDataReader = cmd.ExecuteReader(CommandBehavior.SequentialAccess)
Do While dr.Read()
   Dim pub_id As String = dr.GetString(0)
   Dim pr_info As String = dr.GetString(1)
   Dim buffer() As Byte = DirectCast(dr.GetValue(2), Byte())
   ...
Loop
```

```csharp
// [C#]
SqlCommand cmd = new SqlCommand("SELECT pub_id,pr_info,logo FROM pub_info", cn);
SqlDataReader dr = cmd.ExecuteReader(CommandBehavior.SequentialAccess);
while ( dr.Read() )
{
    string pub_id = dr.GetString(0);
    string pr_info = dr.GetString(1);
    byte[] buffer = (byte[]) dr.GetValue(2);
    ...
}
```

28.28 Process large binary and text fields in chunks

Process large binary and text fields in chunks if they are larger than 8 KB.

Why: Reading a large string or byte array in memory in its entirety affects the scalability of your application. (This is especially true for server-side applications and components.)

More details: A good rule of thumb is to use chunks that are as large as the value you've assigned to the PacketSize property (see rule 28.8).

Example: The following BlobToFile reusable method reads the N-th field of a DataReader and saves it to a file. It works with any ADO.NET provider.

```vb
' [Visual Basic]
Public Sub BlobToFile(ByVal dr As IDataReader, ByVal fldIndex As Integer, _
      ByVal fileName As String)
    Const ChunkSize As Integer = 1024      ' Change as you wish.
    Dim buffer(ChunkSize - 1) As Byte
    Dim fs As New FileStream(fileName, FileMode.Create)
    Dim index As Long = 0
    Try
        Do
            ' Get the next chunk, exit if no more bytes.
            Dim length As Integer = CInt(dr.GetBytes(fldIndex, index, buffer, 0, ChunkSize))
            If length = 0 Then Exit Do
            ' Write to file and increment index in field data.
            fs.Write(buffer, 0, length)
            index += length
        Loop
    Finally
        fs.Close()
    End Try
End Sub
```

```csharp
// [C#]
public void BlobToFile(IDataReader dr, int fldIndex, string fileName)
    const int ChunkSize = 1024;            // Change as you wish.
    byte[] buffer = new byte[ChunkSize];
    FileStream fs = new FileStream(fileName, FileMode.Create);
    long index = 0;
    try
    {
        while ( true )
```

```
        {
           // Get the next chunk, exit if no more bytes.
           int length = (int) dr.GetBytes(fldIndex, index, buffer, 0, ChunkSize);
           if ( length == 0 )
              break;
           // Write to file and increment index in field data.
           fs.Write(buffer, 0, length);
           index += length;
        }
     }
     finally
     {
        fs.Close();
     }
}
```

Here's an example that uses the BlobToFile method. It assumes that cn is an open SqlConnection object that points to the Pubs database.

```
' [Visual Basic]
Dim cmd As New SqlCommand("SELECT TOP 1 logo FROM pub_info", cn)
Dim dr As SqlDataReader = cmd.ExecuteReader(CommandBehavior.SingleRow)
If dr.Read() Then
   BlobToFile(dr, 0, "C:\TestLogo.bmp")
Else
   Console.WriteLine("No record found.")
End If
dr.Close()
```

```
// [C#]
SqlCommand cmd = new SqlCommand("SELECT TOP 1 logo FROM pub_info", cn);
SqlDataReader dr = cmd.ExecuteReader(CommandBehavior.SingleRow);
if ( dr.Read() )
   BlobToFile(dr, 0, @"C:\TestLogo.bmp");
else
   Console.WriteLine("No record found.");
dr.Close();
```

28.29 Resultset pagination

Implement a pagination mechanism to display the result of a query in groups of 50 rows or fewer.

More details: Implementing a good pagination mechanism isn't a trivial task. You can implement a simple pagination algorithm based on overload of the DataAdapter's Fill method, as in this code that assumes that pageSize is the number of rows in each page, pageNum is the one-based number of the page you want to read, da is the DataAdapter, ds is the destination DataSet, and tableName is the name of the destination DataTable:

```
' [Visual Basic]
da.Fill(ds, (pageNum - 1) * pageSize, pageSize, tableName)
```

```
// [C#]
da.Fill(ds, (pageNum - 1) * pageSize, pageSize, tableName);
```

The problem with this approach is that the DataAdapter reads and then discards all the rows before the first row you're interested in; therefore, this technique can't be used with results of more than a few hundreds rows.

A more efficient technique is based on the TOP keyword, available with Access and SQL Server. The following pseudocode shows how you can read any page from a database table that has a unique index on a column named keyName:

```
SELECT * FROM tableName WHERE keyName IN
    (SELECT TOP pageSize keyName FROM tableName WHERE keyName IN
        (SELECT TOP pageSize*pageNum keyName FROM tableName ORDER BY keyName)
        ORDER BY keyName DESC)
    ORDER BY keyName
```

The approach based on nested SELECT statements isn't especially efficient with large result-sets. When the table has more than a few thousand rows, you should adopt more sophisticated techniques based on server-side cursors, temporary tables, or auxiliary columns that contain the row number.

See also: You can read more about the ADO.NET and the pagination technique based on nested SELECT statements in a sample chapter from Francesco Balena's *Programming Microsoft Visual Basic .NET* (Microsoft Press, 2002), available at *http://www.dotnet2themax.com/goto/programmingvbnet.aspx*.

28.30 Batch commands for SQL Server queries

Stuff multiple commands in a semicolon-delimited list when sending a query to SQL Server.

Why: This technique reduces the number of roundtrips to the database. It assumes that cn is an open SqlConnection object that points to the Northwind database:

```
' [Visual Basic]
Dim sql As String = "SELECT * FROM Customers; SELECT * FROM Orders"
Dim cmd As New SqlCommand(sql, cn)
Dim dr As SqlDataReader = cmd.ExecuteReader()
Do
    Do While dr.Read()
        ' Process the current resultset...
    Loop
    ' Read next resultset, exit if no more results.
Loop While dr.NextResult()
dr.Close()

// [C#]
Dim sql As String = "SELECT * FROM Customers; SELECT * FROM Orders");
SqlCommand cmd = new SqlCommand(sql, cn);
SqlDataReader dr = cmd.ExecuteReader();
do
{
    while ( dr.Read() )
    {
```

```
        // Process the current resultset...
    }
    // Read next resultset, exit if no more results.
} while ( dr.NextResult() );
```

28.31 DataSet names

Use the DataSet suffix for strong-typed DataSet classes.

Example: PubsDataSet.

28.32 DataTable names

Use DataTable names that match the name of the corresponding database table. If the DataTable doesn't correspond to a database table, use the plural of the noun of the entity described by each row in the table. Avoid spaces, symbols, and underscores in these names.

Why: A DataTable name that matches the database table makes the code more readable and less ambiguous. If the name doesn't have embedded punctuation symbols within it, the DataTable can be referenced in the same way both using the DataSet.Tables collection and the dot syntax (in a strongly typed DataSet). Notice that, even if the underscore is a valid character in both Visual Basic and C# identifiers, it should be avoided in table names because it can cause confusion when creating DataRelation objects (see rule 28.33).

28.33 DataRelation names

Use the *ParentTable_ChildTable* name convention for DataRelation objects.

Example: The DataRelation object that ties the Customers and Orders tables should be named Customers_Orders.

28.34 Strong-typed DataSet classes

Use strong-typed DataSet objects rather than untyped ones.

Why: This technique reduces the amount of code to write, simplifies usage of the DataSet (thanks to IntelliSense), avoids runtime exceptions caused by misspelled table or column names, and produces code that is more efficient in some cases.

28.35 DataSet vs. DataTable objects

Don't use a DataSet object if a DataTable is all you need to carry out a given operation.

More details: You absolutely need a DataSet in the following cases:

   a. You read data from multiple tables.

   b. You create a relation with another table.

    c. You save the data on a local file, in binary or XML format.

    d. You pass the data to a remote application.

In most other cases, you can just use a DataTable and save some memory.

28.36 The DataSet and DataTable Locale property

Explicitly set the Locale property of any DataSet or DataTable object that your code instantiates.

Why: The Locale property affects the storage format of dates, numbers, and currency values. If you neglect to assign this property explicitly, its default value is the current culture. If the DataSet or DataTable is to be shared with other users who might be using different regional settings, as might happen in an ASP.NET application, you should set this property to the invariant culture.

```
' [Visual Basic]
Dim ds As New DataSet
ds.Locale = CultureInfo.InvariantCulture

// [C#]
DataSet ds = new DataSet();
ds.Locale = CultureInfo.InvariantCulture;
```

28.37 The DataAdapter's autoconnect feature

Don't rely on the DataAdapter's autoconnect feature, that is, the capability to automatically open a connection that is currently closed. Instead, always explicitly open the connection before reading and updating a database table, and close it immediately afterward. (Adopt this behavior even if you are reading or updating an individual database table.)

Why: This technique ensures that the connection is opened only once even if you later read or update more than one table (as you can see in rule 28.41.)

```
' [Visual Basic]
' (cn is a closed connection, ds is a DataSet.)
Dim da As New SqlDataAdapter("SELECT * FROM Orders", cn)

' *** Wrong
da.Fill(ds, "Orders")

' *** Correct
Try
   cn.Open()
   da.Fill(ds, "Orders")
Catch ex As Exception
   ' Deal with errors here.
   ...
Finally
   cn.Close()
End Try
```

```
// [C#]
// (cn is a closed connection, ds is a DataSet.)
SqlDataAdapter da = new SqlDataAdapter("SELECT * FROM Orders", cn);

// *** Wrong
da.Fill(ds, "Orders");

// *** Correct
try
{
    cn.Open();
    da.Fill(ds, "Orders");
}
catch ( Exception ex )
{
    // Deal with errors here.
    ...
}
finally
{
    cn.Close();
}
```

28.38 CommandBuilder objects

Never use CommandBuilder objects, either to populate a command's Parameters collection or to initialize Command objects in a DataAdapter instance. Instead, create the collection of parameters and assign the DataAdapter commands either manually or using Visual Studio .NET RAD features.

Why: The CommandBuilder object requires a roundtrip to the database to read the information it needs; real-world applications can't afford this overhead.

28.39 Autoincrementing identity columns

Set the AutoIncrementSeed property to –1 and the AutoIncrementStep property to –1 for autoincrement columns that correspond to identity fields in Access and SQL Server.

Why: When you update the database using a DataAdapter object, the local value of the auto-incremented column is ignored. However, if the DataAdapter.InsertCommand's UpdateRowSource property is set to a value other than None, the column receives the identity value that has been generated by the database engine. If the new value happens to match a value that is already present in the DataTable and the column has a unique constraint, ADO.NET throws an exception. By using negative values for both the AutoIncrementSeed property and the AutoIncrementStep property, you can ensure that identity values received from the database never match identity values that have been generated locally.

Example: For an example of what can happen if you don't follow this rule, consider this scenario. You read all rows from the Orders table and find that you have 200 records; thus, you set the AutoIncrementSeed property equal to 201 and the AutoIncrementStep property equal to 1. You then insert two records, which are assigned a local identity field equal to 201 and 202. By the time you invoke the DataAdapter.Update method, however, another user has inserted a row in the Orders table; thus, the record you added first (whose local identity field is 201) receives the value 202 from the database. Unfortunately, this value is already present in the local Orders DataTable and ADO.NET throws an exception.

28.40 DataSet serialization

Be aware of inefficiencies when serializing a DataSet object. Avoid passing large DataSet objects to remote components, and consider all the alternatives you have.

More details: When you save a DataSet instance by means of the BinaryFormatter or pass it to another layer of your application using remoting or COM+, data in the DataSet is actually serialized as XML text (see Figure 28-1). When the DataSet contains more than a few hundred rows, this mechanism can impact performance significantly.

In many cases, you can save bandwidth and CPU time by passing a DataSet that contains only the rows that have been inserted, deleted, or updated in the original DataSet. (You create such a DataSet by means of the GetChanges method.). This technique is especially effective in multitiered applications when all database operations are performed by a set of data objects.

See also: Read more about DataSet serialization and surrogate types in the MSDN article by Dino Esposito at *msdn.microsoft.com/msdnmag/issues/02/12/cuttingedge*, and also view an interesting code sample at *support.microsoft.com/default.aspx?scid=kb;en-us;829740*.

Figure 28-1   The file produced by serializing a DataSet with the BinaryFormatter; the file contains a short binary header followed by data in XML format.

28.41 Reading master-detail tables

Open an ADO.NET or COM+ transaction whose level is set to serializable when reading two or more tables in a master-detail relationship.

Why: This technique ensures that you read consistent results also under heavy concurrency. Without a serializable transaction, another user might add or remove rows to the master table after you've read it and you would end up with orphaned rows in the detail table. (Such rows would throw an exception if you've established a relation between the master and the child DataTable objects.)

28.42 Advanced SQL Generation Options dialog box

Unless you have a specific reason not to do so, leave both the Use Optimistic Concurrency and the Refresh The DataSet options checked in the Advanced SQL Generation Options dialog box of the DataAdapter configuration wizard (see Figure 28-2).

Why: The Use Optimistic Concurrency option ensures that the WHERE clause in UPDATE and DELETE SQL commands fail if another user has modified one of the columns in that row. The Refresh The DataSet option ensures that values in the DataTable object match current values in the database so that the client code can retrieve the value of identity columns, calculated columns, and columns modified by triggers.

Why not: Both these options, especially the Refresh The DataSet option, might impact execution speed.

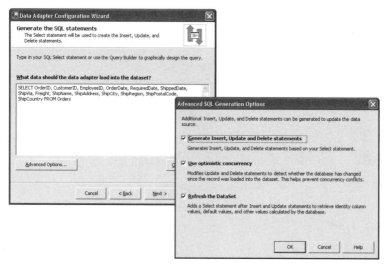

Figure 28-2 The Advanced SQL Generation Options dialog box that you can reach from the Data Adapter Configuration Wizard

28.43 TimeStamp fields for optimistic concurrency

When using optimistic concurrency to update the database, consider adding a TimeStamp column to the database table to enable you to quickly detect when another user has updated one or more rows.

How to: Unfortunately, you can't use Visual Studio .NET code generation features to create commands that take advantage of TimeStamp fields; thus, you must create these commands manually.

The following code assumes that you have added a TimeStamp column named LastUpdate to the Authors table in the Pubs database and that cn is an open SqlConnection object that points to this database.

```vb
' [Visual Basic]
Dim cmdDelete As New SqlCommand( _
    "DELETE FROM Authors WHERE au_id = @au_id And LastUpdate=@LastUpdate", cn)
cmdDelete.Parameters.Add("@au_id", SqlDbType.VarChar, 11, "au_id")
' Timestamp columns are of VarBinary type (they map to a Byte array).
cmdDelete.Parameters.Add("@LastUpdate", SqlDbType.VarBinary, 8, "LastUpdate")
da.DeleteCommand = cmdDelete

Dim cmdUpdate As New SqlCommand("UPDATE Authors SET au_fname = @au_fname,"  _
    & "au_lname = @au_lname WHERE au_id = @au_id AND LastUpdate = @LastUpdate", cn)
' Arguments for the SET clause use new field values.
cmdUpdate.Parameters.Add("@au_fname", SqlDbType.VarChar, 20, "au_fname")
cmdUpdate.Parameters.Add("@au_lname", SqlDbType.VarChar, 40, "au_lname")
' Arguments in the WHERE clause use original field values.
cmdUpdate.Parameters.Add("@au_id", SqlDbType.VarChar, 11, _
    "au_id").SourceVersion = DataRowVersion.Original
cmdUpdate.Parameters.Add("@LastUpdate", SqlDbType.VarBinary, 8, _
    "LastUpdate").SourceVersion = DataRowVersion.Original
da.UpdateCommand = cmdUpdate
```

```csharp
// [C#]
SqlCommand cmdDelete = new SqlCommand(
    "DELETE FROM Authors WHERE au_id = @au_id And LastUpdate= @LastUpdate", cn);
cmdDelete.Parameters.Add("@au_id", SqlDbType.VarChar, 11, "au_id");
// Timestamp columns are of VarBinary type (they map to a Byte array).
cmdDelete.Parameters.Add("@LastUpdate", SqlDbType.VarBinary, 8, "LastUpdate");
da.DeleteCommand = cmdDelete;

SqlCommand cmdUpdate = new SqlCommand("UPDATE Authors SET au_fname = @au_fname,"
    + "au_lname = @au_lname WHERE au_id = @au_id AND LastUpdate = @LastUpdate", cn);
// Arguments for the SET clause use new field values.
cmdUpdate.Parameters.Add("@au_fname", SqlDbType.VarChar, 20, "au_fname");
cmdUpdate.Parameters.Add("@au_lname", SqlDbType.VarChar, 40, "au_lname");
// Arguments in the WHERE clause use original field values.
cmdUpdate.Parameters.Add("@au_id", SqlDbType.VarChar, 11,
    "au_id").SourceVersion = DataRowVersion.Original;
cmdUpdate.Parameters.Add("@LastUpdate", SqlDbType.VarBinary, 8,
    "LastUpdate").SourceVersion = DataRowVersion.Original;
da.UpdateCommand = cmdUpdate;
```

28.44 Transaction duration

Close a transaction as soon as possible. Neither accept user input while a transaction is open nor allow the user to decide whether a transaction should be committed or rolled back.

Why: While a transaction is active, one or more rows (or tables) in the database are locked and other users can't access them. Using short transactions is the key to scalability in enterprise-level applications.

28.45 Resolving update conflicts

Don't rely on the default behavior of the DataAdapter object for managing update conflicts.

Why: The default behavior of the DataAdapter object leaves the database in an inconsistent state if an update conflict occurs because ADO.NET throws an exception in the application but doesn't restore the original state of the database.

How to: Either set the DataAdapter.ContinueUpdateOnErrors property to true (the default is false), or wrap the update in a transaction and roll back the transaction if any conflict occurs, as shown in the following example. (It assumes that cn is an open SqlConnection object and da is the DataAdapter ready to perform the update.)

```
' [Visual Basic]
Dim tr As SqlTransaction = cn.BeginTransaction()
' Enroll all DataAdapter commands in the transaction.
da.UpdateCommand.Transaction = tr
da.DeleteCommand.Transaction = tr
da.InsertCommand.Transaction = tr

Try
    ' Do the update here. Commit the transaction if OK.
    ...
    tr.Commit()
Catch ex As Exception
    ' Roll back the transaction in case of error.
    tr.Rollback()
End Try

// [C#]
SqlTransaction tr = cn.BeginTransaction();
// Enroll all DataAdapter commands in the transaction.
da.UpdateCommand.Transaction = tr;
da.DeleteCommand.Transaction = tr;
da.InsertCommand.Transaction = tr;

try
{
    // Do the update here. Commit the transaction if OK.
    ...
    tr.Commit();
}
catch ( Exception ex )
{
    // Roll back the transaction in case of error.
    tr.Rollback();
}
```

See also: See rule 28.46 for more details on transactional updates.

28.46 Using the DataSet in transactional updates

When updating the database inside a transaction, use the DataSet.GetChanges method to create a new DataSet that contains only added, deleted, and modified rows, and pass this new object to the DataAdapter.Update method instead of passing the original DataSet. After completing the update successfully, you should invoke the AcceptChanges method on the original DataSet.

Why: Performing all database updates from inside a transaction ensures that changes are rolled back if an update conflict occurs. However, when this happens, all DataRow objects that have been updated already are marked as Unmodified because the DataAdapter has already invoked their AcceptChanges method. By working with a separate DataSet object and by invoking the AcceptChanges method manually only at the end of a successful update, you ensure that the original DataSet is synchronized with the database and contains coherent data regardless of whether the update was successful.

However, if the database table includes any identity column, calculated column, or column assigned by a trigger or a stored procedure, you should pass the new DataSet object to the Merge method of the original DataSet.

Example: The following code assumes that cn is an open SqlConnection object, tr is a transaction inside which all updates execute, ds is the DataSet containing the Orders and Customers table, and daOrders and daCustomers are the corresponding DataAdapter objects.

```vb
' [Visual Basic]
Try
    ' Get a copy of the DataSet, use it to update both tables.
    Dim dsCopy As DataSet = ds.GetChanges()
    daOrders.Update(dsCopy, "Orders")
    daCustomers.Update(dsCopy, "Customers")
    ' Commit the transaction if everything went well.
    tr.Commit()
    ' Update the old DataSet with up-to-date data.
    ds.Merge(dsCopy)
Catch ex As Exception
    ' Roll back the transaction in case of error.
    tr.Rollback()
End Try
```

```csharp
// [C#]
try
{
    // Get a copy of the DataSet, use it to update both tables.
    DataSet dsCopy = ds.GetChanges();
    daOrders.Update(dsCopy, "Orders");
    daCustomers.Update(dsCopy, "Customers");
    // Commit the transaction if everything went well.
    tr.Commit();
    // Update the old DataSet with up-to-date data.
    ds.Merge(dsCopy);
}
catch ( Exception ex )
{
    // Roll back the transaction in case of error.
    tr.Rollback();
}
```

If the update operation fails, you might want to merge the result of the dsCopy.GetChanges method with the original DataSet so that the end user can see which row caused the problem.

(This technique is especially useful if a DataGrid is bound to the DataSet because the row that failed to update is marked with a red circle.)

See also: Read rule 28.45 for an example of a transactional update and rule 28.47 for a guideline about updating tables in master-detail relationships.

28.47 Updating master-detail tables

Always follow this order when updating two DataTable objects in a master-detail relationship:

1. Insert and update commands on the parent table.

2. Insert, update, and delete commands on the child table.

3. Delete commands on the parent table.

Why: If the corresponding database tables are tied by a master-detail relationship and if referential integrity rules are active, trying to delete a parent row before deleting all its child rows would cause an error.

Example: The following code assumes that cn is an open SqlConnection object, ds is the DataSet containing the Publishers and Titles tables, and daPub and daTit are the corresponding DataAdapter objects.

```
' [Visual Basic]
Dim dtPub As DataTable = ds.Tables("Publishers")
Dim dtTit As DataTable = ds.Tables("Titles")
' 1. Process modified and inserted rows in parent table.
daPub.Update(dtPub.Select(Nothing, Nothing, DataViewRowState.ModifiedCurrent _
    Or DataViewRowState.Added))
' 2. Process all updates in child table.
daTit.Update(dtTit)
' 3. Process deleted rows in parent table.
daPub.Update(dtPub.Select(Nothing, Nothing, DataViewRowState.Deleted))

// [C#]
DataTable dtPub = ds.Tables["Publishers"];
DataTable dtTit = ds.Tables["Titles"];
// 1. Process modified and inserted rows in parent table.
daPub.Update(dtPub.Select(null, null, DataViewRowState.ModifiedCurrent
    | DataViewRowState.Added));
// 2. Process all updates in child table.
daTit.Update(dtTit);
// 3. Process deleted rows in parent table.
daPub.Update(dtPub.Select(null, null, DataViewRowState.Deleted));
```

Notice that the same update sequence must be applied recursively if the detail table is in turn the master table of another DataRelation.

Chapter 29

ASP.NET Web Forms Applications

ASP.NET is the main reason many developers switch to the Microsoft .NET Framework. Creating an ASP.NET Web site or application is one order of magnitude easier than using older technologies such as Active Server Pages (ASP). In spite of this great simplicity, however, authoring *good* ASP.NET applications still requires much attention, a lot of self-discipline, and many hours spent reading the official documentation as well as Microsoft Knowledge Base and support articles.

In this chapter we have gathered nearly 70 guidelines that are related to ASP.NET Web Forms applications and, to an extent, to Web service projects as well. (Web services use the same ASP.NET infrastructure as Web Forms.) We have included naming guidelines, simple tips about common properties, and suggestions about the preferred techniques to keep state between page postbacks and to pass data to other pages. We have devoted many guidelines to ASP.NET security, which is likely to be the least understood topic in ASP.NET programming. There is so much to say about ASP.NET—and there are so many programming mistakes you can make in an ASP.NET application—it's no surprise this is the longest chapter in the book.

Note One or more code examples in this chapter assume that the following namespaces have been imported by means of *Imports* (Visual Basic) or *using* (C#) statements:

```
System.Collections
System.Data
System.Data.OleDb
System.Data.SqlClient
System.Globalization
System.IO
System.Text.RegularExpressions
System.Threading
System.Web
System.Web.Caching
System.Web.Configuration
System.Web.Security
System.Web.SessionState
System.Web.UI
System.Web.UI.HtmlControls
System.Web.UI.WebControls
System.Xml
```

29.1 Web Forms control names

Use a prefix from Table 29-1 for Web Forms control names.

Example: ddlCountries, btnOK.

More details: When possible, we have listed a prefix for a Web Forms control that is the same as the prefix for the corresponding Windows Forms control (see rule 27.4).

Table 29-1   Suggested Prefixes for Web Forms Controls

Prefix	Type	Prefix	Type
adrot	AdRotator	mpag	MultiPage
btn	Button	pnl	Panel
cal	Calendar	phld	PlaceHolder
chk	CheckBox	rad	RadioButton
clst	CheckedListBox	rlst	RadioButtonList
vacmp	CompareValidator	varng	RangeValidator
ctrl	Control	vareg	RegularExpressionValidator
crv	CrystalReportViewer	rep	Repeater
dgr	DataGrid	repi	RepeaterItem
dgrc	DataGridColumn	vareq	RequiredValidator
dgri	DataGridItem	tbl	Table
dls	DataList	tcel	TableCell
dlsi	DataListItem	trow	TableRow
ddl	DropDownList	tab	TabStrip
hyp	HyperLink	txt	TextBox
img	Image	tba	Toolbar
ibtn	ImageButton	tvw	TreeView
lbl	Label	vasum	ValidationSummary
lbtn	LinkButton	xml	Xml
lst	ListBox	xpwin	XpWindow
lit	Literal		

29.2 HTML control names

Use a prefix from Table 29-2 for HTML control names.

Example: hddlCountries, hbtnOK.

More details: When possible, prefixes for these controls have been built by prepending an *h* character to the prefix used for the corresponding Web Forms control. HTML controls are rarely referenced in code; thus, using longer names is OK.

Table 29-2   Suggested Prefixes for HTML Controls

Prefix	Type	Prefix	Type
hbtn	Button	hlbl	Label
hchk	CheckBox	hlst	ListBox
hddl	DropDownList	hpwd	Password Field
hfil	File Field	hrad	RadioButton
hflp	Flow Layout Panel	hres	Reset Button
hglp	Grid Layout Panel	hsub	Submit Button
hhid	Hidden	htbl	Table
hhor	Horizontal Rule	htxt	TextBox
himg	Image	htxa	Text Area

In general, we don't recommend using HTML controls if there is a corresponding Web Forms control that offers the same (and usually expanded) functionality. However, you might want to use HTML controls to reduce the amount of HTML text sent back to the client and speed up page execution. Controls that display static or read-only data, controls that don't need to preserve data between postbacks, and controls that are never accessed programmatically from inside the page are all good candidates for being rendered as HTML controls.

29.3 Main page properties

Set the pageLayout, targetSchema, and defaultClientScript properties of the page document immediately after creating the Web Forms page.

Why: These properties affect how your application outputs HTML text to the various browsers. Changing these properties in the middle of the development stage usually requires that you recheck how the form behaves and test it again with different browsers.

More details: You can also set these properties in the Designer Defaults page of the Project Properties dialog box to have all new Web Forms inherit them automatically (see Figure 29-1).

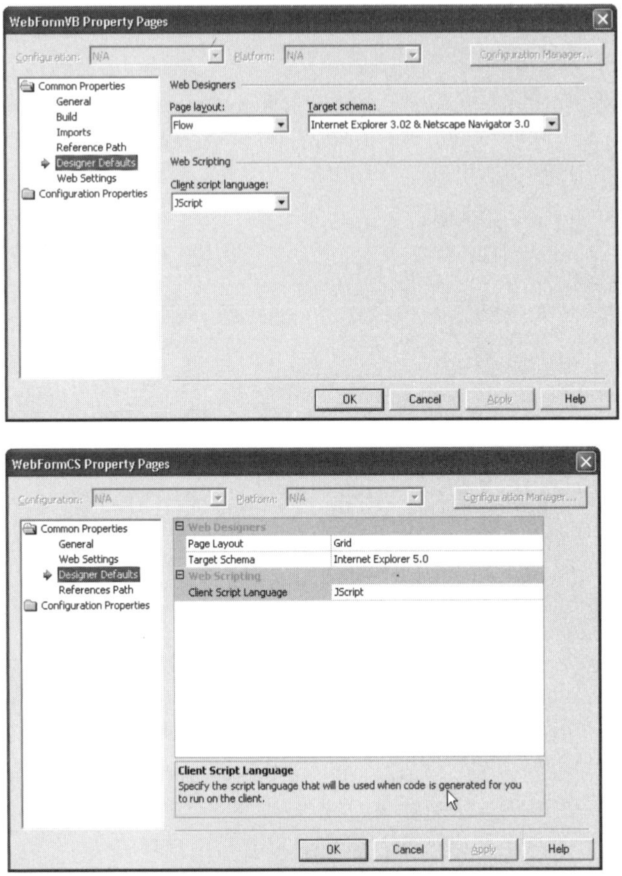

Figure 29-1   The Designer Defaults page of the Project Properties dialog box, as it appears in Visual Basic projects (top) and C# projects (bottom)

29.4 The pageLayout property

Set the pageLayout property to the value FlowLayout, rather than using its default GridLayout value.

Why: The FlowLayout setting makes controls on the form behave like the text in a word processor and causes them to move as the browser window is resized. The GridLayout setting uses absolute coordinates for controls placed on the Web Forms page, much like the controls you place on a Windows Form, and might cause visualization problems if the end user resizes the browser or uses a low screen resolution.

Worse, the GridLayout setting is problematic if the height or width of a control isn't known at design time. For example, often you don't know how large a DataGrid control is at run time, so odds are that it will overlap other controls placed to its right or below it. Another reason for not using the GridLayout setting is that it doesn't work well with trace at the page level because trace information would start at the top of the output page and cover all the page contents.

Why not: Using the GridLayout setting is OK for simple data-entry forms that contain controls that have fixed sizes. If you use this setting, however, ensure that all the controls you place on the form's surface can fit the browser's window even at lower screen resolutions.

29.5 The targetSchema property

Set the targetSchema property to Microsoft Internet Explorer 3.02/Navigator 3.0 for Internet sites that should be viewable even with downlevel browsers. Set this property to Internet Explorer 5.0 for Internet sites that require the advanced features offered by the most recent versions of Internet Explorer or for intranet sites if all the computers in the network have Internet Explorer version 5.0 or later installed.

29.6 The SmartNavigation property

Set the SmartNavigation property to true unless you have a good reason to disable this feature. Assign this property by means of configuration files rather than setting page-level properties so that you can easily disable this feature after deployment.

Why: By enabling smart navigation you reduce flickering during postbacks, preserve the scroll position, maintain the input focus, and retain only one item in the browser's history even after multiple postbacks. Smart navigation works only with Internet Explorer 5.0 or later versions, but is ignored for browsers such as Netscape Navigator or earlier versions of Internet Explorer.

Why not: Smart navigation is implemented by means of client-side JavaScript code. At times, this code interferes with your custom client-side scripts. You might want to turn smart navigation off when testing custom JavaScript routines and turn it on once again after you've completed the debugging of those routines to ensure that everything continues to work correctly. Also, we have occasionally noticed weird behaviors in Internet Explorer (including unexplainable crashes) that disappeared when we turned off smart navigation.

More details: You can turn smart navigation on at the page level by setting the SmartNavigation property of the Page object (either in the Properties window or in the HTML editor), but it is preferable to enable it for the entire application by setting the smartNavigation attribute in Web.config as follows:

```
<configuration>
   <system.web>
      <pages smartNavigation="true" />
   </system.web>
</configuration>
```

29.7 The EnableViewState property

Set the EnableViewState property to false for all the controls that don't need to retain their state between postbacks. If no control on the Web page preserves its state between postbacks, set the page's EnableViewState property to false.

Why: Disabling the ViewState for one or more controls reduces the size of the hidden __VIEWSTATE field and decreases the number of bytes sent to the client and back to the server when a postback occurs.

More details: You can safely disable the ViewState at the page level if the page allows leaving the current page only by means of HyperLink controls. If the page includes one or more controls that can fire a postback, or it contains one or more controls that are filled by data binding, or if the code-behind class contains one or more *xxxx*Changed events, then you should leave the ViewState enabled at the page level and disable it only for the controls that don't depend on this feature.

29.8 The page title

The <Title> tag in a Web Forms page should reflect the page contents as closely as possible. This guideline is especially important if you use the same .aspx page to display different content, possibly taken from a database.

Why: In addition to making the page's title more descriptive for the end user, changing the title to reflect the page's content helps search engines correctly index the many variations of the same page.

How to: The simplest way to control the page's title from your code is by entering the following value for the title property in the Properties window:

```
<%= GetTitle() %>
```

which corresponds to manually editing the code in the .aspx file to embed a reference to a method or a property exposed by the code-behind class:

```
<title><%= GetTitle() %></title>
```

The code-behind class must expose a method or a property that returns the desired value, as in the following example:

```
' [Visual Basic]
Public Function GetTitle() As String
   ' ArticleID is the ID of the currently displayed article.
   Return "Article #" & articleID.ToString()
End Function

// [C#]
public string GetTitle()
```

```
{
    // ArticleID is the ID of the currently displayed article.
    return "Article #" + articleID.ToString();
}
```

29.9 Accounting for Web crawlers

Use the Crawler property of the Request.Browser object to detect whether the user agent is a Web crawler and to configure behavior accordingly, for example, by not incrementing pageview counters and stripping client-side JavaScript code snippets.

29.10 Disabling debug mode in production sites

Ensure that you disable debug mode when deploying the ASP.NET application or when profiling or stressing it.

Why: ASP.NET applications compiled in debug mode are larger, take more memory, and run slower.

How to: You can set debug mode on or off at the application level by setting the debug attribute of the <compilation> element in the root Web.config file.

```
<configuration>
   <system.web>
      <compilation debug="false" />
   </system.web>
</configuration>
```

29.11 Deprecated Response properties

Don't use the following deprecated properties of the Response object: CacheControl, Expires and ExpiresAbsolute (use the HttpCachePolicy class), and Buffer (use the BufferOutput property instead).

29.12 Using ViewState vs. manually restoring control's contents

When displaying a lot of data in a list or template control—that is, a DropDownList, ListBox, Repeater, DataList, or DataGrid control—carefully consider the implications of relying on the ASP.NET ViewState mechanism rather than manually reloading data in the control at each postback. In general, favor the ViewState mechanism unless you expect that many clients will browse your application through a slow connection (such as a dial-up connection).

More details: Keep in mind that by disabling the ViewState mechanism you effectively give up many handy features of template controls, such as *xxxx*Changed events, pagination, editing, and so forth. You can estimate the size of the ViewState by turning on ASP.NET tracing (see rule 29.57).

Example: The following example shows how you can shape your code so that it initializes a control named ddlCountries at each postback (if its EnableViewState property is false) or just the first time the page is loaded (if EnableViewState is true). Notice, however, that if you disable the ViewState mechanism for a list control, you should save and then restore the index of the currently selected item by some other means.

```vb
' [Visual Basic]
Private Sub Page_Load(ByVal sender As Object, ByVal e As EventArgs) Handles MyBase.Load
    If Not Me.IsPostBack OrElse Not ddlCountries.EnableViewState Then
        ' Initialize the ddlCountries control here.
        ...
    End If
End Sub
```

```csharp
// [C#]
private void Page_Load(object sender, System.EventArgs e)
{
    if ( ! this.IsPostBack || ! ddlCountries.EnableViewState )
    {
        // Initialize the ddlCountries control here.
        ...
    }
}
```

29.13 AutoPostBack controls

If a Web Forms page contains one or more controls whose AutoPostBack property is set to true, ensure that users can also cause a postback by means of a Button, LinkButton, or Image-Button control. At the very minimum, add a warning to your users that they must enable client-side scripting to navigate your site.

Why: The AutoPostBack feature relies on client-side JavaScript code; if a form contains Auto-PostBack controls and the user has disabled JavaScript support, the user has no means to submit the form unless you also provide one or more button controls.

29.14 Image-based and hyperlink-based controls

Use the following guidelines to decide which kind of image or hyperlink control is more suitable in different cases:

a.   Use an Image control to display an image that doesn't react to clicks.

b.   Use a HyperLink control to display a link to another page, if you don't require that fields on the current form be processed by server-side code.

c.   Use a Button control for push buttons that must fire a server-side event when clicked.

d.   Use a LinkButton control for a hyperlink element that must fire a server-side event when clicked.

e.   Use an ImageButton control for a clickable image that must fire a server-side event.

29.15 User input validation

Always validate user input and all data coming from the client, including posted files, cookies, and the query string.

Why: Failing to validate user input thoroughly makes your application prone to exploits and attacks, including SQL injection attacks and cross-site scripting attacks.

How to: Here's a list of programming techniques you can adopt to reduce exposure to afore-mentioned attacks:

a. Use parameterized ADO.NET Command objects and pass data entered by end users as parameters to such commands (see rule 28.21).

b. If you can't use parameterized Commands—for example, because you are creating SQL code dynamically—use the String.Replace method to double all single quote characters, as in the following:

```
' [Visual Basic]
Dim country As String = txtCountry.Text.Replace("'", "''")
```

```
// [C#]
string country = txtCountry.Text.Replace("'", "''");
```

c. Leave the ValidateRequest page attribute to true, its default value. This setting causes an HttpRequestValidationException to be thrown if the user enters a string containing a <script> tag or other dangerous patterns, thus helping to protect against cross-site script-ing attacks.

d. Always use the Server.HtmlEncode method to encode text extracted from a control, a cookie, the Request.Forms collection, the Request.QueryString property, or a file that was submitted by the client (see rule 29.17). If the text is supposed to represent a URL, use the Server.UrlEncode method instead.

e. Consider stripping characters that can't be part of a legal input value. For example, the following code strips angle brackets (to discard HTML tags), single quotes and dashes (to protect from SQL injection), and percentage symbols (to avoid encoded characters in a URL).

```
' [Visual Basic]
Dim country As String = Regex.Replace(txtCountry.Text, "[<>'%-]", "")
```

```
// [C#]
string country = Regex.Replace(txtCountry.Text, "[<>'%-]", "");
```

f. Avoid using the Response.Write method or the Label or Literal controls to display data that you haven't carefully validated. If in doubt, use the Server.HtmlEncode method to protect against cross-site scripting attacks.

29.16 Formatting and parsing according to user language

Consider using the Request.UserLanguages collection to format numbers and dates according to the user's locale and to change the language used for resource files.

More details: The UserLanguages collection contains all the languages that the remote user has specified in her browser, with the first element in the collection being the preferred language. You can format numbers and dates according to such a language by inserting the following code in the Page_Load event handler:

```
' [Visual Basic]
Dim ci As CultureInfo = CultureInfo.CreateSpecificCulture(Request.UserLanguages(0))
Thread.CurrentThread.CurrentCulture = ci    ' Used for formatting.
Thread.CurrentThread.CurrentUICulture = ci   ' Used for resources.
```

```
// [C#]
CultureInfo ci = CultureInfo.CreateSpecificCulture(Request.UserLanguages[0]);
Thread.CurrentThread.CurrentCulture = ci;    // Used for formatting.
Thread.CurrentThread.CurrentUICulture = ci;  // Used for resources.
```

Notice that you *must* use the CultureInfo.CreateSpecificCulture static method. You can't just pass the first element in the collection to the CultureInfo's constructor because neutral cultures such as "en" or "it" would throw a NotSupportedException. Also note that the preceding code fails if ASP.NET runs as partially trusted code because in this case it doesn't have the permission to change a thread's culture programmatically (see rule 33.17).

You can also set the default culture and UI culture for all the pages in the ASP.NET application by setting two attributes in the Web.config file:

```
<configuration>
   <system.web>
      <globalization culture="en-US" uiCulture="en-US" />
   </system.web>
</configuration>
```

Finally, you can set the culture and UI culture for an individual page by setting the page's Culture and UICulture properties, either in the Property window or in the @ Page directive:

```
<%@ Page Culture="en-US" UICulture="en-US" %>
```

29.17 Displaying data from files or database fields

Always use the Server.HtmlEncode method when displaying data taken from input fields or database fields to an HTML or Web control.

Why: The Server.HtmlEncode method ensures that special characters such as < and > are displayed correctly and prevents malicious users from injecting scripts into your pages by submitting strings that embed <script> elements.

```
' [Visual Basic]
' In a real app this value would be read from a database.
Dim valueFromDB As String = "<b>123</b>"
' Next statement displays "123" in boldface.
lblValue1.Text = valueFromDB
' Next statement displays "<b>123</b>" (no boldface).
lblValue2.Text = Server.HtmlEncode(valueFromDB)

// [C#]
// In a real app this value would be read from a database.
string valueFromDB = "<b>123</b>";
// Next statement displays "123" in boldface.
lblValue1.Text = valueFromDB;
// Next statement displays "<b>123</b>" (no boldface).
lblValue2.Text = Server.HtmlEncode(valueFromDB);
```

29.18 Asking for confirmation before critical operations

If a button control performs a potentially dangerous operation, such as deleting a record, ask the user to confirm the operation.

How to: You can ask for confirmation by attaching a piece of JavaScript code to the button's onclick client-side event. When the user clicks the button, a message box appears (see Figure 29-2). If the user clicks the Cancel button, the button won't perform its default operation (typically a postback).

```
' [Visual Basic]
Dim code As String = "javascript:return confirm('Do you confirm?');"
btnDelete.Attributes.Add("onclick", code)

// [C#]
string code = "javascript:return confirm('Do you confirm?');";
btnDelete.Attributes.Add("onclick", code);
```

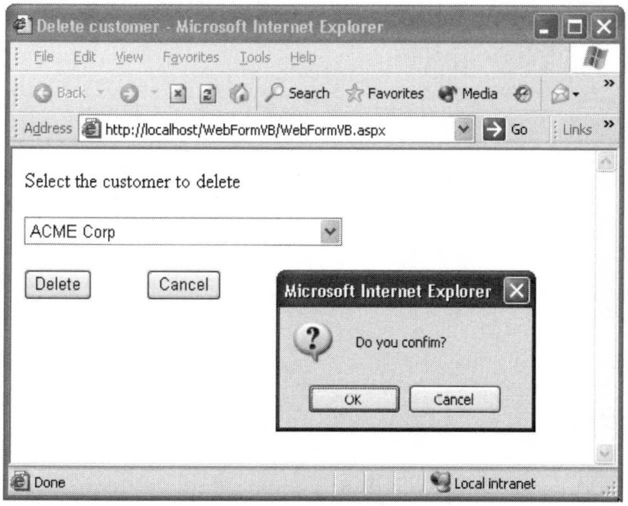

Figure 29-2   A message box displayed when the user clicks a push button

29.19 Client-side and server-side data validation

Validate input data on the client, if possible, by means of ASP.NET validator controls, but always enforce validation on the server as well.

Why: Validating the data on the client makes the application more responsive and more scalable. Performing the validation on the server ensures that malicious users can't enter invalid data in the system by disabling client-side scripts or by saving the HTML file locally and submitting it later after deleting the client-side JavaScript code.

More details: Validation is performed on the server by default; the only way to disable automatic server-side validation is setting the CausesValidation property to false for one or more submit buttons on the page.

You can test the result of this method by means of the Page.IsValid read-only property, which requires that the Page.Validate method has already been invoked. The ASP.NET infrastructure invokes this method after firing the Page_Load event. If you use this property from inside the Page_Load event handler you must invoke the Validate method yourself, though, because the automatic validation hasn't occurred yet.

29.20 Checking mandatory fields

If an empty string is an invalid value for a field, use a RequiredFieldValidator control to validate its value. Don't rely on the fact that you already use another validator control to check the value in the control.

Why: All validator controls except RequiredFieldValidator skip the validation step if the control contains no characters. Therefore, you must test for the empty string case separately, and you need a RequiredFieldValidator to run such a test on the client.

More details: You can invoke the Validate method in the Page_Load event handler before sending the page to the browser for the first time. This action causes all the RequiredFieldValidator controls on the page to display their error message near the corresponding mandatory field. If you assign an asterisk to the ErrorMessage property of these validator controls, the end user has a visual clue of all the fields that must be filled before submitting the form, as shown in Figure 29-3. Interestingly, the asterisk disappears as the user moves to the next field after entering a value in the current control.

```
' [Visual Basic]
Private Sub Page_Load(ByVal sender As Object, ByVal e As EventArgs) Handles MyBase.Load
   ' Force failure of all validator controls.
   If Not Me.IsPostBack Then Me.Validate()
End Sub

// [C#]
private void Page_Load(object sender, System.EventArgs e)
{
   // Force failure of all validator controls.
   if ( ! this.IsPostBack)
      this.Validate();
}
```

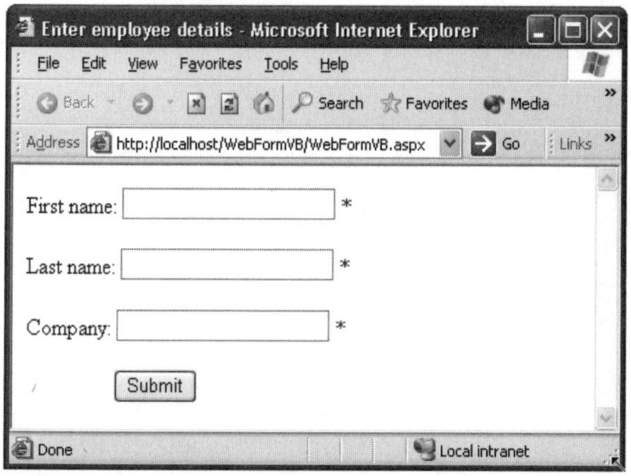

Figure 29-3   Use RequiredFieldValidator controls to mark all the required fields in a Web page.

29.21 Checking data type in input fields

When using the CompareValidator control to compare the numeric or date value of a control with the contents of another control, use an additional CompareValidator or RangeValidator control to ensure that the contents of the other control can be converted to the expected numeric or date value.

Why: If the value in the control specified by the ControlToValidate property of a CompareValidator can be converted to the data type specified by the Type property but the value in the control specified by the ControlToCompare property can't be converted (or is an empty string), the input control mistakenly passes the validation.

See also: See rule 29.20 about the need for an additional RequiredFieldValidation to check that both the control to validate and the control to compare with aren't empty.

29.22 Syntax restrictions in the RegularExpressionValidator control

Don't use Microsoft .NET Framework–specific extensions—for example, the (?i) option for case-insensitive comparisons—in the regular expressions enforced by means of a RegularExpressionValidator control.

Why: The regular expression of a RegularExpressionValidator control is applied both on the client side (using the JavaScript regular expression engine) and on the server side (using the .NET regular expression engine). The JavaScript syntax is a subset of the .NET syntax, so in most cases the same regular expression works well in both cases. However, if the regular expression contains a .NET-specific extension, it isn't recognized by the JavaScript regular expression engine and all values are rejected as invalid.

By avoiding .NET-specific syntax forms that aren't supported by JavaScript, you ensure that the control behaves in the same way both on the client and the server.

> **Note** Never forget that the regular expression you assign to the ValidationExpression property of a RegularExpressionValidator control is visible as clear text in the HTML page; therefore, you should never embed confidential data such as user or account names, passwords, and so forth, in the regular expression pattern.

29.23 Accepting uploaded files from the user

Avoid using the HtmlInputFile control's SaveAs method to store the incoming data to temporary files on the server's hard disk. Instead, read data from the incoming stream and save it directly to the appropriate data store, for example, a database.

Why: The SaveAs method requires that you grant ASP.NET an identity with the permission to write to the server's hard disk. Instead, the technique we recommend simplifies deployment and increases the application's robustness.

How to: File uploads work only if you set the form's enctype attribute to the value multipart/form-data; this attribute doesn't appear in the Properties window and must be entered manually in the .aspx file, after switching to HTML view:

```
<form id="Form1" method="post" runat="server" enctype="multipart/form-data">
```

The following code snippet shows how you can read data uploaded through an HtmlInputFile control without using its SaveAs method:

```
' [Visual Basic]
If Not hfilDocument.PostedFile Is Nothing Then
    ' Read from the incoming stream.
    Dim length As Integer = hfilDocument.PostedFile.ContentLength
    Dim br As New BinaryReader(hfilDocument.PostedFile.InputStream)
    Dim bytes() As Byte = br.ReadBytes(length)
    ' Data is now in the byte array and can be stored in a
    ' database table or a session variable.
    Session("Data") = bytes
Else
    ' No file has been posted.
    ...
End If

// [C#]
if (hfilDocument.PostedFile != null )
{
    // Read from the incoming stream.
    int length = hfilDocument.PostedFile.ContentLength;
    BinaryReader br = new BinaryReader(hfilDocument.PostedFile.InputStream);
    byte[] bytes = br.ReadBytes(length);
    // Data is now in the byte array and can be stored in a
    // database table or a session variable.
    Session["Data"] = bytes;
}
else
```

```
{
    // No file has been posted.
    ...
}
```

More details: Remember to include a submit button (or another control that is capable of causing a postback) on the page that hosts the HtmlInputFile control because this control doesn't raise any server-side event.

29.24 Size and type constraints on uploaded files

Use the maxRequestLength attribute of the <httpRuntime> tag in Web.config to limit the size of the data that a client can upload. The default value for this attribute is 4M, so you should increase it if you expect users legitimately to upload larger files, or decrease it if you expect to receive smaller files. For improved security, check the extension of the file being uploaded to the server to ensure that it is one of the accepted extensions.

Why: These recommendations reduce the risk that a malicious user can upload an executable file on the server or just send large files to consume free space on the server.

How to: Here's a Web.config fragment that decreases the maximum size of uploaded files to 512 KB (size is in Kbytes, default is 4096):

```
<configuration>
    <system.web>
        <httpRuntime maxRequestLength="512" />
    </system.web>
</configuration>
```

The HtmlInputFile's Accept property is a comma-delimited list of MIME encodings. This property doesn't appear in the Properties window; thus, you can set it only by code (for example, in the Page_Load event handler) or directly in the .aspx file. For example, the following settings *should* restrict valid uploads to image and text files:

```
<INPUT type="file" size="64" id="File1" name="File1"
    runat="server" accept="image/*,text/*">
```

Unfortunately, most browsers (including Internet Explorer) don't implement this feature, and they actually ignore the Accept property. For a more robust policy, you should check the file's extension by using code, as in this example:

```
' [Visual Basic]
If Not hfilDocument.PostedFile Is Nothing Then
    Dim ext As String = Path.GetExtension(hfilDocument.PostedFile.FileName).ToLower()
    If ext = ".bmp" OrElse ext = ".jpg" OrElse ext == ".gif" Then
        ' The file is an image—accept it.
        ...
    Else
        lblMessage.Text = "Invalid file extension"
    End If
End If
```

```
// [C#]
if (hfilDocument.PostedFile != null )
{
    string ext = Path.GetExtension(hfilDocument.PostedFile.FileName).ToLower();
    if ( ext == ".bmp" || ext == ".jpg" || ext = ".gif" )
    {
        // The file is an image–accept it.
        ...
    }
    else
    {
        lblMessage.Text = "Invalid file extension";
    }
}
```

29.25 Checking filenames

If the user can enter the name of a file that corresponds to a location on the server, ensure that the file path is relative and can't reference an arbitrary directory on the server's hard disk.

Why: This technique limits the odds that an unauthorized user is allowed to read private data or overwrite files on the server.

How to: You can use a regular expression to filter out filenames that contain an initial backslash, double periods, and colon symbols. You can apply the regular expression either by code or by means of a RegularExpressionValidator control. The following example shows how to accept only relative filenames whose path portions contain only letters, digits, spaces, and underscores.

```
' [Visual Basic]
Dim re As New Regex("^[A-Za-z0-9_ ]+([\\.][A-Za-z0-9_ ]+)*$")
Dim fileName As String = txtFileName.Text
If re.IsMatch(fileName) Then
    ' Filename is relative, you can use it safely.
    fileName = Path.Combine("c:\userdata", fileName)
Else
    ' Filename isn't relative.
    lblMessage.Text = "Invalid file path"
End If
```

```
// [C#]
Regex re = new Regex(@"^[A-Za-z0-9_ ]+([\\.][A-Za-z0-9_ ]+)*$");
string fileName = txtFileName.Text;
if ( re.IsMatch(fileName) )
{
    // Filename is relative, you can use it safely.
    fileName = Path.Combine(@"c:\userdata", fileName);
}
else
{
    // Filename isn't relative.
    lblMessage.Text = "Invalid file path";
}
```

29.26 Opening and closing database connections

Define a page-level connection object, open it at the top of the Page_Load event handler, and close it at the bottom in the Page_Unload event handler.

Why: This coding guideline ensures that code in all the event handlers on the Web page can use an open connection.

```vb
' [Visual Basic]
' The connection to the Pubs database
Dim cn As New SqlConnection(pubsConnString)

Private Sub Page_Load(ByVal sender As Object, ByVal e As EventArgs) Handles MyBase.Load
   ' Open the connection here.
   cn.Open()
   ...
End Sub

Private Sub Page_Unload(ByVal sender As Object, ByVal e As EventArgs) Handles MyBase.Unload
   ...
   ' Close the connection here, if still open.
   If cn.State = ConnectionState.Open Then cn.Close()
End Sub
```

```csharp
// [C#]
// The connection to the Pubs database
SqlConnection cn = new SqlConnection(pubsConnString);

private void Page_Load(object sender, EventArgs e)
{
   // Open the connection here.
   cn.Open();
   ...
}

private void Page_Unload(object sender, EventArgs e)
{
   ...
   // Close the connection here, if still open.
   if ( cn.State == ConnectionState.Open )
      cn.Close();
}
```

29.27 SQL Server authentication in Web applications

Use the following guidelines when deciding whether your Web application should use Microsoft SQL Server authentication or Windows authentication.

    a.   Check the user identity at the IIS level or when the user logs into the application, if possible. After you've authenticated the user, use SQL Server authorization with a connection string that maps to a single SQL Server account or to one of a small set of accounts (depending on the user role). This approach creates a so-called *trusted subsystem*, in which the database trusts the application and assumes that the application has correctly authenticated the user and that the user is authorized to perform the current operation. Here's a connection string that uses SQL Server authentication:

```
Data Source=servername;User ID=username;Password=mypwd;Initial catalog=Pubs
```

b. Use Windows authentication in intranet applications if you need the original user identity to flow to the database, for example, for auditing purposes or to perform authorization at the database object level. Note that you must configure IIS for Integrated Windows authentication and your users must use Internet Explorer to flow their identity to your ASP.NET application and from there to the database. This approach is known as the *impersonation/delegation* model. Here's a connection string that uses Windows authentication:

```
Data Source=servername;Integrated Security=SSPI;Initial catalog=Pubs
```

c. You can't use Windows authentication if there is a firewall between the Web application and the database, or when the application and the database live in nontrusting domains. Also, keep in mind that SQL Server must validate the user identity against the domain's Security Account Manager (SAM); typically, the SAM isn't on the same machine as SQL Server, a detail that can slow down Windows authentication. Finally, you can't use Windows authentication when working with databases other than SQL Server.

d. In general, Windows authentication is more secure than SQL Server authentication because you never need to store the user name and password anywhere or send them in clear text over the network. If your application relies on IIS Integrated Windows authentication, users can be forced by the operating system to use longer passwords and to change them periodically, which makes the mechanism more secure. When using SQL Server authentication, consider using a secure connection between the Web application and the database, for example, using IPSec or Secure Sockets Layer (SSL).

e. Using Windows authentication in ASP.NET applications that impersonate the remote user prevents you from fully leveraging the connection pooling feature. You make the best of connection pooling by either using SQL Server authentication or using Windows authentication with an ASP.NET application that has a fixed identity. In the latter case, you should create a least-privilege Windows account for the ASP.NET application and create a corresponding account on SQL Server. You should create a local account for ASP.NET if the Web application and the database are on the same machine, or a domain account if they are in the same domain or in trusting domains.

f. When using SQL Server authentication, don't use the built-in sa or db_owner accounts; instead, create one or more SQL Server accounts with just the privileges that are needed for a given operation. (This is known as the *least-privilege principle*.) Always use strong passwords that can resist dictionary attacks.

g. In larger, multitiered applications, you should not connect directly to the database from inside the ASP.NET application. Instead, you should put all your data access code in serviced components (COM+ components) stored in a server library. Such components run in a separate process and optionally under a different identity. They can even impersonate a different user by invoking the LogonUser Windows API function, provided that they run under an identity that is granted the permission to call LogonUser. (We recommend that you never call LogonUser from inside ASP.NET; when running on Microsoft Windows 2000 this function requires the Act As Part Of The Operating System option, which indirectly lowers the security bar for the entire system.)

More details: An additional advantage of COM+ server libraries is that the identity under which they run can be set by administrators using the IIS MMC plug-in and that the identity password is stored in encrypted form inside the COM+ catalog. Besides, if the data layer is encapsulated in COM+ server components, it is later possible to move the entire layer to a different machine; this machine might be the only computer that is physically connected to the machine on which SQL Server is installed. (COM+ components might run on the same machine as SQL Server, but we don't recommend this solution unless the computer is powerful enough to host both the database and Component Services effectively.)

See also: For more information on all the points touched on in this guideline, read Chapters 3, 4, 8, and 12 of *Building Secure ASP.NET Applications: Authentication, Authorization, and Secure Communication*, which are available online at *http://msdn.microsoft.com/library/en-us/dnnetsec/html/secnetlpMSDN.asp*.

29.28 Lengthy server-side operations

Consider using the Response.IsClientConnected at the end of (or during) a time-consuming server operation, for example, after a complex database query, to check whether the user has canceled the request. If the client isn't connected any longer, you can invoke the Response.End method and avoid sending data to the client.

29.29 Data binding in Web Forms

Use the following guidelines when performing data binding in a Web Form:

a. If possible, bind to a DataReader rather than a DataSet, DataTable, or DataView object. (Read rule 28.11.)

b. Avoid the Page.DataBind method; instead, invoke the DataBind method for each control that you want to bind to its data source. (The page-level DataBind method must recursively call the DataBind method of all the controls on the page.)

c. When working with template controls—that is, the Repeater, DataList, and DataGrid controls—attempt to keep the names of the container control and its child controls as short as possible. For example, a Label control named lblProductName hosted in a DataGrid named dgrOrderDetails that contains 100 rows generates 100 controls whose names are in the form dgrOrderDetails:_ctl1:lblProductName, producing nearly 7400 characters in the output HTML. (These names appear both in the name and in the id attributes.) By using shorter names such as dgrOd and lblPn, you can save 3800 bytes and make your page render more quickly in the client browser.

 d.   When working on a template control, consider generating HTML code manually for the rows that only display information (as opposed to rows used to edit data). This technique generates less CPU activity on the server and sends fewer bytes to the client (see preceding point). You can also achieve these goals by using HTML controls rather than Web Forms controls, a technique that is more convenient when you need to access the controls from inside an ItemCreated or an ItemDataBind server-side event.

 e.   Define the data binding behavior at design time using the features of Microsoft Visual Studio .NET if possible. For example, bind controls to a DataView in the form's tray area if you want to sort or filter data after reading it from the database.

 f.   In a DataGrid control, use template columns rather than data bound columns because template columns give you more flexibility. After binding the DataGrid control to a DataSet or a DataView at design time, you can use the Columns tab of the DataGrid Properties dialog box to add all the data fields that you wish, you can quickly convert these bound columns into template columns by clicking the Convert This Column Into A Template Column hyperlink at the bottom of the window (see Figure 29-4).

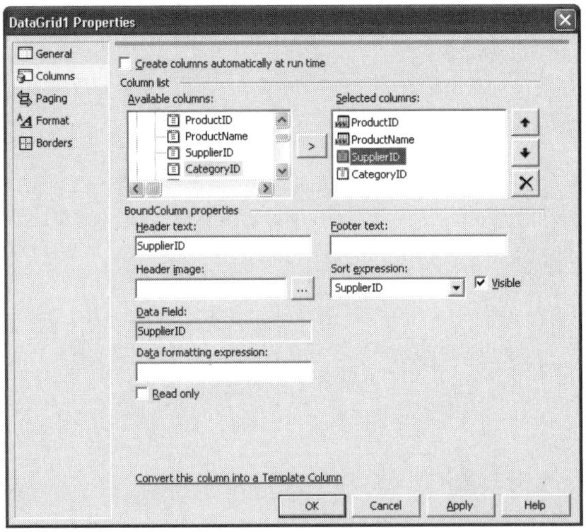

Figure 29-4   The Columns page of the DataGrid Properties dialog box

 g.   Avoid the DataBinder.Eval method because it uses reflection and is therefore slower than strong-typed access. This method should be used only when you don't know in advance to which data source the control will be bound. (See next two points.)

 h.   Cast the Container.DataItem object to a DataRowView object when binding to a DataSet, DataTable, or DataView, or cast to a DbDataRecord object if you are binding to a DataReader.

 i.   When casting to a DbDataRecord object, consider retrieving values by means of a strong-typed method such as GetInt32 or GetDouble, which is slightly faster than the default Item property (Visual Basic) or the indexer (C#). Be aware that these methods take the index of the column rather than its name; therefore, they affect both readability and ease of maintenance negatively.

j. Consider writing code in the ItemDataBound event handler to extract values from the data source manually. This mechanism is more efficient if the control must display the values of multiple fields.

More details: When you use the Visual Studio .NET editor to create a set of template columns in a DataGrid control, this is the kind of code that Visual Studio .NET produces for the .aspx page:

```
<ItemTemplate>
   <asp:Label runat="server"
      Text='<%# DataBinder.Eval(Container, "DataItem.ProductID") %>'>
   </asp:Label>
</ItemTemplate>
```

According to preceding point h, you should modify this code to cast the Container.DataItem object to a specific object, whose type depends on whether you are binding to a DataSet, DataTable, DataView, or a DataReader. In the former case, you must cast to a DataRowView object:

```
' [Visual Basic]
<asp:Label runat="server"
   Text='<%# DirectCast(Container.DataItem, System.Data.DataRowView)("ProductID") %>'>

// [C#]
<asp:Label runat="server"
   Text='<%# (Container.DataItem as System.Data.DataRowView)["ProductID"] %>'>
```

When binding to a DataReader, you must cast to the DbDataRecord object; in this case, you can slightly improve execution speed by using strong-typed methods:

```
' [Visual Basic]
<asp:Label runat="server" Text=
   '<%# DirectCast(Container.DataItem, System.Data.Common.DbDataRecord).GetInt32(0) %>'>

// [C#]
<asp:Label runat="server"
   Text='<%# (Container.DataItem as System.Data.DataRowView).GetInt32(0) %>'>
```

29.30 Displaying multiple database columns in databound list controls

When displaying multiple database fields in a ListBox or DropDownList control, use a proper SQL statement to combine multiple database fields in a single value so that you can directly bind the control to the calculated column.

Example: Run the following code to display last and first names of Pubs authors in a ListBox control. (The code assumes that cn is an open SqlConnection object that points to the Pubs database.)

```
' [Visual Basic]
Dim sql As String = "SELECT au_id, au_lname+', '+au_fname As Name FROM Authors"
Dim cmd As New SqlCommand(sql, cn)
```

```
Dim dr As SqlDataReader = cmd.ExecuteReader()
' Bind the DataReader to the ListBox control.
lstAuthors.DataSource = dr
lstAuthors.DataTextField = "Name"
lstAuthors.DataValueField = "Au_id"
lstAuthors.DataBind()

// [C#]
string sql = "SELECT au_id, au_lname+','+au_fname As Name FROM Authors";
SqlCommand cmd = new SqlCommand(sql, cn);
SqlDataReader dr = cmd.ExecuteReader();
// Bind the DataReader to the ListBox control.
lstAuthors.DataSource = dr;
lstAuthors.DataTextField = "Name";
lstAuthors.DataValueField = "Au_id";
lstAuthors.DataBind();
```

29.31 The ItemCommand event

Don't write code for the ItemCommand to trap clicks on buttons hosted in a Repeater, DataList, or DataGrid control if the button's CommandName property is equal to Select, Edit, Delete, Update, or Cancel. Instead, use the more specific SelectedIndexChanged, EditCommand, DeleteCommand, UpdateCommand, and CancelCommand events.

Why: By using a specific event, you don't need to check the CommandName property from inside the ItemCommand event handler to determine which action should be undertaken. This guideline also ensures that you don't process the click twice, once in the ItemCommand and once in the more specific event.

29.32 State management: The ViewState dictionary

Use the ViewState dictionary to persist variable values between postbacks to the same page.

Why: The ViewState dictionary is stored in a hidden field (named __VIEWSTATE) and works with all browsers, even if the end user has disabled cookie support. Viewstate data is hashed by default and is optionally encrypted, thus users can't easily modify it or even just display it if you enabled encryption.

Why not: You can store only serializable objects in the ViewState. Besides, storing large objects in the ViewState bloats the HTML text that is sent back and forth; for this reason, you should favor Session variables to store these large objects if most clients use a slow connection.

Another important reason for not using the ViewState dictionary is security; the data you pass back and forth is encoded in Base64 format but isn't encrypted by default. In other words, it isn't apparently human-readable, but an expert user can decode it easily, for example, using the Fritz Onion's ViewState Decoder tool (available at *http://www.pluralsight.com/tools.aspx*). For this reason, you shouldn't store sensitive information such as passwords and credit card numbers in the ViewState, or at least you should encrypt the ViewState by means of the ViewStateUserKey property (see rule 29.44).

More details: Always check that a ViewState value isn't a null object reference before using it. The following code illustrates the correct way to increment a variable stored in the ViewState dictionary:

```
' [Visual Basic]
Dim count As Integer = 0
Dim o As Object = ViewState("Count")
If Not o Is Nothing Then count = CInt(o)
ViewState("Count") = count + 1


// [C#]
int count = 0;
object o = ViewState["Count"];
if ( o != null )
   count = (int) o;
ViewState["Count"] = count + 1;
```

See also: See rule 29.41 about wrapping a ViewState variable in a property.

29.33 State management: The in-process Session dictionary

Use the in-process Session dictionary to store values that must be shared among all the pages in an application running on a single server computer.

Why: The Session dictionary enables you to store values on the server and doesn't bloat the HTML page, so it is a good alternative to the ViewState dictionary for slow connections, even for preserving values between postbacks to the same page. The in-process Session dictionary is the most efficient kind of session.

Why not: The in-process Session dictionary has a number of disadvantages, even though ASP.NET offers a reasonable solution for most of them:

- In-process Session dictionaries don't work with applications running on Web gardens and Web farms. These larger applications should use out-process Session dictionaries, as explained in rules 29.34 and 29.35.

- By default, Session dictionaries of any type (not just in-process Sessions) require cookie support; if you can't guarantee that all client browsers support cookies, you should enable support for cookieless Sessions by setting the cookieless attribute of the <sessionState> element in Web.config as follows:

  ```
  <configuration>
     <system.web>
        <sessionState mode="InProc" cookieless="true" timeout="20" />
     </system.web>
  </configuration>
  ```

- Storing large objects in the in-process Session dictionary consumes memory on the server and affects scalability negatively; if scalability is an issue, use out-process Session dictionaries.

- If the current ASP.NET application crashes or is recycled, all in-process Session values are lost; again, you can improve reliability by resorting to out-process Session dictionaries.

An ASP.NET process can be recycled because it has met one of the conditions you stated in Web.config (such as its memory threshold) or because the Web.config, the Global.asax file, or a file in the Bin directory has been modified. Some antivirus programs can scan and modify one of these files and therefore they might indirectly start a process recycling. For this reason, you should disable antivirus software or at least configure it so that it doesn't modify these files.

More details: Always check that a Session value isn't a null object reference before using it, as in the following example:

```
' [Visual Basic]
Dim count As Integer = 0
Dim o As Object = Session("Count")
If Not o Is Nothing Then count = CInt(o)
Session("Count") = count + 1

// [C#]
int count = 0;
object o = Session["Count"];
if ( o != null )
   count = (int) o;
Session["Count"] = count + 1;
```

See also: See rule 29.35 about storing nonserializable objects in a Session dictionary.

29.34 State management: The service-based Session dictionary

Use the Session dictionary but enable support for out-process Windows service-based Session dictionaries in applications that run on a Web garden (multiple instances of an ASP.NET application running on the same machine) or a Web farm (multiple instances of an ASP.NET application running on different computers).

Why: Out-process Session dictionaries can be shared by all the processes in a Web garden and all computers on a Web farm.

Why not: Out-process Session dictionaries are slower than standard (in-process) Session dictionaries, even though the advantages of out-process collections usually compensate for their lower speed. Also, you can't store nonserializable objects in out-process Session dictionaries. Finally, service-based Session dictionaries might be a single point of failure for the entire Web farm, and if the computer hosting it crashes, all the clients that are currently logged on to the application lose their Session state.

How to: You enable support for Windows service-based Session dictionaries by using the following attributes in the <sessionState> tag in the application's Web.config file:

```
<configuration>
   <system.web>
      <sessionState mode="StateServer"
         stateConnectionString="tcpip=192.168.0.4:42424"
         stateNetworkTimeout="20" />
   </system.web>
</configuration>
```

The stateNetworkTimeout attribute enables you to decide how many seconds an ASP.NET application waits for a response from the state server; this attribute is optional and defaults to 10 seconds.

To activate out-process sessions based on a Windows service, you must start the Windows service named aspnet_state, which is installed with ASP.NET. You can use the NET START command from the command prompt to launch aspnet_state:

```
net start aspnet_state
```

In production sites, however, you'll probably want to run this service automatically when the server reboots. You can do this by setting the startup type setting for this service to Automatic in the Properties window of the Services snap-in for Microsoft Management Console (see Figure 29-5).

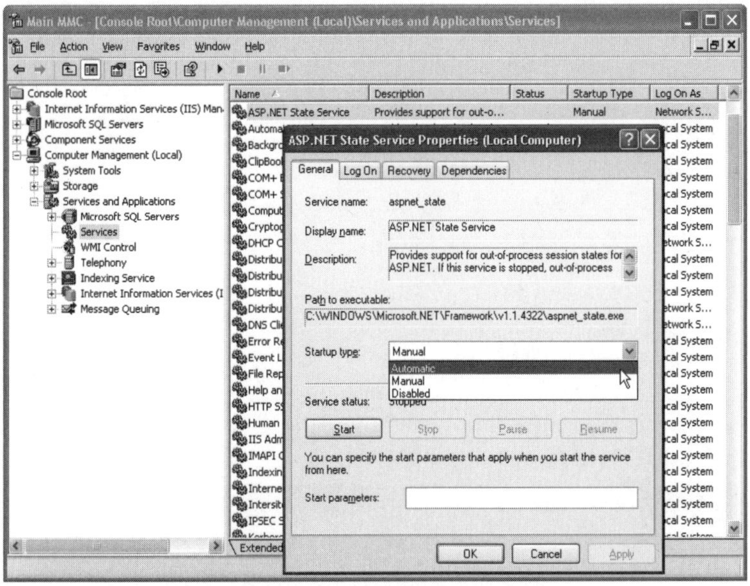

Figure 29-5   Setting the properties of the aspnet_state service

More details: The aspnet_state service doesn't require authentication, and all traffic between the ASP.NET application and the service isn't encrypted; thus, it is recommended that you run the state service on a computer that is behind a firewall. Also, consider using an encrypting protocol such as IPSec for improved security.

By default, the aspnet_state service listens to port 42424, so this is the port number you specify in the stateConnectionString attribute. (And you can omit it if you want.) You can configure the service to use a different port by editing the Port value under the HKEY_LOCAL_MACHINE\SYSTEM\CurrentControlSet\Services\aspnet_state\Parameters key in the registry. You shouldn't change the default port unless you have a good reason to do it, such as if the default port is already being used by another application.

See also: Read rule 29.59 for information about encrypting and storing the stateConnectionString value in the registry.

29.35 State management: The SQL Server–based Session dictionary

Use the Session dictionary but enable support for out-process SQL Server–based Session dictionaries for applications that run on a Web garden or a Web farm.

Why: SQL Server–based Session dictionaries have all the advantages and disadvantages of Windows service–based Sessions, plus the ability to survive system crashes. Additionally, you can run SQL Server on a cluster and avoid the single point of failure problem that you have with state-based Session dictionaries.

Why not: Sessions based on SQL Server are the slowest way to store Session data. Also, if your application doesn't use SQL Server for its own purposes, installing SQL Server just to support out-process Session dictionaries might be too expensive of a solution.

How to: You enable support for SQL Server–based Session dictionaries by using the following attributes in the <sessionState> tag in the application's Web.config file:

```
<configuration>
  <system.web>
    <sessionState
        mode="SqlServer"
        sqlConnectionString="data source=127.0.0.1;user id=sa;password=" />
  </system.web>
</configuration>
```

Before you can use ASP.NET sessions based on SQL Server, you must run either the InstallSqlState.sql or the InstallPersistSqlState.sql script in the C:\WINDOWS\Microsoft.NET\Framework\v1.1.4322 directory. You can run these scripts by dragging them inside the SQL Query Analyzer program (see Figure 29-6) or running them from the command prompt using the OSQL utility.

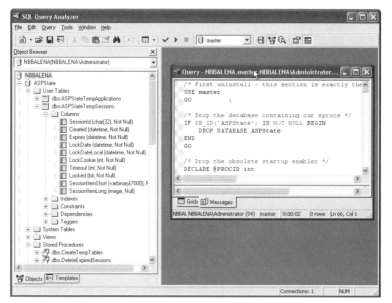

Figure 29-6   Installing and browsing the structure of the ASPState database

The InstallSqlState.sql script creates a new database named ASPState, containing all the stored procedures that ASP.NET requires to enable the SQL Server-based Session dictionary. It also installs a startup procedure named ASPState_Startup, which ensures that all the necessary TempDB tables used for storing session data are correctly re-created when SQL Server restarts. Because TempDB is used, write operations are slightly faster, but session data won't survive a reboot.

The InstallPersistSqlState.sql script performs the same sequence of actions, except that session variables are persisted in the ASPState database, and therefore they live even after the computer is restarted. ASP.NET also comes with the UninstallSqlState.sql script, should you wish to remove this database and all related stored procedures.

More details: If the connection string specified in the configuration file uses Integrated Windows security, your ASP.NET application must impersonate the identity of a user that is granted access to the database. (See rule 29.27 for more details.)

SQL Server–based Session dictionaries can be configured to work on a failover cluster, that is, a group of two or more identical and redundant Web servers that store session data on a SQL Server database running on a different computer. When working on a failover cluster, the <machineKey> element in the configuration file must have the same value for all the Web servers.

See also: Read rule 29.59 for information about encrypting and storing the sqlConnection-String value in the registry.

29.36 State management: Cookies

Use persistent cookies only for small amounts of user data that isn't critical from a security perspective and that must be preserved between visits to the Web site. You can also use either persistent or transient (in-memory) cookies to share data with Active Server Pages (ASP) and other non-ASP.NET applications running from the same Web site. In all other cases, don't use in-memory cookies to preserve temporary state during the user's session.

Why: Cookies are the simplest way to persist information between consecutive visits to the Web site. They work with Web gardens and Web farms and survive an application crash or recycling. They also offer a simple way to force expiration of data after a given number of minutes, hours, or days.

Why not: Cookies travel with each page request; therefore, a large number of cookies (or just a few cookies that carry large pieces of information) can slow down both HTTP requests and page rendering. Also, persistent cookies are stored on the client computer's hard disk (in the c:\Documents and Settings*username*\Cookies folder), and users can view, delete, and tamper with them; thus, consider whether you should encrypt data stored in cookies. Never forget that an unauthorized user might access cookies created by other users, depending on the operating system and on whether the file system supports Access Control Lists (ACLs), a detail server-side ASP.NET applications have no control over.

Finally, most browsers set a limit on the number of cookies per domain and their size: don't store more than 4 KB of data in each cookie and don't create more than 20 cookies for each domain. (You can overcome the latter limitation by storing multiple values in each cookie, though.)

How to: The following code snippets show how to create a cookie, remove a cookie, and read the value of all the cookies received from the client:

```vb
' [Visual Basic]
' Create a cookie with a given name and value.
Dim cookie As New HttpCookie("color", "red")
' Set its expiration date (2 weeks from now).
cookie.Expires = Now.AddDays(14)
' Send it to the client.
Response.Cookies.Add(cookie)

' Remove the "color" cookie.
Dim cookie2 As New HttpCookie("color")
' Set its expiration date to yesterday.
cookie2.Expires = Now.AddDays(-1)
' Send it to the client.
Response.Cookies.Add(cookie2)

' Read the value of all cookies.
For Each cookieName As String In Request.Cookies.AllKeys
    ' Get the cookie with a given name. (Assumes all cookies are single-valued.)
    Dim cookie As HttpCookie = Request.Cookies(cookieName)
    ' Use the cookie as needed.
    Dim val As String = cookie.Value
    ...
Next
```

```csharp
// [C#]
// Create a cookie with a given name and value.
HttpCookie cookie = new HttpCookie("color", "red");
// Set its expiration date (2 weeks from now).
cookie.Expires = DateTime.Now.AddDays(14);
// Send it to the client.
Response.Cookies.Add(cookie);

// Remove the "color" cookie.
HttpCookie cookie2 = new HttpCookie("color");
// Set its expiration date to yesterday.
cookie2.Expires = DateTime.Now.AddDays(-1);
// Send it to the client.
Response.Cookies.Add(cookie2);

// Read the value of all cookies.
foreach ( string cookieName in Request.Cookies.AllKeys )
{
    // Get the cookie with a given name. (Assumes all cookies are single-valued.)
    HttpCookie cookie = Request.Cookies[cookieName];
    // Use the cookie as needed.
    string val = cookie.Value;
    ...
}
```

More details: If security and cookie size are issues, consider storing all user-related data in a database on the server and use a cookie just to maintain the key of the row that corresponds to the user's data. (Basically, this is what ASP.NET does for you when you adopt SQL Server–based Session dictionaries.)

If you use cookies to exchange information with legacy ASP applications, remember that ASP and ASP.NET deal with cookies that don't have a specific path in a slightly different way. If you omit the cookie path, ASP assigns it the Web application name (such as "/AppName"), whereas ASP.NET assigns the path equal to the server name (that is, "/"). You should explicitly set the cookie path to have ASP.NET behave like ASP, as in this example:

```
' [Visual Basic]
cookie.Path = "/AppName"
```

```
// [C#]
cookie.Path = "/AppName";
```

29.37 State management: Hidden fields

Avoid using hidden fields as a means of storing data between page postbacks.

Why: Hidden fields offer the same benefits and drawbacks of using the ViewState dictionary (which in fact is held in the hidden field named __VIEWSTATE). Unlike hidden fields, the ViewState dictionary can hold multiple items and can be encrypted; therefore, there are very few good reasons for manually storing data in hidden fields.

Exceptions: Hidden fields are OK when posting data to another Web application that expects data in HTML controls. Also, you can use hidden fields to store results from calculations performed in JavaScript code when you want those results to be sent to the server when the page is posted.

29.38 State management: The Application dictionary

Avoid using the Application dictionary for storing application-wide variables that should be shared among all users. Instead, use global static variables or the Cache object. If opting for the Application dictionary anyway, use it only for data that is mostly read-only. Always compare values with *Nothing* (Visual Basic) or *null* (C#) before using them, and ensure that you bracket statements between calls to Lock and UnLock methods.

More details: Values in the Application dictionary are lost when the application is restarted, which can happen because of a fatal error or, more simply, because the ASP.NET process is recycled. If you want to preserve Application variables across process restarts, you should use the Application_OnEnd event to save all the values in the collection and restore them in the Application_Start event.

Example: The following code illustrates the correct way to increment an Application variable named Count.

```vb
' [Visual Basic]
Application.Lock()
Dim count As Integer = 0
Dim o As Object = Application("Count")
If Not o Is Nothing Then count = CInt(o)
Application("Count") = count + 1
Application.UnLock()
```

```csharp
// [C#]
Application.Lock();
int count = 0;
object o = Application["Count"];
if ( o != null )
   count = (int) o;
Application["Count"] = count + 1;
Application.UnLock();
```

See also: See rule 29.39 on global static variables, rule 29.54 on the Cache object, and rule 29.33 for more information about ASP.NET process recycling.

29.39 State management: Global static variables

Use global static variables instead of the Application dictionary to store application-wide values that should be shared among all users.

Why: Static variables defined in a class in your ASP.NET application can be referenced faster than Application variables (they don't require a lookup in the collection) and don't need to be cast (because they are strongly typed).

More details: Because your code is compiled and runs inside an ASP.NET working process (that is, aspnet_wp.exe under Microsoft Windows 2000 and Windows XP, w3wp.exe under Microsoft Windows Server 2003) until the process is shut down or recycled, any static variable in your project preserves its value between client requests.

An informal benchmark shows that references to a global static integer variable can be up to 500 times faster than referencing an integer value stored in the Application collection.

```vb
' [Visual Basic]
Public Class Globals
   ' Used for locking purposes
   Public Shared GlobalLock As New Object
   ' Application-level variables
   Public Shared PageViewCount As Integer = 0
   Public Shared Count As Integer = 0
End Module
```

```csharp
// [C#]
public class Globals
{
   // Used for locking purposes
   public static object GlobalLock = new object();
   // Application-level variables
```

```
   public static int PageViewCount = 0;
   public static int Count = 0;
}
```

Notice that the Globals class contains a GlobalLock object variable that you can use for locking purposes, as in this code that increments both variables as an atomic operation:

```
' [Visual Basic]
SyncLock Globals.GlobalLock
   Globals.PageViewCount += 1
   Globals.Count += 1
End SyncLock

// [C#]
lock ( Globals.GlobalLock )
{
   Globals.PageViewCount += 1;
   Globals.Count += 1;
}
```

Visual Basic developers can also define a module instead of a class. However, using a class forces prefixing the variable with the name of the class, which makes the code more readable because it emphasizes that you're referencing a global variable rather than a local or page-level variable.

29.40 Disabled and read-only sessions

Disable the Session dictionary in the root Web.config file if you don't use it anywhere in your application. Alternatively, set the Page's EnableSessionState property to false if you don't access the Session dictionary in a given page, or set it to ReadOnly if you read values in the Session dictionary but don't modify them.

Why: ASP.NET builds the Session dictionary and reads its values from memory, from the aspnet_state service, or from SQL Server just before loading a page. When the page unloads, ASP.NET stores Session values back to the storage medium. By setting the EnableSessionState property to ReadOnly, you skip the latter operation; by setting the EnableSessionState property to false, you skip both of them. By disabling session support in the root Web.config file, you skip these two operations for all the pages in the current application.

Here's another reason for using read-only Session dictionaries or disabling them altogether: ASP.NET locks the Session dictionary while the page is being rendered; therefore, other requests from the same user—for example, requests from a different frame or a different window—can't be served until the page completes its execution. This mechanism can cause delays, timeouts, or even deadlocks.

How to: The following line shows how to disable session support at the application level:

```
<sessionState mode="Off" />
```

29.41 ViewState and Session elements as properties

Wrap each ViewState and Session variable in a property with the same name and consistently access those variables only through the property. Add validation code in the set block and throw an exception if the value being assigned isn't valid.

Why: This technique enables you to access the ViewState or Session variable in a strongly typed fashion and ensures that you never store and use an invalid value. Besides, you can later change the storage medium for the variable without affecting the remainder of the code on the page. (For example, you can decide to implement a Session variable as a ViewState variable, or vice versa.)

```
' [Visual Basic]
Public Property UserName() As String
   Get
       Dim o As Object = Session("UserName")
       If o Is Nothing Then
          Return ""
       Else
          Return DirectCast(o, String)
       End If
   End Get
   Set(ByVal Value As String)
       If Value Is Nothing OrElse Value.Length = 0 Then
          Throw New ArgumentException("UserName can't be empty")
       End If
       Session("UserName") = Value
   End Set
End Property

// [C#]
public string UserName
{
   get
   {
      object o = Session["UserName"];
      if ( o == null )
         return "";
      else
         return (string) o;
   }
   set
   {
      if ( value == null || value.Length == 0 )
         throw new ArgumentException("UserName can't be empty");
      Session["UserName"] = value;
   }
}
```

29.42 ViewState, Session, Application, and Cache element names

Use PascalCase for cookies and for ViewState, Session, Application, and Cache item names. Don't create two or more items whose names differ only by character casing.

Why: ViewState, Session, and Cache items should be wrapped by properties (see rule 29.41 and rule 29.54) and should follow the same naming convention of properties. Besides, ViewState item names are case-sensitive, whereas Session items aren't; thus, avoiding names that differ only by their casing ensures that you can transform a ViewState variable into a Session variable without having to change names.

29.43 The EnableViewStateMac property

Set the Page.EnableViewStateMac property to true to have ASP.NET encrypt and validate the contents of the ViewState. (The default value for this property in machine.config is true; therefore, in practice we recommend that you never change it to false.)

Why: This technique ensures that end users can't change the value of internal variables by manipulating the contents of the hidden __VIEWSTATE field. Setting the EnableViewStateMac property to true forces ASP.NET to check that the ViewState field was generated on the same server that is processing the current request; therefore, it prevents attacks in which a malicious user manufactures a phony page and submits it to the server.

Why not: Validating the ViewState adds a little overhead to page processing, even though this overhead can rarely be a good reason not to use this feature.

Another potential problem is that the validation process makes matters more complicated when the ASP.NET application is running on a Web farm because the ViewState generated on a computer in the farm isn't recognized when the postback is handled by another computer. Read rule 29.46 for a solution to this issue.

See also: Read rule 29.47 for more information about this property and how it can interfere with Server.Transfer methods.

29.44 The ViewStateUserKey property

Assign a nonempty string to the Page.ViewStateUserKey property to increase the security of the ViewState mechanism and to prevent one-click attacks from malicious users. (In this kind of attack, a hacker manually builds an HTML page or uses the HTML page received by another user to submit invalid data to the server.)

Why: Setting this property to a string that is different for each logged-on user prevents a user from posting the HTML received by another user.

How to: Assign the value returned by the Session.SessionID property or the user's authenticated name to the ViewStateUserKey property of the Page object. It's essential that you do the assignment in the Page_Init event handler before ASP.NET creates the ViewState. Doing the assignment in the Page_Load event is too late and throws an exception.

```
' [Visual Basic]
Private Sub Page_Init(ByVal sender As Object, ByVal e As EventArgs) Handles MyBase.Init
    InitializeComponent()
    Me.ViewStateUserKey = Session.SessionID
End Sub
```

```csharp
// [C#]
private void Page_Init(object sender, EventArgs e)
{
    this.ViewStateUserKey = Session.SessionID;
}
```

29.45 ViewState validation and encryption in Web gardens

Omit the IsolateApps modifier in the <machineKey> section of the machine.config file when running multiple instances of the same ASP.NET application on a given server machine (the so-called Web garden configuration).

More details: The default machine.config file installed with ASP.NET 1.1 contains the following section:

```xml
<configuration>
   <system.web>
      <!-- *** Wrong if Web gardens are used -->
      <machineKey
         validationKey="AutoGenerate,IsolateApps"
         decryptionKey="AutoGenerate,IsolateApps"
         validation="SHA1" />
   </system.web>
</configuration>
```

The IsolateApp modifier makes ASP.NET combine the validation key value (or the random value, if AutoGenerate is used) with the application identity to generate the actual validation key used for the ViewState and the forms authentication cookie. The default setting makes it simpler to configure isolated applications on shared servers, but at the same time it makes it impossible to share ViewState or use forms authentication across different applications on the same machine, including different instances of the same application (as it happens when you have a Web garden). Dropping the IsolateApp modifier solves the problem:

```xml
<!-- *** Correct also with Web gardens -->
<machineKey
   validationKey="AutoGenerate"
   decryptionKey="AutoGenerate"
   validation="SHA1" />
```

You can also decide to encrypt the contents of the ViewState in addition to validating it against a hash value. This is necessary when the ViewState contains sensitive information, such as passwords or credit card numbers. You can encrypt the ViewState of all the applications running on a server computer by assigning Triple-DES (3DES) to the validation key, as in the following code:

```xml
<machineKey validationKey="AutoGenerate" decryptionKey="AutoGenerate" validation="3DES" />
```

If you need to share ViewState or authentication cookies among different applications on the same (or different) machines, use specific keys in individual Web.config files. (See rule 29.46.)

29.46 ViewState validation and encryption in Web farms

Use explicit values for validationKey and encryptionKey attributes in the <machineKey> element in the configuration file if the ASP.NET runs on a Web farm.

More details: By default, ASP.NET automatically generates two random keys and uses them to validate ViewState data and cookies used in the forms authentication process. Different computers use different random keys, which prevent multiple instances of the same ASP.NET application from correctly sharing data in Web farms. Using explicit values for these attributes in Web.config is therefore necessary when working with Web farms, but we recommend it also for applications running on a single server that might later scale out to a Web farm.

```
<configuration>
   <system.web>
      <!-- Enter the next two lines as a single physical line -->
      <machineKey validationKey="457877D05E19BDBAB16397E15D2E9DD8A0882BDAD620D1012432
0528A6CC1B10861B1B267FB01D7BD8C3EEF53D2C4523A55799B5D583925F1B24A4E3F1F44C6C"
         decryptionKey="B048BAFD721A049BD95911D972B8E5A263C4DCBB5DE1542D"
         validation="3DES"
      />
   </system.web>
</configuration>
```

More details: The validationKey value should be between 40 and 128 hex characters, corresponding to a key of 20 to 64 bytes. (The recommended length is 128 characters.) The decryptionKey value should be 16 characters long when using Data Encryption Standard (DES) encryption and 48 characters long when using 3DES encryption. Recall that ASP.NET encrypts all ViewState data when you select the 3DES validation algorithm (see rule 29.45). ASP.NET can use 3DES only on computers on which 128-bit encryption is available.

You can easily generate these random values for all three encryption algorithms that ASP.NET supports—namely, SHA1, MD5, and 3DES—by means of a nifty utility that you can download from this address: *http://www.consonica.com/solutions/generatemachinekey/*.

29.47 Redirecting to another page

Use the Server.Transfer or Server.Execute method to redirect execution to another page in the same ASP.NET application; use the Response.Redirect method only to redirect execution to a page belonging to another Web application.

Why: The Response.Redirect method sends a status code to the client, specifying that the requested page can be found at a different URL; the Server.Transfer method performs the redirection without a round-trip and is therefore more efficient.

Why not: The Server.Transfer method doesn't update the URL value in the browser's address field; thus, the end user can't bookmark the target page. Also, the Server.Transfer method doesn't work correctly if you have installed any custom HTTP filter. (You can read more about the latter issue and an available fix at *http://support.microsoft.com/?id=814206*.)

More details: If you pass true in the second argument of the Server.Execute method, the target page can access the QueryString property and the Form collection of the sender page. However, if the target page's EnableViewStateMac property is set to true, an error "ViewState is invalid for this page" occurs because ASP.NET mistakenly believes that the ViewState has been tampered with. For this reason, we suggest you always pass false in the second argument of Server.Execute (or just use the version that takes only one argument) and that target pages retrieve control values by one of the techniques shown in rules 29.49 and 29.50. Read the Microsoft Knowledge Base article at *http://support.microsoft.com/default.aspx?id=kb;en-us;Q316920* for more details.

Likewise, you shouldn't pass true to the second argument of the Response.Redirect method, but for a completely different reason. When you pass true in this argument, the current page terminates immediately (as if you had invoked the Response.End method) and you might lose values that you've assigned to Session variables, among other things. For the same reason, you should be very careful when invoking the Response.End method.

29.48 Passing data between pages: The query string

Consider using the query string as a means for passing small amounts of data that don't include secret information to another page, including pages managed by non-ASP.NET applications.

Why: Using the query string is a good choice when you want to offer users the option to bookmark the page and save state information together with the bookmark or when you want other sites to link to your page and pass parameters to it in the URL.

Why not: You can't use the query string to pass complex data or serialized .NET objects. Also, you can't pass more than 4096 characters on the query string because some browsers might truncate longer strings.

More details: Characters such as ?, &, /, and spaces might be truncated or corrupted by some browsers; thus, you should use the UrlEncode method of the Server object when you pass the target page's URL to the Response.Redirect method, store it in an <A> tag, or assign it to the NavigateUrl property of a HyperLink control.

For the same reason, you should always use the Server.UrlDecode method when reading data passed on the query string. (Both the UrlEncode and UrlDecode methods are also exposed by the HttpUtility type.)

```
' [Visual Basic]
' (Inside the page that creates the data to be passed)
Dim text As String = "Are you ready for .NET?"
' Encode it (displays as "Are+you+ready+for+.NET%3f").
text = Server.UrlEncode(text)
' Redirect to the other page.
Response.Redirect("http://www.contoso.com/showdata.aspx?Data=" & text)
```

```
' (Inside the page that reads the data)
If Not Request.QueryString("Data") Is Nothing Then
    Dim text As String = Server.UrlDecode(Request.QueryString("Data").ToString())
    ...
End If
```

```
// [C#]
// (Inside the page that creates the data to be passed)
string text = "Are you ready for .NET?";
// Encode it (displays as "Are+you+ready+for+.NET%3f").
text = Server.UrlEncode(text);
// Redirect to the other page.
Response.Redirect("http://www.contoso.com/showdata.aspx?Data=" + text);

// (Inside the page that reads the data)
if ( Request.QueryString["Data"] != null )
{
    string text = Server.UrlDecode(Request.QueryString["Data"].ToString());
    ...
}
```

29.49 Passing data between pages: The Context.Items collection

Use the Items collection of the Context object to pass data to a page that you invoke with a Server.Transfer or Server.Execute method.

Why: The Context.Items collection is better than the Session dictionary when passing values between pages because the Items collection is automatically cleared at the end of the current request. (By comparison, elements in the Session dictionary should be removed manually after they have been read in the receiving page.) Also, the Context.Items collection works regardless of whether the client browser supports cookies, without forcing you to use cookieless sessions.

More details: In an ASP.NET application, you frequently need to pass one or more values from one page to another, typically when you navigate to another page by means of a Server.Transfer method. You can pass these values by leveraging one of the many state management techniques that ASP.NET provides for you—for example, Session variables. However, the majority of these techniques require that you clear the data after the new page has read the values—for example, by removing them from the Session dictionary so as not to consume memory unnecessarily. The Context.Items collection doesn't suffer from this problem.

How to: The following code snippets show how you can store data in the Context.Items collection before transferring the execution flow to another page and how the receiver page can read it:

```
' [Visual Basic]
' (In the sender page)
Me.Context.Items("quantity") = 12
Server.Transfer("ReceivingPage.aspx")

' (In the receiver page)
Dim quantity As Integer = CInt(Me.Context.Items("quantity"))
```

```csharp
// [C#]
// (In the sender page)
this.Context.Items["quantity"] = 12;
Server.Transfer("ReceivingPage.aspx");

// (In the receiver page)
int quantity = (int) this.Context.Items["quantity"];
```

29.50 Passing data between pages: The Context.Handler property

When defining a page containing many input fields that should be processed in a different page (invoked by using the Server.Transfer method), wrap all the field values in public read-only properties and access those properties in the receiver page by means of the Context.Handler property.

How to: The Context.Handler property returns a reference to the sender page. ASP.NET Web pages are objects; therefore, the receiver page can read any public variable or property in the first page. Your sender page might look like this:

```vb
' [Visual Basic]
' (In the SenderPage.aspx code-behind class)
Private Sub btnTransfer_Click(ByVal sender As Object, ByVal e As EventArgs) _
      Handles btnTransfer.Click
   Server.Transfer("ReceiverPage.aspx")
End Sub

' The property that wraps the value of a control
Public ReadOnly Property Total() As Double
   Get
      Return CDbl(txtTotal.Text)
   End Get
End Property
```

```csharp
// [C#]
// (In the SenderPage.aspx code-behind class)
void btnTransfer_Click(objet sender, EventArgs e)
{
   Server.Transfer("ReceiverPage.aspx");
}

// The property that wraps the value of a control
public double Total
{
   get
   {
      return Convert.ToDouble(txtTotal.Text);
   }
}
```

The receiver page can grab a reference to the sender page by means of the Context.Handler property after casting it to the specific type of the sender page:

```
' [Visual Basic]
' (In the ReceiverPage.aspx code-behind class)
Private Sub Page_Load(ByVal sender As Object, ByVal e As EventArgs) Handles MyBase.Load
    If Not Me.IsPostBack Then
        If TypeOf context.Handler Is SenderPage Then
            Dim sp As SenderPage = DirectCast(context.Handler, SenderPage)
            Dim total As Double = sp.Total
            ' Use the retrieved value here...
            ...
        End If
    End If
End Sub

// [C#]
// (In the ReceiverPage.aspx code-behind class)
void Page_Load(object sender, EventArgs e)
{
    if ( ! this.IsPostBack )
    {
        SenderPage sp = this.Context.Handler as SenderPage;
        if ( sp != null )
        {
            double total = sp.Total;
            // Use the retrieved value here...
            ...
        }
    }
}
```

29.51 Passing local URLs to another application

If you have a URL pointing to a page in the current application, use the ApplyAppPathModifier method of the Response object when passing this URL to another Web application, regardless of whether the other application is an ASP.NET application.

Why: This method ensures that the URL is correct even if cookieless Sessions are enabled. Even if you don't currently use cookieless Sessions, this guideline ensures that you can enable them any time in the future without any impact on existing code.

More details: An external application might require a return URL passed on the query string or in a hidden field. (This return URL points to a page in the current application where the user is redirected when the external application completes its chores.) The following code snippet shows how to correctly pass this URL:

```
' [Visual Basic]
' The URL you want to pass (the current page's path, in this case)
Dim url As String = Request.Url.ToString()
' Transform it (in case cookieless sessions are enabled).
url = Response.ApplyAppPathModifier(url)
' Encode for being passed on the query string.
url = Server.UrlEncode(url)
' Redirect to the other page.
Response.Redirect("http://www.contoso.com/showdata.aspx?returnUrl=" & url)
```

```
// [C#]
// The URL you want to pass (the current page's path, in this case)
string url = Request.Url.ToString();
// Transform it (in case cookieless sessions are enabled).
url = Response.ApplyAppPathModifier(url);
// Encode for being passed on the query string.
url = Server.UrlEncode(url);
// Redirect to the other page.
Response.Redirect("http://www.contoso.com/showdata.aspx?returnUrl=" + url);
```

See also: See rule 29.48 about passing data on the query string.

29.52 Using COM and COM+ legacy components

Consider the following guidelines when authoring ASP.NET pages that instantiate or use Single-Threaded Apartment (STA) COM components, such as those compiled with Visual Basic 6, or COM+ 1.0 components that require access to unmanaged ASP objects through the ObjectContext object.

   a.   Set the page's aspCompat attribute to true. This setting ensures that all the events in the page run in STA mode and use one thread taken from a special pool of STA threads. Because both the page and the component run in the same thread, no thread switch is necessary when invoking a method of the legacy component. (Notice, however, that the page constructor doesn't run in an STA thread, as explained in the following point c.)

   You can set this attribute in the Visual Studio .NET Properties window or add it to the @ Page directive. (The two methods are equivalent.) Here is an example of the latter technique:

```
' [Visual Basic]
<%@ Page Language="vb" AutoEventWireup="false" Codebehind="WebFormVB.aspx.vb"
    Inherits="CodeArchitects.WebFormVB" aspCompat="True"%>
```

```
// [C#]
<%@ Page language="c#" Codebehind="WebFormCS.aspx.cs" AutoEventWireup="false"
    Inherits="CodeArchitects.WebFormCS" aspCompat="True"%>
```

   b.   Don't store an instance of a legacy component in a variable that can be accessed from other pages, such as a Session variable. Even if the other page were marked with the aspCompat attribute, each method invocation from that page might cause a thread switch and add significant overhead to your application.

   c.   Don't instantiate the legacy component in the page's constructor or by means of a field initializer. (Visual Basic and C# compilers translate these field initializers into variable assignments in the page's constructor.) If multiple methods in the page must access a given legacy component, declare the variable at the page level, but instantiate it in one of the page event handlers, not in the constructor.

More details: Page constructors always run in a Multiple-Threaded Apartment (MTA) thread. The ASP.NET runtime uses a single STA thread (known as *host STA*) for all STA components created from MTA threads; therefore, all the legacy components created inside the constructor of any page in the application share the same STA thread and can block each other. In addition to this serious issue, you would also experience other performance problems because other event handlers in the page will run in an STA thread that is surely different from the thread that created the legacy component; therefore, there would be a thread switch each time your code invokes a method in the component.

```vb
' [Visual Basic]
' *** Wrong: a field initializer is used.
Private word As New Word.Application

' *** Wrong: the component is created in the constructor.
Private word As Word.Application
Sub New()
   word = New Word.Application
End Sub

' *** Correct: the component is created in the Page_Load event.
Private word As Word.Application
Private Sub Page_Load(ByVal sender As Object, ByVal e As EventArgs) Handles MyBase.Load
   word = New Word.Application
End Sub
```

```csharp
// [C#]
// *** Wrong: a field initializer is used.
private Word.Application word = new Word.Application();

// *** Wrong: the component is created in the constructor.
private Word.Application word;
private WebForm1()
{
   word = new Word.Application();
}

// *** Correct: the component is created in the Page_Load event.
private Word.Application word;
void Page_Load(object sender, EventArgs e)
{
   word = new Word.Application();
}
```

29.53 Caching the page's contents

Favor the Response.Cache object over the @ OutputCache page directive when you want to cache the entire contents of the current page.

Why: The methods of the Response.Cache object allow more flexibility and you can read their arguments from configuration files, something you can't do with the @ OutputCache page directive. Also, you can't use the @ OutputCache directive to have the cached content expire at a given date or time value.

Example: The following code corresponds to an @ OutputCache page directive whose Duration attribute is set to 20 seconds.

```
' [Visual Basic]
' Use the cached page for the next 20 seconds.
Response.Cache.SetCacheability(HttpCacheability.Server)
Response.Cache.SetExpires(DateTime.Now.AddSeconds(20))
```

```
// [C#]
// Use the cached page for the next 20 seconds.
Response.Cache.SetCacheability(HttpCacheability.Server);
Response.Cache.SetExpires(DateTime.Now.AddSeconds(20));
```

29.54 The Cache object

Use the ASP.NET Cache object to store data that is read from a file or database if the data doesn't become stale in a short period and can be shared among all users.

How to: There's only one instance of the Cache object for each AppDomain, and this instance is shared by all the users of the application. When you're inside an ASP.NET page, you can reach this instance through the Cache property of the Page object. When you're inside Global.asax or when you have no Page available, you can use the Cache property of the Context object.

In the simplest scenario, you use the Cache object as you'd use the Application object: you check whether an object is already in the cache and load it if necessary. Unlike the Application object, though, you can enforce quite a sophisticated expiration policy for cache items, for example, to refresh the item after a given timeout or when a file is modified.

Example: The following code shows how you can use the Cache object to store an XmlDocument object that stores the Document Object Model (DOM) of a given XML file in such a way that the cache element would be automatically removed when the file is modified and the next read operation would read in the cache again. To make the caching process transparent to the application, all the implementation details have been wrapped in a read-only property.

```
' [Visual Basic]
' A read-only property that wraps the cached contents of an XML file
Public ReadOnly Property DataDocument() As XmlDocument
    Get
        Const CacheItemName As String = "DataDocument"
        Dim xmldoc As XmlDocument = DirectCast(Cache(CacheItemName), XmlDocument)
        If xmldoc Is Nothing Then
            ' Read the XML document if the data isn't in the cache.
            Dim fileName As String = Server.MapPath("~/data.xml")
            xmldoc = New XmlDocument()
            xmldoc.Load(fileName)
            ' Add to the cache, making it dependent on the specified filename.
            Cache.Insert(CacheItemName, xmldoc, New CacheDependency(fileName))
        End If
        ' Return the cached data.
        Return xmldoc
    End Get
End Property
```

```csharp
// [C#]
// A read-only property that wraps the cached contents of an XML file.
public XmlDocument DataDocument
{
    get
    {
        const string CacheItemName = "DataDocument";
        XmlDocument xmldoc = (XmlDocument) Cache[CacheItemName];
        if ( xmldoc == null )
        {
            // Read the XML document if the data isn't in the cache.
            string fileName = Server.MapPath("~/data.xml");
            xmldoc = new XmlDocument();
            xmldoc.Load(fileName);
            // Add to the cache, making it dependent on the specified filename.
            Cache.Insert(CacheItemName, xmldoc, new CacheDependency(fileName));
        }
        // Return the cached data.
        return xmldoc;
    }
}
```

More details: The constructor of the CacheDependency object is overloaded and enables you to specify more than one file, in which case the element is removed from the cache when any of these files are updated.

You must synchronize access to the Cache object when you're performing multistep operations that should be considered as atomic. You can use any of the synchronization methods described in Chapter 26, including the *SyncLock* (Visual Basic) or *lock* (C#) statement, the Monitor object, and the ReaderWriterLock object.

See also: Read rule 29.42 for naming guidelines for Cache elements.

> **Note** If your application relies heavily on the Cache object, selecting a memory limit for the ASP.NET process is a critical decision because the cache can use up to 20 percent of the available memory. For more information about how to configure this value, read Chapters 6 and 17 of the excellent *Improving .NET Application Performance and Scalability*, available online at *http://msdn.microsoft.com/library/en-us/dnpag/html/scalenet.asp*.

29.55 Global error handlers

Always define a global error handler in the Global.asax file to recover gracefully from an unhandled exception that occurred in the current ASP.NET application.

Why: Having a central error handler saves you from trapping the Error event in each page and enables you to implement a common error recovery strategy for the entire application.

More details: The code inside the application's Error event can use the Server.GetLastError property to access the exception object thrown most recently. This property always returns an HttpUnhandledException object, and you must query the InnerException property of this object to retrieve the actual exception that was thrown. The code inside the Error event handler can access all the usual properties in the Request object to help you understand what went wrong and the methods of the Response object to send an alternative error message (see Figure 29-7).

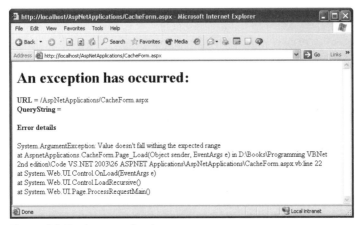

Figure 29-7   An example of a custom error page

```vb
' [Visual Basic]
' (Inside the Global.asax.vb file)
Private Sub Application_Error(ByVal sender As Object, ByVal e As EventArgs) _
      Handles MyBase.Error
   ' Prepare an error report.
   Response.Clear()
   Response.Write("<H1>An exception has occurred:</H1>")
   ' Display information on the page being processed.
   Response.Write("<b>URL = </b>" & Request.Path & "<br />")
   Response.Write("<b>QueryString = </b>" & Request.QueryString.ToString() & "<p>")
   Response.Write("<b>Error details</b><p>")

   ' Display information on the (real) error that occurred.
   Dim ex As Exception = Server.GetLastError.InnerException
   Dim errMsg As String = Server.HtmlEncode(ex.ToString)
   errMsg = errMsg.Replace(ControlChars.CrLf, "<BR />")
   Response.Write(errMsg)
   Response.End()
End Sub

// [C#]
// (Inside the Global.asax.cs file)
private void Application_Error(object sender, EventArgs e)
{
   // Prepare an error report.
   Response.Clear();
   Response.Write("<H1>An exception has occurred:</H1>");
   // Display information on the page being processed.
   Response.Write("<b>URL = </b>" + Request.Path + "<br />");
   Response.Write("<b>QueryString = </b>" + Request.QueryString.ToString() + "<p>");
   Response.Write("<b>Error details</b><p>");
```

```
    // Display information on the (real) error that occurred.
    Exception ex = Server.GetLastError().InnerException;
    string errMsg = Server.HtmlEncode(ex.ToString());
    errMsg = errMsg.Replace("\n", "<BR />");
    Response.Write(errMsg);
    Response.End();
}
```

You can redirect the execution to another .aspx page by using a Response.Redirect method. In general, the standard error page that ASP.NET displays when an unhandled exception is thrown contains a lot of detailed information, so as a rule you shouldn't override it while testing and debugging an application. However, the Error event can be a precious resource in a production site for logging error information to a file or the system log. For example, code in the global error handler might use the SmtpMail object to send an e-mail to the administrator.

29.56 Custom errors

Never use the Off value for the mode attribute of the <customErrors> element in Web.config.

Why: Disabling custom errors also for remote users would let ASP.NET expose important details to the outside, including pieces of source code. Instead, use the RemoteOnly default value to display rich error information when testing the application on the local machine and hide this rich information from remote users.

How to: Here are the recommended ways to use the <customErrors> element in the configuration file:

```
<customErrors mode="RemoteOnly" defaultRedirect="ErrorPage.aspx" >
    <error statusCode="500" redirect="InternalError.htm"/>
    <!-- Add other statusCode/redirect pairs here -->
</customErrors>
```

where ErrorPage.aspx is the page that handles all the errors that aren't associated with one of the statusCode values. Of course, you should use the value On for the mode attribute if you are working on the local server and you want to see how custom error pages appear to remote users.

29.57 Application-level tracing

Enable application-level tracing by setting the proper attribute in the Web.config file rather than by setting the Trace attribute of the @ Page directive or the Trace property of the Page object in the Properties window.

Why: Using trace settings in the configuration file enables you to turn tracing on and off for the entire application without editing individual .aspx files.

How to: Use the following attributes in Web.config to control trace settings. You can use them in the root configuration file to affect application-level tracing or in a secondary Web.config to turn tracing on for all the pages in a folder subtree:

```
<configuration>
   <system.web>
      <trace enabled="true"
         requestLimit="10" pageOutput="false"
         traceMode="SortByTime" localOnly="true" />
   </system.web>
</configuration>
```

If the pageOutput attribute is false, trace information can be viewed by navigating to the trace.axd page; if the attribute is true, trace information is appended to each page's output (see Figure 29-8). The remaining attributes enable you to control other tracing details. The request-Limit attribute is the number of requests whose details are cached by ASP.NET when not in page mode. (Default is 10.) By default, localOnly is set to true to prevent users on remote machines from viewing trace information, but you can set it to false if you're tracing the application from another computer. The traceMode attribute can be SortByTime (default) or Sort-ByCategory and affects the order in which trace information is displayed.

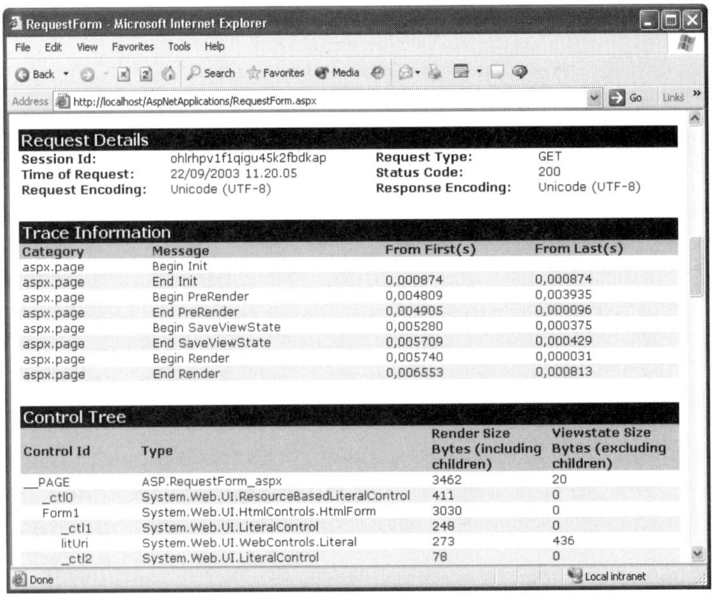

Figure 29-8   An example of trace information

More details: You can also control trace features programmatically by means of the IsEnabled and TraceMode properties of the TraceContext class. You can retrieve an instance of such a class by means of the Page.Trace property or the HttpContext.Current.Trace property. (The latter property enables you to control tracing from outside page classes.)

```
' [Visual Basic]
' Enable tracing and send a warning.
HttpContext.Current.Trace.IsEnabled = True
HttpContext.Current.Trace.Warn("Out of range ID value")
```

```
// [C#]
// Enable tracing and send a warning.
HttpContext.Current.Trace.IsEnabled = true;
HttpContext.Current.Trace.Warn("Out of range ID value");
```

29.58 ASP.NET identity

For intranet sites, enable ASP.NET impersonation if the application must behave differently for each connected user. For Internet sites, run ASP.NET under a user account that you created for this purpose and that is used only for the current application.

Why: You should use a different identity for each different ASP.NET application running on the server so that you can apply more granular security using ACLs, for example, by granting access to a given directory only to applications that actually need it. Conversely, by running applications under the default ASPNET identity (under Windows 2000, Windows XP, and IIS6 running in IIS5 isolation mode) or the Network Service account (under IIS6 running in IIS6 isolation mode), all ASP.NET applications have the same privileges.

How to: Use the following attributes in the root Web.config file to turn impersonation on and run the ASP.NET application under the identity of the user who submitted the current request:

```
<configuration>
  <system.web>
    <identity impersonate="true" />
  </system.web>
</configuration>
```

You can run an ASP.NET application under a specific account (regardless of the current user's identity) by adding the userName and password attributes to the <identity> element:

```
<identity impersonate="true" userName="MyAppUsername" password="MyAppPassword" />
```

It is essential that the identity under which ASP.NET runs has full access to the directory for temporary files (whose name is stored in the TEMP environment variable) and the C:\WINDOWS\Microsoft.NET\Framework\v1.1.4322\Temporary ASP.NET Files directory. The ASP.NET identity must also have Read and Execute, List Folder Contents, and Read permissions on the physical root of the Web site, on all its virtual folders, on the C:\WINDOWS\Microsoft.NET\Framework\v1.1.4322 directory, and on the C:\WINDOWS\Microsoft.NET\Framework\v1.1.4322\CONFIG directory.

See also: Read rule 29.59 for information on how you can encrypt ASP.NET credentials and store them in the registry.

29.59 Encrypted credentials and connection strings in Web.config

Encrypt the user name and password used for the ASP.NET account as well as the connection strings used for state-based and SQL Server–based Session dictionaries.

Why: Even though IIS correctly refuses to send the Web.config file in response to a user agent request, users with access rights for the configuration file might read the name and password of the account you've created for ASP.NET or the connection string used in the <sessionState> element when using sessions based on Windows services or SQL Server. If you think that storing these credentials as clear text in the configuration file might compromise the security of the ASP.NET application, you should take advantage of the ability to store them in the registry in an encrypted form.

How to: Here's how to proceed to store the credentials of the ASP.NET application in the registry in an encrypted format. (Read on for details on how to store connection strings.)

Download the aspnet_setreg.exe utility from the following location on the Microsoft site: *http://support.microsoft.com/default.aspx?scid=kb;en-us;329290.*

Run the aspnet_setreg.exe utility, using the -k: option to specify which registry key should be used to store the encrypted data, the -u: option to specify the user name, and the -p: option to specify the password. For example, here's how you can encrypt and store the values MyAppUsername and MyAppPassword in two registry values under the HKEY_LOCAL_MACHINE\SOFTWARE\MyAspnetApp\Identity registry key:

```
aspnet_setreg -k:Software\MyAspnetApp\Identity -u:MyAppUsername -p:MyApppPassword
```

Run the Regedt32.exe utility to modify the permissions associated with the registry key you've just created so that the ASP.NET process has Read access to this registry key (see Figure 29-9).

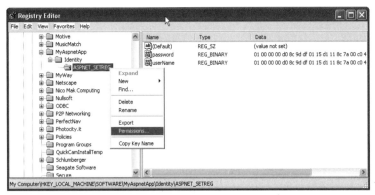

Figure 29-9   Using the Regedit32 utility to change the permissions of the registry keys created by aspnet_setreg

Modify the Web.config file so that the userName and password attributes of the <identity> element point to the new registry values:

```
<configuration>
  <system.web>
    <identity impersonate="true"
        userName="registry:HKLM\Software\MyAspnetApp\Identity\ASPNET_SETREG,userName"
        password="registry:HKLM\Software\MyAspnetApp\Identity\ASPNET_SETREG,password" />
  </system.web>
</configuration>
```

More details: The aspnet_setreg.exe tool supports the -c: option to specify a SQL Server connection string and the -d: option to specify a state connection string, for example:

```
aspnet_setreg -k:Software\MyAspnetApp\SessionState
   -c:"Data Source=.;User id=myuser;Password=mypassword"
```

You must then update the Web.config file to make it point to the new registry key. (In the following listing, the text in boldface has been split on two lines for typographical reasons only. It should be entered on the same physical line.)

```
<configuration>
  <system.web>
    <sessionState mode="SqlServer" cookieless="false" timeout="20"
        sqlConnectionString="registry:HKLM\Software\MyAspnetApp\
SessionState\ASPNET_SETREG,sqlConnectionString"
    />
  </system.web>
</configuration>
```

See also: See rules 29.34 and 29.35 for more information about service-based and SQL Server–based session state, respectively.

29.60 URL authorization

When using URL authorization, append a <deny> element to the end of the list to explicitly deny access to any user who hasn't been authorized by a previous <allow> element. Also, insert a <deny> element to prevent access by anonymous users if the application should be used only by authenticated users.

```
<configuration>
  <system.web>
    <authorization>
       <!-- Reject anonymous users. -->
       <deny users="?" />
       <!-- Add here one or more <allow> tags, as in next line. -->
       <allow roles="managers" />
       ...
       <!-- Deny access to all remaining users. -->
       <deny users="*" />
    </authorization>
  </system.web>
</configuration>
```

29.61 Configuration settings for forms authentication

Use custom settings when enforcing forms authentication for an ASP.NET application.

Why: Validating, encrypting, and renaming the cookie makes it harder for malicious users to spoof its contents. (The default name for this cookie is .ASPXAUTH.)

How to: Here's the portion of the Web.config file that stores details about forms authentication. You should specify all values and not rely on their defaults.

```
<configuration>
   <system.web>
      <authentication mode="Forms">
         <forms loginUrl="/LoginPage.aspx" name="cookiename"
            path="/Reserved" protection="All"  timeout="10" />
      </authentication>
      <authorization>
         <deny users="?" />
         <allow users="*" />
      </authorization>
   </system.web>
</configuration>
```

The loginUrl attribute is the URL of the login page, cookiename is the name for the cookie used to store the authentication ticket, path is the name of the virtual directory that contains the resources that must be protected by forms authentication (default is /, which protects the entire site), protection is the protection level used for the cookie (use All to both encrypt and validate the cookie), timeout is the number of minutes of inactivity after which the cookie expires (default is 30 minutes).

More details: A path for the cookie other than "/" requires that all the links to pages in the reserved section—for example, the NavigateUrl property in HyperLink controls or href attributes in <a> tags—are in the correct case because a few browsers compare paths in case-sensitive mode and don't send the cookie when they access a URL in the wrong case.

See also: See rule 29.46 about encrypting forms authentication cookies in Web farms.

29.62 Custom forms authentication

Implement a custom forms authentication mechanism based on a database table to replace the built-in mechanism.

Why: A custom forms authentication mechanism gives you much more flexibility than the built-in forms authentication method.

How to: You can use the following helper routines to replace built-in methods in the Forms-Authentication type with custom validation and authentication techniques. This code uses the OLEDB .NET Data Provider (instead of the more specific SQL Server .NET Data Provider) for the purpose of being as generic as possible; in a real-world application, you should use the native provider for the database that stores user data.

```
' [Visual Basic]
' This routine works like FormsAuthentication.Authenticate,
' but validates against a database.

Function AuthenticateUser(ByVal username As String, ByVal password As String) As Boolean
   Return AuthenticateUser(username, password, Nothing)
End Function
```

```vb
' This overload fills a hash table with columns read from the database.

Function AuthenticateUser(ByVal username As String, ByVal password As String, _
      ByVal userData As Hashtable) As Boolean
   ' Modify these constants as required.
   Const ConnString As String = "Provider=SQLOLEDB.1;Data Source=.;" _
      & "Integrated Security=SSPI;Initial Catalog=UserData"
   Const Users_TableName As String = "Users"
   Const UserName_FieldName As String = "UserName"
   Const Password_FieldName As String = "Password"

   Dim authenticated As Boolean = False
   Dim cn As OleDbConnection
   Dim dr As OleDbDataReader

   Try
      ' Open the connection to the database holding user names and passwords.
      cn = New OleDbConnection(ConnString)
      cn.Open()
      ' Read the record for this user.
      Dim sql As String = String.Format("SELECT * FROM {0} WHERE {1}=?", _
         Users_TableName, UserName_FieldName)
      Dim cmd As New OleDbCommand(sql, cn)
      cmd.Parameters.Add("username", username)
      dr = cmd.ExecuteReader(CommandBehavior.SingleRow)

      ' Read the row, compare the password in case-sensitive mode.
      If dr.Read() AndAlso dr(Password_FieldName).ToString() = password Then
         ' The user has been authenticated.
         authenticated = True

         ' If provided, fill the hash table with configuration values.
         If Not userData Is Nothing Then
            For i As Integer = 0 To dr.FieldCount - 1
               userData.Add(dr.GetName(i), dr(i))
            Next
         End If
      End If
   Finally
      ' Close the DataReader and the connection.
      If Not dr Is Nothing Then dr.Close()
      If Not cn Is Nothing Then cn.Close()
   End Try

   ' Return true if the user was authenticated.
   Return authenticated
End Function

' A custom routine that works like FormsAuthentication.RedirectFromLoginPage
' but lets you control the authentication cookie's expiration date.
' Set expirationDays = -1 for a cookie that never expires.

Sub RedirectFromLoginPage(ByVal username As String, ByVal persistentCookie As Boolean, _
      ByVal expirationDays As Integer, ByVal cookiePath As String, _
      ByVal secureCookie As Boolean)
   ' Get the URL of the requested resource.
```

```
    Dim url As String = FormsAuthentication.GetRedirectUrl(username, persistentCookie)
    ' Create the authentication cookie.
    FormsAuthentication.SetAuthCookie(username, persistentCookie)

    ' Get a reference to the cookie just created and set its path.
    Dim cookie As HttpCookie = Response.Cookies(FormsAuthentication.FormsCookieName)
    If cookiePath <> "" Then cookie.Path = cookiePath

    ' Set its expiration date, if so desired.
    If persistentCookie AndAlso expirationDays > 0 Then
        cookie.Expires = Now.AddDays(expirationDays)
    End If
    ' Let ASP.NET send the cookie only over secure connections.
    If secureCookie Then cookie.Secure = True

    ' Redirect to the resource that was requested originally.
    Response.Redirect(url)
End Sub


// [C#]
// This routine works like FormsAuthentication.Authenticate,
// but validates against a database.

public bool AuthenticateUser(string username, string password )
{
    Hashtable userData = null;
    return AuthenticateUser(username, password, userData);
}


// This overload fills a hash table with columns read from the database.

public bool AuthenticateUser(string username, string password, Hashtable userData)
{
    // Modify these constants as required.
    const string ConnString = "Provider=SQLOLEDB.1;Data Source=.;"
        + "Integrated Security=SSPI;Initial Catalog=UserData";
    const string Users_TableName = "Users";
    const string UserName_FieldName = "UserName";
    const string Password_FieldName = "Password";

    bool authenticated = false;
    OleDbConnection cn = null;
    OleDbDataReader dr = null;

    try
    {
        // Open the connection to the database holding user names and passwords.
        cn = new OleDbConnection(ConnString);
        cn.Open();
        // Read the record for this user.
        string sql = string.Format("SELECT * FROM {0} WHERE {1}=?", Users_TableName,
            UserName_FieldName );
        OleDbCommand cmd = new OleDbCommand(sql, cn);
        cmd.Parameters.Add("username", username);
        dr = cmd.ExecuteReader(CommandBehavior.SingleRow);
```

```
        // Read the row, compare the password in case-sensitive mode.
        if ( dr.Read() && dr[Password_FieldName].ToString() == password )
        {
            // The user has been authenticated.
            authenticated = true;

            // If provided, fill the hash table with configuration values.
            if ( userData != null )
            {
                for ( int i = 0; i < dr.FieldCount; i++ )
                    userData.Add(dr.GetName(i), dr[i]);
            }
        }
    }
    finally
    {
        // Close the DataReader and the connection.
        if ( dr != null )
            dr.Close();
        if ( cn != null )
            cn.Close();
    }
    // Return true if the user was authenticated.
    return authenticated;
}


// A custom routine that works like FormsAuthentication.RedirectFromLoginPage
// but lets you control the authentication cookie's expiration date.
// Set expirationDays = -1 for a cookie that never expires.

public void RedirectFromLoginPage(string username, bool persistentCookie,
    int expirationDays, string cookiePath, bool secureCookie)
{
    // Get the URL of the requested resource.
    string url = FormsAuthentication.GetRedirectUrl(username, persistentCookie);
    // Create the authentication cookie.
    FormsAuthentication.SetAuthCookie(username, persistentCookie);

    // Get a reference to the cookie just created and set its path
    HttpCookie cookie = Response.Cookies[FormsAuthentication.FormsCookieName];
    if ( cookiePath != null && cookiePath.Length > 0 )
        cookie.Path = cookiePath;

    // Set its expiration date, if so desired.
    if ( persistentCookie && expirationDays > 0 )
        cookie.Expires = DateTime.Now.AddDays(expirationDays);
    // Let ASP.NET send the cookie only over secure connections.
    if ( secureCookie )
        cookie.Secure = true;

    // Redirect to the resource that was requested originally.
    Response.Redirect(url);
}
```

The following code shows how you can use these routines in a forms authentication login page to validate a user. If validation succeeds, all data about the user (preferred layout, colors, and so on) is stored in Session variables. This code assumes that the login form contains one TextBox control for the user name, one TextBox control for the password, and a CheckBox control that lets the user decide whether the authentication cookie should be stored permanently on the local hard disk (see Figure 29-10).

```vb
' [Visual Basic]
Dim userData As New Hashtable
If AuthenticateUser(txtUsername.Text, txtPassword.Text, userData) Then
   ' Store user data in Session variables.
   For Each key As String In userData.Keys
      Session(key) = userData(key)
   Next
   ' Create the cookie and redirect to the requested page.
   RedirectFromLoginPage(txtUsername.Text, chkRemember.Checked, -1, Nothing, False)
Else
   lblMessage.Text = "Invalid user name or password"
End If
```

```csharp
// [C#]
Hashtable userData = new Hashtable();
if ( AuthenticateUser(txtUsername.Text, txtPassword.Text, userData) )
{
   // Store user data in the Session dictionary.
   foreach ( string key in userData.Keys )
      Session[key] = userData[key];
   // Create the cookie and redirect to the requested page.
   RedirectFromLoginPage(txtUsername.Text, chkRemember.Checked, -1, null, false);
}
else
{
   lblMessage.Text = "Invalid user name or password";
}
```

Figure 29-10 The typical login page you use with forms authentication

For added security you might decide not to store user passwords as clear text in the database. Instead, you might store a one-way hash of the password, using the following approach:

```
' [Visual Basic]
' Use a different (possibly longer) salt value in your application.
Dim salt As String = "JM3SYmPzSi95"
Dim hashedPassword As String = FormsAuthentication.HashPasswordForStoringInConfigFile( _
   password & salt, "SHA1")
```

```
// [C#]
// Use a different (possibly longer) salt value in your application.
string salt = "JM3SYmPzSi95";
string hashedPassword = FormsAuthentication.HashPasswordForStoringInConfigFile(
   password + salt, "SHA1");
```

When authenticating a user, you should hash the entered password and compare the result with the value stored in the database.

29.63 Forms authentication cookies

If using forms authentication to protect only a physical or virtual folder (as opposed to the entire Web site), set the cookie Path property equal to the folder name. Also, consider making the login page and the protected directory accessible only through HTTPS.

Why: By setting the cookie's Path property, you tell the end user's browser to send the cookie only when navigating to a page in the protected virtual folder, which improves the site's security and slightly improves performance.

How to: Here's how you tell ASP.NET that the login page should be reachable only by using HTTPS:

```
<configuration>
   <system.web>
      <authentication mode="Forms">
         <forms requireSSL="true"
            loginUrl="https://www.tailspintoys.com/protected/login.aspx" />
      </authentication >
      <authorization>
         <deny users="?" />
      </authorization>
   </system.web>
</configuration>
```

The following code builds on the custom AuthenticateUser and RedirectFromLoginPage methods (see rule 29.62) to create a forms authentication cookie with a path and that can be sent only on a secure connection:

```
' [Visual Basic]
If AuthenticateUser(txtUsername.Text, txtPassword.Text) Then
   RedirectFromLoginPage(txtUsername.Text, chkRemember.Checked, -1, "/protected", True)
Else
   lblMessage.Text = "Invalid user name or password"
End If
```

```
// [C#]
if ( AuthenticateUser(txtUsername.Text, txtPassword.Text) )
{
    RedirectFromLoginPage(txtUsername.Text, chkRemember.Checked, -1, "/protected", true);
}
else
{
    lblMessage.Text = "Invalid user name or password";
}
```

See also: For more information on using SSL with forms authentication, read the Knowledge Base article at *http://support.microsoft.com/default.aspx?scid=kb;EN-US;813829.*

29.64 Robust password policy

Enforce a robust policy for passwords entered by users. For example, accept only passwords that are at least 8 characters long and that contain a combination of digits and uppercase and lowercase characters. Always ask users to retype the password in a second TextBox control when they are creating a user account, and use a CompareValidator control to ensure that the two values match.

Why: A robust password policy makes your application more resistant to dictionary attacks.

How to: You can use a CustomValidator control to enforce the policy on the client side as well as on the server side. First, include this routine in the .aspx file:

```
<script language="javascript">
function CheckPassword(source, args) {
    var pwd = args.Value;
    var minLen = 8;                   // Change minimum length as required.
    var re1 = new RegExp("[A-Z]+");
    var re2 = new RegExp("[a-z]+");
    var re3 = new RegExp("[0-9]+");
    args.IsValid = pwd.length >= minLen && re1.test(pwd) && re2.test(pwd) && re3.test(pwd);
}
</script>
```

Add a RequiredFieldValidator and a CustomValidator control and set the ControlToValidate property of both validator controls equal to the password field. (You need a RequiredFieldValidator control because a blank password doesn't trigger the custom validation routine.) Next, set the CustomValidator control's ClientValidationFunction property equal to CheckPassword and complete the validation by enforcing the password policy also in the ServerValidate server-side event.

```
' [Visual Basic]
Private Sub CustomValidator1_ServerValidate(ByVal source As Object, _
      ByVal args As ServerValidateEventArgs) Handles CustomValidator1.ServerValidate
    Dim pwd As String = args.Value
    Dim minLen As Integer = 8                  ' Change minimum length as required.
    Dim re1 As New Regex("[A-Z]+")
    Dim re2 As New Regex("[a-z]+")
```

```
    Dim re3 As New Regex("[0-9]+")
    args.IsValid = pwd.Length >= minLen AndAlso re1.IsMatch(pwd) _
       AndAlso re2.IsMatch(pwd) AndAlso re3.IsMatch(pwd)
End Sub

// [C#]
private void CustomValidator1_ServerValidate(object source, ServerValidateEventArgs args)
{
    string pwd = args.Value;
    int minLen = 8;                      // Change minimum length as required.
    Regex re1 = new Regex("[A-Z]+");
    Regex re2 = new Regex("[a-z]+");
    Regex re3 = new Regex("[0-9]+");
    args.IsValid = pwd.Length >= minLen && re1.IsMatch(pwd)
        && re2.IsMatch(pwd) && re3.IsMatch(pwd);
}
```

29.65 Client-side scripts

Use script include directives for all the script routines on the page.

Why: Include directives reduce the number of bytes sent to the client because the browser can cache them and reuse them in subsequent requests without downloading them again from your Web sites. Also, keeping all the scripts in a central repository enables you to update and improve them without having to modify each individual .aspx page.

Example: Here's a directive that includes all the routines in the validation.js file in the scripts folder under the root folder:

```
<script language="javascript" src="/scripts/validation.js" />
```

29.66 Centralized configuration files

Consider using the <location> element to place critical settings in machine.config or in the application's main Web.config, and use ACLs to prevent unauthorized users from reading or editing these files. (But ensure that ASP.NET *can* read them.)

How to: The following example shows how you can edit the root Web.config to make the entire site accessible only to the the system administrator, with the exception of the /Public folder (which is accessible to all users, including anonymous ones):

```
<configuration>
    <system.web>
        <authorization>
            <allow roles="MyDomain\Administrator" />
            <deny users="*" />
        </authorization>
    </system.web>
```

```
      <location path="/Public">
        <system.web>
          <authorization>
            <allow users="?" />
          </authorization>
        </system.web>
      </location>
</configuration>
```

You can also use a <location> element in machine.config to affect settings in individual ASP.NET applications and their subdirectories. In this case, the path attribute's value must begin with the IIS site name, as it appears in the MMC snap-in. For example, here's how you can enable tracing for the .aspx files in the /MyApp virtual directory of the default Web site:

```
<location path="Default Web Site/MyApp">
   <system.web>
      <trace enabled="true" localOnly="true" pageOutput="true" />
   </system.web>
</location>
```

Some ASP.NET settings are so critical that the system administrator should prevent them from being changed by individual applications. This ability is especially crucial for servers that host multiple applications written by different developers. In this case, the administrator can prevent undesired changes by adding an allowOverride attribute to the <location> element and setting it to false:

```
<location path="Default Web Site/MyApp" allowOverride="false">
   <system.web>
      <authorization>
         <allow roles="MyDomain\Administrator" />
         <deny users="*" />
      </authorization>
   </system.web>
</location>
```

More details: We have occasionally noticed that the mechanism described with this guideline isn't perfect. For example, in some cases, ASP.NET ignores the settings specified in the <location> element; in others, Visual Studio .NET refuses to run a project whose settings are stored in machine.config. We suggest that you use centralized configuration files only after you've completed the debug and test phase, and be ready to restore standard configuration files if you discover that your application begins to behave errantly.

29.67 Removing unused HTTP modules

Consider removing any ASP.NET HTTP module that you don't use in the current application.

Why: Each ASP.NET module defined in machine.config corresponds to a step in the sequence that all client requests must traverse to be processed. You can make your Web application more responsive by removing all the HTTP modules that you don't use.

More details: The machine.config file installed with version 1.1 of the .NET Framework contains the following section, which lists all the standard ASP.NET HTTP modules (some elements have been split onto two lines for typographical reasons):

```
<httpModules>
    <add name="OutputCache" type="System.Web.Caching.OutputCacheModule" />
    <add name="Session" type="System.Web.SessionState.SessionStateModule" />
    <add name="WindowsAuthentication"
       type="System.Web.Security.WindowsAuthenticationModule" />
    <add name="FormsAuthentication" type="System.Web.Security.FormsAuthenticationModule" />
    <add name="PassportAuthentication"
       type="System.Web.Security.PassportAuthenticationModule" />
    <add name="UrlAuthorization" type="System.Web.Security.UrlAuthorizationModule" />
    <add name="FileAuthorization" type="System.Web.Security.FileAuthorizationModule" />
    <add name="ErrorHandlerModule" type="System.Web.Mobile.ErrorHandlerModule,
       System.Web.Mobile, Version=1.0.5000.0, Culture=neutral, PublicKeyToken=b03f5f7f11d50a3a" />
</httpModules>
```

For example, you should comment out (or physically remove) the PassportAuthentication entry if you never use Passport authentication in your ASP.NET applications.

```
<!-- <add name="PassportAuthentication"
    type="System.Web.Security.PassportAuthenticationModule" /> -->
```

Alternatively, if a given feature is used by some ASP.NET applications but not all of them, you can remove a specific module by means of a <remove> tag in the application's web.config file:

```
<httpModules>
    <remove name="PassportAuthentication" />
</httpModules>
```

In addition to the seldom-used PassportAuthentication module, good candidates for this optimization technique are the ErrorHandlerModule, FormsAuthentication, and UrlAuthentication modules.

Chapter 30
ASP.NET Web Services

Many developers seem to believe that ASP.NET is just a technology to build Web sites and intranet portals. In reality, ASP.NET also enables you to connect computers on the Internet and let them exchange information even without any user interaction. This magic is made possible by Web services. Strictly speaking, you don't need ASP.NET to create Web services, but in practice it would be foolish not to take advantage of this superb infrastructure.

In this chapter, we have gathered several guidelines related to Web services, together with a few code examples. However, Web services is an evolving technology; therefore, our recommendation is that you periodically pay a visit to the MSDN Web site (*http://www.msdn.microsoft.com/webservices/*) and check for service packs and updates. This is especially important if you are using Web Service Enhancements (WSE) techniques in your application (see rule 30.13).

Note One or more code examples in this chapter assume that the following namespaces have been imported by means of *Imports* (Visual Basic) or *using* (C#) statements:

```
System.Collections
System.Configuration
System.Data
System.Globalization
System.Net
System.Web.Services
System.Web.Services.Protocols
System.Xml.Serialization
```

30.1 Name of .asmx files

The name of the .asmx file should be equal or similar to the Web service class that it hosts.

Example: Store a Converter class in a file named Converter.asmx.

30.2 The WebService attribute

Use a WebService attribute to decorate a Web service class with a description and namespace.

Why: The description you set by means of this attribute appears in the page that ASP.NET generates dynamically to describe the Web service and to let users test its methods. (See Figure 30-1.)

```
' [Visual Basic]
<WebService(Description:="A web service for converting currencies", _
   Namespace:="http://www.codearchitects.com/") > _
```

```
Public Class Converter
    Inherits System.Web.Services.WebService
    ...
End Class

// [C#]
[WebService(Description="A web service for converting currencies",
    Namespace="http://www.codearchitects.com/")]
public class Converter : System.Web.Services.WebService
{
    ...
}
```

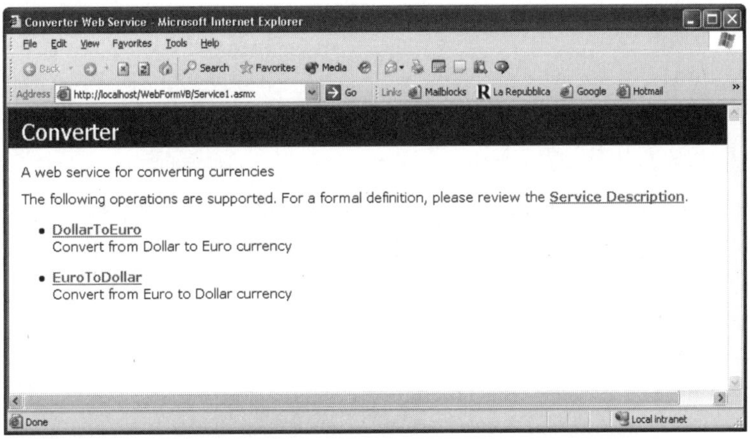

Figure 30-1   The Web Service description page is automatically generated by the ASP.NET infrastructure.

30.3 The WebMethod attribute

Provide a meaningful description in the WebMethod attribute.

Why: The description you set by means of this attribute appears on the page that ASP.NET generates dynamically to describe the Web service and to let users test its methods.

```
' [Visual Basic]
<WebMethod(Description:="Convert from Euro to Dollar currency")> _
Public Function EuroToDollar(ByVal amount As Decimal) As Decimal
    ' The GetEuroToDollarConversionRate method is defined elsewhere in the application.
    Return amount * GetEuroToDollarConversionRate()
End Function

// [C#]
[WebMethod(Description="Convert from Euro to Dollar currency")]
public decimal EuroToDollar(decimal amount)
{
    // The GetEuroToDollarConversionRate method is defined elsewhere in the application.
    return amount * GetEuroToDollarConversionRate();
}
```

30.4 The SoapInclude attribute

Use the SoapInclude attribute to force the inclusion of one or more types in the WSDL contract if the type never explicitly appears in any Web method signature. Note that you must also use the SoapRpcMethod attribute when you use the SoapInclude attribute.

Why: This technique ensures that these types are marshaled correctly from the client to the Web service and back.

More details: The WSDL document that Microsoft Visual Studio .NET creates contains the definitions of all the types that appear in all the methods that are marked with the Web-Method attribute. There are cases, however, when a Web service can return an object whose definition doesn't explicitly appear in any method. An example of such cases is when the method takes or returns an interface pointer or a base class reference; another case is when a method takes or returns a generic collection (such as an ArrayList or a Hashtable) whose elements contain objects that don't appear in any method's signature.

Example: The following example assumes that the Invoice and PurchaseOrder types inherit from the Document class, and that the collection passed to the BuyBooks method contains one or more Book objects:

```
' [Visual Basic]
<WebMethod(),SoapRpcMethod(),SoapInclude(GetType(Invoice)), _
    SoapInclude(GetType(PurchaseOrder))> _
Function GetDocument(ByVal docname As String) As Document
    Select Case docname.ToLower
        Case "invoice"
            Return New Invoice()
        Case "purchaseorder"
            Return New PurchaseOrder()
        Case Else
            Throw New ArgumentException("Unknown document type")
    End Select
End Function

<WebMethod(),SoapRpcMethod(),SoapInclude(GetType(Book)) > _
Sub BuyBooks(ByVal books As ArrayList)
    ...
End Function
```

```csharp
// [C#]
[WebMethod]
[SoapRpcMethod]
[SoapInclude(typeof(Invoice))]
[SoapInclude(typeof(PurchaseOrder))]
public Document GetDocument(string docname)
{
   switch ( docname.ToLower() )
   {
      case "invoice":
         return new Invoice();
      case "purchaseorder":
         return new PurchaseOrder();
      default:
         throw new ArgumentException("Unknown document type");
   }
}

[WebMethod]
[SoapRpcMethod]
[SoapInclude(typeof(Book))]
public void BuyBooks(ArrayList books)
{
   ...
}
```

30.5 Caching method results

If possible, assign a suitable value to the CacheDuration option of the WebMethod attribute to cache the result from a Web service method for a given number of seconds.

```vb
' [Visual Basic]
<WebMethod(CacheDuration:=60)> _
Public Function GetPublishers() As DataSet
   ...
End Function
```

```csharp
// [C#]
[WebMethod(CacheDuration=60)]
public DataSet GetPublishers()
{
   ...
}
```

30.6 Proxy class namespace

Always use a meaningful namespace for the proxy class.

How to: You can select a namespace other than the default localhost in the Add Web Reference dialog box that Visual Studio .NET displays when you add a Web reference to the current project (see Figure 30-2).

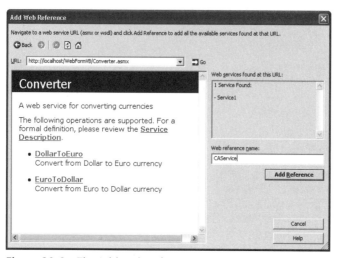

Figure 30-2   The Add Web Reference dialog box lets you change the Web reference name, which in turn affects the namespace in which Visual Studio .NET creates the client proxy class.

30.7 Synchronous invocations

Call a Web service synchronously only from inside a Web Forms application, a server-side component and, more generally, from a program that has no user interface (see rule 30.8).

How to: Always set the Timeout property of the Web service proxy class and wrap the method call in a *Try* (Visual Basic) or *try* (C#) block when calling a Web service synchronously.

```
' [Visual Basic]
' (In client's proxy class)
Dim service As New CAService.SampleService
Try
    ' Set a timeout of 5 seconds.
    service.Timeout = 5000
    ' Invoke the method.
    Dim result As Integer = service.Eval(123)
Catch ex As WebException
    If ex.Status = WebExceptionStatus.Timeout Then
        ' The operation timed out.
        ...
    End If
Catch ex As Exception
    ' Another exception has occurred.
    ...
End Try

// [C#]
// (In client's proxy class)
CAService.SampleService service = new CAService.SampleService();
try
{
    // Set a timeout of 5 seconds.
    service.Timeout = 5000;
```

```
   // Invoke the method.
   int result = service.Eval(123);
}
catch ( WebException ex )
{
   if ( ex.Status == WebExceptionStatus.Timeout )
   {
      // The operation timed out.
      ...
   }
}
catch ( Exception ex )
{
   // Another exception has occurred.
   // ..
}
```

30.8 Asynchronous invocations

Call a Web service asynchronously from inside Windows Forms clients.

Why: A call to a Web method would freeze the user interface if performed synchronously from the UI thread.

How to: Use the following code as a guideline for correctly calling a Web service asynchronously.

```
' [Visual Basic]
Sub CallAsyncMethod()
   Dim service As New CAService.SampleService
   ' (Note that the proxy object is passed in the third argument.)
   Dim ar As IAsyncResult = service.BeginEval(123, AddressOf MethodCallback, service)
End Sub


' This is the callback method.
Sub MethodCallback(ByVal ar As IAsyncResult)
   ' Retrieve the proxy object from the AsyncState property.
   Dim service As CAService.SampleService = DirectCast(ar.AsyncState, _
      CAService.SampleService)
   ' Complete the method call and process the result.
   Dim result As Integer = service.EndEval(ar)
   ...
End Sub

// [C#]
void CallAsyncMethod()
{
   CAService.SampleService service = new CAService.SampleService();
   // (Note that the proxy object is passed in the third argument.)
   IAsyncResult ar = service.BeginEval(123, new AsyncCallback(MethodCallback), service);
}

// This is the callback method.
void MethodCallback(IAsyncResult ar)
```

```
{
   // Retrieve the proxy object from the AsyncState property.
   CAService.SampleService service = (CAService.SampleService) ar.AsyncState;
   // Complete the method call and process the result.
   int result = service.EndEval(ar);
   ...
}
```

Keep in mind that the callback method runs in a non-UI thread; therefore, you can't access the form and its controls directly from this method. For more information, see rule 26.15.

30.9 Support for proxy servers

When implementing a Windows Forms application that invokes a Web service, provide support for clients that run from behind a proxy server.

How to: You can include a key in the configuration file, as in the following example:

```xml
<?xml version="1.0" encoding="utf-8"?>
<configuration>
   <appSettings>
      <add key="ProxyUrl" value="http://proxyserver:80" />
   </appSettings>
</configuration>
```

The following code retrieves the address of the proxy server from the configuration file and assigns it to the Proxy property of the Web service proxy class:

```vb
' [Visual Basic]
' Read the ProxyUrl value from configuration file.
Dim settings As New AppSettingsReader
Dim proxyUrl As String = settings.GetValue("ProxyUrl", GetType(String)).ToString()
' Create the proxy object and set its Proxy property.
Dim service As New CAService.SampleService
If proxyUrl.Length > 0 Then
   ' True means we want to bypass the proxy for local addresses.
   service.Proxy = New WebProxy(proxyUrl, True)
End If
```

```csharp
// [C#]
// Read the ProxyUrl value from configuration file.
AppSettingsReader settings = new AppSettingsReader();
string proxyUrl = settings.GetValue("ProxyUrl", typeof(string)).ToString();
// Create the proxy object and set its Proxy property.
CAService.SampleService service = new CAService.SampleService();
if ( proxyUrl.Length > 0 )
{
   // true means we want to bypass the proxy for local addresses.
   service.Proxy = new WebProxy(proxyUrl, true);
}
```

30.10 The CookieContainer property

Always set the CookieContainer property of proxy classes. This step is mandatory to work with Web services that access the Session dictionary.

Why: Even when calling a Web service that you authored and that doesn't (currently) use the Session dictionary, this technique ensures that all the clients you're creating will work correctly if you later decide to store values in Session variables.

How to: There are two approaches for setting the CookieContainer property. In the simpler technique, you set it immediately after creating an instance of the proxy class.

```
' [Visual Basic]
Dim service As New CAService.SampleService
If service.CookieContainer Is Nothing Then
   service.CookieContainer = New CookieContainer
End If
```

```
// [C#]
CAService.SampleService service = new CAService.SampleService();
if ( service.CookieContainer == null )
   service.CookieContainer = new CookieContainer();
```

Alternatively, you can define a type that derives from the proxy class and that sets the Cookie-Container property in its constructor.

```
' [Visual Basic]
Public Class CAServiceProxy
   Inherits CAService.SampleService

   Public Sub New()
      MyBase.New()
      Me.CookieContainer = New CookieContainer
   End Sub
End Class
```

```
// [C#]
public class CAServiceProxy : CAService.SampleService
{
   public CAServiceProxy() : base()
   {
      this.CookieContainer = new CookieContainer();
   }
}
```

It is recommended that you don't modify the source code of the proxy class generated by Visual Studio .NET because your edits are overwritten when you refresh the type definition.

30.11 SOAP headers

Use SOAP headers for "out-of-band" information that isn't directly related to the method you are calling, for example, the identity of the user who is making the call, routing instructions for the Web service, and the like.

Why: SOAP headers simplify the structure of individual methods calls, make the code more maintainable, and enable you to modify the structure of the Web service and its clients easily to add new functionality.

How to: You define a SOAP header by authoring a class that inherits from the System.Web.Services.Protocols.SoapHeader class and that exposes one or more public fields, one field for each piece of information to be transported in the SOAP header.

```vbnet
' [Visual Basic]
Public Class UserInfoHeader
   Inherits SoapHeader
   ' Culture and time zone info for the caller. We use a floating-point value
   ' to account for time zone offsets that are a noninteger number of hours apart.
   Public Culture As String = ""
   Public TimeOffset As Single = 0
End Class
```

```csharp
// [C#]
public class UserInfoHeader : SoapHeader
{
   // Culture and time zone info for the caller. We use a floating-point value
   // to account for time zone offsets that are a noninteger number of hours apart.
   public string Culture = "";
   public single TimeOffset = 0;
}
```

Next, add to the Web service class a public field typed after the SOAP header class and add a SoapHeader attribute to all the Web methods that want to read the header; the argument of this attribute is the name of the public field. The following sample Web service uses the SOAP header in a method named GetClientTime, which returns the client's local time formatted according to the client's culture. The client passes the locale information and the offset from the Universal Time Coordinates (UTC) in an instance of the UserInfoHeader class:

```vbnet
' [Visual Basic]
Public Class SampleService
   Inherits System.Web.Services.WebService
   ' This is the Public variable that receives the userInfo header.
   Public userInfo As UserInfoHeader

   <WebMethod(), SoapHeader("userInfo")> _
   Public Function GetClientTime() As String
      ' The server's local time in Coordinated Universal Time
      Dim serverTime As Date = Date.Now.ToUniversalTime()
      ' Convert to client's time zone.
      Dim clientTime As Date = serverTime.AddHours(userInfo.TimeOffset)
      ' Create a CultureInfo object with proper locale information.
      Dim ci As New CultureInfo(userInfo.Culture)
      ' Return the time formatted using client's formatting rules.
      Return clientTime.ToString(ci)
   End Function
End Class
```

```csharp
// [C#]
public class SampleService : System.Web.Services.WebService
{
   // This is the Public variable that receives the userInfo header.
   public UserInfoHeader userInfo;
```

```
[WebMethod()] [SoapHeader("userInfo")]
public string GetClientTime()
{
    // The server's local time in Coordinated Universal Time
    DateTime serverTime = DateTime.Now.ToUniversalTime();
    // Convert to client's time zone.
    DateTime clientTime = serverTime.AddHours(userInfo.TimeOffset);
    // Create a CultureInfo object with proper locale information.
    CultureInfo ci = new CultureInfo(userInfo.Culture);
    // Return the time formatted using client's formatting rules.
    return clientTime.ToString(ci);
}
}
```

When you produce the WSDL contract and use it to generate the proxy class, the client definition of the UserInfoHeader class is generated as well, so the client code can create an instance of this class and initialize it as required. Moreover, the proxy class is extended with a field named *HeaderClass*Value–UserInfoHeaderValue in this example–so the client can assign the UserInfoHeader object to this field. Here's how you call a Web service method that takes a SOAP header:

```
' [Visual Basic]
Dim userInfo As New CAService.UserInfoHeader()
userInfo.Culture = "it-IT"      ' Italian culture
userInfo.TimeOffset = 1         ' Time offset for Italy
Dim service As New CAService.SampleService()
' Assign the header to the special xxxxValue field.
service.UserInfoHeaderValue = userInfo
Dim res As String = service.GetClientTime()
```

```
// [C#]
CAService.UserInfoHeader userInfo = new CAService.UserInfoHeader();
userInfo.Culture = "it-IT";     // Italian culture
userInfo.TimeOffset = 1;        // Time offset for Italy
CAService.SampleService service = new CAService.SampleService();
// Assign the header to the special xxxxValue field.
service.UserInfoHeaderValue = userInfo;
string res = service.GetClientTime();
```

More details: Under version 1.1 of the Microsoft .NET Framework, SOAP headers are optional and clients can omit them if they wish; therefore, either you must ensure that the code in the Web service method works well even if the client doesn't send a header or you must throw an exception if the client didn't send a header that is strictly necessary to process the method call.

By default, headers are sent to the Web service but aren't returned to the client, to save bandwidth. In other words, the header object works as an input-only argument for the Web service method. You can change this default behavior by means of the Direction argument of the SoapHeader attribute: its default value is In, but you can set it to InOut or Out. You can combine one of these three values with the Fault value if you want to return the SOAP header to the client even when the Web service throws an exception.

```
' [Visual Basic]
<WebMethod(), _
 SoapHeader("userInfo", Direction:=SoapHeaderDirection.InOut)> _
Public Function GetClientTime() As String
   ...
End Function

// [C#]
[WebMethod()]
[SoapHeader("userInfo", Direction=SoapHeaderDirection.InOut)]
public string GetClientTime()
{
   ...
}
```

30.12 One-way Web service calls

Consider implementing one-way Web service calls for lengthy methods that neither return a value nor take a by-reference argument.

Why: Calls to one-way methods return immediately to the client as soon as ASP.NET has completed the deserialization of the SOAP request. Essentially, you can implement asynchronous, fire-and-forget calls by simply applying an attribute to the Web service method.

Why not: Exceptions in one-way methods aren't reported to clients. Also, code inside a Web service method can't access its HttpContext object, and accessing any property of the Web service class returns a null reference.

How to: You can mark a Web service method as a one-way method by applying a SoapDocumentMethod attribute whose OneWay property is set to true:

```
' [Visual Basic]
<WebMethod(), _
 SoapDocumentMethod(OneWay:=True)> _
Public Sub LogMessage(ByVal text As String)
   ...
End Sub

// [C#]
[WebMethod()]
[SoapDocumentMethod(OneWay=true)]
public void LogMessage(string text)
{
   ...
}
```

30.13 Web Service Enhancements (WSE)

Use the most recent version of Web Service Enhancements (WSE) to implement advanced functions such as the following:

- **Security**   WSE offers a great security infrastructure that enables you to exchange credentials in a safe way, optionally using Kerberos tickets and X.509 certificates.

- **Messaging**   WSE supports a lightweight mechanism for exchanging messages, and applications can use the TCP protocol to exchange SOAP messages without a Web server. (A Web server is required only to handle HTTP requests.)

- **Attachments**   WSE supports file attachments that are sent outside the SOAP envelope, in binary format, and without undergoing a costly XML serialization.

- **Transactions**   WSE enables you to implement distributed transactions using Web Services, similar to what you can achieve with serviced components.

- **Policy**   WSE honors settings in configuration files, thus simplifying the administration of the Web service.

Unfortunately, in practice most of these advanced features are supported only when connecting to other Web services based on ASP.NET and don't interoperate well with services based on non-Microsoft technologies.

As of this writing, you can download version 2.0 of WSE from *http://msdn.microsoft.com/webservices/building/wse*, where you can also read many articles on this technology.

Chapter 31

Serviced Components

Serviced components are Microsoft .NET Framework objects that run under Component Services and can leverage the full range of COM+ services, including just-in-time activation (JITA), automatic transactions, synchronization, object pooling, role-based security (RBS), and programmatic security. You can run a serviced component as a library component (in the client's process) or a server component (in a different process, possibly running on a different computer), even though a few COM+ services are available only in server libraries.

If you aren't familiar with serviced components and their benefits, you can read the whole story at *http://msdn.microsoft.com/library/en-us/cpguide/html/cpconwritingservicedcomponents.asp*. If you have already worked with serviced components, we're sure you'll find some interesting tips in this chapter.

> **Note** One or more code examples in this chapter assume that the following namespaces have been imported by means of *Imports* (Visual Basic) or *using* (C#) statements:
>
> ```
> System.Data.SqlClient
> System.EnterpriseServices
> ```

31.1 COM+ transactions vs. ADO.NET transactions

Carefully consider the pros and cons of using transactional serviced components to implement COM+ transactions as opposed to using standard ADO.NET transactions.

Why: Implementing transactions in serviced components (COM+ transactions) offers several advantages, including the support for distributed databases, a higher degree of independence from the database, and a cleaner object-oriented design (for example, you can use attributes to select the transaction isolation level).

Why not: COM+ transactions use the Microsoft Distributed Transaction Coordinator (MS DTC). DTC-based transactions can be from 10 to 50 percent slower than ADO.NET transactions. When working with a single database server, you might decide to use ADO.NET transactions from inside a standard .NET class rather than encapsulating the database code in a serviced component.

More details: Another factor to consider when deciding which type of transaction to adopt is that serviced components running under Microsoft Windows 2000 can use only the Serializable isolation level; therefore, an ADO.NET transaction can give you more flexibility. Under Microsoft Windows Server 2003, you can use the Transaction attribute to select the actual isolation level (see rule 31.8).

In some cases, you can reduce the overhead of COM+ transactions from inside serviced components by turning off automatic enlistment of an ADO.NET connection. If you're using the Microsoft SQL Server .NET Data provider, you can disable automatic enlistment by setting the Enlist attribute to false in the connection string, as follows:

```
Data Source=.;Integrated Security=SSPI;Initial Catalog=Pubs;Enlist=false
```

31.2 Static members

Avoid public static members (*Shared* in Visual Basic) in types that inherit from System.EnterpriseServices.ServicedComponent.

Why: .NET serviced components support remote method invocation of their instance methods only. Also, COM+ interception doesn't work with static members; thus, the transactional context doesn't flow correctly through static methods calls.

31.3 Library vs. server components

Follow these rules when deciding whether to implement a library or a server COM+ component:

   a. Server components can run remotely, on a computer other than the client's machine, and therefore can improve the application's scalability.

   b. Server components can easily impersonate an identity other than the client's identity.

   c. Server components live inside separate applications that can be restarted automatically under certain conditions.

   d. If you don't need the security, scalability, and fault tolerance features of server COM+ components, use client components to achieve better performance.

   e. All the arguments passed to and returned from a method defined in a server component must be either marked as serializable or derive from MarshalByRefObject.

   f. Server components can run inside a Windows service.

   g. Both library and server components must reside in strong-named assemblies. In addtion, server components must be registered in the GAC.

How to: You decide between a server or library COM+ component by marking the assembly with a suitable ApplicationActivation attribute (see example in rule 31.4).

31.4 Assembly-level attributes

Assign a value to the ApplicationName, ApplicationID, ApplicationActivation, and Description attributes for assemblies that contain serviced components.

Why: The ApplicationName attribute is the name that identifies the application in the Component Services administration snap-in; the Description attribute is used to describe the application itself. The ApplicationID attribute assigns an explicit ID to the application. (If omitted, this ID is generated automatically when the component is registered.) The ApplicationName and ApplicationID attributes affect what you see in the General tab of the application's Properties window.

More details: An explicit ApplicationID value is especially useful for having multiple assemblies share the same COM+ application (and therefore the same server-side process), which in turn optimizes cross-component communication and marshaling. However, keep in mind that this attribute prevents you from using COM+ 1.5 partitions; thus, you must omit it if you plan to use partitions.

```vb
' [Visual Basic]
<Assembly: ApplicationName("BankMoneyMover")>
<Assembly: Description("Components for moving money between accounts")>
<Assembly: ApplicationID("F088FCFF-6FF0-496B-9121-DC9EB9DAEFFA")>
' This is a library COM+ component.
<Assembly: ApplicationActivation(ActivationOption.Library)>
' Assemblies containing serviced components must have a strong name.
<Assembly: AssemblyKeyFile("c:\codearchitects.snk")>
```

```csharp
// [C#]
[assembly: ApplicationName("BankMoneyMover")]
[assembly: Description("Components for moving money between accounts")]
[assembly: ApplicationID("F088FCFF-6FF0-496B-9121-DC9EB9DAEFFA")]
// This is a library COM+ component.
[assembly: ApplicationActivation(ActivationOption.Library)]
// Assemblies containing serviced components must have a strong name.
[assembly: AssemblyKeyFile(@"c:\codearchitects.snk")]
```

Configuration attributes are important especially in the developing and test phase because they help to register the serviced component correctly on the first launch and therefore support XCOPY deployment (this is known as *dynamic* or *lazy registration*). However, most attributes related to serviced components are used only if the COM+ application doesn't exist yet. On the customer's site, the application might be first launched by a user without administrative privileges and the installation would fail. For this reason, you should always rely on the regsvcs tool to register the component.

The only attributes that are always read from the metadata in the component and that supersede the attributes in the COM+ catalog are JustInTimeActivation, AutoComplete, and ObjectPooling, plus the SecurityRole attribute when used at the method level. The ObjectPooling attribute in source code can enable or disable object pooling, but COM+ always uses the pool size defined in the COM+ catalog.

31.5 The ClassInterface attribute

Apply the ClassInterface attribute to all serviced components to make them expose a dual interface if you don't need to apply role-based security (RBS) at the method level.

Why: If you omit this attribute, the Component Services MMC snap-in doesn't list the component's individual methods. Also, late-bound calls from unmanaged clients would ignore the AutoComplete attribute, and you'd be forced to commit or abort the transaction explicitly by using code.

Why not: You can't apply this attribute when you need to apply method-level RBS, as explained in rule 33.17.

```
' [Visual Basic]
<ClassInterface(ClassInterfaceType.AutoDual)> _
Public Class MoneyMover
   Inherits ServicedComponent
   ...
End Class
```

```
// [C#]
[ClassInterface(ClassInterfaceType.AutoDual)]
public class MoneyMover : ServicedComponent
{
   ...
}
```

31.6 The JustInTimeActivation attribute

Mark serviced components with the JustInTimeActivation attribute.

Why: A JIT-activated component is more scalable and resource-savvy because the COM+ infrastructure instantiates it only when one of its methods is invoked and destroys it when the method completes, assuming that the method signals that the task has been completed or is marked with an AutoComplete attribute (see rule 31.7). Also, pooled objects should always be marked with the JustInTimeActivation attribute (see rule 31.11).

Why not: The JustInTimeActivation attribute should be used only for components that are designed to be used in a stateless fashion. You can't just add this attribute to a nontransactional component that you have already tested because the attribute changes the component's lifetime and, consequently, the way clients should use the component.

Another potential problem of JIT-activated components: the server must keep alive a wrapper of the component. Such a wrapper might take a significant amount of memory on the server; therefore, unnecessarily using this attribute can affect the application's performance and scalability negatively.

The JustInTimeActivation attribute is mainly useful to prevent clients from using a stateless component in an incorrect way. If you're using a nontransactional component, you can usually get better performance by omitting this attribute and letting the client release the object explicitly. If the client is itself stateless (for example, it's an ASP.NET Web Forms application), using this attribute is superfluous and might be avoided with nontransactional and nonpoolable components.

More details: A transactional type, that is, a class flagged with the Transaction attribute, is also implicitly a JIT-activated component. However, you should apply an explicit JustInTimeActivation attribute even to transactional types to make the code more readable and avoid problems if you later decide to remove the Transaction attribute.

```
' [Visual Basic]
<Transaction(TransactionOption.Required), JustInTimeActivation()> _
Public Class MoneyMover
    Inherits ServicedComponent
    ...
End Class

// [C#]
[Transaction(TransactionOption.Required)]
[JustInTimeActivation]
public class MoneyMover : ServicedComponent
{
    ...
}
```

31.7 The AutoComplete attribute

Control the outcome of a transaction by applying the AutoComplete attribute rather than by invoking the SetComplete or SetAbort methods. Explicitly throw exceptions if the transaction should be aborted and avoid catching exceptions (unless you rethrow them) when calling other components or methods exposed by .NET Framework objects.

Why: A serviced component should throw an exception whenever something goes wrong. Using the AutoComplete attribute helps you enforce this rule and makes your code more concise and easier to debug.

```
' [Visual Basic]
<AutoComplete()> _
Public Sub TransferMoney(ByVal accountID As Integer, ByVal amount As Decimal)
    ...
End Sub

// [C#]
[AutoComplete]
public void TransferMoney(int accountID, decimal amount)
{
    ...
}
```

31.8 The Transaction attribute

As a rule, use the default Serializable value for the Transaction attribute.

Why: Sticking to the default isolation level makes the component more easily reusable and avoids several potential problems.

Why not: You can usually achieve better performance by using a different isolation level. (You can set a nondefault value only in Microsoft Windows XP and Windows Server 2003 platforms.)

More details: The isolation level of a transaction is determined by the root component—that is, the first transactional component in the call chain. If this root component calls a child component whose isolation level is equal to or higher than the root's isolation level, every-thing works smoothly; otherwise, the cross-component call will fail with an E_ISOLATION-LEVELMISMATCH error.

You can set the transaction support and the isolation level also from the Component Services MMC snap-in, as shown in Figure 31-1.

See also: See rules 31.1, 31.9, and 31.10 for exceptions to this rule.

```vb
' [Visual Basic]
<Transaction(TransactionOption.Required, _
 Isolation:=TransactionIsolationLevel.Serializable)> _
Public Class MoneyMover
    Inherits ServicedComponent
    ...
End Class
```

```csharp
// [C#]
[Transaction(TransactionOption.Required, Isolation=TransactionIsolationLevel.Serializable)]
public class MoneyMover : ServicedComponent
{
    ...
}
```

Figure 31-1   The Transactions page of a serviced component's Properties dialog box

31.9 Isolation level for nonroot components

Consider using the TransactionIsolationLevel.Any value as the isolation level for nonroot components.

Why: This special value forces the component to use the isolation level set by the component that is the root of the current transaction and offers a simple mechanism for making the component reusable in different situations.

```
' [Visual Basic]
<Transaction(TransactionOption.Supported, Isolation:=TransactionIsolationLevel.Any)> _
Public Class MoneyMover
    Inherits ServicedComponent
    ...
End Class

// [C#]
[Transaction(TransactionOption.Supported, Isolation=TransactionIsolationLevel.Any)]
public class MoneyMover : ServicedComponent
{
    ...
}
```

31.10 Types with methods that require different isolation levels

If a type exposes methods that require different isolation levels, consider creating a facade component that uses two (or more) types marked with different Transaction attributes.

Example: Let's say that you have one method that updates a database and requires the Serializable level, whereas another method performs a read operation for which a ReadCommitted level would be enough. If a component exposes both these methods, the best you can do is mark the component with a Transaction attribute that specifies a Serializable isolation level and accept the unnecessary overhead that results when the latter method is invoked. To avoid this overhead, you can create two additional classes: one that performs all the write operations at the Serializable level, and one that performs all read operations at the ReadCommitted level. The original component would have no Transaction attribute and would be responsible only for dispatching calls to one of the two types, depending on whether it's a write or a read operation.

31.11 Poolable objects

Override the CanBePooled method to ensure that the object is returned to the pool as soon as it has completed its job. Remember that pooled objects should be marked with the JustIn-TimeActivation attribute (see rule 31.5).

Why: Object pooling enables you to use resources effectively if clients create many objects and these objects take a significant time to initialize. In addition, pooling gives you the ability to configure the maximum number of objects that can be running at any given time. You need to employ the technique described in this guideline because serviced components aren't poolable by default.

Why not: You might decide not to use object pooling for objects that initialize very quickly. Also, object pooling shouldn't be used to implement a singleton model by forcing the maximum size of the pool to one.

How to: You can make a component poolable by marking it with an ObjectPooling attribute. You can also specify the minimum and/or the maximum number of objects in the pool, even though the values entered in the Component Services MMC snap-in have higher priority than those specified in the ObjectPooling attribute (see Figure 31-2). However, keep in mind that the higher value you assign to the MinPoolSize property, the longer the first instantiation of the component will take.

```vb
' [Visual Basic]
<ObjectPooling(True, MinPoolSize:=4, MaxPoolSize:=20), _
 JustInTimeActivation()> _
Public Class MoneyMover
    Inherits ServicedComponent

    Protected Overrides Function CanBePooled() As Boolean
        Return True
    End Function
End Class
```

```csharp
// [C#]
[ObjectPooling(true, MinPoolSize=4, MaxPoolSize=20)]
[JustInTimeActivation()]
public class MoneyMover : ServicedComponent
{
    protected override bool CanBePooled()
    {
        return true;
    }
}
```

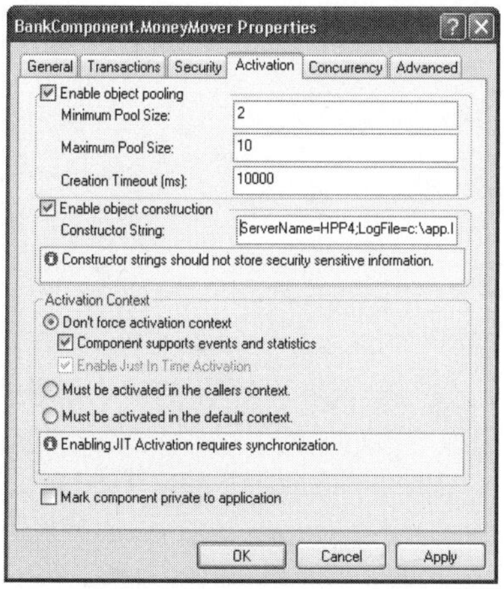

Figure 31-2   The Activation tab of the Properties page of a COM+ component enables you to change object pooling settings.

31.12 The ApplicationAccessControl attribute

Add an assembly-level ApplicationAccessControl attribute to enable COM+ role-based security and to enforce checks at the process and component level.

More details: In .NET Framework version 1.1, the COM+ security is enabled by default if the ApplicationAccessControl attribute is omitted; in version 1.0, COM+ security was disabled by default. Explicitly adding this attribute is recommended to improve readability.

```
' [Visual Basic]
<Assembly: ApplicationAccessControl(True, _
   AccessChecksLevel:=AccessChecksLevelOption.ApplicationComponent)>
```

```
// [C#]
[assembly: ApplicationAccessControl(true,
   AccessChecksLevel=AccessChecksLevelOption.ApplicationComponent)]
```

31.13 The authentication level

In server applications, set the authentication level to Privacy, unless it is safe to use less severe settings.

More details: The authentication level of a library component is inherited from the client process. The Authentication property of the ApplicationAccessControl attribute lets you decide how a server component authenticates data coming from the caller. Setting the authentication level to Privacy ensures that COM+ authenticates the caller's credentials and encrypts each data packet, thus providing the most secure type of authentication but affecting performance negatively. If data sniffing isn't an issue, you might decide to use a more efficient setting, such as Connect (authenticates credentials only when the connection is established), Call (authenticates credentials on each call), Packet (authenticates credentials and ensures that all packets are received), or Integrity (authenticates credentials and ensures that no data packet has been modified).

```
' [Visual Basic]
<Assembly: ApplicationAccessControl(True, _
   AccessChecksLevel:=AccessChecksLevelOption.ApplicationComponent, _
   Authentication:=AuthenticationOption.Privacy)>
```

```
// [C#]
[assembly: ApplicationAccessControl(true,
   AccessChecksLevel=AccessChecksLevelOption.ApplicationComponent,
   Authentication=AuthenticationOption.Privacy)]
```

Remember that the actual authentication level used by a COM+ component depends also on the authentication level set by the client. When the component's and the client's authorization levels differ, COM+ uses the higher level of the two. If the client is an ASP.NET application, you can configure its authentication level by means of the comAuthenticationLevel attribute in the <processModel> element in machine.config.

31.14 The impersonation level

In server applications, set the impersonation level to Identify, unless you need to enable impersonation or delegation.

More details: The impersonation level of a library COM+ component is inherited from the client process and can't be changed. The ImpersonationLevel property of the ApplicationAccessControl attribute lets you decide whether another component called by the current COM+ component can discover the identity of the caller and can impersonate the caller when calling services running on different computers. The available settings are Anonymous (the component is unaware of the caller's identity and can't access local or remote resources on the caller's behalf), Identify (the component can determine the caller's identity), Impersonate (the component impersonates the caller when accessing local resources, or even resources on a different computer if the caller resides on the same machine as the component), and Delegate (the component impersonates the caller when accessing resources on the local computer as well as any remote server; this setting requires the Kerberos authentication services and that the Active Directory directory service is configured on both the client and the server machine).

When using the Identity setting, the called COM+ component can use the SecurityCallContext object to determine the caller's identity (the DirectCaller property) and whether the caller is in a given role (the IsCallerInRole method), but the component can't impersonate the caller when accessing a database or other resources, either on the same machine or on a remote server. Because the trusted subsystem is recommended in multitiered architectures (see rule 29.27), impersonation and delegation are usually neither necessary nor desirable.

```
' [Visual Basic]
<Assembly: ApplicationAccessControl(True, _
   AccessChecksLevel:=AccessChecksLevelOption.ApplicationComponent, _
   Authentication:=AuthenticationOption.Privacy, _
   ImpersonationLevel:=ImpersonationLevelOption.Identify)>
```

```
// [C#]
[assembly: ApplicationAccessControl(true,
   AccessChecksLevel=AccessChecksLevelOption.ApplicationComponent,
   Authentication=AuthenticationOption.Privacy,
   ImpersonationLevel=ImpersonationLevelOption.Identify)]
```

31.15 The ComponentAccessControl attribute

Add a class-level ComponentAccessControl attribute to enable security checks for that component.

More details: This attribute is ignored if access checks are enabled only at the application level (see rule 31.12).

```
' [Visual Basic]
<ComponentAccessControl(True)> _
Public Class MoneyMover
Inherits ServicedComponent
   ...
End Class
```

```
// [C#]
[ComponentAccessControl(true)]
public class MoneyMover : ServicedComponent
{
   ...
}
```

31.16 The SecurityRole attribute

Add one or more assembly-level SecurityRole attributes that define all the user roles recognized by the application. Always include a SecurityRole attribute that adds the Everyone user to the Marshaler role if you plan to enable method-level security.

More details: You can apply the SecurityRole attribute at the assembly, class, and method level. When applied at the assembly level, it defines which users can activate any component in the application, provided that you've applied an ApplicationAccessControl(true) attribute. When applied at the class level, it defines which users can call any method in that class, provided that you have applied a ComponentAccessControl(true) attribute to the class. You apply the SecurityRole attribute to individual methods only when you enable security at the method level, as explained in rule 31.17.

The registration process adds all the roles that you specify in SecurityRole attributes in the COM+ catalog. By default, these roles contains no users, but you can add the Everyone user to a role by passing true in the second argument (which corresponds to the SetEveryoneAccess property). Users other than Everyone can be added to a role only by means of the COM+ explorer or by using an administrative script.

```
' [Visual Basic]
' Accountants can launch this application; all users are in this role.
<Assembly: SecurityRole("Accountants", True)>
' Create the Managers role, but don't add any users to it.
<Assembly: SecurityRole("Managers")>
' Prepare the application for security at the method level.
<Assembly: SecurityRole("Marshaler", True)>

<SecurityRole("Readers", True, Description:="Users who can read")> _
Public Class MoneyMover
Inherits ServicedComponent
   ...
End Class

// [C#]
// Accountants can launch this application; all users are in this role.
[assembly: SecurityRole("Accountants", true)]
// Create the Managers role, but don't add any users to it.
[assembly: SecurityRole("Managers")]
// Prepare the application for security at the method level.
[assembly: SecurityRole("Marshaler", true)]

[SecurityRole("Readers", true, Description="Users who can read")]
public class MoneyMover : ServicedComponent
{
   ...
}
```

31.17 COM+ role-based security at the method level

Follow these steps to correctly enable role-based security (RBS) at the method level:

1. Ensure that you marked the assembly with an ApplicationAccessControl(true) attribute (see rule 31.12) and the serviced component class with a ComponentAccessControl(true) attribute whose AccessChecksLevel property is set to ApplicationComponent (see rule 31.15).

2. Add an assembly-level SecurityRole attribute that adds the Everyone user to the Marshaler role (see rule 31.16).

3. Mark the serviced component class with the SecureMethod attribute.

4. Define the methods to be secured in a separate interface and have the serviced component class implement the interface.

5. Apply the SecurityRole attribute to methods in the class, specifying which role can call which method, or use the MMC snap-in to perform this step from the user interface as shown in Figure 31-3. (Alternatively, you can add the SecurityRole attribute at the class level to configure all methods in the class for that role.)

```vb
' [Visual Basic]
<Assembly: ApplicationAccessControl(True, _
    AccessChecksLevel:=AccessChecksLevelOption.ApplicationComponent)>
<Assembly: SecurityRole("Marshaler", True)>

Public Interface IMoneyMover
    Sub MoveMoney(ByVal accountID As String, ByVal amount As Decimal)
End Interface

<ComponentAccessControl(True), SecureMethod()> _
Public Class MoneyMover
Inherits ServicedComponent
    Implements IMoneyMover

    <SecurityRole("Accountants", True)> _
    Public Sub MoveMoney(ByVal accountID As String, ByVal amount As Decimal) _
        Implements IMoneyMover.MoveMoney
        ...
    End Sub
End Class
```

```csharp
// [C#]
[assembly: ApplicationAccessControl(true,
    AccessChecksLevel=AccessChecksLevelOption.ApplicationComponent)]
[assembly: SecurityRole("Marshaler", true)]

public interface IMoneyMover
{
    void MoveMoney(string accountID, decimal amount);
}
```

```
[ComponentAccessControl(true)]
[SecureMethod()]
public class MoneyMover : ServicedComponent, IMoneyMover
{
    [SecurityRole("Accountants", true)]
    public void MoveMoney(string accountID, decimal amount)
    {
        ...
    }
}
```

Notice that the SecureMethod attribute at the class level isn't strictly required if you use a SecurityRole attribute at the method level, but we recommend that you keep both attributes for increased readability.

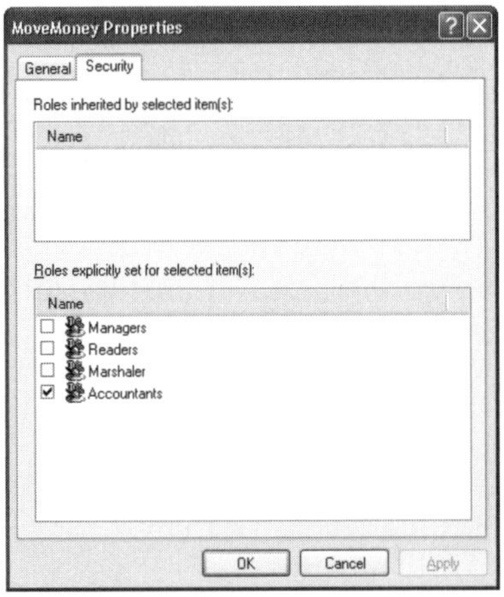

Figure 31-3   You can enforce which roles can call the component using the Security page in the Properties dialog box of individual methods.

31.18 Programmatic security

Use the SecurityCallContext object to perform programmatic security and always explicitly test that the IsSecurityEnabled property is true. Don't use the ContextUtil class to implement programmatic security.

Why: The SecurityCallContext object exposes a more complete set of security-related methods than the ContextUtil class. However, IsCallerInRole and other methods return true even if role-based security (RBS) is disabled; thus, you should always explicitly check that RBS is enabled by testing the IsSecurityEnabled property, as follows:

```
' [Visual Basic]
Dim scc As SecurityCallContext = SecurityCallContext.CurrentCall
If Not scc.IsSecurityEnabled Then
   Throw New Exception("This method requires role-based security")
ElseIf scc.IsCallerInRole("Managers") Then
   ...
End If
```

```
// [C#]
SecurityCallContext scc = SecurityCallContext.CurrentCall;
if ( ! scc.IsSecurityEnabled )
   throw new Exception("This method requires role-based security");
else if ( scc.IsCallerInRole("Managers") )
   ...
```

31.19 Component identity

Run a server COM+ component under the identity of a least-privileged specific account. Never run the component under the interactive user's identity, and avoid using predefined system accounts.

Why: Running the component under the identity of the interactive user is OK only during the development phase because this setting enables you to display message boxes and other diagnostic messages. In real applications, you should always define an ad-hoc account that has only the privileges that the application strictly requires, for example, access to certain directories and registry keys. This technique gives you more granular security than the one offered by predefined system accounts such as Local Service, Network Service, and Local System.

31.20 Disposing of a serviced component

The client application should dispose of all serviced components that aren't JIT-activated as soon as it is finished with them. The recommended way to do so is by calling the component's Dispose method, rather than by means of the ServicedComponent.DisposeObject static method.

```
' [Visual Basic]
' *** OK
ServicedComponent.DisposeObject(obj)
' *** Better
obj.Dispose()
```

```
// [C#]
// *** OK
ServicedComponent.DisposeObject(obj);
// *** Better
obj.Dispose();
```

For performance reasons, a serviced component should never implement the Finalize method because such a method would be called through reflection. Instead, override the protected Dispose(disposed) method and place all finalization code there.

31.21 WebMethod attributes in serviced components

Never mark a public method of a serviced component with a WebMethod attribute to make it callable through the Web service infrastructure.

Why: Both serviced components and Web services offer remote clients the ability to call methods in a .NET component. However, these two remoting technologies might conflict with each other because of the way they enable the transaction and context flow from the client and the component; therefore, you should never mix the two techniques in the same component.

Chapter 32
Remoting

The Microsoft .NET Framework offers as many as three distinct technologies that enable developers to instantiate a component running on a different computer: Web Services, serviced components, and .NET remoting. We covered Web services in Chapter 30 and serviced components in Chapter 31; in this chapter, we complete the guidelines related to remoting technologies available to .NET developers.

Before you build a solution on a specific remoting technology, however, it is of paramount importance that you fully understand the benefits and limitations of each one of them. Here's the short version of the story:

- Web services are the preferred choice when interoperating with non-.NET applications or, more generally, applications running on platforms other than Microsoft Windows. They don't support a native model for security and transactions, even though these additional services are available in version 2.0 of Web Service Enhancements (WSE), as mentioned in rule 30.13. Currently, Web services are touted as the best choice to implement Service Oriented Architectures (SOAs).

- Serviced components are the richest in terms of functionality because they support declarative synchronization and transactions, JIT activation, object pooling, authentication, and encryption. However, they are based on an unmanaged technology (COM+) and can interoperate only with applications running the Windows operating system.

- .NET remoting is the most efficient of the three technologies and is especially recommended for cross-AppDomain and cross-process communications. It supports a native model for authentication and encryption when hosted in Microsoft Internet Information Services (IIS), and you can use custom sinks that supplement .NET remoting with additional features. At this time, however, you can use .NET remoting only to communicate with other .NET applications.

You can read more about remoting technologies at *http://msdn.microsoft.com/library/en-us/ dnpag/html/scalenetchapt11.asp*. You can also find a very useful article and FAQ list at *http:// www.thinktecture.com/Resources/RemotingFAQ/default.html*.

Note   One or more code examples in this chapter assume that the following namespaces have been imported by means of *Imports* (Visual Basic) or *using* (C#) statements:

```
System.Collections
System.Reflection
System.Runtime.Remoting
System.Runtime.Remoting.Channels
System.Runtime.Remoting.Channels.Http
System.Runtime.Remoting.Channels.Tcp
System.Runtime.Remoting.Contexts
System.Runtime.Remoting.Lifetime
System.Runtime.Remoting.Messaging
```

32.1 Remotable types

Abide by the following guidelines when authoring types to be used in a .NET remoting scenario:

a. Use MarshalByRefObject-derived (MBR) classes for objects that expose methods that must be called remotely. (This is a requirement of the .NET remoting architecture.)

b. Avoid static members in classes that inherit from MarshalByRefObject type. (Only instance methods can be invoked by using .NET remoting.) If you need to expose static fields to remote clients, wrap those fields in instance properties.

c. Avoid fields and properties and define stateless MBR objects, if possible, so that you can expose them as SingleCall Server-Activated Objects (SAOs).

d. Favor *chunky* interfaces over *chatty* interfaces in MBRs if you can't define stateless objects. In other words, implement methods that take many arguments so that clients can complete a task with a fewer method calls.

e. Use thread synchronization to protect resources from multiple requests occurring at the same time from clients. (Synchronization is required only for singleton remote objects; see rule 32.5.)

f. Define serializable classes for objects that must be passed as arguments or returned from remote methods; these are known as Marshal-By-Value (MBV) objects.

g. Mark MBV objects with the Serializable attribute but don't have them implement the ISerializable interface unless it's strictly necessary. Ideally, MBV objects should consist only of fields or properties returning primitive types. (Read about problems caused by nonprimitive types in rule 32.10.)

Note   All the code samples in this chapter assume that you have created a class library project named RemoteComponents, containing a MarshalByRefObject-derived type named Calculator that exposes a method named Add.

32.2 Host applications for .NET remoting

Use the following guidelines when selecting which type of application should host your remotable components:

a. Host remotable components in IIS when you need improved security. IIS provides support for secure communications over SSL and can authenticate users (see rules 32.18 and 32.19).

b. Host remotable components in IIS when you need better scalability and fault tolerance. You can easily create a Web farm and use multiple servers in a Network Load Balancing (NLB) configuration.

c. Host remotable components in a Windows service when you expose objects to clients in a trusted environment and you don't need the security, scalability, and fault tolerance features that IIS offers.

d. Host remotable objects in Windows Forms applications if you use .NET remoting as a communication medium among different applications running on the same computer or running on different computers in a trusted environment.

More details: Using IIS to host your remotable objects is the simplest and recommended choice. This hosting technique complies with XCOPY deployment: you can install a .NET remoting solution simply by copying a directory tree from your system to the end user's machine. In addition, all the traffic with clients flows through port 80 (the default port used by HTTP), so you rarely need to configure your firewall when you expose remote objects through IIS. The IIS solution is also very flexible because you can change a setting in the configuration file and the new values will be applied immediately, without the need to explicitly restart the IIS application. Hosting inside IIS gives you another important benefit: security. You can use Basic authentication and Integrated Windows authentication, and you can even encrypt data flowing to and from clients by using an HTTPS channel.

The only serious drawback of IIS as a host for your remotable objects is performance. IIS supports only the HTTP channel and prevents you from using the more efficient TCP channel. You can mitigate this problem by adopting a binary formatter, however; but you can't go as fast as a plain TCP channel. On the other hand, only IIS can benefit from using the server garbage collector, and this factor can partially compensate for the overhead introduced by the HTTP channel. (See rule 23.12 for more information about server and workstation garbage collectors.) For this reason, only accurate benchmarks can help you make an informed decision about which host you should choose when performance is an issue.

See also: Read rule 32.12 for more guidelines about hosting .NET remoting objects under IIS.

32.3 Port numbers

When not using IIS as a host for remotable objects, specify a port number equal to or higher than 1024 to avoid clashes with ports used by common protocols such as HTTP (port 80) or FTP (port 21). Even better, you should use a number equal to or higher than 48152 to stay clear of ports used by other commercial software such as Microsoft SQL Server (port 1433).

```vb
' [Visual Basic]
Dim channel As New TcpChannel(50000)
ChannelServices.RegisterChannel(channel)
```

```csharp
// [C#]
TcpChannel channel = new TcpChannel(50000);
ChannelServices.RegisterChannel(channel);
```

32.4 URI extensions

Use only URIs that have either the .rem or .soap extension.

Why: Using URIs with the .rem or .soap extension is mandatory when you host remotable objects in IIS. The URI doesn't require an extension when you host the remote object in a Windows service or a custom application. If you follow this guideline, however, you can later decide to host these objects inside IIS with minimal or no changes in remote clients.

32.5 Server-Activated vs. Client-Activated Objects

Use the following guidelines when deciding whether you should implement a remote object as a Client-Activated Object (CAO) or a Server-Activated Object (SAO) and whether you should opt for a SingleCall or a Singleton SAO:

a. Favor SAOs over CAOs because SAOs can be instantiated on any available server and are more scalable than CAOs.

b. Use SingleCall SAOs when you don't need to retain state between calls. These objects live only while the method call is in progress and are immediately destroyed afterward. They don't pose any synchronization problem and are extremely scalable.

c. Use Singleton SAOs when you need to share state among different clients or when the server needs to control the object's lifetime. Calls to Singleton objects are served by the threads in the thread pool; thus, you must use thread synchronization to deal correctly with simultaneous calls from clients.

d. Use CAOs only when the object must preserve the state between calls from a given client and when clients need to control the object's lifetime. CAOs are bound to a specific server for their entire lifetime and can be a serious obstacle to creating scalable solutions.

Note   Any MBR object returned by a call to a remote object is treated as a CAO and is therefore subject to all scalability problems of CAOs.

32.6 Declarative vs. programmatic configuration

Favor registration of channels and remote objects by means of configuration files to programmatic registration.

Why: Configuration files give you the option to change .NET remoting settings without recompiling the application. In addition, if you use a configuration file to register your server-side objects, you can later decide to host the objects inside IIS with minimal changes.

Why not: You might decide not to use configuration files and instantiate remote objects by means of the Activator.GetObject method because this method enables you to specify the actual server where the object should be created. (See rule 32.16 for an example that uses this method.)

Example: The following configuration file registers a server-side channel on port 50000 and a Singleton SAO using the Calculator.rem URI:

```
<configuration>
   <system.runtime.remoting>
      <application>
         <channels>
            <channel ref="tcp" port="50000" />
         </channels>
         <service>
            <wellknown type="RemoteComponents.Calculator, RemoteComponents"
               mode="Singleton" objectUri="Calculator.rem" />
         </service>
      </application>
   </system.runtime.remoting>
</configuration>
```

The <wellknown> tag registers an SAO and takes three attributes: type (the type of the object being published), mode (which can be Singleton or SingleCall), and objectUri (the URI where this object can be found). To register a CAO, you use an <activated> tag, which takes only the type attribute. For both SAOs and CAOs, the type attribute is in the format *namespace.classname, assemblyname* if the remotable object is in a private assembly. If the assembly has a strong name, the reference to the assembly must include version, culture, and publisher key values.

The <application> element can include an optional name attribute, as in the following:

```
<application name="RemoteComponents" >
```

If a name is provided, the URL used by clients to refer to the remote object is in the form *protocol://domain/applicationname/objectUri*—for example, *http://localhost/RemoteComponents/Calculator.rem*. The name attribute must be omitted when you use IIS to host the remote object: in that case, the virtual directory name is used instead of the application name.

> **Note**   All the configuration file portions shown in the remainder of this chapter are meant to
> be included inside the following XML elements, unless they include a <configuration> ele-
> ment:
>
> ```
> <configuration>
>    <system.runtime.remoting>
>       <application>
>          <!-- Insert configuration file fragments here. -->
>          ...
>       </application>
>    </system.runtime.remoting>
> </configuration>
> ```

The following configuration file portion shows how to expose an object in a strong-named
assembly as a CAO:

```
<service>
   <!-- Next line has been split in two to fit the page width. -->
   <activated type="RemoteComponents.Calculator, RemoteComponents,
      Version=1.0.0.0, Culture=neutral, PublicKeyToken=c89a5D5de938e0ab"/>
</service>
```

Assuming that the Calculator has been exposed as an SAO over a TCP channel, a client application can access it by means of a configuration file similar to this one:

```
<channels>
   <channel ref="tpc" />
</channels>
<client>
   <wellknown type="RemoteComponents.Calculator, RemoteComponents"
      url="tcp://localhost:50000/Calculator.rem" />
</client>
```

The previous configuration file assumes that the server application is running on the same
computer; otherwise, you should replace localhost with the domain name or the IP address of
the remote machine. Again, if the assembly containing the definition of the remote component is strong named, the type attribute must include the assembly's version, culture, and
publisher key.

Notice that the client application must have a reference to a DLL where the type (RemoteCom-
ponents.Calculator, in this example) is defined. This DLL can be the same assembly used on
the server, a metadata-only assembly generated with the Soapsuds utility, or, more frequently,
an assembly that contains the definition of one or more shared interfaces (see rules 32.16 and
32.17).

To register a remote CAO on the client, you use an <activated> tag instead of a <wellknown>
tag. All the CAOs used by the client application use the URL defined in the <client> tag. (This

URL is ignored by remote SAOs.) Here's an example of a client-side configuration file that defines a remote CAO:

```
<client url="tcp://localhost:50000" >
   <activated type="RemoteComponents.Calculator, RemoteComponents" />
</client>
```

You can read more about .NET remoting configuration files at *http://msdn.microsoft.com/ library/en-us/dndotnet/html/remotingconfig.asp.*

32.7 Loading a .NET remoting configuration file

Consider loading a configuration file in the Main method of all your applications, even if the application doesn't use remoting and the configuration is empty. This will enable you to later deploy some of the objects remotely by simply editing the configuration.

```
' [Visual Basic]
Sub Main()
   Dim configFile As String = [Assembly].GetExecutingAssembly().Location & ".config"
   RemotingConfiguration.Configure(configFile)
   ...
End Sub

// [C#]
static void Main()
{
   string configFile = Assembly.GetExecutingAssembly().Location + ".config";
   RemotingConfiguration.Configure(configFile);
   ...
}
```

More details: When the client is an ASP.NET application, you should place .NET remoting settings in a file other than Web.config and register this file from within the Application_Start event handler in Global.asax. For more details, read the MSDN Knowledge Base article at *http://support.microsoft.com/default.aspx?scid=kb;en-us;323490.*

32.8 TCP vs. HTTP channel

Use the following guidelines to select the most appropriate type of channel and formatter to be used in a .NET remoting scenario:

   a.   Use IIS, and therefore the HTTP channel, when you need security, scalability, and fault tolerance (see rule 32.2).

   b.   When you aren't using IIS as a host, use the TCP channel and a binary formatter for the best performance.

   c.   Use the TCP channel only in untrusted environments, such as when you are implementing cross-process communication on the same machine and when there is no firewall between the client and the server. (See also rule 32.9.)

    d. Regardless of whether you use a TCP or an HTTP channel, always use a binary formatter for the best performance. Also, consider that the SOAP formatter in.NET Framework version 2.0 (in beta as of this writing) doesn't support a few features that the binary formatter supports, such as generics; therefore, the binary formatter appears to be a wiser choice for the future.

More details: The HTTP channel uses the SOAP formatter by default, but you can get better performance by forcing it to use a binary formatter. Here's how you can register an HTTP channel that uses a binary formatter by means of the configuration file on the server:

```
<channels>
   <channel ref="http" port="50000" >
      <serverProviders>
         <formatter ref="binary" />
      </serverProviders>
   </channel>
</channels>
```

The following code shows how you can achieve the same result programmatically:

```
' [Visual Basic]
' An HTTP channel on port 50000 that uses a binary formatter
Dim props As New Hashtable
props("port") = 50000
Dim channel As New HttpServerChannel(props, New BinaryServerFormatterSinkProvider)
ChannelServices.RegisterChannel(channel)
```

```
// [C#]
// An HTTP channel on port 50000 that uses a binary formatter
Hashtable props = new Hashtable();
props["port"] = 50000;
HttpServerChannel channel = new HttpServerChannel(props,
new BinaryServerFormatterSinkProvider());
ChannelServices.RegisterChannel(channel);
```

If you register a server channel that uses a nondefault formatter, you must also register a client channel of the same type and that uses the same type of formatter. Here's the registration of the HTTP client channel that uses a binary formatter in the configuration file:

```
<channels>
   <channel ref="http" >
      <clientProviders>
         <formatter ref="binary" />
      </clientProviders>
   </channel>
</channels>
```

The client-side code that registers the channel programmatically follows. Notice that in this case the names of the channel class and of the formatter class contain the string Client rather than Server:

```
' [Visual Basic]
' Register an HTTP client channel that uses a binary formatter.
Dim props As New Hashtable
props("port") = 0              ' port=0 is used for client channels.
Dim channel As New HttpClientChannel(props, New BinaryClientFormatterSinkProvider)
ChannelServices.RegisterChannel(channel)

// [C#]
// Register an HTTP client channel that uses a binary formatter.
Hashtable props = new Hashtable();
props["port"] = 0;             // port=0 is used for client channels.
HttpClientChannel channel = new HttpClientChannel(props,
new BinaryClientFormatterSinkProvider());
ChannelServices.RegisterChannel(channel);
```

32.9 The rejectRemoteRequests attribute

When using .NET remoting for cross-AppDomain calls or cross-process calls on the same computer, specify a rejectRemoteRequests attribute in the <channel> tag to reject all connections that don't originate from the local computer.

How to: Use the following configuration file on the server to reject requests from other computers. (You can use the rejectRemoteRequests attribute only with the TCP channel.)

```
<channels>
   <channel ref="tcp" rejectRemoteRequests="true" />
</channels>
```

32.10 The typeFilterLevel attribute

Omit the typeFilterLevel attribute in the <formatter> tag (or use its default value of Low) if you are marshaling only primitive types and types associated with the most basic remoting functionality. Use the Full value only to permit marshaling of all types and to allow the server to call back the client.

More details: This attribute has been introduced in version 1.1 of the .NET Framework with the purpose of protecting server applications from deserialization attacks coming from remote clients. (The attribute is also available in .NET Framework version 1.0 Service Pack 3.) When you select the default Low setting, the remoting architecture supports only the marshaling of simple types, including primitive types, types that implement the ILease interface, and types marked as serializable that don't implement ISerializable or that implement ISerializable with a reduced permission set. More complex objects—such as ObjRef objects passed as parameters and objects that implement the ISponsor interface—require the Full security setting. Because the default security level changed in the transition from version 1.0 to 1.1, many existing applications ceased to work properly and threw a SerializationException object.

How to: Use the following configuration file on the server to allow deserialization of all types as well as callbacks to the client:

```
<channels>
   <channel ref="tcp" port="50000" >
      <serverProviders>
         <formatter ref="binary" typeFilterLevel="Full" />
      </serverProviders>
   </channel>
</channels>
```

Use the following configuration file on the client to accept callbacks from the server:

```
<channels>
   <channel ref="tcp" port="0" >
      <clientProviders>
         <formatter ref="binary" typeFilterLevel="Full" />
      </clientProviders>
   </channel>
</channels>
```

32.11 The <customErrors> tag

Prevent remote clients from seeing detailed error information by using appropriate settings for the <customErrors> tag in the configuration file.

Why: Filtering out critical information such as the exception message and the stack contents when the exception was thrown makes it harder for malicious clients to attack the server application.

How to: By default, the remoting infrastructure in version 1.1 of the .NET Framework sends detailed error information only to clients running on the same computer as the application that hosts the remotable objects. During the test phase, you might need to relax this limitation by setting the mode attribute of the <customErrors> tag to off, but you should restore the attribute to remoteOnly (default) or on before deploying the application. (In the latter case, all clients receive filtered error information, including local clients.)

```
<configuration>
   <system.runtime.remoting>
      <customErrors mode="on" />
   </system.runtime.remoting>
</configuration>
```

32.12 Hosting remoting objects in IIS

Follow these instructions when hosting an object inside IIS.

1. Create an appropriate configuration file for the remote objects, and save it as Web.config in a directory on your local hard disk. (IIS configuration files must have this name.) Remember that you can specify an HTTP channel but omit the port number, and you must omit the application name.

2. Create a directory named bin as a subdirectory of the directory that contains the Web.config file; save the DLL exposing the remoting objects (RemoteComponents.dll in our example) into this bin directory. Alternatively, you can sign the assembly with a strong name and register it in the GAC. (If you do so, remember that the configuration file should refer to the assembly using its complete name, including version, culture, and publisher key.)

3. Use the IIS MMC snap-in to create the virtual directory that maps to the physical directory that contains the Web.config file by right-clicking the Default Web Site element and choosing the Virtual Directory command from the New submenu. (In this example, we assume that this virtual directory is named RemoteComponents.)

4. Right-click the new virtual directory to display the Properties dialog box, switch to the Directory Security tab, and then click the Edit button in the Authentication And Access Control area. This action displays the Authentication Methods dialog box, where you should verify that the Enable Anonymous Access check box is selected. (See rules 32.18 and 32.19 for more information about authentication in IIS.)

5. Right-click the Web site element to display the Properties page, and clear the Enable HTTP Keep-Alives check box (see Figure 32-1).

More details: When used with standard Web applications, the Enable HTTP Keep-Alives option enables you to improve performance because it enables browsers to retrieve all the elements in a page (HTML text and graphics) without opening and closing the HTTP connection for each individual element. This sort of optimization isn't necessary with .NET remoting, however, because each call is a self-contained request. By disabling this option, you enable IIS to close the connection and release all related resources as soon as the method call completes. Unfortunately, you can specify this option only at the Web site level, not at the folder level.

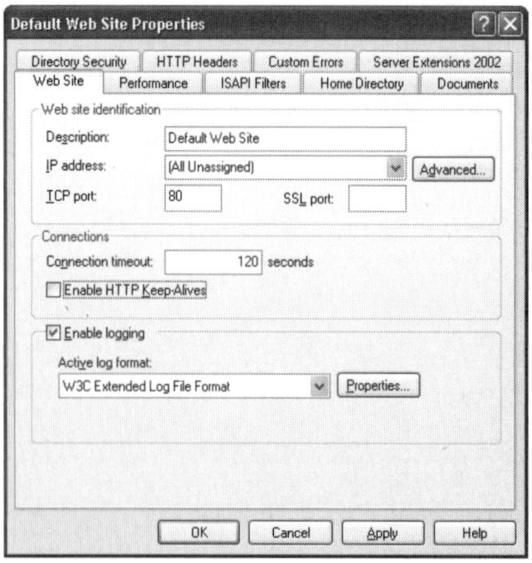

Figure 32-1 The Web site's Properties dialog box

Example: Here's an example of a Web.config file that you can deploy together with the RemoteComponents.dll assembly. You can use the .soap extension for the objectUri attribute of the <wellKnown> tag to emphasize the fact that the object will be serialized through SOAP. (You can use the .rem extension without any problem, however.)

```
<service>
   <wellknown type="RemoteComponents.Calculator, RemoteComponents"
      mode="Singleton" objectUri="Calculator.soap" />
</service>
```

More details: You can drop the <channels> section entirely, unless you need to specify a binary formatter or some other custom attribute for the HTTP default channel.

Very few changes are necessary in the client application to enable it to use a remote object hosted in IIS. In practice, assuming that the application is already configured to use the HTTP channel, the only significant change is in the URL that references the remote object. The new URL doesn't specify the port number, but it must include the name of the virtual directory that you've created for the object. Here's an example of the configuration file that the client can use to reach the object exposed with the Web.config file listed in the previous section:

```
<client>
   <wellknown type="RemoteComponents.Calculator, RemoteComponents"
      url="http://localhost/RemoteComponents/Calculator.soap" />
</client>
```

32.13 Never-expiring Singleton objects

Provide a null object reference as a lease for Singleton SAOs so that the object is never released.

Why: Singleton SAOs are often used to share information among different client applications, so it's necessary to keep their instance alive until the server application terminates. Even if the Singleton object isn't used to share state, keeping a single instance alive on the server doesn't actually affect scalability negatively.

More details: Keep in mind that Singleton objects are destroyed if the server machine crashes or if IIS recycles the host process; therefore, these objects should be used with caution to communicate with computers across the network or with multiple servers in an NLB scenario.

```
' [Visual Basic]
Public Class Calculator
   Inherits MarshalByRefObject

   Public Overrides Function InitializeLifetimeService() As Object
      Return Nothing
   End Function
End Class
```

```csharp
// [C#]
public class Calculator : MarshalByRefObject
{
    public override object InitializeLifetimeService()
    {
        return null;
    }
}
```

32.14 One-way remoting calls

Consider applying the OneWay attribute to a remote method that doesn't return a value and doesn't take a by-reference argument.

Why: When a client invokes a method marked with the OneWay attribute through the .NET remoting infrastructure, the call returns immediately to the client. Essentially, this attribute enables you to implement asynchronous, fire-and-forget remote calls in a very simple way. (For example, this attribute is perfect for methods that perform logging operations.)

Why not: This attribute doesn't work well with Windows Forms applications and, more in general, with applications marked with the STAThread attribute because it can lead to memory leaks. Read *http://www.thinktecture.com/Resources/RemotingFAQ/Handling_Events_Hangs_Application.html* for more details.

```vbnet
' [Visual Basic]
<OneWay()> _
Public Sub LogMessage(ByVal text As String)
    ...
End Sub
```

```csharp
// [C#]
[OneWay]
public void LogMessage(string text)
{
    ...
}
```

32.15 The Soapsuds tool

Avoid using the Soapsuds tool to generate the metadata-only assembly to be deployed on client computers if you are to marshal complex types, such as typed DataSet objects. If using the Soapsuds tool, always include the /nowp option to prevent the tool from creating a wrapped proxy. For two alternatives to using Soapsuds, see rules 32.16 and 32.17.

Why: The Soapsuds tool isn't really reliable when it generates metadata for complex and nested types, such as DataSets. A wrapped proxy isn't recommended because it can reach the remote object only through SOAP over an HTTP channel, and so you can't use the more efficient binary formatter (not to mention the TCP channel). A wrapped proxy is also less flexible because the URL of the remote object is burnt in the proxy assembly. You must regenerate the wrapped proxy and redeploy it on all your clients if you want to move the remote object to another server.

You can read more about Soapsuds's shortcomings at *http://www.thinktecture.com/ Resources/RemotingFAQ/SoapSudsOrInterfaces.html.*

More details: A wrapped proxy is a local class that the client application can use in lieu of the remote class because all its methods and properties automatically dispatch the call to the remote object. A client application that uses a wrapped proxy doesn't even need to register the object as remote.

Example: Here's an example of how you can launch the Soapsuds tool to extract metadata from an assembly named remotecomponents.dll and create a metadata-only assembly named localmetadata.dll; the /sn switch is recommended because it assigns a strong name to the new assembly:

```
SOAPSUDS /ia:remotecomponents /oa:localmetadata.dll /sn:mykeyfile.snk /nowp
```

If you don't have the RemoteComponents DLL available, you can still use the Soapsuds tool to generate metadata from objects running on the server by using the following syntax:

```
SOAPSUDS /url:http://localhost/RemoteComponents/Calculator.soap?wsdl /oa:localmetadata.dll
  /sn:mykeyfile.snk /nowp
```

32.16 Using shared interfaces with SAOs

When working with Server-Activated Objects (SAOs), use assemblies containing only interface definitions and deploy these metadata-only assemblies on both the server and the client computers. The remote component implements the interface, and the client can access the remote component by means of interface variables.

Why: Using shared interfaces gives you the maximum flexibility and control on how remote objects are instantiated and used.

Example: Let's say you want to provide access to a remote Calculator class exposed as an SAO by means of shared interfaces. Begin with creating a new class library project named Remote-Types, and add the ICalculator interface to it, as shown in the following code:

```
' [Visual Basic]
' (In the RemoteTypes project)
Public Interface ICalculator
    Function Add(ByVal n1 As Double, ByVal n2 As Double) As Double
End Interface

// [C#]
// (In the RemoteTypes project)
public interface ICalculator
{
    double Add(double n1, double n2);
}
```

Compile the project, create the RemoteTypes.dll assembly, and deploy it to both the server and the client computers. Next, switch to the project that contains the Calculator class, add a reference to the RemoteTypes.dll, and extend the Calculator class to implement the ICalculator interface.

```vbnet
' [Visual Basic]
Imports RemoteTypes

Public Class Calculator
    Inherits MarshalByRefObject
    Implements ICalculator

    Function Add(ByVal n1 As Double, ByVal n2 As Double) As Double _
          Implements ICalculator.Add
       Return n1 + n2
    End Function
End Class
```

```csharp
// [C#]
using RemoteTypes;

public class Calculator : MarshalByRefObject, ICalculator
{
    public double Add(double n1, double n2)
    {
        return n1 + n2;
    }
}
```

Next, open the client project, add a reference to the local RemoteTypes.dll, and use the following code to instantiate the remote object and call its methods:

```vbnet
' [Visual Basic]
' This code assumes that the remote object is exposed as an SAO and that the RemoteTypes
' namespace has been imported at the top of current source file.
Dim url As String = "http://localhost/RemoteComponents/Calculator.soap"
Dim calc As ICalculator = DirectCast(Activator.GetObject( _
    GetType(ICalculator), url), ICalculator)
' Use the remote calculator.
Dim result As Double = calc.Add(10, 20)
```

```csharp
// [C#]
// This code assumes that the remote object is exposed as an SAO and that the RemoteTypes
// namespace has been imported with a using statement.
string url = "http://localhost/RemoteComponents/Calculator.soap";
ICalculator calc = (ICalculator) Activator.GetObject(typeof(ICalculator), url);
// Use the remote calculator.
double result = calc.Add(10, 20);
```

Remember that the Activator.GetObject method doesn't require that the remote object be registered on the client—either by code or by using configuration files—so the structure of the client application is simpler. You can read more about this topic at *http://www.thinktecture.com/ Resources/RemotingFAQ/UseInterfacesWithConfigFiles.html*.

> **Note**   You can use shared base class definitions instead of shared interfaces. In this case, the remote component inherits from the shared base class and the client can access the remote component by means of a variable typed after the base class. All the pros and cons of shared interfaces apply to shared base classes as well, and the code you need to write is very similar.

32.17 Using shared interfaces and factory methods with CAOs

When working with Client-Activated Objects, use an SAO exposing factory methods that return an instance of the required CAO. These factory methods should be invoked by means of shared interfaces.

More details: This technique works because all objects returned by remote methods are marshaled to the client as CAOs.

Example: This example extends the example shown in rule 32.16 and shows how to provide access to a remote Calculator CAO object. Begin with extending the RemoteTypes project with a new IRemoteFactory interface, as in the following code:

```
' [Visual Basic]
' (In the RemoteTypes project)
Public Interface IRemoteFactory
   Function CreateCalculator() As ICalculator
End Interface

// [C#]
// (In the RemoteTypes project)
public interface IRemoteFactory
{
   ICalculator CreateCalculator();
}
```

(In a real-world application, this interface would contain one factory method for each remote object, such as CreateInvoice, CreateOrder, and so on.) The interface must be compiled in the RemoteTypes.dll assembly and must be accessible to both client and server applications. Next, switch to the RemoteComponents project containing the Calculator type and add the following code. (Remember that RemoteFactory must derive from MarshalByRefObject because it is accessed remotely as a Singleton SAO.)

```
' [Visual Basic]
Public Class RemoteFactory
   Inherits MarshalByRefObject
   Implements IRemoteFactory

   ' This object will live forever.
   Public Overrides Function InitializeLifetimeService() As Object
     Return Nothing
   End Function
```

```
   Public Function CreateCalculator() As ICalculator _
      Implements IRemoteFactory.CreateCalculator
     Return New Calculator
   End Function
End Class
```

```
// [C#]
public class RemoteFactory : MarshalByRefObject, IRemoteFactory
{
   // This object will live forever.
   public override object InitializeLifetimeService()
   {
      return null;
   }

   public ICalculator CreateCalculator()
   {
      return new Calculator();
   }
}
```

The server application must register the RemoteFactory class as a remote object, either programmatically or with the following elements in the configuration file:

```
<service>
   <wellknown type="RemoteComponents.RemoteFactory, RemoteComponents"
      mode="Singleton" objectUri="RemoteFactory.soap" />
</service>
```

Here's the code that runs on the client and uses the RemoteFactory class to create remote objects:

```
' [Visual Basic]
' Get a reference to the remote factory class.
' (You can cache this reference for future calls.)
Dim url As String = "tcp://localhost:50000/RemoteComponents/RemoteFactory.soap"
Dim factory As IRemoteFactory = _
   DirectCast(Activator.GetObject(GetType(IRemoteFactory), url), IRemoteFactory)
' Create an instance of the remote Calculator as a CAO.
Dim calc As ICalculator = factory.CreateCalculator()
Dim result As Double = calc.Add(10, 20)
```

```
// [C#]
// Get a reference to the remote factory class.
// (You can cache this reference for future calls.)
string url = "tcp://localhost:50000/ RemoteComponents/RemoteFactory.soap";
IRemoteFactory factory = (IRemoteFactory) Activator.GetObject(typeof(IRemoteFactory), url);
// Create an instance of the remote Calculator as a CAO.
ICalculator calc = factory.CreateCalculator();
double result = calc.Add(10, 20);
```

Notice that you can easily extend this technique to support constructors with parameters.

32.18 Integrated Windows security in IIS

When using IIS to expose remote objects to clients running in the same domain (or a trusted domain), secure the IIS virtual directory by means of Integrated Windows authentication.

How to: Use the MMC tool to bring up the Properties dialog box of the virtual directory that exposes the remotable object, switch to the Directory Security tab, click the Edit button in the Authentication And Access Control box, and ensure that the Enable Anonymous Access check box is disabled and that the Integrated Windows Authentication check box is enabled (see Figure 32-2). If the client machine is in the same domain or in a trusted domain, you can authenticate the client application by just adding the useDefaultCredentials attribute to the <channel> tag in the client's configuration file:

```
<channels>
   <channel ref="http" useDefaultCredentials="true" />
</channels>
```

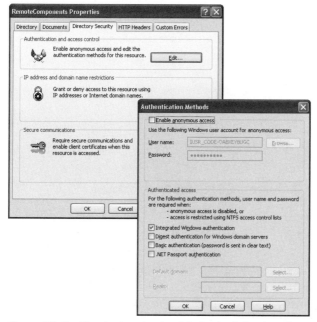

Figure 32-2   The Authentication Methods dialog box for an IIS virtual directory

32.19 Basic authentication security in IIS

When using IIS to expose remote objects to clients that aren't running in the same domain or a trusted domain (which is the case when your objects can be reached from the Internet), secure the IIS virtual directory by means of Basic authentication.

How to: You must enable Basic authentication by using a procedure similar to the one described in rule 32.18. The following code shows how the client application can pass its credentials to the server using Basic authentication:

```
' [Visual Basic]
' Create an SAO.
Dim calc As New Calculator
' Specify user name and password in the channel properties.
Dim props As IDictionary = ChannelServices.GetChannelSinkProperties(calc)
props("username") = "myusername"
props("password") = "mypassword"
' Register the channel.
Dim channel As New HttpClientChannel(props, New BinaryClientFormatterSinkProvider)
ChannelServices.RegisterChannel(channel)
' Use the object as usual.
Dim result As Double = calc.Add(10, 20)

// [C#]
// Create an SA
Calculator calc = new Calculator();
// Specify user name and password in the channel properties.
IDictionary props = ChannelServices.GetChannelSinkProperties(calc);
props["username"] = "myusername";
props["password"] = "mypassword";
// Register the channel.
HttpClientChannel channel = new HttpClientChannel(props, new BinaryClientFormatterSinkProvid
er());
ChannelServices.RegisterChannel(channel);
// Use the object as usual.
Calculator calc = new Calculator();        // An SAO object
double result = calc.Add(10, 20);
```

32.20 Exchanging data between different time zones

Take into account the problems that might arise when exchanging date/time information when the host and the client applications reside in different time zones. If the client sends the host an object that contains one or more DateTime fields or properties, these values will be relative to the client's time zone and a number of problems can arise. For example, if a European client places an order at 1:00 A.M. (local time), a U.S. host application would receive an order with tomorrow's date and might reject it.

How to: The simplest way to account for this problem is to normalize all dates to Universal Time Coordinate (UTC) using the DateTime.ToUniversalTime method. (You can later convert a UTC value back to local time by means of the DateTime.ToLocalTime method.)

See also: Read rule 24.14 for additional problems related to serialization of DateTime values when using the SOAP formatter.

Chapter 33
Security

Many of the guidelines in this book are about creating secure code that can withstand attacks from ill-intentioned hackers, especially in applications that are exposed to the outside through the Internet. However, we still needed a chapter where we could discuss several security-related topics, such as Code Access Security (CAS) techniques, cryptography, and hashing.

The good news is that you rarely have to worry about CAS if you aren't authoring a class library or a program that might run as a partially trusted application. (A partially trusted application is any Microsoft .NET Framework program that is not launched from a local disk.) If you *are* working on a class library, though, we recommend that you apply a Strong-NameIdentityPermission attribute so the only untrusted applications that can access the library are those produced by your company (see rule 33.15), unless of course you plan to sell the library to other developers. If you are building a class library that is meant to be used by other software companies, you might still avoid getting involved with CAS by requesting that only fully trusted applications use the library (see rule 33.4). Finally, if you are designing a class library that might be used by partially trusted applications, it is *absolutely mandatory* that you apply the CAS guidelines explained in this chapter. Failing to do so might open up huge security holes in your .NET software.

> **Note** One or more code examples in this chapter assume that the following namespaces have been imported by means of *Imports* (Visual Basic) or *using* (C#) statements:
>
> ```
> System.Diagnostics
> System.IO
> System.Security
> System.Security.Cryptography
> System.Security.Permissions
> System.Security.Policy
> System.Security.Principal
> System.Reflection
> System.Runtime.InteropServices
> System.Runtime.Serialization
> System.Text.RegularExpressions
> System.Threading
> ```

33.1 Assembly-level permission requests

Mark assemblies with permission attributes specifying suitable RequestMinimum, Request-Optional, and RequestRefuse actions.

Why: This guideline ensures that the assembly has only the permissions that it strictly needs for its chores. By reducing the permission set assigned to the assembly, you make it harder for malicious code to exploit your assembly to access protected resources.

More details: The RequestMinimum action specifies the permissions that are necessary for the assembly to work correctly; if the .NET runtime can't grant these permissions, the assembly won't be loaded and a PolicyException is thrown. The RequestOptional action specifies the permissions that the assembly would like to use but that aren't crucial for its operations; if one of these permissions isn't granted, the assembly loads all the same, but its user interface should disable or hide all commands that would perform a prohibited action (see rule 33.2). The RequestRefuse action specifies permissions that the .NET runtime should never grant to the assembly.

The permission set granted to the assembly consists of all the permissions marked with the RequestMinimum action, plus all the permissions marked with the RequestOptional action, minus all the permissions marked with the RequestRefuse action. In all cases, however, an assembly won't be given permissions that aren't granted by the policy level and the code group the assembly belongs to.

The RequestMinimum and RequestOptional actions create a so-called *white list* that contains the only permissions that the assembly asks for. The RequestRefuse action creates a *black list* that contains the permissions that should be explicitly denied to the assembly. In the security realm, it's always preferable to reason in terms of white lists rather than black lists; therefore, it is recommended that you define your security needs by means of RequestMinimum and RequestOptional rather than RequestRefuse.

Example: The following code shows the attributes that can be applied to an assembly that requires permission to create user interface elements and access files by means of common file dialogs, that wants to be granted permission to use performance counters (but that can run without them), and that explicitly refuses to receive the permission to call unmanaged code:

```
' [Visual Basic]
<Assembly: UIPermission(SecurityAction.RequestMinimum, Unrestricted:=True)>
<Assembly: FileDialogPermission(SecurityAction.RequestMinimum, Unrestricted:=True)>
<Assembly: PerformanceCounterPermission(SecurityAction.RequestOptional, Unrestricted:=True)>
<Assembly: SecurityPermission(SecurityAction.RequestRefuse, UnmanagedCode:=True)>

// [C#]
[assembly: UIPermission(SecurityAction.RequestMinimum, Unrestricted=true)]
[assembly: FileDialogPermission(SecurityAction.RequestMinimum, Unrestricted=true)]
[assembly: PerformanceCounterPermission(SecurityAction.RequestOptional, Unrestricted=true)]
[assembly: SecurityPermission(SecurityAction.RequestRefuse, UnmanagedCode=true)]
```

Notice that the previous code snippet could be simplified by dropping the RequestRefuse action on the SecurityPermission object because this permission isn't in the set of permissions implied by the RequestMinimum and RequestOptional actions and therefore the permission to call unmanaged code will be denied anyway.

33.2 Demand permissions at application startup

Demand all the permissions that the application might require during its lifetime and disable all the user interface elements corresponding to actions that aren't allowed.

Why: It's preferable that users know as early as possible that some actions are forbidden. For example, no sane user would appreciate an application that enables her to work for hours on a document and then raises an error when she attempts to print the document or save it to disk.

Example: You can easily encapsulate Demand methods in reusable procedures that enable you to test whether a given permission is granted:

```vb
' [Visual Basic]
Public Function IsFilePermissionGranted() As Boolean
   Try
      Dim filePerm As New FileIOPermission(PermissionState.Unrestricted)
      filePerm.Demand()
      Return True
   Catch ex As Exception
      Return False
   End Try
End Function
```

```csharp
// [C#]
public bool IsFilePermissionGranted()
{
   try
   {
      FileIOPermission filePerm = new FileIOPermission(PermissionState.Unrestricted);
      filePerm.Demand();
      return true;
   }
   catch
   { return false; }
}
```

33.3 Declarative vs. imperative security actions

Favor declarative demands over imperative Demand, Deny, and PermitOnly security actions.

Why: Declarative actions are easier to use and understand, can be used at the class level, and can be detected by reflection-based tools such as PermView. Imperative actions should be used only when they are based on dynamic information (for example, file paths) that isn't available at compile time.

```vb
' [Visual Basic]
<ReflectionPermission(SecurityAction.PermitOnly, _
   Flags:=ReflectionPermissionFlag.TypeInformation)> _
Public Class ReflectionDemo
   ' All procedures in this class have only the permission to use
   ' reflection to access type information.
   ...
End Class
```

```
// [C#]
[ReflectionPermission(SecurityAction.PermitOnly,
    Flags=ReflectionPermissionFlag.TypeInformation)]
public class ReflectionDemo
{
    // All procedures in this class have only the permission to use
    // reflection to access type information.
    ...;
}
```

More details: Recall that class-level security attributes protect the class and all its members, but don't protect nested types. You need to mark nested types explicitly with appropriate security attributes, if necessary.

33.4 The AllowPartiallyTrustedCallers attribute

Abide by the following guidelines when applying the AllowPartiallyTrustedCallers (APTC) attribute.

   a. Apply this attribute only to strong-named assemblies that are meant to be called from partially trusted assemblies. (By default, strong-named assemblies can be called only by fully trusted assemblies.)

   b. Methods in assemblies marked with the APTC attribute should call methods in another assembly only if the other assembly is also marked with the APTC attribute. This guideline ensures that untrusted assemblies can't use the assembly marked with APTC to call into an assembly that isn't supposed to be available to untrusted callers.

   c. Methods in assemblies marked with the APTC attribute should always demand one or more permissions from callers; exceptions to this rule are sometimes necessary, but you should carefully review your code to ensure that untrusted assemblies can't use your public methods to perform dangerous actions.

   d. Types in assemblies marked with the APTC attribute shouldn't derive from types defined in assemblies that aren't marked with the APTC attribute. (By default, public and protected types in strong-named assemblies are protected with an InheritanceDemand, but the APTC attribute disables this protection.)

More details: If you are developing a strongly named assembly, you must decide whether to use the AllowPartiallyTrustedCallers attribute. If you omit it, your library can't be invoked by partially trusted assemblies and you don't have to worry about CAS. If you apply the attribute, you are implicitly telling the .NET Framework that you understand that your library might be used by untrusted (and potentially dangerous) code and that you have taken all the necessary precautions to prevent callers from tricking your code into doing anything harmful to your system. (This kind of attack is known as a *luring attack*.)

This attribute has no effect if applied to assemblies that lack a strong name and are therefore private to an application (because these assemblies can't be accessed by untrusted code outside the application itself). An application that is launched from a network drive can always access a private assembly that is stored in the application's directory or another subdirectory that is searched by the .NET runtime through probing.

Example: The following example shows the security issue that occurs when a type in an assembly marked with the APTC attribute inherits from a type in another assembly that isn't marked with this attribute and that is supposed to contain private data:

```vb
' [Visual Basic]
' This type contains private data in an assembly that is NOT marked with APTC attribute.
Public Class LoginData
    Public ReadOnly Name As String = "John Smith"
    Public ReadOnly Password As String = "mypwd"
End Class


' This type is placed in an assembly marked with APTC attribute.
Public Class PersonalData
    Inherits LoginData
    Public Overrides Function ToString() As String
        Return Me.Name & ", " & Me.Password
    End Function
End Class


' The main assembly isn't fully trusted but can read private data.
Sub Main()
    Dim data As New PersonalData
    Console.WriteLine(data)      ' Displays "John Smith, mypwd"
End Sub
```

```csharp
// [C#]
// This type contains private data in an assembly that is NOT marked with APTC attribute.
public class LoginData
{
    public readonly string  Name = "John Smith";
    public readonly string  Password = "mypwd";
}


// This type is placed in an assembly marked with APTC attribute.
public class PersonalData: LoginData
{
    public override string ToString()
    {
        return this.Name + ", " + this.Password;
    }
}


// The main assembly isn't fully trusted but can read private data.
static void Main()
{
    PersonalData data = new PersonalData();
    Console.WriteLine(data);      // Displays "John Smith, mypwd"
}
```

> **Note**   This is the complete list of .NET Framework 1.1 assemblies that are marked with the APTC attribute: Accessibility.dll, IEExecRemote.dll, Microsoft.VisualBasic.dll, Mscorlib.dll, System.dll, System.Data.dll, System.Drawing.dll, System.Web.dll, System.Web.Mobile.dll, System.Web.Services.dll, System.Web.RegularExpressions.dll, System.Windows.Forms.dll, and System.Xml.dll.

33.5 Assert security actions

Abide by the following rules when asserting a permission:

   a.   Assert a permission before performing multiple operations on a resource that is subject to CAS.

   b.   Precede any Assert method with a Demand method on the same permission object.

   c.   Keep methods as short as possible so that the permission is asserted for a limited time only.

   d.   If you need to assert a different permission in the same method, use the CodeAccess-Permission.RevertAssert static method to cancel the effect of the most recent Assert method. (There can be only one active asserted permission in a given method.)

   e.   Exercise extra care when asserting special permissions that might give untrusted code the ability to circumvent the security system. Such dangerous permissions include ReflectionPermission (gives the ability to call private members) and most permissions in the SecurityPermission object, such as UnmanagedCode, SkipVerification, Control-Principal, and ControlEvidence.

Why: Asserting a permission is a simple and effective way to optimize performance because asserting reduces the depth of stack walks. However, you should assert a permission only after demanding it to ensure that callers have the right to call the code that accesses the resource.

```
' [Visual Basic]
Public Sub ProcessDataFiles()
   Dim filePerm As New FileIOPermission(PermissionState.Unrestricted)
   ' Ensure that all callers in the stack have this permission.
   filePerm.Demand()
   ' Tell the .NET runtime that you have checked.
   filePerm.Assert()
   ' File operations from now on fire a *partial* stack walk.
   ...
   ' (No need to revert the assertion before exiting.)
End Sub
```

```csharp
// [C#]
public void ProcessDataFiles()
{
    FileIOPermission filePerm = new FileIOPermission(PermissionState.Unrestricted);
    // Ensure that all callers in the stack have this permission.
    filePerm.Demand();
    // Tell the .NET runtime that you have checked.
    filePerm.Assert();
    // File operations from now on fire a *partial* stack walk.
    ...
    // (No need to revert the assertion before exiting.)
}
```

33.6 Deny and PermitOnly security actions

Avoid using Deny and PermitOnly security actions.

Why: You typically use the Deny and PermitOnly methods on a permission object before calling an assembly that you don't trust. However, it is quite impractical to deny all the permissions that you consider potentially dangerous and it is difficult to anticipate all the permissions that the untrusted assembly might legitimately require.

More details: The PermitOnly action defines a white list containing only the permissions that you want to grant, whereas the Deny action defines a black list containing all the permissions that you don't want to grant. As explained in rule 33.1, white lists are preferable to black lists, hence you should favor the PermitOnly action over the Deny action. Also, when denying access to a resource that takes a path (such as the file system), multiple notations to reference the same path might be available, for example, \\server\mydir and z:\mydir, in which case using the Deny method requires that you deny access to all of them.

See also: See rule 33.7 for a case when the Deny and PermitOnly methods might be useful.

```vbnet
' [Visual Basic]
' From now on, deny UI operations.
Dim uiPerm As New UIPermission(PermissionState.Unrestricted)
uiPerm.Deny()
' UI is not permitted now.
...
' Undo the effect of the Deny method.
CodeAccessPermission.RevertDeny()
' UI is permitted again from now on.
```

```csharp
// [C#]
// From now on, deny UI operations.
UIPermission uiPerm = new UIPermission(PermissionState.Unrestricted);
uiPerm.Deny();
// UI is not permitted now.
...
// Undo the effect of the Deny method.
CodeAccessPermission.RevertDeny();
// UI is permitted again from now on.
```

33.7 Security in event handlers and delegates

Carefully scrutinize your code to ensure that event handlers don't contain dangerous code and can't be exploited by malicious clients. At the very minimum, use private or protected scope for all your event handlers. (Fortunately, Microsoft Visual Studio .NET generates event handlers with private scope by default.)

Why: Don't mistakenly believe that a Demand security action can successfully protect your event handlers from being misused. The Demand security action checks whether an untrusted caller is in the call stack but can't check whether the handler was added to the event source by untrusted code; also, the permission might be asserted at the time the event is raised. Therefore, malicious clients might attach your event handler to an event source so that your handler unknowingly executes dangerous code on behalf of the untrusted client.

More details: Delegates pose a security risk similar to event handlers, which isn't surprising because events are based on delegates. When your code raises an event, it calls one or more delegates that might be pointing to any method. If the delegate's target method resides in a trusted assembly, the method executes under the highest privileges.

For example, let's say that your trusted assembly has a method that deletes all the files in a directory and a System.Timers.Timer object that ticks every second; an untrusted assembly might attach the method to the timer's Elapsed event so that the trusted assembly will later perform the delete operation on behalf of the untrusted code. To avoid this sort of security issue, consider using Deny and PermitOnly actions before calling a delegate received from untrusted code.

33.8 Security in exception handlers

Always add a *Catch* (Visual Basic) or *catch* (C#) clause that traps all exceptions if the code in the *Try* or *try* block modifies any property of the current thread in a way that might be exploited by malicious code, for example, by impersonating a user with higher privileges.

More details: A little-known detail about exception handlers is that an exception filter—that is, a *When* clause in a Visual Basic program—might execute before the *Finally* (Visual Basic) or *finally* (C#) block. Consider this code:

```vb
' [Visual Basic]
Public Class MyTasks
    Public Shared Sub PerformTask()
        Try
            ' Impersonate a different, more privileged user here.
            ...
        Finally
            ' Revert to original user.
            ...
        End Try
    End Sub
End Class
```

```csharp
// [C#]
public class MyTasks
{
    public static void PerformTask()
    {
        try
        {
            // Impersonate a different, more privileged user here.
            ...
        }
        finally
        {
            // Revert to original user.
            ...
        }
    }
}
```

Next, suppose that the PerformTask method is invoked from the following untrusted Visual Basic code (in a different assembly):

```vbnet
Sub Main()
    Try
        MyTasks.PerformTask()
    Catch ex As Exception When ExceptionFilter(ex)
        ...
    End Try
End Sub


Function ExceptionFilter(ByVal ex As Exception) As Boolean
    ' This code runs under the impersonated user identity.
    ...
    Return True
End Function
```

As counterintuitive as it might appear, the code in the ExceptionFilter method runs before the code in the *finally* clause in the PerformTask method; therefore, it runs while the code is impersonating a more privileged account and can perform actions that would otherwise be prohibited.

The solution to this problem is to wrap the exception handler in an additional *Try...Catch* (Visual Basic) or *try...catch* (C#) block and rethrow the exception from that block:

```vbnet
' [Visual Basic]
Public Shared Sub PerformTask()
    Try
        Try
            ' Impersonate a different, more privileged user here.
            ...
        Finally
            ' Revert to original user.
            ...
        End Try
    Catch
        Throw
    End Try
End Sub
```

```
// [C#]
public static void PerformTask()
{
   try
   {
      try
      {
         // Impersonate a different, more privileged user here.
         ...
      }
      finally
      {
         // Revert to original user.
         ...
      }
   }
   catch
   { throw; }
}
```

33.9 LinkDemand security actions

Abide by the following guidelines when using the LinkDemand security action:

a. Favor a full Demand security action over a LinkDemand action because the former offers better protection against malicious code.

b. Use the LinkDemand action only if your benchmarks prove that the full stack walk caused by a regular Demand action affects performance significantly.

c. Use the LinkDemand action at the class level if you want to protect all the properties and methods of a class.

d. Don't expose public fields in types that you protect with a LinkDemand action because this action protects only properties and methods. If an assembly without all necessary permissions can grab a reference to an instance of a type protected with a LinkDemand action, the assembly can freely access all the public fields.

e. Don't access members protected with a LinkDemand action from members that aren't protected with a similar LinkDemand action.

f. Don't rely on the LinkDemand action to protect virtual (*Overridable* in Visual Basic) properties and methods. A malicious client might wait until a trusted assembly invokes (and indirectly JIT-compiles) the protected method and then instantiate an object that derives from the secured type but overrides the virtual member. (See rule 33.10 for the most appropriate way to deal with this issue.)

g. If you override a method marked with a LinkDemand security action, the method in the derived type should be marked with the same LinkDemand security action.

h. Always use a full Demand imperative or declarative security check for methods that use types or methods protected only by a LinkDemand action.

i. Don't use a type-level LinkDemand action in a value type or a LinkDemand action in the constructor of a value type (see rule 33.13).

j. Always protect interfaces with LinkDemand actions. If you use LinkDemand to protect a method that implements an interface method, a malicious client might circumvent the check by casting the object to an interface variable; in this case, only the LinkDemand action on the interface can protect the method from misuse.

More details: Unlike the Demand security action, which checks the permissions of all the callers in the stack, the LinkDemand action checks only the permissions of the immediate caller and does it only when the method is JIT-compiled (rather than at each method call). This behavior can improve performance but opens up a few security risks. You should use the LinkDemand action only when performance improvements are significant, and you should use the guidelines illustrated in this section to mitigate such risks.

Example: The following code shows how you can use the LinkDemand action to require that a type be used only by fully trusted assemblies.

```vb
' [Visual Basic]
<PermissionSet(SecurityAction.LinkDemand, Name:="FullTrust")> _
Public Class LoginData
    ...
End Class
```

```csharp
// [C#]
[PermissionSet(SecurityAction.LinkDemand, Name="FullTrust")]
public class LoginData
{
    ...
}
```

33.10 InheritanceDemand security actions

Use a type-level InheritanceDemand action for any nonsealed type that is marked with a Link-Demand action if the type has one or more virtual (*Overridable* in Visual Basic) methods. Alternatively, use the InheritanceDemand action for each virtual method. (The InheritanceDemand action has no effect on nonvirtual members.)

Why: Protecting an overridable member with a LinkDemand action isn't sufficient if the type isn't sealed because malicious code might wait until a trusted assembly invokes (and indirectly JIT-compiles) the protected method and then instantiate an object that derives from the secured type but overrides the virtual member.

```vb
' [Visual Basic]
<RegistryPermission(SecurityAction.InheritanceDemand, Unrestricted:=True)> _
Public Class RegistryFunctions
    ...
End Class
```

```csharp
// [C#]
[RegistryPermission(SecurityAction.InheritanceDemand, Unrestricted=true)]
public class RegistryFunctions
{
    ...;
}
```

33.11 The SuppressUnmanagedCodeSecurity attribute

Abide by the following guidelines in applying the SuppressUnmanagedCodeSecurity attribute:

a.   Avoid using the SuppressUnmanagedCodeSecurity attribute at the type level in public or protected types.

b.   Avoid applying the SuppressUnmanagedCodeSecurity attribute to public and protected members.

c.   Methods marked with the SuppressUnmanagedCodeSecurity attribute should always demand more specific permissions to prevent untrusted callers from performing dangerous actions.

d.   Apply the SuppressUnmanagedCodeSecurity attribute to all methods marked with the DllImport attribute, but use a Demand security action to check required permissions (see previous point).

e.   Always double-check arguments passed to unmanaged code to ensure that they have a valid length and can't cause buffer overruns, that filenames are in canonical form, and that strings don't include hex or Unicode escape sequences, extra null chars, or other invalid characters. You should also account for both long and short filenames and ensure that special NTFS file system stream names (such as filename::$DATA) can't defeat your security checks.

f.   Clearly mark methods that call unmanaged code and that aren't completely safe with the Unsafe prefix to draw programmers' attention to the extra care they must use when dealing with such methods. The .NET Framework exposes several members with this prefix, for example, BinaryFormatter.UnsafeDeserialize and ThreadPool.Unsafe-QueueUserWorkItem.

Why: By default, the .NET Framework makes a full Demand for methods that call unmanaged code through PInvoke or COM Interop services. If you mark the method (or its enclosing type) with the SuppressUnmanagedCodeSecurity attribute, the .NET Framework makes a LinkDemand for the unmanaged code permission. For this reason, you should adopt for this attribute the same precautions illustrated for the LinkDemand security action (see rule 33.9).

Example: The following snippet illustrates the recommended way to declare an external method that you can invoke by using PInvoke. The method uses the SuppressUnmanaged-CodeSecurity so that it can be called even when untrusted callers are in the call stack but explicitly demands the permission to interact with the Clipboard.

```
' [Visual Basic]
<DllImport("User32"), SuppressUnmanagedCodeSecurity(), _
   UIPermission(SecurityAction.Demand, Clipboard:=UIPermissionClipboard.OwnClipboard)> _
Private Shared Function OpenClipboard(ByVal hWnd As IntPtr) As Integer
End Function
```

```
// [C#]
[DllImport("User32")] [SuppressUnmanagedCodeSecurity()]
[UIPermission(SecurityAction.Demand, Clipboard=UIPermissionClipboard.OwnClipboard)]
private static extern int OpenClipboard(IntPtr hWnd);
```

33.12 Mixing type-level and method-level imperative security

If you apply the same declarative security action to both a type and one of its methods, the permission checked at the method level should be more restrictive than the permission checked at the type level. (This guideline doesn't apply to LinkDemand actions.)

Why: If you mark both a type and one of its methods for the same security action but for a different range of permissions, the two permissions aren't combined together. Instead, the type-level permission is ignored and only the method-level permission is applied. (However, attributes of the same type defined at the class and method levels combine their effect if their SecurityAction argument is different.)

If you don't follow this guideline, malicious code might bypass the more restrictive type-level permissions by obtaining an instance of the type by some other means—for example, using a factory method exposed by a trusted assembly—and then invoke the method without any security exception.

Example: The following code illustrates the issue described in this guideline:

```
' [Visual Basic]
<FileIOPermission(SecurityAction.Demand, Unrestricted:=True)> _
Public Class FileFunctions
    ' *** Wrong: method-level permission is less restrictive than type-level one.
    <FileIOPermission(SecurityAction.Demand, Read:="C:\Data")> _
    Public Function GetFileText(ByVal fileName As String) As String
        ...
    End Function
End Class
```

```
// [C#]
[FileIOPermission(SecurityAction.Demand, Unrestricted=true)]
public class FileFunctions
{
    // *** Wrong: method-level permission is less restrictive than type-level one.
    [FileIOPermission(SecurityAction.Demand, Read="C:\\Data")]
    public string GetFileText(string fileName)
    {
        ...
    }
}
```

33.13 Security checks in value types

Don't protect a value type, or its nondefault constructor, with an imperative Demand or LinkDemand security action. Instead, use public properties to wrap private fields and protect all the methods and properties of the value type with appropriate security actions.

Why: The .NET Framework allocates and initializes value types by means of their default (parameterless) constructor, and then executes any constructor with parameters explicitly invoked by the caller. If such a constructor is protected with a Demand or LinkDemand security action and the caller doesn't pass the security check, the .NET Framework throws an exception, but the instance of the value type still exists (as initialized by the default constructor) and its members can be used freely.

33.14 Types implementing the ISerializable interface

Abide by the following guidelines in types that implement the ISerializable interface:

a. Use private scope for the constructor implied by the ISerializable interface or protected scope if the class isn't sealed.

b. Protect the constructor implied by the ISerializable interface with the same security actions used to protect other constructors.

c. Protect the GetObjectData method by demanding SerializationFormatter permissions.

Why: Failing to follow these guidelines might result in a security risk because a malicious caller might serialize an instance obtained through a factory method exposed by a trusted assembly and then create a copy of it at a later time, or it might manufacture a stream of data containing arbitrary values and use it to create an invalid instance of the type.

```vbnet
' [Visual Basic]
Public Class PersonalData
   Implements ISerializable

   <SecurityPermission(SecurityAction.Demand, ControlPrincipal:=True)> _
   Sub New(ByVal name As String)
      ...
   End Sub

   ' *** OK: serialization constructor demands same permissions as regular constructors.
   <SecurityPermission(SecurityAction.Demand, ControlPrincipal:=True)> _
   Private Sub New(ByVal info As SerializationInfo, ByVal context As StreamingContext)
      ...
   End Sub

   ' *** OK: GetObjectData demands SerializationFormatter permissions.
   <SecurityPermission(SecurityAction.Demand, SerializationFormatter:=True)> _
   Public Sub GetObjectData(ByVal info As SerializationInfo, _
   ByVal context As StreamingContext) Implements ISerializable.GetObjectData
      ...
   End Sub
End Class

// [C#]
public class PersonalData : ISerializable
{
   [SecurityPermission(SecurityAction.Demand, ControlPrincipal=true)]
   public PersonalData(string name)
```

```
{
    ...
}

// *** OK: serialization constructor demands same permissions as regular constructors.
[SecurityPermission(SecurityAction.Demand, ControlPrincipal=true)]
private PersonalData(SerializationInfo info, StreamingContext context)
{
    ...
}

// *** OK: GetObjectData demands SerializationFormatter permissions.
[SecurityPermission(SecurityAction.Demand, SerializationFormatter=true)]
public void GetObjectData(SerializationInfo info, StreamingContext context)
{
    ...
}
}
```

33.15 The StrongNameIdentityPermission attribute

Use the StrongNameIdentityPermission attribute to ensure that a type and its members can be called only by another specific assembly or by all the assemblies of your company. (This attribute protects only from untrusted callers, though.)

How to: Use the SN tool to extract the public key of an assembly with a strong name:

```
SN -Tp CodeArchitects.Functions.dll > key.txt
```

You can then load the key.txt file into Notepad and paste the public key as in the following code:

```
' [Visual Basic]
Module Constants
    Public Const CodeArchitectsPublicKey As String = _
        "002401200480FD43940000000602000000240000525341310004000001000105bdc6c040bf307f7" _
        & "2d6eb0c5890122f9db5b7a71e9b03fe26203671abdb3d97238f2872d774c5469e0a89ae71fc3290c" _
        & "a722229c08ec73e513f0f9d82dd1e461e947e418b5c043f1d728ca358ab988b54d389d01e63646c4" _
        & "f3a26fBD56f7d989ba5148c9caa5b17e0e468c47a5d78654a87285502358ac41a79fb16864210f65"
End Module

<StrongNameIdentityPermission(SecurityAction.LinkDemand, _
    PublicKey:=CodeArchitectsPublicKey)> _
Public Class MyTasks
    ...
End Class

// [C#]
public class Constants
{
    public const string CodeArchitectsPublicKey =
        "002401200480FD43940000000602000000240000525341310004000001000105bdc6c040bf307f7"
        + "2d6eb0c5890122f9db5b7a71e9b03fe26203671abdb3d97238f2872d774c5469e0a89ae71fc3290c"
        + "a722229c08ec73e513f0f9d82dd1e461e947e418b5c043f1d728ca358ab988b54d389d01e63646c4"
        + "f3a26fBD56f7d989ba5148c9caa5b17e0e468c47a5d78654a87285502358ac41a79fb16864210f65";
}
```

```
[StrongNameIdentityPermission(SecurityAction.LinkDemand,
    PublicKey=Constants.CodeArchitectsPublicKey)]
public class MyTasks
{
    ...
}
```

More details: This technique has no effect if CAS has been disabled at the machine level; therefore, the StrongNameIdentityPermission attribute is good only to prevent unauthorized *untrusted* assemblies from using your libraries because any full trust assembly can disable CAS at the application level simply by running this code:

```
' [Visual Basic]
SecurityManager.SecurityEnabled = False
```

```
// [C#]
SecurityManager.SecurityEnabled = false;
```

See also: See rule 33.16 for a more robust way to ensure that a method can be invoked only by an assembly signed with your company's public key token.

33.16 Protect libraries from unauthorized use

Use the StackTrace object to walk the call stack and check the identity of the immediate caller (or all the callers in the stack) if you want to prevent your DLLs from being used by unauthorized clients.

Example: The following code shows how you can ensure that the *immediate* caller of a dangerous method is an assembly signed with your company's public key token:

```
' [Visual Basic]
Private Const COMPANY_PUBLICKEYTOKEN As String = "688997da81cf9c98"

Public Sub DangerousMethod()
    ' Retrieve full name of immediate caller.
    Dim st As New StackTrace
    Dim fullname As String = st.GetFrame(1).GetMethod().ReflectedType.Assembly.FullName
    ' Extract public key token, throw exception if not found or doesn't match.
    Dim m As Match = Regex.Match(fullname, "PublicKeyToken=(.{16})")
    If Not m.Success OrElse m.Groups(1).Value <> COMPANY_PUBLICKEYTOKEN Then
        Throw New SecurityException("Unauthorized caller")
    End If
End Sub

// [C#]
private const string COMPANY_PUBLICKEYTOKEN = "688997da81cf9c98";

public void DangerousMethod()
{
    // Retrieve full name of immediate caller.
    StackTrace  st = new StackTrace();
    string fullname = st.GetFrame(1).GetMethod().ReflectedType.Assembly.FullName;
```

```
    // Extract public key token, throw exception if not found or doesn't match.
    Match m = Regex.Match(fullname, "PublicKeyToken=(.{16})");
    if (! m.Success || m.Groups[1].Value != COMPANY_PUBLICKEYTOKEN )
        throw new SecurityException("Unauthorized caller");
}
```

33.17 Policy level for ASP.NET applications

Use the <trust> element in web.config to grant an ASP.NET application the level of trust that it most exactly needs so that ASP.NET code can't be tricked by remote users into performing dangerous actions. Don't change the contents of .config files stored in C:\Windows\ Microsoft.NET\Framework\v1.1.4322\Config.

More details: The policy level applied to an ASP.NET application is based on a mechanism that allows Internet service providers (ISPs) to run multiple ASP.NET applications on the same machine without interfering with each other or with the system. The web.config files (at both the application and directory levels) and the machine.config file can include a <trust> element that specifies the policy level for all the ASP.NET applications, a specific application, or a portion of an application:

```
<trust level="Levelname" originUrl="Url"/>
```

Levelname can be Full, High, Medium, Low, or Minimal under .NET Framework 1.1, and *Url* can be any well-formed URL. Each level corresponds to a different .config file stored in the C:\Windows\Microsoft.NET\Framework\v1.1.4322\Config folder, for example, the High level corresponds to the policy stored in the web_hightrust.config file. The Full level is special because it assigns full trust to all ASP.NET applications and doesn't correspond to any .config file. This is the default policy level for a brand-new installation of ASP.NET. Each successive level, from High to Minimal, grants fewer permissions:

- The High level grants unlimited access to the file system, environment variables, and Web sites. Applications can use the default printer, access the Microsoft SQL Server .NET Data Provider, and assert permissions. Reflection permissions are limited to the ability to emit code dynamically.

- The Medium level grants unrestricted use of isolated storage, read/write access to files in the application's directory, read access to a few environment variables, access to the default printer, the permission to assert, and the permission to connect back to the URL specified in the originUrl attribute. Applications can use the SQL Server .NET Data Provider, but it is required that the user password be nonblank.

- The Low level grants only 1 MB of isolated storage and read access to files in the application's directory.

- The Minimal level grants only execution rights.

See also: See rule 24.10 for more information about isolated storage.

33.18 Setting the principal policy

Invoke the SetPrincipalPolicy method on the current AppDomain for all applications that enforce role-based security policy.

Why: If you omit this step, the Thread.CurrentPrincipal property returns a GenericPrincipal object, which contains information on an unauthenticated user and doesn't expose any significant information about the current user. Setting the principal policy is the prerequisite for using role-based security (see rule 33.19).

More details: The SetPrincipalPolicy method should be invoked before accessing the Principal object; otherwise, it has no effect (and no exception is thrown). Also, you should bracket the call to this method in a *Try* (Visual Basic) or *try* (C#) block because calling this method fires a stack walk demanding a SecurityPermission object with the ControlPrincipal flag. (Only fully trusted code has this permission.)

```vb
' [Visual Basic]
Try
    ' Change the security policy for the current AppDomain.
    AppDomain.CurrentDomain.SetPrincipalPolicy(PrincipalPolicy.WindowsPrincipal)
    Dim ip As IPrincipal = Thread.CurrentPrincipal
    ' Cast to Object to retrieve its Type.
    Console.WriteLine(CObj(ip).GetType)
                       ' Displays System.Security.Principal.WindowsPrincipal.
    Console.WriteLine(ip.Identity.Name)                 ' MyMachine\BenSmith
    Console.WriteLine(ip.Identity.IsAuthenticated)      ' True
    Console.WriteLine(ip.Identity.AuthenticationType)   ' NTLM
Catch ex As Exception
    Console.WriteLine("Unable to change principal policy.")
End Try
```

```csharp
// [C#]
try
{
    // Change the security policy for the current AppDomain.
    AppDomain.CurrentDomain.SetPrincipalPolicy(PrincipalPolicy.WindowsPrincipal);
    IPrincipal ip = Thread.CurrentPrincipal;
    // Cast to object to retrieve its Type.
    Console.WriteLine((ip as object).GetType());
               // Displays System.Security.Principal.WindowsPrincipal.
    Console.WriteLine(ip.Identity.Name);                // MyMachine\BenSmith
    Console.WriteLine(ip.Identity.IsAuthenticated);     // true
    Console.WriteLine(ip.Identity.AuthenticationType);  // NTLM
}
catch ( Exception ex )
{
    Console.WriteLine("Unable to change principal policy.");
}
```

33.19 Role-based security

Use the PrincipalPermission type to enforce role-based security on specific methods or all the members in a type. Favor declarative over imperative demands, and ensure that you set the principal policy before programmatically testing the name or the role of the current user (as per rule 33.18).

How to: The following code shows how you can use the PrincipalPermission type in declarative and in imperative fashions:

```vb
' [Visual Basic]
Public Class MyTasks
    Sub TestImperativeSecurity()
        Dim pp As New PrincipalPermission(Nothing, "BUILTIN\Administrators")
        pp.Demand()
        ...
    End Sub

    <PrincipalPermission(SecurityAction.Demand, Role:="BUILTIN\Administrators")> _
    Sub TestDeclarativeSecurity()
        ...
    End Sub
End Class
```

```csharp
// [C#]
public class MyTasks
{
    public void TestImperativeSecurity()
    {
        PrincipalPermission pp = new PrincipalPermission(null, @"BUILTIN\Administrators");
        pp.Demand();
        ...
    }

    [PrincipalPermission(SecurityAction.Demand, Role=@"BUILTIN\Administrators")]
    public void TestDeclarativeSecurity()
    {
        ...
    }
}
```

More details: A PrincipalPermission attribute at the type level protects all the members in the type except those marked with another PrincipalPermission attribute.

You can demand both a user name and a role, but in practice you should avoid demanding a user name because you don't want to burn the name of a user in code. You can use the Union method to combine multiple permissions together:

```vb
' [Visual Basic]
Dim pp1 As New PrincipalPermission(Nothing, "BUILTIN\Administrators")
Dim pp2 As New PrincipalPermission(Nothing, "BUILTIN\Power Users")
pp1.Union(pp2).Demand()
```

```csharp
// [C#]
PrincipalPermission pp1 = new PrincipalPermission(null, @"BUILTIN\Administrators");
PrincipalPermission pp2 = new PrincipalPermission(null, @"BUILTIN\Power Users");
pp1.Union(pp2).Demand();
```

Windows Forms applications can use the Thread.CurrentPrincipal property to retrieve the WindowsPrincipal object representing the current user and then invoke the IsInRole method to implement sophisticated security policies. For example, the following code throws an exception if a user without administrative privileges attempts to run the application on Sundays:

```vb
' [Visual Basic]
AppDomain.CurrentDomain.SetPrincipalPolicy(PrincipalPolicy.WindowsPrincipal)
Dim wp As WindowsPrincipal = DirectCast(Thread.CurrentPrincipal, WindowsPrincipal)
If DateTime.Today.DayOfWeek = DayOfWeek.Sunday AndAlso _
    Not wp.IsInRole("BUILTIN\Administrators") Then
        Throw New SecurityException("Access denied")
End If
```

```csharp
// [C#]
AppDomain.CurrentDomain.SetPrincipalPolicy(PrincipalPolicy.WindowsPrincipal);
WindowsPrincipal wp = (WindowsPrincipal) Thread.CurrentPrincipal;
if ( (DateTime.Today.DayOfWeek == DayOfWeek.Sunday AndAlso) &&
    ! wp.IsInRole(@"BUILTIN\Administrators") )
        throw new SecurityException("Access denied");
```

The argument you pass to the IsInRole method can be a string in one of the following formats: BUILTIN*groupname* (for built-in roles), *machinename\groupname* (for machine-specific roles), or *domainname\groupname* (for domain-specific roles). You can also use an overloaded version of the method that takes a WindowsBuiltInRole enumerated value, which can be one of the following: AccountOperator, Administrator, BackupOperator, Guest, PowerUser, PrintOperator, Replicator, SystemOperator, or User.

33.20 Applying ACLs for configuration and data files

Always use ACLs to protect configuration and data files so that unauthorized users who have access to the computer can't read or modify them. This guideline is especially useful with files containing serialized objects (see rule 33.23).

33.21 Encrypting data

Consider protecting data files with encryption.

More details: The .NET Framework offers several abstract and concrete classes that enable you to perform both symmetric and asymmetric encryption. All symmetric algorithms require that you define both the Key property (corresponds to the password) and IV property (the initialization vector used to scramble encrypted data and make decryption even harder), both of which are Byte arrays. The length of the key depends on the algorithm being used; it can be 128, 192, or 256 bits in the case of Rijndael, or 192 bits for Triple DES.

You can either assign the Key and IV properties manually, or you can use the values that the .NET Framework generates automatically when you instantiate an object that derives from SymmetricAlgorithm. In the latter case, you must store the autogenerated key in a secure and durable medium, such as an ACL-protected file, because you need it when decrypting data. (Burying the key in code isn't a safe practice because .NET assemblies can be decompiled easily.) You don't need to keep the IV array in a safe place even though it is essential that you use the same initialization vector when you decrypt data.

How to: The following reusable routines show how you can encrypt and decrypt data coming from a stream and store the result in another stream. The includeIV argument enables you optionally to include the initialization vector in the output.

```
' [Visual Basic]
Sub EncryptData(ByVal encr As SymmetricAlgorithm, ByVal inStream As Stream, _
        ByVal outStream As Stream, ByVal includeIV As Boolean)
    Dim cs As CryptoStream
    Const BUFFERSIZE As Integer = 4096
    Try
        ' Write the (unencrypted) IV to output stream, if so requested.
        If includeIV Then outStream.Write(encr.IV, 0, encr.IV.Length)
        ' Create the CryptoStream that encrypts data and writes it to file.
        cs = New CryptoStream(outStream, encr.CreateEncryptor(), CryptoStreamMode.Write)

        Dim bytes(BUFFERSIZE - 1) As Byte
        Do
            ' Read bytes from source file, exit if no more bytes.
            Dim bytesRead As Integer = inStream.Read(bytes, 0, bytes.Length)
            If bytesRead = 0 Then Exit Do
            ' Encrypt and write bytes to the destination file.
            cs.Write(bytes, 0, bytesRead)
        Loop
        cs.FlushFinalBlock()            ' This is VERY important.
    Finally
        If Not inStream Is Nothing Then inStream.Close()
        If Not cs Is Nothing Then cs.Close()
        If Not outStream Is Nothing Then outStream.Close()
    End Try
End Sub

Sub DecryptData(ByVal encr As SymmetricAlgorithm, ByVal inStream As Stream, _
        ByVal outStream As Stream, ByVal includeIV As Boolean)
    Dim cs As CryptoStream
    Const BUFFERSIZE As Integer = 4096
    Try
        ' Read the (unencrypted) IV from source file, if so requested.
        If includeIV Then
            Dim iv(encr.IV.Length - 1) As Byte
            inStream.Read(iv, 0, iv.Length)
            encr.IV = iv
        End If
        ' Create the CryptoStream that can read and decrypt data from source stream.
        cs = New CryptoStream(inStream, encr.CreateDecryptor(), CryptoStreamMode.Read)
```

```
        Dim bytes(BUFFERSIZE - 1) As Byte
        Do
            ' Read and decrypt bytes from source file, exit if no more bytes.
            Dim bytesRead As Integer = cs.Read(bytes, 0, bytes.Length)
            If bytesRead = 0 Then Exit Do
            ' Write decrypted bytes to the destination file.
            outStream.Write(bytes, 0, bytesRead)
        Loop
    Finally
        If Not outStream Is Nothing Then outStream.Close()
        If Not cs Is Nothing Then cs.Close()
        If Not inStream Is Nothing Then inStream.Close()
    End Try
End Sub

// [C#]
void EncryptData(SymmetricAlgorithm encr, Stream inStream,
    Stream outStream, bool includeIV)
{
    CryptoStream cs = null;
    const int BUFFERSIZE = 4096;
    try
    {
        // Write the (unencrypted) IV to output stream, if so requested.
        if ( includeIV )
            outStream.Write(encr.IV, 0, encr.IV.Length);
        // Create the CryptoStream that encrypts data and writes it to file.
        cs = new CryptoStream(outStream, encr.CreateEncryptor(), CryptoStreamMode.Write);

        byte[] bytes = new byte[BUFFERSIZE];
        while (true)
        {
            // Read bytes from source file, exit if no more bytes.
            int bytesRead = inStream.Read(bytes, 0, bytes.Length);
            if ( bytesRead == 0 )
                break;
            // Encrypt and write bytes to the destination file.
            cs.Write(bytes, 0, bytesRead);
        }
        cs.FlushFinalBlock();          // This is VERY important.
    }
    finally
    {
        if ( inStream != null )
            inStream.Close();
        if ( cs != null )
            cs.Close();
        if ( outStream != null )
            outStream.Close();
    }
}

void DecryptData(SymmetricAlgorithm encr, Stream inStream,
    Stream outStream, bool includeIV)
{
```

```
CryptoStream cs = null;
const int BUFFERSIZE = 4096;
try
{
   // Read the (unencrypted) IV from source file, if so requested.
   if ( includeIV )
   {
      byte[] iv = new byte[encr.IV.Length];
      inStream.Read(iv, 0, iv.Length);
      encr.IV = iv;
   }
   // Create the CryptoStream that can read and decrypt data from source stream.
   cs = new CryptoStream(inStream, encr.CreateDecryptor(), CryptoStreamMode.Read);

   byte[] bytes = new byte[BUFFERSIZE];
   while (true)
   {
      // Read and decrypt bytes from source file, exit if no more bytes.
      int bytesRead = cs.Read(bytes, 0, bytes.Length);
      if ( bytesRead == 0 )
         break;
      // Write decrypted bytes to the destination file.
      outStream.Write(bytes, 0, bytesRead);
   }
}
finally
{
   if ( outStream != null )
      outStream.Close();
   if ( cs != null )
      cs.Close();
   if ( inStream != null )
      inStream.Close();
}
}
```

Here's how you can use these routines to encrypt a file. (Decrypting a file is similar.)

```
' [Visual Basic]
Dim encr As Rijndael = Rijndael.Create()
' Either assign the Key property or save the autogenerated key on a durable medium.
...
' Encrypt C:\Data.txt into C:\Data.enc, appending the initialization vector.
Dim inFs As New FileStream("C:\data.txt", FileMode.Open)
Dim outFs As New FileStream("C:\data.enc", FileMode.Create)
EncryptData(encr, inFs, outFs, True)
```

```
// [C#]
Rijndael encr = Rijndael.Create();
// Either assign the Key property or save the autogenerated key on a durable medium.
...
// Encrypt C:\Data.txt into C:\Data.enc, appending the initialization vector.
FileStream inFs = new FileStream(@"C:\data.txt", FileMode.Open);
FileStream outFs = new FileStream(@"C:\data.enc", FileMode.Create);
EncryptData(encr, inFs, outFs, true);
```

33.22 Hashing data files

Consider hashing files, database fields, and other sources that contain data that shouldn't be tampered with.

More details: The .NET Framework exposes several types that implement hashing algorithms. These objects let you analyze a block of data to compute its hash value, which could be considered the signature of the data. Even though two different blocks of data—for example, two files—might coincidentally provide the same hash value, in practice the chance that this will happen is negligible. More important, the hash function can't be reversed; in other words, it's virtually impossible to create a block of data that corresponds to a given hash value. This feature ensures that you can detect any change in a file whose original hash value is known.

How to: All objects that derive from HashAlgorithm expose the ComputeHash method. This method exposes three overloaded versions, which can take a Byte array, a portion of a Byte array, or a stream. The return value from the ComputeHash method is another Byte array that represents the hash value for the data. The following code shows how to use the SHA1 type to compute the hash code of a file. (For simplicity's sake, we haven't included error handling.)

```
' [Visual Basic]
Dim sha1 As SHA1 = SHA1.Create()
Dim fs As New FileStream("C:\Data.txt", FileMode.Open)
Dim hash() As Byte = sha1.ComputeHash(fs)
fs.Close()
```

```
// [C#]
SHA1 sha1 = SHA1.Create();
FileStream fs = new FileStream(@"C:\Data.txt", FileMode.Open);
byte[] hash = sha1.ComputeHash(fs);
fs.Close();
```

The hash value should be kept in a safe place; otherwise, a malicious user might modify both the data and its hash. Alternatively, you can employ a keyed hash algorithm (see rule 33.23).

33.23 Protecting serialized objects

Always encrypt or hash data files and database fields that contain the deserialized state of an object to protect your application against deserialization attacks.

More details: Encrypting and hashing files and database fields holding the serialized state of an object is the best line of defense against a type of exploit known as a *deserialization attack*. The conditions under which such an attack can occur aren't common—which partly explains why deserialization attacks aren't as popular as SQL injection and cross-site scripting attacks—but the potential damage is very high.

Let's suppose that you have a fully trusted application that deserializes an object from a file or a database field using either the BinaryFormatter or the SoapFormatter. A malicious user who can't run the application directly—for example, because it is password- or ACL-protected—but who can access the data file or the database field might replace a serialized object (say, Trust-edType) with data coming from a different type (say, HarmfulType) that the malicious user has defined in a separate DLL and deployed in the application's directory. When the trusted application deserializes the data, a HarmfulType object is instantiated instead of the expected TrustedType object. A hacker can leverage this security hole by having HarmfulType implement the IDeserializationCallback interface so that the DLL can execute code in the context of the trusted application when the object is deserialized. Worse, if the HarmfulType class derives from TrustedType, the application can successfully cast the result of the serializer's Deserialize method to a TrustedType variable and might never realize that it has been hacked.

For this reason, you should always protect serialized objects from tampering. For example, you can add a *keyed hash value* signature and check the hash before attempting to deserialize the stream of data. (Unlike regular hash values, keyed hash values depend on a secret key that you provide so that hackers can't re-create the hash value easily.) Also, serialize only sealed types if possible.

See also: This rule is a corollary of rule 33.22 but is listed as a separate guideline because failing to abide by it can open more dangerous security holes. For more information about keyed hash values, read the documentation of the System.Security.Cryptography.HMACSHA1 type at MSDN.

33.24 Storing user passwords

Don't store user passwords as clear text in a file or a database, if possible. Instead, just compute and store the hash value for each password. If storing the hash values isn't a viable solution, at least encrypt all passwords.

Why: Storing the hash values of passwords ensures that passwords aren't compromised if a malicious user manages to access the file or the database where you store your hash values. Also, sending hash values to remote computers, although not recommended, is much safer than sending passwords in clear text.

Why not: If you store just the hash value of a password, you can't implement a mechanism that enables users to recover their passwords if they forget them.

See also: See rule 33.22 for more information about hashing data.

33.25 Random data for cryptographic purposes

Use the RNGCryptoServiceProvider class whenever you need to generate truly random data.

More details: Many of the cryptographic classes in the .NET Framework require a key containing random bytes. For obvious reasons, the more random the key is, the more secure the encryption. For a robust encryption mechanism, you should never use the System.Random class to generate random keys because this class generates sequences of values that are reproducible and aren't random enough for cryptographic purposes. Instead, you should use the RNGCryptoServiceProvider class, which wraps the CryptoAPI library.

```
' [Visual Basic]
' Generate 64 random bytes.
Dim rng As New RNGCryptoServiceProvider
Dim randomData(63) As Byte
rng.GetBytes(randomData)

// [C#]
// Generate 64 random bytes.
RNGCryptoServiceProvider rng = new RNGCryptoServiceProvider();
byte[]randomData = new byte[64];
rng.GetBytes(randomData);
```

33.26 Random data from user passwords

Use the PasswordDeriveBytes class when you need to generate random data based on a user password.

More details: A common way to generate a key to be used for encryption purposes is to derive it from a textual password. For example, you can ask your user for a readable password such as "ILoveCodeArchitects," and your program can then generate a seemingly random sequence of bytes using some sort of transformation of each character in the string. This technique makes an attacker's job much harder while enabling the end user to use a human-readable password.

How to: You can easily transform a human-readable password into an apparently disordered sequence of bytes by means of a PasswordDeriveBytes object. The constructor for this object takes a string and a Byte array. This Byte array is known as the *salt*, and it has more or less the same purpose that initialization vectors have with symmetric encryption algorithms: it helps hide any recognizable pattern in the input data.

The following code shows how to create the same 32-byte sequence for each given password (provided that you use the same salt array, of course).

```
' [Visual Basic]
Dim password As String = "ILoveCodeArchitects"
Dim salt() As Byte = {3, 45, 78, 123, 9, 77}
Dim pdb As New PasswordDeriveBytes(password, salt)
Dim randomData() As Byte = pdb.GetBytes(32)

// [C#]
string password = "ILoveCodeArchitects";
byte[] salt = new byte[] {3, 45, 78, 123, 9, 77};
PasswordDeriveBytes pdb = new PasswordDeriveBytes(password, salt);
byte[] randomData = pdb.GetBytes(32);
```

33.27 Obfuscating code

Consider using an obfuscator to prevent reverse engineering of your application.

Why: Microsoft .NET applications can easily be decompiled by products such as Anakrino (*http://www.saurik.com/net/exemplar*) or Reflector (*http://www.aisto.com/roeder/dotnet*). Even without such products, often you can understand what a given type or method does simply by disassembling the application with the Ildasm tool. If you believe that the real value of your application is in the algorithms it uses, you should obfuscate your code so that decompiling it doesn't offer many hints about its inner workings.

More details: An obfuscator tool changes the name of all private methods, fields, properties, and types so that the result of decompilation can't reveal the meaning of each member. Obfuscators can also encrypt string constants so that users can't easily peek at sensitive data (such as passwords) buried in your code, but be aware that this option might slow down execution speed because all strings must be decrypted at run time. In some cases, the obfuscator is even able to change the sequence of the IL opcodes generated by the Visual Basic or C# compiler in such a way that some decompilers can't rebuild the original code. An additional benefit of most obfuscators is that they remove unnecessary metadata and use shorter names for methods and properties, so the size of an obfuscated assembly can be significantly smaller than the original one, which means that the assembly loads faster and consumes less memory.

There are several obfuscators available on the market. The least expensive choice is the Dotfuscator Community Edition, which is included in Visual Studio .NET (see Figure 33-1), or you can purchase a commercial obfuscator that offers some additional options, for example, the excellent Demeanor for .NET (*http://www.wiseowl.com/products/products.aspx*).

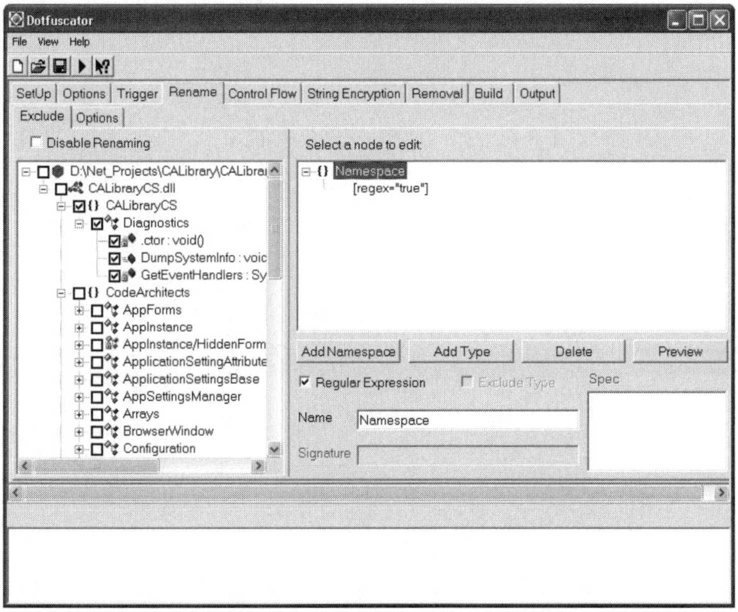

Figure 33-1 The Dotfuscator Community Edition, provided for free with Visual Studio .NET

Appendix A

Test

You've completed your application, at last. It seems to be working fine, doesn't crash unexpectedly, and performs as intended. What comes next? Well, it's time to get serious about testing it. In this short appendix, we've gathered a few obvious and not-so-obvious suggestions and recommendations for how you can test your applications before you release them in the wild world of end users.

1. Use NUnit in the design and test phase of your class library applications. (See *http://www.nunit.org* for more information about the NUnit free tool.)

2. Test the application under different versions of Microsoft Windows. We suggest that you create virtual machines using a product such as Microsoft VirtualPC (*http://www.microsoft.com/windows/virtualpc/default.mspx*) or VMWare Workstation (*http://www.vmware.com/products/desktop/ws_features.html*).

3. Test the application under different (and possibly nonstandard) Windows configurations—for example, with an antivirus program installed, without an installed printer, and so forth.

4. Run the application under less-privileged user accounts. (Tip: right-click the executable in Windows Explorer, and select the Run As command.)

5. Run the application under different regional settings. (See rule 21.24 about overriding the current regional settings through code.)

6. Run the application under different localized versions of the operating system. (Use virtual machines or, more simply, assign the CurrentUICulture property of the current thread, as explained in rule 4.10.)

7. Test the application under different screen resolutions, color depths, and font sizes. Optionally, account for rotated screen configurations to make Tablet PC users happy. (See rule 27.31 for how to detect screen resolution changes.)

8. Test the application under different color schemes and different Windows XP themes.

9. Test Windows Forms application and DLL libraries in a partially trusted context to annotate which functions aren't available in that context. (The easiest way to do so is to have an assembly-level PermissionSet attribute with a RequestRefuse action that refuses FullTrust permissions.)

10. Test your application with the computer's speakers turned off to ensure that no important information is conveyed by means of sound exclusively.

11. Ensure that the end user can access all features by means of the keyboard and that a mouse, a trackball, or another pointing device is not strictly required to operate your application.

12. Consider creating and using one or more custom performance counters to simplify performance tuning after the application has been deployed on the end user's system.

13. Use the event log details to record significant events in your application's lifetime, such as logins and logouts (including failed logins), security alerts, and fatal errors.

14. When benchmarking code, ensure that you start with a "clean" system—for example, by forcing a garbage collection before the test. Repeat your tests at least five times, and discard the best and worst timings (so that you won't account for JIT compilation); always call the Dispose or Close method of disposable objects and include these calls in the results. Differences in timing of less than 5 percent aren't significant.

Appendix B
The FxCop Tool

If you are serious about coding guidelines, you should absolutely try Microsoft FxCop. This great tool is free and can be downloaded from *http://www.gotdotnet.com/team/fxcop/*. FxCop analyzes your compiled EXE and DLL assemblies and prepares a detailed report that flags all the portions that violate one or more guidelines. (You can exclude the rules that you don't want to enforce.) You can even run FxCop from the command line and have it produce a text file, a very useful option if you use the tool in an automated environment.

Using this tool couldn't be simpler. You start by creating an FxCop project. You select which assembly (or assemblies) you want to analyze and which set of rules you want to use, in addition to the default set; click the Analyze button on the toolbar; and wait a few seconds for the results. (See Figure B-1.) We suggest that you use the Options command in the Project menu to enable control flow analysis; this option slows down the analysis step but provides a richer report. For example, control flow analysis can spot string concatenations and other slow operations if they are used in a loop.

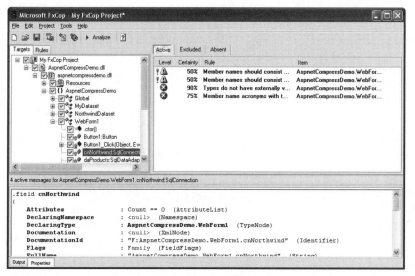

Figure B-1 The FxCop main window shows all the project elements (in the left pane) and which rules those elements don't meet (in the right pane).

The analysis engine is sophisticated: it uses both reflection and a proprietary technique known as introspection. FxCop comes with an SDK, which lets you write rules that leverage the reflection engine and that can expand the default set of rules. (Alas, as of this writing, the documentation doesn't offer many details on the more promising introspection technique.) You can get a taste of how to create custom rules in two great articles by John Robbins, which you can download from *http://msdn.microsoft.com/msdnmag/issues/04/06/Bugslayer/default.aspx* and *http://msdn.microsoft.com/msdnmag/issues/04/09/Bugslayer/default.aspx*. To stay up-to-date on FxCop and its new functionalities, just read the FxCop team's blog at *http://weblogs.asp.net/fxcop/archive/2004/01/19/60319.aspx*.

Appendix C
Source Code and Other Goodies

You can download all the source code examples from this book's "official page" on a Microsoft Press site, at *http:/www.microsoft.com/learning/books/products/8198/* as well as from our own site, at *http:/www.dotnet2themax.com/goto/practicalguidelines.aspx*. At *dotnet2themax* address, you'll also find an update page, where we'll post more samples and any errata found after the book goes to print. You can be informed of any addition to this page by simply subscribing to our free newsletter (which, incidentally, always contains many interesting articles and tips).

One more item you can find at the *dotnet2themax* address is a checklist that summarizes all the guidelines in this book. Each item in the list is a short description of the rule, specifies which language or project type it applies to, and references the rule number where you can find the longer description and a code example.

Not all rules apply to all projects. For example, you don't need a list of ASP.NET guidelines if you're writing a Windows Forms project, and you don't want to be distracted by remoting or COM+ best practices if the application you're working on doesn't use those technologies. For this reason, we provide the guideline checklist in the form of a Microsoft Word document that you can edit to fit your needs. (See Figure C-1.) You can delete those rules you don't want to follow and decide which version you want to adopt if an alternative rule exists. Also, we are using Word styles so that you can easily customize the checklist's look before printing it.

Although we believe that this checklist can be a great tool during the development stage as well as during code reviews, we also won't be surprised if it can be improved. Please let us hear your suggestions and, more generally, how we can make *Practical Guidelines and Best Practices for Microsoft Visual Basic .NET and C# Developers* even better and more useful, by sending a note to *fbalena@codearchitects.com* or *gdimauro@codearchitects.com*.

	3. Comments			
☐	Spell checks comments		3.1	
☐	Standardize on U.S. English (or your national language) for comments		3.2	
☐	Use imperative style for comments		3.3	
☐	Use descriptive style for comments		3.3	alternate
☐	Place comments immediately before the code they refer to, at the same indent level and with no intervening blank lines		3.4	
☐	Use XML comments to document all public types and methods in a class library; use standard comments in all other cases	C#	3.5	
☐	Use XML comments to document all types and methods, regardless of scope and project type	C#	3.5	alternate
☐	Use <include> tags to point to XML comments in external files		3.6	optional
☐	Use NDoc to produce technical documentation		3.7	
☐	Use XML comments instead of regular comments, using the Use the VBCommenter add-in	VB	3.8	optional

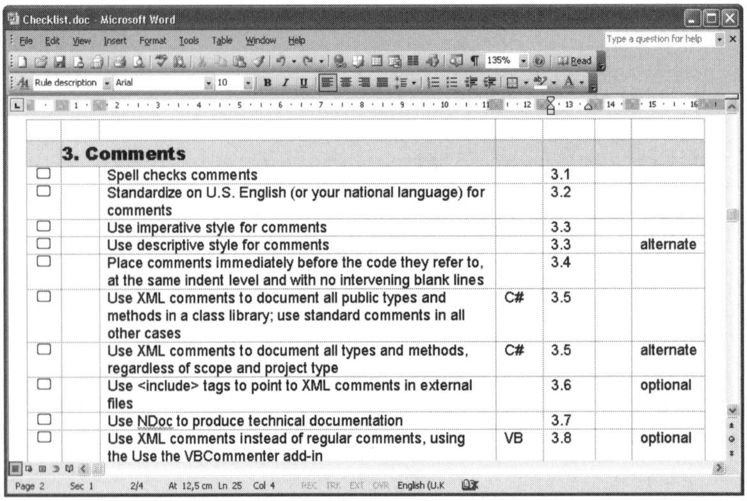

Figure C-1 The Code Architects Guideline Checklist can be customized to fit your coding style.

Index

Francesco Balena

Francesco Balena began writing software in the late 1970s, when the PC had yet to be invented. Since then, he has spoken at many conferences for developers and has written hundreds of articles for programming magazines, including *MSDN Magazine* and *Visual Studio Magazine*. He has authored or coauthored four Microsoft Press books, including the best selling *Programming Microsoft Visual Basic 6.0* and *Programming Microsoft Visual Basic .NET Version 2003*, and about a dozen books for Italian publishers. He founded an Italian magazine for developers (*Visual Basic & .NET Journal*), a popular Web site for developers (*www.vb2themax.com*, now *www.dotnet2themax.com*), and cofounded Code Architects. Francesco is one of two MSDN Regional Directors for Italy. He lives in Bari with his wife Adriana and his son Andrea.

Giuseppe Dimauro

Giuseppe Dimauro has been writing C and C++ code for nearly two decades and has worked with Microsoft Windows since version 1.0. He specializes in Microsoft SQL Server and distributed n-tiered architectures based on COM+, remoting, and Web services. He has written dozens of articles for Italian programming magazines and the Italian MSDN Web site and speaks at many large conferences for developers. He cofounded the www.vb2themax.com Web site and the Code Architects software company. Giuseppe has been MSDN Regional Director for Italy since 2001 and routinely consults for Microsoft Italy and its larger customers. He lives in Santeramo in Colle, with his wife Francesca and his daughter Lucia.

Form Maximizer for .NET

Soup up your Windows Forms apps. No code Required.

- for C#, VB.NET, and any .NET language
- no need to modify existing forms
- royalty free

Form Maximizer **for .NET**

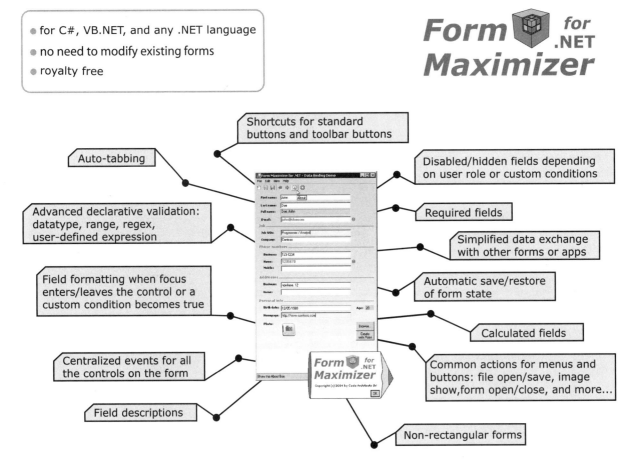

- Shortcuts for standard buttons and toolbar buttons
- Auto-tabbing
- Disabled/hidden fields depending on user role or custom conditions
- Advanced declarative validation: datatype, range, regex, user-defined expression
- Required fields
- Simplified data exchange with other forms or apps
- Field formatting when focus enters/leaves the control or a custom condition becomes true
- Automatic save/restore of form state
- Calculated fields
- Centralized events for all the controls on the form
- Common actions for menus and buttons: file open/save, image show, form open/close, and more...
- Field descriptions
- Non-rectangular forms

Form Maximizer for .NET is a set extender controls that add new properties to all Windows Forms built-in controls as well ad most third-party controls. Full C# source code is available.
Single-developer license at only $129.

Read more at ***http://www.dotnet2themax.com/formmaximixer/***

Www.dotnet2themax.com

- Read hundreds of tips and full-length articles by Francesco Balena, Giuseppe Dimauro, Dino Esposito, and many other .NET experts.

- Download freeware utilities, Visual Studio .NET add-ins, ready-to-use classes and routines. All code samples are both in Visual Basic .NET and C#.

- Learn more about future versions of the .NET Framework and explore .NET 2.0 without installing it, with our online .NET Inspector.

Subscribe to the free News-2-the-Max newsletter for even more technical content, special offers, and more.

Download sample chapters from the best .NET books and demos from Code Architects programming tools

What do you think of this book?
We want to hear from you!

Do you have a few minutes to participate in a brief online survey? Microsoft is interested in hearing your feedback about this publication so that we can continually improve our books and learning resources for you.

To participate in our survey, please visit:

www.microsoft.com/learning/booksurvey

And enter this book's ISBN, 0-7356-2172-1. As a thank-you to survey participants in the United States and Canada, each month we'll randomly select five respondents to win one of five $100 gift certificates from a leading online merchant.* At the conclusion of the survey, you can enter the drawing by providing your e-mail address, which will be used for prize notification *only.*

Thanks in advance for your input. Your opinion counts!

Sincerely,

Microsoft Learning

Microsoft | Learning

Learn More. Go Further.

To see special offers on Microsoft Learning products for developers, IT professionals, and home and office users, visit: *www.microsoft.com/learning/booksurvey*